P9-BZC-699

THE MEDIA AND THE PEOPLE

Charlene J. Brown
Indiana University

Trevor R. Brown
Indiana University

William L. Rivers
Stanford University

With all our love,
Charly
Trevor

Holt, Rinehart and Winston

New York   Chicago   San Francisco   Atlanta   Dallas
Montreal   Toronto   London   Sydney

To Trevor Laurence
and our parents

To Sarah

Editor   Roth Wilkofsky
Senior Project Editor   Marjorie Marks
Production Manager   Robert de Villeneuve
Art Director   Arthur Ritter

Library of Congress Cataloging in Publication Data

Brown, Charlene J.
  The media and the people.

  Bibliography: p. 439
  Includes index.
  1. Mass media—Social aspects—United States.
  2. Mass media—Political aspects—United States.
  I. Brown, Trevor R., joint author. II. Rivers,
  William L., joint author. III. Title.
  HN90.M3B76   301.16'1   77-27977

ISBN 0-03-019056-8

Copyright © 1978 by Holt, Rinehart and Winston
All rights reserved
Printed in the United States of America
8 9 0 1   090   9 8 7 6 5 4 3 2 1

Acknowledgments

page 1 Yeats epigraph: Reprinted with permission of Macmillan Publishing Co., Inc., from "The Old Stone Cross," *Collected Poems,* by William Butler Yeats. Copyright 1940 by Georgie Yeats, renewed 1968 by Bertha Georgie Yeats, Michael Butler Yeats, and Anne Yeats.

page 433 Eliot epigraph: From "Choruses from 'The Rock'" in *Collected Poems 1909—1962* by T. S. Eliot, copyright 1936, by Harcourt Brace Jovanovich, Inc.; copyright © 1963, 1964 by T. S. Eliot; And from "Choruses from 'The Rock'" in *Collected Poems 1909—1935* by T. S. Eliot (London: Faber & Faber Limited, 1961).

Selections from *The Image* by Daniel J. Boorstin. Copyright © 1961 by Daniel J. Boorstin. Reprinted by permission of Atheneum Publishers and George Weidenfeld & Nicolson Ltd. Page numbers are the same as the Harper & Row edition.

Preface

"Communication study has moved so fast that it has seldom stood still for its portrait," Wilbur Schramm wrote in 1971; "in the middle of change it is hard to sum up change." Schramm puts our predicament with admirable succinctness. Not only has the pace of scholarship in communications accelerated but so has the rate of technological change, blurring the present and future of the mass media.

Basing our book on *The Mass Media and Modern Society,* written by one of our number, William L. Rivers, with Theodore Peterson and Jay W. Jensen, we sought to draw on the insights of Professors Jensen and Peterson's literate and persuasive description and analysis of mass communication while reorganizing the contents to reflect the changes in the mass media of the late 1970s. We have retained the interpretative and essayist style and that book's strong historical approach to providing students, both those who plan careers in the mass media and those who do not, with an understanding of the evolution of the mass media in the United States. No citizen can understand or intelligently evaluate or participate in the mass media without learning how they have developed in this society. A judicious historical perspective on the mass media is likely to give us our most sensitive feelers into the future. Similarly, the mass media are such a significant part of our society that no citizen can understand that society without understanding the mass media.

We have quoted Wilbur Schramm here and throughout this book. We have long admired the grace and clarity of his writing and his unmatched ability to synthesize findings relevant to communications from a half-dozen or more disciplines. We are indebted to him for his contribution as scholar, colleague, and teacher to the intellectual lives of all of us.

We would like to thank our colleagues at Stanford University and

Indiana University for the stimulating environments they provide. For their help, we also wish to thank Paul G. Ashdown, Western Kentucky University; Carol C. Basile, Florida State University; William B. Blankenburg, University of Wisconsin; Bert Cross, University of Idaho; Frank Deaver, University of Alabama; Donald M. Gillmor, University of Minnesota; Gerald L. Grotta, University of Oklahoma; Brooks Hamilton, University of Maine; Vernon Keel, University of North Dakota; Ralph L. Lowenstein, University of Florida; Randall L. Murray, Ohio University; Charles A. Oliphant, Memphis State University; William Payden, Los Angeles Valley College; Charles C. Russell, Cornell University; William K. Schwienher, Purdue University. Frances Goins Wilhoit has made the library in the School of Journalism of especial value to students and faculty at Indiana University. We appreciate the contribution to this book of her annotated compilation of *Periodicals about Mass Media.* Readers will find it a valuable tool for pursuing current information on the mass media. Special thanks are due, too, to Gail Rivers for her fine work on the index.

Bloomington, Indiana   CHARLENE J. BROWN
                                                                                        TREVOR R. BROWN
Stanford, California   WILLIAM L. RIVERS
January 1978

Contents

1

The Media and the People: An Introduction

A statesman is an easy man
He tells his lies by rote;
A journalist makes up his lies
And takes you by the throat;
So stay at home and drink your beer
And let the neighbors vote. . . .

W. B. YEATS

People do not respect institutions which are servile; people only respect a society which makes demands on them, which insists that they become better than they are.

IRVING KRISTOL

$\mathbf{I}$n a letter quoted too often and too uncritically, Thomas Jefferson wrote to Edward Carrington in January 1787, " . . . [W]ere it left to me to decide whether we should have a government without newspapers

1

or newspapers without a government, I should not hesitate a moment to prefer the latter."

Taken literally, Jefferson's statement is absurd, but the mass media, increasingly pressured in the 1960s and 1970s by public and governmental criticism of their principles, performance, and power, have often cited it in their defense. Reverence for Jefferson's hyperbole tends to have two effects: It reinforces journalists' romantic view of their role in society, and it contributes to the public's unrealistic expectations of the media and distorted perception of the media's actual power. When Spiro Agnew, the former Vice President of the United States, declared in an interview on the National Broadcasting Company's "Today" show in May 1976 that "the mass media *are* the government," he was expressing a visceral but widely held view. His statement was just as absurd as Jefferson's.

In the social and political turmoil of the 1960s and 1970s, a period when the civil rights movement, an unpopular war, and the downfall of a corrupt government bitterly divided Americans, one of many strange phenomena was the public's turning to the mass media as much as to government for redress of its grievances and for healing of its agonies. The public's expectations flattered the media's view of themselves and later fed the public's disillusionment with its champion. Public opinion fluctuated between visions of the mass media as savior and as devil, as the scourge of society's ills and as the cause of them.

This chapter discusses some common misperceptions of media power, which, though exaggerated, is indeed formidable, and suggests that an informed and responsible citizenry can help make the media responsive and responsible. A democratic society like ours imposes obligations upon the media *and* the citizenry. To a great extent, therefore, the media's imperfections reflect the imperfections of citizens who approve or ignore them.

We are not suggesting, however, that the media should automatically respond to all citizen criticism and demands, that they should merely reflect the wishes of their audiences. By informed and responsible citizens, we mean citizens who understand the roles that our democratic society expects citizens and the media to play and who hold themselves and the media to those roles. By responsive media, we mean media attentive to their audiences' wants and complaints but not subservient to them. By responsible media, we mean media exercising their informed judgment about what people need to know to fulfill their role as citizens and to protect their individual rights and interests—even if such judgment goes against their audiences' wishes.

In this respect, we agree with David Broder, Pulitzer Prize-winning political columnist for *The Washington Post*. Broder argued that the limits of what reporters do ought not to be defined by what is acceptable to the society in which they operate. " . . . [I]f you begin to play that game," said Broder, "then you're in serious trouble. I think you define your role as a reporter in terms of what you understand the role of a reporter to be. And if that incurs a degree of popular wrath, then that's just a consequence of it."[1]

The Nature of Mass Media Power

THE MEDIA'S POWER OF SELECTION: SETTING THE AGENDA

Spiro Agnew's assertion was not altogether absurd. The media do not govern, but they do have enormous power. As media critic Ben Bagdikian wrote in *The Information Machines:*

> Where once priests and kings decided what the populace would hear, the proprietors of the mass media now decide. As men gather in ever larger interdependent masses, communications technology becomes more important and increases the power of those who control it. In an isolated village of 50 persons who meet frequently, community events are learned in face-to-face contacts more effective than any formal medium. But in a country of 200 million self-conscious human beings, the power of news systems is infinitely greater: it is a source of reality itself. For most of the people of the world, for most of the events of the world, what the news systems do not transmit did not happen. To that extent, the world and its inhabitants are what the news media say they are.[2]

Although the media have the kind of power Bagdikian has identified, their power is not monolithic or conspiratorial, as the constant generalizations about "the mass media" and "the news media" suggest. Those phrases are a convenient shorthand and we shall use them, but it is necessary to keep the diversity of the media in mind.

The world and its inhabitants may be what the news media say they are, but the news media do not have exclusive control over our view of reality. Journalists' selection of information and their control over the agenda for public discussion are influenced by a number of factors, including (1) the sources on which they rely for information; (2) events of such impact and consequence that they cannot be ignored.

Consider, for example, the reporting of the Vietnam War.

Reporting Vietnam

In the early years of American involvement in Vietnam, most American reporters depended on the Pentagon for access and transport to battle zones and for information about the war. The view of reality journalists communicated to the American people was that of the U.S. military and of the Kennedy and Johnson Administrations. With exceptions such as David Halberstam of *The New York Times,* Malcolm Browne of the Associated Press, and Charles Mohr of *Time,* journalists presented an optimistic official account of successful American and South Vietnamese military operations. Most reporters did not conspire to ignore nonofficial sources.

Washington journalist Peter Lisagor described the reporters' predicament this way: "We were largely at the mercy of the Administration then. We had no touchstones on the war. And we were less skeptical on the war than we were on other things. There was a tendency to believe more because they were supposed to have the facts and you didn't, and we were more inclined to accepting an official's word on something as cosmic as a war."[3] The point is that the government rather than the media, or the government with the largely helpless cooperation of the media, was shaping our view of reality, was setting the agenda for public discussion.

Then, in January 1968, the Viet Cong mounted an unexpectedly massive attack on Saigon and the U.S. Embassy and laid siege to the U.S. forces at Khe Sanh, exposing the inadequacy of the government's facts and opinions. All the face-saving efforts of the U.S. government could not obscure the essential success—more psychological than military—of the Viet Cong's Tet offensive. This event shattered the confidence of journalists and many other Americans in the government's view of the war, and journalists began to seek other sources and information, which presented a pessimistic and critical view of American involvement. A "credibility gap" opened between President Lyndon Johnson and the public, contributing to his decision not to run for the Presidency in 1968. Thus an event of impact and consequence that journalists could not ignore and government could not explain away influenced the selection of information journalists made and the view of reality they communicated.

President Richard Nixon came to power in 1969 promising to end the war, and indeed began gradually to withdraw American troops. Journalists' emphases shifted accordingly, away from battle stories to accounts of American withdrawal. The impression created was that the worst was over, at least for the United States, an impression the Nixon Administration worked to cultivate and one, no doubt, that the American press and public wanted to believe. Again the government rather than reporters was shaping our view of reality.

Despite the credibility gap the Tet offensive had opened, most journalists had not shaken off their largely uncritical dependence on official sources. On March 17, 1968, for example, *The New York Times* had reported on the front page that American soldiers of the Americal Division, with artillery and helicopter support, had attacked the village of Mylai the previous day, killed between 100 and 200 enemy, detained a dozen suspects, and captured some weapons. These were the facts issued in the Americal Division newsletter, and the news media were not inclined to doubt them.

It was not until 20 months later that Seymour M. Hersh, a 33-year-old freelance reporter, began to doubt the official account when he learned that the military was planning to court-martial an officer at Fort Benning, Georgia, for the murder of about 75 Vietnamese civilians. The Philip Stern Fund for Investigative Journalism awarded Hersh a $2000 travel grant, and he traveled more than 30,000 miles by air locating and interviewing witnesses to the Mylai incident. When he felt that he knew the story behind the military's decision to charge Lieutenant William L. Calley, Jr., with the murder of 109 civilians at Mylai, Hersh offered the story to *Life* and *Look* magazines (Hersh said he knew that "newspapers would be the last to believe it"). Both rejected Hersh's story, so he gave it to the floundering Dispatch News Service operated by his friend and neighbor, David Obst. Of about 50 newspapers contacted, 36 ran the first story of Hersh's series on

October 13, 1969. Only *The New York Times* followed up with its own investigation.

Hersh pursued further witnesses, and newspapers paid more attention to his second Dispatch story in late November. They began to play the story prominently. "It all had suddenly become much more credible," Hersh commented, "when the army announced in late November that Calley had indeed been charged with the murder of 109 Vietnamese civilians. . . . The newspaper industry, in one of those collective changes of mind that can only be found in the business, decided each man's testimony was important enough to play all over the front pages. The indiscriminate use of eyewitness statements was amazing to me. . . ."[4]

Once again the news media abandoned their dependence on official sources to seek another view of reality when they could no longer ignore an event they had apparently first disbelieved.

Reporting Watergate

The news media showed an initial indifference similar to that Hersh had experienced when reporters Bob Woodward and Carl Bernstein of *The Washington Post* began their investigation of Watergate in June 1972. The *Post's* first story ran three days after five men were arrested in the Watergate apartment complex in Washington for burglarizing and bugging the Democratic National Committee's offices. Washington correspondent James McCartney wrote:

> Following the Watergate burglary, on June 17, 1972, the *Post* was the first to make a connection between the burglary and the White House; the first to show that Nixon campaign funds were involved; the first to describe "laundering" of campaign money in Mexico; the first to involve former Atty. Gen. John Mitchell; the first to involve former presidential appointments secretary Dwight Chapin; the first to explain that political espionage and sabotage were an intrinsic part of the Nixon campaign; the first to trace the Watergate affair to the very doors of the president's Oval Office—to his White House chief of staff, H. R. Haldeman. It had unloaded these salvos over a period of months, beginning only three days after the burglary and reaching a climax in October, a few weeks before the election.[5]

Because so few other news media pursued the stories, the Watergate affair was not a topic on the political agenda for the 1972 election. The *Post* could not by itself put it on the agenda, and President Nixon was reelected with one of the largest margins in American history. It is perhaps not surprising that the major news media ignored a freelance reporter using a relatively unknown news service to distribute a story few Americans wanted to believe. But it is bewildering that the news media ignored a respected and influential paper like the *Post* with a story of such staggering implications. Clearly there was no media conspiracy to ignore Mylai and Watergate; equally clearly there was no monolithic effort to put these events on the public agenda—only a few newspapers tried to do that.

John Dean III, former Counsel to President Nixon, testifies at the Senate Watergate hearings. The Washington *Post* could not by itself put Watergate on the public agenda. (United Press International photo)

It took these events so long to secure a place on the public agenda largely because of the nature of the news-gathering process and of the sources on which journalists typically rely. Gathering the information and a variety of interpretations of it for a remote event such as Mylai or a complex one such as Watergate requires more time, effort, and money than reporters with daily deadlines can usually afford. Their limited resources force them to depend largely on official sources as an efficient way of gathering information. In any case, most journalists are inclined to the belief that the public has a right to hear what its elected and appointed officials have to say.

Government bureaucracies at all levels serve their public responsibilities, aid the media, and try to promote the view of reality they want by generating masses of information every day. They issue press releases and handouts and hold press conferences and briefings. Whatever their limitations, these informational efforts are invaluable to reporters who would otherwise exhaust their limited time ferreting out routine information. To a great extent the news media in their coverage of government do not so much gather information as process it. This practice occurs not only in covering the Pentagon and the White House but also in covering an accident or a crime in a local community.

The media do not have exclusive control, then, of our view of reality, but they do have considerable control. Obviously journalists cannot report everything their sources tell them. They must decide what they think is important and interesting, what they think is newsworthy. And, again, journalists do not make these decisions conspiratorially or monolithically.

Because of professional consensus about what news is and because of the competitive nature of the news-gathering process, the news judgments of the major print and broadcast media are remarkably similar each day. Nevertheless, news is the product of a series of individual judgments. What is selected and how prominently it is displayed differs to some extent from one news institution to another.

For example, Agnew's comment that the news media are the government was virtually all that NBC's "Nightly News," on May 11, 1976, selected from a 15-minute interview of Agnew on the morning's "Today" show. The audience of between 15 and 20 million watching NBC's "Nightly News" heard no amplification of his comment nor anything of the various topics he discussed. The 806,000 subscribers of *The New York Times* on May 12, 1976, could read a more complete news report of the interview and extensive excerpts from the broadcast transcript of the "Today" interview. Yet neither the reporter's news story nor the excerpts included Agnew's comment on media power, the only item that NBC's "Nightly News" selected.

Reality for some of NBC's "Nightly News" audience on May 11 differed from that of some of the *Times'* readers on May 12. Some viewers of NBC and readers of the *Times* would be the same people, and therefore able to complement the broadcast with the print account. Still other people who rely on daily media that did not report the Agnew interview may have been among the 2.9 million subscribers to *Newsweek* who could read the magazine's summary of and reaction to it. And a core of people will have seen the "Today" show and the "Nightly News" and read the *Times* and *Newsweek*.

THE MEDIA'S POWER OF PERSUASION

What the various media report, particularly when they report essentially the same information, clearly does influence the climate of opinion. For example, when the official view of Vietnam prevailed in the media, most Americans approved the government's conduct of the war. And when most of the media accepted the Nixon Administration's denial of the *Post's* Watergate stories without further investigation, most Americans approved the Nixon Presidency. Then when Tet and Mylai forced the media to seek other views of reality, public opinion turned against the war. When the seven men involved in the Watergate break-in were convicted in January 1973 and U.S. District Judge John J. Sirica succeeded in pressuring one of them, James McCord, into revealing the story behind Watergate, the revelations vindicated the *Post*. All the news media began to cover the story, the public turned against the Nixon Administration, and President Nixon eventually resigned.

Clearly other factors affected public opinion, but the important point for our purposes is that, without acting as advocates of a point of view or consciously trying to persuade, the mass media do influence public opinion

by the selection of information they report, by the view of reality they
communicate. That is perhaps the media's most formidable power. We
must be careful to distinguish this power to influence public opinion through
their delivery of information from the power many people think the media
have when they try consciously to persuade their audiences to a particular
point of view. Research shows that the media's power as deliberate persuaders is much more limited than is commonly believed.

In a famous speech in November 1969 attacking media power, Spiro
Agnew expressed this tenacious misperception of the media's persuasive
power. His attack was prompted by television network treatment of a
speech by President Nixon on the Vietnam War carried live the same
month, without selection or editing, by all three television networks. Agnew
complained:

> The audience of seventy million Americans gathered to hear the President of the
> United States was inherited by a small band of network commentators and self-
> appointed analysts, the majority of whom expressed, in one way or another,
> their hostility to what he had to say.

Agnew continued:

> Now every American has a right to disagree with the President of the United
> States and to express publicly that disagreement. But the President of the United
> States has a right to communicate directly with the people who elected him, and
> the people of the country have the right to make up their own minds and form
> their own opinions about a Presidential address without having a President's
> words and thoughts characterized through the prejudices of hostile critics before
> they can even be digested.[6]

Apparently because broadcast technology had so penetrated the whole
mass of the people that a President and a handful of hostile critics could
reach 70 million people, those people were helpless to form their own
opinions. That seemed to be Agnew's analysis of media power. It is a
common one. Ask an American whether he is helpless to make up his mind
about an issue after listening to or reading analysis of it by media commentators. Of course not, he will say. Typically, however, he is convinced that
others are helpless, that such commentators are determining what other
Americans think.

Agnew revealed the same kind of fractured logic in his speech. He
argued that the views of the majority of network commentators and producers "do not—and I repeat, not—represent the views of America." He
continued:

> That is why such a great gulf existed between how the nation received the
> President's address and how the networks reviewed it. Not only did the country
> receive the President's address more warmly than the networks, but so also did
> the Congress of the United States.

The people confronted a choice and apparently made up their own minds and formed their own opinions, "self-appointed analysts" notwithstanding.

Agnew's analysis of media power was flawed by the existence of what scholars have called "the obstinate audience," by the diversity of experience and attitudes that individuals bring to their encounters with the media. Although scholars today are not inclined to accept uncritically the nineteenth-century libertarian's faith in people's innate desire to seek and discern truth through the exercise of reason, their research has shown that the media cannot easily shape attitudes and opinions. They may be able to do so on matters new or unfamiliar to citizens, or on matters about which citizens have not taken the trouble to inform themselves.

A Press for the Masses

Jefferson's preference for newspapers over government carried with it an obligation for citizens and set certain conditions. The people, said Jefferson, should be given "full information of their affairs thro' the channel of the public papers" and "those papers should penetrate the whole mass of the people. . . . [E]very man should receive those papers and be capable of reading them."

In the eighteenth and early nineteenth centuries, however, newspapers scarcely penetrated the people at all. They were partisan, financially precarious, and expensive organs of opinion produced, for the most part, by gentlemen for gentlemen. It is true that during the revolutionary period the initiative for change was taken by a group of "ungentlemanly," activist editors such as Benjamin Edes and John Gill of the *Boston Gazette,* who vividly expressed the people's grievances against the government and the ruling class and helped throw the tea into Boston Harbor. The *Gazette's* circulation of 2000 was a record for the period, and Governor Thomas Hutchinson lamented in 1770, "The misfortune is that seven-eights of the people read none but this infamous paper."[7] The populist concerns of radical editors indeed broadened the appeal of newspapers during the revolutionary period, but after the War of Independence the initiative in public affairs passed back to the wealthier, propertied classes who used newspapers as organs for the several factions disputing for power.

THE MEDIA AND THE FIRST AMENDMENT

A cheap, mass press was not possible until the vision of America Jefferson so abhorred—an urban, industrial economy—came into being. Yet long before the crucial conditions of mass media penetration were met, Jefferson's assertion of newspapers' importance was reflected in the First Amendment to the Constitution adopted in 1791: "Congress shall make no law . . . abridging the freedom of speech, or of the press." In restricting the

power of government, and, indirectly, of the people, to abridge press
freedom, the First Amendment has been a vital safeguard of all civil liberties.
It has also inhibited efforts to regulate and restructure print and broadcasting
media in a complex industrial economy the Founding Fathers could not fully
anticipate.

The mass media have always been costly to establish and operate. The
printing technology capable of producing the thousands of newspapers
needed daily to reach every literate person was not available until the
middle of the nineteenth century. But although the technology of mass
production makes for certain economies, the costs of investing in it and
operating a newspaper enterprise were high then and have since risen
dramatically. Not until 1833 was it discovered by Benjamin Day that if he
made his New York *Sun* appealing to as many people as possible, he could
persuade advertisers to pay the bulk of the costs. By doing so, Day could cut
the price of a newspaper from sixpence to a penny, a sum that most
Americans could afford. Government and wealthy backers subsidized the
eighteenth- and early nineteenth-century press; advertising has subsidized it
since. Now advertisers have a wide choice of commercial media—newspapers, magazines, radio, and television.

A single communications medium can rarely command the exclusive
attention of an advertiser. Rising costs and competition for the advertising
dollar largely explain the contemporary decline in newspaper competition
and the concentration of media ownership in fewer and fewer hands. The
growth of vast, corporate, multimedia enterprises and the comparative
inability of government restrained by the First Amendment to regulate them
has led to the kind of public frustration voiced in Spiro Agnew's comment,
"the mass media *are* the government." At the root of this frustration is a
feeling that a gulf is widening between the people and the increasingly
centralized media institutions, some of which are so large that they invite
comparison with other power centers such as business and government.

Modern mass media are not merely institutions comparable with business. They are themselves business enterprises seeking profit. Because of
their special constitutional protection, they suffer a peculiar tension. Increasingly their privileged position has been interpreted to mean that they are
obligated to perform in the public interest, that they must fulfill certain social
responsibilities which may be financially unprofitable. Unfortunately for the
media, public consensus about what the media *ought* to do does not
necessarily lead to majority support or interest when the media do as
consensus says they ought.

For example, few citizens disagree that it is the media's responsibility to
check on government. Yet the media's gradual, painstaking investigations
into the corruption of the Nixon Administration irritated, even outraged, a
considerable number of citizens. Not until the accumulation of facts was so
formidable that members of the Nixon Administration were convicted in
court and the President himself felt it necessary to resign did majority
opinion conclude that the media were heroes. Then the media's investiga-

tive zeal after Watergate seemed to irritate many citizens once more and to raise a dark murmur against what was perceived as the massive, unrestrained power of the press.

THE MEDIA AS ENTERTAINERS

Vast and impersonal though the mass media may be, the economics of their operations make them in great measure responsive to their perceptions of what pleases the kind of audience they and their advertisers want. The mass media's emphasis on entertainment illustrates this point. Discussion thus far has focused on the media as news institutions. In fact, the public spends far more time with the media as entertainers than as informers. That is one of democracy's dilemmas. Democracy's early theoreticians assumed that citizens would be innately impelled to seek information and ideas about their elected representatives and about government's policies and actions. The Founding Fathers considered institutions such as education and the media vital to the creation and maintenance of an informed electorate. In his Farewell Address, President George Washington said:

> Promote, then, as an object of primary importance, institutions for the general diffusion of knowledge. In proportion as the structure of government gives force to public opinion, it is essential that public opinion should be enlightened.

Surveys indicate, however, that only a minority of citizens takes a serious and committed interest in the daily business of government and public affairs. Majority preference has been for entertainment. Because the mass media must survive and make a profit in a basically free enterprise environment, they not only provide a heavy diet of explicit entertainment but also try to make the news as interesting and entertaining as possible. Although journalism tradition ordains the separation of news from entertainment, increasing competition within and among the media has often blurred the division.

Charles Dana, who introduced a crisp and lively newswriting style into journalism when he took over the New York *Sun* in 1868 and elevated the human interest story to a place of prominence on the front page equal to that of news of public affairs, demanded that his reporters "Be interesting!" To one of his competitors, Edwin Godkin at the New York *Evening Post,* this kind of journalism was trivial and foolish, particularly when it was taken to sensational extremes by Joseph Pulitzer and William Randolph Hearst during the period of yellow journalism in the 1890s. Godkin wrote in 1896:

> The note of the press today which most needs changing is childishness. Even if the papers are clean and decent, they are fit only for the nursery. The pictures are childish; the intelligence is mainly for boys and girls. . . . We laugh over everything; make fun of everybody, and think it will "all come out right in the end," just like ill-bred children who hate to have their games interrupted.[8]

But such journalism sold millions of newspapers, and the amusing stories, comics, games, and crossword puzzles that today make up a signifi-

cant proportion of the daily newspaper can be traced back to the innova-
tions of Dana, Pulitzer, and Hearst.

Because of the intense competition within the television medium, television news is even more concerned than print news to be interesting.
Information is selected and presented as much for its dramatic, narrative
value as for its importance to citizens. Television news, on which Americans
are increasingly relying, is affected too by the fact that since its inception
television has been perceived as primarily a medium of entertainment.

In 1977, 97 percent of American homes had at least one set, and the
average set was on for more than six hours a day. Although surveys show
that an increasing number of Americans rely on television for news and
information, most of those six hours are spent on entertainment. Fred
Friendly, the former president of the CBS news division who resigned
because, among other reasons, the network decided to broadcast a fifth
rerun of "I Love Lucy" rather than carry live coverage of the Senate Foreign
Relations Committee hearings on Vietnam for a third day in February 1966,
summarizes television's dilemma neatly: "Because television can make so
much money doing its worst, it often cannot afford to do its best."[9]

The networks confronted this dilemma again soon after all three began
daily coverage of the Senate Watergate hearings in May 1973. Station
affiliates and their audiences protested the interruption of daytime serials
and game shows, and the networks shifted to a rotational system, each
network in turn being responsible for a day's coverage. At the end of the first
phase of the hearings (May 17–August 7, 1973: 181 hours of hearings
spread over 37 days), *Broadcasting* magazine reported: "The best available
estimates put the combined coverage costs to ABC-TV, CBS-TV and NBC-
TV—in terms of reduction of profits—at no less than $7 million and possibly
as much as $10 million."[10] Station affiliates also lost money, a medium-
market station, it is estimated, losing $3000 a week because of preempted
national spot and local commercials. In the Presidential election year of
1976, the three networks were estimated to have lost $30 million because of
their political coverage—of the primaries, the political conventions, the
television debates between Democratic nominee Jimmy Carter and Republican nominee Gerald Ford and between their running mates, election
specials, and election night itself.

Because more people want to watch daytime serials and game shows
and prime-time police shows and comedies than public affairs programing,
broadcasters can make more money from entertainment than from news.
For example, William S. Paley, chairman of CBS, told stockholders in April
1976 that CBS had set new first-quarter records in 1976 with estimated net
income reaching $27.8 million, up 14.8 percent from the previous first-
quarter high mark set in 1975. How had CBS done so? By adhering to the
"primary rule," said Paley, of trying "to appeal, for the most part, to the
largest number of people, while at the same time being mindful of the
interests and expectations of significant minority segments of the public."[11]

The networks spend fabulous sums to appeal to the largest number of people likely to be interested in the advertisers' products. *Broadcasting* described as conservative its estimate that the three television networks would pay more than $600 million to their various program suppliers for all the 73 regularly scheduled shows in their 1977–1978 prime-time line-ups. That was $80 million more than they paid for comparable programing the previous year.[12]

Nevertheless, Robert T. Bower has concluded from his 1970 survey of viewers designed as a follow-up to one conducted by sociologist Gary A. Steiner in 1960 that by the 1970s the honeymoon between the American public and television was over. Bower noted that the very large group of television "superfans" who gave enormously favorable reactions to television in 1960 had sharply decreased. The attitudes of the much better educated 1970 population, he said, "were being modified into a general approval away from the extreme enthusiasm that sometimes attaches to new gadgets."[13] Although viewing has gone up—from between four and five hours a day in 1960 to just over six hours in 1977—it seems that Americans are watching more but enjoying it less.

In fact, criticism of television the entertainer has been much sharper and more organized than criticism of television the informer.

A Case History: Family Viewing Time

Unlike the print media, the broadcast media *must* fulfill certain social responsibilities. Because the physical limitations of the broadcast spectrum restrict the number of broadcasters—there is not spectrum space for everyone to be a broadcaster—Congress has declared the air waves to be a public resource. Broadcasters are licensed as trustees for the public and must program "in the public interest, convenience and necessity" or risk losing their license. The 1927 Radio Act established a commission, which became the Federal Communications Commission (FCC) with the passage of the 1934 Federal Communications Act, to oversee the broadcasting industry.

Few institutions outside of government, however, have been as persistently criticized as television. Public criticism has concentrated particularly on sex and violence in programing. The concern has been that because Americans, especially children, spend so much time watching television, and because so much of what they watch contains violent action or sexual suggestion, they will learn and imitate violent or antisocial behavior, become more tolerant of violence, become more fearful as they identify with the victims of televised violence, or become morally corrupt.

VIOLENCE ON TELEVISION AND IN REAL LIFE

In October 1973 Boston ghetto teenagers forced a woman to pour gasoline over herself, then burned her to death. Boston police pointed out that her death resembled a scene in *Fuzz,* a movie that had been broadcast on ABC two nights before. In March 1973 *The Marcus-Nelson Murders,* a television movie, showed the stabbing deaths of two women. Two weeks later a 17-year-old Atlanta boy admitted killing a young woman in the same way as depicted in the movie, which he had memorized in precise detail.

These horrific examples of imitative violence are exceptional. But they are used by those who argue there is a causal relationship between media violence and violence in society to dramatize statistics like these: It has been estimated that the average American child will witness 1300 video murders per year between ages 5 and 15. In the mid-1970s nearly 60 percent of prime-time programing was devoted to violence-oriented shows. Milton S. Eisenhower, chairman of the National Commission on the Causes and Prevention of Violence that reported to President Nixon in 1970, has commented: "From about 1900 to 1960 the rate of violent crime per 100,000 population was downward, which tends to diminish the argument that we have always been a violent people and always will be. But in the 1960s it began to go up sharply. We went haywire. The rate of violent crime doubled."[14] Few thoughtful people blamed this dramatic rise in violent crime exclusively on violent television programing. Research scholars disagree on whether a direct causal relationship exists between television violence and real-life violence. But to many people common sense suggests a connection.

The history of society's response to such statistics, summarized by Douglass Cater and Stephen Strickland in *TV Violence and the Child*,[15] reveals the interaction of the public, the media, and the government, particularly the catalytic role that concerned citizens can play. The media will respond to citizen pressure, but the response is limited by majority tastes. The media will respond to government pressure, although that response is complicated by the existence of the First Amendment.

Soon after television took off as a mass medium in the early 1950s, parents and educators objected so vociferously to violent programing that Senator Estes Kefauver, chairman of the Subcommittee on Juvenile Delinquency, conducted an investigation in 1954. The Kefauver subcommittee concluded that violent programing in large doses was potentially harmful to young viewers. The television industry promised to do something about the situation. Again pressured by parents dissatisfied with the industry's response, the Senate Subcommittee on Juvenile Delinquency surveyed program content in 1961 and 1964. The subcommittee reported "that the extent to which violence and related activities are depicted on television . . . remains greater than it was a decade ago."

The alarm over urban riots, campus unrest, and assassinations in the 1960s prompted President Lyndon Johnson to appoint the National Commission on the Causes and Prevention of Violence in 1968. The commission reported in 1969:

> We believe it is reasonable to conclude that a constant diet of violent behavior on television has an adverse effect on human character and attitudes. Violence on television encourages violent forms of behavior, and fosters moral and social values about violence in daily life which are unacceptable in a civilized society.

The commission criticized the unfulfilled promises of the television industry. More important, it added:

> The public has tremendous powers to bring about changes in mass media content that are held by no governmental agency. The source of the public's power derives directly from the fact that modern mass media organizations are economic in nature and orientation and are directly dependent upon the public their economic welfare.[16]

Realizing that the commission would not be able to investigate the causal relationship between televised violence and violence in society, Senator John Pastore of Rhode Island, chairman of the Senate Subcommittee on Communications, recommended in 1969 that the Surgeon General appoint a committee of distinguished men and women "from whatever professions and disciplines deemed appropriate" to conduct a study to "establish scientifically insofar as possible what harmful effects, if any, [television] programs have on children."

After three years' work at a cost of $1.8 million, the Surgeon General issued his Scientific Advisory Committee's Report in January 1972. The committee's conclusions were cautious. It found "a preliminary and tentative indication of a causal relation between viewing violence on television and aggressive behavior." Pastore held Senate hearings on the Report's findings, as a result of which the television industry was told that it should take steps to remove "gratuitous violence" from programs children watch.

SEX: A NEW PROBLEM FOR TELEVISION

Until recently sex had not been one of broadcasting's major problems. Sex was there, but it was broadcast late at night or it was suggestive rather than explicit. Most evident in advertising (it seemed that every product from toothpaste to floor wax would improve the viewer's love life), sex was kept out of prime-time programing. On television Elvis Presley's hips were edited from view, and married couples slept in separate beds.

In 1973 there was a flurry of concern over "topless radio," afternoon call-in talk shows that traded in titillation. But broadcasting—particularly television—has been relatively restrained, rarely coming close to the boundaries of obscenity defined by the U.S. Supreme Court.

Its restraint has been a form of self-regulation, a recognition by broadcasters that they are guests in the consumer's home, that they operate media to which children have easy access unaided by an adult, that it doesn't pay to offend the customer. The President's Commission on Obscenity and Pornography even exempted broadcasting from its model statute to protect young people because, it said in its 1970 report, "Industry self-regulation in the past has resulted in little need for governmental intervention." The President's Commission left the matter to the FCC to deal with if times and broadcasting were to change.[17]

Times have changed. Broadcasting is responsive to the marketplace, and in the marketplace more and more interest in sexual themes appeared.

The trend in movies toward greater nudity and frankness presented problems for network censors trying to sanitize films like *M*A*S*H* (in which Army surgeons in the Korean War spend as much time in sexual as in medical endeavors) or *Klute* (which told the story of a call girl threatened by a sadistic murderer).

In October 1974 *Broadcasting* reported that such movies were drawing some of the biggest audiences of the fall season and that "[s]ponsors and affiliated stations [had] been almost surprisingly tolerant of this season's wave of sexuality. . . ." One of the exceptions to the tolerance, although not an exception to the high audience ratings, was an NBC made-for-TV movie, *Born Innocent.* In the film a 14-year-old girl is committed to a reformatory and there violated with a broom handle by a group of other girls. This *sex and* violence was too much for some—at least when shown in the 8 p.m. Eastern Time slot, which translates to 7 p.m. in the Central and Mountain zones (times when many children in the nation are still watching television). An NBC official admitted that the early start "caused a certain amount of the adverse reaction we got to that show."[18] (NBC was later sued for $11 million after two young girls were attacked in the manner depicted in *Born Innocent* three days after the movie was aired.)

THE FCC AND THE NETWORKS REACT

The public was putting pressure on Congress and the FCC. The FCC reported that the number of complaints it received about violent or sexually oriented programs rose from 2000 in 1972 to almost 25,000 in 1974, although many of the latter appeared to be produced by organized campaigns.

The people upset by sexual content were not necessarily the same ones upset by violence. In an FCC public meeting held in Chicago in October 1974, a young man from downstate Illinois asked why the FCC could not rid the airwaves of the likes of *The Last Picture Show,* a movie about growing up in a small Texas town that he found offensive because it included a teenager's affair with the high school coach's wife. The young man preferred John Wayne movies. For others it is the John Wayne western and war movies or the Clint Eastwood and Charles Bronson violence extravaganzas that are upsetting.

Conscious of public pressure, Congress pressured the FCC. During its 1974 budget review of the agency, Senate and House appropriations committees demanded a report from the FCC by the end of 1974 on what it was doing to reduce the amount of sex and violence on the airwaves.

It then appeared to many that FCC Chairman Richard Wiley put the pressure on the broadcasters, calling them to account in a private meeting in November 1974. Because of the FCC's life-or-death power over broadcast licenses, some critics charged that even meeting in private signaled indirect, if not direct coercion.

Wiley said, "No," there was no pressure. He said that he had met with the networks and with officials of the National Association of Broadcasters

(NAB) to *learn* what the broadcasters were planning. Wiley credited then CBS President Arthur Taylor with originating the family viewing period idea.

In the report delivered to Congress in February 1975, Wiley said that broadcasters rather than government should protect children from undue sex and violence on television, because

> The adoption of rules [by the FCC] might involve the government too deeply in programing content, raising serious constitutional questions, and judgments concerning the suitability of particular types of programs for children are highly subjective.[19]

It was clear, however, that the FCC felt broadcasters should be concerned to limit sexual or violent material that would be inappropriate for children even though such material might not be illegal.

There was some dispute over what pressure had been exerted and by whom, but after the meeting with Wiley, each network developed guidelines for its programing. They differed in details, but all contained a provision limiting the first hour of network entertainment programing in prime time to material that would be suitable for family viewing. In April 1975 the television board of NAB voted to adopt family viewing standards for inclusion in the NAB television code. Programs "inappropriate for viewing by a family audience" were excluded not only from the first network hour of prime time but from the immediately preceding hour as well (that is, from 7 to 9 p.m., Eastern time). Warnings were to be used when programs contained "material that might be disturbing to significant segments of the audience." The family viewing standards went into effect for the 1975–1976 television season. They did not apply to broadcasters who were not members of the NAB.

That was not the end of the battle, however. To protect their First Amendment and their financial interests, a group of writers, directors, and producers (the Writers Guild of America) and Norman Lear's Tandem Productions (home of "All in the Family") sued the television networks, the NAB, and the FCC. The complainants sought to eliminate Family Viewing Time, which they referred to as the "prime-time censorship rule," on the grounds, among others, that the requirement violated the First Amendment, that the FCC's participation in its genesis constituted unconstitutional government intrusion in television programing, that the FCC had violated the federal Administrative Procedure Act by imposing a new industry policy without giving the public the opportunity to participate in the regulatory process. In addition, Tandem sought compensation for the financial consequences allegedly caused by CBS's decision to move "All in the Family" out of Family Viewing Time.

The case (*Writers Guild of America et al. v. FCC et al.*) is a collection of ironies. The defendants—the NAB, the networks, *and* the FCC—were strange bedfellows. Federal District Court Judge Warren Ferguson ruled against them *all* with a strikingly strong affirmation of broadcasters' First Amendment rights. Ferguson held that although broadcasters have a *responsibility* to program in the public interest, they have a *right* to exercise their judgment without government pressure. Family Viewing Time, in and of itself, was not unconstitutional, but the way in which it was instituted was unlawful. To bow to government pressure was an abdication of broadcasters' rights and a denial of the First Amendment rights of the public and the writers, producers, and directors. The networks found themselves in the curious position of appealing a decision that encouraged their independence.[20]

Although much of the pressure against sex and violence on the air has come directly or indirectly from the public, two major citizens' groups, the National Citizens Committee for Broadcasting (NCCB) and Action for Children's Television (ACT), supported the Writers Guild and Tandem's challenge of Family Viewing Time. Particularly offensive to these citizens' groups was the exclusion of the public from the development of a solution to the violence problem. (As debate over television programing continued, public attention was focused predominantly, although not exclusively, on violence. Sex took a back seat.)

NCCB encouraged public participation by providing lists of most and least violent programs and lists of the sponsors of most and least violent programs. Nicholas Johnson, NCCB chairman and former FCC commissioner, explained NCCB's stand:

> While the First Amendment should guarantee broadcasters the right to choose and disseminate programs in a free marketplace, it does not give them the right to conduct their business and their decision-making processes behind closed doors with arrogant disregard for the tastes, needs, concerns of an informed public. Our Violence Project allows the public to interact with broadcasters and advertisers from a position of strength, knowledge, and conviction.[21]

And, indeed, that interaction did occur. In November 1976 the National Parent-Teachers Association launched an antitelevision violence program that was to include research, the monitoring and evaluation of programs, local or national boycotts of programs or products advertised during violent programs, a national letter-writing campaign, seminars, public hearings, and visits to local stations, networks, sponsors, and legislators.

In the summer of 1976, the American Medical Association (AMA) house of delegates called "TV's massive daily diet of symbolic violence and crime" an environmental hazard that should be declared "a risk factor threatening the health and welfare of young Americans." The AMA called on physicians and their patients actively to oppose violent programing and offered suggestions for research and education. The AMA provided funds for NCCB's continuing research on violent programing and questioned major advertisers about their sponsorship of such programing.

A group of more than 150 churches owning stock in various corporations won promises from some and were encouraging others not to place advertising in programs with "excessive or gratuitous violence." Although the church group did not own controlling interest in any corporation, its intention to introduce the violence issue in stockholders' meetings did get the attention of corporate officials.

Advertisers were asking themselves whether violent programing was a hospitable context for selling products and services. In March 1977 the American Association of Advertising Agencies joined in the growing chorus of public concern about the impact of violence on society and recommended that member agencies "examine the wisdom of placement of commercials in television programs which emphasize violence."

Although in the early months of 1977 Congress held hearings on television sex and violence, most of the pressure being exerted by private and governmental groups was directed toward encouraging self-regulation. All the activity seemed almost a national consciousness-raising seminar for broadcasters. The volume and repetition of public criticisms at least had an impact on broadcaster rhetoric. There were promises that change was already underway. Alfred R. Schneider, vice president of ABC Inc., told an advertising workshop:

> We are not about to ban violence from the airwaves totally. At the same time we are not about to permit the portrayal of violence for the sake of violence itself, or as a device to titillate the viewers, to shock, or to sensationalize a story line. We will not permit writers who have written themselves into a corner to extricate themselves quickly with a little bloodshed. We will require that when violence is portrayed, it will be responsibly portrayed to the extent to which its consequences are adequately depicted in depth. . . .[22]

Opinion will differ on whether current television fare represents an adequate response to 20 years of citizen pressure to reduce sex and violence in television programing. Whether or not broadcasters live up to the promises made in the spring and summer of 1977, the Family Viewing Time case history illustrates that citizens can get the attention of large institutions such as the FCC, the Congress, and the television networks. Typically, however, issues such as sex and violence generate crosscurrents of opinion, and fragment the pressure on these institutions. And in large measure it is the size and intensity of support citizens' groups can mobilize that influence representative government and commercial industries operating in a marketplace economy. The case history illustrates, too, the agonizing slowness of the democratic process. And it illustrates that in the United States, almost any governmental response to citizens' demand for action against the media is complicated by the First Amendment.

It also illustrates how solutions to one problem can generate new problems. The encouragement of advertiser influence on program content was especially troubling. General Motors backed out of sponsoring a two-part Easter week (1977) telecast on the life of Christ, "Jesus of Nazareth," because of pressure from fundamentalist religious groups. General Motors, one of the companies identified with violent programing by NCCB, had perhaps lost its enthusiasm for controversial programing. NBC did find another sponsor, and the program was broadcast as scheduled.

When Greyhound Corporation announced that it would not only not buy commercials in programs with excessive violence but also would not buy commercials in ones that treated religious, political, social, or other subjects in a controversial manner, NCCB chairman Nicholas Johnson suggested the FCC should prohibit *any* advertising by a corporation that followed so sweeping a policy. He pointed out that broadcasters were *required* by the FCC's Fairness Doctrine to program controversial issues and warned that policies like Greyhound's could undermine broadcasters' enthusiasm for carrying out their Fairness Doctrine responsibilities.[23]

It seems highly unlikely that such prohibition by the FCC would be constitutional, but Johnson did focus on a real concern. By educating advertisers to their power to discourage violent programing, did citizens' groups remind advertisers of their power to discourage other types of programs? Could pressure from groups of various persuasions discourage anything but pap?

PROGRAMING AND AUDIENCE PREFERENCES

Finally, and perhaps most significantly, the Family Viewing Time case history reveals much about ourselves and our use of the mass media. For several years George Gerbner of the University of Pennsylvania has been analyzing the amount of violence on television. His "Violence Profile No. 7," issued in April 1976, showed that the networks, especially CBS, did reduce violence during the Family Viewing Time. But the networks appeared to have redistributed violence, taking it out of the Family Viewing Time and inserting it elsewhere. Violence on weekend children's programs increased sharply, with the result that the overall level of violence remained about the same in fall 1975 as in previous years. But it rose in 1976, to the highest level in all the years that Gerbner had compiled his "Violence Profile." Gerbner's report for 1976 showed that each network had increased violent content and the level of violence had risen most sharply in Family Viewing Time. According to the report, the rate of violent episodes increased from 8.1 per hour in 1975 to 9.5 in 1976; the number of killings dropped slightly.

Gerbner's definition of violence has been controversial.* Broadcasters criticize him for defining violence too broadly, for failing to distinguish between violence in a humorous or fantasy context and violence in a dramatic or socially realistic context. The problem of definition continues to be vexing. Agreement among broadcasters, scholars, politicians, and the public as to what precisely constitutes violence—Popeye bashing Brutus as well as thugs beating a victim on a police show?—is unlikely. But however

---

*Gerbner defined a violent action as: an overt expression of physical force (with or without weapon) against one's self or other; a compelling action against one's will on pain of being hurt or killed, and/or an actual hurting or killing. An action to be considered violent must be plausible and credible and must include human or human-like characters. It may be an intentional or accidental action, humorous or serious or a combination of both as long as the previous conditions are satisfied.

violence was defined, the increasingly organized opinion was that there was too much of it.

Why, in the face of citizen, Congressional, and government agency pressure, did the networks persist in including so much violence in television programing? To Robert D. Wood, former president of CBS Television, "It's quite obvious that if everybody just hated police shows and everybody said there's too much violence, and that was demonstrated by the people who research and report on television, like Nielsen, those shows probably wouldn't be on the air."

"I wonder," Wood asks, "how come nobody acknowledges the characteristics, the behaviors, the viewing patterns and the preference of the audience. Maybe somebody ought to do a critique of the audience."

However much we may discount a degree of self-serving rhetoric in his comments, Wood makes a pertinent point. All the mass media, not only television, to a great extent respond to and reflect their perception of majority wishes. A continuing refrain in the Family Viewing Time suit was the networks' concern to act in concert so as not to put themselves at a competitive disadvantage. To be responsible alone did appear to be self-inflicted jeopardy. In essence, the networks seemed to be saying that if one of us can make money on people's interest in sex and violence, all of us should have the chance to try.

New Media and the Future

Frustrated with the present media of communications, many Americans look to the new electronic media. More than simple faith in new technology is at work. There is rich promise in the extraordinary capabilities of cable television and computer technologies. Kas Kalba, a lecturer at Harvard and president of a communications consulting firm, summarizes the capabilities in this way:

> . . . tomorrow's household will contain a facsimile copier to capture the day's news; a remote learning and shopping terminal; a videotape recorder for delayed playback of entertainment and cultural programing; special terminals to give access to computational services, bank accounts and office files; a wall-size TV screen for viewing abstract art or baseball games; monitoring systems that will prevent burglaries and heart attacks; a television camera for two-way video conferences. . . .[24]

Through these means viewers can become more selective about when or what they watch. Programers can become more selective about whom they reach. The viewer will also be able to talk back to the source of the information or programs. Finally, through data banks, viewer and programer will have access to vastly increased storage capability. What is promised, then, is not only more, but more individualized information and programing, available at the viewer's convenience and transmitted much more quickly.

Every new medium of communications has been heralded with hope and argument that *this* one will bring about the millenium, will inform and educate with more depth and insight, will entertain with most taste and creativity, will better reflect the diversity of cultures and views of America, so producing wiser, more cultivated citizens and a more perfect democracy. The same hopes attended the advent of film as a mass medium at the turn of the century, attended radio in the 1920s and television in the 1940s, as now attend the new medium of cable television tied to computer technology.

Whether media technologies and institutions and the people who control them respond to the best within us depends to a great extent on our understanding of the media's evolution, of the philosophies and legal principles that guide the ethics and performance of media professionals, and of the economics of their operations, which often work in tension with ideals. The rest of this book is designed to help provide that understanding and to correct the sometimes unrealistic expectations of these large institutions' power to resolve the agonizing problems of a troubled society.

Notes

1. Timothy Crouse, *The Boys on the Bus: Riding with the Campaign Press Corps* (New York: Ballantine, 1972), p. 102.
2. Ben H. Bagdikian, *The Information Machines: Their Impact on Men and the Media* (New York: Harper & Row, 1971), pp. xii–xiii.
3. Jules Witcover, "Where Washington reporting failed," *Columbia Journalism Review,* Winter 1970–1971, p. 9.
4. Seymour M. Hersh, "The Story Everyone Ignored," in Alfred Balk and James Boylan (eds.), *Our Troubled Press: Ten Years of the Columbia Journalism Review* (Boston: Little, Brown, 1971), p. 123.
5. James McCartney, "The Washington 'Post' and Watergate: How Two Davids Slew Goliath," *Columbia Journalism Review,* July/August 1973, pp. 8–9.
6. The text of Spiro Agnew's speech on November 13, 1969, to the Midwest Regional Republican Committee in Des Moines, Iowa, can be found in a number of places including Francis and Ludmila Voelker (eds.), *Mass Media: Forces In Our Society* (New York: Harcourt, 1972), pp. 263–269.
7. Willard Grosvenor Bleyer, *Main Currents in the History of American Journalism* (Boston: Houghton Mifflin, 1927), p. 82.
8. Bleyer, pp. 287–288.
9. Fred W. Friendly, *Due to Circumstances Beyond Our Control* (New York: Vintage, 1967), p. xii.
10. *Broadcasting,* August 13, 1973, p. 15.
11. *Broadcasting,* April 26, 1976, p. 41.
12. *Broadcasting,* June 6, 1977, p. 34.
13. "How America Sees Television," interview of Robert Bower in *TV Guide,* July 14, 1973. The full results of the surveys were published in Gary A. Steiner, *The People Look At Television* (New York: Knopf, 1963), and Robert T. Bower, *Television and the Public* (New York: Holt, Rinehart, and Winston, 1973).

14. Quoted in syndicated article by Richard Starnes, Bloomington-Bedford, Indiana, *Sunday Herald-Times,* June 1, 1975.
15. Douglass Cater and Stephen Strickland, *TV Violence and the Child* (New York: Russell Sage Foundation, 1975).
16. Commission quotes reported in Cater and Strickland, p. 13.
17. *The Report of the Commission on Obscenity and Pornography* (New York: Bantam, 1970), p. 65.
18. *Broadcasting,* October 14, 1974, pp. 32–33.
19. *Broadcasting,* February 24, 1975, p. 25.
20. *Writers Guild of America, et al. v. FCC et al.,* 38 RR2d 1409 [CD Calif., 1976]. NBC is appealing only that portion of the opinion granting Tandem the opportunity to recover damages.
21. *Media Watch* (newsletter of the National Citizens Committee for Broadcasting), December 1976, p. 4.
22. *Broadcasting,* February 7, 1977, p. 69.
23. Nicholas Johnson, "Beyond Violence," *access,* June 1977, p. 8.
24. Kas Kalba, "The Electronic Community: A New Environment for Television Viewers and Critics," in *Television as a Social Force: New Approaches to TV Criticism* (New York: Praeger, 1975), p. 142.

2

The Media Environment

To say that any technology or extension of man creates a new environment is a much better way of saying that the medium is the message.

MARSHALL MCLUHAN

Television is another kind of car, a windshield on the world. We climb inside it, drive it, and it drives us, and we all go in the same direction, see the same thing.

JOHN LEONARD

In 1948 Harold Lasswell, a political scientist and pioneer in the study of communications, described the act of communication by breaking down the process into a series of questions:

Who
Says What
In Which Channel
To Whom
With What Effect?[1]

Early communication theorists devised models that reflected this one-directional description of the act, diagraming it along these lines:

source → message → channel → receiver

Working here was both public and scholarly concern about the persuasive power of Nazi, Fascist, and Communist propaganda. The perception that the act of communication was something that someone did to someone else profoundly influenced our way of thinking about communication. Research concentrated on theories of persuasion.

As the mass media, and particularly television, pervaded our lives, concern intensified that the messages of the media were irresistible, that they invaded and conquered our defenseless minds and shaped our behavior. For many people that concern persists. But research has long shown that the act of communication is not one-way, nor is it simple. Rather it is a complex relationship, an act of sharing to which, as Wilbur Schramm has written, "each participant brings a well-filled life space, funded and stored experience, against which he interprets the signals that come to him and decides how to respond to them."[2]

FEEDBACK AND NOISE

The idea of a passive audience has been replaced in communication theory "by the concept of a highly active, highly selective audience, manipulating rather than being manipulated by a message—a full partner in the communication process."[3] Receivers talk back—most directly in face-to-face communication situations, by smiling, frowning, or yawning as well as by speaking. They talk back much less directly to the mass media, by buying certain publications and not others and by turning to certain channels rather than others. A small minority of the audience does talk back directly to the media, by writing and calling editors and station managers. By these and other means people inform one another and the mass media whether or not messages are getting through and are being understood, whether or not people are interested or bored, delighted or offended. Communication scholars call these responses "feedback," and as competition among the media has intensified and the public has become more selective, media owners have actively solicited feedback by investing increasing amounts of time and money in audience research.

Such research is concerned not only with discovering who and how many are reading, listening to, and watching what. Like any communicator, the media want to know what difficulties may be interfering with the reception of their messages. Communication scholars call these difficulties "noise," a term embracing actual noise—children yelling, dogs barking, brakes screeching—and a variety of distractions—a mumbling actor, an ungrammatical writer, a misleading headline, an irritating commercial.

Awareness of the communication act as one of sharing has produced complex models of the process. Schramm's is one of the more concise. He pictures "A" communicating a message to "B" in this way (in Schramm and Roberts, 1971):[4]

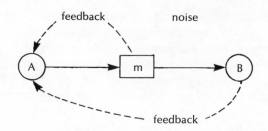

Because large organizations and large audiences are involved, mass communication is more complicated than interpersonal communication. Some of the messages of the media reach audiences through the opinion leaders of individuals or groups by a process of retransmission that has been called the "two-step or multi-step flow."[5] Typically, noise is greater and feedback weaker in the mass communication than in the interpersonal situation. But the essential process of communication is similar. Moreover, mass media communication and interpersonal communication tend to function concurrently, one affecting the other.

"People come to the media, as to other messages," Schramm observes, "seeking what they want, not what the media intend them to have."[6] People do not take everything the media offer. As Steven Chaffee, a communications scholar, has pointed out, "There is far more information to be found in the news columns and broadcasts of the media than in the minds of the audience."[7] Because the act of communication involves individual persons—two or more people conversing, a journalist informing or entertaining a reader, listener, or viewer—generalizations about the media's power or effects tend to be inconclusive, heavily qualified, or contradictory. We can document with some certainty the number of newspapers, magazines, radio, and television stations, and cable systems in existence at a particular time; we can calculate with less certainty the size and nature of the media's audiences; we can estimate the amount of time the mythical "average" American spends with each medium, and we can try empirically and experimentally to measure the effects of these "facts" on society, on particular groups, and on individuals. But no theory of communication, no study of communication or media effects, is likely to be able to account for the full range of individual human differences.

Although individual scholars and theorists may speak with assurance, you should expect inconclusiveness and possibly contradiction in discussion of the theories, speculations, and research findings on communication and society and on the media's effects on society. One way to build a tolerance for frustration in this field is to regard the confusion as a measure of the triumph of human individuality over all efforts to generalize convincingly about human beings in the mass. Tolerance is valuable, because scholars have produced provocative insights and increased our understanding of the complex act of communication.

Communication(s)

The terms *communication* and *communications* need clarification. One
way of distinguishing them is this: *Communication* is the process of communicating, while *communications* is the technical means used to carry out the
process, although the term can also be used to describe the messages
conveyed.

Communication, then, is a central fact of human existence and social
process. It is all the ways by which one person influences another and is
influenced in return. The ways may be direct and personal, as when a friend
talks to a friend, or indirect and impersonal, as when a tom-tom or a
television station carries the message. Communication is the carrier of the
social process; it makes interaction within humankind possible and enables
people to be social beings. It includes not only verbal communication, but
also nonverbal communication, what some have called body language—
the raised fist, the raised eyebrow, the frown that contradicts the pleasant
greeting.

The plural communications is usefully given a much narrower meaning.
It embraces all the technical means of indirect or "mediated" communication, from tribal drums, smoke signals, and stone tablets to telegraphy,
printing, broadcasting, and satellites.

The distinction between the two words has real historical and sociological importance, Edward Sapir pointed out some years ago, because all
mankind is blessed with the primary processes of communication, but only
relatively advanced civilizations have developed sophisticated secondary
techniques.[8]

All secondary techniques have two things in common. First, even though
they can be as physically different as a painting and television, or a book and
a satellite, their main task is to extend communication by language or
gesture to situations in which face-to-face exchange is impossible. Second,
they do not communicate by themselves; they can do so only when people
use them.

By creating, improving, and multiplying these technical means, people
have virtually freed the communication process from the limitations of time
and space. We can communicate not only with our contemporaries but with
unborn generations. We can quickly contact others in distant places. Moreover, the communications system has made it possible for acculturation to
take place over great distances in parts of the world physically remote from
one another, so that societies take on similarities not shared by the peoples
of regions adjoining them. Geographical contiguity has lost much, though
not all, of its importance. Today, the "scientific community," which has no
clear-cut location on the map, shares common values, attitudes, and beliefs.
In general, so does the "democratic world" or the "Christian world" or the
"socialist" world or the "youth culture" and so on.

The mass media are technical extensions of speech and gesture—much

as the shovel and pile driver are technical extensions of the human arm—
which, just by existing, have altered the fundamental structure of society.
People often misread the role of the mass media in their lives. Some, for
instance, see the media as a kind of accidental by-product of technology that
has been taken over by hucksters, propagandists, and manipulators. That
view has some truth in it, but neglects the objective relationships between
the mass media and society, relationships that seem to exist quite apart from
the motives and interests of owners, managers, editors, writers, and others.

Communication by Symbols

Traditionally philosophers have set people apart from other animals on the
basis of our powers of reason. But another faculty distinguishes us from
other animals—our ability to communicate by symbols. We are the only
creatures who react not only to the real physical environment but also to a
symbolic environment of our own making. A hungry dog reacts to food by
eating it. People may react in the same way, but we may also have more
complicated reactions, which depend on symbolic considerations. We may
avoid some foods for fear of offending the deity; we may eat other foods for
their reputed curative powers; we may even eat some foods, such as caviar,
primarily for status.

What all this means is that people have an environment far different
from that of other creatures. Most creatures live largely in physical environments. They receive stimuli; they respond to them. They have little or no
sense of past or future; as Kenneth Boulding, an economist who has written
about communication, reminds us, a dog has no conscious idea that there
were dogs on earth before it arrived and that there will be dogs here after it
has gone. But people, by creating a symbolic world, have given reality a
dimension known only to the human species. Between the mere stimulus
and response of other creatures, we have erected a symbolic system that
transforms the whole of human life and sets it apart from the life of all other
animals. This distinctive mark of human life is not necessarily related to our
rationality (or to our irrationality, for that matter). It is a remarkable achievement that has taken us out of a merely physical universe and put us into a
symbolic universe of language, art, and myth.

People do not confront reality firsthand. Instead of always dealing with
things themselves, as other animals do, we develop *ideas* about things. We
so envelop ourselves in linguistic forms, in artistic images, in mythical
symbols, or in religious rites that we cannot see or know anything except
through our symbolic system. As the Stoic philosopher Epictetus said,
"What disturbs and alarms man are not the things, but his opinions and
fancies about the things." A modern political strategist made a similar point
while trying to develop a plan for winning a Presidential election: ". . .
[W]hat we have to deal with now is not the facts of history, but an image of

history. The history we have to be concerned with is not what happened, but what's remembered, which may be quite different. Or, to put it another way, the historical untruth may be a political reality."[9]

Reality, of course, contains all the things that reach us through our senses; but the framework and structure of reality are not something that we can touch or directly see. They are intellectual, and we can perceive them only indirectly through symbols. Sapir and others have argued our perceptions are conditioned by language. Sapir wrote:

> Human beings . . . are very much at the mercy of the particular language which has become the medium of expression for their society. It is quite an illusion to imagine that one adjusts to reality essentially without the use of language and that language is merely an incidental means of solving specific problems of communication or reflection. The fact of the matter is that the "real world" is to a large extent unconsciously built up on the language habits of the group. . . . We see and hear and otherwise experience very largely as we do because the language habits of our community predispose certain choices of interpretation.[10]

To understand Sapir's point fully one only needs to reflect on how such words as "ripoff," "uptight," "withit," *"chutzpah,"* "psychedelic," "honky," and "freak out" have changed our world view.

Animals react to outside stimuli either directly or not at all. People, on the other hand, respond largely in a cerebral way, producing images, notions, figments of all sorts, as symbols for ideas about things. A cat may cower under a porch during a thunderstorm; only a human being would interpret the storm as a sign of a god's wrath. For us as symbol makers, then, the world is mainly a pseudo-world, a web of symbols, of our own making.

Yet this pseudo-world is not sheer fantasy. Mathematics, language, and the formula $E = mc^2$ are examples of our rational and practical efforts to deal with experience. They are attempts to organize our sensations and to build up around them symbolic systems that give meaning to our existence.

MASS MEDIA AND THE PSEUDO-ENVIRONMENT

Walter Lippmann's *Public Opinion,* although first published in 1922, is still one of the most provocative and insightful books ever written on human communication. In it Lippmann painted a clear portrait of the pseudo-environment. "For the real environment," Lippmann said, "is altogether too big, too complex, and too fleeting for direct acquaintance. We are not equipped to deal with so much subtlety, so much variety, so many permutations and combinations. And although we have to act in that environment, we have to reconstruct it on a simpler model before we can manage with it."[11]

In their heads people make for themselves a more or less trustworthy picture of the world outside. Thus they behave not on the basis of direct and certain knowledge of the real world but on pictures they have made or derived from others. What people do depends on those pictures in their heads.

Public Opinion begins with the matter-of-fact power that informs all of Lippmann's writing:

> There is an island in the ocean where in 1914 a few Englishmen, Frenchmen, and Germans lived. No cable reaches the island, and the British mail steamer comes but once in sixty days. In September it had not yet come, and the islanders were still talking about the latest newspaper which told about the approaching trial of Madame Caillaux for the shooting of Gaston Calmette. It was, therefore, with more than usual eagerness that the whole colony assembled on the quay on a day in mid-September to hear from the captain what the verdict had been. They learned that for over six weeks now those of them who were English and those of them who were French had been fighting in behalf of the sanctity of treaties against those of them who were Germans. For six strange weeks they had acted as if they were friends, when in fact they were enemies.[12]

Lippmann goes on to show how little the world as it really is conforms to the picture of the world that we carry in our heads. He defines our stereotypes:

> For the most part we do not first see, and then define, we define first and then see. In the great blooming, buzzing confusion of the outer world we pick out what our culture has already defined for us, and we tend to perceive that which we have picked out in the form stereotyped for us by our culture. . . . That is why the accounts of returning travellers are often an interesting tale of what the traveller carried abroad with him on his trip. If he carried chiefly his appetite, a zeal for tiled bathrooms, a conviction that the Pullman car is the acme of human comfort, and a belief that it is proper to tip waiters, taxicab drivers, and barbers, but under no circumstances station agents and ushers, then his odyssey will be replete with good meals and bad meals, bathing adventures, compartment-train escapades, and voracious demands for money.[13]

This internal picture-making process inevitably colors the messages that people get from the world outside. People use stored-up images, preconceptions, prejudices, motivations, and interests to interpret the messages, fill them out, and in turn direct the play of attention and the vision itself. These interpretations and expansions become patterns, or stereotypes. And these stereotypes, Lippmann wrote, determine human action. Originally a stereotype was the plate made by taking a mold of a printing surface and casting type metal from it. According to Lippmann the minds of people are also poured into molds—their pictures of the world outside. The minds then reproduce ideas and react to stimuli according to the patterns of the molds.

Lippmann was writing only of the relationship between public opinion and newspapers. However, his concept can profitably be extended to all mass media. As a major source of information, the media provide people with messages from the outside world with which they have no direct experience. People use these messages to form mental pictures of the world of public affairs. The mass media, then, can be viewed as creating a kind of pseudo-environment between people and the objective "real" world, enveloping us in a kind of ersatz reality.

Historian Daniel Boorstin has suggested a refinement of the idea of the pseudo-environment. In *The Image* he is concerned chiefly with what he calls "pseudo-events." He characterizes the pseudo-event as follows:

> It is not spontaneous, but comes about because someone has planned, planted, or incited it. Typically, it is not a train wreck or an earthquake, but an interview.
>
> It is planted primarily (not always exclusively) for the immediate purpose of being reported or reproduced. . . . Its occurrence is arranged for the convenience of the reporting or reproducing media. Its success is measured by how widely it is reported.
>
> Its relation to the underlying reality . . . is ambiguous.
>
> Usually it is intended to be a self-fulfilling prophecy.[14]

That is, to say that something is true, or to act as if it were, leads to the general belief that it is true.

Although pseudo-events invade virtually all aspects of our lives, nowhere are they more evident than in politics. Modern communications technology has put new tools at the disposal of politicians, but they have long attempted to manipulate our perceptions of events to their greater benefit. Citizens learning to maximize their impact on the political process

A master of psuedo-events, Senator Joseph McCarthy could multiply headlines by calling a morning press conference to announce an afternoon press conference. (CBS photo)

also learn to plan and to plant information. A Congressman schedules a press conference to announce support of a tax reform measure to suit the deadline of *The New York Times*. A citizens' group alerts the local television station that its members will be picketing city hall. The media don't always appear as commanded, but some groups and individuals are skillful or charismatic enough to be almost irresistible. Senator Joseph McCarthy in the Cold War era could multiply headlines by calling a morning press conference to announce an afternoon press conference.[15]

In any event, those with political ambitions rarely leave their fate to the natural course of events.

Immediately after the 1972 Presidential election, aides sent then Georgia Governor Jimmy Carter a lengthy memorandum that *Newsweek* described as laying out a "blueprint for winning the 1976 Democratic nomination" for the Presidency.

The memo, written by Hamilton Jordan, warned that Carter "will . . . have to convince press, public and politicians that he knows how to run a government," and it organized his image year by year. In 1973 he was to promote his accomplishments as governor. In 1974 he was to be portrayed as a leader in the Democratic Party who could revitalize it. In 1975 he would be served up as a "heavyweight thinker, leader in the party who had some ideas for running the country." All this to ensure that by 1976 there would be no doubt that he would be not only a credible Presidential candidate but *the* Democratic Presidential candidate.

Jordan mapped out this strategy for dealing with the press:

It is necessary that we begin immediately to generate favorable stories and comments in the national press. . . . Stories in *The New York Times* and *Washington Post* don't just happen, but have to be carefully planned and planted.

Carter was advised to

compile a list of regional and national political editors and columnists who you know or need to know [*New York Times* columnist Tom Wicker, *Washington Post* publisher Katharine Graham, and some sixteen other major media figures were suggested as specific targets.] You can find ample excuse for contacting them—writing a note complimenting them on an article or column and asking they come to see you when convenient. . . . Like it or not, there exists an Eastern liberal news establishment which has tremendous influence in this country all out of proportion to its actual audience. The views of this small group of opinion-makers and the papers they represent are noted and imitated by other columnists and newspapers throughout the country and the world. Their recognition and acceptance of your candidacy as a viable force with some chance of success could establish you as a serious contender worthy of the financial support of major party contributors. They could have an equally adverse effect, dismissing your effort as being regional or an attempt to secure the second spot on the ticket. . . . Fortunately, a disproportionate number of these opinion-makers are Southerners by birth and tradition and . . . they would be fascinated by the prospect of your candidacy. . . .[16]

In the 1972 Presidential campaign, *Washington Post* reporters Carl Bernstein and Bob Woodward have reported, some staffers at the Nixon White House and the Committee to Re-elect the President mounted a campaign of "dirty tricks" that went beyond the run-of-the-mill pseudo-event.

One of the most damaging "tricks" was a letter that surfaced in William Loeb's Manchester (N.H.) *Union Leader* in the days before the New Hampshire primary. The letter, supposedly sent from Florida, said that Senator Edmund Muskie of Maine, then the front-running Democratic candidate for the Presidency, had condoned the use of the term "Canuck," a slur on Americans of French-Canadian ancestry, of whom there were many eligible to vote in New Hampshire. Loeb published the letter and a front page editorial attack on Muskie on February 24.

On February 25, he published a two-month-old *Newsweek* piece that was unflattering to Muskie's wife, Jane.

The next morning Muskie, standing on a flatbed truck outside the *Union Leader* offices with snow falling heavily, attacked Loeb. More important, he cried, and television provided a close-up of Muskie's tears for voters in New Hampshire and around the nation. For some candidates it might have been an acceptable reaction, but as Woodward and Bernstein point out in *All the President's Men:*

> It shattered the calm, cool, reasoned image that was basic to Muskie's voter appeal, and focused the last-minute attention of New Hampshire voters on the alleged slur against the French-Canadians who would be a formidable minority of voters in the Democratic primary.[17]

Perhaps in part as a result of this and other political pranks, Richard Nixon faced in the Presidential election the candidate he wanted to face, the one he was most confident he could beat: Senator George McGovern of South Dakota.

This is not to condemn all planned events and planted information. There are other things more important to our political and social lives than earthquakes and train wrecks; and interviews, despite Boorstin's insight into their artificial nature, are a valuable tool for eliciting ideas, attitudes, and information that are central to social organization.

The Functions of a Communication System

In every society, from the most primitive to the most complex, the communication system performs four broad tasks. Harold Lasswell had defined three of these as surveillance of the environment, correlation of the components of society in responding to the environment, and transmission of the social heritage. Wilbur Schramm has used simpler terms: watcher, forum, and teacher. Charles Wright, in developing a sociological perspective on mass communication, added a fourth task: entertainment.

Every society has its watchers who provide other members with information and interpretation of events. They survey the environment and report on the threats and dangers as well as on the good omens and opportunities. A watcher may be the elder in the tribe who complains that the younger generation is showing less and less respect for ritual or the foreign correspondent who reports political tension in the Middle East and interprets its significance or the local newspaper that reports the school board will be discussing new textbooks Tuesday night or the "shopper" that alerts the consumer to this week's grocery bargains.

When a consensus is necessary for dealing with threats or opportunities, society uses its communication system as a forum. Simple societies may reach their consensus from face-to-face discussion, complex industrial ones may rely heavily on the mass media. Information for decision-making may be supplied by government officials, community leaders, reporters, members of the public, or others. The value of one decision over another is argued. Through persuasion or manipulation a society settles on a course of action or inaction. Troubled times may allow no consensus and may cause a breakdown of social organization. On the other hand, no disagreement within a society could lead to stagnation.

The communication system can also serve as a forum for information about the economic system, as a marketplace facilitating the exchange of goods and services and as a forum for decisions about economic policy.

Society uses its communication system as a teacher to pass the social heritage from one generation to the next. As the mass communication system can be compared to the tribal council or the New England town meeting in its function of correlating responses to the environment, so it can be compared to the institutions of home, church, and school in its role as teacher.

A society awash in troubling news, challenged to solve a multitude of seemingly insoluble problems may find entertainment an essential respite, an ingredient in our lives that helps us cope. Although when we think of entertainment we usually think of programs presented for that purpose, one researcher reported recently that two-thirds of the respondents to his survey said that newscasters' jokes "make the news easier to take."[18]

Indeed, the functions of the communication system of a society are often interrelated as in the folk tale that entertains while educating the young to the values of their society. In discussing television, Gary Steiner suggested that entertainment is essential not only because it amuses but also because it provides palatable learning situations. Whether their *purpose* is entertainment or instruction, the entertainment programs the media provide educate us to social roles, social relationships and social values—of course, not all of them are desirable. Most worrisome in a mass communications system is that the distance between the communicator and the audience attenuates any sense of responsibility for what is delivered. In fact, because entertainment programs are often meant only to divert and amuse, the producers of the programs may feel no sense of responsibility for what is *taught*.

The Media and Social Change

Harold Innis, a Canadian economist who became a communication theorist, argued that the technology of communication was central to all other technology and influenced strongly the social organization of a society. He noted a medium-induced myopia: "The significance of a basic medium to its civilization is difficult to appraise since the means of appraisal are influenced by the media, and indeed the fact of appraisal appears to be peculiar to certain types of media. A change in the type of medium implies a change in the type of appraisal and hence makes it difficult for one civilization to understand another."[19]

Innis, breaking out of the myopia of his own civilization, analyzed history in terms of epochs dominated by different media of communication.

Christianity exploited the advantages of parchment for maintaining the old order. The durability of parchment gave the Church a means of preserving a nucleus of ideas over many centuries; the scarcity of parchment limited the guardianship of those ideas to a few and for a long time left the Church relatively free from challenge or dissent. Innis pointed out that the secular state, on the other hand, used cheap paper for disseminating knowledge widely, thus challenging the traditional order and extending control over large areas.

When faced with barbarian invasions and the ambitions of the kings and princes, the Church tried to maintain a monopoly of knowledge, stressing stability and continuity through dependence on a limited body of scriptural writings in Latin. The Church's control of ideas and opinions helped it to defend itself against ideological challenge.

However, Innis theorized, the Church's monopoly over knowledge was gradually destroyed in the competition for people's minds that followed the increased use of paper and the renaissance of classical learning, especially Greek science and philosophy. The invention of printing and increasing supplies of cheap paper supported the Reformation and the growth of vernacular literature, both of which became important in determining the character of the new nation-state.

The industrial revolution and the application of steam power to the printing and paper industries were similarly important. They profoundly influenced the rise to power of the middle class and the emergence of liberal democracies in Western Europe and America. Indeed, contemporary forms of society, democratic or totalitarian, would not be possible without high-speed presses and electronic media for rapid communication with large numbers of people over vast areas.

Whereas Innis saw communication technology as principally affecting social organization and culture, his disciple, Marshall McLuhan, who is also a Canadian, sees its effect on sensory organization and thought as most significant.

McLuhan holds that in the Electric Age, which was first established with the invention of the telegraph, a network of electric circuitry was built that now links the world in a web of instant awareness. In effect, the world has become a tribal village.

McLuhan agrees with Innis that people, when they discovered movable type, did not merely find a new tool for mass-producing communication; they changed their own essence. McLuhan builds on this to suggest that in the age before the alphabet, the ear was dominant in communication— hearing was believing. Then the new medium of the phonetic alphabet and the beginning of reading forced a change to a new sensory balance centered in the eye. The invention of movable type and the vast spread of literacy required that people begin to comprehend in linear, connected fashion, taking one thing after another in slow progression. When the Electric Age annihilated space and time, the new media—especially television, which involves most of the senses simultaneously—took over from print. From such beliefs McLuhan derives his aphorism, "the Medium is the Message," which means simply that society is shaped more by the media through which people communicate than by what they communicate. That is, print itself is more important than anything or everything that has ever been printed. Television is more important than anything or everything shown on television.

McLuhan has filled several books with elaborations of such ideas, which are concerned only in part with the mass media. Indeed, he speaks of "media" as all the "extensions" of people—including automobiles, clothing, clocks, and a disparate collection of other items. He takes his ideas about changing eras to the point of holding that the linear sense that developed in response to movable type is directly responsible for the assembly line and for the Newtonian and Cartesian philosophies of the universe as a mechanism in which it is possible to locate a physical event in time and space. The all-at-once Electric Age, McLuhan argued, would see the triumph of football, in which everything happens at once when a play starts, over baseball, which is a one-thing-at-a-time, linear sport.

One need not accept all McLuhan's scattershot speculations—he calls many of them "probes" rather than theories and serenely refuses to try to substantiate them, saying "I explore, I don't explain"—to consider his central idea provocative. If the medium is not the message, it is quite obviously something more pivotal than a mere tool for multiplying audiences. For example, it is feared that the pervasiveness of television is, indeed, having an effect on sensory organization and thought—to their detriment. There is talk of a "television-conditioned" society. McLuhan has announced that television has ended the literary culture. Other social critics and educators blame a number of institutions, including the school system and almost invariably television. Educators warn that people who cannot write are not equipped to think, and people cannot learn to write unless they read. Thus when young Americans watch television instead of read, educators worry.

Neither McLuhan nor Innis saw all changes in communications technology as social progress. The question that remains is this: If we are alerted to the ways in which changes in media technology change our society, can we alter the outcome?

The Media and Social Control

Some theorists, who are not willing to go as far as Innis and McLuhan in assigning influence to the media, nevertheless consider mass communications an arm of the ruling order of society and a strong agency of social control—at least in the long run. This is a sharp break with libertarian theory, which sees the media as freeing people from the tyranny of ignorance and inherited superstition and as thus enabling them to govern themselves by reason and individual conscience.

Social control through the mass media is so extensive and effective, some observers believe, that it is the chief characteristic and function of the media. For instance, Joseph Klapper described the "engineering of consent"—a term for the process of social control—as the most significant feature of the mass media. Attempts to engineer consent are neither new nor limited to those with sinister motives, of course. One function of communication has always been to engineer consent, which is necessary for a stable society. But never before, according to some social scientists, has there been engineering on such a vast scale, with the mass media working in such unison that there is little counter-engineering. Sociologist C. Wright Mills listed the media of mass communications along with universal compulsory education among the "historically unique instruments of psychic management and manipulation" available to the power elites of contemporary American society. Indeed, Mills saw some of the higher agents of the media as among those power elites. Mills dismissed the media's "apparent variety and competition" as misleading, finding that the media "seem to compete more in terms of variations on a few standardized themes than of clashing issues." He warned in the 1950s: "The freedom to raise issues effectively seems more and more to be confined to those few interests that have ready and continual access to these media."[20]

Critiques of the limited world view of the mass media became more strident in the turmoil of the 1960s. The so-called "underground" press drew its energy in part from the perceptions of sub-cultures and political dissidents that the mass media were part of the establishment and thus incapable of exploring alternatives not advanced by the mainstream of American society. And there are still pressures to win for members of the public a legal right of access to present their views in the established media of mass communications. Advocates of a right of access argue that only such a system would provide alternatives to the narrow vision of the mass media.

MASS MEDIA AS AN ADJUNCT OF THE INDUSTRIAL ORDER

Whether big or little, the mass media in America are businesses; they are oriented to marketing; they are, as George Gerbner has said, "the cultural arm of American industry.'' One must understand this in order to grasp the essential meaning of the media and their relationship to the American social order.

A similar understanding is necessary for analysis of the Soviet communications system. To grasp the essential meaning of the Soviet mass media and their relationship to Communist society, one must first recognize that the Soviet communications system is an arm of the political order, as it is in any authoritarian society.

In the United States the industrial order, which directly and indirectly controls the mass media, is concerned largely with preserving the status quo. It does not wish to encourage revolutionary changes in a social system that provides it with abundant freedom and benefits. It has no more interest in doing so than the ruling political order in an authoritarian society has in furthering dissent. To that end it seeks to intensify and mold certain existing tendencies of the system, to nurture sanctioned values and beliefs, and to sharpen public attitudes and desires so as to produce particular actions in the market place. The media are an important means of realizing those objectives.

This is not to say that business interests have conspired to control the policy and content of the mass media for their own selfish ends. Deliberate, organized, and calculated propaganda in support of the existing system and against social change is insignificant. There is no plot, no cabal, no organized effort to preserve the status quo, but the media serve the industrial order nonetheless.

The strategic policy and the bulk of content of the mass media work toward engineering consent in favor of the existing order because commercial control of the media and the resulting need to please the largest possible audience virtually assure that they will. Media operators seek to saturate the market they have cut out for their product in order to hold down unit costs and, if they accept advertising, to justify high rates for space or time. To attract a huge following, the media must stick to majority views, reflect prevailing values, and reinforce the primary assumptions of the social order. The more completely their content reasserts the form and character of existing society, the more efficiently the mass media perform as an adjunct of the industrial order. To depart from the popularly sanctioned path is often to invite economic disaster.

CONTROL OF SOCIETY'S AGENDA

Current research, taking a more measured view of the influence of the mass media on society, has focused considerable attention on the media's impact on society's agenda. Although the concept of agenda-setting draws on the rich literature on stereotyping, pseudo-environment, and media functions, no one has stated the concept more strikingly than political scientist Bernard Cohen did in 1963:

[The] media may not be successful much of the time in telling people what to think, but [they are] . . . stunningly successful in telling [their audiences] . . . what to think *about.*

> . . . For most of the foreign policy audience, the really effective political map of the world—that is to say, their *operational* map of the world—is drawn by the reporter and the editor, not by the cartographer. (Latin America, for instance, takes up a lot of space on the cartographer's map, but it scarcely exists on the political map delineated by most newspapers in the United States.) And if we do not see a story in the newspapers (or catch it on radio or television), it effectively has not happened so far as we are concerned.[21]

This is not to say that there is a cabal or conspiracy that chooses the items for the agenda. Researchers have investigated the influence on the media's agenda of publishers, "newsmakers," professional norms, technology, economic and political constraints, media philosophies, and even the interests of the audience itself. It seems unlikely that any single factor determines the media's agenda. More likely, as with all complex institutions, it is a confluence of many factors. In fact, it is undoubtedly more appropriate to speak of agendas, because different media outlets offer different agendas.*

In 1972 Maxwell McCombs and Donald Shaw were the first to demonstrate empirically the validity of the agenda-setting theory, and they have been joined by a large group of scholars whose research refines Cohen's insight. As David Weaver and his colleagues have summarized the research:

> While behavioral scientists have not discovered that media have all the power ascribed to them by conventional wisdom, there is considerable evidence that [the media] . . . play an important part in shaping perceptions of reality. Audiences not only learn about public issues . . . through the media, they sometimes also learn how much importance to attach to an issue from the emphasis placed on it by the mass media. In other words, the media set the agenda for public opinion, without necessarily determining the direction that opinion will take.[22]

But Weaver has also pointed out,

> . . . [T]he conveying of the importance of political issues to an audience does not hold uniformly for all kinds of audience members or for all kinds of topics. . . .
>
> Although audiences sometimes seem to learn how much importance to attach to various public issues from the emphasis placed on these issues by the mass media, . . . the aggregate agenda-setting effect of the mass media seems similar in some respects to other media effects—it holds only under certain conditions.[23]

Los Angeles Times reporter David Shaw studied the front pages of the *Los Angeles Times, The New York Times,* and *The Washington Post* for the first five months of 1977 and found that "20% of the time—33 days—there was not one single story that appeared on the front page of all three papers—and only 32 days did the three front pages have more than two stories in common. Thus, 60% of the time, the front pages of these three papers had only one or two of their eight or 10 stories in common." Shaw's interesting account of his research appeared in the *Los Angeles Times,* June 24, 1977.

Weaver encourages the development of a transactional research model, suggesting we should attend to what people do *with* media in combination with what the media do *to* people.

It is always worth keeping the complexity of humankind in mind when attempting to ascribe profound influence to institutions like the media. Our perceptions of people's receptiveness and resistance to the influence of the media are in constant flux as researchers unveil more and more nuances in this process of communication. As we examine the media's development and performance, we should not let our fascination with them blind us to the larger context of our society.

Notes

1. Harold Lasswell, "The Structure and Function of Communication in Society," in Wilbur Schramm and Donald F. Roberts (eds.), *The Process and Effects of Mass Communication,* Revised Edition (Urbana, Ill,: University of Illinois Press, 1971), p. 84.
2. Wilbur Schramm, *Men, Messages, and Media: A Look at Human Communication* (New York: Harper & Row, 1973), p. 43.
3. Wilbur Schramm, "The Nature of Communication between Humans," in Schramm and Roberts, p. 8.
4. Schramm, "The Nature of Communication between Humans," in Schramm and Roberts, p. 27. © 1971 by The Board of Trustees of the University of Illinois.
5. Elihu Katz, "The Two-Step Flow of Communication," *Public Opinion Quarterly,* 21, 1957, pp. 61–78.
6. Schramm, "The Nature of Communication between Humans," in Schramm and Roberts, p. 51.
7. Steven H. Chaffee, "The Diffusion of Political Information," in Steven H. Chaffee (ed.), *Political Communication: Issues and Strategies for Research* (Beverly Hills, California: Sage Publications, Inc., 1975), p. 101.
8. Edward Sapir, "Communication," in Bernard Berelson and Morris Janowitz (eds.), *Reader in Public Opinion and Communication,* Second Edition (New York: The Free Press, 1966), pp. 162–166.
9. November 28, 1967, memorandum written by Ray Price, planning strategy for Presidential campaign of Richard Nixon, reprinted in Joe McGinniss, *The Selling of the President 1968* (New York: Pocket Books, 1970), p. 203.
10. Edward Sapir, "The Status of Linguistics as a Science," *Language,* 5, 1929, pp. 209–210.
11. Walter Lippmann, *Public Opinion* (New York: The Free Press, 1965), p. 11.
12. Lippmann, p. 3.
13. Lippmann, pp. 54–5, 65.
14. Daniel J. Boorstin, *The Image: A Guide to Pseudo-Events in America* (New York: Harper & Row, Publishers, 1964), pp. 11–12.
15. Richard H. Rovere, *Senator Joe McCarthy* (Cleveland, Ohio: The World Publishing Company, 1960), pp. 163–164.
16. Accounts and portions of the memo can be found in Jules Witcover, *Marathon: The Pursuit of the Presidency 1972–1976* (New York: The Viking Press, 1977), pp. 110–115, and in *Newsweek,* May 10, 1976, pp. 28–9.
17. Carl Bernstein and Bob Woodward, *All the President's Men* (New York: Simon and Schuster, 1974), p. 127.

18. *Broadcasting,* April 11, 1977, p. 38.
19. Harold A. Innis, *Empire and Communications,* Revised Edition (Toronto: University of Toronto Press, 1972), p. 9.
20. C. Wright Mills, *The Power Elite* (New York: Oxford University Press, 1965), pp. 310–311, 313–314.
21. Bernard C. Cohen, *The Press and Foreign Policy* (Princeton, New Jersey: Princeton University Press, 1969), p. 13.
22. David H. Weaver, Maxwell E. McCombs and Charles Spellman, "Watergate and the Media: A Case Study of Agenda-Setting," *American Politics Quarterly,* 3, October 1975, pp. 459–460.
23. David H. Weaver, "Voters' Need for Orientation, Media Use and Gratifications, and the Learning of Issue Saliences During the 1976 Presidential Campaign," paper presented to the Mass Communication Division, Speech Communication Association, Washington, D.C., December 1977, p. 1.

3

The Rise of Mass Media

If any man was to ask me what I would suppose to be a perfect
style or language, I would answer, that in which a man speaking
to five hundred people, of all common and various capacities,
idiots or lunatics excepted, should be understood by them all.

DANIEL DEFOE

On September 30, 1975, the contracts of nine craft
unions expired at the Washington *Post*. In the early hours of October 1
pressmen of Local 6, the Newspaper and Graphic Communications Union,
smashed the *Post*'s nine presses with knives, crowbars, and torches. They
jammed the automatic firefighting equipment, started fires, severely beat a
foreman who tried to stop the destruction, then left the building to go on
strike.

The pressmen's desperation and violence dramatized the human and
institutional agonies of a long-established industry beset by technological
change. Computer editing and printing technologies and miniaturized
videocameras were vastly increasing the speed and sophistication with
which the news media could gather, store, process, and distribute information. The savings and efficiencies and the sheer magic of the gadgetry were
irresistible. In fact, because of soaring costs in labor and material, it was
doubtful that the media of the 1970s could survive economically if they

The strike at the Washington *Post* in September 1975 dramatized the human and
institutional agonies of technological change. (Wide World photo)

continued to work with technologies developed in the nineteenth century to
meet the demands of mass industrialized society.

The cost of shifting from old to new technology, however, is particularly
high for large news enterprises. Since 1969 the *Post* had been preparing for
the shift, and during the 4½-month strike that followed the pressmen's
violence the *Post* installed a front-end computer system with 22 video
display terminals for preparing and editing copy.

Although this new technology eliminates the need for certain manual
skills, it cannot replace the skills of gathering, analyzing, communicating,
and commenting on the news. Reporters and editors, then, have been
sandwiched between labor and management in the dispute over new
technology and jobs. The increasing formal educational background and
professionalization of journalists make it difficult for them to identify fully
with pressmen, yet their professional ideals and conventions separate them
from management and its business orientation.

The pressmen's strike thus virtually destroyed the morale at the *Post* so
recently boosted by the reporting of Carl Bernstein and Bob Woodward on
Watergate. The *Post*'s 800 news and commercial workers who belonged to
the American Newspaper Guild, organized in 1933 "to preserve the voca-
tional interests of the members and to improve the conditions under which
they work by collective bargaining," had to decide whether to cross a picket

line. Three times a majority voted to cross and continue working. They were able to work because of management's improvisations during the strike. Copy for a stripped-down 24-page paper was flown by helicopter from the roof of the *Post* building to newspapers in Maryland and Virginia willing to risk a strike for printing the *Post.* Advertising and clerical workers and members of management did double shifts as production workers. Katharine Graham herself, the publisher of the *Post,* and her chauffeur, her secretary, and one of her granddaughters, helped wrap papers, although, said one reporter who captured the ambivalence of the journalists' position, "It was a little obscene that she wore those $300 or $400 dresses in the mailroom."

Behind the scenes the strike also dramatized the dilemma of large media corporations torn in the 1970s between the instinct to unite in protection of their corporate interests and profits and the concern to promote the economic and libertarian benefits of competition.

As soon as she learned of the pressmen's destruction of the *Post*'s presses, Katharine Graham asked her competitor, Joe L. Allbritton, publisher of the Washington *Star,* to help print the *Post,* telling him that putting out *no* newspapers would be better than competing in such a crisis. Allbritton refused. A self-made Texas millionaire, he had only recently entered the newspaper business. In 1974 when he took over the *Star,* Washington was one of a handful of cities in the United States that still had newspaper competition, but the *Post*'s booming success had brought its only competitor, the *Star,* almost to bankruptcy. *Star* stockholders allowed Allbritton to buy stock in the Star holding company and take control of the paper's management. Allbritton also loaned the *Star* $5 million. Despite his efforts, the *Star* was losing between $750,000 and $1 million a month when the strike began at the *Post.*

Because of its success, particularly in its coverage of Watergate, the *Post* had become the major competitor of the New York *Times* in national and international prestige and respect. Yet on October 2, 1975, Arthur O. ("Punch") Sulzberger, the publisher of the *Times,* tried to persuade Allbritton to risk a strike and help print the *Post.* Sulzberger later told *The New Republic* magazine that "he merely wanted to let Allbritton know what had happened in New York when papers had been 'whiplashed back and forth between the unions' until they realized they had to stick together."[1] But Allbritton was in no position not to take whatever advantage he could of his competitor's predicament.

Because he was a new owner of a multimedia corporation—unlike Graham and Sulzberger of the long-established and profitable Post and Times enterprises—Allbritton was among the first to suffer society's mounting concern about the concentration of media ownership in a few families and corporations. In an effort to break up cross-media combinations, the Federal Communications Commission (FCC) had adopted a rule in January 1975 forbidding a single owner to operate a newspaper and broadcast station in the same market, a rule applying primarily to new and newly purchased broadcast-publishing combinations. The Star holding company had owned not only the Washington *Star* but also WMAL – TV and WMAL AM and FM, three Washington broadcast stations. Convinced that the broadcasting profits were vital to the newspaper's survival, Allbritton bought the broadcast properties as well as the paper. Such changes in broadcast ownership, however, are subject to FCC approval. Allbritton petitioned the FCC to waive its new cross-ownership rule so that newspaper competition, according to Allbritton, could *survive* in the nation's capital. The FCC refused and Allbritton agreed to divest himself of the Washington broadcast properties within three years.

Much of the predicament of the multimedia Post and Star corporations is explained by the forces that have shaped the rise of the mass media in the United States. At the heart of their dilemma is the need to balance American democracy's expectations of press responsibility and performance and the economic arrangements necessary to meet those expectations. The expectation that the press must give society full information of its affairs and those of other nations and readers' desire to be variously entertained have impelled news enterprises toward ever larger units so as to concentrate resources and take advantage of economies of scale. The increasing demand in the twentieth century that the press fulfill the responsibility to inform alluded to by the Founding Fathers but never clearly defined in the Constitution or the First Amendment has been based on the notion that the press must perform in the public interest in return for its freedom. Regrettably, what has been thought to constitute the public interest has not always coincided with what has interested the public. And as business enterprises the news media cannot ignore what interests the public.

The News Business

The virtual extinction of newspaper competition, the chumminess of corporate executives in a crisis, the vastness and diversity of media enterprises they control and government efforts to break them up, and the struggle between labor and management as automated technology threatens jobs— all familiar aspects of twentieth-century mass media—would be incomprehensible to an American publisher in the eighteenth century, bewildering to one in the nineteenth. During those 200 years publishing has gone from the relative simplicity of a cottage industry to big, corporate business.

But there is much in common across the centuries. We should not be misled by the romance of the eighteenth-century printer's fight for press freedom. He, too, operated a business, however primitive by comparison. But because no First Amendment protected his enterprise, political philosophy was of more lively, immediate concern to a colonial printer than to a twentieth-century publisher.

The Massachusetts legislature jailed James Franklin for a month in 1722 for the gentle sarcasm of this news item in his *New England Courant* concerning government inaction against pirates operating up and down the coast: "We are advised from Boston, that the Government of Massachusetts are fitting out a ship to go after pirates, to be commanded by Captain Peter Papillon, and 'tis thought he will sail some time this month, wind and weather permitting."[2] The *Courant* had to improvise to survive in James' absence. His 16-year-old brother and apprentice, Benjamin, took over and, as a response to government harassment, reprinted "Cato's Letter" on freedom of speech.

When Benjamin Franklin bought the Pennsylvania *Gazette* in Philadelphia in 1729 and became a publisher in his own right, it turned out that he was more businessman than philosopher. He won the government printing contract and the postmastership from his rival, Andrew Bradford, publisher of the *American Weekly Mercury,* then delivered his paper at the public's expense while denying the mails to his competitor. The device was unwor-

FRANKLIN THE PRINTER.

The colonial printer did everything with little help. (Library of Congress)

thy of Franklin's genius. The greatest journalist of his day, some would say the greatest American journalist ever, Franklin beat out his rival because he was a gifted printer, writer, and editor. But talent alone does not explain how Franklin could make a fortune out of publishing and retire to a career in science and statesmanship at age 42.

Joe Allbritton's need for other profitable businesses like broadcast stations to sustain the Washington *Star* would have been very familiar to colonial printers. Newspapering was a precarious enterprise and postmasterships, government printing contracts, job printing, the operation of a bookshop, perhaps even a coffeeshop, were vital to a colonial printer's economic survival.

The sight of a publisher wrapping newspapers would have caused no comment in colonial times. The printer did everything with little help. But a woman publisher was unusual, although the widows of Andrew Bradford, John Peter Zenger, and others managed their husbands' printing businesses. Women did not enter journalism in any numbers until the last decades of the nineteenth century, and even in the 1970s a top female media executive was rare. He would have been awed by any publisher, man or woman, who had taken over a family business with revenues of $85.5 million in 1963 and transformed it into a public corporation owning the Washington *Post,* the Trenton *Times, Newsweek,* part of the *International Herald Tribune,* half of a national news service, six broadcast stations, and most of a newsprint company and earning $309.3 million in revenues in 1975.

The transition from the financial improvisations of a Benjamin Franklin to the corporate sophistication of a Katharine Graham has occurred because of three main forces that have shaped American society and institutions: the rise of democracy, the industrial and technological revolution, and urbanization. Democracy's rise reflected the powerful influence of theory and ideas, industrialization and urbanization reflected the equally powerful influence of practical economics, and a lively, sometimes bitter tension between philosophy and economics has shaped the structure and development of the mass media in America.

The Rise of Democracy

THE EXTENSION OF THE FRANCHISE

Jefferson stipulated that newspapers could play a vital role in democracy only if they penetrated the whole mass of the people and those people could read. Jefferson might also have emphasized an even more vital condition both for the operation of democracy and for stimulating the people's interest in their affairs through the press: that people should have the right to vote, to participate in their own government. To give the people full information of their affairs through newspapers is valuable only if they can then use that information to judge their representatives through the ballot. As Governor of

Virginia from 1779 to 1781 Jefferson had broadened the franchise, but when he wrote his letter to Edward Carrington in 1787, the vote in Virginia was still restricted to landowners. Qualifications for the vote and for holding office varied from state to state, but despite the idealism of the Declaration of Independence and of the Constitution, much of the population was denied the right to vote and to hold public office until the first half of the nineteenth century.

The rapid spread of landownership did enfranchise many Americans, and the influence of new states with liberal constitutions led to the liberalization of the franchise in the older states. For example, between 1810 and 1820 six new states entered the union with constitutions that required no property qualifications for voting. With the rise of the common people, privilege was in retreat. James Fenimore Cooper wrote: "The pretense has been that none but the rich have a stake in society." Cooper disagreed. "Every man who has wants, feelings, affections, and character has a stake in society."[3] As significant as the extension of the franchise was the increasing interest in exercising it. Historians have noted that "from 1828 to 1848 the number of Americans in the nation as a whole who exercised their right to vote increased 2½ times—an increase far greater than that of the population itself."[4]

By the outbreak of the Civil War adult white males could vote, generally without further qualification. The extension of the franchise to other groups has been gradual. In 1870 the Fifteenth Amendment to the Constitution guaranteed the vote to adult male blacks. Early feminists such as Elizabeth Cady Stanton and Lucretia Mott first seriously proposed the vote for women in 1848, and most early feminists advocated abolition as well. When the Fifteenth Amendment gave the vote to black males but not to the women who had helped win it for them, women concentrated on the struggle for the vote. It was not until 1920 that the Nineteenth Amendment granted nation-wide suffrage to women.

Out of the anti-Vietnam war and campus ferment of the 1960s pressure increased to lower the voting age from 21 to 18, one argument being that if 18-year-olds were mature enough to fight for the country, they were mature enough to vote. In 1972 the Twenty-Sixth Amendment guaranteed the vote for 18-year-olds. The right to vote had taken at least a century, then, to reach into the mass of the people, most of whom had been literate enough to read newspapers for much of that period.

THE SPREAD OF EDUCATION

All the early theoreticians of democracy emphasized that an informed electorate was crucial if democracy were to work, and they put great faith in education. The Founding Fathers, after all, were among the most educated people of their generation anywhere in the world. At least a dozen universities and colleges had been founded before the Declaration of Independence, among them prestigious Ivy League universities such as Harvard,

Yale, Princeton, Columbia, Brown, the University of Pennsylvania, and Dartmouth.

More important to the common people was the spread of free public education. Henry Barnard and Horace Mann led the movement to reform the nation's common schools in the 1830s and 1840s, and after the Civil War the high school system expanded dramatically. In 1870 about 7 million pupils were enrolled in more than 300 public high schools; by 1900 an estimated 15½ million pupils were enrolled in about 6000 high schools. Opportunities for a university education increased with President Lincoln's signing of the Morrill Act in 1862 granting federal lands to the states for the establishment of colleges. Few women had been admitted to college, and the feminist movement in the mid-nineteenth century spurred the establishment of women's colleges such as Mt. Holyoke (1837), Elmira (1853), Vassar (1861), Wellesley and Smith (both in 1871), and Bryn Mawr (1881). A reinvigorated women's movement in the 1960s opened prestigious men's universities to women, and in 1976, 340 years after it was founded, Harvard graduated its first woman valedictorian.

National concern for the expansion of formal education from the elementary to the university level was reflected in less formal ways, too. Between 1836 and 1857 William McGuffey compiled six McGuffey Eclectic Readers. Constantly revised, the readers maintained their place for nearly two generations and sold an estimated 122 million copies. These educational advances not only helped make a mass press possible, but inexpensive newspapers also played a part in educating the population, especially the immigrants flowing into the cities. Between 1820 and 1930 about 38 million immigrants entered the United States, settling mainly in the northeastern cities. Despite this influx of largely non–English-speaking people, illiteracy had dropped to 11 percent by 1900. By 1910 it had dropped to 7.7 percent for persons aged 10 or older.

Studies in the 1970s suggested, however, that a rising proportion of the population was *functionally* illiterate. That is, they could not complete such tasks as taking a driver's test, filling out an income tax statement or a job application, understanding the labels in a supermarket, or interpreting an airline schedule. A 1975 study by the U.S. Office of Education found that in terms of these criteria 22 percent of Americans over age 17 were functionally illiterate and another 32 percent were marginally literate. Critics were quick to point out, as Melvin Maddocks did in the *Christian Science Monitor,* that "what functional illiterates can't read isn't always English but bureaucratese or academese or journalese masquerading as English in everyday life." Maddocks commented: "If even understanding a tax form— to say nothing of filling it out—is the national standard of adult competence, there are PhDs in classical philology who are in serious trouble."[5]

Understanding gobbledygook may not be a meaningful test of literacy, but there was increasing alarm in the mid-1970s that reading and writing skills were declining. Verbal scores on the Scholastic Aptitude Test, a national standardized test required of applicants to most universities, had been dropping for 10 years. This decline was occurring at a time when more Americans were graduating from high schools and universities than ever before in the nation's history. We have been arguing that literacy was vital to the establishment of a mass press. The coincidence, therefore, of an apparent decline in literacy and a drop of 2.5 million, or 4 percent, in daily newspaper circulation between 1973 and 1975 not surprisingly concerned newspaper publishers more than anyone else. Were Marshall McLuhan's "probes" so devastatingly correct?

In the 1960s McLuhan had asked if the rebellion of children in classrooms against books had anything to do with the electronic age in which we live. He observed:

> Before us are two utterly incongruous objects: a South Sea mask representative of primitive culture and pre-literate man; and a television set, representative of post-literate, electronic man. Between these two extremes exists the Gutenberg Galaxy, five centuries of print resulting from a thousand years of phonetic alphabet.

McLuhan concluded:

> Apparently, education is now facing a tremendous problem of transition between two worlds. In fact, they both coexist. Making a transition from one vast embracing technology to another would seem to call for the utmost attention, offering the utmost challenge to human understanding.[6]

It was a challenge newspapers were slowly beginning to comprehend in the mid-1970s. The diffusion of education in the nineteenth century had made their extremely profitable enterprises possible. Now more Americans were in high schools and universities than ever before, but they seemed to be shifting from newspapers to the electronic media. Who was the enemy? Permissive educational philosophies? Inadequate high school and university curricula and instruction? Electronic media? Or traditional definitions of news and methods of reporting it?

One solution being considered in the 1970s was a merger of newspapers and electronic media. A wide range of print and audiovisual services can be concentrated in the home through the linkage of cable television and computers. Industrial technology had permitted newspapers in the mid-nineteenth century to respond to the needs of a literate, enfranchised population. New technologies in the 1970s seemed one way that print media could again respond to the challenge of change.

The Industrial Revolution and Urbanization

Vernon Parrington has described the America of Jefferson's day as

> . . . a simple world, with a simple domestic economy. More than ninety percent were plain country folk, farmers and villagers, largely freeholders, managing their

local affairs in the traditional way. There were no great extremes of poverty and

The Industrial
Revolution and
Urbanization

51

wealth, no closely organized class groups.[7]

It was a world of which Jefferson approved. To him, "Those who labor in the earth are the chosen people of God, if ever he had a chosen people, whose breasts he has made his peculiar deposit for substantial and genuine virtue." He feared the rise of great industrial cities, and bitterly fought Alexander Hamilton, his Federalist opponent, who planned a centralized, industrial, capitalist state. Jefferson wrote:

> While we have land to labor then, let us never wish to see our citizens occupied at a work-bench, or twirling a distaff . . . for the general operations of manufacture, let our work-shops remain in Europe. It is better to carry provisions and materials to work-men there, than bring them to the provisions and materials, and with them their manners and principles. . . . The mobs of great cities add just so much to the support of pure government, as sores do to the strength of the human body.[8]

If newspapers were as important to democracy as Jefferson said they were, if to play their part they had to penetrate the whole mass of the people, then the urban, industrial state he loathed was vital. Dense, urban populations earning wages from businesses and factories and buying the goods of mass production technology were basic to the development of a mass press. Such an economy generated the income newspapers needed to free themselves from financial dependence on government and political factions so that they could perform the function Jefferson had specified: to check on government. The industrial cities concentrated mass readerships for newspapers and created living and working conditions crusading editors such as Joseph Pulitzer could profitably investigate and deplore. Jefferson was right. Because of their living and working conditions, the mobs of the great cities did become sores on the body politic. Their situation did not perturb Alexander Hamilton, the major architect of the American industrial state, who planned to run the country as a business. He was convinced that manufacturers' interests were identical with the national interest, and as George Washington's Secretary of the Treasury he instituted economic and political measures that shored up the position of the commercial and industrial barons and shaped America far more than Jefferson's democratic idealism. Hamilton shared none of Jefferson's concern for the common people and was candid about exploiting them. He wrote, for example:

> It is worthy of particular remark, that, in general, women and children are rendered more useful, and the latter more early useful, by manufacturing establishments, than they would otherwise be.[9]

A pioneering example of the corporate future was set by Francis Lowell, Patrick Jackson, and Nathan Appleton, who formed the Boston Manufacturing Company in 1813. In six years they spent $600,000 to build the first wholly integrated cotton-manufacturing plant in the world. Everything from the unbaling of raw cotton to the dyeing and printing of raw cloth was done under one roof. Always attentive to new technology, they introduced power looms and spindles. Most of their workers were young women, aged 18 to 22, whom they sheltered in a company town. Between 1821 and 1835 they opened up nine companies in Massachusetts and New Hampshire, each specializing in a textile product. They founded insurance companies and banks to concentrate capital, real estate companies to take over the best company land, and water-power companies to control dams and to harness the power of rivers.

By the outbreak of the Civil War there were 140,000 industries of all types; by 1900 there were more than 500,000, served by an expanding communications network, exchanging the agricultural produce of the West and South for the manufactured goods of the East. Private road construction had started in the 1790s, and between 1800 and 1840 more than 10,000 miles of turnpike were built. In 1806 Congress chartered a "National Highway," and by the 1850s the federally funded road stretched from Philadelphia to Vandalia, Illinois. The Erie Canal, which contributed substantially to the spectacular rise in importance of New York City, was completed in 1825, and by 1840 canals connected almost all the seaboard states with the West. With the spread of canals and the development of the steamboat, water travel became infinitely more comfortable than torture by stage coach.

In the 1830s railroads supplemented canals and rivers, and in 1832 the federal postal system began to shift from stage coach to rail. In 1869 the Union Pacific and Central Pacific railroads met at Promontory Point in Utah, and the continent was joined by rail. In 1844 Samuel Morse demonstrated the practicability of his telegraph to Congress by transmitting the message, "What God hath wrought," over a wire from Washington to Baltimore. The first telegram to California was transmitted in October 1861, so leading to the end of the Pony Express. A permanent telegraphic cable crossing the Atlantic was laid in 1866.

Transportation developments increased the mobility of an already restless people. The factories attracted farm laborers, and after the Napoleonic Wars immigrants poured into the United States. An estimated 150,000 entered in the 1820s; that number increased 12-fold in the 1840s. Most settled in the northeastern cities, swelling the proletariat Jefferson feared. By 1890 one-third of the country's population was living in communities of 4000 people or more and providing the markets for the standardized goods of mass production.

THE MERCANTILE PRESS

In the first decades of the nineteenth century the mercantile, political papers of the cities made no effort to appeal to the urban masses. It was no accident that the word "Advertiser" appeared in many of their titles. In New York the *Commercial Advertiser,* the *Mercantile Advertiser,* and the *Daily Advertiser* devoted most of their space to commercial announcements of interest only to the mercantile class. They paid no attention to local news, except for marine and shipping news. Historian Frank Luther Mott writes: "It was said that the New York *Commercial Advertiser* would ignore floods, earthquakes, and wars; but if the editor missed a single ship clearance he had to be restrained from blowing out his brains."[10]

The mercantile class these papers served for the most part shared Hamilton's indifference to the plight of the working people, who could not afford the sixpence it cost to buy a paper anyway. To combat this indifference mechanics and independent artisans began to organize craft unions in the 1820s. Six craft unions joined in 1834 to form the National Trades Union, and in the next three years craft union membership soared from 27,000 to 300,000. Unions conducted at least 175 strikes in this period. Workers organized politically. In 1828 Philadelphia unions formed the American Working Men's Party to campaign for a 10-hour day and free public education for their children. It was a platform Joseph Pulitzer and William Randolph Hearst would endorse and promote in the 1890s, partly out of conviction, partly out of an unabashed concern for circulation and profit.

The Rise of a Mass Press

THE PENNY PRESS

The urban masses' hardships, petty crimes, grievances, and desire for escape from daily toil in factories were gradually to enter into the nineteenth-century editor's definition of news. Among the first to see the masses as potential readers was Benjamin Day. With the help of a compositor and a boy and a hand press capable of turning out 250 sheets an hour, Day launched his four-page New York *Sun* in September 1833.

Day virtually ignored political and commercial news and editorials. The *Sun* was devoted mainly to stories of local crimes and accidents, murders, criminal trials, executions, fires, foreign and domestic, clipped from other papers. He hired George Wisner at $4 a week to cover the police court and to produce punchy items like these:

> William Luvoy got drunk because yesterday was so devlish warm. Drank 9 glasses of brandy and water and said he would be cursed if he wouldn't drink 9 more as quick as he could raise the money to buy it with. He would like to know what right the magistrate had to interfere with his private affairs. Fined $1.

> Sudden death—Ann McDonough, of Washington Street, attempted to drink a pint of rum on a wager, on Wednesday afternoon last. Before it was half swallowed, Ann was a corpse. Serve her right!"[11]

Day sold the *Sun* for a penny; its cheapness and the popularity of its contents led to a daily circulation of 10,000 in one year, 15,000 in two years. In the last week of the *Sun*'s second year, Day ran a seven-article series by Richard Locke on "Great Astronomical Discoveries, lately made by Sir John Herschel at the Cape of Good Hope." Locke reported that through his immense telescope Herschel had seen these inhabitants on the moon:

> They averaged four feet in height, were covered, except on the face, with short and glossy, copper-colored hair, and had wings composed of a thin membrane, without hair, lying snugly upon their backs from the top of the shoulders to the calves of the legs.

Locke's final article described the Great Temple of the Moon:

> It was open on all sides, and seemed to contain neither seats, altars, nor offerings, but it was a light and airy structure, nearly 100 feet high from its white glistening floor to the glowing roof, and it stood upon a round, green eminence on the eastern side of the valley.[12]

Edgar Allan Poe explained that he had stopped work on the second half of "The Strange Adventures of Hans Pfaall" because he felt that he had been outdone. The *Sun*'s celebrated "moon hoax" pushed circulation to 19,000, which Day claimed was a world record, surpassing the 17,000 of the London *Times*.

In 1838, although circulation had reached an astonishing 30,000, Day sold the *Sun*. In less than five years, then, the 23-year-old Day had achieved the largest circulation in the world, had bought two Napier double-cylinder presses capable of turning out 4000 sheets an hour, had built up an enterprise with an annual budget of $93,000, and had sold the business for $40,000 before he was 30 years old.

Although the *Sun* had made a dramatic start in penetrating the whole mass of the people, it clearly did not comply with Jefferson's requirement that a paper give the people full information of their affairs. Day's successful appeal had been to emotions, not reason. Nevertheless, by breaking free of a dependence on government and political party, Day paved the way for a financially stable, independent press to fulfull its function of checking on government for all the people. His greatest contribution was to mass media economics rather than to the implementation of libertarian press philosophy.

Day was the first media owner effectively to get into the business of selling large audiences to advertisers. By so doing, he could keep the cost of his product for the consumer below the cost of producing it. Advertisers paid the bulk of his costs. The technique was to develop an editorial formula that would appeal to the largest number of people possible, hence his rejection of stuffy commercial and political news and editorials in favor of titillating items on crime and disaster. The sale of his readers to advertisers not only produced income to cover his operating costs but generated the capital for investment in the printing technology needed to produce thousands of newspapers daily.

The relationship among editorial formula, circulation, and advertising that Day "discovered" profoundly affected the structure and development of American mass media. Such a relationship was not possible before the forces of urbanization and industrialization had coalesced to provide him with an accessible mass readership, the technology of mass production to serve it, and a system of marketing to finance his enterprise. The system whereby a grocer weighed out a sack of beans from a barrel or a druggist poured medicine from a jug was giving way to one where packaged goods replaced bulk goods. The manufacturer's trademark or brand name was becoming an important means for identifying the product for consumers and giving the manufacturer a share of the market. In the early 1840s Volney Palmer formed the first advertising agency. His agency, and others that followed, bought large blocks of space in newspapers and magazines and sold it in smaller units to advertisers. Advertising was on its way to becoming an institution in its own right, and the media's dependence on it would later raise questions about the media's ability and willingness to maintain a critical distance from it.

THE RISING COST OF COMPETITION

Day's exploitation of the relationship among editorial formula, circulation, and advertising gave him an enormous competitive advantage over the sixpenny papers. As has happened throughout American media history, a successful formula was quickly imitated. The costs of competing, however, rose geometrically. The entry cost for James Gordon Bennett was small. He started his New York *Herald* in 1835 in a Wall Street basement with no more than $500, a plank across two flour barrels for a desk, and an aging press. But to catch up with Day's circulation required extraordinary enterprise. At first Bennett disdained police news as "trash," because he intended to appeal, as he put it, to "the merchant and man of learning, as well as the mechanic and man of labor." He soon discovered, as editors have since, that an interest in trivia, crime, sex, and scandal is fairly evenly distributed among persons of all classes and economic and educational levels. Within weeks he was advertising for "a Police Reporter, of genius and education."

Bennett's major contribution to journalism was to stamp the gathering and reporting of news rather than the expression of views and opinion as the primary function of newspapers. He was willing to spend royally to get the news, and was especially alert to the value of each communications advance. To outdo his rivals he maintained boats to meet incoming ships and chartered special trains to secure foreign news from ships in Boston. He used the Pony Express to collect news from Washington until the development of the telegraph. Then he wrote:

> By means of the electric telegraph the local advantages of the Washington papers are transferred to this metropolis, and the superior enterprise and pecuniary means of the journals here will enable them to turn these advantages to the best account.

He foresaw, too, the effect of the transatlantic cable on newspapers:

> There can be no doubt that the telegraphic communication with Europe will revolutionize the newspaper business on both continents. It will tend to produce

a condensation of style in newspaper articles. . . . The telegraph will bring us
back to that succinct, simple and condensed method of expressing our ideas
which prevailed in ancient times.[13]

Bennett expanded the definition of news to include coverage of Wall
Street, Washington, foreign capitals, religion, theater, society, sports, and a
variety of local news. When he started, he wrote all the news and editorials,
accepted the advertising, and transacted all of the paper's business himself.
But the expansion of his news-gathering enterprise soon involved the hiring
of many reporters. He spent about $500,000 to cover the Civil War and had
between 30 and 40 correspondents assigned with tents and wagons to every
army corps.

THE SEPARATION OF NEWS-EDITORIAL AND MANAGEMENT

Bennett defined the scope and nature of the news business in such a
way that anyone wishing to compete had to have considerable resources. It
cost Horace Greeley $2000 to start the New York *Tribune* in 1841. Like
Bennett, he tried to do everything himself but had neither time nor expertise
to run both the management and editorial sides of the business. Thomas
McElrath took over management, freeing Greeley to become one of the
most influential editorial writers in American journalism history. That division between news-editorial and management has characterized major mass
media organization ever since.

When Henry Raymond, a former assistant to Greeley, started the New
York *Times* in 1851 with banker George Jones as his partner in the business
office, he found it necessary to enter competitive New York with $100,000.
Day had started with nothing, Bennett with $500, Greeley with $2000, and
Raymond with $100,000, an astonishing rise in less than 20 years. By the
1850s, then, no publisher could enter a major city with several competing
newspapers without the capital to invest in the printing technology to
produce thousands of papers daily and to cover the costs of employing a
growing staff of reporters and managerial employees until he could win a
large enough readership to attract advertisers.

SENSATIONALISM AND COMPETITION FOR CIRCULATION AND ADVERTISING

By the end of the century entry costs in major cities were prohibitive to
all but the rich. Joseph Pulitzer entered New York in 1883 not by starting a
new paper but by buying an old one. Even though the New York *World* was
struggling against the competition, Pulitzer had to pay financier Jay Gould
$346,000 for the tottering concern. Pulitzer revived it with a flamboyant
sensationalism derived from Bennett, all the while professing the highest
ideals for journalism in a democratic society. A newspaper, he said, should
be:

An institution that should always fight for progress and reform, never tolerate
injustice or corruption, always fight demagogues of all parties, always oppose

privileged classes and public plunderers, never lack sympathy with the poor, always remain devoted to the public welfare, never be satisfied with merely printing news, always be drastically independent, never be afraid to attack wrong, whether by predatory plutocracy or predatory poverty.[14]

Pulitzer's schizophrenic *World,* with a front page of crime, sex, scandal, and corruption and an editorial page cogently expressing Pulitzer's idealism, might have mellowed into a more harmonious mix of serious news and opinion had not William Randolph Hearst entered New York publishing in 1896.

Hearst began his New York *Journal* with the mind-boggling millions of his family's mining fortune behind him and an apparent willingness to spend every cent to outdo Pulitzer's *World.* At Harvard Hearst, who was rumored to receive a weekly allowance in gold nuggets, showed no interest in anything other than outrageous pranks and a hearty good time until the editors of the chronically strapped humor magazine, the Harvard *Lampoon,* sought his help. They expected no more of him than his father's money, but Hearst was determined to put the *Lampoon* on a sound financial footing. He walked the streets for ads, the magazine covered its costs for the first time in its history, and Hearst developed an obsession for journalism.

Pulitzer's *World* fascinated Hearst, and he persuaded his father to let him manage the San Francisco *Examiner* and rescue the ailing newspaper by experimenting with Pulitzer's sensational methods. Historian John Tebbel describes how the *Examiner*'s city editor, Arthur McEwen, reacted to Hearst's experiments:

> . . . when he looked at the *Examiner*'s front page, he said, "Gee, whiz!" When he looked at the second page, it elicited an astonished "Holy Moses!" and the third page produced a bellowing "God Almighty!"[15]

The period of lurid yellow journalism Hearst provoked in competition with Pulitzer in New York exposed the fallacy of the libertarian's assumption that if truth and falsehood are permitted to grapple in a free and open encounter, truth will triumph, that vigorous newspaper competition will lead to the press' fulfillment of its democratic functions. Pulitzer had dignified his front page of sex and scandal by arguing that it was necessary to seduce readers into his serious editorial columns. "I want to talk to a nation," he said, "not to a select committee." Hearst had no such pretensions. He went for the masses with shrieking sensationalism and dragged the ailing but competitive Pulitzer down with him. To attract the largest possible audience and advertising revenue, both had in differing degree allowed what interested the public far to outweigh what was in the public interest.

Other publishers of their time—Edwin Godkin of the New York *Evening Post,* and William Rockhill Nelson of the Kansas City *Star,* for example—struck a more responsible balance. But as businesses in a competitive, free enterprise system, newspapers could not avoid trading a portion of what they perceived to be in the public interest for what interested the public, a portion of responsibility for responsiveness.

PUBLIC EXPECTATIONS OF NEWS

Understanding the evolution of mass newspapers in the last three-quarters of the nineteenth century is vital to an understanding of the contemporary press. During those years journalists developed reporting, writing, and editing skills, ethics, conventions, and assumptions that have had a lasting effect on the news media. Even as journalists responded to what interested the public, so they also shaped the public's expectations of newspapers and news.

Daniel J. Boorstin expresses the effect of those years vividly, though with some overstatement. When the first American newspaper, Benjamin Harris' *Public Occurrences,* appeared in 1690, Boorstin writes, "The responsibility for making news was entirely God's—or the Devil's. The newsman's task was only to give 'an Account of such considerable things as have arrived unto our Notice.'" That, says Boorstin, is now a very old-fashioned way of thinking.

> We need not be theologians to see that we have shifted the responsibility for making the world interesting from God to the newspaperman. We used to believe there were only so many "events" in the world. If there were not many intriguing or startling occurrences, it was no fault of the reporter. He could not be expected to report what did not exist.
>
> Within the last hundred years, however, and especially in the twentieth century, all this has changed. We expect the newspapers to be full of news. If there is no news visible to the naked eye, or to the average citizen, we still expect it to be there for the enterprising newsman. The successful reporter is one who can find a story, even if there is no earthquake or assassination or civil war. If he cannot find a story, then he must make one—by the questions he asks of public figures, by the surprising human interest he unfolds from some commonplace event, or by "the news behind the news."[16]

Boorstin summarizes public expectations this way: "There was a time when the reader of an unexciting newspaper would remark, 'How dull is the world today!' Nowadays he says, 'What a dull newspaper!'" In their evolution from government- or party-controlled and subsidized media of information and persuasion to corporate enterprises catering to mass audiences, newspapers took on some of the characteristics of a commercial product sold in the marketplace. And in a comparatively free marketplace, the public has a low tolerance of dullness. Public acceptance of dullness is greater in closed societies, where government tightly controls the economy, the flow of information, and the range of choice.

When other media began to compete with newspapers for audiences and advertising in the United States, they changed as newspapers had done. The major magazines of the nineteenth century—*Scribner's, Harper's,* and *The Century*—were serious, literary publications of limited appeal selling for 35 cents. For the mass audience they were expensive and dull. Like the penny newspaper publishers of the 1830s and 1840s, magazine publishers

Frank Munsey, Sam McClure, and William Randolph Hearst took advantage in the 1890s of the existence of a public with increasing education, income, and leisure and of a growing system of national marketing to produce cheap, entertaining magazines. The lavishly illustrated popular fiction and human interest stories in *Munsey's, McClure's,* and *Cosmopolitan* sold for 10 cents, and a magazine's circulation jumped from thousands to hundreds of thousands. Unlike newspapers, these magazines appealed far beyond the confines of local communities, and they were admirable vehicles for advertisers trying to sell packaged goods with brand names such as Ivory Soap, Baker's Chocolate, Kodak, and Gillette.

Magazines, too, had to be responsive to what interested the public. When *McClure's* published three articles in a single issue in January 1903 by Ida Tarbell, Lincoln Steffens, and Ray Stannard Baker exposing corruption and malpractice in big business, city government, and labor, the magazine discovered an unanticipated depth of public concern and interest. A decade of investigative journalism, which President Theodore Roosevelt called "muckraking," followed as other magazines mined this rich vein of public interest. But when the public tired of gloom and a depressing view of society, *McClure's* and others returned to popular fiction and human interest stories.

Some will criticize the publishers—as did Steffens and Baker, who left *McClure's* in protest against the shift—for exchanging significance for triviality. But publishers of mass or general-interest magazines in the United States are businesspeople seeking a profit, and significance may be a luxury they cannot always afford. The wants and tastes of the majority inevitably define the limits of their endeavor, although they may be able to play some part in shaping those wants and tastes.

In its first two decades of development there was a chance that radio would be less responsive to majority taste. Radio was initially perceived as a message-sending device of particular value in ship-to-shore communication, and the U.S. Navy urged after World War I that radio be declared a government monopoly. But when Congress decided that radio was to be an arena of business competition subject to limited government regulation and the broadest industry turned in the 1920s to advertising to finance programing, U.S. broadcasting became as responsive as the other media to the marketplace, except where government regulation directed otherwise.

COMPETITION AMONG MEDIA FOR AUDIENCES AND ADVERTISING

Students of the effects of a new medium upon an older have at their disposal masses of statistics. Certainty and precision, therefore, should follow. Not so. Communication is not like transportation. Statistics are eloquent about the effect of the steam engine on the horse, even of automobiles and airplanes on trains. The balance sheets of Wells Fargo Stagecoach and the Pennyslvania Railroad say it all. But new communications media do not so much replace as displace old—at least among a people of plenty who can afford to accommodate and support them all. The competition of each new medium, moreover, has apparently stimulated rather than reduced use of existing media.

The immediate or short-term effects of a new medium on others are usually dramatic and readily identifiable, but when the novelty wears off, and people adjust to it and the media to one another, complexity returns. Radio and television rapidly saturate the population, print media sustain remarkable stability. All, that is, learn to perform slightly different functions, advertisers discover what these are and deploy their dollars accordingly, and people to a great extent use them all. James Reston, political columnist of the New York *Times,* summarized this process succinctly in 1966:

> Everybody seems to be poaching on everybody else's preserve. The newspapers are now getting into the periodicals' field of "news significance"; the periodicals are invading the fields of both news and sociology, once dominated by the book publishers; the book publishers are producing "instant" paperback books on important news events; the television networks are bidding for the services of newspaper reporters, magazine writers, and historians; and all are engaged in a savage struggle for the advertising dollar.[17]

Affluence has sustained all the media. But, except for books and movies, people have not paid directly for the full costs of media content. Advertising has been a vital subsidizer of the mass media in the United States.

The Institution of Advertising: Is It Essential?

Few observers have analyzed advertising more acutely than the historian David Potter. In *People of Plenty,* he points out that:

> . . . advertising is not badly needed in an economy of scarcity, because total demand is usually equal to or in excess of total supply, and every producer can normally sell as much as he produces. It is when potential supply outstrips demand—that is, when abundance prevails—that advertising begins to fulfill a really essential economic function. In this situation the producer knows that the limitation upon his operations and upon his growth no longer lies, as it lay historically, in his productive capacity, for he can always produce as much as the market will absorb; the limitation has shifted to the market, and it is selling capacity which controls his growth.[18]

What this kind of emphasis on consumption means, Potter suggests, is that radio and television programs and newspaper and magazine articles "do not attain the dignity of being ends in themselves; they are rather means to an end; that end, of course, is to catch the reader's attention so that he will then read the advertisement or hear the commercial, and to hold his interest until these essential messages have been delivered."[19]

If this view is the correct one, surely the judgment made in *A Study of Four Media,* published by the Alfred Politz Research Company, is also correct in its flat assertion that "the delivery of an audience for the advertiser is the fundamental function of any medium." These views suggest the force of economic reality, but there are, of course, other perspectives. Although most of those who work in the mass media must think always of large audiences, it is doubtful that any writer of a news story or magazine article, any reporter for a radio or television news program, or even a director of a situation comedy, ever weighs the possible effect of the work on the advertiser's ability to sell another Chevrolet or another case of Pepsi.

Not all media depend on advertising. There is nothing inherent in the nature of the media that requires them to depend on advertising for the large share of their income. Newspapers survived without any great amount of it for two centuries, and so did magazines. Books and motion pictures have never depended on advertisers. In many parts of the world, the media today put nowhere near the reliance on advertising support as in the United States. Even television, which in the United States is dominated by advertising, has other means of support in some countries.

Indeed, when radio sets began to make their entry into American homes, there was little thought that broadcasting would become married to advertising. Quite the contrary, there was a feeling that it should be protected from commercialization. Even David Sarnoff, who later became chairman of the Radio Corporation of America, saw broadcasting as a public institution free from commercial taint.

Printer's Ink, a voice of the advertising business, held in 1923:

> Any attempt to make radio an advertising medium . . . would, we think, prove positively offensive to great numbers of people. . . . Imagine the effect, for example, of a piano sonata by Josef Hoffman followed by the audible assertion, "If you are under forty, four chances in one you will get pyorrhea." "Pickle Bros. are offering three-dollar silk hose for $1.98." Exaggerated, no doubt, yet the principle is there. To break in upon one's entertainment *in his own house* is quite likely intolerable, and advertising as a whole cannot be the gainer by anything of the sort.

Even if the American mass media did not depend on advertising, however, it is doubtful that their content would be dramatically different. Virtually all of the media are under pressure to saturate the market they have chosen for their product. This compulsion to maximize their chosen audience may have been encouraged by the growth of advertising, but mainly it has been a concomitant of mass production.

For any medium many of the costs of doing business are fixed. However, once the medium passes the breakeven point, it may pile up profits rapidly. So even a medium without advertising strives for an audience large enough to take it past the breakeven point and deep into the realm of profit.

But a large audience may influence what a medium carries and what it does not. To attract and hold its audience, a medium ordinarily cannot risk alienating any substantial part of it, so it usually stays close to the tastes, interests, and values of the great majority.

Consider *The Reader's Digest.* From its founding in the basement of a

Greenwich Village speak-easy in 1922 until April 1955, it carried no advertising whatsoever. If advertising is the corrupting influence in mass communication, *The Reader's Digest* should have been a cultural monument
during the first 33 years of its life. Free from the taint of the advertiser, it
should have been an enlightened, sophisticated, literate, courageous magazine. It was not. And the fact that it was trying to please more than 10 million
readers was pivotal. That fact also influenced the *Digest*'s decision in 1955
to accept advertising.

It is extraordinarily difficult for most media to survive the competition
within and among media, to sustain the largest possible audience of the kind
they want, and to meet the rising production costs without advertising
support. Even movie producers expect to recover some costs by selling their
movies finally to commercial television. Rarely can a medium convince its
audience to bear the full costs of production. The ordeal of public broadcasting, or educational broadcasting as it was first called, shows just how difficult
it is to finance a medium outside the commercial system in the United
States.

PUBLIC BROADCASTING

Public broadcasting's founding rationale was precisely to escape the
constraints of commercial competition by deriving its financial support from
a mix of tax revenues, foundation grants, and viewer subscriptions. Freed
from dependence on advertising, from the necessity to attract the largest
possible audience by programing for the lowest common denominator,
public broadcasting would supplement commercial broadcasting. It would
offer programing of sufficient diversity and excellence to satisfy the general
public and particularly the minorities and subpublics within it.

From the inception of educational radio in 1919 and of educational
television in 1953, however, public broadcasting has limped along as
commercial broadcasting's poor relation, a chronic victim of financial mal-
nutrition. Public broadcasting has tried, therefore, to persuade business and
industry to contribute to the funding mix by "underwriting" programs, that
is, by sponsoring programs without directly advertising particular programs
or services.

The distinction between underwriting and advertising is important to
public broadcasting's original purpose and self-image, but it is a distinction
at the border where advertising and public relations blur and requires
uncomfortable rationalizations. Typically a potential underwriter wants
some assurance of visibility, of a respectably large audience. That is pressure
public broadcasting was designed to escape. Educational broadcasting's
pioneers abhorred any participation in the numbers game, and government
agreed. Ratings were out. In the 1970s, however, the American Research
Bureau and the A. C. Nielsen Company were regularly surveying the
audiences of public broadcasting programs, partly to please underwriters,
partly to reassure Congress, which was voting larger and larger appropria-

Audiences of the Mass Media

The impulse to measure the audiences of the media has been both practical and theoretical. The media producers and advertisers want to know how many people are reading, listening, or watching and what their age, sex, income, and other characteristics are so as to match the editorial formula or program with the people advertisers want to reach. Communication researchers are interested in these questions, too, but they are more interested in why certain individuals or groups use the media and what gratifications they get.

Research shows that although their audiences overlap considerably, each of the mass media has a tendency to draw its most devoted following from a somewhat different sector of the population. Each medium offers a particular combination of characteristic contents which tend to divide into two broad categories: fantasy-escape and information-education. Research shows, too, that certain demographic attributes characterize the different sectors of the population who use different media. From the many studies of audiences, general principles of communications behavior have emerged.

Paul Lazarsfeld and Patricia Kendall remarked on what they called the all-or-none aspect of communications behavior, the tendency for a person who is above average in exposure to one medium to be above average in exposure to all. Lazarsfeld and Merton saw the all-or-none principle as springing from interest and opportunity. That is, a person interested in escapist material may find it in books, in magazines, or on the air. Similarly, one interested in public affairs will probably seek information in newspapers, books, and magazines. In short, people can best satisfy their interests by using more than one medium. And people who have little opportunity to use one medium—because of the demands of jobs, hobbies, or other activities—will probably have little opportunity to use any.

In general, studies indicate that the better educated people are, the more use they will make of the media. The amount of newspaper reading tends to increase with education, as does serious use of the paper. The typical magazine reader is likely to have well over five years' more schooling than the person who does not read magazines. Moreover, the number of magazines read rises swiftly as the level of education goes up. The better-educated read more books than the rest of the population.

Use of the media increases as income increases, although this principle seems to apply more strongly to the print than to the broadcast media. Not only does newspaper reading increase with economic status, but so does attention to serious content such as editorials or material about public affairs, social problems, economics, and science. People with high incomes are more likely to read magazines than those with low incomes: about 90 percent of those in the high-income group are magazine readers; only about half of those in the low-income group are. Those with large incomes tend to read more magazines as well. And the number of books read also increases as income rises.

These general principles apply more to the print media than to broadcasting, particularly television. Television quickly established itself as the mass medium, the one used by people of all educational, income, and age levels. An early conclusion was that people tend to use print media mainly for information, broadcasting media mainly for entertainment. Surveys in the 1960s and 1970s showed, however, that although its programing was mostly entertainment, television was becoming an important source of news and information, particularly of national and international news. Certainly television was the most popular medium. Without distinguishing the category of content attended to or the demographic characteristics of the audiences, the Television Bureau of Advertising reported its finding that between 1970 and 1975 adults increased their use of newspapers, magazines, radio, and television by almost an hour a day, from 289 to 341 minutes a day. The increased time was distributed as follows:

Television: up 40 minutes, from 139 to 179 minutes a day
Radio: up 16 minutes, from 93 to 109 minutes a day
Newspapers: down 4 minutes, from 36 to 32 minutes a day
Magazines: no change, 21 minutes a day

Age, sex, education, and income do influence the reasons why people turn to the media and to some extent explain their patterned, predictable communications behavior. But profiles of audiences and of the different emphases in content in the various media do not fully explain peoples' media choices. More subtle factors—attitudes, aspirations, hopes, fears, needs, wants—also affect people's use of the media and complicate the task of identifying generalizable principles to explain media use.

Wilbur Schramm has suggested two general principles to explain peoples' selection and use of the media: the principles of least effort and promise of reward.

By "least effort" Schramm meant that the reader, listener, or viewer takes the route of least resistance in choosing communications offerings. Several factors explain this aspect of communications behavior. One is availability. All other things being equal, people help themselves to whatever communications are at hand. Expense is another factor. Money spent on one medium may prevent expenditure on another. Time affects communications behavior. Leisure time comes at different periods for different people and affects media selection and use. Role, habit, and custom may also affect media choices, for it is easier to continue behavior patterns than to change them. Communications behavior, in fact, becomes a part of social behavior, and some selection of media fare is really just a habitual social act.

Schramm interpreted "promise of reward" to mean that people choose from the available communications whatever they think will give them the greatest reward. Schramm classified rewards into two general types: immediate and delayed. Content that pays its rewards at once may relax tensions or help in problem solving. Content that pays its rewards in the future may promise information useful for social effectiveness.

The notion that much communications behavior is habitual suggests that it is passive and purposeless. The emphasis in Schramm's principles, however, is that communications behavior is active, conscious, rational, and goal-directed. But this rational behavior may not occur in quite the way Schramm suggested. He was inclined to conclude that fantasy-entertainment material was in the category of immediate rewards, information-education material in that of delayed rewards. Research shows, however, that the same media content may satisfy a variety of audience needs and functions, "that almost any type of content may serve practically any type of function." McQuail, Blumler, and Brown wrote in 1972 that

> . . . the relationship between content categories and audience needs is far less tidy and more complex than most commentators have appreciated. . . . One man's source of escape from the real world is a point of anchorage for another man's place in it.[20]

For some an objective account of the charge by Elizabeth Ray in 1976 that Congressman Wayne Hays of Ohio paid her $14,000 a year out of public funds to serve as his mistress may provide vital political information prior to voting for their Congressional representative. For some the account may titillate and entertain. For others the news item may momentarily brighten their habitual and largely uncritical practice of reading a newspaper or watching television news.

Some may watch the television comedy series "M*A*S*H" merely as a form of diversion from daily routines and problems, as a way to relax and kill time. Some may watch it to learn how to cope with pain and suffering. For some the cast of familiar and perhaps much loved characters may provide a form of companionship. And others may watch the show as a way of spending time with their families.

Media content, then, is not the only source of a variety of gratifications. Exposure to the media, the act of reading, listening, or watching itself, can be its own reward. The social context in which exposure to different media typically occurs rather than a medium's actual content gratifies some individuals and groups. Some adolescents go to the movies to escape the home and be with their peers or to date the opposite sex. *What* is on the screen may not matter.

Growing awareness of the diversity of peoples' uses and gratifications has not only afforded a richer understanding of communications behavior, it has been used to justify content that some consider objectionable and of dubious value. Harold Mendelsohn, a communications researcher and a member of the Surgeon General's Scientific Advisory Committee on Television and Social Behavior, has noted:

> Thus "gossip" columns can flourish under the pretense of meeting the public's "need to know." Explicit sex films can be purveyed as affording "everything you wanted to know about sex—but were afraid to ask." And blatant one-sided propaganda of all sorts can be presented as satisfying the "information" needs of various publics.[21]

In a subjective and unscientific way, the media have also speculated about audience needs and wants and have based their editorial formulas and programing on their instinctive evaluations. That is why media content continues to change as audiences change, why media adjust to the presence and approach of other media as well as to the measured and assumed changes in audiences. As Mendelsohn has observed, "Neither the media nor media audiences are cemented in place for all time."

The shifting nature of audiences and of their needs and wants, the shifting nature of media functions and capabilities as new technologies develop, and a relatively competitive free enterprise system explain the pluralism of American media. Nevertheless, they are united in their diversity by common purposes. All are concerned in differing degree to inform, educate, persuade, and entertain, and most hope to make as much profit as possible doing so. Because the media's services and purposes are essentially similar, economies of scale have stimulated centralization and consolidation within and across media and multimedia ownership.

CENTRALIZATION AND CONSOLIDATION

Soon after cheap newspapers striving for mass circulations entered into vigorous competition with one another, publishers recognized the need for some cooperative news gathering to cut costs. In 1848 six New York papers joined in an informal cooperative association to share the cost of procuring foreign news by telegraph from ships arriving in Boston. This organization was to grow eventually into the Associated Press. The Midwestern publishers, Edward and James Scripps, had a chain of papers served by three press associations, which they merged in 1907 into the United Press Association. In 1909 William Randolph Hearst formed his own press association, the International News Service. It later merged into Scripps' association to become what we know today as United Press International. These two wire services, AP and UPI, now supply about 99 percent of American newspapers and most American radio and television stations with a daily mix of news, photographs, and features.

Newspaper syndicates began in 1884. The first ones distributed fiction and feature material, mainly for women. Edward Bok, later editor of the *Ladies' Home Journal,* observed that "the American woman was not a newspaper reader," and he built up a clientele of 90 newspapers around the country for his syndicated material of interest to women. Today there are four main syndicates: AP Newsfeatures, United Features, King Features, and NEA Service.

The main purpose of these news associations and syndicates is to offer news and features at costs much lower than individual media would have to pay to gather the material themselves. Such savings helped sustain the extraordinary number of competing newspapers in major American cities at the turn of the century (in 1890, New York had 15 daily newspapers, eight morning and seven afternoon papers). But no centralized or cooperative enterprise could compensate in the end for the crippling competition engaged in by wealthy publishers such as Pulitzer and Hearst, nor could advertising sustain the large number of often weak and mediocre papers in the same city, not when other media were becoming available. In this century, then, newspapers have been merged, killed, or have died; by 1977, less than 3 percent of American cities with daily newspapers had local daily newspaper competition. Moreover, the surviving newspapers had to a great extent been bought up by chains, which by 1977 owned 60 percent of all American daily newspapers.

Centralization of resources occurred early in the development of the electronic media. Few radio stations could afford to pay the high programing costs to attract and hold audiences who quickly came to expect a variety of fare: drama, comedy, concerts, news, and sports. In 1926 the Radio Corporation of America (RCA) formed a subsidiary, the National Broadcasting Company (NBC), to hire top talent and to produce and distribute news and entertainment programing to a network of affiliate stations. Affiliate stations in effect sold their audiences to the central network, which then sold the total audience to advertisers, so covering its programing costs and making its profits. The Columbia Broadcasting System (CBS) began to compete with NBC in 1927. Under pressure from the Justice Department, which was concerned about its monopolistic practices, NBC sold one of the two networks it operated in 1943, and a new network, the American Broadcasting Company (ABC), was born. When television took off as a mass medium of news and entertainment in 1952, the three radio networks were well established to become the major producers and distributors of programing in the new industry.

The accelerating centralization of news and entertainment sources and concentration of ownership in this century early alarmed persons concerned that a basic libertarian and democratic principle, the free marketplace of ideas in which as wide a diversity of ideas and information as possible could clash and compete, was in jeopardy.

MULTIMEDIA OWNERSHIP AND CONGLOMERATES

Of even greater contemporary concern has been the growth of cross-media ownership and conglomerates. Until about 1960 the communications businesses stuck rather single mindedly to their specialty of communicating. A magazine publisher might bring out a new magazine or add a line of paperback books. A newspaper publisher might add another daily to the chain or buy a broadcasting station. But it was usually low-key and had little effect on the large world of mass communication.

Today the scope, style, and substance of media ownership has changed. Many communications businesses are expanding into other areas, and others are being taken over by huge conglomerates. Consider these examples in 1977:

The Times Mirror Company published the Los Angeles *Times, Newsday,* and the Dallas *Times Herald,* owned the New American Library paperback company and cable television systems in New York and California, and had subsidiaries that produced telephone directories, Bibles, law books and medical journals, road maps for oil companies, and navigational charts for airlines.

RCA, which owned NBC, also owned RCA Victor records, Random House books and its several subsidiaries, and Hertz car rental. RCA manufactured a wide range of electronic hardware for defense and space industries and through its RCA Global Communications, Inc., controlled telecommunications in 200 countries.

In addition to its broadcasting enterprises, CBS owned the Holt, Rinehart and Winston publishing company, Fawcett Publications, at least six magazines, Creative Playthings, Steinway pianos and X-acto tools, and operated businesses in 30 countries.

ABC owned 277 theaters, a water-bottling company, Word, Inc., which produced religious materials of all kinds, and had substantial recording enterprises.

Keeping track of the mergers and acquisitions involving communications properties is a formidable task. In 1972 Robert Bishop made these calculations: "The combined holdings of groups, cross-media owners, conglomerates, and firms related to the mass media encompass 58 percent of daily newspapers, 77 percent of TV stations, 27 percent of AM, and 29 percent of FM stations."[22]

The reasons for the development of conglomerates are various. One obviously is to broaden the financial base. Because magazine publishing is rarely a highly lucrative enterprise, for instance, some publishers want alternative sources of income. Another is to capitalize on the swiftly expanding educational market by providing the textbooks, teaching aids, programmed learning materials, and other elements of the curriculum from kindergarten through college. Yet another is recognition of the revolution in communications technology, which is already blurring the distinction between the printed and electronic media. When Time Inc. acquired $17.7 million worth of Metro-Goldwyn-Mayer stock in 1967, it did so on the basis of a 200-page staff report titled *Information Technology: An Overview of the 70s.* Time Inc. was attracted to M-G-M not only for its movie-making potential but also for its diversified holdings in such fields as TV programing, music, and recordings. Said the executive in charge of corporate develop-

ment: "Such new and soon-to-come electronic techniques as satellite communications, CATV, pay-TV, video tape and video disc are part of the new
world of communications, and this is what Time Inc. is interested in."

All this is profoundly disturbing to a number of thoughtful observers. The
almost inevitable conflict of interest of these diversified conglomerates, it is
feared, may inhibit the free flow of information and comment about affiliated companies through the news media units of their enterprises. Nicholas
Johnson, an FCC commissioner from 1966 to 1973, reviewed the conglomerate record of mass communications and concluded:

> . . . the wave of renewed interest in the impact of ownership on the role of the
> media in our society is healthy. All will gain from intelligent inquiry by Congress,
> the Executive, the regulatory Commissions—and especially the academic com-
> munity, the American people generally, and the media themselves. For, as the
> Supreme Court has noted, nothing is more important in a free society than "the
> widest possible dissemination of information from diverse and antagonistic
> sources." And if we are unwilling to discuss *this* issue fully today we may find
> ourselves discussing none that matter very much tomorrow.[23]

Clearly we should be concerned about these concentrations of ownership and power in media organizations and conglomerates. The potential
threat to basic principles of libertarianism and American democracy is real.
But it is not necessarily so that news media owned by large corporate
enterprises ignore their responsibilities while smaller, independently owned
news media competing in a wide, diverse marketplace carry out theirs.
Neither media concentration nor media competition is inevitably good or
bad. As the period of yellow journalism showed, competition can produce
thoroughly irresponsible journalism. Freed from the temptation to sensa-
tionalize in situations of intense competition, news media in situations of
near monopoly may find it easier to perform more responsibly, to use their
concentrated resources in the public interest, and to exercise responsible
leadership rather than respond to public whim. Nor is the media's massive
size necessarily a disadvantage. The size and power of government and its
intrusion into our daily lives have grown formidably in this century, particularly since the 1930s. If the media are to serve as effective watchdogs of
burgeoning government, they may often need considerable resources. It is
doubtful that a small newspaper or local radio or television station could
have sustained the lengthy investigation of the Nixon Administration in
1972 and 1973 and could have endured the administration's counterattack
as did the Washington *Post*.

Whatever reservations we may have about the corporate behavior of the
Post as revealed through its handling of the strike in 1976, and clearly such
behavior deserves the closest scrutiny, we should acknowledge the value to
democratic society of powerful media institutions when they use their power
in the public interest.

Notes

1. Eliot Marshall, "Striking Facts about the Post," *The New Republic,* October 25, 1975, p. 11.
2. Frank Luther Mott, *American Journalism* (New York: Macmillan, 1947), p. 20.
3. Richard Hofstadter, William Miller, and Daniel Aaron, *The American Republic,* Volume One (Englewood Cliffs, N.J.: Prentice-Hall, 1959), p. 390.
4. Hofstadter *et al.,* pp. 391–392.
5. Syndicated article by Melvin Maddocks, *The Louisville Courier-Journal & Times,* November 16, 1975.
6. Gerald Emanuel Stearn (ed.), *McLuhan: Hot & Cool* (New York: Signet Books, 1967), pp. 143, 150.
7. Vernon L. Parrington, *Main Currents in American Thought,* Volume One (New York: Harcourt, 1927), p. 361.
8. Parrington, p. 353.
9. Parrington, p. 311.
10. Mott, p. 197.
11. New York *Sun,* July 4, 1934, quoted in Mott, p. 223.
12. New York *Sun,* August 25–28, 1835.
13. Willard Grosvenor Bleyer, *Main Currents In The History Of American Journalism* (Boston: Houghton Mifflin, 1927), pp. 198, 206.
14. Edwin Emery, *The Press and America: An Interpretative History of the Mass Media,* Third Edition (Englewood Cliffs, N.J.: Prentice-Hall, 1972), p. 311.
15. John Tebbel, *The Media In America* (New York: New American Library, 1974), p. 288.
16. Daniel J. Boorstin, *The Image: A Guide to Pseudo-Events in America* (New York: Harper & Row, 1964), p. 8.
17. James Reston, *The Artillery of the Press: Its Influence on American Foreign Policy* (New York: Harper & Row, 1966), p. 81.
18. David M. Potter, *People of Plenty: Economic abundance and the American character* (Chicago: University of Chicago Press, 1968), pp. 172–173.
19. Potter, pp. 181–182.
20. Quoted in Jay G. Blumler and Elihu Katz (eds.), *The Uses of Mass Communications: Current Perspectives on Gratifications Research* (Beverly Hills: Sage Publications, 1974), p. 28.
21. Harold Mendelsohn, "Some Policy Implications of the Uses and Gratifications Paradigm," in Blumler and Katz, pp. 303–304.
22. Robert L. Bishop, "The rush to chain ownership," *Columbia Journalism Review,* November/December 1972, p. 10.
23. Nicholas Johnson, *How to talk back to your television set* (New York: Bantam, 1970), p. 69.

4

The Print Media: Newspapers, Magazines, and Books

Formerly life's bitterest misfortunes enriched only the hearts of wretches or were of spiritual value exclusively. But now any frightful event may be a gold mine. I'm sure that if and when poor Thaxter makes it, if they release him, he will strike it rich by writing a book. Hundreds of thousands of people who at this moment don't give a single damn about him will suffer with him intensely.

SAUL BELLOW, *HUMBOLDT'S GIFT*

The message of McLuhan in the 1960s was that electronic communications were killing print. That judgment has proved wrong or at least premature. True, the antenna of the media picked up tremors in the mid-1970s indicating that Americans' reading and writing skills were declining, and by concentrating public attention on alarming statistics and assertions of decline, the media moved the tremors up the Richter scale. Popular and expert opinion quickly blamed television as a major villain, particularly as the apparent decline coincided with a drop in newspaper circulation. Then analysts so explained the statistics as to raise doubts that the decline was real; experts disagreed about whether or not a problem in fact existed, and if it did, just how serious it was; and historians pointed out that concern about declining literacy had surfaced before and seemed cyclical in nature. Nevertheless, the message through the media was that indeed Johnny could not read or write, and schools and universities were put on notice to do something. Then the media picked up other tremors in society and moved on.

Because it lacked dramatic visual appeal, the "story" of declining literacy lent itself more to examination by the print than the electronic media, so illustrating an important point. Although the media all perform the same functions, they cannot in every instance perform them equally well. To some extent their competition for audiences and advertisers is at one another's expense, but each possesses sufficiently unique attributes for supplementary and complementary roles to survive. This chapter, then, discusses a dynamic not a dying communications technology.

The Newspaper Industry

CHAIN OWNERSHIP

The creation of mass markets, which only large and costly units could service efficiently, has led inevitably to a contraction of ownership in many cities and towns and thus to the development of newspaper chains. The high point in the number of newspapers published in the United States came in 1909, when there were 2600 daily publications. On this situation, magazine publisher Frank Munsey commented, "There is no business that cries out so loud for organization and combination as that of newspaper publishing. For one thing, the number of newspapers is at least 60 percent greater than we need."[1]

Munsey dreamed of a national chain of 500 newspapers and tried to start it by buying newspapers in New York, Washington, Boston, Baltimore, and Philadelphia. Although his chain failed, he pioneered an accelerating trend in twentieth-century publishing.

In the first half of the twentieth century, more than 2000 new daily newspapers (including those changing from weekly to daily) were started. But, during the same period, 1947 daily newspapers suspended publication to become weeklies, 547 disappeared through merger or consolidation, and at least 302 local combinations took place. At the same time the number of newspaper chains increased from three, publishing 62 newspapers, to 70, publishing 386, with more than two-fifths of the daily and one-half of the Sunday circulation. In the 1950s there were scarcely more than 100 cities with competing daily newspapers. Of the 1500 cities with daily newspapers in 1977, only 2.5 percent—fewer than 40—had competing newspapers. By then the nation's 168 chains owned three-fifths of the nation's 1756 daily newspapers and controlled 71 percent of the circulation.

Professor Paul Jess of the University of Kansas reported[2] that as of December 31, 1976, the leading chains were

In terms of numbers of newspapers owned:

Gannett	73	Harte-Hanks	24
Thomson	57	Scripps League	20
Knight-Ridder	34	Worrell	19
Walls	32	Cox	18
Newhouse	30	Stauffer	18
Freedom	25		

In terms of daily circulation:

Knight-Ridder	3,725,000	Times Mirror	1,750,000
Newhouse	3,530,000	Dow Jones	1,700,000
Chicago Tribune	2,995,000	Hearst	1,550,000
Gannett	2,940,000	Cox	1,200,000
Scripps-Howard	1,750,000	N.Y. Times Co.	1,005,000

According to journalism historian Frank Mott, consolidation of newspapers is not a strictly recent tendency; it can be found in all periods. But since World War I, the skyrocketing cost of newspaper publication has been a strong influence in accelerating the tendency to consolidate.

Melville E. Stone established the Chicago *Daily News* in 1876 with a few thousand dollars capital; in 1925 it sold for $13 million. In 1963 two Omaha dailies were sold for $43 million, and in 1967 Newhouse Newspapers bought the Cleveland *Plain Dealer* for $53.4 million. Knight Newspapers paid $55 million for two Philadelphia papers in 1969. In 1976 Rupert Murdoch, the Australian press baron, paid, according to *Folio* magazine's estimate, $30 million for the New York *Post* at a time when all three New York dailies were losing circulation (between March 1974 and September 1976, the *Times* dropped from approximately 910,000 daily to 802,000, the *Daily News* from 2.12 million to 1.93 million, and the *Post* from 650,000 to 489,000).

In the typical American town in earlier days, more newspaper publishing ventures were attempted than the economy could support. Some newspapers—for example, those founded solely as voices of political parties or other interest groups—went out of business simply because they could not win general community support. Others were founded by people who went into the business apparently on the assumption that to make money it was only necessary to "buy newsprint white and sell it black." They soon discovered that, aside from the problems of editing a mass medium, such factors as rigid advertising and circulation rates made newspaper publishing a dubious enterprise at best. For the new entrant today the problems are even more formidable, particularly in metropolitan areas. Not only has population shifted increasingly to the suburbs, with businesses and service industries in pursuit, but inflation in the 1970s was forcing more and more families to stop subscribing to more than one newspaper.

Both in procuring their raw material and in marketing their products, newspaper publishers exhibit the familiar behavior of monopoly and oligopoly. As buyers they use the customary pressures for keeping down costs; as sellers they maintain rigid advertising and circulation rates, discriminate by rate differentials, and practice block selling of space in morning and evening newspapers in combination. The typical newspaper pays out for newsprint roughly one-third of its revenues, which is just about what it receives in circulation revenue. Practically all newsprint is sold in carload lots under long-term contracts, mostly to large publishers. Those who cannot afford carload lots get their newsprint from jobbers, brokers, and paper merchants at open market prices, which are sometimes higher by 10 percent or more than the carload rates.

Procuring syndicated features and wire services is no less difficult for the new entrant. The syndicated feature business is dominated by four major companies: AP Newsfeatures, King Features, NEA Service, and United Features. Most franchises provide for exclusive territories. Furthermore, package selling enables large publishers to buy up rights to more features than they print. Oligopoly is similarly a chief trait of the two wire services.

The new newspaper is confronted in many markets by chain organization. Chains, especially of large newspapers, have certain special advantages: Notably, they make wider use of editorial and feature writers; it is easier for them to obtain new funds from the capital market; they engage in block merchandising of space to national advertisers, in centralized and large-scale research, and in bulk purchases of newsprint, ink, and equipment; they are better able to make maximum use of specialized technical and managerial services, and of electronic automation—central computers can serve all papers in the chain.

THE LOCALISM OF U.S. NEWSPAPERS

Despite these centralizing tendencies, American news institutions, and newspapers in particular, have been local rather than national because of "a peculiarity in American political organization and the prevailing pattern of family money spending." Ben Bagdikian has written:

> More governmental functions are left to the local level in the United States than in other developed countries. Schools, property taxes, land use, public health, large areas of business regulation, and many other political and social activities are controlled by locally elected and locally controlled bodies. . . . These locally controlled policies have maximum immediate impact on family life, such as schooling for children, design and location of homes, routes of local highways, and rates of personal property taxes. Such decisions are made by a complicated but highly localized set of political bodies.[3]

The United States has no national newspapers. The closest approxima-
tions are the *Wall Street Journal,* which in 1977 reached across the nation to
1.46 million people interested mainly in financial news, and the New York
Times, one quarter of whose 854,000 daily subscribers in 1977 lived more
than 100 miles from New York City. To a much lesser extent, the Washington *Post* also reached beyond the capital, but it did not compete seriously in
national and international circulation with the *Times.* In the late 1970s the
Times was spending $35 million a year (the *Post* was spending $19 million)
to support the world's largest full-time news staff—641 journalists (550 in
New York, 40 in Washington, 19 scattered throughout the United States,
and 32 abroad). There are fatter American newspapers than the *Times* (the
average "news hole"—the space devoted to editorial words—of the *Times*
in 1977 was 160 columns a day; the Washington *Star* printed 185 and the
Chicago *Tribune* 218 columns a day), but they rely typically on wire service
and syndicated material for much of their content. Almost everything in the
Times is staff written.

These huge newspapers with an impact beyond their cities of publication
form a tiny minority of American daily newspapers; only half a percent of all
dailies have more than 500,000 circulation. Seventy percent of U.S. dailies
have circulations of 25,000 or less; 53 percent are published in cities with
populations less than 25,000. Although the New York *Times* has an
influence in the United States and abroad out of all proportion to its size, the
statistics in the tables below present a clearer perspective on the newspaper
industry as a whole and vividly make Bagdikian's point about the localism of
newspapers.

As Americans' disposable income has risen, retail stores and service
enterprises have kept pace at the local level in competing for this income,
typically by advertising through the local newspaper. In 1976 advertisers
spent $33.6 billion in all media. Newspapers got $10.2 billion or 30 percent
of that, 25.6 percent local, only 4.4 percent national. Television got $6.6

Circulation of U.S. Daily Newspapers for 1976 by Population Groups†

Population 1970 U.S. Census	Morning	Evening	Total	Percent	Circ. in Mill.
*More than 1,000,000	16	12	27	1.5	11.3
500,001 to 1,000,000	25	24	49	2.8	10.1
*100,001 to 500,000	90	125	211	12.0	16.8
*50,001 to 100,000	69	174	237	13.5	8.0
*25,001 to 50,000	64	252	310	17.6	6.4
*Less than 25,000	62	848	928	52.7	8.3
	346	1,435	1,762	100.0	61.0

†Derived from 1977 *Editor & Publisher International Year Book,* p. 23.
*19 "All-Day" newspapers included in these figures, for which adjustments have been made in
the totals.

Circulation of U.S. Daily Newspapers in 1976 By Circulation Groups†

Circulation As of Sept. 30, 1976	Morning	Evening	Total	Percent	Circ. in Mill.
500,001 and over	7	2	9	.5	7.2
*250,001 to 500,000	14	14	27	1.5	9.9
100,001 to 250,000	40	43	83	4.7	13.0
*50,001 to 100,000	65	68	131	7.4	8.8
*25,001 to 50,000	71	202	266	15.1	9.4
*10,001 to 25,000	76	449	518	29.4	8.3
*5,001 to 10,000	47	402	447	25.4	3.3
*Less than 5,000	26	255	281	15.9	1.0
	346	1,435	1,762	100.0	61.0

†Derived from 1977 *Editor & Publisher International Year Book*, p. 23.
*19 "All-Day" newspapers included in these figures, for which adjustments have been made in the totals.

billion or 19.7 percent of the total, 14.7 percent network and spot, only 5 percent local. An example of the impact on newspapers of family spending in the 1970s was the coupon war arising out of competition among local retail stores, particularly supermarkets. The Nielsen Company reported that 20 percent more manufacturers' coupons were issued in 1975 than in 1974 and that 65 percent of all U.S. households used coupons in 1975 compared to 58 percent in 1971. Newspapers had the biggest share of coupons—55.9 percent in 1975, compared to 51.8 percent in 1971. In fact, it has been argued that the money a family saves by clipping coupons more than pays for subscribing to a local newspaper.

SHOPPERS

Because of family spending patterns, the population shift to the suburbs, and the mushrooming suburban shopping centers, a relatively new newspaper category has emerged: the shopper's guide or shopper or throwaway. A typical daily newspaper has a ratio of about 65 percent advertising content to 35 percent news and feature content. Shoppers, by contrast, contain 75 percent or more advertising content, and many are distributed free. And their numbers are growing. The U.S. Suburban Press, Inc., had 850 of these shoppers with a total circulation of 11.3 million in early 1976.

To curb shoppers' eating into their advertising revenues, established newspapers were supporting efforts by some states to exclude shoppers from the tax privileges enjoyed by "traditional" newspapers. In New Jersey state tax officials were struggling to come up with a satisfactory definition of "newspaper." The rise of the suburban press, whether as traditional newspaper or shopper, challenged the domination of major metropolitan newspapers, many of which began developing their own suburban or zone editions in the 1970s to compete for readers and advertisers.

The localism of newspapers and their efforts to attract and hold readers in a competitive market have made the newspaper in many respects a more direct descendant of the early magazine of the nineteenth century than is the contemporary magazine. The word "magazine" is derived from the French word *magazin,* meaning "storehouse," and early magazines were miscellanies of information and amusement. In its growing consumer orientation and emphasis on "news you can use," today's local newspaper is very similar. Readers of all ages can usually find something to interest them in the paper's coverage of local events and activities, in its local and syndicated features, comics, and games, and in its local retail ads and listing of local entertainment. Even the large metropolitan newspapers that concentrate on public affairs and appeal to a readership far beyond their cities of publication—the New York *Times,* Washington *Post,* the *Wall Street Journal,* and the *Christian Science Monitor*—publish a miscellany of serious and entertaining content more diverse than that of a general-interest magazine.

In fact, it seemed in the late 1970s that newspapers had to publish more of such "soft" news and feature material to stave off circulation declines. By adding a section three days a week in 1976 and 1977—Living, a section on food and wine, on Wednesdays, Home, on furniture, interior decorating, and gardening, on Thursdays, and Weekend, a guide to entertainment and the arts, on Fridays—the New York *Times* reversed its circulation decline, increasing circulation from a daily average of 821,000 in 1976 to 854,000 in 1977. Not only did more people buy the *Times* on the days with added sections—35,000 more than on unsupplemented days—more advertisers bought space. The *Times* sold more advertising in May 1977 than in any previous month in its history.

STANDARDIZATION

To some extent their local orientation offsets the standardization of American newspapers. Yet whatever character a publisher or editor or the community itself confers on a local newspaper, economy dictates a heavy reliance by almost all on wire and news services for national and international news and on syndicates for features, columns, and comics. Studies have long shown that the comics sections, and particularly the Sunday comics, are among the best-read sections in the paper. A study reported by N. W. Ayer and Company in 1976 found that more than 50 million copies of Sunday comics are distributed to American homes every week, where they are read by over 100 million people. And two organizations, Metro Sunday Comics and the Puck Group, supply over 76 percent of those copies.

Not only do these centralized sources of news and entertainment make for an essential similarity in newspaper content from place to place, but the newswriting techniques and formulas of the wire services—typically a summary lead paragraph followed by the facts in order of decreasing importance—have influenced reportorial style in such a way that even local stories read alike. The chemistry of the city council members and the nature of the issues they discuss may differ dramatically between Lompoc, California, and

Brunswick, Maine, but the way in which the Lompoc *Record* and the Brunswick *Times Record* report them is unlikely to differ much. Researchers have argued, in fact, that because of professional norms concerning definitions of news and the inverted pyramid style of reporting, reporters ignore the color, flavor, and very human disorder and tedium of city council discussion in favor of a concise, objective account of the decisions taken. The effect of this approach, the researchers argue, is to shore up the authority of local government by creating the impression that it is consistently acting decisively and rationally.

Even though the great majority of daily newspapers—approximately 85 percent—have circulations under 50,000, and may therefore appear small enough to serve as personal vehicles for strong-minded, colorful publishers who can stamp the newspaper with their own personalities, the forces of industrialization and urbanization accelerating after the Civil War virtually killed the dominance of flamboyant publishers like Bennett, Pulitzer, and Hearst whose papers were personal, idiosyncratic extensions of themselves. Most newspapers today are corporate and impersonal enterprises.

PERSONAL JOURNALISM

Examples of the colorful breed of the nineteenth century survive, of course. In New Hampshire, William Loeb, the publisher of the Manchester *Union Leader,* uses his statewide newspaper with vigorous partisanship against political candidates of whom he disapproves. Rupert Murdoch, the Australian publisher of the New York *Post,* seems a reincarnation of much of the best and worst of Pulitzer and Hearst.

In Las Vegas, Herman M. Greenspun, publisher of the Las Vegas *Sun,* has carried an adventurous life into his paper. *Editor & Publisher* gives this account of the extraordinary derring-do of his fight for Israel's survival in 1948. He plundered a naval depot in Hawaii, and, posing as an agent for Generalissmo Chiang Kai-Shek, seized a yacht at gunpoint. He then filled a ship at Tampico Bay with 6000 tons of contraband rifles, machine guns, howitzers, cannons, and tons of ammunition, and sailed to Israel. He was convicted in 1950 of violating the U.S. Neutrality Act and stripped of his civil rights. President John Kennedy pardoned him in 1961. Before becoming publisher of the *Sun,* Greenspun worked as publicity director for the Flamingo casino, owned by hoodlum Bugsy Siegel, who was later gunned down. Since then Greenspun has campaigned against gangsters in Las Vegas, and as a result of his investigative journalism and his trenchant front-page column, "Where I Stand," has been hit with more than 100 lawsuits, so becoming the most sued publisher in the nation. He was one of the first publishers to attack Joseph McCarthy, the anti-Communist senator from Wisconsin in the early 1950s; he was the only newsman to testify before the Senate Watergate committee—he said he knew of a $100,000 campaign contribution to Richard Nixon from billionaire recluse Howard Hughes.

Newspaper publishing has other characters, but the generalization holds: Most newspapers are impersonal, corporate enterprises that reflect the

Rupert Murdoch, the Australian publisher of the New York *Post:* A modern day Hearst? (United Press International photo)

middle-class values of their mainly middle-class owners. Not only does the scale of their enterprise distance many publishers from the daily operation of the newspaper, but the professionalization of journalists also sets publisher and reporter apart. The rise of journalism education and of organizations such as the Newspaper Guild and the Society of Professional Journalists, Sigma Delta Chi, has to some extent institutionalized journalists' ethics and reinforced conventions such as objective reporting, adherence to which has given reporters a measure of independence from publishers' whims.

THE UNDERGROUND PRESS

Largely to protest middle-class values and accepted journalistic responsibilities and conventions and to express their protest in vivid, unrestrained language, an "underground" press flowered in the late 1960s and early 1970s, giving the lie fleetingly to the generalization that newspapers are impersonal, middle-class businesses. There were only four in 1965, but Robert Glessing counted approximately 3000 underground papers that had published at one time or another between 1965 and 1972.

Some underground papers built circulations in the tens of thousands, among them the highly successful *Berkeley Barb.* In 1969 wrangling between the owner, Max Scherr, and his staff became public, revealing just how lucrative such an operation can be. It also revealed that, like the capitalists of the commercial press, some underground journalists are money-conscious. A large group of Scherr's helpers broke away and began to publish the *Berkeley Tribe,* but not before their negotiations to buy the *Barb* had reached figures in the hundreds of thousands.

It will not do to assign sweeping significance to the underground press. Ray Mungo, one of the founders of the Liberation News Service, which provided material for underground newspapers, has written:

> Lots of radicals will give you a very precise line about why their little newspaper or organization was formed and what needs it fulfills and most of that stuff is bullshit, you see—the point is they've got nothing to do, and the prospect of holding a straight job is so dreary that they join the "movement" and start hitting up people for money to live, on the premise that they're involved in critical social change blah blah blah. And it's really better that way, at least for some people, than finishing college and working at dumb jobs for constipated corporations; at least it's not always boring . . . that's why we decided to start a news service— not because the proliferating underground and radical college press really needed a central information-gathering agency staffed by people they could trust (that was our hype), but because we had nothing else to do.[4]

At the same time, it is important to recognize the real strengths of this new journalism. It provided a forum for ideas that were not considered, or not considered adequately, in conventional media. The undergrounders also provided a view of a different life style and afforded different and valuable perspectives.

What this new journalism proved was that a vast distance stretched between the conventional media and important segments of the public. There was a time when a newspaper or magazine served its own small public. The circulation was relatively slender, but editors spoke directly to the central interests of their readers, and they could usually count on reader loyalty. Anyone who cherished another point of view might attack, and a publication that posed a threat might be destroyed—the abolionist papers, for example—but most people simply subscribed to publications that squared with their own prejudices and idiosyncrasies.

When the conventional media became large and few, however, and editors were trying to attract mass audiences, separate voices could no longer be raised so readily in a free marketplace of ideas.

Many underground papers succeeded in building close relationships with their readers, at least in part because they revived the art of speaking to a relatively homogeneous audience. One important technique was to present news in heavily subjective prose: "A growing revolt against the selfish and reactionary American Medical Association came to a head here," began an article in *Open City,* a Los Angeles paper. "Objectivity is a farce," said Thorne Dreyer of Liberation News Service. Jeff Shero, former editor of *The Rat,* said, "We make our biases clear. That frees our writers to talk about their guts."

Perhaps the strongest challenge to conventional journalism was this "gut reporting." The underground press had a marked distaste for the roots of journalism: the search for verifiable facts.

THE BLACK PRESS

The underground press, like the revolutionary press of the eighteenth century, was a phenomenon of a period of protest and discontent. It faded for a variety of reasons: because the Vietnam War eventually ended; because the issues diminished in intensity, were resolved, or forgotten; because money and energy ran out; because the journalists turned 30. By contrast, the black press in the United States has struggled and survived by keeping one foot in conventional newspaper publishing and another in militancy and protest.

In 1976 the 325 black newspapers listed in *Editor & Publisher International Year Book* published mainly in metropolitan areas where black population concentrates, and competed with white metropolitan newspapers for readership and advertising. Only two of these black newspapers were dailies, the Atlanta *Daily World* and the Chicago *Defender;* a few published twice a week; most published weekly.

Their need for the advertising support of white-owned businesses and industries forced upon them a conservatism in editorial approach at a time when blacks had become increasingly militant, so creating a tension between publisher and readers. For example, John Sengstacke, publisher of the Chicago *Defender,* was delighted when Marshall Field and Company agreed to advertise in the *Defender.* But Marshall Field is not a store that many blacks can afford to patronize. Nor can Sengstacke afford to take too militant a stance on issues of concern to blacks if he wishes to retain the support of advertisers like Marshall Field. Sengstacke not only confronts this dilemma but must also compete for middle-class black readers, and also for black reporters, with the Chicago *Daily News,* the *Sun-Times,* and the *Tribune.* And he must compete for more militant black readers with *Muhammad Speaks,* published in Chicago by the Black Muslims, and with such other militant organs in Chicago as *Black Truth,* the *Observer,* and the *Black Liberator.*

The militant black organs fit comfortably into the tradition of the black press in this country. Historically it has been a press of protest, ever since John B. Russwurm and the Rev. Samuel Cornish started the nation's first black newspaper, *Freedom's Journal,* in 1827, to fight slavery. But today major black newspapers, such as the *Defender,* the Baltimore *Afro-American,* and the Pittsburgh *Courier,* which seek to survive in the commercial world by reflecting the interests mainly of middle-class blacks, tend to be more informational organs than organs of protest. And they have had to face the rising costs of the industry as a whole with little of the advertising support on which white newspapers have been able to count. Typically, therefore, these papers have had to scale down their enterprises. In 1945, the Pittsburgh *Courier,* with a circulation of 257,000, the Chicago *Defender,* with a circulation of 202,000, and the Baltimore *Afro-American,* with a circulation of 137,000, were national weeklies. In the 1970s all three were local newspapers with much reduced circulations. In 1976 the *Courier* was circulating about 20,800 copies a week; the *Afro-American,* which published biweekly, was circulating 26,000 on Tuesdays and 28,000 on Saturdays; and the *Defender,* which became a daily in 1956, was circulating 20,000. Some consolidation and concentration in ownership has also occurred. For example, John Sengstacke bought the *Courier* chain in 1967, so acquiring 10 newspapers in nine states. By 1976 his chain had been reduced to five papers publishing in four states.

The black press as a whole, however, had expanded. In 1945, 150 black newspapers were publishing in the United States with an estimated circulation of 1.6 million. In 1976, 325 black newspapers were publishing with an estimated circulation of 7 million.*

Although the number of black newspapers has expanded, the number of white newspapers has been remarkably constant for decades despite the consolidation and mergers and decline in competition. The rise in educational and economic opportunities for blacks and their increasing militancy in securing those opportunities, often by starting newspapers to express their grievances, explains the expansion of the black press. But the black press in the mid-1970s was showing the same characteristic that explains the stability in numbers of the white press: an emphasis on localism. The major black national papers of the 1970s, *Muhammad Speaks* and the *Black Panther,* differed from the early national weeklies—they are organs of religious or political movements rather than of news and information. Most black newspapers, like most white papers, were directed at local communities. As white populations left the metropolitan areas, so contributing to the decline in competing dailies, suburban dailies replaced them to respond to the needs of suburban readers and advertisers.

THE CHALLENGE OF BROADCASTING

Coverage of their immediate localities and in-depth, interpretive journalism became the major functions of newspapers after radio and television took over the function of reporting up-to-the-minute spot news. As newspapers lost advertising to radio in the 1930s, newspapers tried briefly to contain broadcast news competition. In 1933 the American Newspaper Publishers Association (ANPA) persuaded the press associations to suspend service to broadcasters. With the support of the radio networks, the Press Radio Bureau was formed in 1934 to edit the files of the press associations and to release news twice daily for no more than five minutes each. The news broadcasts could not be sponsored. But some radio stations refused to abide by the bureau's rules and a new press service, the Trans-Radio Service, was started to sell news directly to radio. By 1940 the ANPA capitulated, allowing the major wire services to sell news to radio and allowing radio to seek sponsors for news. Radio and television can get breaking news to their audiences almost instantly, and the time-consuming

---

Editor & Publisher International Year Book, 1976, shows that only a handful of the black newspaper circulations it reports were verified by the ABC. At least 20 percent of the total circulation of 7 million was free rather than paid circulation.

background, in-depth, interpretive journalism of newspapers is their adjustment to broadcasting's technological strengths. Because broadcast news is
constrained by FCC regulations such as the fairness doctrine and because
broadcasters are vulnerable to the government's licensing procedures,
broadcast news is typically not as penetrating and controversial as print
news. Broadcasters simply do not enjoy protection of the First Amendment
equal to that enjoyed by newspapers. This is partly why newspapers rather
than broadcasters tackled such controversial, complex, and largely nonvi-
sual stories as the Pentagon Papers and Watergate. In the American system
of media economics, space is more elastic and less expensive than time. And
because of the new electronic technologies in print journalism, particularly
the integration of computer technologies into the editing process, newspapers in the 1970s were saving time in a way that enabled them to make
more flexible and intelligent use of their space.

Newspapers, then, have survived the formidable competition of broadcasting and, to a much lesser extent, of magazines, by adjusting their
functions and by retaining an independence from government and from
direct advertising influence. Because many newspapers are local monopolies, advertisers tend to need newspapers more than newspapers need
particular advertisers, although their mutual need is obviously great. How
intensely readers feel they need newspapers is not really known, although
the decline in daily circulation in the mid-1970s suggests that the sense of
need was diminishing. Years of readership surveys have produced a profile
of newspaper buyers that Ben Bagdikian summarized in 1971 as follows:
". . . the best educated; those in skilled professional, technical, managerial
white-collar jobs; the wealthiest; those who live in urban areas; those who
are married; and people between the ages of thirty and fifty-four." But in a
speech at the Allied Daily Newspapers annual meeting in Seattle on May 15,
1975, Robert G. Marbut, president of Harte-Hanks Newspapers, Inc.,
reflected on these items: daily newspaper circulation was declining; the ratio
of daily newspaper circulation to the number of households had declined
steadily over the past decade; and the dependence on newspapers by
younger people—the ones 20–35 who are among the prime targets of
advertisers—appeared to be declining. Marbut asked:

> How are these trends possible? Just the opposite should be true. As people
> become better educated and more affluent, they should be more prone to be
> loyal newspaper readers. And, since current trends indicate that we do have a
> larger number of better educated and more affluent people, why isn't the
> number of newspapers sold per household *increasing* rather than *declining?*

He warned the industry that unless each publisher produced "[t]hat
unique package of news, opinion and other information designed for the
specific needs of a particular market," someone else would do so. And he
pointed to the growing number of hungry competitors:

> Just look at the number of other media chipping away at what newspapers used
> to consider safely within their franchise. Whether it be the television sales staff

going after local advertisers like never before, or the blanket coverage shopper, or the direct mail pennysaver, or the preprint being delivered by a private delivery service, or the Government's setting up regional computerized job data banks, or in the future a computerized data bank connected to the home by bidirectional cable—all of these vehicles are supplying information to *our* markets—in what used to be *our* domain.

No profile of the typical newspaper buyer, then, no generalization about the newspaper's typical functions seems to fit precisely in the flux of the 1970s.

The Magazine Industry

The modern magazine succeeded as a mass medium chiefly because of its original role as an adjunct of the marketing system. Like the newspaper, it was able, over the years, to appeal to an expanding range of tastes and interests. But, unlike other media, most magazines were designed for homogeneous audiences or special-interest groups. And, in contrast to the newspaper, their circulation was nationwide. Thus, although many magazines were directed to specialized audiences, magazines in general developed as a mass medium in the sense that they appealed to large numbers in a national market that cut across social, economic, and educational class lines.

Early in the twentieth century, some magazine publishers, notably those of pulps and digests, derived their income from a small unit profit on a high turnover of copies instead of from advertising. Still others relied on trade associations, fraternal organizations, and professional groups to make up any deficit. But with the rise of national advertising, the great majority— both in numbers and circulation—were bound closely to the marketing system. In effect, magazine publishing became fundamentally a matter of the publisher's deciding on a consumer group that advertisers wanted to reach, devising an editorial formula to attract and hold that group, and then selling advertisers access to it.

In terms of originating a market for the advertiser, the relationship of magazines generally to their audiences is quite different from that of other media. Some magazine publishers have first developed a publication and then let both readers and advertisers seek out the magazine. But the typical magazine follows a less risky strategy. It devises an editorial formula that can be counted on to attract a homogeneous and relatively small special-interest group; then it assembles advertisers who want to address that audience.

In *Magazines of the Twentieth Century,* Theodore Peterson notes four threats to magazines in the first half of the twentieth century: the automobile, radio, movies, and television. Yet magazines have enjoyed virtually uninterrupted growth in numbers, circulation, and revenue since 1900. There were well over a thousand more magazines in the United States in the mid-1970s than in 1900; per-issue circulation rose over 98 million between 1950 and

1970, a gain of 44 percent; and advertising revenue tripled between 1950 and 1974, from $458.5 million to $1.5 billion. Peterson ascribes most of magazines' prosperity to population increase, more particularly to rising income levels and the expansion of the middle class, to the spread of popular education, and to the increase in leisure time. Typically magazines, like other print media, have been read by richer, better-educated Americans whose increase has sustained print against the competition of radio and television.

MASS MAGAZINES AND THE DEATH OF *LIFE*

In the 1950s and 1960s, however, some of the major magazines did not merely rely on this group but challenged television on its own ground. They went for the mass audience, by direct mail campaigns and subscription offers at bargain rates. The massive circulations of such magazines as *The Reader's Digest,* the *Saturday Evening Post, Life,* and *Look* resulted. Stung by television, these magazines lost sight of their real source of strength, the selective market. Now only the *Digest* survives in its original form, ranking second after *TV Guide* in total circulation in the United States.

Try as they might, the mass magazines could not adapt to change, could find no identity for themselves as other media displaced them. How *Life,* far and away the biggest revenue producer of all magazines before it died, tried tells us much about the structure and functions of the media in general and of the magazine industry in particular. *Life*'s struggle shows that, despite opinion to the contrary, media structure and functions are not fixed but bend to the needs and wants of their constituencies.

Thirty-six years after its founding, *Life,* the last great mass-circulation, general-interest picture magazine, died in December 1972. Because of its status as something of a national institution, *Life*'s passing was mourned with more emotion than sense. Loyal readers and some staffers accused management of murder; *Life* could and should have been saved. So presumably could other mass magazines, such as *Collier's,* which died in 1956, the *Saturday Evening Post,* which died in 1969, and *Look,* which died in 1971. Chris Welles, a *Life* editor from 1965 to 1968, is more persuasive. He studied *Life* in its death throes in 1971, then conducted a postmortem in 1973, concluding: "The collapse of *Life*'s profit-oriented *raison d'être* derived from its increasing inability to fill the needs of its two essential constituencies—advertisers and readers."[5]

Increasing affluence, education, and leisure time had fragmented the mass audience and enabled people to pursue a variety of interests to which hundreds of specialized magazines responded. Television satisfied mass tastes. And advertisers followed the audiences they wanted wherever they could be reached most effectively.

Henry Luce created *Life* in 1936 in the middle of the depression, "[t]o see life; to see the world; to eyewitness great events," and to see them positively. *Life* was to combat the national gloom and to correct what Luce considered journalism's distorted priorities: "That evil makes big news and good makes little or no news." What particularly annoyed him was the press' interest in scandal. In a speech in September 1937, he said:

> . . . if there is one fact about our society which is shouted daily to the people of America it is that rich folk get into trouble with chorines and gigolos, steal each other's wives and husbands, indulge in orgies, and are otherwise licentious. . . . On the relevant issue of whether the press has presented a fair picture to the public of an aspect of American life, the criticism should be turned around. For if there *are* a number of rich or solvent people who live reasonably decent lives, never get more than moderately drunk and are not sexual monsters—then *that* is the fact which the capitalist-controlled press has failed to establish.

With something of the awe of discovery, Luce argued that "The photograph . . . turns out to be an extraordinary instrument for correcting that really inherent evil in journalism which is its unbalance between the good news and the bad." He explained how *Life* was using the camera as corrective:

> A few weeks ago *Life* published a picture essay on wheat—I mean wheat, growing and being happily harvested. The article had nothing to do with any frantic row in Congress over a farm bill, nothing to do with the horrors of drought and dying cattle. And it was the lead article and ran for nine pages. Now can you imagine any non-photographic magazine, intended to interest millions of readers, daring to devote its first nine pages to a descriptive contemplation of the fruitful and normal and quiet labors of farms and horses and harvesters and the wheat itself ripening beneath the sun? And yet it is precisely the kind of thing which *Life* is doing.[6]

But no power of positive thinking could blind *Life* to the ugly realities of the 1960s and early 1970s. Its magnificent photographers produced some of the most searing and moving pictures of the Vietnam War, around which the discontent of the decade had gathered. Its reporters investigated the troubles prominent people get into. William Lambert reported on Supreme Court Justice Abe Fortas' agreement to accept a fee of $20,000 yearly for life from the Wolfson Foundation (Louis Wolfson was twice indicted for stock fraud). Fortas resigned in May 1969, the only justice ever to resign from the Supreme Court under pressure.

Curiously for a picture magazine, *Life* was in the vanguard of aggressive investigative reporting when it died. But *Life*'s change in editorial formula did not impress advertisers, who in the 1970s could pursue the audience they wanted through the massive, undifferentiated reach of television and the concentrated, selective reach of specialized magazines. Because of this competition, *Life*'s huge audience—it was said that in its prime 70 million adults read each issue of *Life*—began to fade away.

Life's mass circulation survived longer than that of its deceased rivals partly because it acquired a million and a half subscribers from the dying *Saturday Evening Post*. Circulation was sustained mainly by cheap subscriptions and low newsstand prices. A study not long before *Life* died estimated that the average *Life* reader paid only 12 cents for a magazine costing 41 cents to edit and print. Advertisers had to make up the remaining 70 percent of publishing costs at ad rates as high as $64,000 a color page. Advertisers found that they could reach more people more cheaply on prime time television. In 1971 the advertising cost per thousand persons reached by *Life* was about $7.71; by television, about $3.60. Advertisers questioned *Life*'s identity and argued that people no longer cared enough for *Life* to pay a reasonable share of the costs. Advertisers withdrew. Between 1966 and 1972 *Life*'s advertising revenues dropped from $170 to $91 million. Its only consistently dependable advertisers were cigarette and liquor manufacturers, who were banned from advertising on television. Publishing costs meanwhile were soaring. Paper prices were expected to double within five years, and postal rates were expected to rise 142 percent within the same period. *Life* tried for a more affluent, educated audience by allowing its circulation to drop by attrition from 8½ to 5½ million between 1970 and 1972, by charging higher subscription rates, and by experimenting with different editorial formulas such as an emphasis on investigative reporting. Readers still drifted away. Newstand sales averaged only 184,000 an issue for the first six months of 1972, a 20 percent drop from 1971 and lower than the sales of *Weight Watchers*. In its last five years *Life* lost $35 million; another $30 million loss was projected for 1973 and 1974. Confronting that, and fading reader and advertiser interest, *Life* elected euthanasia.

Perhaps more imaginative and sharply focused editorial formulas could have saved *Life,* but it is doubtful that *Life* could have survived as a mass magazine. As advertisers were quick to see, the times were out of joint for that medium.

Today American magazines reflect virtually every shade of thought and opinion, virtually every interest, of their readers. They cover everything from hot rodding, coin collecting, yachting, hunting and fishing, and preparing to be a bride to gourmet dining and calorie counting.

Despite the fierce competition and the uncertainties, magazine publishing on a small scale is perhaps the communication most accessible to the new investor. What counts most is the idea. If the entrepreneur has a fresh idea for a magazine, there are likely to be persons willing to finance it. If the magazine can be sustained while it seeks acceptance by readers and advertisers, there is always some chance that it will achieve a modest success. And there is a remote chance that it will wind up in the company of giants.

The ease of entry into the magazine industry, in contrast to the formidable obstacles encountered in newspaper publishing, broadcasting, and motion pictures, explains why the industry today is dotted with relatively small units, small staffs, and modest offices with little equipment. Magazine publishers ordinarily do not invest in presses and equipment, but instead let out their printing on contract. A publisher who does not wish to compete with large-circulation leaders can still launch a successful magazine on a million dollars or so—a comparatively small sum for starting a national medium. Some that began as regional publications started with far less. Jann Wenner began *Rolling Stone* as a rock music magazine with less than $20,000 and aimed it at San Francisco Bay Area readers. Then he expanded to national distribution, diversifying content to include top New York writers Truman Capote, Tom Wolfe, and Norman Mailer. In 1977 Wenner, then only 30 years old, moved *Rolling Stone* to New York. Its circulation was up to 450,000; Wenner wanted it up to a million by 1980.

IMITATORS

Factors that make it easy for one publisher to enter the industry also make it easy for competitors to enter. Successful magazines invariably breed imitators, for publishers cannot hide their formulas for success, forced as they are by the nature of publishing to exhibit their best ideas in public.

What Hugh Hefner chose to exhibit in public in *Playboy* soon stimulated imitators, most formidably Bob Guccione's *Penthouse.* Hefner had attracted readers with his centerfolds of nude women, the blemishes and too intimate parts of their voluptuous bodies discreetly airbrushed. Guccione disdained touching up his photographs and successfully challenged *Playboy* with candid frontal nudity. For decades DeWitt Wallace had been trying through his *Reader's Digest* to keep America at moral attention; Hefner and Guccione claimed to be liberating America from its sexual taboos. Whatever the validity of their claim, their magazines reflected the sexual permissiveness of the 1970s.

Both their contents and their distributional methods violated normal publishing conventions. Most magazines rely heavily on advertising; typically about 60 percent of a magazine's contents is advertising, 40 percent is editorial. *Playboy* and *Penthouse* virtually reversed the ratio, charging the reader the entire cost of the magazine. Advertising, therefore, was almost pure profit. Their distributional costs were lower than those of most major magazines because they relied more on newsstand sales than on subscriptions, which involve solicitation and distribution of sales through the increasingly expensive postal system. Compare these circulation figures for 1970, when *Life* was still living:

	Subscription	Newsstand	Total
		(figures in millions)	
The Reader's Digest	15.8	1.7	17.5
Life	8.3	0.2	8.5
Time	4.0	0.2	4.3
Playboy	1.3	4.0	5.3
TV Guide	5.2	10.1	15.3

In the mid-1970s *Penthouse,* which claimed a worldwide circulation of 5.3 million, was selling over 90 percent of its copies at newsstands. Note that

Magazines more than any other medium reflect the pluralism of American society.
(Kenneth Karp)

the vast bulk of *Time*'s circulation sells via subscription, although occasional
striking covers may well increase sales dramatically. *Playboy* took malicious
pleasure in July 1976 in pointing out that *Time* was not above using nudity
(*Playboy* mentioned *Time*'s putting the entertainer Cher in a see-through
dress on the cover of a best-selling issue) to sell magazines even though in a
cover story, "The Porno Plague," in April 1976, *Time* had criticized *Playboy* "and its far crasser imitators" for the practice. In a period of escalating
postal rates, *Time*'s reliance on subscriptions for approximately 95 percent
of its circulation was a crippling expense. In October 1975, therefore, *Time*
began an experiment in three cities whereby subscribers received their *Time*
from a newspaper carrier rather than a mail carrier. Delivery by carriers of

cooperating newspapers was expected to be considerably cheaper than postal delivery.

Competition by imitation is usually a Darwinian process. The fittest survive. Black publisher John H. Johnson has made a success of imitation because he has not competed with his models. He modeled *Black World,* titled *Negro Digest* until 1970, on *The Reader's Digest. Jet,* a news weekly, copied the format of the Cowles magazine *Quick. Tan* copied the true confession magazines. In 1945 Johnson launched *Ebony* as a monthly and sensational version of *Life.* He toned down the sensationalism in the 1950s, and *Ebony* became a magazine for middle-class blacks. In the militant 1960s *Ebony* abandoned its earlier cautiousness and tackled black grievances. An entire issue in 1965, for example, was devoted to "The White Problem in America." Johnson explains that "*Ebony*'s goal is to reflect the attitudes and opinions of our readership as well as to lead. We don't go too far ahead, but we're always pushing for more."

Special Interest Magazines

WOMEN'S MAGAZINES

Because newspapers cater mainly to a heterogenous local community and television mainly to the national undifferentiated mass, the magazine has become the vehicle of the aspirations or ideologies of special-interest groups, one of the means by which they push for more. For decades men dominated the publishing of women's magazines, so reinforcing, it was charged, stereotypes of women as mothers and homemakers. In 1973 journalist Pamela Howard described her professional goals this way: "Ten years ago, I dreamed about becoming editor-in-chief of a woman's magazine. Accordingly, I went to work at one of the largest in the country, only to find that all the Katharine Hepburn roles were filled by short men."[7]

A man, Cyrus Curtis, founded the *Ladies' Home Journal* in 1883. Although his wife, Louisa Knapp, edited it for six years, it was editor Edward Bok who took the magazine's circulation over a million in 1903. Bok, it was said, had no affection for women, but succeeded with his readers by emphasizing the concept of service for women. And not only for women, apparently. During World War I the *Journal* ranked third among magazines most demanded by soldiers. Despite their emphasis on serving women, however, magazines like the *Journal* and *McCall's* have not led the women's movement as they have led women's magazines in circulation. Helen Gurley Brown gave new direction to women's magazines when she became editor of the Hearst Corporation's *Cosmopolitan* and dealt candidly with the nonhousewifely aspirations and sexuality of women, particularly young single women.

Essence, founded for black women in May 1970, was torn in its first two years by internal strife, caused, some said, by the fact that it was run by men.

Initially intended strictly as a fashion and beauty magazine, it had to convince potential advertisers that black women had sufficient buying power to make them a worthwhile market. Advertisers had also to be educated to *Essence*'s requirement that ads in no way demean black women. Moreover, *Essence* requires that all ads show a black woman, although it will accept ads that show a white woman and a black woman. Marcia Gillespie, who started as managing editor in November 1970, became *Essence*'s fourth editor-in-chief in May 1971 and began to change the magazine. "I had wanted to combat the negative imagery which for centuries had been foisted on Blacks," she said. "Forever, it seems, we Blacks have heard how we are stupid, lazy, shiftless, unable to build family units. . . . I didn't want little Black girls growing up as I had thinking only white women were beautiful. I wanted them, through *Essence,* to see and to feel what Black women really are—incredibly vital people who have been boxed in intellectually, creatively and emotionally."[8] Marcia Gillespie's approach has been immensely successful. Circulation has grown from 75,000 in 1970 to 550,000 in 1977; between 1970 and 1976 advertising revenue rose from $208,000 to $3.8 million.

When Gloria Steinem and Elizabeth Forsling Harris decided in 1971 to publish *Ms.* magazine, they were determined to keep women in control. Steinem was to be editor and president, Harris publisher and chairwoman of the board. *Ms.* was a deliberate protest against the conventional women's magazines (while working at the *Ladies' Home Journal,* Steinem was handed a story by an editor and told, "Pretend you're a woman and read this"). For too long, Steinem declared, women have been "sanitized, deodorized, slicked up, and fixed up" in magazines. According to Harris, the purpose of *Ms.* was to "communicate the commonality of feeling among women around the country." Pamela Howard described *Ms.* as "a forum for women who are exploring new ways of living."[9]

Womensports, founded by tennis star Billie Jean King, promotes and celebrates one of these new ways, a career as a female athlete. In the great variety of women's magazines, a shared purpose has united them, symbolized in July 1976 by a meeting of 30 women's magazines to discuss how best to ensure passage of the Equal Rights Amendment to the Constitution.

JOURNALS OF OPINION

These women's magazines are comparatively new special-interest magazines of narrow focus. Many of their individual concerns have been forthrightly discussed, advocated, or condemned for years in such journals of opinion, comment, and controversy as *Ramparts, The Nation, National Review, New Leader, The New Republic,* and *Progressive.* Their emphasis is on ideas rather than on reportage, and their positions are rarely neutral.

Most of the journals since the turn of the century have been organs of liberal thought, although a few, such as the *National Review,* founded in 1955, have spoken for conservatism. In their agitation for political reform and social justice, the magazines have often been far ahead of popular thinking. For that reason and others, their way has always been difficult; their circulations have been counted in the thousands instead of in the millions of the general interest magazines, their advertising volume has been lean or non-existent, and their financial position has ever been precarious. Yet they seem to have wielded an influence all out of proportion to their circulations, for they have aimed at opinion leaders instead of the great mass audience. Frank P. Walsh once remarked that he had written an article about railroads for the *Nation* in the days when its circulation was about 27,000 and a series on the same subject for the Hearst newspapers when their total circulation was around 10 million. No one ever commented on the newspaper series, he said, but as soon as the *Nation* article appeared, his phone jangled with calls from persons of importance. Charles Beard has credited the journals of opinion with contributing to such reforms as women's suffrage, old-age pensions, social security legislation, wages-and-hours laws, public housing, and public ownership of hydroelectric sites.

PHOTOJOURNALISM AND *PEOPLE* MAGAZINE

Despite the magazine industry's response via specialized magazines to the political beliefs, social concerns, and leisure activities and hobbies of an audience with increasingly diverse interests, a role for the general interest magazine survived in the mid-1970s.

One bold test of this notion was Time Inc.'s launching of *People* magazine in February 1974. Conventional wisdom was that *Life* died in 1972 partly because television had killed the relevance and appeal of the still photograph, at least in news.

The *National Geographic* was still a haven for lovers and practitioners of photography, but it was not concerned with the timeliness of its contents. Rather it captured in magnificent color what relatively unexplored and exotic peoples and places remained in the world, or it glamorized the familiar. Somewhat like *The Reader's Digest,* the *Geographic* contrived a timelessness for each issue. It was not a publication read on the run and discarded. Bookshelves around the world groan under the weight of back issues of the *Geographic.*

Photojournalism, in fact, has struggled for its less than a century of existence to overcome journalism's bias toward print. It was not until the 1880s that the halftone photoengraving process was perfected, not until the 1890s that a way was developed to run off photographs on a rotary press, making it possible to print photographs in newspapers and mass magazines. Unfortunately, these developments coincided with the yellow journalism of Pulitzer and Hearst, who used photographs unscrupulously and sensationally. Then in the 1920s the tabloids outdid Pulitzer and Hearst, selecting, retouching, and faking pictures for maximum sensational impact. Long after it was technologically possible to use photographs, therefore, many newspapers shied away from them or used them sparingly. When the Associated Press Managing Editors Association decided in 1935 to devote its next session to photography, many editors protested, arguing that photography would lower the dignity of the American press, that photography should not encroach on print.

The damage that yellow journalism inflicted from the 1890s through the 1920s on the respectability and perceived value of photojournalism and graphics cannot be overestimated. By reinforcing the arrogance of print, yellow journalism set back intelligent analysis of what information is best communicated verbally, what visually, and of how words and pictures can be used most effectively to enhance each other's shared purpose—to communicate. In this respect, the advertising industry, typically scorned by journalists, has been light years ahead in its imaginative use of photography, graphics, color, and design to communicate its messages. Magazines have long had to compete for readers' attention with the color and allure of advertisements beside their articles and have been much more visually innovative than newspapers. It was about the time that newspaper editors in the APME were deciding to dignify photojournalism by assigning a session to the topic that Henry Luce discovered the positive power of the camera and *Life* was born. And *Life*'s photography did much to make photojournalism respectable for newspapers. So when *Life* died and television was seen as an accessory before the fact, many concluded that the day of the general-interest picture magazine was dead.

Yet *People* is basically a picture magazine; some have described it as television in print. It runs about 15,000 words an issue; *Time* runs three times that many. Despite requiems for the picture magazine, *People* was paying its way within 20 months of its launching in 1974, a remarkable achievement in contemporary publishing. Photojournalists have criticized the magazine as a prostitution of *Life,* as an exploitation of the form rather than an extension of it, and some have sought their professional future in newspapers rather than in magazines. *People* showed that a picture magazine can still draw a huge audience. *People* offered a flashy, quick look and read into the lives of celebrities. Gossip? No more than a high-class fan magazine? "We do not run gossip," says Managing Editor Richard B. Stolley. "Everything is checked for accuracy. Instead of concentrating on the issues, we look at the personalities behind them. Our policy is to tell you new things about personalities you already know. We also include unknown people doing things we think are exceptional." *People*'s Washington correspondent Clare Crawford reported in late 1975: "The Fords love this magazine. The President has told me that he hopes we don't 'mess it up' with pictures of blood vessels and hearts, the way they did with *Life*. And that's the key to *People*'s success. Nobody from Presidents on down can resist reading about other people."

GRAPHICS AND *NEW YORK* MAGAZINE

Superficially this marriage of people and pictures has characterized *New York* magazine, launched by Clay Felker in 1968. In fact, *New York* is a mix of serious journalism and lively, imaginative graphics which has had considerably more than local impact on publishing. Early on it became a vehicle for the "new journalism" of writers like Tom Wolfe, Jimmy Breslin, and Gail Sheehy, who were applying the literary techniques of the short story and novel—dramatic scene, dialogue, interior monologue—to the presentation of thoroughly researched journalism. Their writing styles, which reflected much greater sensitivity to the visual sense, to all the senses, than just-the-facts-ma'am objective reporting, and the magazine's bright, provocative graphics gave a pace and excitement to *New York* that other magazines soon imitated. Milton Glaser, *New York*'s design director, said, "[t]he magazine is not designed to look beautiful, but to convey a sense of energy, compression, density, information. We want it to be fast-paced like the city, easily accessible, undemanding. We want people to get in and out of it very easily."[10]

In almost every respect, then, it was the antithesis of the staid, dignified *New Yorker,* which has never been concerned to hurry its readers through the magazine. Rather, *The New Yorker* communicates an aura of decorous quiet, of leather upholstery and muted paneling, of civilized, reflective conversation by the elegantly styled and coiffed people in the ads it carries. Tradition weighs heavily on *The New Yorker,* which cherishes the character given it by its founder Harold Ross and by writers James Thurber and E. B. White.

New York, by contrast, has been as mercurial as its founder Clay Felker and as the times it has reflected. In the early 1970s critics condemned its articles as poorly researched, sensational, vulgar, superficial, and trendy. *Newsweek* dismissed the magazine as "a tedious collection of pop trivia." As Watergate spread gloom in the nation and New York City's bankruptcy depressed the inhabitants, the magazine's breeziness was almost unseemly. Investigative journalism was in vogue, and, although still graphically colorful and irreverent, *New York* became a more conservative, solidly researched magazine—until the Australian, Rupert Murdoch, bought it in January 1977. Murdoch, who then owned 88 newspapers, 11 magazines, and some television properties in Australia, England, and the United States, is known for a "blood, guts, and girls" formula, and *New York* admirers were concerned that the magazine would succumb to Murdoch's earthy sensationalism.

Before Murdoch's takeover, *New York* seemed to be going through a process Clay Felker had described soon after he started *New York:*

> There appears to be an almost inexorable life-cycle of American magazines that follows the patterns of humans: a clamorous youth eager to be noticed; vigorous, productive middle-age marked by an easy-to-define editorial line; and a long slow decline, in which efforts at revival are sporadic and tragically doomed.[11]

In the post-Vietnam and -Watergate trauma of the mid-1970s, national nostalgia had revived a pale version of the *Saturday Evening Post. Life* was publishing special issues such as "The Year in Pictures" and was talking of a comeback. Some magazines came and went with the public's whims and fads. Many kept pace with society's elemental concerns, and, despite the inexorable life-cycle Felker describes, survived.

We have glanced at only a selection of the diverse range whose covers blaze from newsstands and supermarket racks. As a whole, magazines more than any other medium reflect the pluralism of American society and the multifarious interests, serious and trivial, perennial and passing, that affluence and leisure enable it to indulge.

Book Publishing

Like other communications industries, book publishing is a business seeking profit. Like the news media, however, it acknowledges certain responsibilities to the cultural life of the nation: to support and promote scholarship and literature, to influence and elevate taste, to teach and delight. And these responsibilities may transcend, perhaps limit, profit. To some extent, it is easier for the book publishing industry than for the news media to meet its responsibilities. Unlike newspapers, magazines, and broadcast programs, books are not subsidized by advertisers. The news media must please two constituencies—audiences and advertisers. Book publishers must please only one—readers.

In the United States, however, books are not as popular with the mass of Americans as the products of the other media of communication. In 1975 book publishing industry sales amounted to $3.8 billion, $1.5 billion of which, or 40 percent, was spent on educational materials for schools and colleges. But the buying of educational materials is not usually discretionary. In fact, such a minority of Americans chooses to buy books that, strictly speaking, book publishing is not a mass industry. A national best seller may sell between 2 and 3 million copies, which may be read by twice that number of persons. The New York *Daily News* sells almost 2 million copies daily to New Yorkers; *Time* magazine sells more than 4 million copies a week; *Family Circle* sells more than 9 million a month; *The Reader's Digest* more than 18 million a month; and readership for each of these publications is probably three times circulation. A reasonably popular network television show can expect an audience of between 20 and 30 million on a single night. Even the exception, a best seller, then, cannot rival the reach of the other media. The average hardbound trade book may sell no more than 10,000 copies, the average mass market paperback no more than 100,000.

"Mass market" is a misnomer. Although literacy is almost universal in the United States, the American masses do not yet read books. It was the implication of Marshall McLuhan's pronouncements in the mid-1960s that they never would because the advent of the electronic media had signaled the death of print. In fact, the 1960s were boom years for book publishing. From 1963 to 1969, industry sales rose 59 percent. So far from killing print, the electronic media seem instead to have stimulated reading. Book sales slowed in the 1970s, but retained solid growth. Between 1971 and 1975, years of recession and retrenchment in the American economy, book sales rose 30.8 percent. Hard times particularly affected education, the source of much of the demand for books. Enrollments in schools and colleges declined or leveled off, and taxpayers and their elected representatives at the local, state, and federal levels cut school and college appropriations.

Moreover, book publishing was especially vulnerable to the increasing use in schools, colleges, and libraries of the Xerox and other copying machines. Until 1976 U.S. copyright law had been virtually unchanged since 1909, long before the invention of the automatic copier. For years copyright bills to protect the rights of authors were mired in complexity and controversy in Congress. The bill that finally passed in 1976 still permitted some copying for educational purposes without compensation to authors.

Book publishing managed the recession of the 1970s relatively well largely because the industry was a part during the boom years of the 1960s of multimedia merger and consolidation. RCA bought Alfred Knopf, Pantheon Books, and Random House. CBS bought W. B. Saunders and Holt, Rinehart and Winston, itself created by mergers. Time Inc., bought Little, Brown; ITT bought Bobbs-Merrill and Howard Sams; and the Times Mirror Company, publisher of the *Los Angeles Times,* bought a number of book publishing enterprises.

John P. Dessauer comments that these mergers and consolidations

> . . . made resources available without which the industry could probably not have capitalized on its opportunities and fulfilled its obligations to educational and consumer audiences alike. They brought new management and new business acumen to the field which had been seriously lacking and which, in many instances resulted for the first time in orderly budgeting, forecasting, planning, and fiscal arrangements.[12]

But, Dessauer adds, the mergers and consolidations "also placed the power of ultimate decision and policy making in the hands of people unfamiliar with books, their peculiarities, and their markets."

The estimated book publishing industry sales, 1971–1975, issued by the Association of American Publishers (AAP), show the wide range of book types and suggest some of the ways books are sold. See the table on page 97.

The R. R. Bowker Company, which keeps statistics on the book publishing industry, lists 12,000 book outlets of all kinds in the United States. Of these

> . . . 6700 . . . handle new books; 900 are department store book departments; 2900 are college bookstores; 7300 handle paperbacks; 1700 carry law, medical, technical, and scientific titles; 4000 sell religious books; 3000 handle juveniles; 1300 are rare book dealers; and 1000 are secondhand dealers.[13]

The book industry refers to these retail outlets as "traditional trade stores," some of which sell books exclusively, others of which sell them only as a sideline. In addition, there are more than 90,000 mass market outlets— newsstands, drugstores, and supermarkets. From early in this century, books have also been sold directly to the reader, by mail order and by book clubs. The first book clubs, the Book-of-the-Month Club and the Literary

Estimated Book Publishing Industry Sales, 1971–1975

	Millions of Dollars					Percent Change	
	1971 $	1972 $	1973 $	1974 $	1975 $	1974– 1975	1971– 1975
Trade (total)	422.7	442.0	460.1	522.7	549.2	5.1	29.9
Adult hardbound	242.0	251.5	264.8	308.2	313.4	1.7	29.5
Adult paperbound	69.6	79.6	86.7	97.3	111.2	14.3	59.1
Juvenile	111.1	110.9	108.6	117.2	124.6	6.3	12.1
Religious (total)	108.5	117.5	124.7	130.6	154.6	18.4	42.5
Bibles/testaments, hymnals/prayer books	54.4	61.6	66.5	67.5	76.6	13.5	40.8
Other religious	54.1	55.9	58.2	63.1	78.0	23.6	44.2
Professional (total)	353.0	381.0	405.4	466.3	501.2	7.5	42.0
Technical/scientific	122.3	131.8	138.4	158.2	175.5	10.9	43.5
Business/other professional	178.3	192.2	206.2	236.3	242.3	2.5	35.9
Medical	52.4	57.0	60.8	71.7	83.4	16.3	59.2
Book clubs	229.5	240.5	262.4	283.6	303.4	7.0	32.2
Mail order publications	194.6	198.9	221.2	247.0	279.8	13.3	43.8
Mass market paperback	228.8	252.8	285.9	293.6	339.6	15.7	48.4
University presses	39.3	41.4	42.6	46.1	48.8	5.8	24.2
Elementary/secondary texts	496.6	497.6	547.9	598.8	643.1	7.4	29.5
College texts	371.5	375.3	392.2	453.4	530.6	17.0	42.8
Standardized tests	25.3	26.5	28.8	34.2	36.7	7.3	45.0
Subscription reference	301.0	278.9	262.2	280.2	258.1	−7.9	−14.2
Other	141.0	154.8	164.2	176.0	164.9	−6.3	16.9
Total	$2911.8	$3007.2	$3197.6	$3532.5	$3810.0	7.8%	30.8%

SOURCE: Extracted from AAP, "1975 Industry Statistics," Table S2. Reprinted from the February 14, 1977, issue of *Publishers Weekly,* published by R. R. Bowker Company, a Xerox company. Copyright © 1977 by Xerox Corporation.

Guild, founded in the 1920s, appealed to people who could not easily get to a bookstore or who wanted advice on the latest books, and offered them free books and considerable savings on those the club selected. With the increase in affluence and leisure, the book clubs—like the magazine industry—have become increasingly specialized, catering now to the special interests of readership groups: the American Garden Guild Book Club, Antiques Book Club, Detective Book Club, the Movie Book Club, and the Nostalgia Book Club, among others.

Magazine publishers have been the leaders in mail order publishing, an enterprise they began in the 1950s. Time Inc., *The Reader's Digest, Newsweek,* and *Playboy,* which are some of the largest organizations involved, prepare and publish their own books and try to sell them, for the most part, to the subscribers to their magazines.

From this variety of publishing sources and through this variety of distribution methods, an ever-larger number of books are published each year competing for the attention of a comparatively small number of

Americans interested in buying books. The number of new books and new editions published between 1960 and 1974 was as follows:

1960	1965	1970	1973	1974
15,012	28,595	36,071	39,951	40,846

And during those years the prices of books, hardcover and paperback, have soared. Between 1965 and 1976, the average prices of books were

	1965	1970	1973	1974	1975	1976
Hardcover	$7.65	$11.66	$12.20	$14.09	$16.19	$16.32
Paperback						
Mass market	.62	.95	$1.17	$1.18	$1.46	$1.60
Trade	$2.50	$4.81	$3.73	$4.38	$5.24	$5.53

Typically the direct forms of advertising in which publishers engage—in publishers' catalogues and in ads in the important trade publications of the industry, *Publishers Weekly* and *Library Journal*—have nothing like the impact on potential readers as the "free" advertising that books receive in the review columns of newspapers and magazines. The most influential of these include the *New York Review of Books, Saturday Review, Time, Newsweek, Harper's,* and the *Atlantic Monthly.* The most important review medium is unquestionably the *New York Times Book Review.* But all of these combined, and the other newspapers and magazines that review books, cannot review more than a fraction of the books published each year. With all the space it tries to give book reviews, the *New York Times Book Review* criticizes and comments on less than 3000 books a year. Moreover, the reach of these publications is limited to a relatively small number of people, who tend to be wealthier and better educated than the average. None of these review media is as effective, therefore, as the brief appearance an author may be lucky enough to secure on a network talk show such as Johnny Carson's "Tonight" show on NBC.[14]

Book publishing has "used" the other media of communication to secure sales in more dramatic ways. The growth of the paperback industry has enabled publishers to rush to press with the news in book form. Bantam was one of the first to experiment with "instant publishing" when it published the *Report of the Warren Commission on the Assassination of President Kennedy* in book form 80 hours after the official government commission report was released to the public in September 1964. (Normally a book takes about six months from completion of the manuscript to publication date.) So successful was its first attempt—the book was an instant best seller, selling over a million copies within weeks—that Bantam published 56 "instant books," or "extras" as the company calls them, in the next 10 years.

In the 1970s, then, the oldest of the American media, like the other print media, had adjusted to the popularity of the electronic media. It had yielded much of its earlier concentration on fictional entertainment to the movies and television. During the first paperback revolution in publishing, in the 1840s and 1850s, and on through the enormous success of the sensational "dime novel" of the 1870s and 1880s to the romantic historical and family novels of the early 1900s, fiction dominated book publishing. The trend toward nonfiction began after World War I and has accelerated since. In 1960, 16 percent of the new books or new editions published were fiction; in 1974, less than 9 percent were fiction.

Much of the nonfiction exploited sensation and trivia in the news, but the public's taste for these ephemera subsidized the book industry's commitment to the less profitable or unprofitable publication of what the 19th century poet and critic Matthew Arnold called "the best that is known and thought in the world."

● ● ●

Newspaper circulation was recovering in the late 1970s; by proliferating ever more specialized publications, the magazine industry sustained overall circulation; and although the boom in book sales of the 1960s leveled off in the 1970s, the book industry managed modest growth. Print survived the doom prophesied for it partly because owners of print media were alarmed enough to invest heavily in audience research, partly because new technologies enabled quicker, more flexible responses to what the public wanted. Print survived mainly, one suspects, because the written word gives information and ideas, fact and fiction, a life that the electronic media with all their dazzling visual appeal cannot supplant. Significantly, the passion and energy of the generation of the 1960s, the first generation to be dominated since birth by television and one excited by McLuhan's probes, took concrete though not always coherent form in print, in the underground press. The competition between print and electronic media has been a healthy stimulus to fruitful and profitable coexistence rather than a fight to the death that print was destined to lose.

Notes

1. Edwin Emery, *The Press and America: An Interpretative History of the Mass Media,* 3rd ed. (Englewood Cliffs, N.J.: Prentice-Hall, 1972), p. 450.
2. Quoted by Ben H. Bagdikian, "Newspaper mergers—the final phase," *Columbia Journalism Review,* March/April 1977, p. 19.
3. Ben H. Bagdikian, *The Information Machines: Their Impact on Men and the Media* (New York: Harper & Row, 1971), pp. 72–73.
4. Raymond Mungo, *Famous Long Ago: My Life and Hard Times with Liberation News Service* (New York: Pocket Books, 1971), p. 10.
5. Chris Welles, "Lessons from *Life,*" in Michael C. Emery and Ted Curtis Smythe (eds.), *Readings in Mass Communication: Concepts and Issues in the Mass Media,* (Dubuque, Ia.: Wm. C. Brown Company, 1974), p. 250.
6. Speech by Henry Luce to the Institute of Human Relations in Williamstown, Mass., on September 2, 1937; published in John K. Jessup (ed.), *The Ideas of Henry Luce* (New York: Atheneum, 1969), pp. 44–45.
7. Pamela Howard, "*Ms.* and the Journalism of Women's Lib," *Saturday Review,* January 8, 1972, p. 43..

8. Marjorie McManus, "An Interview with Editor-In-Chief Marcia Ann Gillespie," *Folio,* December 1976, p. 28.

9. Pamela Howard in *Saturday Review,* January 8, 1972, p. 44.

10. A. Kent MacDougall, "Clay Felker's New York," *Columbia Journalism Review,* March/April 1974, p. 42.

11. Clay S. Felker, "Life Cycles in the Age of Magazines," in Francis and Ludmila Voelker (eds.), *Mass Media: Forces in Our Society* (New York: Harcourt, 1972), p. 91.

12. John P. Dessauer, *Book Publishing: What It Is, What It Does* (New York: R. R. Bowker Company, 1974), p. 8.

13. Dessauer, p. 103.

14. See Ross Drake, "Book-of-the-Mouth Club: The talk-show circuit is a must for sales-hungry authors," *TV Guide,* October 30, 1971.

5

The Electronic Media: Radio, Television, Cable Television, and Movies

We have to give most of the people what they want most of the time. That doesn't mean anything cheap or tawdry. Popular programing to me is programing of high quality. Popular programing brings a lot of joy and happiness and fun to millions and millions of people throughout this country.

WILLIAM S. PALEY

Whatever their capabilities, however forceful they may be as leaders, the men in television are lashed to the system.

But the public is not lashed to it, and hope for the medium survives in that implicit freedom. The freedom of the public, in fact, is the time bomb in television.

LES BROWN

The Electronic
Media: Radio,
Television, Cable
Television, and
Movies

102

In May 1977 William Sargent, a Los Angeles promoter, offered the National Football League $400 million for control of the NFL's championship play-offs and Super Bowl for the next five years. Sargent wanted to include football among the permanent 52-week cycle of closed-circuit live entertainment events—rock concerts, Broadway plays, operas, ballet, nightclub performances—for which he was trying to lease about 500 movie theaters around the country. His idea was not new. Heavyweight boxing champion Muhammad Ali had made millions by selling tickets to theaters that showed his major title fights on closed-circuit television.

Sargent's competitors for the Super Bowl, of course, were the national television networks which had been paying the NFL between $57- and $60-million a year to televise *all* the NFL games, including post-season contests. The money was worth paying. Football commanded huge audiences. In fact, until the extraordinary success of ABC's televising of Alex Haley's best-seller *Roots* on eight consecutive nights in January 1977, the six Super Bowl games from 1972 to 1977 had all been among the 10 programs watched by the largest audiences in American television history (seven episodes of "Roots" had displaced all but the 1977 Super Bowl from the top 10 as of June 1977).

To the networks' relief, the NFL was not inclined to take Sargent's offer seriously. To have done so would have been to court a public relations disaster, perhaps even mob violence. The anger of 80 million football fans deprived for the first time in a decade of seeing the Super Bowl free on television is terrifying to contemplate. But the prices sports organizations were charging the networks were escalating to a point where alternatives such as Sargent's scheme had the force of economic logic. ABC had paid $13.5 million for the 1972 Olympics in Munich and $25 million for the 1976 Olympics in Montreal; NBC had to pay the Soviet Union $85 million to cover the 1980 Olympics in Moscow. In 1977 the NFL itself was raising its price for network coverage of the football season, from about $60 to $80 million a year.

Although most Americans expected to see such events free on television, enough were willing to pay to see them on their home screens to alarm the broadcast industry. In April 1975, Home Box Office (HBO) in New York launched a national pay cable television network. Via a combination of satellites, earth stations, and microwave relays, HBO in 1977 was sending a daily program package dominated by current movies, live sports events and nightclub acts to 750,000 cable television homes. For a monthly fee, subscribers were receiving between 60 and 70 hours of programing a week. To limit this kind of threat to the interests of commercial over-the-air broadcasting and to assure that the public did not have to pay for what it had formerly received free, the FCC adopted what it called "antisiphoning" regulations in 1970. These were designed to protect over-the-air television from losing feature films and sports events to pay cable. But in March 1977 the U.S. Court of Appeals in Washington, D.C., overturned the FCC's pay cable rules on the grounds that the commission had failed to present evidence to support the need for regulation and that the rules as amended in 1975 violated the First Amendment.

Sargent's offer dramatized what could happen if no regulations restrained pay television. Sargent's plan, said Vincent Wasilewski, president of the National Association of Broadcasters, "demonstrates that a very small percentage of the market is all that is needed for pay-TV to outbid commercial television" and "confirms the potential for the suppliers of sports programing to sell to the highest bidder."[1] The scenario Wasilewski sketched would seem to violate neither the basic philosophy of the American free enterprise system nor the general understanding of the First Amendment. Movie producers and book publishers must often bid against competition for material of potential interest to large audiences. Yet in May 1977, Rep. Lionel Van Deerlin (D-Calif.), chairman of the House Communications Subcommittee, and Rep. Louis Frey Jr. (R-Fla.), the ranking minority member of the subcommittee, announced that they were working on legislation to protect conventional television against the siphoning of sports programs by any pay medium, including pay cable.

By means of tax exemptions, second class postal rates, and the Newspaper Preservation Act, government gives economic assistance to the print media, but no legislation protects the content of newspapers, magazines, books, and movies from the competition of other communications technologies. Why should broadcasters expect and the FCC and influential members of Congress of both parties agree that over-the-air commercial television was entitled to protection from what would seem to be the normal competition of another technology?

The concerns of these constituencies for what they perceived or described as the public's interest in this instance cannot be understood without first considering radio's early development and particularly the dispute between government and the private sector over who was going to control broadcasting in the United States and for what purposes.

Two problems slowed the early development of broadcasting as a mass medium of news and entertainment in the United States: chaos in the broadcast spectrum space and the financing of programing. How these problems were resolved profoundly affected the structure and functions of radio and television in the United States, giving American broadcasting a character different from the broadcast systems of most other countries.

Radio and Television

RADIO'S EARLY DEVELOPMENT

From 1895, when the Italian physicist Guglielmo Marconi transmitted a message across his father's estate in Bologna, until 1916, when David Sarnoff, a young radio engineer working for the American Marconi Company, predicted the major outlines of radio as a mass medium, radio was perceived of mainly as a dot-dash message-sending device. During those

The Electronic
Media: Radio,
Television, Cable
Television, and
Movies

104

years, as thousands of amateurs tinkered with primitive crystal sets, Marconi moved to England, formed a company, and began to install his equipment on British ships. In 1899 he came to the United States, formed the Marconi Wireless Company of America and tried to persuade the U.S. Navy to use his equipment. But local leaders were emerging from the ranks of the amateur experimenters. Lee de Forest, an Iowan, formed the De Forest Wireless Telegraph Company, made a sale to the War Department and the Navy, and began to compete strongly with American Marconi. In 1910 and 1912 radio laws were passed requiring ships of specified types to carry wireless equipment. Radio amateurs delighted in talking to ships at sea but jammed official messages. The Army and the Navy demanded regulation, and in 1912 Congress passed the first radio licensing law. The law empowered the Secretary of Commerce and Labor to assign wavelengths and time limits, but he could not refuse a license.

In World War I the government financed and the Navy directed radio's technological development, drawing in major companies such as American Telephone and Telegraph (AT&T), General Electric, Westinghouse and American Marconi to help the war effort. Because of the war, David Sarnoff's memorandum in 1916 to his superiors at American Marconi was put aside. He had seen radio as a "household utility," a "Radio Music Box" arranged for several different wavelengths over which music, lectures, news, sports, concerts, and recitals could be transmitted into the home. The Navy had another vision. At war's end in 1918 Secretary of the Navy Josephus Daniels testified in Congress in favor of a bill that, he said,

> . . . will secure for all time to the Navy Department the control of radio in the United States, and will enable the Navy to continue the splendid work it has carried on during the war.[2]

But in an act of major significance for the development of broadcasting in this country, the House Committee on Merchant Marine and Fisheries tabled the bill, mainly because it saw exclusive control by the Navy as a dangerous monopoly.

The committee's decision not only had momentous implications for the future of American broadcasting, it was filled with irony. Within a decade the main conglomerates, which have dominated American broadcasting ever since, had come into being and would themselves be perceived as dangerous monopolies. When the Navy lost out to the private sector, radio was defined as an "arena of business competition" rather than a public medium of communication. In most countries different definitions have been formulated for the control of broadcasting, either as an exclusive government controlled public medium, or as a combination of public and private control, with the public usually dominant.

Although the Navy had been defeated in its bid to control radio, it did not withdraw from influencing the direction of radio's development. If government could not control radio, then the Navy favored a commercial monopoly instead, but not a British one. The growth of the British based

Marconi companies particularly alarmed the Navy, and Owen D. Young of General Electric skillfully fostered the Navy's fear. Young wanted an American-dominated system of world communications. In his history of American broadcasting, Erik Barnouw comments:

> This objective could be viewed in a variety of ways: in idealistic terms—*let nation speak to nation;* in isolationist terms—*end the British monopoly;* in business terms—*we can undersell the cables;* in patriotic terms—*give America a voice;* in military terms—*we need it.*[3]

With the support of the Navy, Young led General Electric in October 1919 to form the Radio Corporation of America (RCA). In November 1919 American Marconi transferred all its assets and operations to RCA. Owen Young became chairman of the board and Rear Admiral W. H. G. Bullard was named the government representative on the board. In early 1920 General Electric and RCA negotiated an alliance with AT&T and its subsidiary, Western Electric, to share one another's patents. AT&T bought a block of RCA stock. The huge conglomerate had taken shape in less than a year, and the only major company excluded from it was Westinghouse. Its plant was geared to wartime production, but after the war its rival, General Electric, had secured control of marine and transoceanic communication through RCA.

Westinghouse encouraged its employees to continue experimenting with ways to use the company's wartime production capacity, reluctantly permitting, among many experiments, Vladimir Zworykin to pursue his work in television. Another employee, Frank Conrad, was experimenting in his garage in Wilkinsburg, Pennsylvania, transmitting phonograph records irregularly to the neighborhood. Amateur radio fans began to request particular records; Conrad started regular Saturday evening "concerts"; a Westinghouse vice president learned of the broadcasts and recognized a market "of limitless opportunity." The company invited Conrad to build a stronger transmitter on the roof of the Westinghouse plant in East Pittsburgh. The Department of Commerce assigned the call letters KDKA to the station, which was launched dramatically by reporting the election returns in Warren Harding's win over James Cox for the Presidency in 1920. David Sarnoff's vision was being realized, but by another company. General Electric was "amazed at our blindness. . . . We had everything except the idea." RCA had had the man and the idea but ignored them. Now all the major companies rushed to follow Westinghouse and KDKA into broadcasting. In June 1921 Westinghouse joined the patent alliance. Among them the GE-RCA-AT&T-Westinghouse alliance controlled approximately 2000 patents.

Government had not only largely financed the massive alliance's technological development, it had actively encouraged the alliance's oligopolist tendencies. In 1919 Congress had denied a monopoly to the Navy partly because, said Congressman William Greene, the proposal violated the aims of anti-trust laws. In March 1923 Congress asked the Federal Trade Com-

The Electronic
Media: Radio,
Television, Cable
Television, and
Movies

106

mission to investigate the radio industry to find out if it was violating anti-trust laws. But although the government was to have some success breaking up the giant it had helped create, it had launched a process substantially beyond its control. In the 1970s the Justice Department was still trying to dismember the same giant.

CHAOS IN THE SPECTRUM AND GOVERNMENT REGULATION

In terms of the 1912 act Commerce Secretary Herbert Hoover had designated 360 meters as the band where any licensed radio operator could broadcast "news, lectures, entertainment, etc." Weather and crop reports could be broadcast on the 485 meter wavelength. So popular was radio that manufacturers of home receivers lagged hopelessly behind demand. In 1923 alone Americans spent $136 million for sets. But the proliferation of stations in response to public demand soon caused chaos in the unregulated spectrum space. The more than 500 major stations broadcasting regularly and the approximately 1,400 smaller stations of low wattage broadcasting haphazardly were operating so close to one another that interference became intolerable. In the absence of any active legal authority, stations ignored their own informal agreements dividing available time. Having achieved the supremacy of private over public control, the radio industry appealed to the Department of Commerce to regulate frequencies. Hoover

Listening was a family affair in the early days of radio. (Wide World photo)

asking the industry leaders

... to advise the Department of Commerce as to the application of its present powers of regulation, and further to formulate such recommendations to Congress as to the legislation necessary.[4]

Although Hoover was understandably concerned to secure the support of the industry before proposing regulation, the manner of his approach is important. In effect Hoover was asking the very business he proposed to regulate how it should be regulated. Partly he took this approach because he was inclined to believe that what was good for business was good for the public. But we must also remember that radio was in its infancy and few could foresee the nature and scope of its development. It is not surprising, then, that Hoover should ask the experts, the industry itself, for guidance. Consequently, however, the notion that the regulatory agency should regulate in the interest of the public rather than of the regulated industry itself has battled to survive. Today the FCC is still criticized as the handmaiden of the broadcasting industry.

After four radio conferences in Washington between 1922 and 1925, Congress enacted the Radio Act of 1927, which established a vital principle: The airwaves belong to the people. The act provided for "the use of such channels [of radio transmission], but not the ownership thereof, by individuals, firms, or corporations, for limited periods of time, under licenses granted by Federal authority." The Federal Radio Commission (FRC) established by the act was empowered to grant or revoke licenses when it was in the public interest, convenience, or necessity to do so. An important principle the licensing authority was required to protect was that of localism. The FRC, said the act, shall

... make such distribution of licenses, bands of frequency of wave lengths, periods of time for operation, and of power among the different States and communities as to give fair, efficient, and equitable radio service to each of the same.[5]

In 1934 the Federal Communications Act replaced the FRC with the FCC and broadened its authority. The 1934 act with amendments has become the principal regulatory instrument of the U.S. broadcasting industry. One subtle but significant extension of the FCC's authority was this general power: The FCC shall

Study new uses for radio, provide for experimental uses of frequencies, and generally encourage the larger and more effective use of radio in the public interest.[6]

Congress could not anticipate the extraordinary potential of cable television which was to rise in the 1960s and 1970s as a formidable competitor to over-the-air broadcasting by radio and television. When the FCC took on

The Electronic
Media: Radio,
Television, Cable
Television, and
Movies

108

the responsibility for regulating cable, therefore, it felt itself obliged never-theless to protect the interests of broadcasting. Some critics have felt that in its adjudication of the competing interests of broadcasting and cable, the FCC has been too wedded to the interests of an industry and a technology that had been surpassed by another in its potential for serving the public interest.

THE FINANCING OF PROGRAMING

Although government had early surrendered control to private industry, it recovered a measure of control through its licensing power and the vaguely defined statutory requirement that stations broadcast in the public interest, convenience and necessity. Implicit was some notion of enforceable social responsibility; because of that power, broadcasting has never enjoyed protection of the First Amendment equal to that enjoyed by the print media. But government lacked a power to control broadcasting that governments in most countries possess—the power of the purse. Some form of tax revenue funds most countries' broadcasting systems, which are typically administered either directly by government or through a public corporation, such as the British and Canadian broadcasting corporations. In the United States the broadcasting industry had yielded to government regulation of the spectrum, but it retained financial control.

In the early 1920s the major companies could afford to finance programing for their own stations from the sale of radio sets, but small stations had no such resources. Between March and July 1923, 143 stations went out of business. David Sarnoff had predicted that "Philanthropists would eventually come to the rescue of a hard-pressed industry." Sarnoff was partly right. Philanthropy has contributed to the financing of a public broadcasting system in the United States, but not to commercial broadcasting. A committee of New York businessmen tried to persuade listeners to pay for top quality talent to perform over a New York station. Most decided that they would rather listen free and the experiment failed. That stance has characterized the public's attitude ever since; most Americans are reluctant to pay directly for broadcast programing.

Government officials, industry leaders, and many groups of citizens deplored any advertising on radio. "It is inconceivable," said Herbert Hoover at the first radio conference, "that we should allow so great a possibility for service, for news, for entertainment, and for vital commercial purposes to be drowned in advertising chatter." But in 1922 WEAF had sold radio time for a Long Island real estate agent to sell lots. Major companies began to sponsor programs without directly selling their products; programs merely identified the sponsoring company by name. Sociologist Melvin DeFleur explains why the idealistic position of Hoover and others was doomed:

With listeners more interested in "free" entertainment than quality programming; with government playing only a technical role, primarily to keep frequencies unscrambled; with ownership of the media in the hands of profit-seeking companies and corporations, the noble views of the Secretary of Commerce and his supporters were not consistent with the value system, the political structure, and the economic institution of the society within which the medium was developing. The same socioeconomic forces that led newspapers to turn to selling space to advertisers so they could sell their products to a mass audience were to result in a parallel pattern for radio.[7]

NETWORKING

Parallel, too, was the development of centralized sources of news and entertainment. As the print media had developed wire services for news and syndicates for comics and features, so radio moved to centralized networks to concentrate financing for the production of high-quality programing. In 1926 RCA formed the National Broadcasting Company (NBC) as a subsidiary. It was owned by RCA (50 percent), GE (30 percent), and Westinghouse (20 percent), leased wires from AT&T, and operated two networks, the red and the blue. In 1927 the United Independent Broadcasters was formed, becoming the Columbia Broadcasting System (CBS) later in the year.

These networks evolved a system whereby they contracted with stations for time, then sold that time to advertisers anxious to reach the broad national audience networking afforded. In return for the time they sold to the network, individual stations received programing of a quality they could not possibly finance themselves. Moreover, they were paid to carry the networks' shows and could also sell time to local advertisers in spots the networks left open for that purpose. The contractual arrangements differed from network to network, but in broad outline that is how the system operated.

The networks quickly signed up with stations anxious to affiliate with them to enjoy the benefits of the arrangement. In 1927 NBC had 48 affiliates; CBS had 16. In 1946 NBC had 159 affiliates, CBS 162. As individual publishers or corporations bought up chains of newspapers, so the networks began to acquire stations by ownership as well as by affiliation. Networks also bought up control of radio talent. NBC created Artists' Service in 1926 and acquired Civic Concert Service, Inc., in 1935. CBS formed Columbia Artists, Inc., and Columbia Concerts Corporation in 1930. Such centralization of power in broadcasting began to alarm government, but its regulatory agency, the FCC, had limited control over networks. This fact is vital to an understanding of the American broadcasting system. The FCC licenses stations, not networks, and has regulatory control over networks not as networks per se but only insofar as they are owners of stations.

Nevertheless, pressured by the antitrust emphasis of President Franklin Roosevelt's New Deal, the FCC began a study of chain broadcasting and monopoly problems in 1938. The FCC completed its report in 1941, recommending, among other proposals: that the two NBC networks be

The Electronic
Media: Radio,
Television, Cable
Television, and
Movies

110

divorced; that because stations had no right to surrender control of time to networks, network options to station time be limited to specific hours; and that affiliate stations had the right to reject network programs in favor of other programs whenever they felt that rejection would serve the public interest.

Not only did the networks attack the proposed rules, but Congress turned on the FCC and its chairman, James Fly. Rep. Martin Dies, chairman of the House Committee on Un-American Activities, said that the FCC harbored subversives. Rep. Eugene Cox, a member of the House rules committee, said that Fly was "the most dangerous man in Washington," who was turning the FCC into "a Gestapo, the equal of which has never been seen under a free government."[8] Fly stood his ground against incredible invective and pressure, and in 1943 the Supreme Court upheld the FCC against suits by NBC and CBS seeking to enjoin the enforcement of the FCC's Chain Broadcasting Regulations. In terms of these regulations the FCC had carried out its statutory responsibility to ensure that the principle of localism survived the forces of centralized power in the industry. And it had caught hell for doing so.

In 1943 RCA sold one of its networks, and in 1945 this network became the American Broadcasting Company (ABC). Thus an invigorated system of government regulation and frequency control and a system of program financing through advertising and networking were in place, not only for radio's golden age in the 1930s and 1940s, but also for television's development.

Experimentation in television had been going on even as radio was still developing. Vladimir Zworykin demonstrated a crude, partly electronic television system for Westinghouse in 1923; Philo Farnsworth patented a dissector tube in 1927, the year that car radios appeared; and in 1928 station WGY telecast the first television drama production. Franklin Roosevelt became the first President on television when his opening of the New York World's Fair in 1939 was telecast. At the fair RCA displayed sets with 5- and 9-inch tubes at prices ranging from $200 to $600. By May 1940, 23 stations were telecasting in the United States. Then World War II switched television production to the war effort, particularly to the development of radar. Most stations left the air, and television sets disappeared from the market. After the war, television picked up once more, but in 1948, after it had issued about 100 licenses, the FCC put a freeze on licenses so that it could study interference problems. The FCC lifted the freeze in 1952, was instantly pressed by 700 applicants for channels, and television took off. It took radio almost 25 years to penetrate into 40 million homes; television accomplished as much in 10.

RADIO AND TELEVISION: PROGRAMING AND FUNCTIONS

The 1930s and 1940s were radio's golden age. In 1922, there were 400,000 radio sets in American homes; in 1930 there were 13 million sets; and, despite the Great Depression during the 1930s, Americans owned 51 million sets in 1940, an average of almost 1½ sets per household. During those years radio was America's source of entertainment, its escape from the horrors of the depression. During the day, serials dominated. By the end of 1938, for example, 38 sponsored serials were being broadcast daily. Sociologist Herta Herzog found that the average serial listener listened to 6.6 serials daily. Many listeners confessed to strong dependence on the serials as a guide to solutions of their own problems, and as a source of friendship and emotional support. In the evenings comedy and variety, with stars such as Bob Hope, Jack Benny, Fred Allen, and Bing Crosby, provided what Barnouw called "universal therapy." Contest and quiz shows were almost as popular; in the late 1930s drama became a serious competitor for the mass audience.

After the American Newspaper Publishers Association failed to restrict radio's news programing (see Chapter 4), radio was able to report news with a drama and immediacy that riveted audiences. H. V. Kaltenborn covered

Edward R. Murrow, a pioneer in radio and television news reporting and commentary. (Wide World photo)

The Electronic
Media: Radio,
Television, Cable
Television, and
Movies

112

the Spanish Civil War and broadcast via shortwave the actual sounds of war. Renting cars at his own expense, he penetrated the areas held by the government and by Francisco Franco's forces and reported back to the United States over the CBS network. In 1937 CBS sent Edward R. Murrow to Berlin as the network's European director. To help him, Murrow hired William L. Shirer. Following a call from Shirer in March 1938 that the German army had crossed into Austria, Murrow chartered a plane from Berlin to Vienna, took a streetcar into the city, and described the city's fall to Hitler for American listeners. During the Munich crisis in September 1938 Americans heard the actual voices of all the leaders involved—Hitler of Germany, Chamberlain of England, Mussolini of Italy, Benes of Czechoslovakia—while Kaltenborn translated and interpreted for American listeners. Murrow's reporting from London during the Blitz moved Americans as few commentators have done before or since. "You burned the city of London in our houses," said the poet Archibald MacLeish, "and we felt the flames that burned it. You laid the dead of London at our doors and we knew the dead were our dead . . ."[9]

Back in the United States Herbert Morrison of WLS in Chicago persuaded his station to let him cover the arrival in 1937 of the giant German dirigible, the airship *Hindenburg,* in Lakehurst, New Jersey. Morrison, an airship enthusiast, communicated his excited anticipation as the balloon came into view. Then just as it was anchoring at the mooring mast, the *Hindenburg* burst into flames, burning the passengers. Overcome, Morrison wept at the sight and struggled to control himself enough to make the report. At the time both NBC and CBS forbade the use of recordings; all programs were produced live. But Morrison's broadcast was so moving that NBC suspended its policy and broadcast a recording of Morrison's emotional account of the disaster over the blue network.

In his poetic rendering of the effect of Murrow's reporting from London, MacLeish captured the nature of radio's power in news, a power actor-director Orson Welles was to exploit in his radio production of H. G. Wells' *War of the Worlds* in October 1938. Welles' story was adapted so that the Martians landed in New Jersey. With increasing frequency and specificity, authentic-sounding newscasts interrupted a palm court orchestra broadcasting from a downtown New York hotel. Finally an eye witness was able to clarify the confusing bulletins from New Jersey; he reported seeing a creature emerging from an object that had landed on a New Jersey farm. All over the United States panic broke out among groups of listeners convinced that the CBS drama was real. People called police stations and newspapers for help. AP sent a bulletin to its subscribers explaining what was happening. Some listeners swore that they had seen the Martians.

Because most of us have grown up with the electronic media, because radio and television have been so pervasive a part of our lives, radio's early impact in news and drama may be incomprehensible now. One who was quick to see and exploit its power and intimacy was President Franklin Roosevelt. His famous "fireside chats," begun in 1933, alerted politicians to the new medium's potential. It enabled them to bypass the editing practices of newspapers and to speak directly to the people. Via networks they could talk to a nation. Before long an ability to present themselves effectively on radio, and then television, became a critical skill for politicians, and particularly for the President.

Radio's share of advertising kept pace with its popularity. Radio had 6.5 percent of all advertising in 1935, 10.5 percent in 1940, and 14.6 percent in 1945. In 1950, radio's share dropped to 10.7 percent. Television had arrived. In 1965, radio's share dropped to 6.1 percent; television had 11.2 percent. In 1976, radio had 6.7 percent of all advertising; television had 19.7 percent. Advertising share is a crude but effective measure of a medium's popularity and salience. Where radio had been the focus of attention of millions of Americans, day and night, through the 1940s, television thereafter took away much of its programing, some of its stars, and most of its audience. As newspapers had had to adjust to radio's speed in communicating up-to-the-minute news, so radio had to adjust to television.

The 7,331 AM and FM commercial radio stations licensed in August 1977 functioned mainly as a background medium, something to which people listen while they are occupied with other activities—driving to and from work, doing household chores, studying, lying on the beach. Most radio programing is music, but radio has shown itself more versatile than the mass medium of television in attracting specialized audiences. Thus in major markets there will be stations appealing to a variety of musical tastes— classical, pop, rock, rhythm and blues, country and western, and so on. It has been a medium of effective appeal to minorities because, like the specialized magazine, radio can be financially viable by paying exclusive attention to a particular audience.

For the most part radio news is confined to interrupting disc jockeys on the hour or half hour with short bulletins on breaking news supplied by the radio wires of AP and UPI and to providing local traffic and weather information. CBS has operated all-news radio stations successfully in a few major cities, but NBC's more ambitious venture failed. In 1975 NBC signed up 27 stations for its 7-days-a-week 24-hour News and Information Service (NIS). By September 1976, 72 stations were subscribing to the service, but after losing more than $10 million in two years, NBC terminated NIS in May 1977.

A remarkable development in radio as a technology, one reminiscent of radio's early appeal to amateur experimenters, has been two-way Citizens Band (CB) radio. Popular with truckers who broke the monotony of cross-country driving by chatting with fellow truckers and warning them of the whereabouts of the police, CB radio spread rapidly in the 1970s to the public at large. By June 1977 the FCC had issued 11 million licenses to operate CB radios since CB began in 1958, and it was estimated that more than 50 million CB radios would be in use by 1980. Early celebrated for its value in mobilizing relief efforts during emergencies such as floods and

The Electronic
Media: Radio,
Television, Cable
Television, and
Movies

114

tornados and in helping stranded motorists, CB was causing concern in the late 1970s because of its use as a law-evader's tool, as a device for effectively monitoring and frustrating police efforts to apprehend law-breakers or to control riots and disturbances.

CB kept broadcasting in touch with its roots, with a time when radio had been little more than a technological marvel for destroying distance between people and enabling them to talk to one another. It harked back to a time before the rise of great corporate institutions had turned broadcasting into big business, and CB's popularity was perhaps an indication of the potential implicit in the two-way communication promised by the linkage of cable television and computers.

THE RISE OF TELEVISION

Radio had prepared the structure and technology for television's development, and the postwar boom fueled its take-off. Television quickly displaced radio as the *mass* medium. Equally quickly, the television industry discovered its vulnerability. Its timidity as a government-licensed industry made it vulnerable to powerful interests and politicians; its greed made it vulnerable to advertisers. Because the economics of its operations required it to be immensely popular, television failed from the first to secure a sure sense of its own identity. No medium could rival its capacity to entertain mass audiences. But the FCC required it also to inform a society that often preferred to be entertained. Thus television has had difficulty resisting the temptation to blur its functions as a mass medium of news, entertainment, and commerce. Most of its newscasters have no confusion about their professional identity. In the intensely competitive environment in which they work, however, some newscasters entertain rather than inform. And others also sell floor wax and deodorants and dog food.

Part of television's problem was a severe case of nerves at birth; it was born in the hey-day of America's hysterical anti-Communism. In May 1947 former FBI employees founded *Counterattack,* a newsletter listing celebrities alleged to be Communists or subversives. *Counterattack* began to pressure the broadcasting industry and its advertising sponsors to purge suspect producers, writers, and actors. In 1950, *Red Channels* appeared, listing 151 persons as Communists or subversives, among them the best-known and most admired members of the industry. At the same time Joseph McCarthy, the junior senator from Wisconsin, made his meteoric rise to prominence by attacking Communists and by shrewdly manipulating the media to promote his efforts. In the process of this anti-Communist crusade careers were scarred, some forever ruined, and the broadcast industry itself, like other institutions, was profoundly intimidated. Not until March 1954 did television confront the menace. Then Edward R. Murrow exposed McCarthy's tactics of the smear and half-truth to the mass audience of CBS's news documentary series, "See It Now," and contributed dramatically to ending McCarthy's career. But a year later the career of "See It Now" itself had ended. After some 200 controversial, hard-hitting broadcasts in four years, television's most outstanding journalism was in effect replaced by a newly popular force.

In the half-hour immediately preceding the weekly "See It Now" broadcast, "The $64,000 Question" quiz show had started. Within months there were eight or nine almost equally popular imitators. Alcoa Aluminum, sponsor of "See It Now," had been paying $50,000 for each half-hour of the series; Revlon, sponsor of "The $64,000 Question," paid $80,000 for the quiz show. The virtual replacement of news with entertainment and the difference in the price the sponsors paid explain much about television's identity and functions. As a commercial enterprise concerned to make a profit, television discovered that its audience and advertisers found entertainment more appealing than public affairs. Controversial journalism like "See It Now" angered interest groups, who pressured sponsors, and politicians, who pressured the FCC and threatened station licenses.

Today television has recovered a sense of balance between news and entertainment that it seemed to be losing in the mid-1950s, but had it not been for a scandal in 1958–1959, one wonders just how television might have developed. The quiz shows were drawing massive audiences and making celebrities of contestants. Television's sense of the difference between entertainment and journalism, between show business celebrities and journalists, was most clearly revealed by the use NBC made of Charles Van Doren, a Columbia University English instructor. Van Doren became a star as a contestant on the quiz show "Twenty-One," briefly holding the record for the highest winnings—$129,000. Although Van Doren had no journalism background, NBC made him host of its morning news-magazine show, "Today," as a summer replacement. It turned out that Van Doren had neither journalism background nor the ethics one expects of a journalist. A New York grand jury was investigating rumors and charges that the quiz shows were fixed. Van Doren, among others, denied the charges. In Congress the House subcommittee on legislative oversight began to look into the allegations. Then Van Doren confessed. The producer of "Twenty-One" had prepared Van Doren with the answers before each program, coaching him in ways to build suspense. Other witnesses told the House committee that Revlon had often instructed producers which contestants on "The $64,000 Question" should be "beaten" and removed.

The industry responded quickly to the uproar and the collapse of its image. CBS, which had just dropped "See It Now," instituted a new documentary series, "CBS Reports." NBC launched a similar documentary emphasis in its news division. The major quiz shows were dropped, and new Hollywood series such as "The Untouchables," "Bonanza," and "Twilight Zone" took their place. But this reassertion of the importance of television news did not permanently solve television's identity crisis. As late as mid-1976 television revealed its blurred identity as simultaneous entertainer-informer when ABC lured Barbara Walters, co-host of NBC's "Today" show, away to anchor ABC's evening news with Harry Reasoner. Walters was offered a salary of $500,000, about $100,000 more than the salary of

The Electronic
Media: Radio,
Television, Cable
Television, and
Movies

116

such major anchorpersons as Walter Cronkite and David Brinkley. She was offered a further $500,000 to anchor four prime-time specials and occasionally to host "Issues and Answers." Although an outstanding news interviewer, Walters clearly was not being paid $1 million only for her journalistic skills but also, perhaps mainly, for her "show biz" qualities. Walters was as much a star as a journalist.

Walters was not the first woman to anchor a national news program. In Britain Angela Rippon had been co-anchoring the British Broadcasting Corporation's evening newscast since 1975. Rippon was paid the standard BBC reporter's salary of less than $14,000 a year, plus a $127 annual clothing allowance. "I'm delighted for Barbara Walters," *Time* magazine quoted Rippon as saying, "But things are on a different scale here. We're not in the personality industry. We are journalists, not performers."[10]

Although ABC enjoyed spectacular success with its entertainment programs in the 1976–1977 season, far outstripping CBS and NBC in the ratings, its gamble on Barbara Walters fizzled. ABC's "Evening News" lagged way behind the evening news on CBS and NBC in the ratings. Nor did ABC's resolution of this problem allay the fears of those who saw the always precarious balance between news and show biz tipping fast in favor of entertainment. In May 1977 ABC named ABC Sports president Roone Arledge head of the network's news division as well. Recognized as television's most innovative sports broadcaster, Arledge had no experience in news. But he rejected any analogy between his appointment and the satirical point of the popular 1976 movie *Network* in which screenwriter Paddy Chayefsky portrayed a network news division as willing to offer whatever vulgarity, crudity, or absurdity that titillated audiences and won rating points. Interviewed by *Newsweek,* Arledge said his proudest achievement had been "the degree of journalism that we have brought to sports." On the Walters hiring, however, his strictly journalistic values were not clear. He would have been in favor of hiring Walters from NBC, he said, "because I think that Barbara is a unique personality."[11]

These examples suggest the ambiguities in commercial television's functions. Although an increasingly important source of news for Americans—some surveys show people regard it as more important and credible than newspapers—television's initial appeal was as a visually exciting medium of entertainment and it has not been able fully to separate news from show business as journalistic convention requires. This fuzzing of function is increased by the commercial and competitive rules commercial television plays by. Although competition between newspapers in the same city is virtually extinct, television is intensely competitive.

THE STRUCTURE OF THE TELEVISION INDUSTRY

Of the 963 television stations licensed to broadcast in August 1977, 242 were educational or public stations and 721, or almost 75 percent, were commercial stations. Approximately 85 percent of the commercial stations were affiliated to or owned by networks, which serve as the affiliates' brokers in selling audiences to advertisers and acquiring programs from the

Television Finances 1975–1976 (In Millions of Dollars)

Broadcast Revenues	1976	1975*	% Increase 1975–1976
3 Networks	2,117.5	1,673.8	26.5
15 Network Owned and Operated Stations (all VHF)	486.9	395.6	23.1
All other Stations			
477 VHF	2,231.1	1,762.2	26.6
188 UHF*	363.0	262.6	38.2
Subtotal	2,594.1	2,024.7	28.1
Industry Total	**5,198.5**	**4,094.1**	**27.0**
Broadcast Expenses			
3 Networks	1,821.9	1,465.3	24.3
15 Network Owned and Operated Stations (all VHF)	327.9	290.0	13.1
All other Stations			
477 VHF	1,500.4	1,306.1	14.9
188 UHF*	298.2	252.7	18.0
Subtotal	1,798.5	1,558.8	15.4
Industry Total	**3,948.3**	**3,314.1**	**19.1**
Broadcast Income (before Federal income tax)			
3 Networks	295.6	208.5	41.8
15 Network Owned and Operated Stations (all VHF)	159.0	105.7	50.4
All other Stations			
477 VHF	730.7	456.1	60.2
188 UHF*	64.8	9.9	557.1
Subtotal	795.6	465.9	70.7
Industry Total	**1,250.2**	**780.0**	**60.3**

*The 1975 data represent 177 UHF stations.
NOTE: Last digits may not add to totals because of rounding.

Reprinted from Public Notice 87928, August 29, 1977, Federal Communications Commission, Washington, D.C.

major Hollywood movie studios and other program suppliers and syndicates. The dominance of U.S. commercial television by the three major networks, NBC, CBS, and ABC, is shown in the table above. For example, the revenues of the networks and their 15 owned-and-operated stations accounted in 1976 for half of the television industry's total revenues.

Contrary to what many people think, the product of commercial television stations is not programs but audiences. They try to make as much profit as possible by selling audiences to advertisers at prices that are listed in dollars per thousand viewers per minute of commercial time. Advertisers buy two kinds of audiences—national and local. Advertisers wanting to reach the national audience buy from the television networks. Advertisers wanting to reach selective local audiences with what is called national spot

The Electronic
Media: Radio,
Television, Cable
Television, and
Movies

118

advertising buy directly from individual local stations. And local businesses with only local sales buy from local stations. Commercial stations use programs, then, to attract, hold and sell as many viewers as is economically profitable without violating FCC regulations or their own codes of responsibility.

THE RATINGS

As advertisers finally required an independent agency, the Audit Bureau of Circulation, to certify the circulations of the print media, so television has rating agencies. The major ratings services are the A. C. Nielsen Company and the American Research Bureau (ARB). In rating network programs, Nielsen places audimeters in a national sample of 1,200 homes to indicate which channels are being watched at any time of day. The audimeter information produces two numbers, rating and share, that can mean life or death for an entertainment show, prosperity or unemployment for a news director.

Rating is a percentage of the total possible audience measured in households. If CBS gets a rating of 19 for "The Carol Burnett Show" in prime time, this means that 19 percent of the more than 72 million American homes equipped with television were tuned to the show. According to Les Brown in *Televi$ion: the Business Behind the Box,* "[a] national score of 17.0 is generally satisfactory in prime time, and expensive programs which fall below that level rarely are able to produce a profit."[12] For a local program, the rating measures the percentage of homes in the local area tuned to a show.

Share is a comparative measure. If, at 8 p.m. on Saturday, CBS's "The Jeffersons" earns a share of 34, NBC's "Emergency" earns 28, and ABC's "Good Heavens" earns 32, the figures mean that of all the sets actually in use at the time, 34 percent of them were tuned to CBS, 28 percent to NBC, and 32 percent to ABC. It also means that "Emergency" is likely to be canceled, for, says Les Brown, "It is considered reasonable to require a 30 share from a network show as the lowest measure of success."[13]

In addition to the 1200 audimeters, Nielsen places 2200 diaries in a sample of homes reflecting different income and educational levels. The diarists record the viewing by all family members for a week—the time, the program, the channel number, the number of family members watching, and the age and sex of each. Combined with the audimeter information, the diary information gives advertisers a demographic breakdown of the audiences for the various programs, so telling them whether the audience is of the kind they are trying to reach. The actual size of the audience, then, may not be as important to an advertiser as the kind of persons being reached. Les Brown comments:

One of the myths about American television is that it operates as a cultural democracy, wholly responsible to the will of the viewing majority in terms of the programs that survive or fade. More aptly, in the area of entertainment mainly, it

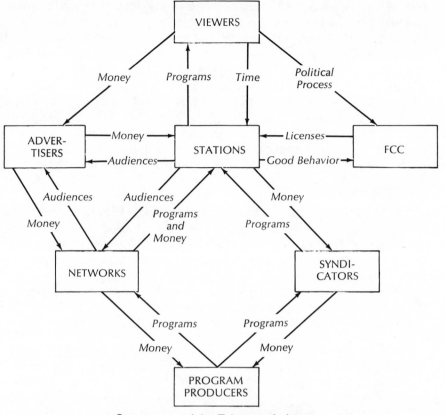

Organization of the Television Industry

Reprinted by permission of the publisher, from *Television Economics* by Bruce M. Owen,
Jack H. Beebe, and Wilard G. Manning, Jr. (Lexington, Mass.: Lexington Books, D. C. Heath
and Company, 1974).

is a cultural oligarchy, ruled by a consensus of the advertising community. . . .
This emphasis on the popularity of shows has made television appear to be
democratic in its principles of program selection. In truth, programs of great
popularity go off the air, without regard for the viewers' bereavement, if the
kinds of people it reaches are not attractive to advertisers.[14]

Television news plays by less savage rules mainly because stations do
not have the option of canceling news shows that are not drawing audiences. Stations must broadcast in the public interest, convenience, or
necessity, and the FCC has interpreted this vague language to mean that
stations must present news if they wish to retain their licenses. Stations can
schedule news at a different time, they can reduce or expand the time for
news, but they cannot avoid reporting it. In 1976 Norman Lear's soap
opera-comedy hit, "Mary Hartman, Mary Hartman," nicely illustrated television's dilemma. ABC put up the money to develop the show, then
withdrew. CBS funded a pilot, then rejected the series. Then NBC, and

The Electronic
Media: Radio,
Television, Cable
Television, and
Movies

120

ABC again, decided not to buy it. None of the 15 network-owned-and-operated stations bought it. So the 101 stations around the country who bought it in 1976 showed it at different times, almost half of them late at night, often opposite local news shows. In Chicago "Mary Hartman" was beating the NBC affiliate's news show in the ratings, was close to the CBS affiliate's news show, and was losing badly only to the ABC affiliate's "happy news" show. "Mary Hartman" was having similar success in New York and Los Angeles. Thus these news shows were not only competing intensely in the ratings against one another but also against a major entertainment hit. It is important to note that in these major cities "Mary Hartman's" strongest competitor was a so-called "happy news" show.

HAPPY NEWS

In the mid-1960s a minor industry was growing—television consultants. These individuals or firms analyzed stations' television news programs, reported their findings, and suggested changes. Increasingly in that decade of violence and turmoil they recommended a more informal, upbeat, and lively approach to the news. They did not necessarily recommend that accuracy and significance be rejected in favor of more cheerful, entertaining news, but usually they recommended that the manner of presentation be changed, in the direction, it seemed, of show business rather than of

"We'll be back in a minute with Harlan Harris's Sports Extra, Jules Bernmeier and the weather, Jimmy Cunningham's Entertainment Plus, Judith Enright's Fashion Notes, Grady O'Toole's Celebrity Interview, Maria Dellago's Budget Center, Murray Vaughn's Mr. Fix-It Shop, and me, Biff Brogan, with a note on the news."

Drawing by Ziegler; © 1977 The New Yorker Magazine, Inc.

professional journalism. All over the country, and particularly in the intensely competitive major markets, newscasters took a joshing, chatty approach to one another and to the news. In extreme examples of the format, the hijinks and elaborate props of the weather reporter drowned news of tragedy and disaster, of significant public affairs. The reporters appeared to be having a good time and the hope, apparently, was that viewers would too.

Ron Powers, who won a Pulitzer Prize for television criticism in 1973, blamed the choreographed bonhomie of happy news on the dictates of consultants and audience research. Powers wrote that if the late Edward R. Murrow had seen this "cybernetic news," he "might have noticed that in very few cases was there a sense of *mission* about the TV newscasts: a sense of continuity in the life of the city (or 'market') covered; a palpable willingness to perform the vigorous, adversary, check-on-government, intervening role that American journalism has traditionally performed."[15]

Powers' condemnation of television's responsiveness to researcher guidelines—"toward the end of gratifying the audience's surface whims, not supplying its deeper informational needs"—could be extended to newspapers in the late 1970s. Confronting declining circulations, caused in part by the visual and experiential appeal of television news, the newspaper industry was investing increasingly in audience research and turning toward more feature and consumer-oriented content.

To survive and make a profit, all commercial media of news and entertainment must, above all, please as many people as possible of the kind advertisers want to reach. The mix of information and entertainment, of news and show business values, has therefore fluctuated with audience and advertiser preferences and, in broadcasting, with the regulatory zeal of FCC commissioners. But because the First Amendment inhibits government tampering with freedoms of speech and press and because the broadcast industry had established its commercial nature before inviting government regulation, Congress and the FCC have had difficulty reordering the priorities that ratings and advertiser perceptions of majority taste dictate. A certain cultural and journalistic idealism in broadcasting statute and regulation does restrain the commercial and democratic imperatives of majority will. But however zealously the FCC has tried to assure a judicious balance between profit and the public interest, diversity and excellence in the programing of commercial broadcasting are ultimately at the mercy of mass taste—or of broadcasters' own sense of responsibility.

Regrettably, however, broadcast leadership is rarely uplifting in matters of public concern that may affect industry profits. In a January 1977 speech he titled, apparently without deliberate irony, "A New Spirit for Broadcasting," Julian Goodman, chairman of the board of NBC, announced:

Next fall [1977], NBC will be deemphasizing programs with violent content. Of the 50 pilot programs we are considering for the coming season, 21 are

The Electronic
Media: Radio,
Television, Cable
Television, and
Movies

122

Your Guide to Happy Viewing

By now you've noticed that local television news programs aren't what they used to be—carbon copies (or videotape recordings, for that matter) of each other. Knowing you might like to discuss this phenomenon at future cocktail parties or other gatherings journalists attend, we give you this glossary of terms to facilitate discussion. It is by no means complete, since producers could come up with something revolutionary at any time. It also does not suggest that every news program will fall neatly into one category because 1) journalists hate labels, 2) some stations think a combination of previously successful formats have a synergetic effect, 3) some stations haven't decided they want to go with any of them, or 4) all of the above. If you find none of the terms suffice, make something up.

FORMAL FORMAT [*nearly obsolete*]—1. Godlike, Doomsday 2. Olympian 3. Format in which the anchorman sits in front of the camera and reads the news, the sportscaster and weatherman do same 4. No conversation between on-air personalities 5. No nonsense 6. No off-the-cuff or scripted remarks about recent haircuts, vacations, cute stories, etc.

EYEWITNESS NEWS—1. Format in which station proves it had a reporter on the scene and the news did not come from wire services or the newspaper 2. Reporter has two minutes on camera to tell the story, preferably with appropriate background (on berm of highway for road construction story, knee-deep in water on floods, on street during lunch hour if interviewing the mayor, etc.); or reporter can be brought on newsroom set to tell anchorman the story *(see In-the-Newsroom Set)*

IN-THE-NEWSROOM SET—1. On-air personalities reporting from their natural working habitat—the busy newsroom (include cluttered desks, ringing phones and clacking wire machines) 2. Appears to the viewer to be actual newsroom, but can be staged.

INFORMAL FORMAT—1. On-air personalities may show they have personality 2. On-air personalities permitted to look at each other and exchange comments. 3. Weatherman may wear appropriate clothing to aid viewers in choosing proper garb should they wish to dash outdoors midway through the broadcast (discretion is urged when reporting on extremely warm weather) 4. Weatherman must also qualify as fall guy.

HAPPY TALK [*derogatory*]—1. Of the ha ha school of journalism 2. Jokes, slap-stick and other comedy spiced up with occasional news reports 3. More good news than bad with marshmallow commentaries and vaudeville atmosphere.

TABLOID NEWS [*very derogatory*]—1. Story or film value based on sex, sin, blood, vulgarity or deviance 2. Variation of Happy Talk whereby jokes are written by former burlesque comedians 3. No news makes good news.

Halina J. Czerniejewski, Associate Editor, *The Quill,* published by The Society of Professional Journalists, Sigma Delta Chi, May 1974.

comedies and most of the rest are variety shows, family programs, and dramas that shun violence. We are going to try new programming approaches, because if the public has had enough violence, we have too.[16]

This happy coincidence of public and private interest should not mislead us into viewing commercial broadcasting as submissive by nature. When its private interests are threatened, commercial broadcasting—like all the communications media—not only has a ready command of First Amendment and public interest rhetoric, but, through one of the most powerful lobbying groups in Washington, the National Association of Broadcasters, to which the networks and most stations belong, can be very persuasive in Congress and the FCC.

CABLE TELEVISION

Cable television, the FCC announced in 1970, "offers the technological and economic potential of an economy of abundance." Such overripe rhetoric had been a familiar part of the atmospherics buzzing around cable for a decade. Brainstorming in universities and think tanks, electronics and communications experts and sundry futurologists had conjured visions of a time when the marvels of cable and computer linked in a broad-band communications network throughout a wired nation would handle all of an individual's communication needs. People would learn, shop, correspond, and converse, be entertained and informed, perhaps even work, all at the press of a button that would flash into homes or offices whatever services of the store, newspaper, library, government, and entertainment industry were wanted.

This wizardry did not excite the telephone and broadcasting industries, which statute required the FCC to regulate in the public interest, convenience, and necessity. They saw disappearing customers and viewers and advertisers, for what had begun in the late 1940s as a supplement to over-the-air broadcasting had emerged in the 1960s as a head-on competitor. At first the FCC rejected broadcasters' request to regulate this competition, then shifted to intrude its jurisdiction over cable on behalf of the interests of broadcasting. By the early 1970s, when the frustrated cable industry and concerned citizens finally broadened the FCC's perspective, FCC regulation had retarded cable's development long enough to have secured protection for broadcasters.

The broadcast, television programing, and cable industries, which had been contending before the FCC, Congress, and the courts since 1959, came to a consensus agreement in 1972. In return for the opportunity to compete against over-the-air television in all markets, cable agreed with the broadcast industry to accept certain restrictions on its carriage of local and distant television signals, and with the suppliers of television programing to pay copyright fees for the use of their products. The FCC itself was quite clear about the equality of its priorities in resolving these issues: "[O]ur basic objective is to get cable moving so that the public may receive its benefits, and to do so without jeopardizing the basic structure of over-the-air television."[17] How and why had this compromise come to pass?

When cable transmission began in the late 1940s, it by no means alarmed the infant over-the-air commercial television industry, whose expansion the FCC had frozen between 1948 and 1952. The technological and economic demands of commercial television—the need imposed by

The Electronic
Media: Radio,
Television, Cable
Television, and
Movies

124

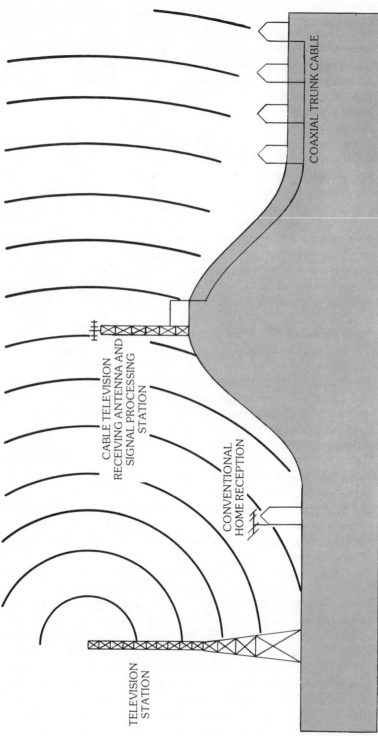

COAXIAL TRUNK CABLE

CABLE TELEVISION
RECEIVING ANTENNA AND
SIGNAL PROCESSING
STATION

CONVENTIONAL
HOME RECEPTION

TELEVISION
STATION

Typical arrangement of a cable television system centers on a receiving antenna that is at a place, such as a hilltop, where the signals broadcast by a television station come in clearly. A separate antenna is used for each station that the cable system picks up. Signals thus received are sent to subscribers' homes by coaxial cable.

From "Cable Television" by William T. Knox, *Scientific American*, October 1971. Copyright © 1971 by Scientific American, Inc. All rights reserved.

limited signal range for densely populated "markets" attractive to advertisers—confined television broadcasting mainly to large cities. Distance or obstructions prevented many small towns and rural areas from receiving a television signal—until the development of the coaxial cable.

The simplest way to provide a cable television signal is to erect an antenna to pick signals out of the air from the nearest television station and transmit them through a cable to the home. It was through this system, called "community antenna television" or CATV, that people in rural or mountainous areas received television in the 1950s. The added viewers delighted commercial broadcasters; cable television did not compete with but extended over-the-air commercial broadcasting. Then other methods of cable transmission killed this chummy relationship.

Cable operators can not only provide or improve reception from nearby television stations, but they can import distant signals from stations in cities hundreds of miles away. The signal is then transmitted from the antenna by long-distance microwave or cable link. By erecting an antenna near enough to Los Angeles to pick up the city's television signals, an enterprising cable operator in San Diego was able in 1961 to offer subscribers four independent Los Angeles television stations in addition to the three network affiliate stations broadcasting in San Diego. Because viewers were willing to pay for the importation of distant signals and more programing choice, cable television began to pose a competitive threat to local commercial broadcasters.

The development of color television provided a further incentive for city dwellers to sign on for cable service. VHF signals bounce off obstacles such as tall buildings, so producing interference, particularly on color sets. Because it bypasses these obstacles, cable offered viewers high-quality color pictures over-the-air television could not match. The willingness of viewers to pay for better pictures made cable systems financially attractive enterprises in large cities, and the alarm of commercial broadcasters began to grow.

Finally, cable operators can originate and transmit their own programing, by buying it from others, by producing it themselves in their cable television facilities, or by covering entertainment, special, and sports events not carried by local broadcasters. They might offer this programing as part of the system's regular service or require that subscribers pay a program or channel fee in addition to the regular monthly cable service charge. The national pay cable network, Home Box Office, which in 1977 was transmitting between 60 and 70 hours of current movies, live sports, and nightclub acts a week, was an example of this supplementary pay cable TV service.

In 1952 the cable television industry as a whole served 14,000 subscribers; in 1971 it served 5.5 million; in 1977 almost 10 million in more than 6000 communities. In the 1960s the average cable system served 1000 subscribers; in the late 1970s it served 4000. Commercial broadcasters had few grounds for complaint about cable's technological appeal to people who had poor over-the-air reception or none at all. But when cable began to seduce viewers by importing distant commercial television signals to offer

The Electronic
Media: Radio,
Television, Cable
Television, and
Movies

126

more programing choice, broadcasters cried "Foul!" and in 1959 asked the FCC to assert jurisdiction over CATV.

Although the FCC was sympathetic enough to the broadcasters to recommend that Congress require cable operators to get permission from stations whose signals they imported and to carry the signals of local stations at their request, the FCC found no basis for asserting its jurisdiction over CATV. In essence, it said, "the broadcasters' position shakes down to the fundamental proposition that they wish us to regulate in a manner favorable toward them vis-a-vis any nonbroadcast competitive enterprise."[18]

Then the FCC began gradually to abandon this noninterventionist view for two reasons: It was persuaded that cable's importation of distant signals would fragment the audience of local stations and possibly eliminate them, thus endangering a basic principle of American broadcasting—localism— and that cable's use of distant broadcast signals without payment gave it an unfair competitive advantage over local television stations, which had to pay copyright holders. Failure to pay copyright would jeopardize the markets of copyright holders.

In the mid-1960s the FCC shifted its concern from cable's competitive threat to small local stations to cable's threat to the development of the UHF spectrum in major markets. Arguing that it was of the utmost importance to the public interest that cable and television broadcasting have complementary rather than conflicting roles, the FCC ruled in 1966 that cable operators must prove that importation of distant signals into a top 100 market would not adversely affect UHF development in that market. The effect of the rule was to prevent cable operators from entering major markets. Cable companies challenged the FCC's authority to regulate cable, but the U.S. Supreme Court in 1968 and 1972 upheld the FCC's jurisdiction. Largely because it lost these battles in the courts, and even though it had won copyright battles in the Supreme Court, the cable industry came to terms with broadcast interests in the consensus agreement that preceded the FCC's comprehensive rulings in 1972.

After resolving the issues dividing the private commercial interests of the cable and broadcast industries with its rules on carriage of local and distant broadcast signals and on copyright, the FCC addressed the public interest in cable's potential. It is appropriate, the FCC said, "that the fundamental goals of a national communications structure be furthered by cable—the opening of new outlets for local expression, the promotion of diversity in television programing, the advancement of educational and instructional television, and increased informational services of local governments."[19]

The FCC ruled, therefore, that cable systems starting operations after March 31, 1972, and serving more than 3500 subscribers must provide capacity for 20 channels and two-way transmission. Cable systems must also provide "one dedicated, noncommercial public access channel available without charge at all times on a first-come, first-served nondiscriminatory basis." The cable operator was to proscribe "obscene or indecent matter," but could not censor or control program content in any other way. The cable system also had to provide one channel for educational use and another for local government use.[20]

So much optimistic, even apocalyptic rhetoric has attended cable's development, and so much prophecy of doom for conventional broadcasting and for newspapers as we know them, that these media seem to have put a deposit on the future by buying into cable interests. Although FCC regulation prohibits a telephone company or a television station from owning a cable system in the same market and prohibits networks from owning cable systems at all, *Broadcasting* reported that media interests had ownership holdings in approximately three-quarters of all cable firms: over 35 percent of the systems had ties with broadcast interests, almost 25 percent with program producers, and almost 15 percent with newspapers.[21]

In promoting cable's promise of "an economy of abundance," the FCC has had the difficult task of fulfilling its statutory obligations and of arbitrating the contending interests of citizen groups, commercial broadcasters and their program suppliers, and cable entrepreneurs. Because it has fumbled toward a regulatory policy for cable that offers something for each group, the extent of the FCC's responsiveness to public or private interests is much debated. In the late 1970s, cable and broadcasting coexisted profitably, citizens had a right of access to local cable television, and the public had a wider range of program choice through regular and pay cable service. The technology was available to carry the informational services and program diversity whose prospect had so dazzled for a decade.

Yet the programing preferences of most subscribers in the late 1970s were hardly innovative—movies and sports. That is why people hopeful that cable's multichannel capacity would free it from the economics of mass-oriented commercial broadcasting, so enabling more enriching and penetrating cultural and public affairs programing for specialized audiences, were disillusioned. Hopes for culturally diverse and ambitious programing seemed still to lie with a noncommercial public telecommunications system.

PUBLIC BROADCASTING

In August 1977 there were 893 licensed educational radio stations (about 11 percent of all U.S. radio stations) and 242 licensed educational television stations (about 25 percent of all U.S. television stations). Some were licensed to states, some to local school districts, some to colleges and universities, and some to nonprofit community corporations. They were funded in varying proportions from the same mix—federal, state, and local taxes, foundation grants, business and industry contributions and underwriting (sponsorship), and individual subscriptions. The FCC, which licenses all stations, commercial and noncommercial, requires noncommercial broadcast stations to be licensed only to nonprofit educational organizations for educational purposes. Although their programing emphases differ with the nature of their ownership—university and community stations spend more time on cultural and public affairs programing, for example, than do state and school district stations—all stations broadcast instructional programing

The Electronic
Media: Radio,
Television, Cable
Television, and
Movies

128

that extends teaching services beyond the classroom. In addition to their locally originated programing, stations receive programs from regional and national networks.

This broad, complex structure developed along with the evolution of radio and television as mainly commercial media. From radio's earliest days, colleges and universities had taken an interest in radio, for experimentation in the technology and for extending teaching services. By the end of 1922, for example, 74 colleges and universities were broadcasters; by the end of 1924, 151. But from then on into the 1930s their numbers declined. Frequency problems, financing difficulties, and pressure from commercial stations to sell thinned the ranks of educational broadcasters. By the mid-1930s their number had dwindled to about 30, and the FCC showed little disposition to rescue them from oblivion. After hearings in fall 1934, the FCC reported to Congress that commercial broadcasters were eager to use some of their time for educational and nonprofit needs, so there was really no need to reserve channels for education.

When television took off in the late 1940s the educators organized more carefully this time to ensure that the new medium's educational potential was realized. In FCC Commissioner Frieda Hennock they had an energetic ally, and in 1952 the FCC reserved 242 VHF and UHF channels for education; more would be reserved later. Generous though the reservations may seem, however, the UHF channels could not be received by most television sets, so educational television had problems developing an audience. But its main problem, one that persists, was financing. Historian Erik Barnouw describes an educational license as no more than "a license to beg." Had it not been for the generosity of the Ford Foundation, which poured millions into the system for station construction and for establishing a program service throughout the 1950s, it is unlikely that the educational stations would have survived.

After a comprehensive study of the system, the Carnegie Commission on Educational Television articulated in 1967 what it felt the goals of the system should be, how many stations were needed to service the nation, what the cost would be, and how the system should be funded. After identifying the limited goals of commercial television, the commission reported that society was still confronted with "the obligation to bring that technology [television] into the full service of man." Public television, said the commission, is capable of becoming "the clearest expression of American diversity, and of excellence within diversity," of being "a civilized voice in a civilized community." The commission recommended a broadened interpretation of "education":

> Education is not always somber or laborious. It is co-extensive with the full range of human experience and includes joy and gaiety as well as hard intellectual endeavor. Educational television should be no less.[22]

To spread these benefits across the nation, the commission reported, would require 380 television stations at a construction cost of $621 million. These would cost $270 million annually to operate. The commission recommended that an excise tax on sets provide the funds to operate the system, which was to be based on the bedrock of localism, the local station. In the Congressional hearings that followed the commission's report, almost everyone thought the commission's vision was splendid—but limited. The term "public" replaced "educational," the vision was extended to include radio as well as television, and in 1967 the Public Broadcasting Act was passed with remarkable speed and enthusiasm. The act created the Corporation for Public Broadcasting (CPB) to promote, plan, and develop the system as a whole by assisting national interconnection and program development. It would also administer the federal funds dedicated to the system. In 1969 CPB created the Public Broadcasting Service (PBS) to select, schedule, and distribute quality television programing across the nation. In the same year CPB studied public radio and created National Public Radio (NPR), a national program production and distribution service. Very quickly, then, it seemed that the Carnegie Commission's splendid vision was being realized. But the system had no money. The commission had insisted on a massive infusion of federal money over the long term and properly insulated from the political process to ensure that television realized its potential. No support for a dedicated tax was forthcoming in Congress, which appropriated only $5 million in fiscal 1969. By 1972, five years after the 1967 act, the appropriation had risen to only $35 million, which meant that with all its other financial sources public broadcasting was able to spend 84 cents per head of population to provide programs; commercial television spent $15.89 per person that year.

But money was not public broadcasting's only problem. The change from "educational" to "public" invited the system to tackle public affairs programing. With Ford Foundation support a National Public Affairs Center for Television was established in Washington and was just getting into its stride when it, and the public system as a whole, fell victim to the Nixon Administration's general onslaught on the press. The Nixon Administration attacked what it saw as excessive centralization of the system in clear violation of the "bedrock of localism" philosophy and argued that public affairs programing was inappropriate in a federally supported system. Tension had long beset the cumbersome, poverty-stricken system, and the Nixon attack brought the animosities to the surface. As a result a new and no less complex structure has emerged, and only gradually in the mid-1970s was public broadcasting recovering its confidence in public affairs broadcasting lost in the Nixon years. It had retained some of its stature in educational and cultural programing through such acclaimed children's programs as "Sesame Street," "The Electric Company," and "Zoom," and such dramatic and historical series as "Masterpiece Theater" and "The Adams Chronicles," but was having difficulty funding the kind of penetrating, controversial public affairs broadcasting envisioned in the early 1970s.

In the mid 1970s these were the methods used to place television programs on the PBS network:

The Electronic
Media: Radio,
Television, Cable
Television, and
Movies

130

1. Propose a program to PBS, pay all production costs, and charge the network nothing. Institutions making such proposals include private corporations, federal agencies, and foundations. In 1975, for example, there were 14 corporate sponsored shows (eight of them sponsored by oil companies), three federally funded shows, four nonprofit foundation shows, and eight CPB shows. PBS reviews all these proposals and decides which ones to put on the network.

2. Sell a show to local stations through the station program cooperative (SPC). The stations select programs on the basis of a written proposal in a catalogue and on a program pilot. The selecting stations share the costs of the program. Of the nearly $50 million spent on programs PBS distributed in the 1974–1975 season, 25 percent were financed through the SPC.

3. Offer a program or a package of programs to stations at a lower per-station cost than the single-buyer purchase price. PBS acts as the stations' agent. This system, called the Station Acquisition Market (SAM), was started in 1975 and bypasses the bidding and voting process of the SPC in which programs compete against one another for station support.

All three methods are designed to contribute to a more "democratic" system in which the stations themselves have more power over what the network feeds than had been so before the Nixon Administration's attack on the centralized power of CPB and PBS. As means for helping to fund quality programing, the various devices can work only to the extent that local stations have money to invest in programs. As the federal government has

Public television's "Sesame Street" proved learning could be fun. (courtesy of Children's Television Workshop)

increased its funds to the public system (from $5 million in fiscal 1969 to almost $103 million for fiscal 1977), stations have had more programing funds. But the relativity of that statement must be emphasized. In the 1974–1975 season the public broadcasting system spent about $50 million on news and entertainment programs distributed nationally by PBS. The three commercial networks spend about $500 million for their national entertainment programing alone; that is, each network spends at least three times as much as the public system for programs. Although the public system concentrates a proportion of its programing directly on minority groups in a way the commercial system does not, increasingly both the public and the commercial system seem to be competing for the same mass audience. Public broadcasting was originally designed to avoid that competition, but financial insecurity and a still unclear vision of precisely how it is to supplement the commercial system seem to be pushing it closer to the source it was to depart from.

Anne Branscomb, a communications lawyer and vice president of a communications consulting firm, commented in 1976 that public broadcasting's dilemma

> . . . is the result of a too "benign neglect" by federal agencies, coupled with a schizophrenia of the public broadcasting entities as to their proper roles, a myopia concerning their potential for development, and a certain lack of self-confidence in their survival quotient.[23]

The continuing conflict between CPB and PBS particularly threatened the energy and morale of the system. PBS objected to CPB's intrusion into programing decisions (CPB maintained a 17-person programing staff at a cost of $660,000 in 1977); CPB argued that PBS failed to recognize CPB's legislatively mandated role to promote the full development of public broadcasting. Other critics complained of the two entities' expensive and wasteful duplication of functions. In May 1977 the House Communications Subcommittee, which was to consider public broadcasting in hearings in September 1977 on proposed revision of the 1934 Communications Act, recommended that functions of CPB and PBS be combined. President Jimmy Carter was expected to send legislative proposals on public broadcasting's structure and funding to Congress in September 1977. Then in June 1977, the Carnegie Corporation of New York announced the formation of a new Carnegie Commission on the Future of Public Broadcasting to conduct a $1-million, 18-month-long study of every aspect of public broadcasting—structure, funding, the application of new communications technologies, and programing.

At the end of 1977, then, the heartening prospect was that public broadcasting's cumbersome organizational structure and bureaucracy would be trimmed. That the system's persistent bickering about its philosophy and programing principles, bickering that had the endurance of an interminable soap opera, would thereby be eliminated was less certain.

The Electronic
Media: Radio,
Television, Cable
Television, and
Movies

132

Movies

If you're tired of life, go to the picture show,
If you're sick of troubles rife, go to the picture show;
You'll forget your unpaid bills, rheumatism and other ills,
If you'll stow away your pills, and go to the picture show.

So ran an advertising jingle 15 years after the world's first Kinetoscope parlor opened on Broadway in New York City on April 14, 1894. It is easier to understand why Universal Pictures spent $1.8 million on advertising and publicity to promote the movie *Jaws* in 1975, why Dino De Laurentiis spent $10 million to promote *King Kong* in 1976, than to understand the need to persuade people to go to the picture show 65 years ago. Then everyone, it seems, went to the movies in somewhat the same largely uncritical way everyone now watches television.

In 1911 between 5 and 7 million people daily went to the movies in the country's 13,000 theatres. In film's first 20 years the audience expanded from immigrants and blue-collar workers paying a penny to stand and peep one at a time at a 10- or 20-second movie in the Kinetoscope machine developed by William Dickson in Thomas Edison's New Jersey laboratory to middle-class families paying 5 or 10 cents to sit in a nickelodeon theater and watch an hour's miscellany of adventure, comedy, or fantasy films projected on a screen by Edison's Vitascope or Dickson's Biograph. All classes, all ages, went to the movies. The challenge was less to persuade them to go than to produce and distribute at least two new movies a week for those thousands of theaters and millions of people. In 1911, for example, Chicago's 400 theaters showed 3255 different movies.

Quantity is no longer the challenge. The industry that developed to feed film's voracious appetite for more movies, an appetite for material like television's, now has to lure an audience away from cheaper, more accessible media of mass entertainment and from the many pastimes available to a people of plenty. Although the U.S. population more than doubled between 1914 and 1977, weekly movie attendance dropped by half. In 1914, when the population was approximately 98 million, 49 million people a week went to the movies. In 1977, when the population was approximately 214 million, only 20 million people a week went to the movies. A weekly network television series that commanded only 20 million viewers would be considered in ratings trouble and would probably be cancelled.

The contemporary movie audience tends to be the younger and better-educated members of the population: 65 percent of Americans with at least a year of college education go to the movies frequently or occasionally. Only 50 percent of those with a high school education and 25 percent without a high school diploma attend the movies regularly. Sixty-three percent of those without a high school diploma never go to the movies.

The younger, more educated group has always gone to the movies, as much for social contact with peers and escape from the home as for any pleasure intrinsic in the movies themselves. The mass has been more fickle, losing early its enthusiasm for film's technological novelty. It has been lured back by technological innovation, by sound in 1927, by 3-D and the large curved screen of Cinerama and Cinemascope in the early 1950s. But technology's appeal has been fleeting. The boom-bust pattern of mass attendance seems to have been linked more directly to the boom-bust pattern of the economy itself than to technological innovation.

After the initial shock of the Great Depression—when average weekly attendance dropped from 80 million in 1929 to 60 million in 1932 and 1933, major companies went into the red, some into receivership, and many theatres closed—people returned to the movies in spite of the appeal of radio. In spite of the appeal of television, and television movies, people went to the movies during the recession of the early 1970s; in 1974 box-office receipts rose to an all-time record of $1.9 billion, the highest since 1946.

Nevertheless, the financial health of the film industry in the late 1970s depended more on the spectacular success of a few movies than on a renewed appeal of movies in general. *Jaws,* for example, surpassed *The Godfather* as box-office champion by earning $125 million at home and abroad in less than 90 days of release. In 1977 *Star Wars* promised to do better than *Jaws. New Yorker* film critic Pauline Kael commented in 1975: "It's becoming tough for a movie that isn't a big media-created event to find an audience, no matter how good it is. And if a movie has been turned into an event, it doesn't have to be good; an event . . . draws an audience simply because it's an event. You don't expect Mount Rushmore to be a work of art, but if you're anywhere near it you have to go."[24] That's why Universal's $1.8 million for publicity for *Jaws,* why De Laurentiis' $10 million for *King Kong* was money well spent.

In 1977 competitors criticized filmmaker Joseph E. Levine for paying stupendous salaries—$9 million of the film's $25 million budget—for his World War II epic, *A Bridge Too Far.* Levine retorted, "As far as I'm concerned it was good business to pay Robert Redford $2 million for four weeks work in *A Bridge Too Far.* After all, he's the world's number one film idol—and with him in the cast I've been able to get a hell of a lot better deal from distributors."[25] What Levine managed was the simultaneous opening of *Bridge* in 1000 movie houses in the United States and Canada for June 15, 1977, including at least 30 klieg-light premieres.

Such costly and contrived hoopla, with which television cannot compete, has seemed vital to attract the attention of the mass audience to the movies in the 1970s. Yet the mass audience may still not go. One of the more expensive and most ballyhooed movies of the 1970s, David Merrick's *The Great Gatsby,* fizzled at the box office in 1974 even though the "world's number one film idol," Robert Redford, starred as Gatsby. Because of the combination of F. Scott Fitzgerald's famous and much loved novel and of Redford (helping in the hoopla, *Newsweek* reported in a February 4, 1974, cover story that Redford was appearing in "the most

The Electronic
Media: Radio,
Television, Cable
Television, and
Movies

134

hungrily awaited movie since *The Godfather,* playing the most coveted male role in years"), a month before the movie's release in March 1974, Paramount had taken in more than $18 million from movie exhibitors eager to show the $6.2 million movie in their theaters. No amount of money and press agentry could lure the masses, however. This big, media-created event found no audience.

By contrast, the unheralded *Rocky,* made on a bare-bones $1.1 million budget, shot on a tight 28-day schedule, and written and acted in the title role by unknown Sylvester Stallone for a salary of $25,000, was a huge box office success in 1976 and 1977. It not only quickly passed *King Kong* in earnings, but Stallone became only the third man in movie history to win Oscar nominations for both best screenplay and best acting. Although he won neither, *Rocky* won the Oscar for Best Picture of the Year.

Pauline Kael's point, of course, was not that the *Rocky* phenomenon could not happen, only that it has become increasingly difficult for it to happen. Although successful movies breed temporarily successful imitations, so producing cyclically popular genres—the gangster movie, the western, the musical, the horror movie, the disaster movie, and so on—the movie audience is perhaps the most unpredictable of all the audiences of the mass media. That is why movie making, which is an enormously expensive undertaking, is such a precarious business.

Once the moviegoers had turned *Rocky* into an event, the media were inclined to romanticize struggling actor and screenwriter Stallone's defiance of industry conventions (United Artists offered him $150,000 for his script if, instead of Stallone himself, he would let a name actor play the title role). Stories suggested that *Rocky* was a one-man operation reminiscent of movies such as *Easy Rider* in the late 1960s that had been produced, financed, and distributed by independent enterprises. Not so. Stallone had neither the personal resources nor the professional credentials to raise the money for his movie. He needed a major movie company, United Artists, as do even major, established talents such as Redford, Barbra Streisand, and producer-directors Robert Altman and Francis Ford Coppola. Although each of them has managed a degree of independence in producing the films they want to make, all have had to rely ultimately on the major movie companies to distribute their movies. The Justice Department had broken the stranglehold of the major movie companies over the industry in 1948, but these companies' experience and expertise in the distribution of movies enabled them to retain their stature in the industry over even the most successful independent artists and producers.

David Gordon, an authority on the economics of the film business, explained why:

> . . . [F]ilm distribution is necessarily expensive, and so risky that distributors have
> to exercise some control over what they distribute. It is so expensive because the
> essence of film economics is that the unit of production costs millions of dollars,
> but the return comes back in millions of cents. It is gigantically expensive to get a

film from studio to cinema. Very roughly, out of each $100 of cinema receipts, $60 is for the cinema costs and profit. Of the remaining $40, about $15 is available to cover the negative costs of the film, and the rest is for the overheads and profits of the distributor. In order to get the film into as many cinemas as possible, distributors have to have an international sales organization.[26]

In 1948 the Supreme Court had decided unanimously that the movie majors had engaged in illegal monopolistic practices—block booking, the fixing of admissions prices, unfair runs and clearances, and discriminatory pricing and purchasing arrangements favoring affiliated theater circuits. Following the court's decision, the Justice Department ruled that the major companies could not produce and distribute movies and own theaters as well and must divorce theater ownership from production and distribution functions. By uniting these separate functions—economists call the process "vertical integration"—in the same company in the 1920s, the so-called Big Five—Paramount, Warner Brothers, Twentieth Century-Fox, Loew's, and RKO—had transformed an industry of almost perfect competition between individuals and companies specializing in the separate functions of movie making—production, distribution, and exhibition—into an oligopolist industry that effectively restricted independent filmmaking. The Big Five were the particular target of the Justice Department; so too were the Little Three—Universal, Columbia, and United Artists—for, although they owned no theaters, they had participated in the same price-fixing and monopolistic trade practices as the Big Five. Together these eight companies had accounted for more than 80 percent of American film production before World War II.

The Justice Department's action did lead to a boom in independent film production. The number of independent film companies rose from 40 in 1945 to 165 in 1957; the independents produced almost 60 percent of American films produced in 1957. But the eight majors retained a considerable measure of their power in the industry nonetheless. The Justice Department's action had coincided with the rise of television, which cut into the audience of the movies and sharply reduced movie production. The majors, then, stayed in business partly by helping independent film producers with the financing of their movies and by renting to them their idle studio space and facilities, partly by handling their films—in the way that United Artists helped Sylvester Stallone with *Rocky* in 1976.

THE IMPACT OF TELEVISION

Disdainful at first of television, the majors, and the industry as a whole, had to confront the loss of their audience. Between 1949 and 1954 the number of television sets in use rose from 1 million to 32 million; at the end of the 1950s almost 90 percent of American homes had sets. Annual box office receipts for movies dropped from $1.7 billion in 1946 to $1.3 billion in 1956, a slower percentage decline than that of movie attendance only because movie ticket prices jumped from 35 to 50 cents. More than 4000

The Electronic
Media: Radio,
Television, Cable
Television, and
Movies

136

conventional movie theaters closed during this period. The combined profits of the 10 leading movie companies dropped 74 percent, from $121 million to $32 million. Employment in the movie industry dropped from a high of 24,000 in 1946 to 13,000 in 1956. The movie industry went over to the enemy.

By 1958 the movie companies had sold or leased an estimated 3700 feature movies, most of them made before 1949, to television at an average price of $10,000 a film. In the 1960s and 1970s they were selling recent movie releases to television at ever-escalating prices—$200,000 a movie before 1965, $400,000 a movie that year; in 1966 ABC paid Columbia $2 million for *The Bridge on the River Kwai;* in 1974 NBC paid $10 million for a one-time-only showing of *The Godfather.*

By the early 1960s Hollywood was producing most of television's prime-time programing—drama, comedy and variety. In the late 1960s the television networks began to put up the financing for made-for-television movies—at an average of $1 million for a two-hour movie—which were to be shown first on television, then in movie theaters. In that reversal of the process, television, it seemed, had become the senior partner.

By the end of the 1960s the major movie companies themselves had lost some of their independence. As had happened in all the communications media, movie companies were swallowed up by conglomerates. The Music Corporation of America took over Universal in 1962; Gulf and Western Industries, with interests in steel, hydraulics, mining, and plastics, acquired Paramount in 1966; Transamerica Corporation, an insurance and financial conglomerate, bought United Artists in 1967; Kinney Services, involved in car rentals, parking lots, and funeral parlors, acquired Warner in 1969. The initial concern that the directors of these conglomerates, with no knowledge or experience of filmmaking, would sacrifice whatever art and experimentation American film companies were inclined to engage in to the requirements of profitability has dissipated. The conglomerates have provided vital financial backing to sustain efficiently planned production programs and have used their multinational expertise to secure favorable treatment for American movies in foreign markets where American film companies dominate almost as much as they do in the United States.

THE INTERNATIONAL MARKET

Most of the costs of a movie go toward making the first copy; prints require little additional investment. But the costs for that first copy are immense (as a general rule, a movie must make two-and-a-half times its initial cost before it begins to make a profit), too great to be recovered quickly enough, if at all, in the domestic market alone. From its earliest years, then, and particularly after World War I, the American film industry has exported vigorously. It soon threatened the existence of foreign film industries and the cultural and artistic life of foreign countries, so popular were American movies and, apparently, the values and lifestyle they celebrated.

To lessen U.S. dominance, European governments restricted the importation of American films in the late 1920s to protect their own film industries and cultures. Then World War II devastated the European film industries, offering markets more vulnerable to American film exports than before. About a third of American film companies' revenue came from abroad before the war; more than half did so after 1945. European governments, therefore, imposed stricter protective measures than after World War I. But the Motion Picture Export Association (MPEA), a department of the Motion Picture Association of America to which all the major American film companies belonged, was able in the late 1940s to conclude a series of film trade treaties with foreign countries that evaded some of the restrictions on the importation of American films. The MPEA negotiated these treaties with the help of the U.S. State Department which, in its role as promoter of the American capitalist system and American business interests around the world, has been an invaluable ally of the American film industry abroad. Particularly during the period of the Cold War, the American film industry in turn became something of a cultural arm of the State Department.

Typically the film treaties restricted the amount of film earnings U.S. companies could withdraw from a foreign country in return for the lifting of import restrictions (in terms of the Anglo-American Film Agreement of 1948, for example, American companies could take out no more than $17 million a year of their annual $60 million earnings). These treaties coincided with the decline of American film production at home as television spread and with rising production costs, caused largely by the growing strength of unions in the film industry.

The unions had organized mainly during the Great Depression of the 1930s. By 1933 most of the trades and crafts in the film industry had organized under the jurisdiction of the International Alliance of Theatrical Stage Employees. The Screen Actors Guild became the bargaining agent for actors in 1937, the Screen Writers Guild for writers in 1938, the Screen Directors Guild for directors soon after.

To avoid the high salary scales of Hollywood and to use the earnings frozen abroad, American film companies invested in the production of films made abroad both for the American and foreign market. In the 1960s American films financed abroad rose from 35 percent to 60 percent of all films made by American producers, then dropping to 45 percent in the early 1970s as salaries abroad rose and the dollar was devalued. The situation, then, had been almost reversed. Foreign films that had been heavily subsidized by American film companies were seeking an outlet beyond their own domestic markets, were seeking specifically to penetrate the U.S. market. The British, French and Italian film industries tried to organize their own distribution chains in the United States, but, like American independent producers, found they could not break the control of major American film companies over distribution. In the United States and abroad American distributors continue to handle the biggest box-office attractions.

In their efforts to control American dominance, foreign governments

The Electronic
Media: Radio,
Television, Cable
Television, and
Movies

138

have been torn between the threat that American film companies pose to their own film industries and cultural life and the value of American investment. The short-term gains of tax revenue and jobs have seemed irresistible but these have intensified concerns about American cultural imperialism, particularly as American film companies have become part of multinational conglomerates. They have added their power and expertise to the American film industry's own experience over more than 60 years in exploiting the insecurities of foreign governments.

Thomas Guback, a student of the international film industry, has written: "American film companies have forged a new empire rivaling those of former days based on spices and minerals, an empire in constant evolution, stretching around the world, and worth billions of dollars. Its impact on human minds can hardly be calculated."[27]

CENSORSHIP AND SELF-REGULATION

The impact of movies on human minds had been of concern since movies began. Because the moving picture, with or without sound, can leap the barriers to communication posed by lack of education, income, and social status in a way that mass newspapers and magazines cannot, society's leaders were early wary of the medium's enormous appeal. Movies were to the political and cultural leaders of the first decades of the 20th century what commercial television programs are to some of them today—potentially damaging to right thinking and behavior in politics, sex, religion, art, and human relations in general. As a hugely expensive medium making its commercial way without advertising and, initially, without First Amendment protection—the U.S. Supreme Court had declared in 1915 that movies were "business, pure and simple . . . and not to be regarded as part of the press of the country or as organs of public opinion"[28]—the movies were vulnerable to both government and public pressure.

For more than half a century, a number of states and municipalities have had official movie censorship boards. Chicago was among the first in 1907. Then came New York in 1909, Pennsylvania in 1911, and Kansas in 1913. The Pennsylvania law set the pattern from which most subsequent censorship laws were designed. No movie could be shown in Pennsylvania without the approval of the state board of censors. Except for a few isolated instances, the young movie industry did not fight to enlarge its freedom. Aiming at a mass market, the major producers were much more interested in giving the public what it wanted than in championing the right to dissent. They cooperated with both official and unofficial censors, and they tried to keep screen fare antiseptic.

Darryl F. Zanuck wrote:

> The fear of political reprisal and persecution . . . has prevented free expression on the screen and retarded its development. The loss has not been merely our own. It has been the nation's and the world's. Few of us insiders can forget that shortly before Pearl Harbor the entire motion picture industry was called on the carpet in Washington by a Senate committee dominated by isolationists and

asked to render an account of its activities. We were pilloried with the accusation that we were allegedly making anti-Nazi films which might be offensive to Germany.[29]

Similar pressures have been exerted in every time of tension, especially during the early 1950s, when McCarthyism was rampant. Blacklists of suspected Communists among actors, writers, and directors were circulated through studios. The listed actors and directors could not work; some of the writers prepared scripts under other names. When an Academy Award was announced for a script written by one Robert Rich, no one came forward. "Rich" was actually Dalton Trumbo, a blacklisted writer, one of the Hollywood Ten who had refused as a matter of principle to answer questions put to them by the House Committee on Un-American Activities in 1947, had been cited for contempt of Congress, and had been sent to the federal penitentiary. Fifty leading movie executives announced that the Hollywood Ten had been suspended without compensation and asked Hollywood's talent guilds to help them rid the industry of subversives. The power of the blacklist that the executives thereby originated was to last for almost two decades.

The zeal with which the industry purified its ranks of political undesirables was the product of an unheroic period in American history and passed when the nation recovered its respect for its central freedoms. The industry, however, had consistently tried to purify movie content of anything that offended government or the public. Notorious for a racy lifestyle, Hollywood was hit by scandals in the 1920s and threatened with even more restrictive government censorship than already permitted. The industry responded in 1922 by creating the Motion Picture Producers and Distributors of America (MPPDA), called the Hays Office after its first president, former Postmaster General and Chairman of the Republican National Committee, Will H. Hays.

In 1930 the MPPDA adopted the Production Code, a set of rules governing film properties that members tried to live by until movie attendance dropped in the early years of the Depression. Then members began to introduce salacious material into movies to seduce audiences back into the theaters, so outraging Catholics that they formed the Legion of Decency to classify pictures according to its own standard of acceptability. More than 11 million Catholics pledged to boycott offensive movies. Against so powerful an economic threat, the MPPDA amplified its code in 1934 and ruled that each release must have the Hays Office seal of approval before it could be exhibited in theaters affiliated with MPPDA members. In 1937 the Hays Office reviewed and approved approximately 98 percent of all the movies exhibited that year, sanctifying the so-called "family film" in the process.

MPPDA members abided by the code as long as the family film was profitable. Then television in the 1950s virtually killed their commitment to the code, as had the Depression in the 1930s. At the same time, in *Burstyn v. Wilson* in 1952, usually called *The Miracle* decision, the U.S. Supreme

The Electronic
Media: Radio,
Television, Cable
Television, and
Movies

140

Court moved motion pictures a step closer to freedom by ruling that a state may not ban a film on the censor's conclusion that it is sacrilegious, that motion pictures come under the protection that the Constitution gives the press, and that their importance as an organ of public opinion is not lessened by their preoccupation with entertainment. But the court interpreted the Constitution as not authorizing absolute freedom to show every kind of movie at all times and places. Since sacrilege was the sole standard involved in *The Miracle* case, the court did not pass on other standards whereby states could ban a film.

The 1952 decision established that the movies are entitled to First Amendment protection, an important victory that was consolidated and extended in later cases. Two years later the court held that New York could not ban *La Ronde* and in 1955 that Kansas could not ban *The Moon Is Blue.* In 1959 it rejected a ban that New York had imposed on a movie version of *Lady Chatterley's Lover,* which the censors said seemed to advocate immoral ideas. Justice Potter Stewart remarked that the Constitutional guarantee is not confined to majority opinions: "It protects advocacy of the opinion that adultery may sometimes be proper, no less than advocacy of socialism or the single tax."[30] What these decisions permitted, then, was advocacy of unpopular sexual values, sometimes called "ideological obscenity," but not necessarily the depiction of nudity, explicit sexual acts or language.

To keep pace with the courts' and society's expanding tolerance, the Motion Picture Association of America (MPAA), which had succeeded the MPPDA in 1945, liberalized the Production Code's standards in 1966. The code office was empowered to label films judged unsuitable for children as "Suggested for Mature Audiences." But the MPAA's effort failed to appease persons in government and in the public offended by the movies' exploration of sexual themes and use of some nudity and frank language. In 1968, therefore, the MPAA reluctantly adopted a full-scale rating system.

The MPAA's Code and Rating Office reviews American and foreign films submitted to it—producers and importers cannot be required to submit their films for rating—and assigns one of four designations: "G" (general audience); "PG" (parental guidance suggested); "R" (restricted; persons under 17 may not be admitted unless accompanied by a parent or adult guardian); and "X" (no one under 17 admitted). Producers or importers of films that they do not submit to the MPAA may assign an "X" rating themselves, but they cannot assign any other rating. Political scientist Richard S. Randall reported in 1976:

> Independent studies indicate that about 80 percent of the films in commercial release have been submitted for rating. Because these include most of those of the major producing companies and major importers of foreign features, about 90 percent of the exhibition bookings or "playdates" involve rated films. Further, since most of the largest theaters and biggest circuits play mainly major, rated productions, probably as much as 98 percent of the American moviegoing audience on a given day or night views rated films.[31]

The MPAA has not revealed the criteria on which it bases the ratings, although the erotic and violent content of a movie seem to be central to the rating decision. Randall found:

> Of nearly three thousand films viewed and rated during the system's first six years, 1968 – 74, three-quarters were in the "PG" or "R" categories. . . . Since the first years of the system, the percentage of "R" ratings had increased markedly and "X" ratings slightly. The percentage of "G" ratings has dropped considerably.[32]

Although the MPAA and the National Association of Theatre Owners, the largest exhibition organization, have estimated that about 80 percent of exhibitors in the United States work with the rating system, whether or not it is actually enforced depends on the exhibitor, specifically on the persons on duty at the box office itself. Their rigor may be responsive to community pressure.

In the 1970s such pressure concentrated almost exclusively on alleged obscenity, the area in which movies, and all the media, do not enjoy First Amendment protection and in which the U.S. Supreme Court has empowered state and local community standards, within specified guidelines, to prevail. Because such standards differ from one state or community to another, a film may be obscene in one but not in another. Thus *Deep Throat*, by 1977 the most successful hardcore pornographic movie ever made (in "softcore" pornographic movies sex acts are simulated, in "hardcore" movies they are not), was found to be obscene and not obscene in the same state. In New York City, usually regarded as one of the most liberal of U.S. cities, *Deep Throat* was declared obscene; in Binghamton, N.Y., the movie was found to be not obscene.

A movie does not have to be ostentatiously explicit about sex, deliberately produced for devotees of hardcore pornography, to invite censorial scrutiny. Although Mike Nichols' film adaptation of Jules Feiffer's *Carnal Knowledge* was critically acclaimed and its female lead was nominated for an Oscar, the Georgia State Supreme Court declared it obscene in July 1973. The U.S. Supreme Court unanimously reversed that decision in June 1974, but such unanimity did not resolve movie producers' difficulties in ensuring that their movies meet the standards of every community in the nation.

Nevertheless, movies could take advantage of society's expanded tolerance of sexually explicit content in a way that television could not. Television programing in the late 1970s had reached only into the area of "ideological obscenity" that movies had tackled in the 1950s. The FCC did not interpret the public interest, convenience, and necessity to mean that nudity, actual or simulated sex acts, or frank language could appear on home television screens. But because ultimately most movie producers want to sell their movies to television, this restriction indirectly affects them, too. Although the broadcasting, cable, and movie industries each sought to

The Electronic
Media: Radio,
Television, Cable
Television, and
Movies

142

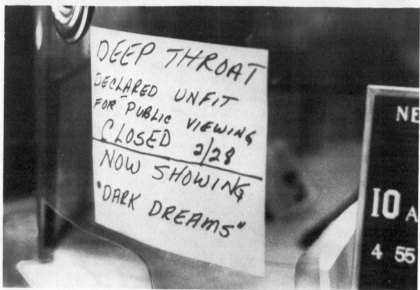

Even within states "community standards" vary—sometimes in surprising ways. *Deep Throat* was declared "obscene" in New York City, but *not* obscene in Binghampton, New York. (United Press International photo)

maintain a separate and competitive identity, the public's love of visual entertainment tangled them uncomfortably, sometimes abrasively, together.

By 1977 they had had barely 25 years to adjust to one another. Nor had society—through Congress, the FCC, and the Justice Department—yet

The Electronic
Media: Radio,
Television, Cable
Television, and
Movies

143

determined what balance best fit the public interest. Consider these developments in 1977, apparently a critical year:

1. Largely in response to complaints by the Westinghouse Broadcasting Company about the television networks' dominance over affiliates and to pending antitrust suits against the networks by the Justice Department, the FCC announced in January 1977 its first major study of network practices since 1957, focusing particularly on the acquisition and distribution of programing. In May 1977 the MPAA and the major movie studios petitioned the FCC as part of the study to review and correct what they called the networks' abusive practices in acquiring programs.

2. In May 1977 the House Communications Subcommittee began its "substantial reappraisal" or "review" of the 1934 Communications Act to make it "compatible with modern communications technology and amenable to new developments" so as "to encourage the greatest diversity of choices by the consuming public at the least possible costs."[33]

3. In June 1977 the Carnegie Commission on the Future of Public Broadcasting was formed to conduct an 18-month study of the public system.

4. Paramount and Universal proposed to establish a "fourth" television network, providing mainly made-for-television movies and starting in spring 1978.

Notes

1. *Broadcasting,* May 30, 1977, p. 20.
2. Quoted in Erik Barnouw, *A Tower in Babel: A History of Broadcasting in the United States,* Vol. I (New York: Oxford University Press, 1966), p. 53.
3. Barnouw, p. 59.
4. Quoted in Barnouw, p. 94.
5. Sec. 4 (c), Public Law No. 632, February 23, 1927, 69th Congress, reprinted in Barnouw, p. 302.
6. Sec. 303 (g), Public Law No. 416, June 19, 1934, 73d Congress, reprinted in Erik Barnouw, *The Golden Web: A History of Broadcasting in the United States,* Vol. II (New York: Oxford University Press, 1968), p. 319.
7. Melvin L. De Fleur, *Theories of Mass Communication,* Second Edition (New York: McKay, 1970), p. 64.
8. Quoted in Barnouw, *The Golden Web,* p. 174.
9. Quoted in Fred. W. Friendly, *Due To Circumstances Beyond Our Control* (New York: Vintage Books, 1968), p. xvi.
10. *Time,* May 31, 1976, p. 39.
11. *Newsweek,* May 16, 1977, p. 103.
12. Les Brown, *TeleviSion: The Business Behind the Box* (New York: Harcourt, 1971), p. 33.
13. Brown, p. 33.
14. Brown, pp. 59–60.
15. Ron Powers, "Eyewitless News," *Columbia Journalism Review,* May/June 1977, p. 18.

The Electronic
Media: Radio,
Television, Cable
Television, and
Movies

144

16. Julian Goodman, "A New Spirit for Broadcasting," speech to the Glasgow, Kentucky, Chamber of Commerce, January 31, 1977. NBC distributed a copy of the speech in pamphlet form.

17. Federal Communications Commission, "Cable Television Service; Cable Television Relay Service," *Federal Register,* Vol. 37, No. 30, February 12, 1972, p. 3259.

18. Quoted by D. Bruce Pearson, "Cable: The Thread By Which Television Competition Hangs," 27 *Rutgers Law Review* 800, 1974, p. 807.

19. Federal Communications Commission, *Federal Register,* Vol. 37, No. 30, February 12, 1972, p. 3269.

20. *Federal Register,* February 12, 1972, p. 3269.

21. *Broadcasting,* April 14, 1975, p. 56.

22. Carnegie Commission for Educational Television, *Public Television: A Program for Action (New York: Bantam, 1967)*

23. Anne W. Branscomb, "A Crisis of Identity: The Future of Public Broadcasting," in *The Future of Public Broadcasting* (New York: Praeger, 1976), p. 8.

24. Pauline Kael, "On the Future of Movies," in Michael C. Emery and Ted Curtis Smythe (eds.), *Readings in Mass Communications,* Third Edition (Dubuque, Iowa: Wm. C. Brown Company, 1977), p. 241.

25. Quoted in syndicated article by Marilyn Beck, *Bloomington-Bedford Sunday Herald-Times,* January 23, 1977.

26. David Gordon, "Why the Movies Are Major," in Tino Balio (ed.), *The American Film Industry* (Madison: The University of Wisconsin Press, 1976), pp. 461–462.

27. Thomas H. Guback, "Hollywood's International Market," in Balio, p. 409.

28. *Mutual Film Corp. v. Ohio,* 236 U.S. 230, 244 (1915).

29. Quoted in William L. Rivers, Theodore Peterson, Jay W. Jensen, *The Mass Media and Modern Society,* 2nd ed. (New York: Holt, Rinehart and Winston, 1971), p. 156.

30. *Kingsley International Pictures Corp. v. Regents,* 360 U.S. 684, 688–689 (1959).

31. Richard S. Randall, "Censorship: From *The Miracle* to *Deep Throat,*" in Balio, p. 447.

32. Randall in Balio, p. 446.

33. *Broadcasting,* May 30, 1977, p. 19.

6

The Intellectual Environment: Libertarianism

[The newspaper] industry serves one of the most vital of all general interests: the dissemination of news from many different sources, with as many different facets and colors as is possible. That interest is closely akin to, if indeed it is not the same as, the interest protected by the First Amendment: it presupposes that right conclusions are more likely to be gathered out of a multitude of tongues, than any kind of authoritative selection. To many this is, and always will be folly; but we have staked upon it our all.

JUDGE LEARNED HAND, IN
UNITED STATES V. ASSOCIATED PRESS (1943)

The mass communications system in the United States, like that in other lands, has been shaped not only by the country's economic and social history but also by its intellectual environment. The communications system in the United States performs as it does to some degree based on our concept of freedom, our attitudes towards free enterprise and private

145

property, and our ideas of what our communications system *should* be and do.

During the American Revolution there was no real freedom of expression in the Colonies. There was freedom to hail the Patriot cause in territory controlled by Patriots, freedom to hail the Tory cause where Tories dominated. Those who advocated the wrong cause in the wrong place were summarily silenced. After the war the states made no attempt to rid themselves of the seditious libel laws on their books or even to amend them.

Although eloquent statements of press liberty were available to the Colonies in the eighteenth century, a true American libertarian tradition did not emerge until after the war, and then it was more a result of bitter political fights than disinterested sentiment. More than 60 years ago Charles Beard, in *An Economic Interpretation of the Constitution,* contended that the Constitution owed far less to abstract concern about rights than to the economic self-interest of the men who drafted it. More recently Leonard Levy, in his *Legacy of Suppression,* has cogently developed the thesis that the generation that adopted the Constitution, the Bill of Rights, and the early state constitutions did not believe in a broad scope for freedom of expression, particularly in political matters. He concluded that there is good reason to believe that the Bill of Rights was more the chance product of expedience than the happy product of principle.

The Bill of Rights was a compromise to allay the fears of those who thought that a strong national government would jeopardize the traditional

The same generation of Americans that wrote the Constitution and the Bill of Rights wrote the Sedition Act of 1798, which made it a crime to publish "false, scandalous, and malicious" writings against the federal government or its officials. (Library of Congress)

rights of individuals and the authority of the states. At the time that the ratification of the Constitution was under consideration the two major political forces at work were the Federalists, who favored a strong national government, and the anti-Federalists, who preferred a league of more or less independent states. Federalists such as Alexander Hamilton held that because the national government was to have only the powers specifically granted it, a bill of rights was superfluous. But the promise of a bill of rights was crucial in securing the necessary votes for ratification by states such as Massachusetts, New York, and Virginia. James Madison drafted what was distilled into the first 10 amendments to the Constitution. The first of those amendments, which states in part that "Congress shall make no law . . . abridging the freedom of speech or of the press . . .," in essence reserved to the states the power to regulate expression.

Indeed, the states did not recognize an unlimited right of expression. For instance, the Pennsylvania constitution of 1790 protected the right of every citizen freely to "speak, write, and print on any subject" but held the citizen responsible "for the abuse of that liberty." It adopted broad protection for the individual in the event of a criminal prosecution for such an abuse, but it did not abolish the possibility of criminal prosecution. Pennsylvania's constitution was among the more generous of state constitutions of the period on the question of press freedom.

The Bill of Rights, because of its focus on restricting the *federal* government, did much less than the furor over the Alien and Sedition Acts of 1798 to push libertarians beyond the conventional and relatively narrow eighteenth-century American vision of press liberty.

In the nineteenth century many of the traditional restraints that had plagued English and Colonial publishers disappeared from the American scene. The press was substantially free of controls for most of the century although the postal and custom services were used to restrain the distribution of obscenity and some political matter, and state laws provided for punishment of libel. To be sure, publishers at times spoke as if the specter of repression haunted them. If Congress proposed increasing the postal rates, if a state legislature considered altering the requirements for publishing legal notices, publishers sometimes sounded as if the republic were in peril. But what concerned them most about such moves was the threat to the profitability of their enterprises rather than any interference with their freedom to speak. The impact of the libertarian philosophy on the press was at least equally balanced by self-interest.

To understand the communications system of any society, one must know what the society expects of it. What are the system's functions? How much freedom does it have? What do we mean by freedom anyway? The answers to these questions come only after one has looked at the basic assumptions the society holds. What view does the society take of the nature of man? What does the society regard as the ideal relation between man and the state? What is the society's idea of truth? Sooner or later, then, the study of a communications system leads to questions of philosophy.

The system in the United States has a strong English heritage, for the

Colonists copied the institutions and culture of England. They modeled their newspapers and magazines on those in the homeland. To keep their press in line, they imported the controls that were used in England. When they revolted, they justified their action by arguing that the mother country was denying them their rights as free-born Englishmen. And when, under their newly won freedom, Americans developed theories of the press, they borrowed from thinkers in England and in Europe.

The Rise of Libertarianism

In the seventeenth century a new concept of the nature of man and of his relationship to the state was emerging. It rejected the authoritarianism that placed the state superior to the individual and that identified priests or kings as the source of all Truth. Scientific and geographic discoveries broadened humanity's understanding of the universe. The rising commercial class disputed the privileges of the nobility and challenged the supremacy of the monarch. The old order was crumbling. When the century began, the authoritarian order seemed secure; when it ended, the Crown was subordinate to Parliament, and liberalism was in the ascendancy. In the eighteenth century in Europe and America the tenets of libertarianism were put to practical test.

LIBERTARIAN GOVERNMENT

From the liberal English and European theorists of the seventeenth and eighteenth centuries came the libertarian philosophy that so strongly influenced the American form of government and the protections granted the freedoms of speech and press. That philosophy conceived of the world as a vast perpetual-motion machine, going timelessly on according to the laws of nature. Libertarians believed that people are guided by reason, not by passion or narrow self-interest. By using reason people could discover the laws of nature that govern the universe, bring their institutions into harmony with these laws, and so build a good and just society.

The early libertarians thought that people are born with certain natural rights, which limit the hand of government and demand protection for the individual's liberty and property. Although tyrants might temporarily abridge these rights, no one can properly take them away, for they are as much a part of the divine scheme as the laws under which the universe operates.

According to this libertarian view, people, in their natural state—before they voluntarily joined together to form governments—existed perfectly free and equal. But in that state of nature, their enjoyment of their rights was in constant danger, because individuals were at the mercy of domineering fellows, who could deprive them by force of their liberty and property.

So, by common consent, people form governments to secure their natural rights. The best way that government can ensure those rights is by leaving the individual as free as possible. The best government, then, is that which governs least. When government fails to protect the liberty and property of its citizens, it has failed in its purpose; and it is the right and duty of the people to establish a new government that does enable them to enjoy their freedom.

The libertarians saw truth as deriving not from authority but from human intellect. People are not to be led and directed toward truth; they are to find it themselves with the reason with which they are endowed. With the free play of their intellects, they can discover the all-embracing truth that unifies the universe and the phenomena in it.

As Carl L. Becker has remarked, modern democracy offers long odds on the capacity and integrity of the human mind. It assumes that people are not only rational beings but moral ones. If people are to be free from all but the most necessary of restraints, their moral sense must enforce those obligations to their fellows that are not specifically covered by law. Human perfectibility, natural rights, and natural reason, then, are three of the key items in the development of the libertarian philosophy.

What is the nature of humanity? People are guided by reason. They are disposed to seek truth and to be guided by it. What is the ideal relationship between the people and the state? People should be governed only with their own consent. The state, by keeping its power at a minimum, should preserve but not infringe upon people's natural rights. What is the nature of truth? Truth is not the monopoly of the few in power, but it is discoverable by all people using their natural intellect; it is the key to understanding the natural order of things so that people can form a harmonious society.

LIBERTARIAN THEORY OF THE PRESS

Those same answers are the base on which the libertarian theory of the press was erected. Let us briefly summarize the theory.

In libertarian theory the press must have a wide latitude of freedom to aid people in their quest for truth. To find truth through reason, people must have free access to information and ideas. Out of the fare the press serves them, they can, by employing their intellects, distinguish truth from falsehood. They find some truth hidden amid falsehood, some falsehood hidden amid truth. Yet with time, if people are faithful to reason, truth will emerge from the unrestrained interplay of information and ideas. Social change will come, then, not from force but from a process of discussion and persuasion.

Because, according to libertarian theory, free expression carries built-in correctives, there need be few restrictions on what people may speak and write. The great majority of people are moral creatures who will use their freedom responsibly in an honest desire to find truth. One need not worry about the small minority who may abuse their freedom by lying and distorting. Others will find it profitable to expose them—and the lies and distortions will be shown up for what they are, because all information and ideas are put to the powerful scrutiny of reason. Therefore, it is unnecessary to require responsibilities in exchange for freedom; most people will assume them without being asked, and the remainder can cause no great harm.

Censorship before publication is an evil for at least three reasons under libertarian theory. First, it violates people's natural right to free expression. Second, it could enable tyrants to perpetuate themselves in power and to make the state a foe instead of liberty's protector. Third, it could temporarily hinder the quest for truth by throwing off balance the delicate process by which truth ultimately emerges. If people are to discover truth, they must have access to all information and ideas, not just those fed to them.

Governments supposedly operating under libertarian theory have permitted restrictions on expression. For instance, some have sanctioned sedition laws to protect government against false criticism and obscenity laws to preserve or elevate the public's morals. Although sanctioned by some libertarians, such laws appear more as evidence of the unavoidable authoritarian tendencies of any government than examples of libertarian theory. Libertarianism has often been held in check by political expediency or by contrary views of the people and the government. And there is always a tension generated by the application of theory to reality.

Shapers of Libertarianism

It is perhaps misleading to speak of *the* libertarian theory of the press. Libertarianism has drawn on the ideas of people of different countries and several centuries, and this richness and diversity must be kept in mind if libertarianism is to be understood.

Libertarian press theory, as it developed abroad and in America, drew on the ideas of more than the few whose names are commonly associated with it. However, some had reputations that gave greater prestige to their teachings; some were more effective than their contemporaries in expressing the ideas current among the thinkers of their times. Whether because of originality, influence, or eloquence, the following men made major contributions to libertarian press theory.

JOHN MILTON (1608–1674)

After the Puritans had fought their way to power in the civil wars that tore England in the turbulent seventeenth century, they perceived, as English monarchs had before them, that regulating the press was one means of stifling dissent and maintaining authority. One method was licensing books, pamphlets, and papers—subjecting them to the review of a censor before they were published and made available to the public. In 1644 a few pamphleteers raised their voices against such regulation. The voice that is remembered was that of the poet John Milton, who had run afoul of authorities with a tract on divorce. His *Areopagitica* has long been regarded as a classic defense of a free press.

The *Areopagitica* offered three major arguments against licensing. One was that licensing was the evil child of evil parents. Licensing was invented by the Roman Catholic Church, an anathema to the Puritans and very definitely to Milton, and used to prohibit anything the church found unpalatable.

Second, licensing was impractical, Milton argued. It simply would not work. Licensing was not broad enough to control the minds of the people because it merely regulated the current output of the press. To do the job effectively, the censor would also have to review everything printed in the past, cut the bad parts out of good books, and strictly regulate *all* activities of the citizens. Licensing assumed infallible and incorruptible censors. Such people would be difficult to find, and if they could be found, licensing would be a waste of their talent and virtue.

Milton's third argument against licensing did not bring an end to censorship in his time, but it is the one that endures in libertarian press theory. Licensing hinders man's search for truth. Milton wrote:

> . . . As good almost kill a man as kill a good book: who kills a man kills a reasonable creature, God's image; but he who destroys a good book, kills reason itself, kills the image of God, as it were, in the eye.[1]

Milton praised the purifying value of confronting evil and falsehood:

> I cannot praise a fugitive and cloistered virtue, unexercised and unbreathed, that never sallies out and sees her adversary, but slinks out of the race, where that immortal garland is to be run for, not without dust and heat. Assuredly we bring not innocence into the world, we bring impurity much rather: that which purifies us is trial, and trial is by what is contrary. . . .
>
> Since therefore the knowledge and survey of vice is in this world so necessary to the constituting of human virtue, and the scanning of error to the confirmation of truth, how can we more safely and with less danger scout into the regions of sin and falsity than by reading all manner of tractates, and hearing all manner of reason? And this is the benefit which may be had of books promiscuously read.[2]

Milton was willing to confront falsehood and evil because he was convinced that truth would always prevail:

> And though all the winds of doctrine were let loose to play upon the earth, so Truth be in the field, we do injuriously by licensing and prohibiting to misdoubt her strength. Let her and Falsehood grapple; who ever knew Truth put to the worse in a free and open encounter?[3]

In this, his most quoted passage, Milton expressed in powerful metaphor what was to be a central faith of libertarianism: The conviction that free expression carries its own correctives. Grant all people the freedom to express themselves and in the clash of ideas that ensues, the true will triumph over the false. If falsehood prevails, it is but a temporary victory. As long as government does not weight the balance, truth *must* prevail. It is man himself whom God trusts "with the gift of reason to be his own chooser."

Although his *Areopagitica* remains magnificent and relevant after three centuries, Milton was a product of his age. He wrote with eloquence of man's rationality, but by temperament he was a scholar and an intellectual aristocrat. His prescriptions for education suggest that he expected only people "judicious, learned, and of a conscience" to make good use of the freedom he advocated. "[A] wise man will make better use of an idle pamphlet than a fool will do of sacred Scripture." Yet he warned in the *Areopagitica* against licensing even to protect "children and childish men."

The *Areopagitica seems* democratic, but Milton put narrow limits on who should be allowed to write without hindrance. He would have denied full freedom of expression to those who disagreed with him on fundamentals—Catholics, for instance, and Royalists (although he would try "to win and regain the weak and misled"). And he could not conceive of suffering that which was impious or absolutely evil, that which was against faith or morals: blasphemy, atheism, and libel. Superficially at least, his idea of press freedom resembles that of the present-day Soviet state, which forbids criticism of the basic assumptions of Communism but does permit some criticism of how the work of the party is carried out.

The freedom he advocated was limited: a freedom from government restriction before publication—quite simply an end to licensing. But he was not a man to shrink from punishing those who abused this generous freedom: "Those which otherwise come forth, if they be found mischievous and libellous, the fire and the executioner will be the timeliest and most effectual remedy that man's prevention can use."

Milton gave the *Areopagitica* a strongly religious cast. Unlike later contributors to the libertarian tradition, who justified free expression as a natural right, Milton justified it on religious grounds. With the removal of the church as the intermediary between God and humanity, people must themselves apply reason and conscience to know God and to discover truth.

That truth for Milton was something outside of humanity, an expression of a higher law—the will of his Puritan God. Man once had it, then lost it:

> Truth indeed came once into the world with her divine Master, and was a perfect shape most glorious to look on; but when he ascended and his Apostles after him were laid asleep, then strait arose a wicked race of deceivers, who . . . took the virgin Truth, hewed her lovely form into a thousand pieces, and scatter'd them to the four winds.[4]

From that sad day onward, friends of Truth have tried to pick up the scattered pieces. Milton encourages the search but warns that the whole will not be reconstructed until Christ's second coming.

It may seem anticlimactic that the *Areopagitica* was not widely circulated and had little effect in its own day and that Milton himself later became a censor of government publications. His contribution to freedom of the press was not realized in his own century, but in the following one.

Libertarians striving to expand the boundaries of freedom in the eighteenth century drew heavily on the ideas of three men who are remembered not for their thoughts on the press but for their ideas on science, government, and economics. The orderly nature of the universe, natural law, natural rights, the rationality of man, the hands-off role of government were ideas expressed by Isaac Newton, John Locke, and Adam Smith to justify curbing the authority of the state and making the individual paramount.

Unifying work done in physics and astronomy, Newton in 1687 gave people a new picture of the universe as an orderly machine, timeless, unchanging, running on according to certain discoverable laws of nature. Newton's discoveries demonstrated the power of human reason. For instance, through their own intelligence people could discern that gravity ensures that apples always fall toward the earth.

Building on Newton, John Locke gave libertarians their picture of humanity and its relation to government. In vindicating the scientific achievements of his age, Locke set out to show that all knowledge comes from experience, from the senses. Although the human intellect does have limits, its powers are great enough to secure happiness for mankind. He proved to the satisfaction of libertarians that people are distinguished by their capacity for creative thought and their essential rationality.

In his essays on civil government, which provided ringing phrases for the American Declaration of Independence, Locke advanced a system of natural rights. Like Newton's discoveries, these rights rest on the unchanging laws of nature. Human beings in a state of nature are free and equal, with certain inalienable, self-evident rights. (He never explained how people who were supposed to use their senses and to demand evidence could accept such fundamentals as self-evident.) They form government by their own consent to protect those rights, and a government that does not protect them has violated its purpose and should be dissolved in favor of one that does.

Libertarian press theory took three of its vital propositions from Locke: the rationality of people, free expression as a natural right, and the well-being of the individual as the ultimate justification of society and government.

Human rationality became inextricably bound up with the self-righting process of Milton. By putting all discussion, spoken or written, to the powerful test of reason, people could discover truth. Newton had given a glimpse of the majestic truth that people could discover—the enduring laws of nature. People could discover those laws, bring their institutions into harmony with them, and thus found an earthly paradise of justice and order.

Locke identified life, liberty, and estate as people's natural rights, which society and government must protect. In libertarianism free expression is accounted one part of our natural liberty, and no one has the authority to deprive anyone else of it. Indeed, it is the right on which all other rights depend, for if people are free to speak their minds, they can rally support whenever the government acts unjustly or arbitrarily.

Locke himself was intolerant of intolerance. He encouraged punishing any who "will not own and teach the duty of tolerating all men in matters of mere religion," but he was less generous toward those who would speak "irreverently or seditiously of the government or governors, or of state matters."

Locke, like Milton before him, distinguished between prior restraint of publication and punishment for publication of false or harmful criticism of government. Like Milton he opposed the licensing system of seventeenth-century England, but as Leonard Levy has pointed out, not a single one of the 18 reasons Locke drafted for the House of Commons in 1694 "was a principled defense of freedom of the press or a philosophical argument for the free mind."[5] The arguments that it was impractical, unnecessary, and a hindrance to the printing trade were more persuasive, however, than Milton's eloquence or principles, and the licensing law was allowed to lapse in 1694.

Unlike Newton's natural law, which was fundamentally descriptive, Locke's system of natural rights was normative as well as descriptive. Locke's system of rights provided a standard by which the morality of man-made law could be judged and those rights limited the authority of society and government. In the nineteenth century the concept of natural rights would cease to have theoretical significance for European libertarians, but the centrality of the individual and the assumption that the protection of private rights would promote the common good would persist. Locke's writing greatly influenced the authors of the American Declaration of Independence and the American Constitution, and his ideas retain their vitality in those documents even though libertarianism has taken on other colorations.

In 1776 Adam Smith showed how economics fit into both Newton's orderly world and Locke's system of natural rights and self-government. He contributed two more propositions to the libertarian theory of the press.

One was that government should assume a negative role in people's affairs, should take a position of laissez faire or "hands off," lest it upset the delicate workings of nature's laws. The idea was an appealing one to libertarians, who had long eyed government as the chief threat to freedom. Here was good reason why the press should be obliged to make its own way in the marketplace. Here, too, was good reason why the government should not sponsor media of its own in competition with private media.

Smith's second contribution was his theory that as each person works for personal gain, he or she serves the welfare of the community—in essence, a variation of the self-righting process. In other words, natural law dictates that the public interest is ensured by everyone pursuing private interests. The press has promoted this idea with conviction and enthusiasm. The idea lies, for instance, behind the remark of the editor who said that readers vote for his newspaper with their coins every time he brings out a new issue. According to this line of thought, the press is accountable to the public, and the public controls the press in its own interests by the choices it makes. If a newspaper, magazine, or broadcasting station serves what people regard as the public interest, they will give it their patronage, and it will flourish. If it fails to serve the public interest, they will not patronize it. In consequence, it will wither and die. By working for personal gain, then, the publisher or broadcaster, in competition with others, automatically gives the public the sort of media it wants. There is an assumption that what it wants is also what it needs.

Smith's idea can be used to justify the publication of virtually anything. The argument can be put something like this: Helping to find the truth is in the public interest. Many ideas and much information are needed for the discovery of truth. What I publish for my own personal profit serves the cause of truth and hence the public interest. For some critics of libertarianism this comes closer to license than liberty. For others, it is a foolish misunderstanding of the way in which the marketplace operates.

"CATO"

Despite Locke's considerable contribution to political theory in his own and subsequent centuries, the most popular source of ideas on political liberty and freedom of expression in the eighteenth-century American Colonies was *Cato's Letters*. Historian Clinton Rossiter describes Cato's writing as "the most popular, quotable, esteemed source of political ideas in the colonial period."[6]

The essays, which were published beginning in 1720 in London newspapers, were widely reprinted and quoted in the Colonies. Benjamin Franklin published Cato's "Of Freedom of Speech" in the *New England Courant* as early as 1721 and "Reflections upon Libelling" in 1722.

But who was Cato? Two English political journalists, John Trenchard (1662–1723) and Thomas Gordon (1685?–1750), jointly used the pseudonym and provided the Colonies with a theory of political liberty that placed freedom of expression at its core. They wrote, "Freedom of Speech is the great Bulwark of Liberty; they prosper and Die together. . . ."

They explained the relationship:

> Without Freedom of Thought, there can be no such Thing as Wisdom, and no such Thing as public Liberty, without Freedom of Speech, which is the Right of every Man, as far as by it he does not hurt or controul the Right of another: And this is the only Check it ought to suffer, and the only Bounds it ought to know.
> This sacred Priviledge is so essential to free Governments, that the Security of Property, and the Freedom of Speech always go together; and in those wretched Countries where a Man cannot call his Tongue his own he can scarce call any Thing else his own. Whoever would overthrow the Liberty of a Nation must begin by subduing the Freeness of Speech; a Thing terrible to publick Traytors.[7]

Government exists to protect the rights of its citizens, but citizens have the responsibility to watch that government fulfills its obligations. To facilitate this, government must be open and receptive to public comment.

Although Trenchard and Gordon admitted that freedom of expression sometimes resulted in unjust libels on government and individuals, they argued that only the guilty need fear such freedom:

> The best Way to prevent Libels, is not to deserve them, and then they always lose their force; for certain Experience shews us that the more Notice is taken of them, the more they are published. Guilty Men alone fear them, or are hurt by them, whose Actions will not bear Examination, and therefore must not be examin'd.[8]

Like Milton they were confident that unfettered truth would always best falsehood and argued that the way to combat falsehood was not with punishment but with truth.

They were willing to suffer wrong, irreligious, or seditious ideas as the unavoidable consequence of freedom because, they argued, if people were not permitted to communicate freely,

> they will know nothing of the Nature of Government beyond a servile Submission to Power, nor of Religion, more than a blind adherence to unintelligible Speculations, and a furious and implacable animosity to all whose Mouths are not form'd to the same Sounds; nor will they have the Liberty or means to search Nature and investigate her Works. . . .[9]

Cato's Letters sounds like nothing so much as an amalgam of Milton and Locke, but Trenchard and Gordon had a more expansive view of freedom of expression than either. Freedom from prior restraint was insufficient protection. Although Trenchard and Gordon did not argue for an unrestrained liberty for people to libel each other or the government, Levy describes their acceptance of England's libel laws as a genuflection to keep on the safe side of the law whereas, in fact, they "thought the law of criminal libel was neither good nor prudently enforced; indeed, that it was quite dangerous to public liberty and to good government."[10]

The great confidence that philosophers had in the inevitability of truth triumphing over falsehood was of little practical help to journalists and printers in the Colonies. The most repressive restriction on expression was criminal prosecution for seditious libel, that is, for criticism of government or government officials. In the common law of England and the Colonies, truth was no defense against a libel prosecution. The law held that the greater the truth, the greater the libel. The object of the law was to protect confidence in government, and that was more likely to be undermined by a truthful revelation than by a false report that could be refuted. Arguing that truth will triumph over falsehood is obviously not the politic answer to such reasoning. Trenchard and Gordon argued not only that truth would triumph but that it should triumph. If the government is a trustee for the public, the public is better equipped with truth than ignorance to evaluate its effectiveness.

In the latter half of the eighteenth century the limits of legal protection for freedom of expression remained almost as narrow as those for which Milton had argued. The principle recognized in England and America was this: Government shall not restrain the press before publication.

Lord Mansfield sat as chief justice on the King's Bench in England from about 1750 to 1790. He held that the government does not have the right to suppress any material before it is published. However, it does have the authority to punish publishers of material that causes damage, as determined by the common law and Parliament. Publishers are free from censorship before publication; they may publish whatever they wish, but they must bear full responsibility for the abuse of their freedom.

Mansfield's ideas were incorporated by Sir William Blackstone into his famous *Commentaries,* an influential statement of the English law of the period. In a much quoted passage Blackstone wrote:

> The liberty of the press is indeed essential to the nature of a free state: but this consists in laying no *previous* restraints upon publications, and not in freedom from censure for criminal matter when published. Every freeman has an undoubted right to lay what sentiments he pleases before the public; to forbid this, is to destroy the freedom of the press; but if he publishes what is improper, mischievous, or illegal, he must take the consequences of his own temerity.[11]

By twentieth-century libertarian standards both men had a narrow view of press freedom. They granted lawmakers the authority to decide what materials constituted abuses and to set the punishments for offenders. In effect, then, they gave lawmakers the authority to decide what should be published. Under such a system the government could easily stifle ideas. It could simply declare the publication of certain materials an abuse of freedom. Or it could make penalties so severe that fear of punishment would discourage publishers from bringing forth certain ideas.

There were many contributors (some of whom we have already discussed) to libertarian theory that made the same basic distinction between prior restraint and subsequent punishment. What makes the contributions of these English jurists significant is timing.

In 1783 the American Colonies signed the treaty ending their War of Independence against England. A constitution was drafted in 1787. The process of its adoption by the states, however, was gradual, and some states refused to join the new nation until the protection of certain fundamental rights was secured against federal encroachment. During its first session the Congress of the United States of America passed a series of amendments to the Constitution. Ten of these amendments were ratified by the states and became part of the law of the land in 1791. The First Amendment in this Bill of Rights reads:

> Congress shall make no law respecting an establishment of religion, or prohibiting the free exercise thereof; or abridging the freedom of speech, or of

the press; or the right of the people peaceably to assemble, and to petition the Government for a redress of grievances.

Some who have tried to fathom what the authors of those words meant by *"the* freedom of speech and of the press" have fastened on Blackstone's statement as the explanation. Blackstone was not, of course, interpreting the American Constitution. Even as a description of English law, his definition of press liberty was dated by the substantial changes worked in English law by the passage of Fox's Libel Act of 1792. Americans have demanded and American courts have granted more protection against subsequent punishment than Blackstone recognized, but the absoluteness of the protection against prior restraint that Blackstone stated has remained an important tenet of libertarianism.

Until the 1930s it was generally accepted that the First Amendment meant at a minimum that there could be no prior restraint on publication. In 1931 the U.S. Supreme Court, in *Near v. Minnesota,* narrowly rejected a Minnesota statute that provided for a permanent injunction against "malicious, scandalous, and defamatory" newspapers or periodicals. The court suggested, however, that there were circumstances when the First Amendment—or at least the Supreme Court—would tolerate prior restraint. Chief Justice Charles Evans Hughes, in his opinion for the majority of five, gave these examples of exceptions:

> [T]he protection even as to previous restraint is not absolutely unlimited. But the limitation has been recognized only in exceptional cases. . . . No one would question but that a government might prevent actual obstruction to its recruiting service or the publication of the sailing dates of transports or the number and location of troops. On similar grounds, the primary requirements of decency may be enforced against obscene publications. The security of the community life may be protected against incitements to acts of violence and the overthrow by force of orderly government. . . .[12]

For two weeks in 1971 *The New York Times* and *The Washington Post* were enjoined by the federal courts from publishing the Pentagon Papers, a classified government account of decision-making during a period of the Vietnam War. Although the newspapers won their case, the Supreme Court again made clear that there would be circumstances—albeit extreme ones—when prior restraint would be tolerated. What was once thought an inviolate principle has been violated frequently in the 1970s.

EARL CAMDEN (1719–1794) AND THOMAS ERSKINE (1750–1823)

By giving the legislature a strong control of the press, Mansfield and Blackstone were at odds with a growing and influential body of libertarians who believed in a minimum of government. Lord Camden and Sir Thomas Erskine were among the Englishmen who had adopted Locke's philosophy of man's reason and natural rights. They broadened libertarian theory by

arguing that the power of the government to interfere with the press should
be severely restricted.

Camden and Erskine believed that the authority of government is limited
by natural law and natural rights. Because free expression is a natural right,
the government should not restrict the press either before or after publication, so long as the material is aimed at peaceful change. Even to save itself,
the government should not interfere with any publication that would change
the existing order by peaceful means or by appeal to the intellect. Here the
scope of freedom is far, far broader than that pleaded for by John Milton,
who would have spared the existing order from public questioning.

THOMAS JEFFERSON (1743–1826)

In America Thomas Jefferson also had an optimistic faith in people's
reason and a pessimistic distrust of government—particularly, in the American context, of a strong federal government. He wrote no unified work on
the press, but his letters are full of scattered references to it. From them one
can piece together his idea of press freedom and the role of the press in a
democratic society. His beliefs arose quite naturally from his political
philosophy.

Like the philosophers of the Enlightenment, Jefferson believed that the
universe had been created in accordance with some orderly plan. Human
beings had been given reason so that they could discover that plan and
bring their lives and institutions into harmony with it. He put strong faith in
the rationality and morality of humanity; people are good unless ignorance
or bad institutions corrupt them. Because people are essentially reasonable,
because they have certain natural rights, they should have a minimum of
governing. Jefferson knew, however, that even under the best form of
government those in public office may become so corrupted by power that
they will stifle the freedom of the people. Therefore, the citizens must be
alert to any attempts to curtail their liberty.

The role of the press followed from that picture of the citizen and the
state. Freedom of the press was not a natural right like freedom of religion
but a tool to accomplish other goals: public enlightenment and the protection of personal liberties.

The press, Jefferson wrote in 1823, is "the best instrument for enlightening the mind of man and improving him as a rational, moral, and social
being."[13] Democracy places a heavy burden on individual citizens. They
must be enlightened in order to govern themselves wisely. The press is an
important auxiliary of government as the means of giving citizens the facts
and ideas they need for intelligent self-government.

The press should also be a check on government, Jefferson said. The
freedom of the individual is the core of democracy, but even a democratic
government can trample the rights of its citizens. An important function of
the press, Jefferson asserted, is to safeguard personal liberties, to serve as a
watchdog and sound the alarm whenever individual rights are threatened or

... it is so difficult to draw a clear line of separation between the abuse and the
wholesome use of the press, that as yet we have found it better to trust the public
judgment, rather than the magistrate, with the discrimination between truth and
falsehood." Thomas Jefferson, 1803. (University of Virginia, painted by Thomas
Scully)

infringed. As a result public officials who rule despotically can be deposed
peaceably by public opinion instead of violently by revolution. The role of
the press as watchdog was on Jefferson's mind when he wrote to George
Washington in 1792:

> No government ought to be without censors; and where the press is free, no one
> ever will be. If virtuous, it need not fear the fair operations of attack and
> defense.[14]

Jefferson's eloquence has generated considerable admiration for his libertarianism, but he was not a consistent advocate—either in his writing or in his activities—of freedom for all political discourse. In 1783 in a draft of a constitution for Virginia, he suggested that the press should be liable "to legal prosecution for false facts printed and published. . . ."[15] He advocated the First Amendment as a necessary limitation on the federal government although he advised James Madison, who was drafting it, that the protection for the press should not be extended to "false facts affecting injuriously the life, liberty, property, or reputation of others or affecting the peace of the confederacy with foreign nations."[16] He wrote to Mrs. John Adams in 1804 that whereas Congress was denied "a right to control the freedom of the press, we have ever asserted the right of the States, and their exclusive right, to do so."[17] And when as President he had to contend with outrageous assaults on his character, he encouraged selective prosecutions by the states to restore the credibility of the press. He suggested to Governor Thomas McKean of Pennsylvania in 1803:

[S]o abandoned are the tory presses . . . that even the least informed of the people have learnt that nothing in a newspaper is to be believed. This is a dangerous state of things, and the press ought to be restored to it's credibility if possible. The restraints provided by the laws of the states are sufficient for this if applied. And I have therefore long thought that a few prosecutions of the most prominent offenders would have a wholesome effect in restoring the integrity of the presses. Not a general prosecution, for that would look like persecution: but a selected one. The paper I now inclose appears to me to offer as good an instance in every respect to make an example of, as can be selected.[18]

Jefferson was strongly committed to the principle that truthful contributions to the public debate should be protected. That alone places him among the more liberal statesmen and philosophers of his day. His exception of falsehood from press liberty and his reliance on state prosecutions to cleanse a malicious and false press should not deny him the credit he enjoys for the contributions he made to libertarianism. The confidence he expressed in free expression during his first inaugural address (1801) is a great tribute to the principles of libertarian theory:

If there be any among us who would wish to dissolve this Union or to change its republican form, let them stand undisturbed as monuments of the safety with which error of opinion may be tolerated, where reason is left free to combat it.[19]

His experience as an active political figure may have led him on occasion to compromise his libertarianism, but he returned repeatedly to that foundation. Although his recognition of the value of the press was tinged with bitterness at its performance during his political life, he wrote in 1823, just three years before his death, that an absolute freedom of the press for political discussion was "essential to the protection of the life, liberty, property, and safety of the citizen. . . . This formidable censor of the public functionaries, by arraigning them at the tribunal of public opinion, produces reform peaceably, which must otherwise be done by revolution."[20]

For much of the eighteenth century the goal of libertarians in America was legal recognition of the principles argued in defense of printer John Peter Zenger in 1735. The Zenger principles were that truth must be accepted as a defense in a criminal libel prosecution and that the jury rather than the judge should decide the criminality of the words.

The Alien and Sedition Acts of 1798 incorporated precisely those principles into a law designed to suppress anti-Federalist and Jeffersonian sentiments. Libertarians awoke to the realization that the Zenger principles offered no true protection. At last it became clear that political truth could not be proved, that the standard of truth offered no protection against criminal prosecution for the dissident citizen. How to measure the truth of opinion? Or the criminal intent or good motives of a publisher? What meaningful standard could a jury apply? Truth as a defense would protect no one but those who adhered to the prevailing passions. The new libertarians, as Levy calls them, men such as Tunis Wortman, John Thomson, and St. George Tucker, rejected the Blackstonian distinction between prior restraint and subsequent punishment and declared that there could be no crime of seditious libel. They advocated an absolute freedom for political expression. Only when political advocacy moved from the realm of expression to conduct could the criminal law be applied.

The new libertarians spoke of press liberty in expansive terms that American law did not reflect until the second half of the twentieth century. And even then, as it won some points, it lost others. As the United States moved into the nineteenth century the Alien and Sedition Acts lapsed, but many states adopted the principles of that much criticized law. The state protection was for truth. And some states added the conditions that truth would be protected only if it were published with good motives and for justifiable ends. It was not until the twentieth century, when state laws were brought under the restrictions of the First Amendment and the U.S. Supreme Court extended constitutional protection to all but malicious falsehood, that law and theory came close to meeting.

JOHN STUART MILL (1806–1873)

In the nineteenth century the nation was more interested in economics than the limits on press freedom, and laws of sedition proved slight restraint on the economic interests of publishers. Although some restrictions were imposed on the press before and during the Civil War, the libertarian tradition strongly predominated in the United States throughout the nineteenth century; viewpoints of all sorts were tolerated, even those that questioned or attacked the beliefs of the majority.

Shortly after midcentury, an English scholar contributed new ideas to libertarian thought. In his essay "On Liberty," John Stuart Mill justified free expression not on the basis of natural rights but on the grounds of utility. All human action, he said, should aim at creating the greatest happiness for the greatest number of persons. This happy state will come about most surely if the individual is free to think and act as he pleases. The individual needs freedom to bring his capabilities to their fullest flower, Mill argued; and as each individual flourishes, society as a whole benefits.

Unlike earlier utilitarians who had reasoned that liberty was secured by limiting government, Mill emphasized that government, the traditional enemy of liberty, was not the sole threat to individual freedom. He warned not about the tyranny of government but the tyranny of the majority which through its intolerance of minority opinion might stifle innovation, insight, and, indeed, truth. As George Sabine, an eminent student of political theory, has observed, "What Mill recognized, and what the older liberalism had never seen, was that behind a liberal government there must be a liberal society."[21]

Fighters for liberty commonly regard the government as their chief enemy, Mill said, and think that they have won the battle when they have thrown off the yoke of government. Yet the majority can tyrannize just as surely as government by imposing its collective opinion on the individual:

> [T]here needs protection also against the tyranny of prevailing opinion and feeling; against the tendency of society to impose, by means other than civil penalties, its own ideas and practices as rules of conduct on those who dissent from them; to fetter the development, and, if possible, prevent the formation, of any individuality not in harmony with its ways, and compel all characters to fashion themselves upon the model of its own.[22]

These major arguments underlie Mill's case for free expression. Liberty is not just a means to the individual's happiness, but a substantive part of it. Only through the exercise of liberty can the individual grow to his or her potential. If the majority silences an opinion—even a minority of one—it may be silencing the truth. Even a wrong opinion may contain a grain of truth necessary for finding the whole truth. Even if the commonly accepted opinion is the whole truth, people will hold it not on rational grounds but as a prejudice unless they are forced to defend it. Unless commonly held opinions are contested from time to time, they lose their vitality, their effect on character and conduct.

Mill wrote in "On Liberty":

> If all mankind minus one were of one opinion, and only one person were of the contrary opinion, mankind would be no more justified in silencing that one person, than he, if he had the power, would be justified in silencing mankind. Were an opinion a personal possession of no value except to the owner; if to be obstructed in the enjoyment of it were simply a private injury, it would make some difference whether the injury was inflicted only on a few persons or on many. But the peculiar evil of silencing the expression of an opinion is, that it is robbing the human race; posterity as well as the existing generation; those who dissent from the opinion, still more than those who hold it. If the opinion is right,

they are deprived of the opportunity of exchanging error for truth: if wrong, they lose, what is almost as great a benefit, the clearer perception and livelier impression of truth, produced by its collusion with error.[23]

For Mill liberty is the right of mature individuals to think and act as they please so long as they harm no one else by doing so. Harm to others is the sole justification for restraint. For its own protection society may try to advise, instruct, and persuade individuals, but it may not coerce them for their or its own good.

OLIVER WENDELL HOLMES (1841–1935) AND LOUIS D. BRANDEIS (1856–1941)

A major weakness in Mill's argument that harm to others was the only justification for restraint of liberty is that society is so easily able to perceive harmful consequences from words. The consequence might be the ruin of an individual's reputation, or the loss of his privacy, or the denial of his right to a fair trial or the disturbance of the public tranquillity or the jeopardizing of the lives of soldiers in wartime. Even a society educated to democracy and libertarianism—and it may be false to assume that those values have pierced the soul of the American public—will not tolerate complete freedom of expression. Words can inflict harm, and when freedom of expression comes in conflict with other cherished values, society demands that some accommodation be reached—usually in the form of restrictions on expression.

The Espionage Acts of 1917 and 1918 were designed to protect the American effort in World War I. The speech and press cases that were brought under those acts presented the American judiciary with the task of preserving civil liberties in the face of the majority's concern to protect the national security at whatever cost.

In 1919 in *Schenck v. United States,* Justice Oliver Wendell Holmes of the U.S. Supreme Court tried to draw the fine line. In his opinion for the court, Holmes upheld Schenck's conviction and refused First Amendment protection to words that constituted a clear and present danger. Holmes wrote:

> The question in every case is whether the words used are used in such circumstances and are of such a nature as to create a clear and present danger that they will bring about the substantive evils that Congress has a right to prevent. It is a question of proximity and degree. When a nation is at war many things that might be said in time of peace are such a hindrance to its effort that their utterance will not be endured so long as men fight and that no Court could regard them as protected by any constitutional right.[24]

Holmes was criticized for providing a rationale that permitted Congress to restrict freedom of expression whenever Congress determined it was necessary to do so. But the clear and present danger test was probably the best that could be hoped for during wartime.

Holmes did not as much reject libertarianism as qualify it. He wrote in
another case in 1919:

Shapers of
Libertarianism

165

> . . . [W]hen men have realized that time has upset many fighting faiths, they may
> come to believe even more than they believe the very foundations of their own
> conduct that the ultimate good desired is better reached by free trade in ideas—
> that the best test of truth is the power of the thought to get itself accepted in the
> competition of the market, and that truth is the only ground upon which their
> wishes safely can be carried out. That at any rate is the theory of our
> Constitution.[25]

For Milton it was an absolute Truth that would emerge from a free and
open encounter with falsehood. For Holmes what is accepted in the marketplace is truth. For Holmes freedom of expression seemed less important as a
means for finding Truth than as a means of accommodating and releasing
social pressures. For both Milton and Holmes it was a self-righting process,
but history presented Holmes with a period in which the dangers seemed
immediate. In wartime society might have to forgo the time-consuming self-
righting process.

Holmes and Louis Brandeis, a fellow Supreme Court justice, argued the
clear and present danger test as a restriction on government as much as a
limitation on personal freedom. In their view there were criteria that had to
be met before the government could punish expression. Perhaps the most
significant of the criteria was the immediacy of the danger. Brandeis, joined
by Holmes, wrote in a 1927 criminal syndicalism case:

> To courageous, self-reliant men, with confidence in the power of free and
> fearless reasoning applied through the processes of popular government, no
> danger flowing from speech can be deemed clear and present, unless the
> incidence of the evil apprehended is so imminent that it may befall before there is
> opportunity for full discussion. If there be time to expose through discussion the
> falsehood and fallacies, to avert the evil by the processes of education, the
> remedy to be applied is more speech, not enforced silence.[26]

Although the phrase "clear and present danger" endures in the popular
vocabulary, the test is seldom used explicitly by the courts except, on
occasion, in cases involving the threat to a criminal defendant's right to a fair
trial. The test was distorted by the Supreme Court in the 1950's, in large
measure in response to the wave of fear of Communism at that time, but
although the court now seems intent on avoiding the label, it has restated its
concern that freedom of expression not be abridged unless the danger it
provokes is immediate. When there is time, the remedy for falsity is more
speech.

HUGO BLACK (1886-1971)

Libertarianism has drawn on the ideas of so many people that it is
difficult to identify the *true* libertarian theory. Supreme Court Justice Hugo
Black's ideas would not match up with those of all the prominent libertarian

theorists, but he advocated as unlimited a freedom of speech and press as any. Black was noted for his "absolutist" view of the First Amendment. He said, "It is my belief that there *are* 'absolutes' in our Bill of Rights, and that they were put there on purpose by men who knew what words meant and meant their prohibitions to be 'absolutes.'"[27]

There have been a number of theories, tests, and doctrines used in the twentieth century to interpret or explain what the authors of the First Amendment meant in the eighteenth century by the words, "Congress shall make no law . . . abridging the freedom of speech or of the press. . . ."

For Black, the First Amendment absolutely prohibited government restraint on the freedoms of speech and press except regulation of the time, place, or manner of the exercise of those freedoms. (Black accepted that government could restrict a person who wished to make a noisy speech at 2 a.m. or in someone else's home or to brace speech with action such as picketing.) According to Black, the First Amendment made obscenity laws, sedition laws, libel laws of any kind, any law that treads on the freedoms of speech or press unconstitutional. In Black's view the time to restrain citizens is when they take action, not when they talk. His confidence in the rightness of the First Amendment and his interpretation of it was sustained, he said, by the "old-fashioned trust in human beings" that he had learned as a country boy.

Alexander Meiklejohn, a highly regarded American educator, interpreted the First Amendment as protecting all *political* speech, leaving intact obscenity laws and the law of libel that protects the private citizen's reputation. His views were very similar to Black's, and Black greatly admired him, but for Black the First Amendment would lose its strength if exceptions were made for restraints on private speech. Black said:

> It is not any trouble to establish a classification so that whatever it is that you do not want said is within that classification. So far as I am concerned, I do not believe there is any halfway ground for protecting freedom of speech and press. If you say it is half free, you can rest assured that it will not remain as much as half free. . . . I realize that there are dangers in freedom of speech, but I do not believe there are any halfway marks.[28]

Black, whether writing in dissent or with the majority, was often joined in speech and press cases by his colleague on the court, William O. Douglas. Although Douglas felt in some areas less bound by the test of the Constitution than Black did,[29] Douglas came very close to mirroring Black's absolutism on the freedoms of speech and press. Douglas was not persuaded that restrictions should be readily accepted even on troublesome expression. Douglas wrote in 1949:

> A function of free speech under our system of government is to invite dispute. It may indeed best serve its high purpose when it induces a condition of unrest, creates dissatisfaction with conditions as they are, or even stirs people to anger. . . . That is why freedom of speech, though not absolute . . . is neverthe-

less protected against censorship or punishment, unless shown likely to produce a clear and present danger of a serious substantive evil that rises far above public inconvenience, annoyance or unrest.[30]

Douglas eventually discarded the clear and present danger test entirely and embraced an absolutism akin to Black's. Black retired from the court in the late summer of 1971 and died soon after. Douglas retired because of ill health in late 1975. Black served 34 years on the court, Douglas 36. Without their influence, the First Amendment would not be as strong a libertarian force as it is today. They were the last justices on the court to hold that "no law" meant *no law*. It may be a long time before we have another.

Libertarian Functions

According to libertarian theory, the underlying purposes of the media are to help discover the truth, to assist in the successful working of self-government by presenting all manner of evidence and opinion as the basis for political and social decisions, and to safeguard civil liberties by providing a check on government. Libertarianism also recognizes that to accomplish these goals the mass media must make a profit, and it recognizes that the media play an important role in servicing the economic system. No one medium is responsible for all these, of course; they are the functions of all the media working together. By looking at how libertarian theorists defined these functions and how they expected them to be carried out, we get a picture of what libertarians thought the media should be and should do.

Libertarian theorists universally regarded public enlightenment as a major function of the press. From the time of Milton, they saw the press as an important partner in the search for truth. The press can feed people the information they need to formulate their own ideas; it can stimulate them by presenting the ideas of others. The press, in short, is one of the most pervasive and inexpensive of educators.

Akin to that first function of the press is the second—servicing the political system. Democratic government places heavy responsibility on both the citizens and the press. To govern themselves wisely in congregation with others, individual citizens must be aware of the problems and issues confronting the state and of their possible solutions and consequences. In a government resting on public opinion, then, the press furnishes the people with the information and ideas they need for making sound decisions.

The third function of the press, safeguarding civil liberties, stems quite naturally from the second. The idea of individual autonomy is the heart of libertarian theory. John Stuart Mill expressed the idea this way: "The only freedom which deserves the name, is that of pursuing our own good in our own way, so long as we do not attempt to deprive others of theirs, or impede their efforts to obtain it. Each is the proper guardian of his own health, whether bodily, or mental and spiritual."[31] As individuals pursue their own good in their own ways, as they freely develop their capacities, libertarians thought, society would be enriched.

But individuals' freedom is threatened. The libertarians generally regarded government as the traditional and chief foe of liberty; even in democratic societies, those in office might use their power capriciously and dangerously. Therefore, libertarians assigned to the press the task of maintaining a constant check on government, of playing the watchdog to warn the public whenever personal liberties are endangered. Tunis Wortman, a New York lawyer and democratic theorist, wrote in 1800:

> The Press is undeniably possessed of extensive influence upon Government. . . . While Society is furnished with so powerful a vehicle of Political Information [as the press], the conduct of administration will be more cautious and deliberate. . . . Ambition cannot fail to dread that vigilant guardian of Public Liberty, whose eye can penetrate, and whose voice be heard, in every quarter of the State.[32]

The press, then, protects not only its own freedom but the freedom of all citizens.

Libertarian ideas on economics lend strong justification to the fourth function of the press—making a profit. According to libertarian theory, only a free press, operating under a private enterprise system as conceived by classical liberal economists, can enlighten the public, service the political system, and safeguard civil liberties. Only a free press, beholden neither to government nor to any faction in society, can serve the cause of truth and ultimately, the rights of individuals and the public interest. Therefore, if the press is to be free to present views and information without fear or favor, it must be a private, independent business enterprise. This line of thought has been used also to justify large communications units, including monopolies and chains and cross-media empires. The argument is that a large, prosperous organization can better withstand pressures than a small, marginal one.

Today, according to disciples of traditional libertarian theory, a free people should strongly resist the government's entry into the communications field. Media owned outright by the government would be more interested in perpetuating the party in power than in encouraging a free trade in information and ideas. Media subsidized by the government would threaten the autonomy of privately owned communications. Moreover, with no compulsion to earn a profit, media of either type would have an unfair economic advantage over the traditional commercial press. Therefore, they would inhibit the operation of the self-righting process inherent in a competitive market of ideas and opinion.

In linking press autonomy with profit making, libertarian theory has borrowed freely from Adam Smith's concept of "the invisible hand" in classical economics. In the economic marketplace, each individual working for his or her own gain ultimately contributes to the wealth of all. In the marketplace of knowledge, each individual freely expressing his or her ideas and opinions furthers the inevitable emergence of truth. Public benefit is virtually guaranteed by the profit motive, which results in a press finely geared to the wants and interests of the community. As the late George Sokolsky once expressed it, "The battle for circulation becomes a battle for the truth." His explanation of that remark is in the best libertarian tradition:

> Some newspapers and some journalists may become subservient to base purposes but in a competitive system, the truth will out. What one seeks to suppress, another will publish. The error of one reporter is corrected by another. The fallacy of one editor is made right by another editor. The attempt to serve some private cause is exposed by a competing newspaper or news service.

By serving their own personal interests in making a profit, then, publishers, as if by deliberate intent, give the community the sort of newspaper it wants and needs.

Contemporary critics of libertarian theory have challenged this. Instead of the invisible hand at work, they see a sort of Gresham's law of journalism, under which bad publications tend to drive out good. For, they argue, a press system devoted to the irresponsible pursuit of profit results not in publications serving the wants and needs of the community but in publications ill equipped to meet the demands of a complex industrial society. Wants are not synonymous with needs. In this complex world the public is not necessarily attuned to its self-interest or to the public interest. The saving point in traditional theory—which most critics disdain—is the libertarian's contention that people are essentially moral; that if the pursuit of profit does not result in responsible journalism, publishers' innate moral sense eventually will cause them to provide it.

Servicing the economic system, the fifth function of the press, is intimately bound up with the task of profit making. It became an accepted function of the media with the rise of modern advertising. From its infancy the American press to some degree served the economic system. Colonial newspapers carried information in their news columns about commerce and shipping; in their advertising columns they carried announcements of merchants and traders. Mercantile dailies, newspapers devoted to specialized commercial information and announcements, were an important segment of the press even after Ben Day and his followers began turning out in the 1830s mass-oriented papers heavy with human interest.

However, as industrialization brought mass production and mass distribution, the media became linked more than ever to the economy and its operation. As always the media report happenings in the business and industrial world, but today they do it on an unprecedented scale. For millions of readers thousands of business, technical, and trade publications cover new ideas and new developments in the specialized areas they serve. General newspapers and magazines carry an impressive load of material about business and economic affairs. Perhaps even more important, through advertising the media play an important role in bringing together the buyers and sellers of goods and services. By doing so they contribute to a high level of consumption, help to allocate the nation's resources, stimulate product variety, and help to make possible prices that are favorable to consumers.

Based on the assumptions of eighteenth-century thought, libertarian theory had to be modified as the media developed. But even today it is a powerful factor in the formulation of policy of public communication. Conceiving of free expression as a natural right essential to individual autonomy and of a free press as indispensable to that prerequisite of a free society, and showing a strong faith in the rationality and essential goodness of people, libertarian theory takes for granted the existence of a self-righting process inherent in a free and open marketplace of knowledge and opinion. Its ultimate and morally persuasive appeal is to a transcendental order of values. Truth (the will of God or the laws of nature) is discovered by rational, moral people in the contest with falsehood. Freedom lies in the knowledge of truth and in living in accordance with the book of nature (or the word of God). The focus of libertarian attention is the individual. The freedom of the press is a universal, personal right. The right to publish is subject only to individual reason and conscience and to the minimal restraints of a free society composed of autonomous individuals with similar and equal rights. Comprehensive and impressive in stature, libertarianism helped to order the development and shape the character of the contemporary media of mass communication in the United States.

Notes

1. *Areopagitica and Other Prose Works of John Milton* (London: J. M. Dent & Sons Ltd., 1927), p. 5
2. *Areopagitica,* pp. 13–14.
3. *Areopagitica,* p. 36.
4. *Areopagitica,* p. 30.
5. Leonard Levy (ed.), *Freedom of the Press from Zenger to Jefferson* (Indianapolis: Bobbs-Merrill, 1966), p. xxii.
6. Clinton Rossiter, *Seedtime of the Republic* (New York: Harcourt, 1953), p. 141.
7. John Trenchard and Thomas Gordon, *Cato's Letters: Or, Essays on Liberty, Civil and Religious,* No. 15, in Levy, pp. 11–13.
8. Trenchard and Gordon, *Cato's Letters,* No. 100, in Levy, p. 23.
9. Trenchard and Gordon, *Cato's Letters,* No. 100, in Levy, p. 22.
10. Levy, p. xxv.
11. Thomas M. Cooley (ed.), *Commentaries on the Laws of England; in Four Books. By Sir William Blackstone,* Third Edition-Revised, Vol. 2, Book IV (Chicago: Callaghan and Company, 1884), p. 151.
12. *Near v. Minnesota,* 283 U.S. 697, 716 (1931).
13. Thomas Jefferson, letter to Adamantios Coray, October 31, 1823, in Levy, p. 387.
14. Paul L. Ford (ed.), *The Writings of Thomas Jefferson,* Vol. VI (New York: G. P. Putnam's Sons, 1895), p. 108.

15. Jefferson, "Draft Constitution for Virginia," 1783, in Levy, p. 332.

16. Jefferson, letter to James Madison, August 28, 1789, in Levy, p. 340.

17. Jefferson, letter to Abigail Adams, September 11, 1804, in Levy, p. 367.

18. Jefferson, letter to Thomas McKean, February 19, 1803, in Levy, p. 364.

19. Jefferson, "First Inaugural Address," March 4, 1801, in Levy, p. 358.

20. Jefferson, letter to Adamantios Coray, October 31, 1823, in Levy, p. 376.

21. George H. Sabine, *A History of Political Theory,* Third Edition (New York: Holt, Rinehart and Winston, 1963), p. 710.

22. John Stuart Mill, "On Liberty" (1859), reprinted in William Ebenstein, *Great Political Thinkers: Plato to the Present,* Third Edition (New York: Holt, Rinehart and Winston, 1963), p. 554.

23. Mill, in Ebenstein, p. 560.

24. *Schenck v. United States,* 249 U.S. 47, 52 (1919).

25. Justice Oliver Wendell Holmes, dissenting, *Abrams v. United States,* 250 U.S. 616, 630 (1919).

26. Justice Louis Brandeis, joined by Justice Holmes, concurring, *Whitney v. California,* 274 U.S. 357, 377 (1927).

27. Hugo L. Black, "The Bill of Rights," *New York University Law Review,* 35, 1960, p. 867.

28. Quoted in Edmund Cahn, "Mr. Justice Black and the First Amendment 'Absolutes': A Public Interview," *New York University Law Review,* 37, 1962, p. 559.

29. In *Griswold v. Connecticut,* Justice Douglas, writing for the court, found that penumbras emanating from the Bill of Rights created a zone of privacy, a Constitutional *right* of privacy. Justice Black dissented from Douglas's opinion on the grounds that the Constitution did not *specify* a "right of privacy." Black acknowledged only those rights, such as the Fourth Amendment's protection "against unreasonable searches and seizures," the framers had *specified.* 381 U.S. 479 (1965).

30. Justice Douglas, writing for the court, *Terminiello v. Chicago,* 337 U.S. 1, 4 (1949).

31. Mill, in Ebenstein, p. 558.

32. Tunis Wortman, extracts from *A Treatise Concerning Political Enquiry, and the Liberty of the Press,* reprinted in Levy, p. 273.

7

The Intellectual Environment: Social Responsibility

... [F]reedom of the press is not an end in itself but a means to the end of a free society. The scope and nature of the constitutional guarantee of the freedom of the press are to be viewed and applied in that light.

JUSTICE FELIX FRANKFURTER

Partly because the First Amendment is a legal tie to a libertarian past, libertarian ideas still guide thinking about the communications system in the United States. However, changes in social and economic conditions, in understanding of human behavior, and in evaluations of media performance and power have generated a new complex of ideas about the freedom, the role, and the responsibilities of the mass media. Some have called this complex of ideas the social responsibility theory of the press. It is less a theory than a body of media and social criticism that harbors a range of ideas about the appropriate relationships between the public, the government, and the media.

The central proposition for all those who stress the social responsibility of the press is this: Whoever enjoys freedom has certain obligations to society. The mass media are guaranteed freedom by the Constitution and are therefore obliged to perform certain essential functions. Although some would disagree, the idea of responsibility or obligation is not inconsistent with the fundamental tenets of libertarianism as long as owners and practitioners of the media define responsibility for themselves. However, those who are impatient with the media argue that if the media fail to live up to the obligations that *society* defines, the media will find that other agencies, including government, will *make* them live up to their responsibilities.

The emphasis on social responsibility has arisen as critics in recent years have challenged the adequacy of press libertarianism and the accuracy of the libertarian description of people and society. The critics have questioned not only the performance of the press but also the underlying assumptions of libertarianism regarding the nature of reality, people, society, and freedom. The revolution in ideas wrought by Darwin with his theory of evolution, Einstein with his theory of relativity, and Freud with his theory of the unconscious has undermined the foundations of libertarianism. The ideas of evolution and modern physics have challenged the Newtonian picture of the universe as a timeless, unchanging order. Modern psychology, with Freud and behaviorism, has laid siege to the fortress of rationalism. Contemporary political science, attacking the tradition of natural law, has declared the doctrine of natural rights to be merely a persuasive slogan of an outmoded ideology. (Indeed, the doctrine of natural rights had already lost its hold on the utilitarian libertarianism of the nineteenth century.) Economists and social scientists, questioning the radical individualism of libertarians, have raised doubts about even the possibility of a free and open marketplace of either commodities or ideas. The self-righting process has been widely rejected as a notion without foundation in reality—a romantic myth; and free exercise of the individual will has been forcefully attacked as often harmful to the community.

Moreover, critics assert, certain social forces and certain developments within the media themselves have so altered the environment of public communication that the media cannot be and cannot do what libertarian theory assumes they can be and do. Most critics cite the three forces described in Chapter 3—the rise of democracy, the economic and technological revolution that produced America's modern industrial culture, and the urbanization of American life. Some mention the development of markets for mass consumption of mass-produced goods and the development of modern advertising, publicity, and public relations for the exploitation of those markets. All those factors, the critics say, have so transformed the character and functions of the media that much of traditional libertarian theory is either obsolete or misguided.

New Theory or Old?

There are those who argue that libertarianism celebrates irresponsibility. That view would not fit well with the intelligence of the great contributors to the libertarian tradition. Milton relied on "good men," men "judicious, learned, and of a conscience." And although he advocated freedom from licensing, he held men responsible for what they published. Trenchard and Gordon would have held the press accountable for libels exposing private and personal failings, but they would not condemn the exposing of public failings and, indeed, reversed the obligation: "The exposing therefore of publick Wickedness, as it is a Duty which every Man owes to Truth and his Country, can never be a Libel in the Nature of Things. . . ."[1] For Jefferson, experience had shown that a free press was a fence "peculiarly efficacious against wrong." Its utility justified its protection, and Jefferson expected a free press to educate the public and act as a check against government injustice. And on more than one occasion he showed himself intolerant of falsehoods in the press. John Stuart Mill would have extended freedom of expression to those who exercised that freedom without harming others.

As George Watson has written in *The English Ideology:*

> The classic mistake about Victorian freedom is to suppose that it was a simple conviction that the power of authority, and notably of central government, ought to be reduced. In fact, it was a conviction and a hope that private discipline would render large areas of public discipline unnecessary. To the extent that men govern themselves, they do not need to be governed. All this puts the doctrine of liberty at the farthest conceivable extreme from mere permissiveness. Liberty is not the right to do as you please: it is the chance to do as you ought.[2]

Within libertarianism there has been a gradual shift *in emphasis* from rights to responsibilities. The rhetoric of libertarianism in earlier centuries was that of a fight to establish what did not exist—the right to freedom of speech and press.

With the increased understanding and recognition of the irrationality and weaknesses of human beings and of the potential for injustice and human suffering in an unrestrained economic and political system, the shift to expressions of responsibility was a natural development. In the twentieth century many libertarians comfortably embrace a social responsibility emphasis because for them it means that media responsibility is defined by the media practitioner and enforced only by the conscience of the media practitioner.

Like libertarianism, what is now called the social responsibility theory of the press is a collection of ideas, criticisms, and interpretations rather than a unified theory. For some, social responsibility theory is no more than a shift in emphasis within libertarianism, for others it is no more than increased accountability through public scrutiny to the public's standards of responsibility, and for still others it is the use of government authority to ensure that the press lives up to its public responsibilities (some critics of this view see such government involvement as no more than not-too-well-disguised authoritarianism). There is virtually a continuum of ideas that call upon the name of social responsibility theory.

In one sense, many of the ideas, beliefs, and values underpinning all these views have evolved from traditional libertarianism. For instance, virtually all who argue for social responsibility accept the libertarian functions of enlightening the public, servicing the political system, and safeguarding civil liberties. They also accept the functions of servicing the economic system and making a profit, but would subordinate those tasks to the more important ones of promoting and protecting democratic processes. Thus the social functions traditionally assigned to the media are accepted, but the ways in which some owners and practitioners have interpreted those tasks and the ways in which the media in general have fulfilled them are scrutinized more closely.

On the other hand, some ideas of some social responsibility advocates contradict fundamental tenets of libertarianism. Such advocates hold that the media, which enjoy a protected and privileged position under American laws and customs, have an obligation to society to carry out certain essential functions in a complex, modern industrial democracy. If the media assume their responsibilities and make them the basis of operational policy, remedies may be unnecessary to ensure the fulfillment of contemporary society's needs. But, as such social responsibility theorists warn, in the areas where the media do not assume those responsibilities, other social agencies, including government, must see that the essential tasks of mass communications are carried out.

Somewhere between the bitter partisanship of the early press and the ostensible objectivity of modern communications, faith diminished in the happy notion that liberty, coupled with reason and conscience, would assure a press adequate to society's needs. Some members of the public are demanding higher standards of performance, threatening to enact legislation if the media do not meet those standards.

A New Emphasis on Responsibility

William Livingston, a libertarian of the eighteenth century, described with profound disgust a printer of his day:

> I could name a Printer, so attached to his private Interest, that for the same of advancing it, set up a Press, deserted his Religion, made himself the Tool of a Party he despised, privately contemned and vilified his own Correspondents, published the most infamous Falsehood against others, slandered half the People of his Country, promised afterwards to desist, broke his Promise, continued the Publication of his Lies, Forgeries and Misrepresentations; and to compleat his Malignity, obstinately refused to print the Answers or Vindications of the Persons he had abused; and yet even this Wretch, had the Impudence to talk of the *Liberty of the Press.*[3]

In reality—rather than in theory—in those early days when publishers were mainly printers who ran newspapers as sidelines, they rarely gave much thought to the ethics of journalism. And in later years when editors were frankly partisan and wedded to political interest, it was useless to expect them to put the public interest above their own. By the middle of the nineteenth century, however, some newspapermen such as Horace Greeley thought that the newspaper should ignore the trivialities of the penny press and the political bondage of the partisan press. The newspaper should not be politically neutral, but it should not serve any political party or faction. It should furnish political leadership by setting the public good above party allegiance.

At midcentury, too, there were men such as Henry Raymond of the New York *Times,* who thought that the newspaper should be free of party but not of principle, that it should give its readers the broadest possible coverage, and that it should actively promote the community welfare. Later in the century men such as William Rockhill Nelson of the Kansas City *Star* saw the newspaper as an aggressive force for community betterment. In all those views there were traces of a growing sense of social responsibility among those actively involved in journalism.

In the twentieth century, professions of public responsibility have become more numerous and more explicit. Increasingly publishers have spoken of the duties imposed on the press by its growing professional spirit and its important role in the progress of society. In 1904 Joseph Pulitzer took nearly 40 pages of the *North American Review* to defend his proposal for a college of journalism. But, as more than a plea for journalism education, his article asked publishers to place duty to the public above duty to the counting room.

> Commercialism has a legitimate place in a newspaper, namely, in the business office. . . . But commercialism, which is proper and necessary in the business office, becomes a degradation and a danger when it invades the editorial rooms. Once let a publisher come to regard the press as exclusively a commercial business and there is an end of its moral power.[4]

Journalism needed moral and courageous people to give newspapers their ideals; for as Pulitzer put it, "Without high ethical ideals a newspaper not only is stripped of its splendid possibilities for public service, but may become a positive danger to the community."[5]

As the decades passed, others reminded their fellow journalists in similar words of the responsibilities that went with freedom. As newspaper ownership became increasingly concentrated and as the number of competing dailies declined, editors and publishers spoke of the special responsibilities of ownership in one-newspaper communities. In time movie makers and broadcasters also picked up the theme of public responsibility.

CODES OF PERFORMANCE

This sense of responsibility has been embodied in codes setting ethical standards for the media. In 1923 the American Society of Newspaper Editors (ASNE), a national organization, adopted its Canons of Journalism, which called upon newspapers to act with truthfulness, sincerity, impartiality, fair play, decency, respect for individual privacy, and responsibility to the general welfare.

The canons were more attuned to libertarianism than were the first codes of the motion picture and broadcasting industries. The newspaper, some three centuries old when the ASNE code was adopted, was deeply attached to the liberal movement of the seventeenth and eighteenth centuries which led to the battle for press freedom. The newspaper canons shared the libertarian's faith in the rationality of people, in their interest in searching for truth, and in their ability to distinguish right from wrong by the power of reason and the dictates of conscience. The canons also shared the traditional faith that the self-righting process will operate in a free marketplace of knowledge and opinion. But the canons also acknowledged that freedom of the press carries a responsibility to the public welfare and that pursuit of selfish interest violates the journalist's "high trust." Most striking was the concession the canons made to government judgment:

> Freedom of the press is to be guarded as a vital right of mankind. It is the unquestionable right to discuss *whatever is not explicitly forbidden by law,* including the wisdom of any restrictive statute. [Emphasis added.]

Nevertheless, the codes of broadcasting are much more attached to the emerging values and beliefs of the social responsibility theory. They reflect not only the intervening changes in intellectual and social climate but also the dark cloud of government intervention and regulation. The radio code of 1937 and the television code of 1952—both of which have been extensively amended—were written under conditions of existing government regulations, which required them to perform "in the public interest, convenience, and necessity." These codes see the broadcasting industries as devoted primarily to producing entertainment, although they do make references to educational functions. The codes also reflect the changing image of people as not altogether rational in their behavior and as highly susceptible to moral corruption. The broadcasting codes are largely concerned, as a matter of social responsibility, with promoting public morals and conforming to accepted standards of good taste in programing and advertising. Only as if by afterthought do they deal with promoting democracy by enlightening the public.

The movie code, which was written in 1930, was merely negative, and set minimum standards of acceptability, not of responsibility. Then, late in the 1960s movie makers began to ignore most of the provisions. To placate critics in the public and to head off increased government regulation, the Motion Picture Association of America amended the code to set up a system of rating movies to prevent the very young from attending movies designed for adults.

All this attention to codes and rating systems is, of course, a sharp break with the individualism of libertarianism. It is in much closer harmony with the assumptions and goals of social responsibility theory.

The Commission on Freedom of the Press

Changing attitudes of media owners and practitioners toward the functions and operations of the media reflect a general drift in the direction of collectivist conceptions of reality, of people, and of society. However, not until 1947, with the report of the Commission on Freedom of the Press, were those attitudes and conceptions organized into what has been described as a new theory of the press.

In 1942, Henry Luce, founder and head of Time Inc., asked Robert M. Hutchins to establish a commission to inquire, as Hutchins described it, "into the present state and future prospects of the freedom of the press." The commission was funded with a grant of $200,000 from Time Inc. and $15,000 from Encyclopaedia Britannica, Inc., although neither institution participated in the work of the commission. Hutchins, the chancellor of the University of Chicago, assembled 12 men from such fields as law, philosophy, economics, history, political science, government, and education. Journalism was the notable omission.

Although the commission drew many of its observations and recommendations from the mass media, the work of the commission was much criticized by them. Luce himself condemned what he called "a doctrine of 'an accountable press,'" for "the most appalling lack of even high school logic. . . ."[6] He did not reject the idea that the media have responsibilities, but he faulted the commission for not attempting to specify *who* is accountable to *whom* for *what*. He also rejected the accuracy of many of the fundamental criticisms the commission made of the press.

The commission, while supporting the legal protections libertarianism had won for the press, presented a philosophically different view of the nature of freedom. The commission advanced the principle that freedom of the press is not a natural right but a moral right. And a moral right, unlike a natural right, is forfeited when "the duty of a man to the common good and to his thought . . . is ignored or rejected." The moral right isn't lost because the speaker is in error as long as he is trying for truth. "What the moral right does not cover is the right to be deliberately or irresponsibly in error," the commission explained.

The commission was unwilling, however, to limit the legal right of freedom of the press to its responsible exercise: "[T]o impair the legal right even when the moral right is gone may easily be a cure worse than the disease. If the courts had to determine the inner corruptions of personal intention, honest and necessary criticisms would proceed under an added peril."[7]

Although not encouraging much extension of government regulation (the commission recommended a law requiring retraction or right of reply as an alternative to traditional libel law), the commission warned that a press which ignored its moral duty would find its legal right in jeopardy. Society would not tolerate as powerful an institution as the press—the control of which was exercised by only a small proportion of the population—behaving irresponsibly. Because the media are so powerful—the commission called them "probably the most powerful single influence" on American culture and public opinion—their performance must measure up to the standards that serve society's interests and needs. The commission listed five things that contemporary society requires of the press. Ironically, these requirements did not originate with the commission; it drew them largely from the professions and practices of the most responsible of those who operate the media.

TRUTH AND MEANING IN THE NEWS

The first requirement of the media in contemporary society, according to the commission, is that they provide "a truthful, comprehensive, and intelligent account of the day's events in a context which gives them meaning." The media should be accurate; they should not lie. Moreover, they should identify fact as fact and opinion as opinion and should separate the two as much as possible. In simpler societies, the commission said, people could often compare accounts of events with other sources of information. Today they can do so to only a limited degree. Therefore, it "is no longer enough to report *the fact* truthfully"—as, for example, an accurate account of a statement made by a politician. "It is now necessary to report *the truth about the fact*"—presumably the motives and interests of the politician and the political situation in which the statement was made.

The media themselves appear to agree with the commission's dictum that they should be accurate and should separate news and opinion. Most newspapers try to adhere to the principle of objective reporting and to relegate expression of opinion to the editorial page. (Some newspapers, such as the Louisville *Courier-Journal,* run Gary Trudeau's comic strip, "Doonesbury," on the editorial pages so that it is clearly represented as opinion—not necessarily the paper's—rather than entertainment.)

Broadcasters take much the same view of their interests and responsibilities, a view reinforced by the Federal Communications Commission's Fairness Doctrine, which requires that broadcasters provide a fair and balanced account of controversial issues. Newscasters, depending heavily on wire service copy and serving large audiences of diverse opinions, seldom deliberately violate the principle of objectivity. There are exceptions, of course, just as there are in newspapers. Paul Harvey introduces his 15-minute broadcasts for the ABC radio network with the words, "Stay tuned for *news*" (emphasis his), but he sprinkles his news with opinion and has perfected the raised-eyebrow, hand-over-the-heart, tear-on-the-cheek, and twinkle-in-the-eye tones of voice. He is, however, less a reporter or announcer than a commentator, and is recognized as such. Most newscasters, when they do make comments on the news, are careful to label them and to separate them from straight news.

With respect to the Hutchins Commission's demand that the media tell the "truth about the fact," the situation is somewhat different. Many newspapers and broadcasting stations are reluctant to go beyond telling what happened or what was said. To attempt to give the reader an understanding of the *why* would be to run the risk of introducing bias and distortion into the straightforward account of events as they happened, of statements as they were uttered.

In *Public Opinion,* Walter Lippmann argued that truth and news are not the same thing and that, indeed, they do not even have the same function. He wrote, "The function of news is to signalize an event, the function of truth is to bring to light the hidden facts, to set them into relation with each other, and make a picture of reality on which men can act."

Lippmann pointed out that there is very little information susceptible to exact proof. Most of what we "know" is opinion.

> There is a very small body of exact knowledge, which it requires no outstanding ability or training to deal with. The rest is in the journalist's own discretion. Once he departs from the region where it is definitely recorded at the County Clerk's office that John Smith has gone into bankruptcy, all fixed standards disappear. The story of why John Smith failed, his human frailties, the analysis of the economic conditions on which he was shipwrecked, all of this can be told in a hundred different ways. There is no discipline in applied psychology as there is a discipline in medicine, engineering, or even law, which has authority to direct the journalist's mind when he passes from the news to the vague realm of truth. . . . His version is only his version.
>
>   . . . . The control exercised over him by the opinions of his employers and his readers, is not the control of truth by prejudice, but of one opinion by another opinion that is not demonstrably less true. . . . [T]he choice has, in large measure, to be governed by the will to believe.[8]

Providing the background and context of events can be costly to the news media not only in manpower and time but in audience reaction. The major elements of the newspaper's market might not find the "truth about the facts" palatable, even if it were attainable. A mismatch between the journalist's and the audience's opinions of truth may do more to undermine the credibility of the journalist than to "correct" the opinions of the audience. Nevertheless, increasingly, many media leaders are encouraging "interpretative" and "depth" reporting because reporting only the bare, verifiable facts is so obviously an inadequate base of information for a self-governing nation.

"COMMON CARRIER" OF IDEAS

A second requirement of the media, said the Commission on Freedom of the Press, is that they serve as "a forum for the exchange of comment and criticism." What this means, the commission said, is that the media should regard themselves as "common carriers" in the realm of public discussion. The choice of words was unfortunate, because "common carrier" has a meaning the commission specifically rejected. The commission did not intend to force the media to publish all messages anyone was willing to pay to distribute, but to provide a vehicle for exchange of important and interesting ideas. The commission urged that the media, without giving up their own proper function of taking a stand, should, as a matter of policy, carry views contrary to their own.

Behind this requirement is the concern for the increasing concentration of media ownership in fewer and fewer hands. The commission argued that because the individual citizen finds access to the facilities of public expression more and more difficult, the media must carry viewpoints that otherwise might not find public circulation.

On this requirement, too, the media seem to agree with the commission. Newspaperman Grove Patterson defined one of the social responsibilities of the press as making sure that "newspapers are representative of the people as a whole and not of special interest." The failure of some editors, publishers, and owners to make their papers truly representative of the people lies in their erroneous belief that freedom of the press belongs to them alone, he said, and added, "A free press is vastly more than a meal ticket for publishers."

Broadcasters, too, speak in their codes of exerting every effort to ensure equality of opportunity in the discussion of public issues. The television code suggests that stations "give fair representation to opposing sides of issues which materially affect the life or welfare of a substantial segment of the public."

As a natural part of the change from journals of opinion in the eighteenth century to gatherers of information in the twentieth, the modern news media through their efforts to be objective (they may not actually succeed, but for the most part they do try) carry by interview and by report a wide range of ideas. Conflict is a prominent element of news. Reporters will seek out the other side to be fair or to be interesting or to be safe—and perhaps even to be all three. The tendency to seek out more than one side may be suppressed by the reporter's or the publisher's bias (although reporters deal with so many issues about which neither they nor their publishers feel strongly), but more often when there is a culprit, it is the deadline.

(Some sources of news are masterful at manipulating reporters with an eye on a deadline. It is difficult for a journalist to resist reporting even an outrageous charge if it comes from a prominent person. The determination not to be beaten by a competitor goads the journalist to report the charge even if the deadline allows no time to get a response from the object of the charge. But if the story runs on the 6 o'clock news, most journalists will work hard to get the response by the 11 o'clock news.)

It has also become common practice among American newspapers to provide a variety of views on the editorial page and op-ed page (the page facing the editorial page). William Buckley is run across from Tom Wicker, George Will next to Russell Baker. Some newspapers even run opposing editorial cartoons. And some newspapers, such as the New York *Times,* the Washington *Post,* the Los Angeles *Times,* and the Chicago *Tribune,* regularly publish articles written by nonprofessional journalists. Most newspapers—and many magazines—routinely run letters to the editor, albeit a *selection* of the mail they receive.

For some publications the effort is not only or primarily to balance conservative and liberal views, or to provide the pros and cons of each and every issue, but, as the Detroit *News* described its op-ed page, to provide "a kind of cafeteria" of viewpoints for readers.[9]

Although some trace the origin of the modern op-ed page to the New York *World* of the 1920s, the practice of devoting space—perhaps a page or more—to comment and opinion from nonstaff writers and in some cases from nonprofessional journalists is really more a phenomenon of the 1960s and 1970s. David Shaw of the Los Angeles *Times* has pointed out that the "complexity and contentiousness" of events in the 1960s led some papers to look outside their staff for expert analysis and commentary.[10] Issues such as the civil rights movement and the Vietnam War provoked national debates on morality, justice, and policy. The decreasing number of cities with competing newspapers led many newspapers—especially those left in a monopoly situation—to publish opinions contrary to the publisher's, out of a sense of social obligation and in an effort to attract diverse audiences.

That this role is indeed socially responsible is challenged by some. The debate is an old one. Ben Franklin wrote in 1731:

> Printers are educated in the Belief, that when Men differ in Opinion, both Sides ought equally to have the Advantage of being heard by the Publick; and that when Truth and Error have fair Play, the former is always an overmatch for the latter: Hence they chearfully serve all contending Writers that pay them well, without regarding on which side they are of the Question in Dispute.[11]

But another libertarian, William Livingston, wrote in 1753:

> A Printer ought not to publish every Thing that is offered him; but what is conducive of general Utility, he should not refuse, be the Author a Christian, Jew, Turk or Infidel. Such Refusal is an immediate Abridgement of the Freedom of the Press. When on the other Hand, he prostitutes his Art by the Publication of any Thing injurious to his Country, it is criminal,—It is high Treason against the State.[12]

Some modern-day publishers argue that they have a responsibility *not* to publish what they know to be false or believe to be foolish.

But critics of the media warn that the increasing concentration of media ownership in fewer and fewer hands and the basic aversion of established, establishment media to controversial ideas means that most citizens have no real opportunity to participate in public debate. Some critics, such as law professor Jerome Barron, argue that the First Amendment prohibition on government restraint does not forbid the government from acting to enhance citizens' opportunities to exercise their freedom of press. Barron argues in favor of a legal right of access for citizens to the mass media.

It is just as easy and probably not much more expensive in the 1970s for an individual to have a thousand copies of a political speech run off by a local printer as it would have been in the eighteenth century. What has changed in the past two centuries is not the ease of publishing an opinion but the difficulty of winning an audience. In the 1970s running off a thousand copies of a political speech provides no opportunity to participate in the national debate and probably not much opportunity to participate in a debate of issues in a small community. The avenue to an audience is through an established *mass* medium—a newspaper, a magazine, a television station.

The 1960s and 1970s have seen the birth and death of many "underground" publications. They served many functions but for the most part they did not provide an avenue for participation in policy-making and policy-changing public discussion. They reached a comparatively small audience that typically already agreed with their views.

The media have fought to retain the right to exercise their editorial judgment on what they publish. They have opposed laws compelling them to accept applicants for space and time or any move by government to regulate their rates. And largely they have been successful. The Supreme Court has deferred to the private newspaper editor's judgment in cases dealing with rights of access. Because broadcasters are licensed by government, they have had to recognize the special, if limited rights of access of political candidates and of persons or groups who have been attacked by broadcasters. But even though the Supreme Court has held the public's right to hear competing views superior to the broadcasters' right to use their frequencies as they wish, the broadcasters as trustees for the public, retain—except in limited circumstances—the right to exercise discretion.

Average citizens do not have much more of an opportunity for access to the media now than they did at the beginning of the 1960s, but it seems that as newspapers seek to maintain circulation and broadcasters face costly legal battles with citizens' groups, the media are more attentive to citizen complaints than they were even 15 or 20 years ago.

A REPRESENTATIVE PICTURE OF SOCIETY

The third requirement is that the media give a representative picture of the various groups that make up society. That is, they should portray accurately all social groups and not perpetuate stereotypes. The Commission on Freedom of the Press urged that the media take into account each group's values and aspirations as well as its weaknesses and vices.

Media performance in meeting this third requirement has been tragically weak. The entertainment media have traded heavily in stereotypical images for comic, dramatic, and commercial effect, and in the news media stereotyping often colors what is supposed to be objective reporting. The difficulty is that all of us naturally rely on stereotypes to organize a confusing world. Whether the media's use of stereotypes is malicious or unconscious, the concern is that such use gives us inaccurate pictures on which we base judgments and actions that may be harmful to social harmony and individual development.

What concerned the commission was not only inaccurate depiction in particular instances but distortion by piling example on example of one kind of behavior and omitting examples of all other kinds of behavior for a particular group. Women have many other roles than that of housewife, but until recently television advertising that didn't depict women as sex symbols most often presented them as empty-headed creatures who couldn't keep their houses clean or buy the groceries without the advice of a man—often a very silly man like the Man from Glad or the Tidy-Bowl Man or the man trying to swap coffees outside the supermarket. Not only were women shown almost exclusively as housewives, but they were made out to be not very good housewives.

Minorities have received similarly limited and misleading treatment by the media. As Ben Bagdikian pointed out in 1968:

> Until the recent past, Negroes appeared in the news most often because of crime. . . . [T]his news treatment of the Negro was more persistent and more pernicious than that of any other low status group. . . . For the average white, Negroes did not go to school, earn scholarships, win election to the hierarchy of the Masons, attend PTA meetings, or die peaceful deaths after laudable or even uneventful lives. One wonders what the effects of this have been on white perception of the Negro, on the Negro's perception of himself, and on the news media's ability to hypnotize itself with its own information.[13]

Such treatment of women and minorities is, in part, a reflection of long-standing, deep-seated views held by media owners and practitioners, who still include few women or minorities in their numbers. The long absence of minority faces in advertising and entertainment programing was, in part, a reflection of economics: Programs and advertising are aimed at those groups thought to have money to spend on advertised products.

In 1975 only two out of approximately 700 commercial television stations and 49 out of more than 7000 commercial radio stations were owned by minorities.[14] Several recent studies of women in newspaper management found few women in top management positions.[15] Statistics compiled for 1975 by the Equal Employment Opportunity Commission show 96.2 percent of "officials and managers" and "professionals" in the newspaper industry were white; 86.8 percent of "officials and managers" and 71.3 percent of "professionals" were white males.[16] Statistics for such decision-makers are, of course, more relevant to charges of bias in programing and coverage than overall industry figures which include clerical workers, laborers and service workers.

In August 1977 the U.S. Commission on Civil Rights released a report, *Window Dressing on the Set: Women and Minorities in Television*, that criticized television for stereotyping minorities and women "in pursuit of higher ratings and higher profits."

The commission found that white males dominated network entertain-

Table 7.1 Employment Patterns in 1975

	Total Employment	Officials and Managers[c]	Professionals	Technicians	Sales Workers	Office and Clerical Workers	Craft Workers	Operatives	Laborers	Service Workers
Newspapers[a]										
(692 units)										
All Employees[*]	100.0%	100.0%	100.0%	100.0%	100.0%	100.0%	100.0%	100.0%	100.0%	100.0%
Male	73.3	90.1	73.9	79.4	67.9	28.7	91.8	85.6	81.6	83.5
Female	26.7	9.9	26.1	20.6	32.1	71.3	8.2	14.4	18.4	16.5
White	91.4	96.2	96.2	93.6	93.2	89.5	95.2	87.6	80.3	60.6
Male	67.1	86.8	71.3	75.0	63.9	25.3	87.5	74.6	63.8	49.1
Female	24.3	9.4	24.9	18.7	29.3	64.3	7.6	12.9	16.5	11.5
Minority[d]	8.6	3.8	3.8	6.4	6.8	10.5	4.8	12.4	19.7	39.4
Male	6.2	3.2	2.6	4.5	4.0	3.4	4.3	10.9	17.8	34.4
Female	2.4	.6	1.2	1.9	2.8	7.0	.5	1.5	1.9	5.0

*All Employees = 246,508

	Total Employment	Officials and Managers[c]	Professionals	Technicians	Sales Workers	Office and Clerical Workers	Craft Workers	Operatives	Laborers	Service Workers
Television[b]										
(40 stations)										
All Employees[**]										
Male	71.15	74.83	71.48	94.97	69.68	17.32	93.0	89.9	100.0	84.06
Female	28.85	25.16	28.53	5.04	30.32	82.69	6.99	10.1	0.0	15.93
White	79.89	88.74	80.74	84.63	83.55	64.11	90.36	63.64	52.0	45.13
Male	59.61	68.34	60.31	81.10	55.81	10.08	83.61	57.58	52.0	38.05
Female	20.28	20.40	20.43	3.53	27.74	54.03	6.75	6.06	0.0	7.08
Minority[d]	20.11	11.25	19.27	15.38	16.45	35.9	9.63	36.36	48.0	54.86
Male	11.54	6.49	11.17	13.87	13.87	7.24	9.39	32.32	48.0	46.01
Female	8.57	4.76	8.1	1.51	2.58	28.66	.24	4.04	0.0	8.85

**All Employees = 8176

[a]Source: Equal Employment Opportunity Commission, *Equal Employment Opportunity Report—1975: Job Patterns for Minorities and Women in Private Industry*, Vol. 1 (Washington, D.C.: U.S. Government Printing Office, 1977), p. 32. The data were drawn from EEO-1 reports, which in 1975 were required of every private employer subject to Title VII of the Civil Rights Act of 1964 (employers affecting commerce) and having 100 or more employees and of federal contractors having 50 or more employees and contracts of at least $50,000. The commission report does not include data from Hawaii.

[b]Source: U.S. Commission on Civil Rights, *Window Dressing on the Set: Women and Minorities in Television* (Washington, D.C.: U.S. Government Printing Office, August 1977), pp. 141–142. The data were drawn from an analysis of the 1975 employment reports of 40 major market television stations. The sample consisted of 15 owned and operated network stations (5 each from ABC, CBS, and NBC), 15 stations affiliated with the networks and 10 public stations. The stations are located in the following cities, each of which has a high proportion of one or more of the minority groups under study (with the exception of Native Americans): New York, Los Angeles, Chicago, Detroit, Philadelphia, San Francisco, Cleveland, Washington, D.C., St. Louis, and Atlanta.

[c]These are the standard job categories used by the Equal Employment Opportunity Commission on its reporting forms.

[d]Data on blacks, Asian Americans, Native Americans, and Spanish origin Americans are combined in the category "minority." A breakdown of employment data into these groups is available in both sources used for this table.

Despite advances by minorities and women, white males still dominate positions of responsibility in the mass media. (United Press International photo)

ment and news programing. Indeed, the commission found that white males took most of the entertainment roles, including most of the villain roles. Examining a sample of network news programs broadcast in 1974 and 1975, the commission found that most of the newsmakers covered—whether public officials or criminals—were white males (a fact that could be accounted for in part by the preponderance of white males in such news-making areas as government) and that white males provided most of the coverage. More than 85 percent of the 85 correspondents reporting during the period studied were white males, only 8.2 percent were white females, 3.5 percent nonwhite females, 2.4 percent nonwhite males.

In an analysis of the 1975 employment reports of 40 television stations, the civil rights commission found 88.74 percent of "officials and managers" were white, 68.34 percent were white males; 80.74 percent of the "professionals" were white, 60.31 percent were white males. Those figures are less lopsided than the figures for newspapers cited above, but the civil rights commission found that "[a]lmost 75 percent of all employees at the 40 stations were classified in the top 4 categories" of which "officials and managers" and "professionals" are two. The commission found little evidence that white women and minority men and women were given decision-making responsibilities appropriate for these upper-level job categories.

The Commission on Civil Rights unnerved broadcasters and officials at the Federal Communications Commission by calling on the FCC to investigate regulating television programing and employment practices to remedy such problems. Of course regulating program content, even for a laudable purpose, raises First Amendment concerns. Ironically, the civil rights commission acknowledged the FCC is the only independent federal regulatory agency to adopt equal employment opportunity rules for those it regulates.

There is a basic issue of fairness in employment practices, news coverage, and entertainment portrayal that needs attention. It does seem unfair to have *any* industry employ a disproportionate number of white males. It also seems possible that the world view of a white male may be different from that of a Latino female or a black male and that such differences can affect news and entertainment program decisions.[17] On the other hand, it would be unfortunate to assume that individuals can only evaluate or report on like-situated people. We have not assumed that the media had to employ burglars to report on burglars, police to report on police, Canadians to report on Canadians. We surely would not want to press the media to hire women to report on women and blacks to report on blacks—at least not exclusively. To respond to the concerns of the Commission on Freedom of the Press requires a broader rather than a narrower perspective.

CLARIFICATION OF THE GOALS AND VALUES OF SOCIETY

The fourth requirement recommended by the Commission on Freedom of the Press is that the media present and clarify the goals and values of society. The commission did not suggest sentimentalizing and manipulating the facts to create a rosy picture. Rather it asked for realistic reporting of the events and forces that work against social goals as well as those that work for them. The media are an educational instrument, perhaps the most powerful one we have; therefore, they must "assume a responsibility like that of educators in stating and clarifying the ideals toward which the community should strive."

The commission encouraged the media to exercise their leadership for the public good, to resist the arguments that to be profitable they must be slavishly responsive to consumer tastes and interests. The commission wrote:

> It has been said that, if the press is to continue as a private business, it can succeed only as other retailers succeed, that is, by giving the customers what they want. On this theory, too, the press is bound by what it believes to be the interests and tastes of the mass audience; these interests and tastes are discovered by finding out what the mass audience will buy. On this theory, if the press tries to rise higher than the interests and tastes of the mass audience as they are revealed at the newsstands or at the box office, it will be driven into bankruptcy, and its existence as a private business will be at an end.
>
> We have weighed the evidence carefully and do not accept this theory. As the example of many ventures in the communications industry shows, good practice in the interest of public enlightenment is good business as well. The agencies of mass communication are not serving static wants. Year by year they are building and transforming the interests of the public. They have an obligation to elevate rather than to degrade them.[18]

What the commission was asking for was the responsible exercise of the editorial function, the antithesis of the common carrier notion that the media serve as no more than a conduit for the flotsam of other people's imagination. What the commission was encouraging was a continuation of the tradition of independent editors who through the agenda that they set for the public direct its attention to the fundamental rather than the foolish. William Hocking, one of the members of the commission, argued that time would prove responsibility profitable.

> The American press has frequently departed from strict business considerations to improve the quality of its work; with almost equal frequency it has found such departure eventually profitable. In any case, it belongs to the professional character of the press to take such risk; as Robert Redfield has put it, "We have to ask the press to be better than its public."[19]

It should not be surprising that the media have not met this requirement to everyone's satisfaction. What may be surprising is that they have met it to the satisfaction of so few. In the 1960s and the 1970s the mass media were criticized by discontented members of society for providing too much support for traditional values, for promoting such values without reexamining if they continue to be valid. The underground press and other instruments of dissent challenged the racism, the sexism, the imperialism, and the materialism that they perceived the media shared with other established institutions.

In contrast, other commentators have criticized the unrelenting negativism of the media. Some charge the news media are nitpicking to death vital American institutions, setting unrealistic goals and destroying the human beings who fail to measure up to impossible ideals.

The complicating problem is that the pluralism of America generates conflicting as well as complementary goals and values. Especially after the turmoil of the 1960s and early 1970s, it is doubtful that a consensus on this society's fundamental goals and values could emerge.

FULL ACCESS TO INFORMATION

The final requirement that the Commission on Freedom of the Press urge is that the media provide "full access to the day's intelligence." The citizens of a modern industrial society, the commission said, need a far greater amount of current information than people needed in any earlier time. Even if all the citizens do not always use all the information they get, the wide distribution of news and opinion is essential to government carried on by consent.

Media leaders surely agree. They are eager, for economic reasons, to reach as wide an audience as possible, but they also accept the obligation, the social responsibility for maintaining what the commission calls "freedom of information." As the media have sought to conquer larger and larger markets and have become more and more imbued with a sense of responsibility to the public, they have urged that the public has a right of access to information, a basic right to be informed.

James Madison and Thomas Jefferson recognized the need to keep the citizens of a democratic nation informed. People who mean to be their own governors must have access to information about the affairs of state or such government is doomed to failure. But the establishment of that need as a right has been difficult to accomplish. The phrase frequently used in contemporary times is that the public has a "right to know." The American judiciary has been most reluctant to include a right of access to information within its interpretation of the freedom of press protected by the First Amendment. Realistically, a right of access cannot be enforced unless *what* the public has a right to know is specified. The public does not have a right to know everything because such an expansive right would run counter to other values cherished by society, values such as personal privacy and national security.

The emphasis on the public's *right* contrasts with traditional libertarianism. The First Amendment was written to protect a medium of opinion and commentary. Society was not so complex and government was an immediate experience. In the twentieth century Americans must rely on the mass media for information of their affairs as well as commentary and opinion about them. Modern Americans also must rely on the media to provide the information they need in time for effective citizen action. Libertarian theory developed in a less rushed and less frantic time, and it assumed that full access to the day's intelligence would be the natural consequence of personal experience and a free and open marketplace of knowledge and opinion. No provision was made for guaranteeing the flow of information when individuals chose to be silent or government chose to be secretive. (As a matter of practicality, our Founding Fathers, who drafted the Constitution in secret so as not to upset the public with premature speculation, were hardly likely to endorse a right of the public to know everything about its government and its governors.) By contrast, in the twentieth century, the media, having taken on the responsibility to provide information as well as opinion, have become active agents in breaking down the barriers of secrecy and silence. The American Society of Newspaper Editors, the Society of Professional Journalists (Sigma Delta Chi), and other professional groups have formed freedom-of-information committees to champion the public's right to know and to help open up the sources of news at all levels of government. Journalists have warned repeatedly of the dangers to democratic government of censorship by suppression of information. Such efforts have been effective. Although the First Amendment still has not been held to incorporate a right of access to all information, Congress has enacted freedom-of-information legislation applying to the executive branch, passed government-in-the-sunshine laws to open up federal agency activities to public scrutiny, and through resolutions opened up its own processes—at least a little—to public gaze. In addition, according to a study published by

Access Reports in December 1975, 49 states and the District of Columbia
have some form of open meeting and/or open records laws on their books.
(Only Rhode Island had neither.)

Libertarian theory saw the media as instruments of individual—as
opposed to public—will. In principle no person was barred from either
acquiring or using the media for individual ends. Libertarian theory tolerated
the selfish use of the media on the assumption that conflict in ideas is a good
in itself. Today, however, the media are exhorted to act as agents not of the
individuals who own and manage them but of the public, which bestows
freedom. The commission urged the press to "take on the community's
press objectives as its own objectives."

Asserting the "public's right to know," the media have presented themselves as the agents of the public. An idea largely unexplored is whether the
public has a right, at least in theory if not in law, to insist the media provide
the information necessary to keep the public well-informed. What recourse
should the public have against a news institution that fails to tell it something
it needs to know—let's say something like the information that a major
industry in the community is dumping health-threatening pollutants in the
water system?

RESPONSIBILITIES AND REMEDIES

The Commission on Freedom of the Press suggested several remedies
for the ills it had diagnosed in the American media. It made recommendations for government, press, and public action, emphasizing that the more
the press and the public would be willing to do, the less would be left for the
state. It encouraged little increased government regulation. Its prescriptions
for government were relatively mild and in some instances directly suppor-
tive of the media. It recommended that the constitutional guarantees of
freedom of the press be recognized to include broadcasting and motion
pictures. It recommended the repeal of legislation prohibiting advocacy of
revolutionary change in our institutions—unless such advocacy presented a
clear and present danger that violence would result. It encouraged the
government to help inform the public by cooperating directly with the media
and, when necessary, employing media of its own. To combat media
concentration the commission recommended:

> that government facilitate new ventures in the communications industry, that it
> foster the introduction of new techniques, that it maintain competition among
> large units through the antitrust laws, but that those laws be sparingly used to
> break up such units, and that, where concentration is necessary in communica-
> tions, the government endeavor to see to it that the public gets the benefit of
> such concentration.[20]

Its strongest recommendation for increased legislation was the suggestion
that legislation be passed that would provide for retraction or right of reply
as an alternative to existing libel laws.

Its most interesting recommendations were those directed at the press and public. The press was encouraged to engage in "vigorous mutual criticism," and to "use every means . . . to increase the competence, independence, and effectiveness of its staff." The commission urged the public to create or use existing "agencies to supplement the press, to propose standards for its emulation and to hold it to its accountability." One of the most interesting aspects of the commission's report is that it did not encourage direct public expression of the public interest or direct public pressure on the media. The commission suggested agencies such as universities and press councils that would insulate the media from the pressures and passions of the general public. The intent was to create a responsible rather than a responsive press.

The fact that so many of the commission's recommendations have been followed may be less an indication of the influence of the commission than its reflection of the sensibilities of the twentieth century. Mutual and self-criticism is now increasingly evident in the press, and the press has joined with educational institutions to improve the competence of its news staffs. There are local media councils around the country and a national news council. Foundations and universities support research on the media and join with government to support nonprofit media. All this activity has not, however, protected the media against public dissatisfaction or government efforts to control the media.

Education for Responsibility

In their early years schools and departments of journalism concentrated largely on supplying the demand for newspaper staff members. Today the best of them provide a professional education, not merely technical training—and many have substituted in their titles "communication" or "communications" to reflect broader and deeper concerns. Most of them give students an overview of the entire range of human communication even as they place their primary focus on the mass media.

Nearly all the schools have broadened their offerings to include more than preparation for newspaper work. Their graduates now go into public relations and public information and take positions with broadcasting stations as script writers, announcers, newscasters, directors, or producers. Still others make careers on magazines—general, technical, trade, professional, company-sponsored—as writers and editors, often after starting as editorial assistants. Some graduates, combining journalism with a speciality, have gone into agricultural journalism, home economics journalism, science writing, consumer journalism, legal journalism, and medical journalism. Some go into positions in many phases of advertising: with agencies as copywriters, layout specialists, researchers; with retail stores and mail-order forms; with newspapers; broadcasting stations; and magazines, both general and specialized. In short, the schools of journalism and communication have come to serve all the media.

Increasingly schools of journalism are offering students instruction on equipment as sophisticated as what they will encounter in the media. (Kenneth Karp)

In the past 25 years graduate as well as undergraduate instruction has, in some cases, reflected a broadening of outlook. Few journalism schools offered academic instruction beyond the master's level before World War II. To be sure, the University of Missouri awarded its first doctorate in journalism in 1934, and a few other institutions offered a journalism minor in combination with a doctorate in some other field, such as political science.

Since World War II more than 20 schools have established doctoral programs in communication. Most of these programs have attempted to apply the methods and disciplines of the various social sciences to the basic problems of communication. They cover such areas as the communication process, the philosophy of communication, policies and structures of communication systems, public opinion and attitude formation, the history and economics of the mass media, mass communications law, and public policy toward the mass media.

Similarly, communication research has flourished during the last 30 years. Before World War II there was comparatively little research, and only a handful of people associated with schools and departments of journalism had earned national stature as scholars. For the most part research on the mass media was left to those in other disciplines—political science, psychology, sociology, for example—who became interested in communication problems as an outgrowth of their other studies. As Wilbur Schramm has observed, communication was a crossroad where many passed but where few tarried. Today some schools that are unable to afford elaborate research departments have at least one staff member whose primary assignment is research. And a few schools or colleges support research centers. Most of these are dedicated to an interdisciplinary approach to the problems of both interpersonal and mass communication; staff members, who may represent such academic specialties as anthropology, economics, linguistics, psychology, political science, history, law, and sociology, have a professional commitment to communication or communications research.

Most of the educational programs for undergraduates demand that no more than 25 percent of the students' time be devoted to journalism courses, thus allowing them the full scope of a broad education. The American Council on Education for Journalism, which accredits journalism education programs, recommends that no more than 25 percent of a journalism student's course work be in journalism and mass communication. And journalism programs are requiring their majors to take not only newswriting and editing courses, but courses in communications law, media history, and professional ethics.

EDUCATION FOR MIDCAREER JOURNALISTS

Opportunities for working journalists to return to the campus for special studies began in the 1930s with the Nieman Fellows Program at Harvard. For decades there was little more than that. Then in the late 1960s the Ford Foundation made grants to Stanford, Northwestern, Columbia, and the Southern Regional Education Board to establish educational opportunities for other working journalists. These programs give journalists the chance to take courses in science, religion, economics, anything but journalism that might enhance their specialties or their understanding of their society. Other universities offer graduate journalism programs suited to those in midcareer who want to learn more about their profession or who want to learn the research methods of law, history, or the behavioral sciences in order to improve their ability to gather or evaluate information. Foundations, professional journalism organizations, and universities offer seminars and workshops on the law, ethics, practices, and techniques of journalism.

Many of those who have participated argue that such programs are essential if the mass media are to meet the challenges of a complex, rapidly changing society. It is doubtful that a communications system can be truly socially responsible without education that will help journalists obtain a wider view of the world and a deeper understanding of their profession.

"VIGOROUS MUTUAL CRITICISM"

The media have been criticized, no doubt, since their beginnings. They have always had the power to make someone unhappy. Thomas Jefferson wrote this to Walter Jones in 1814:

> . . . I deplore, with you, the putrid state into which our newspapers have passed, and the malignity, the vulgarity, and mendacious spirit of those who write for them; and I enclose you a recent sample, the production of a New England

judge, as a proof of the abyss of degradation into which we are fallen. These ordures are rapidly depraving the public taste, and lessening its relish for sound food. As vehicles of information, and a curb on our functionaries, they have rendered themselves useless, by forfeiting all title to belief.[21]

It should not be surprising, however, that those in government would criticize the press when the press spends so much time criticizing government. What is significantly new about media criticism in contemporary times is that as much of it comes from those who are a part of the media.

Early in this century Will Irwin contributed to *Collier's* magazine a series of carefully reasoned, closely argued articles on the influence and failings of the press. He warned that the press had become an integral part of big business, imbued with the business mentality. He warned, too, that the commercial nature of the press and its obeisance to advertisers caused many of its failings. And he alerted his readers to the shift in the influence of the press from its editorial pages to its news columns. In 1919 Upton Sinclair, one of the most prolific muckrakers, attacked what he considered the prostitution of the press to big business in *The Brass Check.* The bitterness of his criticism reflected his anger at the ill treatment he felt he had received from the press. In the 1930s George Seldes, a former head of the Berlin and Rome bureaus of the Chicago *Tribune* and war correspondent in Spain for the New York *Post,* set out to document the corruption of the press. In his *Lords of the Press* (1938) he accused publishers of conspiring against the public welfare:

> . . . in the closed sessions they defend the employment of child labor, they take united action against a Congressional measure which would keep drugmakers from poisoning or cheating the American people, and they gloat over their own strikebreaking department which offers scabs not only to members but to anyone who wants to fight the unions.[22]

A. J. Liebling, a witty and sharp, sometimes shrill, critic of the media, wrote a column called "The Wayward Press" for *The New Yorker* from 1944 to 1963. He described publishers' distance from news in these terms: "Many proprietors . . . have a prejudice against news—they never feel at home with it. In this they resemble racing owners who are nervous around horses."[23] He explained the irrelevance of libertarian theory in the twentieth century in this way:

> The corrective for the deterioration of a newspaper is provided in nine-teenth-century theory, by competition, which is governed equally by nature's abhorrence of a vacuum and Heaven will protect the working girl. Theoretically, a newspaper that does not give news, or is corrupt, or fails to stand up for the underdog, attracts the attention of a virtuous newspaper looking for a home, just as the tarantula, in the Caribbees, attracts the blue hornet. Good and bad paper will wrestle, to continue our insect parallel. Virtue will triumph, and the good paper will place its sting in the bad paper's belly and yell, "*Sic semper* New-house management!" or something of the sort. Then it will eat the advertising content of the bad paper's breadbasket.

This no longer occurs. Money is not made by competition among newspapers, but by avoiding it. The wars are over, and newspaper owners are content to buy their enemies off, or just to buy them. The object of diplomacy is to obtain an unassailable local position, like a robber-castle, in New Orleans or Elizabeth or Des Moines, and then levy tribute on the helpless peasantry, who will have no other means of discovering what is playing at the Nugget.[24]

It was not until the 1960s, however, that formal organs of media criticism, edited and written in large part by journalists, began publication. The oldest, the *Columbia Journalism Review* (*CJR*), published its first issue in October 1961 with a statement of policy that has been carried in every issue:

> . . . to assess the performance of journalism in all its forms, to call attention to its shortcomings and strengths, and to help define—or redefine—standards of honest, responsible service. . . .
> . . . to help stimulate continuing improvement in the profession and to speak out for what is right, fair, and decent.

CJR began regular, quarterly publication in 1962, underwritten by a $35,000 advance from the trustees of Columbia University. It has continued, switching to bimonthly publication in 1971, financed by subscription monies and contributions from private individuals and foundations such as the Ford Foundation and the John and Mary Markle Foundation. It was a matter of policy in the beginning not to accept advertising, but the review now regularly carries ads from such entities as Xerox, The Pharmaceutical Manufacturers Association, General Motors, and State Farm Insurance.

CJR has published articles defending ("The Agnew Analysis: False Premises, Wrong Conclusion") as well as attacking ("How I Tried to Write a Letter to the Times and Found Myself Cut to the Quick") the media and provides, on a continuing basis, some of the most valuable commentary on media performance available. Since the late 1960s a number of gutsy journalism reviews have sprung up—many started on shoestring budgets by journalists interested in reforming their hometown media. Marty Coren described in an article in *CJR* the genesis of one of the most widely appreciated reviews, the *Chicago Journalism Review:*

> [S]hortly after the tumultuous 1968 Democratic Convention, a group of angry Chicago journalists gathered at their favorite drinking place to complain about being turned into liars by their own newspapers' rewriting the history of convention week. As one complaint tumbled over another, someone suggested they do something—picket, meet with the editors, start a journalism review. Being reporters and writers, they picked the natural alternative and started the *Chicago Journalism Review*.[25]

The Chicago review died in 1975. *CJR* mourned the death, attributing it to "lack of funds and business know-how, and, perhaps, . . . flagging will." Many others such as the *Hawaii Journalism Review* have come and gone in the last few years. A few such as *MORE* carry on, although some do so in a constantly precarious financial position. And new ones such as *The Wash-ington Journalism Review* ("the only publication devoted exclusively to coverage of the Washington news scene," according to its direct mail promotion) are starting.

Although many of the journalism reviews were started because of reporters' and editors' dissatisfaction with management policy, there is evidence that the need for criticism and reform is recognized by others, too.

Some citizens' groups support magazines or newsletters which regularly criticize the mass media, for example, *access* and *Media Watch* put out by The National Citizens Committee for Broadcasting. The behavior and insti-tutions of the news media have often become in recent years as gripping a news story as any earthquake, political bribe, or other disaster. Although the media of mass distribution can serve up criticism as hard-edged as Jello, it is possible to find sharply-phrased, biting critiques such as those of the British journalist, Henry Fairlie, in *The New Republic* and witty and insightful analyses such as Michael Arlen's pieces on television in *The New Yorker.*

In 1973 Keith Sanders of the University of Missouri surveyed a sample of daily newspapers in the United States to determine what mechanism, if any, those papers were using to respond to public criticism. Sanders found only 23 percent of the papers he surveyed had no system of accountability. The rest used a variety of techniques from ombudsmen and press councils to standing heads for corrections and "How Are We Doing?" reader evalua-tion coupons.[26] Many editors seem to see such devices as a means not only to improve their papers' performance, but to educate the public about the stresses and strains, the day-to-day problems and procedures of getting out the news.

One of the most interesting approaches to accomplish these ends is the designation of an ombudsman or representative of the public on the news institution's staff. A. H. Raskin wrote in *The New York Times Magazine* in June of 1967, proposing

> that newspapers establish their own Department of Internal Criticism to check on the fairness and adequacy of their coverage and comment. The department head ought to be given enough independence in the paper to serve as an Ombudsman for the readers, armed with authority to get something done about valid complaints and to propose methods for more effective performance of all the paper's services to the community, particularly the patrol it keeps on the frontiers of thought and action.

The same year Barry Bingham, Sr., chairman of the board of the Courier-Journal & Louisville Times Co., and Norman Isaacs, then executive editor of the *Courier-Journal* and the Louisville *Times,* took up Raskin's challenge and designated John Herchenroeder, the assistant to the execu-tive editor, as ombudsman for the two papers. Herchenroeder was much respected in the news business and in the community. That respect is perhaps the key to his success as ombudsman. Isaacs wrote soon after Herchenroeder was appointed, "A newspaper has to be deeply earnest

Reader can select bridge column

QUESTION — It seems that about every third day, in the "Jacoby on Bridge" column, you print a bridge hand that does not match the story above it. Can't that be straightened out somehow? R.T., Bloomington.

ANSWER — The problem was traced to the syndicate which has been sending the Herald-Telephone and other subscribing newspapers a column and hand that do not match as a result of a mix-up in its printing department.

This problem, plus requests from other bridge column readers that the Herald-Telephone purchase a different bridge column, has prompted a search for other bridge columns available.

The readers are being given an opportunity to provide some input into which column is purchased. From the ones listed below rank them 1, 2 and 3 and send your rankings to Bridge Column, Herald-Telephone, P.O. Box 909, Bloomington, Ind. 47401. The column · that receives the most votes will be purchased.

The columns available are: B. Jay Becker, Goren on Bridge, Sheinwold on Bridge and The Aces.

Addresses column

QUESTION — I have thought for some time that you could perform a great service to your readers by publishing some kind of "Addresses" column in the paper. This would include the addresses for local, county, state and federal elected officials; addresses of various bureaucratic agencies at all levels; addresses for radio and television companies received here in Bloomington; and the like. I know that often I have the urge to write but get bogged down at the outset because I don't know the proper address or zip code. Gary Lane, Bloomington.

ANSWER — This is an excellent suggestion that will be implemented beginning next week on the editorial page. There are undoubtedly numerous other readers who share your problem of having easy access to the addresses of various people and organizations.

Back talk

Bill Schrader

Marriage licenses

QUESTION — I have noticed that those filing for marriage licenses in Monroe County have their names printed in the newspaper. Is there any way to avoid having this information made available to the public. G.H., Bloomington.

ANSWER — No.

There are certain public records which the newspaper has determined it should publish, including marriage licenses, court records, property transfers and certain arrest records.

As long as these records are going to be published we feel it is important that they be published in their entirety with no exceptions made.

Once exceptions are made it's impossible to arbitrarily draw the line where they will stop.

To avoid being trapped in this situation all records are published.

EDITOR'S NOTE: If you have a question about newspaper policy, about a story that has been printed or if you have a suggestion for something you would like see included in the newspaper send it to BACK TALK, Herald-Telephone, P.O. Box 909, Bloomington, Ind. 47401.

The Bloomington, Indiana, Herald-Telephone, a paper with a daily circulation of almost 25,000, periodically runs a "Back talk" column in which its editor explains the paper's procedures and responds to reader complaints and suggestions. If the column is any measure, reader suggestions are taken seriously. (Reprinted with permission from the Herald-Telephone, Bloomington, Indiana, July 29, 1977) about the whole thing—and to give the assignment to someone good enough and important enough to make it work."

A major responsibility of the ombudsman in Louisville is dealing with reader complaints about the performance of the papers and suggestions for their improvement. The papers encourage readers to make their concerns known to Herchenroeder, and the papers print corrections of errors as well as descriptions of how some complaints are handled and how the newspapers operate.

The ombudsman job varies from paper to paper. Ben Bagdikian, who early urged newspapers to employ ombudsmen, served a year (1971–1972) as ombudsman for the Washington *Post,* moving from the position of assistant managing editor for national affairs. Bagdikian credits the *Post* with "being the first paper to put a man to work not just to correct errors but to comment publicly and critically on his own paper in his own paper."[27] The responsibilities of the current *Post* ombudsman, Charles Seib, include responding to reader complaints, criticizing the *Post*'s performance through internal memoranda and direct discussion with reporters and editors, and writing a weekly column, "The News Business," which is published in the *Post* and syndicated through the Washington Post Writers Group. The *Post* is not the only news institution under scrutiny in his column. Seib takes on a wide range of topics and media. In Louisville, the responsibility for publicly critiquing the news media falls not to Herchenroeder, but to Bob Schulman, the Louisville *Times*'s media critic.[28]

Not many newspapers can afford or think it worth the price to employ an ombudsman. Sanders found only nine percent of the papers he studied did so. There are many news institutions around the country that consider it no better than foolishness to *pay* someone to criticize them when they already feel victimized by all the criticism so *freely* available.

Broadcasters seem perhaps even more leery of the ombudsman system. In 1975 Accuracy in Media, Inc., (AIM), a citizens' group of conservative leanings and owner of four shares of RCA common stock, proposed at the annual stockholders meeting:

> RESOLVED: that the shareholders ask the Board of Directors of RCA Corporation to take serious note of their wish that NBC be required to employ an ombudsman, or in-house critic, who will be responsible for reviewing NBC's performance in public affairs programming with a view to insuring fairness and balance as well as strict accuracy in the presentation of news and public affairs documentaries.
>
> Under AIM's proposal, the ombudsman would:
> (a) be responsible for receiving and investigating complaints from the public about unfair or inaccurate programs;
> (b) be allotted time on radio and television to report to the NBC audience about action taken on such complaints;
> (c) have direct access to top management of RCA as well as NBC;
> (d) be given responsibility for devising a workable code of ethics for NBC

News, similar to the code adopted and recommended by the Society for Professional Journalists, and

(e) report to the shareholders on his or her activities annually.

The motion was defeated in 1975, and in 1976, and in 1977.

The proposal was not likely to appeal to broadcast corporation management for a number of reasons, not least of which would be the nightmare for any closely regulated industry that the ombudsman would take the "other" side in a legal battle. In addition, regardless of the merits of the proposal, RCA and NBC were unlikely to be positive about the request because of the source. AIM had fought a long legal battle with NBC over whether or not a network documentary on pensions met the requirements of the Federal Communications Commission's Fairness Doctrine. Although NBC won the case, the experience was not likely to generate enthusiasm in RCA corporate offices for AIM.

Media Councils

Some media institutions also consider it no better than foolishness to cooperate with another agency of media criticism that has been organized in recent years—the media council. Mass media councils have been established in the United States, as they have in Europe, to help the media interpret and fulfill their social responsibilities. As the 1970s began, about a dozen local councils were operating in cities across the United States. Although some served only newspapers, a few were concerned with all the local media. All the councils had a similar function: to meet periodically— usually monthly or quarterly—to assess the performance of the media and to advise responsible representatives of local newspapers and broadcasting stations how council members thought the media could improve performance. Often the meetings were more educational for the council members than for the media; some citizens began to learn for the first time what the mass media are and what they are designed to do in a democratic society.

European nations have used media councils for decades. Sweden formed the Press Fair Practices Commission in 1916 to serve as an intermediary between press and public. About 15 other European nations have since set up councils or courts of honor, with the British Press Council probably the most famous and successful. In most of Europe, the council is considered as a protector of freedom of the press and as a channel for dialogue between the newspaper and its readers. J. Edward Gerald of the University of Minnesota has characterized the effective overseas press council:

1. It is a private body designed to ward off government pressures upon the press.

2. It operates as a buffer between the press and the public and between the press and the government.
3. Its membership is composed of balanced representation of the community and the media.
4. It has no statutory power and relies on public support after reporting its deliberations and decisions.
5. It appears to function best in nations where newspapermen avoid all forms of extremism.[29]

In the United States the first suggestion for press council operations seems to have originated in the 1930s with Chilton R. Bush, then head of the Department of Communication at Stanford. He conceived the notion that a newspaper could strengthen itself and its community by establishing a council of citizens who would offer criticisms and suggestions. He developed the idea and promoted it among publishers.

In 1950 William Townes, then publisher of the Santa Rosa, California, *Press Democrat,* decided to try it. Townes chose the members of his "Citizens' Advisory Council" to represent community interests, such as labor, agriculture, education, city government, business, and to include a few outspoken critics of his policies. After telling the council members at the first meeting that he alone would decide publishing policies, Townes emphasized that he would welcome criticisms and suggestions. After a hesitant period at the beginning of the first meeting, the members engaged in lively discussions. Townes spent most of his time listening. It was not even necessary for him to defend his paper against its harshest critic, a judge who had been asked to serve on the council because he was known to oppose the paper, for the other council members were quick to challenge unfounded criticisms. Until Townes left Santa Rosa, he kept the council in operation and said it had helped him to improve his paper. *Editor & Publisher,* the trade weekly of the newspaper business, commented in 1951:

> . . . On the practical side, this particular newspaper reports that Council meetings revealed several important stories that had not been covered. And Council members felt free to visit the newspaper offices thereafter, something many of them might not have thought about previously.
>
> This is an experiment in getting closer to the community which strikes us as valuable. The good points out-weigh the bad, and if conducted properly and regularly can only result to the benefit of the paper.[30]

Nonetheless the press council idea languished in the United States until 1967. It was then that Ben Bagdikian became president of the Mellett Fund, one of the smallest foundations. The Fund was established with a bequest from Lowell Mellett, who had been editor of the Washington *Daily News,* an adviser to President Franklin Roosevelt during World War II, and a syndicated columnist. Part of his estate went to the American Newspaper Guild, and he directed that the money be used to encourage more responsible performance by the press without infringing First Amendment freedoms. He specifically mentioned the hope that his bequest could be used to establish "a relationship between the people and the press whereby full responsibility for its behavior would be met by the press."

These words led Bagdikian to suggest to the Mellett Fund Board that the $40,000 it had in 1967 be used to support university researchers who would establish local councils. A series of small grants led to council experiments in small cities in Oregon, California, and Illinois, and to the setting up of media councils in Seattle and St. Louis. These, in turn, stimulated other councils that were not the direct result of Mellett Fund grants. Some of those who participated in the Mellett Fund councils became enthusiastic proponents of the idea and helped to encourage the establishment of councils in other cities. Robert W. Chandler, editor of the Bend, Oregon, *Bulletin,* the first editor to agree to participate in the Mellett Fund program, was instrumental in convincing newspapers in Hawaii to set up a council. It began operating in 1970. Later, Minnesota newspapers set up a statewide council.

THE NATIONAL NEWS COUNCIL

One of the recommendations of the 1947 Hutchins Commission was the establishment of an agency independent of the government and the press to compare "the accomplishments of the press with the aspirations . . . the people have for it" and to "educate the people as to the aspirations which they ought to have for the press."[31] The local and state media councils are such agencies. However, it was not until 1973 that a national council was established, a council that could review the performance of the national media—the major suppliers of information of international and national affairs.

In 1972 a task force funded by the Twentieth Century Fund, a private research foundation, reported that the credibility and the freedom of the mass media of information were under challenge and that it was essential "[t]hat an independent and private national news council be established to receive, to examine, and to report on complaints concerning the accuracy and fairness of news reporting in the United States, as well as to initiate studies and report on issues involving the freedom of the press."[32]

The task force recommended that the council's attention be limited to the national news suppliers (nationwide wire services, the major "supplemental" wire services, the national weekly news magazines, national newspaper syndicates, national daily newspapers, the national broadcast networks) and that it have no other enforcement power than the power of publicity. The effectiveness of the council would necessarily depend on the cooperation of the national media. Without such cooperation the council would be deprived of the information it would need from targets of criticism to evaluate public complaints and it would be deprived of its major source of influence, widespread reporting of its decisions.

Nine of the 14 members of the task force were from the media, and eight of the 18 members now sitting on the National News Council are from the media. Perhaps partly because of this participation of newspaper and broadcast representatives, the council enjoys what William B. Arthur, the council's executive director, called after its first year of operation, "a heartening amount of cooperation from the media." The disheartening exception, according to Arthur, is the New York *Times,* which has written that the council "could actually harm the cause of press freedom in the United States." Arthur, a former managing editor of *Look* magazine, disputes the *Times'* warning and cites references in a major Supreme Court decision in 1974 that demonstrate, in Arthur's words, "in the eyes of the Supreme Court, at least, the Council is one of the stones in the wall protecting the media's First Amendment rights against government encroachment, and not, as our critics never tire of suggesting, a Trojan horse that somehow has slipped inside the wall."[33] And an evaluation committee set up by the 10 foundations funding the council issued a report in 1976 that recommended the council be continued and expanded because it "provides a public sounding board," because it deflates "unfair criticism of the press," and because "the mere existence of a nongovernmental National News Council can help blunt any drive to restrict press freedom."

In response to recommendations from the evaluation committee, in 1976 the council voted to expand its membership from 15 to 18 and to expand its attention to include examination of "news reporting in all media, whether national or local in initial circulation, if the matter is of national significance as news or for journalism."

COMPLAINTS TO THE COUNCIL

In its first four years the National News Council has dealt with such varied complaints as:

1. Charges by Accuracy in Media, Inc. (AIM) that CBS News by omitting a particular quote had in a program entitled "Castro, Cuba, and the U.S.A." given "viewers the erroneous impression that 'Castro has abandoned his support of violent subversive activity in other countries.'" AIM called this "censorship by omission."

   The council found CBS *had* portrayed "Castro as a revolutionary leader who supports the cause of revolution in Latin America" and the choice of which particular quotes would be used was a matter for CBS's editorial judgment. (Complaint No. 64)
2. Charges by the Consul of Monaco that the *National Star,* a national weekly newspaper, had in two articles published in June 1975 "concocted the thoroughly false impression [that Prince Rainier and Princess Grace of Monaco] . . . are living separate lives." Princess Grace and her brother both wrote letters to the *Star* denying the story.

   The *Star* did not cooperate in providing information as the council would have liked. Based on the information it did have, the council found that the *Star* had abused its privilege of independent exercise of editorial judgment by relying on anonymous sources to convey the impression that the royal couple had "split up." The council also disapproved of the *Star*'s failure to report from sources such as the Princess and her brother, who were willing to be named, after the *Star* had stated it was willing to publish a statement from the Monacan Consul or the Prince and Princess. (Complaint No. 65)

3. Charges by Dr. Stephen Barrett, chairman of the Lehigh Valley (Pennsylvania) Committee Against Health Fraud, Inc., "that a column by James J. Kilpatrick of the Washington Star Syndicate, Inc., contained factual errors regarding Laetrile, an alleged cancer cure which has been banned by the Food and Drug Administration." Dr. Barrett charged that Kilpatrick had implied Laetrile was a "harmless nutrient," when, according to Dr. Barrett, it was harmful because it "may break down into toxic cyanides" and "because it held out false promises of cure to cancer victims."

The National News Council acknowledged it was "obviously . . . not in the position to make medical judgments." But the council found that "from a journalistic perspective, Mr. Kilpatrick was clearly within the bounds of editorial discretion by implying that Laetrile was harmless. As an editorial columnist, Mr. Kilpatrick was expressing his *personal* viewpoint on a controversial public issue." The council noted that Kilpatrick had acknowledged some of the harmful aspects of Laetrile and focused on whether it was appropriate for the government to interfere with "the right of a free citizen to fritter away his money—and his life—if he wants to." In addition, because Kilpatrick had written a second column, one about Dr. Barrett's complaint to the council, Kilpatrick had agreed to distribute a reply from Barrett to the syndicate subscribers who had received the Kilpatrick column. Kilpatrick's voluntary action is consistent with the general recommendation of the National Conference of Editorial Writers, that encourages columnists to aid in the distribution of replies to columns which criticize specific groups or individuals. (Complaint No. 85)

The National News Council has not always waited for complaints to be filed to make its opinion known. It has addressed such issues as the CIA's employment of journalists and the UNESCO proposal to give governments control over news media. In March 1977 the council released a statement on media coverage of terrorism, in which it rejected "as unthinkable any notion that such activities should not be reported because they are perceived as 'contagious.'" The council did, however, urge the media to exercise or at least consider some self-restraint on the questions of live coverage (because it "precludes full context or judicious editing") and the practice of telephoning for interviews with terrorists or hostages during the event. The council offered to become a repository for guidelines and policies on terrorism coverage developed by news institutions that could be circulated among other news organizations.[34]

How to complain to The National News Council

The National News Council has two committees—the Grievance Committee, which takes complaints from anyone, individual or organization, concerning inaccuracy or unfairness in a news report, and the Freedom of the Press Committee, which takes complaints from news organizations concerning the restriction of access to information of public interest, the preservation of freedom of communication, and the advancement of accurate and fair reporting.

The procedure to follow in filing a grievance is simple:

Write to the news organization and send a copy of your letter of complaint to the Council.

If you are not sure to whom to address your complaint at a news organization, send it directly to the Council. A copy will be forwarded to the appropriate news executive.

If your complaint concerns a printed news report, include a copy of the report, the name of the publication, and the date.

If your complaint concerns a radio or television news report, include the name of the station, the name of the network, the date and the time of airing.

Be sure to include as specific information as possible as to why you are complaining.

Complaints to either committee should be addressed to:

> The National News Council
> One Lincoln Plaza
> New York, N.Y. 10023

The National News Council is dependent on the good will of the media for publicity for its decisions, activities, and procedures. AP and UPI have covered every Council meeting. The *CJR* regularly runs this Council notice and the Louisville *Courier-Journal* and *Times* daily invite readers with complaints to contact their ombudsman and, if still dissatisfied, the National News Council.

Also in March 1977 the council released a statement in which it noted "with deep concern the growing problem arising out of the . . . emergence on television of . . . 'docudramas.'" The council worried that such dramas, seeming to be based on fact but written as entertainment, could be confused with historical truth because they were aired by "the same broadcast organizations that also present news and documentaries."[35] The council's challenge to the broadcasters "to assure a proper regard for factual and historical accuracy" would certainly cramp the style of television's Shakespeares, and it highlighted the special problems of media which provide both news and entertainment. Certainly a rash of such docudramas— "Ruby and Oswald" and "The Trial of Lee Harvey Oswald," keying off the events surrounding the Kennedy assassination; "Washington: Behind Closed Doors," based on the novel, *The Company,* by Nixon aide John Ehrlichman (such fiction is mined by readers and viewers for hints of the inside story of the Nixon Administration); a five-hour film on civil-rights leader Martin Luther King, Jr., to name just a few—programed for the

1977–1978 television season gave the council's concern an immediate relevance.

The National News Council has weathered the initial hostility of the news industry. (Its executive director was quoted in late 1976 as saying, "Things are looking up. . . . I haven't seen an editorial attacking us in months.") The council has sought to broaden its activities by engaging in research on restrictions on the media, and its chairman, Norman Isaacs, · expressed optimism that because of the participation of non-journalists on the council, it could speak effectively in defense of press freedom. There are still those who doubt the value of the council. Despite some attention from professional organizations and a decision by *Columbia Journalism Review* to run reports from the council regularly, the council continues to suffer from a problem that, for an institution relying on publicity for impact, is worse than criticism—low visibility.

Rights and Responsibilities

The idea that the media have a responsibility to the public is now widely, if not universally, accepted by practitioners as well as theorists. Many news institutions and organizations have adopted codes of ethics in recent years— from the Milwaukee *Journal* to the Associated Press Sports Editors, from the Newspaper Food Editors and Writers Association to The Society of Professional Journalists (Sigma Delta Chi).

The Code of Ethics adopted by The Society of Professional Journalists in 1973 includes these words: "We believe in public enlightenment as the forerunner of justice, and in our Constitutional role to seek the truth as part of the public's right to know the truth." And it closes with this pledge:

> Journalists should actively censure and try to prevent violations of these standards, and they should encourage their observance by all newspeople. Adherence to this code of ethics is intended to preserve the bond of mutual trust and respect between American journalists and the American people.

In the 1975 revision of the ASNE Canons of Journalism (discussed on pages 176–177) ASNE reinforces the alliance of the press with the public: "The purpose of gathering and distributing news and opinion is to serve the welfare of the people." At the same time it states explicitly and more forcefully its adversary relationship with government: "The American press was made free not just to inform or just to serve as a forum for debate but also to bring an independent scrutiny to bear on the forces of power in the society, including the conduct of official power at all levels of government." The 1923 provision conceding to government the definition of what is outside the realm of legal discussion was replaced with this:

> Freedom of the press is a vital right of all the people. It must be defended against infringement or assault, from any source, public and private. Journalists must be constantly alert to see that the public's business is conducted in public, and must

oppose those who would use the press as a servant of government or any special interest.

In 1976 at the first conference of IRE (Investigative Reporters and Editors), even those who voiced their opposition to a code of ethics for investigative reporters spoke of their responsibility to the public interest. And although the public is often referred to in noble terms, there seems to be a firmly established view among many reporters and editors that what the public wants or attends to is often *not* what it *needs* to know, that what we don't know and aren't interested in *can* hurt us. Such reporters and editors are torn between the economic pressure to cater to public taste and their sense of responsibility to the public interest.

What splits those who recognize that the media have responsibilities is disagreement over the nature of those responsibilities, over who should define those responsibilities, and over who should enforce those responsibilities. It seems evident in the 1970s that the media have lost any exclusive right they might have once felt they had to define and enforce responsibilities for themselves. In this "age of the consumer" there are some members of the public who hold very strong (though not uniform) views on media responsibilities, and they are gaining the sophistication to work the economic and legal systems to their advantage. The government's struggle to control the media may be quiescent at times, but the desire to control the systems of information and social education is an unavoidable characteristic of even the most enlightened government. We turn in the next chapter to the regulation of the media through the legal system.

Notes

1. John Trenchard and Thomas Gordon, *Cato's Letters: Or, Essays on Liberty, Civil and Religious,* No. 32, in Leonard Levy (ed.), *Freedom of the Press from Zenger to Jefferson* (Indianapolis: Bobbs-Merrill, Inc., 1966), p. 15.
2. George Watson, *The English Ideology: Studies in the Language of Victorian Politics* (London: Allen Lane, 1973), pp. 59–60.
3. William Livingston, "Of the Use, Abuse, and LIBERTY OF THE PRESS," in Levy, pp. 81–82.
4. Joseph Pulitzer, "The College of Journalism," *North American Review,* 178, May 1904, p. 659.
5. Pulitzer, p. 667.
6. Henry R. Luce, "Critique of a Commission," in John K. Jessup (ed.), *The Ideas of Henry Luce* (New York: Atheneum, 1969), p. 64.
7. The Commission on Freedom of the Press, *A Free and Responsible Press* (Chicago: University of Chicago Press, 1958), pp. 10–11.
8. Walter Lippmann, *Public Opinion* (New York: Free Press, 1965), pp. 226–227.
9. Hillier Krieghbaum, "The 'Op-Ed' Page Revisited," *Saturday Review,* November 13, 1971, p. 92.
10. David Shaw, "Newspapers Offer Forum to Outsiders," Los Angeles *Times,* October 13, 1975.
11. Benjamin Franklin, "An Apology for Printers," in Levy, p. 5.
12. Livingston, in Levy, p. 81.

13. Ben Bagdikian, "Editorial Responsibility in Times of Urban Disorder," in Charles U. Daly (ed.), *The Media and the Cities* (Chicago: University of Chicago Press, 1968), p. 15.

14. Figures supplied by office of Benjamin Hooks, Federal Communications Commission, Washington, D.C., August 1975, reported in Milan D. Meeske, "Black Ownership of Broadcast Stations: An FCC Licensing Problem," *Journal of Broadcasting,* 20, Spring 1976, p. 261.

15. Dorothy Jurney found women made up only 2.7 percent of the "Directing Editors" (the term the American Society of Newspaper Editors uses in its membership criteria) of newspapers with daily circulations of 40,000 or more. *Media Report to Women,* May 1, 1977, p. 5.

   In 1977 Weaver *et al.* found only 60 women (about 2.4%) in a sample of 2,465 top-level managers from 433 U.S. daily newspapers. David H. Weaver, Christine L. Ogan, Charlene J. Brown, and Mary I. Benedict, "Women in Newspaper Management: Where Are They, Who Are They, How Did They Get There, and How Well Are They Doing?," preliminary report of the Conference on Women in Newspaper Management, Indiana University School of Journalism, May 1977.

   Another 1977 study found, however, that women made up 32.4 percent of the editors in a sample of weekly newspapers. Susan Holly, Master's Thesis, School of Journalism, Indiana University, 1978.

16. Equal Employment Opportunity Commission, *Equal Employment Opportunity Report—1975: Job Patterns for Minorities and Women in Private Industry,* Vol. 1 (Washington, D.C.: U.S. Government Printing Office, 1977), p. 32. The commission notes that the statistics are limited to private employers subject to Title VII and having 100 or more employees, with some exceptions, and federal contractors having 50 or more employees and contracts of at least $50,000. In this report the commission excluded Hawaii from its summary analysis because of the state's ethnic diversity.

17. For example, see Bernard E. Garnett, *How Soulful is "Soul" Radio?* (Nashville: Race Relations Information Center, 1970) or Stuart H. Surlin, "Black-Oriented Radio: Programming to a Perceived Audience," *Journal of Broadcasting,* 16, Summer 1972, pp. 289–298.

18. The Commission on Freedom of the Press, pp. 91–92.

19. William E. Hocking, *Freedom of the Press: A Framework of Principle* (Chicago: University of Chicago Press, 1947), p. 199.

20. The Commission on Freedom of the Press, p. 83.

21. Thomas Jefferson, letter to Walter Jones, January 2, 1814, in Levy, p. 383.

22. George Seldes, *Lords of the Press* (New York: Julian Messner, Inc., 1945), p. 4.

23. A. J. Liebling, *The Press* (New York: Ballantine Books, 1964), p. 6.

24. Liebling, p. 6.

25. Marty Coren, "The Perils of Publishing Journalism Reviews," *Columbia Journalism Review,* November/December 1972, p. 25.

26. Keith P. Sanders, "What Are Daily Newspapers Doing to Be Responsive to Readers' Criticisms?: A Survey of U.S. Daily Newspaper Accountability Systems," *News Research Bulletin* of the American Newspaper Publishers Association, 9, November 30, 1973.

27. Ben Bagdikian, "The Saga of a Newspaper Ombudsman," in Michael C. Emery and Ted Curtis Smythe (eds.), *Readings in Mass Communication: Concepts and Issues in the Mass Media* (Dubuque, Iowa: Wm. C. Brown Company, 1974), p. 74.

28. See Timothy Leland, "In-house Press Critics: A Selection of Recent Work by

Newspaper Ombudsmen," *Columbia Journalism Review,* July/August 1977, pp. 48–53, for just such a selection.

29. J. Edward Gerald, "What the Association for Education in Journalism Can Do with the Press Council Idea," paper presented to the Association for Education in Journalism, Boulder, Colorado, August 29, 1967, pp. 1–3.

30. "Advisory Council," *Editor & Publisher,* July 28, 1951, p. 36.

31. The Commission on Freedom of the Press, pp. 100–101.

32. Twentieth Century Fund Task Force, *A Free and Responsive Press: The Twentieth Century Fund Task Force Report for a NATIONAL NEWS COUNCIL; Background Paper by Alfred Balk* (New York: The Twentieth Century Fund, 1973), p. 3.

33. William B. Arthur, "The National News Council," *Mass Comm Review,* 2, December 1974, pp. 5–6.

34. "National News Council Report," *Columbia Journalism Review,* May/June 1977, p. 81.

35. "National News Council Report," *Columbia Journalism Review,* May/June 1977, p. 85.

8

The Government, the Public, and the Regulation of the Mass Media

What is the liberty of the press? Who can give it any definition which would not leave the utmost latitude for evasion? . . . [W]hatever fine declaration may be inserted in any constitution respecting it, must altogether depend on public opinion, and on the general spirit of the people and of the government.

ALEXANDER HAMILTON

Freedom of expression is not our only liberty. It is, to my mind, our most important liberty, the basis of all others. But it is part of an entire structure. It is entitled to no imperium; it must democratically live with other guarantees and rights.

CHARLES REMBAR

So long as members of this Court view the First Amendment as no more than a set of "values" to be balanced against other "values," that Amendment will remain in grave jeopardy.

SUPREME COURT JUSTICE POTTER STEWART

The Government,
the Public, and the
Regulation of the
Mass Media

210

The most striking element on page 1 of the Sunday, June 13, 1971, issue of the New York *Times* was a picture-book photograph of President Richard Nixon and his daughter Tricia at her White House wedding the day before. To the right of the photo was the low-key headline:

Vietnam Archive: Pentagon Study Traces
3 Decades of Growing U.S. Involvement

The front-page story by Neil Sheehan was part of six pages in that issue devoted to the Pentagon Papers, a Department of Defense study of United States policy making toward Vietnam under four American Presidents. It was an important story even for a paper so accustomed to important stories. By the end of 1971 most of the documents would be available to the public from the U.S. Government Printing Office, but in June the New York *Times* was confronting the government with a massive security leak that the *Times* was sure would provoke legal action against the newspaper.

For almost three months the *Times* had worked on the Pentagon Papers study in secrecy, using security precautions that rivaled those of the Pentagon itself.[1] In late March Sheehan, a *Times* Washington reporter, had obtained copies of roughly 7000 pages of documents from a foreign policy specialist named Daniel Ellsberg, who had made the copies while working at the Rand Corporation. A firsthand look at the war in Vietnam had started Ellsberg's slow transformation from a supporter of American involvement there to a man bitterly opposed to it—a transformation that was accelerated by his first reading of the Pentagon Papers while on the Rand Corporation staff. The *Times* closeted Sheehan and Gerald Gold, an assistant foreign editor, first in a Washington hotel to assess the significance of the material and to determine how much of it had already been published, and later in the New York Hilton with other *Times* personnel to prepare the material for publication. They were told *not* to show up at the *Times* offices. No one at the paper who didn't absolutely have to know what was going on was told anything about their activity.

In May a secret composing room was set up in a vacant office on the ninth floor of the *Times'* own building. On the Saturday afternoon before publication just 10 copies of the page 1 layout were made for the makeup editors and news desks that really needed them. During the months of preparation the *Times* had kept its secret.

But why the concern for secrecy? The *Times* knew that although it was common practice for government officials, including some Presidents, to leak classified information and just as common for the news media to publish classified information, the paper was risking government retaliation either in the form of criminal prosecution or an injunction to halt publication. The Pentagon study was basically historical—there was nothing more recent than 1968, Ellsberg had withheld the most sensitive diplomatic material, and the *Times* itself had deleted anything that might give a foreign

The Goverment
the Public, and the
Regulation of the
Mass Media

211

The government's effort to suppress the Pentagon Papers became a bigger issue than what the Papers revealed. (United Press International photo)

power information about such things as cryptographic codes or troop deployment. But the very volume of material involved raised questions about the ability of the United States to keep its secrets secret, and the substance of the study would at least raise questions about the integrity and intelligence of recent American officials.

To lessen the chance of successful criminal prosecution and no less to preserve its credibility and to meet its own standards of responsibility to the public, the *Times* exercised great care and restraint in its organization and selection of material from the 7000 pages in its possession. The *Times* considered publishing all the articles it had planned for 10 days in a one-day special supplement, so giving the government no opportunity to bring an injunction. For the *Times* editors and reporters, however, the legal arguments were less convincing than the journalistic ones. (Who, even among *Times* readers, would wade through 60 pages on Vietnam?) The *Times* opted for its 10-day series and the more substantial impact and sustained interest a series would deliver.

Journalistic competitiveness also contributed to the *Times*'s efforts to preserve absolute secrecy before publication. The *Times* knew that Senator William Fulbright and the Institute for Policy Studies each had a copy of the study, and, according to Sanford Ungar's account in *The Papers & the Papers,* there was concern that the *Times* would be scooped by either Fulbright or the Institute or that a copy of the study would fall into another paper's hands. Ungar records Max Frankel, the *Times* Washington bureau chief, saying, "We were just tormented by the notion that somebody else would dribble this stuff."[2]

Frankel and the others who had worked on the story waited expectantly

The Government,
the Public, and the
Regulation of the
Mass Media

212

on Sunday for reactions from the government and from other news media. Almost nothing happened. A few papers, including the Washington *Post,* began rewriting the *Times* material for their own publications, but it was not until afternoon that UPI put a story on the wire. AP, the nation's largest news supplier, sent nothing until *Monday* afternoon. Defense Secretary Melvin Laird, that Sunday's guest on CBS's "Face the Nation," had consulted with Attorney General John Mitchell in anticipation of questions on the *Times* material. None were asked. Nor were any asked on ABC's "Issues and Answers" of Senator Húbert Humphrey, who had been Vice President during part of the period covered by the study. Of the networks only NBC carried a story on the Sunday night news.

A number of reasons have been suggested for the reluctance and slowness of so many news institutions to run the Pentagon Papers story. First, the *Times* had downplayed the story in order to avoid charges of sensationalism, and the significance of the material may not have been readily apparent to many. Second, some journalists—including some at the *Times*—strongly opposed the publication of material they thought should indeed be under the control of the government. Third, the Nixon Administration had acted and spoken aggressively against the media, and it is possible that many journalists were afraid to take on the government.

The government's silence, however, was particularly puzzling. The *Times* ran a second installment Monday morning and readied the third. Then at 7:30 Monday evening Robert Mardian, chief of the Internal Security Division of the Department of Justice, phoned the *Times* with the text of a telegram from the Attorney General. The *Times* was asked to cease publication and return the documents. Not without some internal argument, the *Times* refused. On Tuesday morning the government sought an injunction from a federal district court. To preserve the issues for judicial decision a temporary injunction was granted.

The issues were not easy to decide. The First Amendment freedom of the press was pitted against the government's constitutional responsibility and power to preserve the nation's security. The press said that the public had a right to know what its government had been doing in Vietnam. The government said that to tell the public would inflict serious injuries, indeed, irreparable harm on the national interest—in part, because to tell the public would be to tell the world. The First Amendment has suffered from a variety of interpretations, but a presumption common to virtually all of them was that freedom of the press means *at least* freedom from government censorship prior to publication. The issue of prior restraint had been considered by the Supreme Court a very few times before. Although the court had refrained from flatly declaring that prior restraint would necessarily violate the Constitution, in the cases dealing with the print media the press had won. Now the New York *Times* found itself enjoined for what appeared to some to be an effort by the government to reduce the embarrassment of having to explain how more than 40 volumes of top-secret documents could walk out the door. Such embarrassments make other nations hesitate to trust America's ability to negotiate in secret.

A combination of the *Post*'s determination to be in on the story (in part
to overcome its own embarrassment at being left with no more than the job
of rewriting *Times* material, but also to join the battle for press freedom*) and
Ellsberg's determination to get the papers published led to the *Post*'s first
original story and the inevitable injunction—both on Friday. Although other
papers also published original stories based on the Pentagon study and two
were also enjoined, it was the *Times* and the *Post* cases that were eventually
joined into one before the U.S. Supreme Court. The seriousness of the
restraint on press freedom was mirrored in the haste of the court's deliberations. The court accepted the case on Friday, June 25, heard the legal
arguments on Saturday, June 26, and handed down its decision on
Wednesday, June 30. As the dissenters in the 6–3 decision wrote, the issues
deserved more reflection and consideration than could possibly be mus-
tered in six days. In addition to a brief *per curiam* (by the court) order, nine
separate opinions (the maximum possible) were filed. All that the majority of
six had time to agree on was this:

> "Any system of prior restraints of expression comes to this Court bearing a
> heavy presumption against its constitutional validity." . . . The Government
> "thus carries a heavy burden of showing justification for the enforcement of such
> a restraint." . . . The District Court for the Southern District of New York in the
> *New York Times* case and the District Court for the District of Columbia and the
> Court of Appeals for the District of Columbia Circuit in the *Washington Post* case
> held that the Government had not met that burden. We agree.[3]

The *Times* and the *Post* had won, but the court did not say what many
(although not the court) had asserted from the time the First Amendment
was written—that prior restraint was by definition unconstitutional. The
court did say there was a presumption that prior restraint was unconstitutional. A heavy burden of proof was put squarely on the government. *But
the presumption of unconstitutionality could be overcome if the government
could demonstrate an overwhelming need for suppression.* That the government had failed to convince the court this time did not mean that it could
never succeed. And some members of the court came close to inviting the
government to initiate criminal action against the papers. Even in victory the
press was reminded of its vulnerability.

First Principles and Inevitable Dilemmas

The late Supreme Court Justice Hugo Black repeated often his view that
when the Founding Fathers wrote in the First Amendment "Congress shall

---

*The *Times* had expected that some government action would result from its publication of
material from the Pentagon study. But by the time the *Post* got the documents, it *knew* that it
would face at least an injunction. It also recognized that there was a chance that publication
after the *Times* had already been enjoined could be interpreted as disrespect for the judiciary. If
the government later chose to bring a criminal action, the *Post*'s lucrative broadcast licenses
would be jeopardized. The FCC is not likely to consider criminals to have the requisite good
character to hold a broadcast license.

The Government,
the Public, and the
Regulation of the
Mass Media

214

make no law . . . abridging the freedom . . . of the press," they meant to bar all government restrictions on the press. Black's view has appealed to many journalists but few judges. Black would focus on the phrase "no law" and, indeed, there seems no ambiguity in those words. Yet, Justice Black recounted in his Pentagon Papers case opinion, the Solicitor General could make this statement to him in all seriousness:

> "Now, Mr. Justice, your construction of . . . [the First Amendment] is well known, and I certainly respect it. You say that no law means no law, and that should be obvious. I can only say, Mr. Justice, that to me it is equally obvious that 'no law' does not mean 'no law,' and I would seek to persuade the Court that that is true."[4]

There also seems to be no ambiguity in the word "Congress," yet the courts have long held that the freedoms cited in the First Amendment are not protected just against abridgment by Congress but against abridgment by all branches of government. Black accepted *that* disregard of precise writing without hesitation. In absolutes there can be no ambiguity and yet there are ambiguous words in the seemingly simple admonition protecting press freedom. The First Amendment says: "Congress shall make no law . . . abridging *the* freedom of the press. . . ." [Emphasis added.] Does the article "the" denote a defined concept of freedom of the press? Was there a consensus in 1791 that could be designated as "*the* freedom of the press"? Whatever the first Congress meant is not clear and it is certainly not irrelevant, but of more practical significance to the mass media is what contemporary jurists responsible for interpreting those words have said they mean.

In our governmental system the federal Constitution, including its amendments, stands as the supreme authority on the distribution of powers and responsibilities and the protection of fundamental rights in this country. The U.S. Supreme Court is the ultimate arbiter of what that Constitution means. There have been justices on the court who, like Black, have given a preferred status to First Amendment freedoms as the foundation of all other freedoms, but there has never been a majority on the court to hold that press freedom is absolute. Press freedom has its limits. This society, as all others, will not tolerate a totally free press.

THE PROTECTION OF THE LAW

In a speech in New York City during World War II (1944), Judge Learned Hand said:

> I often wonder whether we do not rest our hopes too much upon constitutions, upon laws and upon courts. These are false hopes; believe me, these are false hopes. Liberty lies in the hearts of men and women; when it dies there, no constitution, no law, no court can save it; no constitution, no law, no court can even do much to help it. While it lies there it needs no constitution, no law, no court to save it. . . .

There is merit in what Hand said, but less than might appear on first reading. Although freedom of the press is not secure even with the protection of laws, courts, and constitutions, there would be *no* freedom of press without them. Most basically, a society must have some way other than force of resolving conflict. The press benefits without doubt from the security of the general laws.

In addition, the First Amendment protects the press not only against government but against the public as well. In a representative democracy the government—at least in theory—is an expression of the public will. It is times when public passions are aroused, when the majority is least tolerant, that the First Amendment serves as a brake on legislative responsiveness to the public's desire for repression. It reminds us again of the value of a free press. Thomas I. Emerson, a First Amendment scholar, describes its educational benefits:

> [T]he theory of freedom of expression is a sophisticated and even complex one. It does not come naturally to the ordinary citizen, but needs to be learned. It must be restated and reiterated not only for each generation but for each new situation. It leans heavily upon understanding and education, both for the individual and the community as a whole. The legal process is one of the most effective methods for providing the kind of social comprehension essential for the attainment of society's higher and more remote ideals.[5]

Emerson has also summarized the values and functions of a system of freedom of expression:

> First, freedom of expression is essential as a means of assuring individual self-fulfillment. The proper end of man is the realization of his character and potentialities as a human being. . . . To cut off his search for truth, or his expression of it, is to elevate society and the state to a despotic command over him and to place him under the arbitrary control of others.
>
> Second, freedom of expression is an essential process for advancing knowledge and discovering truth. . . .
>
> Third, freedom of expression is essential to provide for participation in decision making by all members of society. . . . This principle . . . carries beyond the political realm. It embraces the right to participate in the building of the whole culture, and includes freedom of expression in religion, literature, art, science, and all areas of human learning and knowledge.
>
> Finally, freedom of expression is a method of achieving a more adaptable and hence a more stable community, of maintaining the precarious balance between healthy cleavage and necessary consensus. . . . Freedom of expression thus provides a framework in which the conflict necessary to the progress of a society can take place without destroying the society. It is an essential mechanism for maintaining the balance between stability and change.[6]

The reasonableness of Emerson's summary can be lost, however, on the individual whose reputation has been ruined by false reports or on a community wracked by civil disturbance. The inevitable dilemma for a society that values press freedom is what to do when the press jeopardizes other values that society holds dear. Should the rights of the press *always*

The Government,
the Public, and the
Regulation of the
Mass Media

216

take precedence over the public's concern for national security? Domestic tranquility? Reputation? Privacy? Morality? The right to a fair trial? Never? When?

Almost all societies exercise at least four basic controls over freedom of expression: a law designed to protect individuals or groups against defamation, a copyright law to protect authors and publishers, a statute to preserve the community standard of decency and morality, and a statute to protect the state against treasonable utterances. Despite the protection of the First Amendment, the Supreme Court has sanctioned such laws and others as well that impinge on press freedom. For some of these the government is not the antagonist of the media but the arbiter of competing social interests.

PROTECTED AND UNPROTECTED EXPRESSION

In the 1940s the Supreme Court declared that certain categories of expression were so lacking in social value that they forfeited the protection of the First Amendment. Among those categories were obscenity, libel, and commercial advertising.[7] The court has softened its stand on libel and advertising, but obscenity remains unredeemed. Even those categories of expression that fall under the umbrella of the First Amendment receive less than absolute protection. As the Solicitor General said, "'No law' does not mean 'no law.'" Much of the remainder of this chapter will be devoted to describing how press freedom has fared in competition with those other cherished values.

National Security and Domestic Tranquility

Chief Justice Fred Vinson, in a 1950 case dealing with political strikes, reminded that First Amendment freedoms are themselves "dependent upon the power of constitutional government to survive."[8] *All* governments, including constitutional democracies, can be expected to act to protect themselves and preserve the peace.[9]

Americans pride themselves that the reins of power can shift from Republicans to Democrats and vice versa without the losers taking to the streets to prevent the change. (As a nation we are less tolerant of political ideologies that would alter the fundamental nature of the political system.) A basic principle of the system is that if change does come, it must come through peaceful persuasion, not violence, and change that is advocated peacefully must be tolerated. The most difficult question is what to do when violence is advocated in a peaceful manner.

A section of the Alien Registration Act of 1940 (the Smith Act) warns that it is "unlawful for any person . . . to knowingly . . . advocate . . . or teach . . . the desirability . . . of overthrowing . . . any government in the United States by force or violence." There are many state statutes which duplicate that warning. In cases arising out of World War I, Justice Oliver Wendell Holmes attempted to mark out an area of protection for dissent. "The question in every case," he said, "is whether the words used are used in such circumstances and are of such a nature as to create a clear and present danger that they will bring about the substantive evils that Congress has a right to prevent. It is a question of proximity and degree."[10] The essential protection of the "clear and present danger" test was that if there is *time* for discussion, there is no need for restrictions on First Amendment rights.

But in the late 1940s and early 1950s, discussion seemed a luxury in the face of what so many Americans saw as the threat of an international Communist conspiracy and the potential for a Communist takeover in the United States. No matter that a Communist had never won an election in this country. Chief Justice Vinson wrote in a case reviewing the convictions of 11 Communists under the Smith Act:

> Obviously, [the clear and present danger test] cannot mean that before the Government may act, it must wait until the *putsch* is about to be executed, the plans have been laid and the signal is awaited.[11]

In Vinson's view, if the evil is sufficiently grave, the fact that it is not likely to occur in the near future is of little significance.

The court gradually shifted from Vinson's severely limited protection for expression to something much closer to what Holmes had urged. In 1969 the court reversed the conviction of a Ku Klux Klan leader who had been tried under an Ohio criminal syndicalism statute. The conviction had been based on a televised rally at which he had made derogatory remarks about blacks and Jews, had warned of a march on Congress, and threatened "revengeance." The court limited the state's authority to punishing advocacy that is intended to incite or produce *imminent* lawless action and is likely to succeed.[12]

Of course the *mass* media in this country are not in the business of advocating the violent overthrow of the government. Of more pressing concern to them has been the government's determination to control the flow of information relating to the national security and the retaliation they invite by publishing information that the government has designated secret.

With regard to the Pentagon Papers case, Vice President Spiro Agnew said, "The Nixon administration has a great deal more confidence in the judgment of the elected officials of this country than in the New York *Times.*" Not a surprising comment from one of those elected officials. But *Times* associate editor Tom Wicker commented that to advance the argument that the people of the United States would be better off and the national interest further advanced if the study were locked in the Pentagon's vaults "would be to assert that truth has less value than deception and that in a democracy the people ought not to know." The problem is more complex than Wicker admits. There is a need for secrecy in government, and journalists—including those who work for the New York *Times*— accept that need frequently. But the media reserve an independent right to second-guess the government. Part of the journalist's job is to ferret out information the government does not want released because, as Jack

The Government,
the Public, and the
Regulation of the
Mass Media

218

Anderson warns, "If the government were honest about it, most government documents stamped secret would be stamped censored."

The classification system, the machinery of secrecy to protect the national security, is provided for in a series of Presidential orders. They are, in essence, housekeeping orders for members of the executive branch of the federal government that carry no sanction against journalists who disregard them. The prosecution of Daniel Ellsberg for his part in the copying and release of the Pentagon Papers was aborted for reasons relating to the manner in which the government's investigation of him was conducted. No criminal case was ever brought against any of the media that published documents or stories from the Papers, although some members of the Supreme Court seemed almost to encourage one. In fact, it has not been resolved whether or in what circumstances federal espionage laws apply to the distribution of classified information, not to spies or foreign governments, but to the American public.

During the Nixon Administration efforts were made to revise the espionage laws to include an "official secrets act" that would cover behavior such as that of the New York *Times* in the Pentagon Papers episode. Indeed, it seemed that the legislation supported by the Nixon Administration would have made any unauthorized release of information relating to the national defense illegal even if the information were not classified. So far such efforts to revamp the espionage laws have been unsuccessful—but they continue.

"Efficient" Government

Of course, not all information the government attempts to control or conceal relates to national security or political violence. A phenomenon of contemporary government is a massive bureaucracy that, in many instances, finds it safer, easier, and more advantageous to withhold than to release information. (The reluctance to release information officially is not contradicted by the selective leaking of information anonymously.) The errors of a bureaucrat too generous with information to the public or press are public, irreversible errors, errors that put a bureaucrat's job in jeopardy. Not so for the bureaucrat who errs on the side of secrecy. Processing the public's requests for information takes time, time the bureaucrat may feel is better spent on other public objectives. The control of information also conveys a measure of power. The "professionally informed," to use Max Weber's term, seek to maintain and increase their superiority by keeping others less informed. ("You can't possibly judge the correctness of my decision because you don't know all the facts.")

Each day the government makes available hundreds of reports, press releases, texts of speeches, brochures, pamphlets, and so on. Reporters and members of the public willing to plow through them can find some truly valuable information. But the government does not always release at its own initiative the information we most need to evaluate its performance and policies. Thus the media have the task, which they sometimes execute and sometimes don't, of dislodging such information from reluctant officials and agencies.

For all the rhetoric about the public's right to know, the public on its own or through its agents in the media, has a *right* to know much less than it needs to know in order to govern itself intelligently. Of course, it is also evident that we have a right to know more than we will ever pay attention to, which is why we expect the media to call our attention to what we need to know.

One might expect that in a society conceived as a self-governing republic the right of the public to information would be a fundamental stipulation of the Constitution. It is not. Nor has the Supreme Court read any general press or public right to information into the First Amendment. The Pentagon Papers case, for instance, protected the right of media to distribute information already in their possession. It did not extend to the media a right to compel the government to release the documents. The Supreme Court has said that newsgathering is entitled to some protection from the First Amendment, but it would appear that this protection is rather small. According to the Supreme Court, the rights of the press to information are coextensive with those of the public. The First Amendment, for example, does not grant a right of access for the press to grand jury proceedings, Supreme Court conferences, official bodies meeting in executive session, scenes of crime and disaster, or prisons beyond that available to the general public. However, the need for special rights for the media, as representatives of the public, continues to be the object of debate and litigation.

In recent years Congress and many state legislatures have attempted to legislate a public right to know by requiring that the public's business—as the rule rather than the exception—be conducted in public. Many government officials will tell each other, if not you, that it's a bother to do so. S. J. Archibald, who participated in the development of federal access to information legislation, writes, "Government technicians, bureaucrats, and administrators honestly believe they can do a more effective, efficient job of running the government without the help of press or public."[13]

Quite possibly they can, but then dictatorships can be efficient and effective, too. The American Revolution was not fought to secure efficient government, but public participation in government.

As the permanent federal bureaucracy grew after World War II, so did interest in increasing the opportunity for public scrutiny. Through the efforts begun in the 1950s by Representative John Moss of California, other members of Congress, journalists, members of the public, and members of the legal community, Congress passed in 1966 what is commonly called the Freedom of Information (FOI) Act. It is more properly described as a public records law because it deals only with information set down or required to be set down in records. It has nothing to do with public observation of government meetings or the freeing of information that officials retain in their heads but do not set down on paper. The act does not apply to

The Government,
the Public, and the
Regulation of the
Mass Media

220

Congress or the courts, but to the executive branch of the federal government and the independent regulatory agencies: the FBI, the Department of Health, Education, and Welfare, the Federal Communications Commission, the Federal Maritime Commission, the Executive Office of the White House, and so on.

The act does not require the seeker of information to prove a "need to know" before information must be released. Officialdom is required to demonstrate a "need to withhold." This is a major change from the previous federal records law. However, Congress wrote nine exceptions to the new law, nine reasons why officials could (not must) withhold information from the public and the media. The law, as amended in 1974, exempts the following:

1. Information properly classified according to the criteria set out by executive order to protect "the interest of national defense or foreign policy";
2. Information regarding internal agency personnel rules and practices;
3. Information "specifically exempted from disclosure by statute";
4. Trade secrets and privileged or confidential commercial or financial information;
5. Inter-agency and intra-agency memos and letters not available to other parties in litigation with the agency;
6. Personnel, medical, and similar files which if released "would constitute a clearly unwarranted invasion of personal privacy";
7. "Investigatory records compiled for law-enforcement purposes, but only to the extent that the production of such records would (A) interfere with enforcement proceedings, (B) deprive a person of a right to a fair trial or an impartial adjudication, (C) constitute an unwarranted invasion of personal privacy, (D) disclose the identity of a confidential source . . . [or, in some instances, would disclose confidential information supplied only by a confidential source], (E) disclose investigative techniques and procedures, or (F) endanger the life or physical safety of law enforcement personnel";
8. Agency documents relating to the regulation or supervision of financial institutions; and
9. "Geological and geophysical information and data, including maps, concerning wells."

The 1966 legislation had received a great deal of support from the media, but very little use by reporters once it was enacted. It was a clumsy, time-consuming tool for reporters pressured by deadlines. Requests for information could take forever to process even when refused. In some instances ridiculously high fees were charged for search and copying. Agencies bent on being uncooperative could insist that documents be described in such detail that it seemed only someone who already had the documents would know them so intimately.

Amendments passed in 1974 over President Gerald Ford's veto were designed to make the Freedom of Information Act a more effective tool for the media and the public. They were also meant to make it more troublesome for government to withhold information. For example, under the amendments the government must respond to FOI requests within specified time limits. The fees for search and copying must be reasonable, and when the release of information benefits the general public, reduced fees or no fees are to be charged. When the government loses an FOI case, the court may charge the court costs and attorney fees to the government. The court can also request the Civil Service Commission to consider disciplinary action against an official who "arbitrarily or capriciously" withholds information.

In 1976 Congress increased the opportunity for public observation of the federal government in action with the passage of the "Government in the Sunshine Act." Federal government agency meetings must be open to the public and announced in advance. The exemptions to open meetings parallel the exemptions for government records.

The movement to greater openness in government is progressing at the state as well as the federal level, in legislative as well as executive activity. For the most part the full sessions of both houses of Congress have been conducted in the open since the beginning of the republic. Much of the real work of legislation, however, is done in committee meetings, and since 1970 Congress has opened more and more (but by no means all) of those committee meetings.

What is striking about the public's right to know government information is that it is largely a product of legislative definition. But what the legislature defines, the legislature can redefine. The third exemption to the federal FOI act is an open-ended opportunity to define additional exemptions. If the climate is right and the public and media are inattentive, the right could contract as rapidly as it has expanded.

The federal and state sunshine and freedom of information acts are balancing acts. They accommodate pressures for secrecy within a framework of openness. If we reflect on the information the government may have assembled on each of us, we probably all can think of things that we would prefer the government kept secret.

The Public's Right to Know

As champions of the public's right to know, reporters and editors have, ironically, claimed a First Amendment right to *withhold* information. In the late 1960s and early 1970s journalists found themselves the object of a number of government subpoenas, many of them stemming from coverage of the antiwar movement, the civil rights movement, the counterculture, the low-life scene of prostitution, gambling, and drugs, and corruption in high and low places. Journalists had gathered information from all sorts of confidential informants, from those who provided the "dope" on street

The Government,
the Public, and the
Regulation of the
Mass Media

222

crimes and police corruption to government officials blowing the whistle on other government officials. Journalists had sought to withhold a variety of types of information:

1. The identity of confidential sources;
2. Unpublished information provided on a confidential basis;
3. Information not included in stories or edited out before their release, such as that which might be found in "outtakes" (film or tape shot but not used in a final story) or a reporter's notes or drafts;
4. Information gathered through direct observation, such as the witnessing of a political demonstration or a crime; and
5. Physical evidence, such as a letter or tape recording from an underground organization.

The use of the subpoena power to compel testimony or evidence is a well-established right of government acting on the public's behalf; indeed, the Sixth Amendment to the Constitution explicitly guarantees to criminal defendants the right to compel the appearance of witnesses on their behalf and to be confronted with the witnesses against them, although those are not the only circumstances in which the subpoena power can be used. Thus, the public has a right to information not only through the mass media but through established legal processes as well.

The news media's arguments for resisting government process have varied with the type of information withheld. In 1971 Dr. Frank Stanton, then president of CBS, was asked by a congressional subcommittee to provide the outtakes from "The Selling of the Pentagon," a documentary that was controversial not only for its attack on government propaganda but also for CBS's editing of several interviews with Pentagon officials. Stanton's arguments that the editorial discretion of CBS was protected by the First Amendment and that official government examination of the editing process would chill the exercise of First Amendment rights did not dissuade the subcommittee or its parent committee from voting to recommend that he be cited for contempt of Congress, even though they had at their disposal tapes of the interviews made by the Pentagon. Perhaps sobered by the prospect of the public reaction to, and the political consequences of, putting a highly respected head of a national news institution in jail, the full House voted to recommit the contempt recommendation, thus killing it.

In different circumstances journalists have used different arguments to resist government process. When political demonstrators took to the streets, journalists were often there to record their activities. Because it is the job of journalists to take careful notes or to record on film or tape what they have seen, they seemed particularly valuable witnesses to law-enforcement agencies and the courts. But journalists contended that using them in this fashion annexed the media as an investigative arm of government, tying up journalists' time in court and jeopardizing their safety at other demonstrations.

The newsmen's privilege controversy has focused particularly on the protection of the confidential relationships that some reporters find useful in getting information from some sources. Journalists warn that if they are compelled to breach confidential relationships, the public will be denied important information that would not otherwise surface. Probably the best known anonymous source is "Deep Throat" of the Watergate period, although the government never attempted to compel the disclosure of his (or her?) identity. Carl Bernstein and Bob Woodward, the Washington *Post* reporters who figured so prominently in the unraveling of Watergate, even dedicated their book *All the President's Men* to their confidential sources "in the White House and elsewhere."

The Caldwell Case

One of the most significant of the newsmen's privilege cases involved a black reporter from the New York *Times,* Earl Caldwell, who had won the confidence of leaders and members of the Black Panther Party, a black activist political group that in the late 1960s and early 1970s was suspected of criminal activity. Caldwell's access to the party made him a valuable source of information about their activities and ideas. In 1970 he was subpoenaed by a federal grand jury to testify and "bring notes and tape recordings of interviews reflecting statements made for publication by officers and spokesmen for the Black Panther Party concerning the aims, purposes and activities of the organization." Caldwell sought to resist the subpoena on the grounds that everything he was at liberty to disclose could be read in the *Times,* that any cooperation he gave the grand jury would destroy his relationship with the Panthers and would disrupt the flow to the public of information about the Panthers.

Because its proceedings are secret, Caldwell refused even to appear before the grand jury.[14] He knew that if he did go behind closed doors, the Panthers would not know for sure whether he had or had not answered any questions. For refusing to go before the grand jury or for going before it and refusing to testify, Caldwell could have been put in jail and kept there until he agreed to cooperate (or until the grand jury lost interest in the information or its term ended). Unappealing as jail is, if Caldwell had gone behind closed doors and refused to testify, the *worst* thing that could have happened to him as a reporter would have been a decision *not* to cite him for contempt. The Panthers would then have strong reason to suspect that he had violated their confidence and talked. One reporter has suggested that some prosecuting attorneys (often the dominating force in grand jury proceedings) are wily enough to use exactly that technique to punish a difficult reporter.

Caldwell's case was one of three decided together in 1972 by the U.S. Supreme Court. A second involved Paul Branzburg, a reporter for the Louisville *Courier-Journal* who had written stories on the availability of

The Government,
the Public, and the
Regulation of the
Mass Media

224

drugs in the Louisville and Frankfort, Kentucky, areas. The third involved a television reporter-photographer named Paul Pappas, who had been allowed inside a Black Panther headquarters in New Bedford, Massachusetts, in anticipation of a police raid. As a condition of his entry Pappas was not to write on anything but the raid. No raid occurred, and Pappas did not write a story.

None of the arguments of these reporters or the many respected news people who filed briefs on their behalf could persuade a sufficient number of the Supreme Court of the necessity of a privilege based on the First Amendment. Caldwell's lawyers put the broad arguments in these terms:

> [C]onfidential communications to newsmen are indispensable to their gathering, analysis and dissemination of the news; . . . when newsmen are subpoenaed to appear and testify concerning information obtained by them in their professional capacities, their confidential news sources are terrified of disclosure and consequently shut up; . . . the mere appearance of a newsman in secret grand jury proceedings, where what he has told cannot be known destroys his credibility, ruptures his confidential associations, and thereby irreparably damages his ability to function professionally; and . . . the resulting loss of confidence spreads rapidly and widely to other newsmen, thus critically impairing the news gathering capacities of the media and impoverishing the fund of public information and understanding.[15]

Justice Byron White, writing for the majority of the court, called predictions of sources "drying up" no more than speculative and refused to take seriously what he characterized as "the theory that it is better to write about crime than to do something about it." White did not see how the court could grant to the press special First Amendment privileges that the rest of the public, which is also entitled to the rights embodied in the First Amendment, would be denied. How could "newsman" be defined, he asked? Are underground papers entitled to a privilege? Even those that *advocate* violence or disregard of the law? Could not anyone who wanted to avoid testifying merely run to the mimeograph machine? Such questions clearly worried the court, and it remained unconvinced

> that a virtually impenetrable constitutional shield, beyond legislative or judicial control, should be forged to protect a private system of informers operated by the press to report on criminal conduct, a system that would be unaccountable to the public, would pose a threat to the citizen's justifiable expectations of privacy, and would equally protect well-intentioned informants and those who for pay or otherwise betray their trust to their employer or associates.[16]

The court did rule that newsgathering was entitled to some First Amendment protection, but not under the circumstances of these three cases. The decision sent chills down the spines of many in the media. Norman Isaacs, a former Louisville *Courier-Journal* and *Times* editor, warned that the world George Orwell had described in *1984* seemed to be at hand and that we were "in a period of libertarian and journalistic repression."[17] But rather as the press had lost something in the Pentagon Papers case even as it won the actual decision, the reporters in the Caldwell cases won something even as they lost.

The split of the justices in the Caldwell cases can best be described as 4½ to 4½. One of the four justices joining in White's majority opinion wrote a separate, concurring opinion that limited the impact of what White had written. In words that at best can be described as unclear, Justice Lewis Powell acknowledged, it seemed, some protections that were not far from what Caldwell, Branzburg, and Pappas had asked for. He urged that the need for testimony be balanced in each case with the reporter's freedom of the press. Powell's opaque language, taken in conjunction with the opinions of the four dissenters, suggests that a majority of the Supreme Court thought that there was some form of qualified First Amendment privilege, and many lower courts have approached privilege cases on that basis. Thus, journalists have won some cases and lost others, depending in part on whether there was reason to believe they had relevant information that went to the heart of the case, whether other sources for the information had been exhausted, and whether the issues were of such moment to justify overriding the First Amendment.

Shield Laws

In roughly half of the states journalists have an alternative to dependence on the First Amendment—state shield laws. Justice White explicitly stated in the Caldwell decision that Congress or the state legislatures might establish a privilege by statute. Many states had already done so, starting with Maryland in 1896. In the concern that followed the Caldwell decision six states enacted shield laws and four more amended theirs in 1973 alone.[18]

Reliance on legislation is not without its problems, since the statutes vary considerably. Some protect information gathered as well as the identity of confidential sources; others do not. Some protect only the sources of published information; others protect sources whether or not the information is published. Some cover all the media; others do not. And even the most generous can be disregarded by the courts. Kentucky had a strong shield law when Paul Branzburg was subpoenaed, but because he had *witnessed* criminal drug activity, he was considered to be his own source and thus not protected by the statute.

In 1970 the California shield law said that no reporter could be held in contempt by any governmental body for refusing to identify a source of information published or broadcast. No exceptions. Nevertheless, William Farr, who had covered the Manson Family murder trial for the Los Angeles *Herald Examiner,* found himself facing what he termed a life sentence in jail because he would not reveal who had given him copies of a vivid, ghoulish statement by a prospective witness. In the interests of protecting the defendants' Sixth Amendment rights to a fair trial, the judge had placed a restrictive order on attorneys, court personnel, and prospective witnesses,

The Government,
the Public, and the
Regulation of the
Mass Media

226

forbidding the release of proposed trial testimony or any other evidence. Farr admitted that he had obtained copies from three people, at least two of whom were attorneys in the case and subject to the order. It was of no small importance to the court which attorneys had violated the order. Of particular concern was whether the report had been released by the prosecution or the defense (or both).

Farr's case worked its way through both the California and the federal court systems. Despite the shield law and the First Amendment, he lost at virtually every stage. The California courts rejected the right of the legislature to circumscribe the judiciary's powers to protect the integrity of its processes. When the U.S. Court of Appeals, Ninth Circuit, reviewed Farr's case, it went so far as to interpret the Supreme Court's Caldwell decision as granting a First Amendment privilege, but held that when the constitutional right to a fair trial conflicted with the right of a reporter to a constitutional privilege, the First Amendment must give way to the Sixth.[19] Farr served 46 days in jail before the California courts acknowledged it was unlikely he could be coerced to reveal the information. The California shield law had done nothing for Farr except perhaps give him some false hope.

On the heels of the Caldwell decision, when journalists thought the courts would give them nothing, they turned to Congress. Many shield bills were introduced, but none passed. Journalists as well as legislators could not agree on what rights journalists should have.

Some journalists felt that, like everyone else, they should pay their dues as citizens. Some felt that the news media should not take "gifts" from Congress lest Congress expect some favor in return. Some felt nothing short of an absolute shield would be adequate but knew Congress was not likely to be that generous. There were concerns that qualified federal legislation could reduce the protection given by some of the more generous state statutes, that what Congress could give, Congress could take away, and that journalists were inviting a form of licensing by Congress. Some advised that, if the past was any indication of the future, the news media would stand a better chance with the judiciary and the First Amendment than with Congress. As if to prove that point Senators Edward Kennedy and John McClellan in 1977 introduced a revision of the federal criminal code that would, in the analysis of The Reporters Committee for Freedom of the Press, make "it a crime to refuse to obey a court's order to disclose confidential news sources even if, after an appeal, a reporter agrees to identify the source voluntarily" and would make it "a crime to refuse to disclose confidential news sources to police if the source is a criminal suspect."[20]

The newsmen's privilege issue puts both source and journalist in an interesting dilemma. There seems little doubt that there is some form of First Amendment privilege, and in some states there is a statutory shield. Neither offers journalists predictable security. Both can be defeated by some compelling, competing interest such as the right to sue or the right to a fair trial. In the end, the source's confidence must depend on whether it is given to a journalist who will choose to be a martyr if all else fails. Not all journalists would.

Reputation

227

Reputation

An individual's reputation is a precious possession. It is the measure of what other people think of him or her, and it influences whether and under what circumstances other people will associate with or trust him or her. A ruined reputation can mean the end of a good business, the loss of a job, the end of friendships, the loss of respect from the community. The law protects individuals against those who harm their reputations.

The term "defamation" is used to describe expression that exposes individuals to hatred, contempt, or ridicule or causes them to be shunned or avoided or injures them in their business or calling—in short, almost any expression that tends to make others think worse of them. Because the media frequently publish material that is derogatory, unflattering, or critical, they need to be particularly concerned with the very complicated law of defamation.

There are two categories of defamation: slander, which is spoken defamation, and libel, which—generally—is written and considered the more harmful. The distinction predates the invention of radio and television and reflects the now questionable judgment that print has the potential for greater impact because of its wider distribution and greater permanence. Now that spoken words can reach across a continent and beyond instantaneously, the courts have had to reconsider the reasonableness of automatically assuming libel to be more damaging than slander. One court coined the term "defamacast" to describe defamation by broadcast, but it treated the offense as it would have libel. The courts are not unanimous, but a useful rule-of-thumb is that if the broadcast defamation was first written or prepared, as in a script, it is treated as libel. If it is spontaneous, as a comment during a talk show might be, it is slander. Libel is the category of greater concern for the media and the one on which we shall focus.

Libel law is mined with contradictions and ambiguities and hence dangerous even for the prepared journalist. The First Amendment was initially understood to prevent the involvement of the federal government in libel law, but the states did not impose upon themselves the same strict prohibition. The consequence is that the modern journalist is faced with 51 varieties of libel law. The differences pose problems not only for journalists who change states when they change jobs, but for journalists whose work reaches beyond the border of a single state.

Although some states have codified their libel law—that is, written it down in statutes—many states rely in part or in whole on the centuries of accretion of decisions made by judges without the benefit of statutes. The product is not always easy to decipher. Libel began in England as a criminal offense and states have adopted criminal libel statutes, but they are no

The Government,
the Public, and the
Regulation of the
Mass Media

228

longer much used. The preferred action for someone who has been libeled is a civil suit for damages. The civil law is the avenue the state offers to the individual who seeks money in compensation for harm suffered. It should come as no surprise that most persons libeled prefer the financial possibilities of a civil suit to the purely psychic rewards of putting the libeler in jail or seeing him fined (fines go to the government, not the victim). Large damage awards and high legal fees make a civil suit almost as threatening to a news institution as a criminal action.

Although not restrained by the First Amendment when it was passed, many states have not been unmindful of the importance of a free press and have extended protections to enhance the possibility the media would fulfill the responsibilities that society desired. Three of the major protections, recognized by state laws as defenses against libel suits, were truth, qualified privilege, and the privilege of fair comment and criticism. Each in itself is the expression of an expectation of the media.

TRUTH

Should an individual be compensated for the ruin of an undeserved reputation? Some states said no and protected a truthful libel. Some said yes; no one should suffer the damage of his or her reputation unless the libeler published with good motives and justifiable ends.

If truth were to be used as a defense, however, the libel must be true in all its essential facts. It was not enough for a journalist to point to notes and a tape recorder and say that the story accurately reproduced the words of the source. Journalists had to be prepared to prove the truth of their source's words, not the accuracy of their own renditions of the words. Of course, if the truth of the charges were easily proved, the journalist probably wouldn't be in court.

QUALIFIED PRIVILEGE

There are occasions when the law protects even false libels. Participants in official government proceedings or those fulfilling official government responsibilities enjoy an absolute privilege to say what they think necessary without fear of losing a libel suit. Prosecuting attorneys could not do their job without such protection. The accusation of a crime is considered virtually automatically libelous. If prosecutors did not have the protection, every time they failed to convince a jury beyond a reasonable doubt that a defendant had committed the crime charged, they would be flirting with a libel suit.

In order that the public be apprised of what occurs in such proceedings and of what its officials are doing, the media are extended a qualified protection to report on them. What makes the media's privilege qualified rather than absolute is that the report *must* be a fair and accurate report of what transpired. Journalists lose the protection if the report fails to meet those qualifications.

How can a jury judge whether *opinion* is true or false? It can't. Because it can't, the privilege of fair comment and criticism developed as a defense for the media. It was meant to protect criticism of and comments on the public acts of public persons and institutions and on the work offered for the approval of the public by those whose activity affects the public welfare.

A requirement of this defense was that the comment had to be based on true facts and that the opinion must be fair and delivered without malice. The courts seem to have interpreted fairness very loosely. This review of the vaudeville act of the Cherry Sisters was held protected by the defense of fair comment and criticism back in 1901:

> Effie is an old jade of 50 summers, Jessie a frisky filly of 40, and Addie, the flower of the family, a capering monstrosity of 35. Their long skinny arms, equipped with talons at the extremities, swung mechanically, and anon waved frantically at the suffering audience. The mouths of their rancid features opened like caverns, and sounds like the wailings of damned souls issue therefrom. They pranced around the stage with a motion that suggested a cross between the *danse du ventre* and fox trot—strange creatures with painted faces and hideous mien. Effie is spavined, Addie is stringhalt, and Jessie, the only one who showed her stockings, has legs with calves as classic in their outlines as the curves of a broom handle.[21]

The true key to this defense is that the opinion, the commentary, must be directed at public acts. The law would have been less generous if the reviewer had criticized the private lives of the Cherry Sisters with the same enthusiasm.

THE CONSTITUTIONAL MALICE RULE

In 1942 the Supreme Court identified libel as one of those categories of expression so lacking in social utility that it forfeited the protection of the First Amendment. The court had some years earlier ruled that the First Amendment—written originally only as a prohibition on the federal government—applied to the states as well. In 1868, after the convulsion of the Civil War, the United States adopted the Fourteenth Amendment to the federal Constitution to regulate more closely the authority of the states over the fundamental rights of their citizens. Section 1 included these words:

> No State shall make or enforce any law which shall abridge the privileges or immunities of citizens of the United States; nor shall any State deprive any person of life, liberty, or property, without due process of law. . . .

In 1925 the Supreme Court suggested and in 1931 it ruled that the First Amendment was incorporated in the Fourteenth Amendment and that the states could not deprive their citizens of the rights guaranteed by the First Amendment without due process of law.[22] The application of the First Amendment to the state governments did not disrupt the development of libel law because libel law, the court would soon say, fell outside the

The Government,
the Public, and the
Regulation of the
Mass Media

230

protection of the First Amendment. Then, in 1964 the court dramatically reversed that view in one of the most significant media cases ever decided: *New York Times Co. v. Sullivan.*

The *Sullivan* case involved an advertisement placed in 1960 in the New York *Times* by the Committee to Defend Martin Luther King and the Struggle for Freedom in the South. The ad, in part, described events that had occurred at Alabama State College during a civil rights demonstration. It also appealed for funds and support for the student movement, for voting rights, and for the legal defense of Martin Luther King, Jr. The ad carried the signatures of 64 prominent Americans and 16 Southern clergymen although at least some of these people were not aware of the ad before it was published.

There were errors in the ad, some of which related to the handling of the student demonstration by Montgomery, Alabama, police. One of the three police commissioners of Montgomery, L. B. Sullivan, alleged that his reputation had been damaged by the errors even though he had not been named in the ad. He sued the New York *Times* and four black clergymen and was awarded $500,000 in damages. The Alabama Supreme Court upheld the award, and the New York *Times* took the case to the U.S. Supreme Court.

The Sullivan case was one of 12 brought against the *Times* by Alabama state and local officials in the early 1960s—some were based on the ad, some were based on two articles on racial unrest in Birmingham written by Harrison Salisbury. With encouragement from the Alabama attorney general ("My conclusions and recommendations are definite. File a multi-million dollar law suit."), the officials sought $7 million in damages from the *Times.* Five suits against the Columbia Broadcasting System, Inc., based on its civil rights coverage, sought $1.7 million. In addition, Harrison Salisbury was indicted on 42 counts of criminal libel.[23]

In reversing the judgment of the Alabama courts in the *Sullivan* case, the Supreme Court set down a constitutional rule that imposed some measure of uniformity on the libel law of all jurisdictions:

> [The Constitution] prohibits a public official from recovering damages for a defamatory falsehood relating to his official conduct unless he proves that the statement was made with "actual malice"—that is, with knowledge that it was false or with reckless disregard of whether it was false or not.[24]

The court placed at the core of the First Amendment "the principle that debate on public issues should be uninhibited, robust, and wide-open, and that it may well include vehement, caustic, and sometimes unpleasantly sharp attacks on government and public officials."

What was particularly novel about the court's application of the First Amendment to libel law was that the court protected not just truth, but some falsehood as well: "[E]rroneous statement is inevitable in free debate, and . . . it must be protected if the freedoms of expression are to have the 'breathing space' that they 'need to survive.'"[25] The court was concerned that if honestly presented statements are not protected, the news media will hold back—out of fear of being unable to *prove* in a court of law the truth of the statements in *every* particular—from the spirited criticism of and reporting on government and government officials the First Amendment was thought to protect.

Still outside the protection of the First Amendment were defamation directed at people other than public officials and knowing or reckless falsehood about public officials.

In the Sullivan case the Supreme Court limited the use of the malice rule to cases brought by government officials, but over the next seven years the court extended its use to cases brought by ex-public officials, potential public officials, and public figures. In 1971 a plurality of the court applied the rule to a suit brought by a private individual caught up in a public issue—in this case a Mr. Rosenbloom who had been arrested for distributing allegedly obscene books.[26] (The books were declared not obscene and Rosenbloom argued that radio broadcasts about his arrest prejudged his guilt.) It seemed to some as if the law of libel were being wiped out by the Constitution, or, perhaps more correctly stated, by the Supreme Court.

It is extremely difficult to prove that a reporter or editor knew that a piece of information was false or even that either one had entertained serious doubts that it was false. Recklessness and knowledge of falsity are states of mind not easily documented, and so the balance between the interest in reputation and freedom of the press seemed tipped quite decidedly in favor of the press.

Then in 1974 the Supreme Court reconsidered the plight of the defamed private individual. In a case in which a lawyer named Elmer Gertz had been called a "Communist-fronter" in a John Birch Society magazine, the court argued that private individuals are more vulnerable to injury than public officials and public figures, less able to command space or time from the media to rebut false accusations, and also more deserving of recovery.[27]

The court weighed the interests of reputation against the interests of an uninhibited, robust press. The result was a complicated system that returned to the states the *option* of making it easier for private individuals than for public persons to win libel judgments.

PUBLIC OR PRIVATE FIGURES?

The Supreme Court also made it more difficult for the media to distinguish between public and private figures. In 1967 *Time* magazine reported among its "Milestones":

> Divorced, by Russell A. Firestone, Jr., 41, heir to the tire fortune: Mary Alice Sullivan Firestone, 32, his third wife, a onetime Palm Beach schoolteacher; on grounds of extreme cruelty and adultery; after six years of marriage, one son; . . .

Although the divorce court's language was unclear, the grounds for divorce did not include adultery. Indeed, Mrs. Firestone could not have

The Government,
the Public, and the
Regulation of the
Mass Media

232

been awarded alimony under Florida law if adultery had been the grounds for divorce.

The question for the U.S. Supreme Court was whether Mrs. Firestone was a public or a private figure. In *Gertz* the Supreme Court had noted that some people "occupy positions of such pervasive power and influence that they are deemed public figures for all purposes." But, the court said, "[m]ore commonly, those classed as public figures have thrust themselves to the forefront of particular public controversies in order to influence the resolution of the issues involved."[28]

Although Mrs. Firestone had called press conferences on the subject of her divorce, the court ruled that she was not a public figure because the dissolution of her marriage through judicial proceedings was not the sort of "public controversy" referred to in *Gertz*. The Supreme Court seemed to put itself back into the dilemma of deciding what public issues were of legitimate interest to the public—a dilemma the court said in *Gertz* it wished to avoid.

The Supreme Court sent the *Firestone* case back to the Florida courts to decide what standard of responsibility Florida would impose on the media— and whether *Time* had met it.

Firestone and *Gertz* reaffirmed the tremendous protection for the media against defamation suits brought by government officials and public figures, but the two cases also led the media into another era of uncertainty as state courts exercise the option of setting their own standards for private libel cases. Just how careful do reporters and editors have to be in New Mexico? In Minnesota? In Georgia? How many sources have to be checked? How exact must the wording of a headline be? What trade-offs on certainty of accuracy can be made under the press of the deadline?

For the media, the euphoria of *Rosenbloom* has passed.

Privacy

In 1890 two young lawyers, Samuel Warren and Louis Brandeis, published in the *Harvard Law Review* an article entitled "The Right to Privacy." The article is considered by some to be one of the most influential law review articles ever published. It pulled together the threads of existing common law such as the protections against trespass and libel and synthesized them into a new legal concept—a right of privacy. As an intellectual and philosophical concept privacy was not new, but as a complete legal concept it was.

The focus of their concern was newspaper reporting of *true* information that they felt should remain private. The newspapers of Boston were taking more interest in the domestic and social life of the Warren family than Warren considered tolerable. In their words:

The press is overstepping in every direction the obvious bounds of propriety and of decency. Gossip is no longer the resource of the idle and the vicious, but has become a trade, which is pursued with industry as well as effrontery. . . . To occupy the indolent, column upon column is filled with idle gossip, which can only be procured by intrusion upon the domestic circle. . . .[29]

While the concern for the public revelation and distribution of private information continues, privacy as a legal right has taken forms not discussed by Warren and Brandeis.

Seventy years after the publication of this article, legal scholar William Prosser surveyed the evolution of the law of privacy and found that four distinct concepts had developed.[30] Although all have a core concern for the individual's ability to control the collection and distribution of information about himself or herself, the nature of that concern varies considerably from category to category. The U.S. Supreme Court has acknowledged the importance of the distinctions Prosser identified.

One concept was protection against the use of a person's name or likeness for commercial advantage—for instance, the unauthorized use of someone's photograph to advertise shaving cream. A second was protection against intrusion upon a person's seclusion or solitude—for instance, a journalist placing a listening device in someone's apartment. A third was the protection against the public disclosure of embarrassing private facts about a person—very much what Warren and Brandeis had in mind. The fourth was publicity that places a person in a "false light" in the public eye, that is to say, the publication of false information that may not be defamatory, but that misrepresents the person to the public.

Each of these concerns is a reflection of significant changes in our society. What was once a predominantly rural society is now highly indus-trialized and commercial. Advertising is pervasive, using people's names and faces for illustration and endorsement. We employ computers, cameras, tape recordings, electronic bugs, laser beams, microfilm, one-way and parabolic mirrors, and so on to gather, store, and retrieve enormous amounts of information and misinformation relating to very personal aspects of each other's lives. That "we" includes the government, insurance compa-nies, credit agencies, banks, schools, the mass media, and other "informa-tion" institutions. Although we have always had to endure the interest of our neighbors, the mass media extend the reach of gossip beyond the traditional limitations of the human ear, eye, voice, and memory. Government records our progress from birth to taxes to death. Our use of credit cards and checks leaves a history of financial transactions that cash never provided. Informa-tion is distributed beyond our capability to test its accuracy. Where reputa-tions were once built on personal experience, they now depend on credit ratings.

Contemporary American society could not exist without the vast reser-voirs of information that is collected and swapped. The government could not collect taxes, make Social Security payments, or hold an election. Restaurants, airlines, and stores could not extend immediate credit to people they have never seen before. The mass media could not provide

The Government,
the Public, and the
Regulation of the
Mass Media

234

timely information on far-flung places, complicated issues, football scores from across the nation.

As American society has changed, the law of privacy has expanded. It has expanded as a right against government intrusion in our lives and as a right against the intrusion of our fellow citizens, whether they be neighbors, insurance investigators, or reporters. Both the constitutional right of privacy and the right of privacy against our fellows seriously affect the ability of the media to gather and use information.

PUBLIC DISCLOSURE OF PRIVATE INFORMATION

A particularly troublesome area for the news media is the protection against public disclosure of private information. Journalists reveal private information about people all the time—either because they think the public needs to know the information or because they think the information will be interesting to the public. Courts have developed a defense of "newsworthiness" to enable the media to do so safely if the information has news value.

For example, as a child William Sidis had been especially gifted at mathematics, so gifted that at the age of 11 he had lectured to distinguished mathematicians and at the age of 16 he was graduated from Harvard. But after this early display of genius, Sidis shunned all publicity, seeking a life of obscurity as an ordinary clerk. Many years after Sidis had escaped the public life, *The New Yorker* ran a biographical sketch on him under the title, "Where Are They Now?" The U.S. Court of Appeals, Second Circuit, described the article as "merciless in its dissection of intimate details of [Sidis's] life" but found the article did not go beyond what the mores of the community would accept. "Regrettably or not," the court wrote, "the misfortunes and frailties of neighbors and 'public figures' are subjects of considerable interest and discussion to the rest of the population."[31]

The courts have imposed limits, however, on the media's catering to public curiosity. Floating through the court decisions in this area is a concern that the media not publish private information that would "offend the sensibilities of an ordinary person"—an opaque standard at best. Areas of special concern would be medical information, mental health information, information on sexual matters, information about children, particularly deformed, retarded, or delinquent children.

One piece of information long thought to be especially sensitive is the identity of a rape victim. Most news institutions voluntarily refrain from reporting such information. But in 1972 a reporter from a Georgia television station was shown court documents and attended court proceedings in which a rape victim who had died as a result of the attack was named. The television station broadcast the name as part of its news report, and the victim's father sued for invasion of privacy.

In fundamental respects the U.S. Supreme Court's decision, despite the tremendous sensitivity of the issue, is clearcut: Information contained in any official record available to the public is not *private* information.[32] If the reporter had stolen a look at court records not available to the public or had misreported the information, the court would have faced an entirely different issue.

The news media have often had difficulty determining what private information is necessary for the public to know and safe to report. The city councilman who is arrested for drunk driving on the way home from a Saturday night party may consider such arrest information unrelated to his public responsibilities and therefore private, but if the information is contained in a public record, publication is protected. More complicated are questions about aspects of the "private" lives of public people that do not find their way into public records but may affect the performance of public responsibilities: extramarital affairs, alcoholism, senility, ill health. The courts have noted that public officials and public figures are entitled to some area of privacy, but the more important the person, the smaller that area is likely to be.

With only one U.S. Supreme Court decision—on public records—in the area of public disclosure of private information, many questions are left unanswered or are answered in different ways by different states.

INTRUSION

The public taste for information about certain people has led to bizarre behavior by some who wish to satisfy that taste. An aggressive freelance photographer named Ronald Galella has pursued Jacqueline Onassis and her children mercilessly. In 1972 Galella filed a $1.3 million suit and sought an injunction, claiming that Mrs. Onassis and the Secret Service agents guarding her children had prevented him from pursuing his livelihood. Galella's lawyer tried to show that Mrs. Onassis purposely harmed Galella by putting on sunglasses whenever she saw him. Galella complained that her sunglasses made the pictures less salable.

She countersued for $1.5 million in damages and asked that Galella be enjoined from harassing her and her children. The federal district court described Galella's behavior:

> He was like a shadow: everywhere she went he followed her; . . . nothing was sacred to him whether [Mrs. Onassis] went to church, funeral services, theatre, school, restaurant, on board a yacht in a foreign land. . . .
> * * * * *
> When Galella rushed her limousine . . . she was terrified. Galella's pursuit of her and the children at [a] horse show . . . caused her concern and anxiety for fear that his activities would frighten the horse and thereby endanger her children. . . . When Galella crashed about in the tunnel beneath Lincoln Center and tried to push his way through a revolving door with Mrs. Onassis and her children she was frightened that someone would be injured in the door. . . . When Galella cruised around Mrs. Onassis in a power boat as she was swimming . . . , he was so close she was afraid she would be cut by the propeller. . . .
> * * * * *
> His surveillance is so overwhelmingly pervasive that he has said he has not married because he has been unable to "get a girl who would be willing to go looking for Mrs. Onassis at odd hours."

The Government,
the Public, and the
Regulation of the
Mass Media

236

. . . He has intruded into her children's schools, hidden in bushes and behind coat racks in restaurants, sneaked into beauty salons, bribed doormen, hatcheck girls, chauffeurs, fishermen in Greece, hairdressers and schoolboys, and romanced employees.[33]

"In short," said the court, "Galella has insinuated himself into the very fabric of Mrs. Onassis's life and the challenge to this Court is to fashion the tool to get him out." The court set restrictions on the contact Galella could make with Mrs. Onassis and her family, including forbidding him and his agents from coming closer than 225 feet to the children and 150 feet to Mrs. Onassis. Although the distances were shortened by the court of appeals, both courts agreed that the First Amendment was no shield for such unreasonable behavior.

Few reporters are as single-minded or relentless as Galella. But the search for information—some of it of true importance for the public—can lead journalists to intrude on the privacy of others in ways that test the limits of tolerance.

Two *Life* reporters misrepresented themselves in order to gain access to the home of a journeyman plumber named Dietemann who "was engaged in the practice of healing with clay, minerals, and herbs." The reporters, ostensibly seeking "medical" help, carried a concealed camera and a radio transmitter, the signals of which were being recorded in a parked car occupied by another *Life* employee and officials from the District Attorney's Office and the State Department of Public Health. *Life* had undertaken its investigation of Dietemann in agreement with the District Attorney's Office.

That official connection and the importance to the public of information on medical quackery, however, did not prevent a federal court of appeals from deciding that Dietemann was entitled to recover damages. The court observed, "Investigative reporting is an ancient art; its successful practice long antecedes the invention of miniature cameras and electronic devices. . . . The First Amendment is not a license to trespass, to steal, or to intrude by electronic means into the precincts of another's home or office."[34]

Some reporters find it difficult to restrain themselves from doing what is necessary to get the goods on those they consider dishonest or a threat to the public well-being. One investigative reporter admitted that he would do almost anything short of the crime he was investigating, including committing a lesser crime. Of course, his attitude is not accepted by all journalists. When reporters, including a Washington *Post* stringer, broke into the apartment of a man arrested for one of a series of highly publicized New York murders, the managing editor of the Washington *Post* reminded stringers: " . . . [W]e do not 1) break laws, 2) misrepresent ourselves, 3) engage in unethical activities."[35]

"FALSE LIGHT"

Soon after it developed the constitutional malice rule in libel law for public officials, the U.S. Supreme Court applied the same rule to "false light" privacy in a case involving a family of private citizens who became involved in a public event. The James Hill family had been held hostage by three escaped convicts for 19 hours. The Hills shunned publicity, but a book, a play, and a movie were written fictionalizing their experience. A *Life* magazine article on the opening of the play ("True Crime inspires Tense Play") implied that the fictional account matched the Hills' experience. The court ruled that the Hills could not recover damages unless they could prove the responsible employees at *Life* knew the implication was false or were reckless about whether it was false or not.[36]

The court's decision in the *Hill* case seemed consistent at the time with the gradual enlargement of the use of the malice rule in libel. When the court retreated from its application to private individuals bringing libel cases, however, observers expected some adjustment in the privacy area as well, some greater solicitude for *involuntary* public figures, essentially private people like the Hills who through no action of their own are caught up in occurrences that interest the public. The court has not yet taken the opportunity to make that adjustment.[37]

INACCURATE RECORDS

Experience with credit bureaus, agencies of government, and similar organizations has demonstrated that those who collect and store information do not always do so with sufficient care. Computers print out what people put in, reporting with great fidelity erroneous as well as accurate information. As a consequence, individuals have been given greater rights to examine and correct information held by such institutions in order that when reports are made and distributed, they are based on accurate information. Appealing as such rights are for the individual, attempts to extend similar rights against the news media would encounter substantial First Amendment problems.

APPROPRIATION

In a case that has very little to do with the notion of privacy as we would generally think of it, Hugo Zacchini sued Scripps-Howard Broadcasting Company for airing during its 11 P.M. news program a videotape of an act he performs in *public*. Zacchini's act lasts 15 seconds, the time it takes him to be shot from a cannon into a net about 200 feet away. Zacchini, who had been performing as a human cannonball at the Great Geauga County Fair in Burton, Ohio, felt the televising of his entire act denied him his just compensation as a performer. The U.S. Supreme Court agreed, noting that although Zacchini's "state-law right of publicity" had "little to do with protecting feelings or reputation" and although the performance had been broadcast during a *news* program, he had been denied the right "to reap the reward of his endeavors."[38]

While some might seek protection against the embarrassment of having their names or likenesses used to endorse products or services, more often appropriation questions turn not on minimizing or preventing the use of a

The Government,
the Public, and the
Regulation of the
Mass Media

238

person's identity, but the question of "who gets to do the publishing." Or, indeed, whether the individual is adequately compensated for the use of his or her identity. Someone like football star Joe Namath is obviously not camera-shy, but generally the courts have recognized that he is entitled to control the conditions under which his name is used for commercial gain. This right to publicity, particularly the right to the financial gain generated by such publicity, is a major factor in the incomes of such celebrities as Olympic decathlon gold medalist Bruce Jenner, golfers Jack Nicklaus and Arnold Palmer, football star O. J. Simpson, tennis champion Chris Evert, and a host of show business and other sports personalities. Even such dignified heroes as former Senator Sam Erwin have taken advantage of their celebrity to make commercials.

Of course, the news media, like advertisers and the entertainment industry, are engaged in business for commercial gain. Recognizing that the media would be paralyzed if they had to secure consent every time they used a name, photo, or anything else that identified an individual, the courts have generally excluded public affairs and news content from the reach of appropriation suits.

THE CONSTITUTIONAL RIGHT OF PRIVACY

Although the Constitution protects specific rights that contain an element of privacy—for instance, the Fourth Amendment's protection against unreasonable search and seizure by government or the Fifth Amendment's protection against self-incrimination—there is no specific mention of a right to privacy anywhere in the document.

In 1965, however, the U.S. Supreme Court found such right in the penumbras emanating from the Bill of Rights.[39] The parameters of the constitutional right to privacy have yet to be defined, but agencies of government have sought to draw a line by limiting the release of information held by government. Legislation such as the federal Freedom of Information Act is limited by exemptions for privacy and by specific federal privacy legislation. The pressure that has been building for privacy can also be seen in efforts such as those by the federal Law Enforcement Assistance Administration (LEAA) in 1975 to require state courts and police departments receiving money from the agency to develop rules barring access to alphabetically filed criminal records—that is, you could not get access to records by using an individual's name. The media would continue to have access to records filed chronologically, but reporters would have to know the date and nature of the charge in order to make effective use of them. The purpose of the restrictions, according to an LEAA spokesman, "is to make it as difficult as possible for reporters and others to get information."[40] After an avalanche of protests from the media, the LEAA requirements were modified to exempt records of public judicial proceedings, but police blotters, long accessible to reporters, are not to be available unless chronologically organized. The modified regulations, scheduled to go into effect December 31, 1977, are still designed to make it tough for the media to get criminal justice information.

Interest in the rehabilitation of criminal offenders and concern for the reputations of those arrested but never convicted have spawned an interest in the sealing or expunging of criminal records—particularly arrest records. There is an obvious argument to be made for expunging arrest records of people arrested in error or for sealing past criminal records to aid in the successful reintegration into society of those who have been rehabilitated. But sanction for the destruction or sealing of such records means that the criminal justice system can conceal its errors, its inefficiencies, and its misdeeds.

In the long run the media may have more trouble with the concept of privacy than with libel because the concern for privacy affects the gathering as well as the reporting of information, because it affects the standards used in libel cases, and because it provides the foundation for this phenomenon of the twentieth century—the law of privacy.

The Right to a Fair Trial

On the evening of October 18, 1975, local police found six members of the Henry Kellie family murdered in their home in Sutherland, Nebraska, a town of about 850 people. Police released the description of a suspect, Erwin Charles Simants, to the reporters who had hastened to the scene of the crime. Simants was arrested and arraigned in Lincoln County Court the following morning, ending a tense night for this small rural community.[41]

Under the Sixth Amendment* to the federal Constitution, Simants was entitled to be tried by a jury that had not already decided he was guilty. Under the protection of the First Amendment* the news media sought to report to the residents of Sutherland, Nebraska, the danger in their midst: the nature of the crime that had been committed and the likelihood that the police had arrested the right man.

Could the public be informed without destroying Simants' constitutional rights? Could his rights be preserved without restraining the press? The questions are worth keeping in mind as we examine the nature of the conflict between the First and Sixth Amendments, for they are central to it.

A "FAIR" TRIAL

The Sixth Amendment does not explicitly guarantee "fairness." It says that a criminal defendant is entitled to "a speedy and public trial, by an impartial jury," a jury willing and able to make its judgment solely on the basis of evidence and testimony introduced during the trial. It also says that the accused has the right "to be informed of the nature and cause of the accusation" against him, "to be confronted with the witnesses against him," "to have compulsory process for obtaining witnesses in his favor, and to have the Assistance of Counsel for his defence." The Fifth and the Four-

*The protections of the First and Sixth Amendments have been applied against the states through the "due process" clause of the Fourteenth Amendment.

The Government,
the Public, and the
Regulation of the
Mass Media

240

teenth Amendments say that he has a right to "due process of law." These
and other rights contribute to the fairness of the accused's trial. The depriva-
tion of any one of them destroys that fairness. An incompetent judge, an
unprepared lawyer, a lying witness, a biased juror, and, indeed, responsible
as well as irresponsible media can put it in jeopardy.

In this society, the media stand as guarantors of the right to a fair trial as
well as a threat to it. They have a role to play in the criminal justice system,
just as they have a role to play in other aspects of government, checking on
whether government is doing its job. One job of the courts is to ensure
defendants get fair trials.

THE ROLE OF THE MEDIA IN THE CRIMINAL JUSTICE SYSTEM

Public scrutiny through media coverage of police, judicial, and correc-
tional institutions helps protect the individual against governmental harassment, incompetence, and abuse. Media coverage of the criminal justice
system also serves other public interests.[42]

The media expose the existence of crime. They are a particularly
important supplement to official investigation in instances of official corruption. With due regard for the contributions of official sources and the
judiciary, the exposure of the Watergate crimes is testimony to the value of
media enterprise.

By publishing details of crime and descriptions of suspects, *the media
warn the public of danger posed by criminals still at large and aid in their
apprehension.* Reports of the high incidence of rapes and muggings in a
park can be fair warning to stay away from the area until police have
arrested the offenders. Individuals who have information of help to authorities are alerted to that fact by such coverage. The public is apprised of
whether law enforcement agencies are doing an effective job.

*The media reassure the public by reporting the apprehension of sus-
pects.* A community chilled by a grisly crime in its midst will not rest easily
until arrests have been made, and they are assured that there is a reasonable
likelihood the police have arrested the right persons.

*Coverage of the trial itself can educate the public to the way in which the
legal system works* and can explain the "technicalities" that sometimes lead
to controversial outcomes.

*Coverage of the consequences of the law may deter others from
committing similar crimes.* It also focuses the public's attention on the
justness of particular laws. For example, is a 15-year sentence for selling
marijuana too high or too low a price to extract? Does the death penalty
deter, or is execution by the state "cruel and unusual punishment"?

In many respects the public would benefit from more rather than less
coverage of the criminal justice system, but not all coverage is benign or
constructive.

PREJUDICIAL PUBLICITY

In their worst moments the media play to public emotions and prejudices
in ways that have no place in a system of laws and reasoned judgment, but it

is the reporting of *information*—whether to pander to a public taste for details of crime and violence or to respond to the public's need to know about its social environment and its government—that is most problematical for the courts. Under our legal system guilt is properly determined in courts using procedures designed to prevent the conviction of the innocent and to hold government to certain standards of fair conduct. The news media do not always sift evidence with the same attention to constitutional safeguards.

Stanford University law professor Marc Franklin has noted three types of information courts generally exclude:

> [A]n accused's prior record of convictions is not generally admissible in evidence unless the defendant chooses to testify. The fear is that if jurors learn that a defendant has a prior record they may be tempted to convict even though the prosecution may have failed to establish guilt beyond a reasonable doubt in this particular situation.
>
> . . . [C]onfessions made by the defendant before the trial are not admissible in evidence at the trial unless voluntarily made. Even if other evidence shows the confession accurate, to accept a coerced confession would encourage law enforcement authorities to abuse their power.
>
> The third major variety of inadmissible evidence involves items seized in an unlawful search. In these cases, the evidence is almost always trustworthy—and often devastating. Nonetheless, it is excluded if the search was illegal. Again, the point is to discourage the state from engaging in illegal behavior.
>
> In all three situations, since the evidence is inadmissible in the courtroom, the courts seek to keep jurors from gaining access to such information by other means.[43]

These are, of course, the pieces of information the media often wish to report. Does this conflict of interests present the courts—if they are prevented by the First Amendment from restricting the media—with the task of filling jury boxes with ignoramuses or hermits who have never read a newspaper or watched a television news program? How much information can individuals be given before they lose their objectivity and suitability as jurors?*

Though it has changed its standards over the years for what makes a juror impartial, the Supreme Court does not insist the juror be a *tabula rasa*. It looks for specific evidence of prejudicial impact. In 1975 the Supreme Court upheld the conviction of Jack ("Murph the Surf") Murphy even though some jurors were aware of his prior convictions for murder and the theft of the "Star of India" sapphire from the New York Museum of Natural History.[44] The courts have also upheld the convictions of William Calley (the

---

*The research studies of the effects of prejudicial publicity—with a few exceptions—seem to reinforce what some lawyers have argued from practical experience: Exposure to prejudicial information can predispose jurors to judge defendants guilty, but the experience of even mock trials tends to mitigate that influence. Real and role-playing jurors seem to take their duties seriously. When instructed to make judgments based only on trial evidence, they generally do so. For a summary of the research see Rita J. Simon, "Does the Court's Decision in *Nebraska Press Association* Fit the Research Evidence on the Impact on Jurors of News Coverage?," *Stanford Law Review,* 29:515, February 1977. For a lawyer's personal experiences see John Kaplan, "Of Babies and Bathwater," *Stanford Law Review,* 29:621, February 1977.

The Government,
the Public, and the
Regulation of the
Mass Media

242

Mylai Massacre), John Ehrlichman and John Mitchell (Watergate), Sirhan Sirhan (the assassination of Senator Robert Kennedy), and others despite massive, detailed, nationwide publicity. Pretrial publicity, the Supreme Court said in a major case in 1976, "even if pervasive and concentrated, cannot be regarded as leading automatically and in every kind of criminal case to an unfair trial." The court said that it would "take into account what . . . measures were used to mitigate the adverse effects of publicity."[45]

FROM REMEDY TO PREVENTION

On July 4, 1954, Marilyn Sheppard, pregnant with her second child, was bludgeoned to death in an upstairs bedroom of her home in Bay Village, Ohio, by what her husband could only describe as a "form." There followed a grim circus.

From the beginning official and media attention focused on her husband, Dr. Sam Sheppard. "After a search of the house and premises on the morning of the tragedy, Dr. Gerbner, the Coroner, [was] reported . . . to have told his men, 'Well, it is evident the doctor did this, so let's get the confession out of him.'" They didn't get a confession out of him, and the media coverage was impatient, relentless, and sensational. The Supreme Court cited headlines such as these:

"Why No Inquest? Do It Now, Dr. Gerbner"
> headline, page 1 editorial, July 21

"Why Isn't Sam Sheppard in Jail?"
> headline, page 1 editorial, July 30

"But Who Will Speak for Marilyn?"
> 2-inch, page 1 headline run during selection of jury

"Sam Called a 'Jekyll-Hyde' By Marilyn, Cousin to Testify"
> 8-column headline, November 24, during trial

The actual conduct of the trial matched the publicity. The courtroom measured just 26 by 48 feet. To accommodate the news media, the trial judge had a temporary table set up inside the bar, the railing that usually separates participants from spectators. The judge assigned approximately 20 newspaper and wire service reporters to this table. Of the four rows of seats beyond the bar, the first three were assigned to the news media, the last to the families of the victim and the defendant.

The Supreme Court disapproved of these and other "arrangements made by the judge with the news media." As the court described conditions,

> The fact is that bedlam reigned at the courthouse during the trial and newsmen took over practically the entire courtroom, hounding most of the participants in the trial, especially Sheppard. . . . Having assigned almost all of the available seats in the courtroom to the news media the judge lost his ability to supervise that environment. The movement of the reporters in and out of the courtroom caused frequent confusion and disruption of the trial. . . . Participants in the trial, including the jury, were forced to run a gauntlet of reporters and photographers each time they entered or left the courtroom. The total lack of consideration for

The U.S. Supreme Court deplored "the carnival atmosphere" of the 1954 trial of Dr. Sam Sheppard and overturned his conviction. (Wide World photo)

the privacy of the jury was demonstrated by the assignment to a broadcasting station of space next to the jury room on the floor above the courtroom. . . .

* * * * *

. . . The prosecution repeatedly made evidence available to the news media which was never offered in the trial. Much of the "evidence" disseminated in this fashion was clearly inadmissible. The exclusion of such evidence in court is rendered meaningless when . . . news media [make] it available to the public.[46]

The *Sheppard* case illustrates very clearly the basic patterns of many free press/fair trial cases: Cooperation—intended or not—among officials, attorneys and the media. Reporters are rarely the sole cause of unfair trials—even when the problem is unfair publicity.

To remedy the injustice of Sheppard's conviction in such an inflamed atmosphere, the Supreme Court in 1966 granted him a new trial. He was acquitted at that second trial, but he had already spent 10 years in prison. And if Sheppard was innocent, what had the "form" that had bludgeoned Marilyn to death been doing since July 4, 1954?

The *Sheppard* case is noteworthy not only for the bad judgment shown by so many in the summer and fall of 1954. It marks the beginning of an emphasis on *preventing* unfair trials that has been interpreted—or misinterpreted—as encouragement for placing direct restrictions on the media. . . . "[W]e must remember that reversals are but palliatives; the cure lies in those remedial measures that will prevent the prejudice at its inception," the court said in *Sheppard.*

The Government,
the Public, and the
Regulation of the
Mass Media

244

Without stinting in its criticism of the media, the court placed the responsibility for ensuring a fair trial squarely on the judge; and it did so without suggesting any direct *controls* on the media other than those designed to preserve the proper judicial calm in the courtroom itself. It urged the judge to consider such traditional legal tools as sequestering the jury, granting a change of venue or a new trial, insulating witnesses, and so forth. None of these is a direct threat to the First Amendment freedoms of the media, although they can exact a heavy price from others. (Few people enjoy jury duty sequestered from friends, family, and job.) The only control the Supreme Court encouraged on media content was indirect: The trial judge was encouraged to control the release of prejudicial information to the news media by lawyers, defendants, witnesses, and court officials and to request city and county officials to control the release of such information by their employees. The court left open the question of what steps could be taken against a "recalcitrant press" if none of these procedures worked.

"PREVENTION" IN THE 1970S

In response perhaps to the spirit of the *Sheppard* decision and to the door left open in the Pentagon Papers case to prior restraints on the media in exceptional circumstances, trial judges in the 1970s turned to three controversial tools of prevention: the restrictive orders on trial participants the Supreme Court seemed explicitly to encourage in *Sheppard;* restrictive orders ("gag orders," as the media call them) against the media; and closure of portions of the trial process, a tool suggested in somewhat limited terms by the controversial 1968 Reardon Report of the American Bar Association. Although all three affect media content, the most threatening to traditional concepts of press freedom was the increasing use of "gag orders" against the media. The issue of their constitutionality reached the Supreme Court in a case that began with Erwin Charles Simants.[47]

Simants was accused of an extraordinarily gruesome crime. Not only had six members of the Kellie family been murdered, the three female victims had been sexually assaulted after their deaths. It was one of those crimes that is sensational even in the most straightforward accounts. It was also one of those crimes that so frightens a small community such as Sutherland, Nebraska, that the news media can argue they have a responsibility to report details linking the suspect with the murders in order to reassure the public that the right person has been apprehended.

To preserve Simants' right to a fair trial, the county court judge prohibited everyone who attended Simants' preliminary hearing, including the news media, from disseminating to the public information about testimony and evidence produced there. The judge also ordered the media to adhere to the Nebraska Bar-Press Guidelines. The order was striking for its restrictions on the reporting of open court proceedings that any passer-by could attend and for imposing as an *order* what had been drafted as voluntary guidelines (a powerful argument to the media not to cooperate in drafting such documents in the future).

The question the media faced was whether the judge could make a case

that the restrictive order was a *necessary* step under the circumstances of
the Kellie murders. The media had two ways to learn the answer. They
could appeal the court order in the hopes that it would be overturned
quickly, or they could disobey it and appeal the contempt citation they were
sure to face. The second choice was lure for a martyr. In 1971 two reporters
disobeyed a federal district court order not to report evidence presented in
an open court hearing. Faced with a tight deadline and what they considered an important story, the reporters disobeyed the order, were cited for
contempt, and fined. The U.S. Court of Appeals, Fifth Circuit, found the
lower court order clearly unconstitutional, but ruled that court orders—
whether constitutional or not—"*must be obeyed*" (the court's emphasis)
until they are overturned by orderly review. This "Dickinson rule," named
for one of the reporters, looms over reporters faced with court "gag orders."
Although very sympathetic to the reporters, the appellate court offered no
real protection against unconstitutional orders except the requirement that
appeals of such orders must be reviewed promptly.[48]

The Nebraska media chose the second way to test the validity of the
Simants order; they obeyed it and appealed. In a process notable for its
delay, the media remained under one restriction or another (three separate
orders were entered by the Nebraska courts) until Simants went to trial in
January 1976. Six months later, after Simants had been convicted and
sentenced, the Supreme Court ruled that all of the orders of the Nebraska
courts were impermissible prior restraints. Just as it had done in the Pentagon Papers case, it refused to rule *all* prior restraints unconstitutional. It did
say, however, that before trial judges could constitutionally impose such
restrictive orders on the media, they must exhaust all the remedies suggested in *Sheppard* and have a reasonable expectation that the orders will
work to protect the defendant's rights. In Simants' case the Supreme Court
found no evidence that the Nebraska courts had considered any alternative
measures and found considerable evidence that the restrictions on Nebraska
media would be ineffective against local rumor and national coverage. The
Supreme Court's disapproval of "gag" orders on the media was clear if not
absolute.

What was absolute was the court's reiteration that the media cannot be
forbidden to report on open court proceedings or records. By not forbidding
the obvious "next step," however, the court most probably encouraged it:
The sealing of records and the closing of courtrooms to media and public
alike. Such alternatives offer the advantage of being an effective control
over at least some information without directly "gagging" the press. However, secret proceedings and secret records are hardly an advancement in
the cause of justice. One state court has already ruled that when courtrooms
are closed for the purpose of cutting off the flow of information to the media,
the decisions to do so must be subjected to the same scrutiny the Supreme
Court required for direct orders against the media.[49] This area is by no
means settled, and there is likely to continue to be a great deal of litigation.

There will also be, it seems, more cases on restrictive orders against trial
participants. Although the Supreme Court explicitly recommended such

The Government,
the Public, and the
Regulation of the
Mass Media

246

Media-Bar Guidelines

In response to the Supreme Court's decision in *Sheppard v. Maxwell,* a committee of the American Bar Association addressed itself to the free press/fair trial issues and produced in 1968 what is commonly known as the Reardon Report. The most substantial recommendations were directed at the conduct of attorneys and judges, although it did make some suggestions regarding the closing of hearings and the use of the contempt power. The ensuing controversy between media and bar, perhaps surprisingly, produced a considerable amount of cooperation in the form of media-bar guidelines. Strictly voluntary, such guidelines have been drafted by representatives of media and bar in at least 23 states.

Nebraska's guidelines, reprinted here, were incorporated in part in the first and second restrictive orders imposed on the media for the protection of Erwin Charles Simants.

Nebraska Bar-Press Guidelines for Disclosure and Reporting of Information Relating to Imminent or Pending Criminal Litigation

These voluntary guidelines reflect standards which bar and news media representatives believe are a reasonable means of accommodating, on a voluntary basis, the correlative constitutional rights of free speech and free press with the right of an accused to a fair trial. They are not intended to prevent the news media from inquiring into and reporting on the integrity, fairness, efficiency and effectiveness of law enforcement, the administration of justice, or political or governmental questions whenever involved in the judicial process.

As a voluntary code, these guidelines do not necessarily reflect in all respects what the members of the bar or the news media believe would be permitted or required by law.

Information Generally Appropriate for Disclosure, Reporting

Generally, it is appropriate to disclose and report the following information:

1. The arrested person's name, age, residence, employment, marital status and similar biographical information.

2. The charge, its text, any amendments thereto, and if applicable, the identity of the complainant.

3. The amount of conditions of bail.

4. The identity of and biographical information concerning the complaining party and victim, and, if a death is involved, the apparent cause of death unless it appears that the cause of death may be a contested issue.

5. The identity of the investigating and arresting agencies and the length of the investigation.

6. The circumstances of arrest, including time, place, resistance, pursuit, possession of and all weapons used, and a description of the items seized at the time of arrest. It is appropriate to disclose and report at the time of seizure the description of physical evidence subsequently seized other than a confes-

sion, admission or statement. It is appropriate to disclose and report the subsequent finding of weapons, bodies, contraband, stolen property and similar physical items if, in view of the time and other circumstances, such disclosure and reporting are not likely to interfere with a fair trial.

7. Information disclosed by the public records, including all testimony and other evidence adduced at the trial.

Information Generally Not Appropriate for Disclosure, Reporting

Generally, it is not appropriate to disclose or report the following information because of the risk of prejudice to the right of an accused to a fair trial:

1. The existence or contents of any confession, admission or statement given by the accused, except it may be stated that the accused denies the charges made against him. This paragraph is not intended to apply to statements made by the accused to representatives of the news media or to the public.

2. Opinions concerning the guilt, the innocence or the character of the accused.

3. Statements predicting or influencing the outcome of the trial.

4. Results of any examination or tests or the accused's refusal or failure to submit to an examination or test.

5. Statements or opinions concerning the credibility or anticipated testimony of prospective witnesses.

6. Statements made in the judicial proceedings outside the presence of the jury relating to confessions or other matters which, if reported, would likely interfere with a fair trial.

Prior Criminal Records

Lawyers and law enforcement personnel should not volunteer the prior criminal records of an accused except to aid in his apprehension or to warn the public of any dangers he presents. The news media can obtain prior criminal records from the public records of the courts, police agencies and other governmental agencies and from their own files. The news media acknowledge, however, that publication or broadcast of an individual's criminal record can be prejudicial, and its publication or broadcast should be considered very carefully, particularly after the filing of formal charges and as the time of the trial approaches, and such publication or broadcast should generally be avoided because readers, viewers and listeners are potential jurors and an accused is presumed innocent until proven guilty.

Photographs

1. Generally, it is not appropriate for law enforcement personnel to deliberately pose a person in custody for photographing or televising by representatives of the news media.

2. Unposed photographing and televising of an accused outside the courtroom is generally appropriate, and law enforcement personnel should not interfere with such photographing or televising except in compliance with an order of the court or unless such photographing or televising would interfere with their official duties.

3. It is appropriate for law enforcement personnel to release to representatives of the news media photographs of a suspect or an accused. Before

The Government,
the Public, and the
Regulation of the
Mass Media

248

publication of any such photographs, the news media should eliminate any portions of the photographs that would indicate a prior criminal offense or police record.

Continuing Committee for Cooperation

The members of the bar and the news media recognize the desirability of continued joint efforts in attempting to resolve any area of differences that may arise in their mutual objective of assuring to all Americans both the correlative constitutional rights to freedom of speech and press and to a fair trial. The bar and the news media, through their respective associations, have determined to establish a permanent committee to revise these guidelines whenever this appears necessary or appropriate, to issue opinions as to their application to specific situations, to receive, evaluate and make recommendations with respect to complaints and to seek to effect through educational and other voluntary means a proper accommodation of the constitutional correlative rights of the free speech, free press and fair trial.

June, 1970

orders in Sheppard, their form and use have come under challenge. One federal court of appeals has held that "gag" orders on participants are to be tolerated only in circumstances when there is a "serious and imminent threat to the administration of justice,"[50] but generally courts seem to be willing to use them under circumstances that would not support a "gag" order on the press. Although such orders on sources of information are only an indirect restraint on the media, they are direct restrictions on the First Amendment rights of participants. Particularly those who feel themselves unjustly dealt with by the criminal justice system or the political system or who feel the laws in question are themselves unjust would find such restrictions on their right to speak intolerable.

CAMERAS AND RECORDING EQUIPMENT IN THE COURTROOM

At the same time that some courts are shutting off coverage, other courts are experimenting with making their proceedings more accessible to the public through the media.

The American Bar Association after the excesses of the coverage of the 1935 trial of Bruno Hauptmann for the kidnapping and murder of Charles Lindbergh's son recommended in its Code of Judicial Responsibility, Canon 35, that cameras and recording equipment not be used during court proceedings. Part of the concern was that the use of bulky equipment, lights, and flashbulbs disrupted proceedings and detracted from the dignity of the courtroom. The prohibition on cameras and recording equipment was adopted by the federal and most of the state courts around the country. When television became available, it was also excluded.

In 1965 members of the U.S. Supreme Court gave these reasons, among others, for prohibiting television in the courtroom:

1. the potential impact on jurors who are subjected to the pressure of the community through this intense scrutiny;
2. the likelihood that the telecasting would distract jurors' attention from the testimony;
3. the subconscious influence on jurors who see televised reports that emphasize particular points at the expense of others;
4. the impact on potential jurors if a defendant is retried;
5. the impact on the quality of testimony given by witnesses (Television could induce cockiness, overstatement, embarrassment. Witnesses could be influenced by the televised testimony of earlier witnesses);
6. the burden on the judges who would have to supervise the televising of the proceedings in addition to their other responsibilities;
7. the potential that judges, especially elected judges, could attempt to use television to their personal advantage;
8. the impact on the defendant (The court likened telecasting to a form of mental harassment, which "might well transgress his personal sensibilities, his dignity, and his ability to concentrate on the proceedings. . . .").[51]

In the end, the court observed, "A defendant on trial . . . is entitled to his day in court, not in a stadium, or in a city or nationwide arena," and reversed the conviction of Billie Sol Estes because of the televising of pretrial hearings and the trial itself.

In essence, four members of the court felt television could never be anything but disruptive and offensive in the courtroom and thus should be constitutionally banned. The fifth member of the majority, however, was prepared to limit the ruling to the sensational case at hand and others like it and to accept that some day television might be so commonplace in our lives that it would not have the psychological impact the court worried about and that the technology of television might advance to the point where the equipment itself would not be disruptive.

The technology has advanced, and some observers have suggested that the scrutiny of television can hardly be more intimidating than the courtroom and trial itself. Cameras and tape recorders are still generally excluded from courtrooms, but several states have opened their processes, at least on an experimental basis, to television and still photography. In Florida a defendant indicted on embezzlement and narcotics charges requested that the court permit the broadcasting of his trial. He claimed that "only a full and accurate reporting of [the] trial by radio and television [would] cure the damage to [his] reputation, honor and integrity already destroyed by nine months of biased and slanted headlines." His case was not broadcast, but Florida has now opened its proceedings on an experimental basis. When the Washington Supreme Court changed court rules to permit the use of photographic and recording equipment, the Chief Justice said the rule "will give the public an opportunity to have a better idea of what goes on in the courtroom."[52] The perception of broadcasting as an antidote to newspapers

The Government,
the Public, and the
Regulation of the
Mass Media

250

or an educational tool is a far cry from the view the Supreme Court presented in the *Estes* case.

The American Bar Association has revised its Canon 35. In its new code (1972) the ABA continues the general advice that broadcasting, recording, or taking photographs in or near the courtroom should be prohibited, but sanctions exceptions for educational or practical purposes (such as closed circuit television to a press room). If technology is not distracting when used for these exceptions, it does not have to be distracting when used for news. What remains for scrutiny is *how* it is used.

Whatever the appearance, all lawyers and judges do not end up on one side of the free press/fair trial debate and all newspeople on the other. Lawyers and judges have spoken effectively on behalf of the media's First Amendment freedoms even in the fair trial context, and at least some journalists have recognized the need for cooperation and restraint to protect the rights of criminal defendants.

A Moral Society

The pressure to censor obscenity comes from those who are concerned that the unrestricted availability and blatant advertising of sexual material will undermine the morality of American society, incite antisocial sexual conduct (rape, for example), permanently damage the developing character of the nation's children, offend the sensibilities of those who do not wish to be exposed to it, and/or excite "impure thoughts" among those who do. It is relatively easy to regulate the marketing and advertising of obscenity so that it is not thrust upon someone who does not want it. It is more difficult to regulate its availability to children. It is *much* more difficult to regulate its use by willing adults. Will our neighbor accept our judgment when we tell him he is too weak-willed to be trusted with *Hustler?*

There are no hard data to show that use of obscenity will lead to the predicted consequences, and indeed, some evidence to the contrary, but the measurements of the causal relationships are by no means beyond question and many people have made intuitive or religious judgments from which they will not be swayed. In any case, the Supreme Court has considered the *proof* of obscenity's harm unnecessary. Obscenity has been assumed to lack social value, therefore it is not protected by the First Amendment and therefore there is no need to show that it presents a "clear and present danger" to the nation's morality or that it presents any other existing or potential harm.

Because the Supreme Court continues to consider obscenity outside the protection of the First Amendment, it continues to struggle with the problem of defining obscenity. Not all books, or films, or plays, or magazines that treat sexuality are obscene, the court tells us. The trick for the court is identifying which sexual material is obscene and which is protected speech. The line must be clearly drawn so that those who wish to deal with sexual topics will not be "chilled" from exercising their First Amendment rights to

do so because they cannot tell when they might be slipping over into
obscenity, a slip that could put them in jail. Justice Potter Stewart—with
frankness and some insight—wrote in 1964 that he would limit the criminal
laws to hard-core pornography, continuing, "I shall not. . . attempt to define
the kinds of material I understand to be embraced within that shorthand
description; and perhaps I could never succeed in intelligibly doing so. But I
know it when I see it, and the motion picture involved in this case is not
that."[53] The problem is, would anybody else "know" what Stewart knew?

The Supreme Court decided its first test of the constitutionality of
obscenity laws in the landmark case of *Roth v. United States* in 1957. It
upheld the constitutionality of the federal and California state obscenity
statutes involved. It did *not* hold that all jurisdictions must treat obscenity as
illegal. The role of the court is to set the guidelines under which state and
federal legislatures *may* outlaw obscenity if they choose, not to insist that
they do so. Justice William Brennan attempted for the court to define
"obscenity" with these words:

> Whether to the average person, applying contemporary community standards,
> the dominant theme of the material taken as a whole appeals to prurient
> interest.[54]

If it did, the work was obscene.

PRURIENT APPEAL

One definition of "prurient" is "characterized by lascivious or lustful
thoughts." There is considerable ambiguity in Brennan's definition, but he
did clearly limit the term "obscenity" to material that arouses or appeals to
sexual interests. Under dictionary definitions a war can be described as
obscene, but under the Supreme Court's definition it cannot be—unless it is
a war that appeals to someone's sexual sadomasochism.

This limitation to material with sexual appeal has been of no small
importance. Those inclined to use sexual or scatalogical terms in political
debate and discussion have been protected against obscenity convictions by
the court's ruling, for instance, that the phrase "Fuck the Draft" lettered on
the back of a jacket was not a sexual provocation but a political statement.[55]
Although there are bases for prosecuting those who use such words in
situations likely to produce violence, the court has resisted efforts to sanitize
the language. Even efforts to sanitize the language of television and radio,
despite their accessibility to very young children and the difficulty—even for
adults—of avoiding offensive content interspersed in acceptable fare, have
been unsuccessful so far.[56]

Sixteen years and hundreds of cases after *Roth,* the court returned to a
test quite similar to, but more restrictive than *Roth.* The very difficulty of
defining obscenity with sufficient clarity had taken the court during those
years close to abandoning the effort and to extending the protection of the
First Amendment to obscenity. That didn't happen, and a few persons spent

The Government,
the Public, and the
Regulation of the
Mass Media

252

time in jail because they misinterpreted the court's direction. In the 1973 case *Miller v. California* Chief Justice Warren Burger delivered the opinion for a court split 5 – 4, setting down these guidelines for the states:

> The basic guidelines for the trier of fact must be: (a) whether "the average person, applying contemporary community standards" would find that the work, taken as a whole, appeals to the prurient interest, (b) whether the work depicts or describes, in a patently offensive way, sexual conduct specifically defined by the applicable state law, and (c) whether the work, taken as a whole, lacks serious literary, artistic, political, or scientific value.[57]

The *Miller* decision swept the obscenity cases back to the states where the court, no doubt, hoped they would be resolved. The standards to be applied were local or state community standards, not national standards as had previously been asserted. And, as the court made clear in later cases, the jury could rely on what it believed to be its community's standards even if another jury from the same community might perceive different standards.

Unhappy with the burdensome tests of earlier cases, the *Miller* court intended to make criminal convictions easier. In *Roth* Justice Brennan had stated as an assumption that obscenity was "utterly without redeeming social importance." With a slight change of language, Brennan in the *Fanny Hill* case of 1966 turned that assumption into an additional test of obscenity.[58] A book, for instance, could not be judged obscene unless it was found "to be *utterly* without redeeming social value." (Brennan's emphasis.) That meant any book, magazine, or whatever that had even minimal value was not obscene under the law. It would be difficult for a prosecutor to prove the negative, that a book was *utterly* without value. Almost everything has *some* value. John Cleland, the eighteenth-century author of *Fanny Hill,* had celebrated Fanny's sexual experiences with explicit detail, but he had done so with considerable humor and without resorting to one vulgar word. Literary experts testifying at the trial cited the book for its "historical value," "literary merit," and "deliberate, calculated comedy."

The *Miller* court rejected the burden of Brennan's opinion in *Fanny Hill* and held that a work which "lacks *serious* literary, artistic, political, or scientific value" can be considered obscene. (Emphasis added.) The only example of a work with "serious . . . value" Burger offered was a medical textbook.

BRENNAN'S CONVERSION

One of the ironies of the *Miller* cases (five obscenity cases were handed down the same day) was Brennan's abandoning of his own tests. The *Miller* court rejected *Fanny Hill* but salvaged *Roth.* Brennan, the author of both tests, rejected both and confessed that the court had failed to define obscenity with sufficient precision to reconcile its suppression with First and Fourteenth Amendment principles. The overload of obscenity cases on the Supreme Court's docket was testimony, in his view, to the court's inability to draw lines in this area that others could see. He found the regulation of

A Moral Society
waste of society's resources.

With each new obscenity case that comes before the court Brennan reiterates his view of the foolishness of the court's enterprise. One can only wonder at his timing. If he had made his conversion just a few years earlier, when Black was available for a liberal majority, obscenity might now be protected speech—though probably still regulated.*

LOCAL COMMUNITIES' STANDARDS

Although the court had argued over the point, the community standards in pre-*Miller* days were supposed to be those of the national community. Acknowledging the diversity of communities throughout the land, Brennan had pointed out in 1964 that a local community standard could not properly be the test of what is protected by the federal constitution.[59] *Miller,* on the other hand, found a national standard in such a diverse nation a figment and accepted as constitutionally permissible the notion that standards might vary from locale to locale.

As Brennan had warned the acceptance of variable community standards creates substantial problems for the national distributor of films or books or magazines that treat sexual topics. How does one tell whether Wichita, Kansas, has the same community standards as New York City? How does one predict whether Cincinnati, Ohio, has the same standards as Columbus? The calamity of a wrong guess could be a criminal conviction.

The *Miller* case is an invitation to prosecutors in conservative communities to play censor for the nation. Publishers can be seduced (without much resistance) to a jurisdiction in which they stand small chance of beating an obscenity charge. In the summer of 1976 Al Goldstein and his co-publisher were convicted on 11 counts of using the mails to distribute obscene material—and one count of conspiracy.[60] They had mailed their publications, *Smut* and *Screw,* from New York to Kansas. *Smut* and *Screw* were not available on Kansas newsstands and between them had less than 15 subscribers in the state. Goldstein did not really seem to be putting the morals of Kansas in jeopardy, particularly because four of the subscribers were fake names for a New York postal inspector. The inspector had arranged for the subscriptions to be bought through Kansas post offices, then sent back to him unopened. Goldstein's willingness to send his publication to Kansas—and indeed to the other 49 states—made him vulnerable to prosecution wherever the federal government chose. As the prosecutor who brought him to trial in Wichita said, "If they mail to all 50 states, and they make profits in all 50 states, then they should be tried in any of the 50 states, not just New York."[61]

---

*Even as the Supreme Court was extending First Amendment protection to another pariah, commercial advertising, it noted that advertising, "like all public expression, may be subject to reasonable regulation that serves a legitimate public interest." *Bigelow v. Virginia,* 241 U.S. 809 (1975); *Virginia State Board of Pharmacy v. Virginia Citizens Consumer Council, Inc.,* 425 U.S. 748 (1976).

The Government,
the Public, and the
Regulation of the
Mass Media

254

Being tried in Kansas meant more than facing a jury more sheltered from sleaze and sex than New York City might provide. (One female juror was reported to have burst into tears at her first close look at Goldstein's publications.) It meant facing a jury likely to be more religiously and politically conservative. Disagreement with political and social views should not be the basis for obscenity convictions, but the nature of the political and social commentary that Goldstein sent along with the sex in *Screw* was perhaps more likely than the sex to offend Kansans. (For example, a two-page lampoon of the Catholic Church called "Holy Shit.")

Facing trial 1500 miles from New York also added to Goldstein's legal expenses the transportation and living costs for defendants, attorneys, and witnesses. And a conviction could encourage prosecutors in New Mexico, Alaska, or Kalamazoo to try their hand at prosecuting Goldstein.

The original conviction of Goldstein was thrown out because improper issues were raised by the prosecutor in his summation to the jury, but Goldstein was scheduled to be retried—back in Wichita.

The variation in community standards presents problems not only for publishers and distributors. Actor Harry Reems was convicted on federal obscenity and conspiracy charges based on one day's work in the film *Deep Throat.* Although the film was made in Miami, Florida, he and his co-defendants were tried in Memphis, Tennessee, a town he had not been in before the trial. His earnings from the film, $100, were small down payment on his legal fees. Reems had the good fortune of slipping through a loophole, however. He had done his day's work before the 1973 *Miller* decision, but he had been tried by the standards of that case. The trial court granted Reems a new trial after the Supreme Court had held in another case that the tougher *Miller* standards could not be applied retroactively—a reason of little benefit to future offenders. His co-defendants were unable to win new trials because their activities in the production, promotion, and distribution of *Deep Throat* had continued after *Miller.*[62] Reems was saved the expense of another trial when the government decided not to retry him.

"ORGANIZED CRIME" AND THE LIBERAL CONSCIENCE

A full-page newspaper ad protesting the conviction of Larry Flynt began,

> Dissident writers and artists in the Soviet Union and other nations are being villified and imprisoned, and President Jimmy Carter has stated his deep concern. In the wake of recent events, we urge the president to take a closer look at the restrictions of freedom of expression in America itself.

The ad continued with a brief description of the circumstances of Flynt's conviction and closed with these words:

> We the undersigned wish to protect the infringement of Mr. Flynt's rights under the First Amendment because it is a threat to the rights of all Americans. We cannot, under any circumstances, approve of government censorship. Further, we urge President Carter and all our fellow citizens to strengthen their commitment to protecting every American's right to freedom of expression.[63]

The comparison with Soviet dissidents offended many because Flynt's magazine, *Hustler,* a raunchy men's magazine, has not a moment of grace, style, or edification; but it is popular, increasingly so.

Lewis Lapham, the editor of *Harper's,* first agreed to sign the ad and then after buying a copy of *Hustler,* withdrew his support. Lapham wrote in *Harper's;*

> Mr. Flynt doesn't make it easy to quote passages from Milton's *Areopagitica.* . . . In Mr. Flynt's magazine I found myself confronted by the negation of the meaning embodied not only in the First Amendment but also in the idea of civilization. Why should I protect the man who seeks to destroy what I have worked to build? If I found somebody passing out leaflets that demanded my assassination, would I argue for his right to free expression?[64]

The comparison of Flynt's peepshow vulgarity with the threat of assassination was perhaps as much rhetoric as Flynt's likening himself to Soviet dissidents. Nevertheless, Flynt's magazine and Lapham's response to it reflect something of a basic constitutional dilemma. Does the First Amendment apply only to that which we approve? Is there a difference between supporting individuals' right to say or display what they please (and what others wish to buy) and encouraging or approving the transaction? Even if one disapproves of *Hustler,* was Flynt fairly dealt with by the law?

Like Goldstein, Flynt was tried in a jurisdiction in which his magazine was sold (Cincinnati) rather than in the community in which he published (Columbus). In February 1977 he was sentenced to 7 to 25 years in prison and fined $11,000 for pandering* obscenity and for engaging in organized crime in violation of Ohio state law. The crime of pandering obscenity, a misdemeanor, carries a six-months maximum sentence and a $1000 maximum fine. The conviction for engaging in organized crime accounts for the severity of Flynt's punishment. Under Ohio law if five individuals conspire to

---

*The term "pandering" took on legal significance in 1966 when the Supreme Court upheld the conviction of Ralph Ginzburg because he had advertised his magazine *EROS,* a biweekly newsletter, *Liaison,* and *The Housewife's Handbook of Selective Promiscuity* with "the leer of the sensualist."

Many critics of the decision consider the conviction a denial of due process because, as Justice Stewart pointed out in dissent, Ginzburg had been indicted not for pandering but for mailing obscenity. The court "assumed" that the materials were not obscene on their face but found Ginzburg's conduct sufficiently offensive to uphold his conviction with its five-year prison sentence. (The sentence was later reduced to three years; Ginzburg served eight months.) Some characterized Ginzburg's efforts to secure mailing privileges at Blue Ball and Intercourse, Pennsylvania, and Middlesex, New Jersey, as no more than a bad joke. The court, however, found such conduct part and parcel of the "commercial exploitation of erotica solely for the sake of their prurient appeal." The court ruled, "Where the purveyor's sole emphasis is on the sexually provocative aspects of his publications, the fact may be decisive in the determination of obscenity." There is a suggestion from the court that if Ginzburg had limited his appeals to physicians or psychiatrists, who could have used the materials for therapy, his claims of social value would have been more persuasive. *Ginzburg v. United States,* 383 U.S. 463, 86 S.Ct. 942, 16 L.Ed.2d 31 (1966).

Although Justice Stevens considers such "truthful" advertising to be fair warning to an unsuspecting consumer, the court continues to accept the notion that the manner in which a seller represents his wares has a bearing on whether they are to be judged obscene. *Splawn v. California,* 2 Med. L. Rptr. 1881 (1977).

The Government,
the Public, and the
Regulation of the
Mass Media

256

violate an obscenity law, they have committed a felony. Although other people, including Flynt's wife, were indicted, all but Flynt were acquitted. As Robert Yoakum phrased it in CJR, "Flynt became a one-man perpetrator of 'organized crime.'" He has appealed the conviction.

EROGENOUS ZONES

In the 1970s some communities tried to accommodate the interests of those who wanted access to adult entertainment and those who wanted to maintain the quality of community life. Different communities tried different approaches with varying success. Boston limited such entertainment to a two-block area now known as the Combat Zone. The concentration of low-life enterprises has attracted prostitution, other crimes, and violence. Boston's experiment received a particularly bad press when a Harvard football player was stabbed on the street in the area. Boston police were accused of turning the zone over to criminals.

A more popular zoning approach has been the one used in Detroit. As a part of an Anti-Skid Row Ordinance, Detroit in 1972 prohibited any more than two adult theaters, adult book stores, cabarets, bars, taxi dance halls, or similar enterprises within 1000 feet of each other or within 500 feet of a residential area.

The U.S. Supreme Court accepted Detroit's arguments that such restrictions were necessary because the concentration of such businesses within a limited area would almost inevitably lead to a decline in the neighborhood. The court accepted the zoning of protected expression (not all adult entertainment is obscenity) because such regulation did not suppress expression but only affected the *location* of adult businesses.[65]

Other cities responded to this encouragement from the Supreme Court and developed zoning ordinances patterned on Detroit's.

PRIVACY, OBSCENITY, AND CHILDREN

Some argue that in order to protect children, obscenity should be suppressed. Traditionally, the argument was meant to protect children as consumers or audience. The Supreme Court has approved a variable concept of obscenity that distinguishes what can be kept from children and what can be kept from adults, but the court has resisted efforts to limit adults to what children can withstand. Literature need not be reduced to fairy tales.

The concern to protect children took a new turn in the late 1970s, however. A society that had tested what seemed like the outer limits of sexuality and candor—from snuff movies (where the actress is killed or appears to be killed for sexual gratification) to bestiality—turned to a not-so-new but growing obscenity, the sexual use and abuse of children. In an article for *Ms.* a female reporter described with tangible disgust the use of children in pornography. She quoted people in the adult porno business who were contemptuous of those who trafficked in children. But in the end she confessed to "great [personal] conflict on the subject" of legislation to suppress "kid porn." She wrote, "The material is hateful. But to some of us

who dwell in print, the legislative effort seems a perilous step on what has
been called 'the slippery slope,' a fast downhill race toward problems of
capricious censorship. Who is to know whether the test applied to *Moppets*
today will not be used tomorrow on [*Ms.*]." But as another observer she
quoted put it, one has to wonder if "Thomas Jefferson did all that work" so
pornographers could display the sexual organs of little girls and boys.[66]

Another concern of all but the most liberal commentators on obscenity
or pornography is the protection of society's privacy. Adults who willingly
display themselves to the camera's eye and adults who choose to view them
can perhaps be left alone.* There is less tolerance, however, of those who
thrust sexual materials on unsuspecting individuals. "Nothing in the Constitution compels us to listen to or view any unwanted communication,
whatever its merit. . . ." To this end the law has been used to limit the
display and distribution of pornography. For example, some local ordinances require adult bookstores to blacken their windows so that only those
who *choose* to enter the store will encounter what many would consider
offensive. A federal statute permits individuals to define for themselves what
they find obscene—whether it be a sex manual, a sewing catalogue, or a
religious tract—and to enlist the support of the Postal Service in insisting the
mailer stop all future mailings.

The structure for regulating obscenity is complex, monumental, and
costly. Can it ensure a sexually moral society?

Progress and Creativity

If one assumes that the First Amendment is absolute, the very first Congress
violated it by passing a copyright law.

Article I, §8 of the federal Constitution empowered Congress "to promote the Progress of Science and useful Arts by securing for limited Times
to Authors . . . the exclusive Right to their Writings. . . ." With that authority
Congress has fashioned labyrinthine laws that extend a property right—a
copyright—to such intellectual creativity. The challenge to Congress has
been to provide for a copyright without hampering the free exchange of
opinion and information promoted by the First Amendment.

As a property right copyright is rather curious. Although it can be bought
and sold, inherited, divided, or given away, it does not relate to the
ownership of any physical thing. Buying a copy of Saul Bellow's *Humboldt's Gift* does not give any claim to ownership of the copyright of that

---

*The Supreme Court held in *Stanley v. Georgia,* 394 U.S. 557, 89 S.Ct. 1243, 22 L.Ed.2d
542 (1969), that it cannot be a crime for an individual to possess obscene materials in his
home. Justice Thurgood Marshall said for a unanimous court, "If the First Amendment means
anything, it means that a State has no business telling a man, sitting alone in his own house,
what books he may read or what films he may watch. Our whole constitutional heritage rebels
at the thought of giving the government the power to control men's minds." The principle has
not been extended to use outside the home, however.

The Government,
the Public, and the
Regulation of the
Mass Media

258

book. Ownership of the book—even the original manuscript—carries the right to dispose of it, sell it, or give it away, for example. It does not give the right to reproduce it for sale to others or turn it into a movie even if Bellow's authorship is acknowledged. If novelists or biographers can be deprived of the financial benefit of their labor by any enterprising plagiarist, there is little incentive or support for scholarship or artistic effort. The law of copyright does not guarantee financial reward, but it does protect what reward a work might win against those who would unfairly take for their own advantage what others create.

WHAT DOES COPYRIGHT PROTECT?

The 1978 revision* of federal copyright law grants protection to "original works of authorship fixed in any tangible medium of expression . . ." and includes the following categories:

1. Literary works [including books, periodicals, manuscripts, or any work expressed in words or numbers];
2. Musical works, including any accompanying words;
3. Dramatic works, including any accompanying music;
4. Pantomimes and choreographic works;
5. Pictorial, graphic, and sculptural works;
6. Motion pictures and other audiovisual works; and
7. Sound recordings.

Copyright protection can extend to any of the mass media. And, indeed, does apply to much of what you see, read, and hear even though little of it may appear truly original. For a work to qualify as original, it need not be innovative. The law requires only that it not be copied from someone else's work. In fact, the law protects only the manner or pattern of expression; copyright does not protect ideas or concepts or principles or discoveries. A historian cannot copyright history although he or she can copyright an expression of it. The line between manner of expression and ideas is obviously difficult to draw, and a close paraphrase can be considered as much a copyright infringement as a verbatim account.

Subject to some substantial limitations, the owner of a copyright has the right to control the reproduction and distribution of the copyrighted work, the preparation of derivative works, the public performance of a work (for example, for movies, plays, symphonies, choreographed dances), and the display of a work (for example, for sculpture, still photography, individual images of motion pictures, literature, music).

Until the 1978 federal law became effective, unpublished works were protected by the common law of the states. Common law copyright ended only with publication. Because it, in essence, gave control over whether a

---

* The revision, effective January 1, 1978, was passed and signed into law in 1976. See *United States Code Annotated* (U.S.C.A.), Volume 17, 1977.

work would be published or not, it protected privacy as much as financial interests. Under the common law, writers and their heirs could withhold a work from public distribution indefinitely even though another might own a copy of it. For example, the recipient of a letter might own the letter, but the common law gave control over whether even one line of that letter was published to the letter writer.

The 1978 federal law, however, erases all but traces of that common law copyright and limits the copyright for works created after January 1, 1978, to the author's life plus 50 years.[67] Beyond that period the privacy of the creator and any heirs is not so precious as to justify withholding material from public view. For material that is published, a longer period seems unnecessary economic incentive. Copyright scholar Melville Nimmer has observed, "It seems most unlikely that an author, assured of the economic fruits of his labor for his own lifetime, that of his children, and perhaps also his grandchildren, would elect not to engage in creative efforts because his posterity in perpetuity would not also benefit."[68] Although Nimmer was writing of the copyright limits of federal law before 1978, a maximum of 56 years from date of publication, his point remains apt.

FAIR USE

For much of this century the copyright for published works was governed by the 1909 federal copyright statute, which gave to the copyright holder the exclusive right "to print, reprint, publish, copy, and vend the copyrighted work." Because it would, if applied literally, have hampered rather than promoted a desirable exchange of information and ideas, the courts employed a doctrine known as "fair use." Congress incorporated the judiciary's creation in the 1978 law in these terms:

> [T]he fair use of a copyrighted work . . . for purposes such as criticism, comment, news reporting, teaching . . . scholarship, or research, is not an infringement of copyright. In determining whether the use made of a work in any particular case is a fair use the factors to be considered shall include—
> > (1) the purpose and character of the use, including whether such use is of a commercial nature or is for non-profit educational purposes;
> > (2) the nature of the copyrighted work;
> > (3) the amount and substantiality of the portion used in relation to the copyrighted work as a whole; and
> > (4) the effect of the use upon the potential market for or value of the copyrighted work.

Such provisions are essential for intellectual reflection and progress because they permit us to examine and to build on what has gone before. As legal scholar Zachariah Chafee noted, "[A] dwarf standing on the shoulders of a giant can see farther than the giant himself."[69] The exceptions for fair use make it possible for a critic to cite passages from the work being considered, for a scholar to marshal the wisdom of others before moving to the next plateau. Such exceptions, however, are granted with a weather eye on the financial interests of the copyright holder.

The Government,
the Public, and the
Regulation of the
Mass Media

260

The 1978 law offers a wide range of remedies to protect those interests. One who infringes another's copyright can be enjoined from continuing to do so, can find the infringing work impounded and even destroyed, can be sued for profits attributable to the infringement and for money damages to compensate for the harm suffered by the copyright holder. In addition, the person "who infringes a copyright willfully and for purposes of commercial advantage or private financial gain" can be imprisoned and fined.

TWENTIETH-CENTURY TECHNOLOGY

As new technologies have rendered compromises of earlier years inadequate, Congress has had to reconsider the copyright law. Having determined that a substantial revision of the 1909 copyright law was essential, Congress struggled for over a decade to accommodate the multiplying interests produced by the advancing technologies of the twentieth century— photography, movies, photocopying, computers, sound recording, radio, television, cable television.

CABLE AND COPYRIGHT

In 1968 the Supreme Court ruled that cable television systems were not infringing the rights of copyright holders by carrying copyrighted material picked up from broadcast signals. Even though broadcasters had to pay copyright fees and get permission to use copyrighted materials, the Supreme Court ruled that cable functioned as nothing more than a super antenna.[70] In 1974 the court repeated this conclusion in a case involving cable systems importing television signals from distant markets. The antenna would have to be monumental to fit the court's analogy, but the court continued to define cable as a method of transmission of broadcast signals, not as "performance for profit."[71] The court, of course, had to pull its decisions out of a 1909 statute that had been written by legislators who had not contemplated broadcasting, much less cable. The 1909 law gave copyright holders exclusive rights to control "performance for profit" but said nothing of reception.

The court victories were of no small interest to the cable industry, but precisely because they were based on a statute that was clearly outmoded, there were no illusions that those victories would stand forever. Cable had long known that it would have to pay royalties. What was negotiable was "how much" and what could be won in return.

The carriage of distant signals makes the cable copyright problem especially complex. Copyright holders obviously benefit from being paid for the use of their works. If a copyright holder contracts with a major market television station a payment of fees for the right to broadcast a program and if the station signal is picked up by cable systems in other markets, the copyright holder cannot easily require the television station to pay greater fees. The station's ability to earn greater revenues from advertisers is unaffected by the addition of viewers in distant markets. The television station has no control over the cable systems' use of its signal; the station's advertisers may well not be interested in paying increased rates for audiences in other markets. Although the value of the copyright in the initial market is not impaired, the copyright holder has almost no basis for negotiating performance rights in the added markets. Because the copyright owner cannot guarantee exclusivity to a station in an importing market, the station, if interested in the program at all, will be unwilling to pay large sums for the right to duplicate what is already available in that market. Duplication, broadcasters fear, means fragmented audiences and smaller advertising revenues.

The cable industry, on the other hand, has felt that its growth would be stunted if it were relegated to doing no more than improving the signals of local broadcasting stations. Requiring cable systems to negotiate with copyright holders or the originating stations for every program picked up from distant broadcast signal, the cable industry argued, would effectively frustrate their capacity to carry such signals at an economic cost to their subscribers.

The Consensus Agreement

In late 1971 the chairman of the Federal Communications Commission, Dean Burch, and the director of the White House Office of Telecommunications Policy, Clay Whitehead, steered the cable, copyright, and broadcast industries to an agreement that paved the way for major revisions in FCC regulation of the cable industry and the copyright laws. In exchange for the FCC's opening up major markets to cable development, the cable industry agreed to support legislation that would make cable liable for copyright. In addition, cable won the promise that copyright legislation would grant cable "compulsory licenses" for all signals the FCC determined in its initial reregulation of cable that a cable system would be entitled to carry. The provision for compulsory licensing meant that cable, although still limited by exclusivity agreements between broadcasters and copyright holders, would not have to negotiate with copyright holders or broadcast stations on a per-program basis. A standard fee schedule would be established.

The FCC's 1972 cable rules distinguish between "must" carry and "may" carry signals. For instance, a cable system *must* carry all local stations that request to be carried; how many distant signals a system *may* carry varies according to a complex formula that is keyed to the size of the market in which the cable system operates.

The 1971 consensus agreement and the 1972 cable rules were premised on action by Congress to bring copyright legislation in line. Promises had been made that only Congress could keep, but it took Congress until 1976 to pass responsive legislation. That legislation benefits cable much more than the 1971 consensus agreement promised.

Under the new legislation, cable is indeed liable for copyright, but as Michael Botein of Rutgers Law School has pointed out, "the legislation will neither make cable operators poor nor copyright holders rich." A "sound compromise," he suggests.[72]

The Government,
the Public, and the
Regulation of the
Mass Media

262

Under a rather modest schedule of fees, cable systems are granted compulsory licenses for all the signals they are permitted to carry by FCC regulation. However, they are required to pay only for distant signals, and the fees are fixed as percentages of the revenues a cable system generates by delivering broadcast signals. Although most broadcast programing is copyrighted, the law could lead, as Botein points out, to the anomalous situation of cable paying copyright fees for programs that aren't copyrighted merely because they are carried by distant signal and not paying for copyrighted material because it is picked up from local signals.

Only experience with the new legislation will reveal if it is fair in operation.

COPYRIGHT AND THE NEWS

News, like history, cannot be copyrighted. If news *could* be copyrighted, the competition for a scoop would be no enterprise for the faint-hearted. However, as with other types of content, the manner or pattern of expression is protectable. A newspaper can copyright its story on foreign government bribes. It cannot copyright the facts on which the story is based.

Even though the courts acknowledge that the facts of the news cannot be copyrighted, in some instances they have recognized a limited property right in those facts. When the Associated Press sued International News Service for distributing to INS clients news picked up from uncopyrighted AP wire stories, the Supreme Court ruled that such appropriation, though not a violation of copyright law, was a form of unfair competition. The Supreme Court described INS as "endeavoring to reap where it has not sown," and—by selling AP's news to AP's competitors—as "appropriating . . . the harvest of those who have sown."[73]

In other instances the events of the news are so wedded to the manner of expression that First Amendment interests seem to be in direct conflict with copyright. In one of those accidents of history Abraham Zapruder, a private citizen with a home movie camera, managed to film what he thought would be a parade but what turned into the assassination of President John Kennedy. Zapruder made copies of the film available to the Secret Service but sold the original and all copies to *Life* magazine. *Life* used some frames of the film in copyrighted articles and copyrighted the entire film. *Life* denied the use of any frames from the film to Josiah Thompson, an author who had written a careful account of the assassination in book form, despite an offer by his publisher to turn over all profits from the book to *Life*. The author and his publisher had detailed charcoal sketches made from the published frames for use in their book, and *Life* sued for copyright infringement. Under normal circumstances such close copying would amount to a violation, but the federal district court judge incorporated First Amendment arguments in a defense of fair use. He found "a public interest in having the fullest information available on the murder of President Kennedy," and "little, if any, injury to . . . the copyright owner." The judge found no competition between *Life* magazine and the Thompson book and speculated that the book would, "if anything, enhance the value of the copyrighted work."[74] But if Thompson were in direct competition with *Life,* should that mean *Life* had the right to withhold or use only as it chose pictures of such considerable significance? Consider all the speculation in recent years that the assassination was not the act of one man but a conspiracy.

A copyright conveys control over publication of the copyrighted expression. That control poses particularly knotty First Amendment problems when the copyrighted work itself is of tremendous interest or concern to the public and when the ideas conveyed by the work cannot readily be separated from the expression of those ideas. The significance of the Zapruder film inheres in the film itself. The most vivid translation into words could not convey its content adequately or as credibly.

The law of copyright both complements and conflicts with First Amendment interests, and Congress and the courts face a continuing challenge to minimize the conflict and to contend with the human genius to develop confounding new technologies.

Diversity of Ideas

It may seem curious to suggest that diversity of ideas is a value that conflicts with freedom of the press, but the increasing size and concentration of ownership of media institutions in the twentieth century and the technological scarcity of broadcasting have raised doubts about whether protecting the media from government regulation may not defeat rather than encourage the fundamental interests of the First Amendment. As the power wielded by the mass media—whatever its nature may be—has settled in fewer and fewer hands, the concern has grown that the real threat to the public's interest comes not from government but from private enterprise. Was the First Amendment really meant to protect attitudes like those expressed by the late Lord Thomson?: "I buy newspapers to make money to buy more newspapers to make more money. As for editorial content, that's the stuff you separate the ads with."

In the 1960s law professor Jerome Barron argued that the primary interest of those who controlled the mass media was to maximize profit, not discussion. If society was to benefit from the wisdom of its people—those who didn't own the media as well as those who did—and if society wished to avoid the violence generated by the frustration of those who felt closed out of meaningful participation in public debate, then there must be a right of access for the public to the established media forums.

Barron's arguments were clearly influenced by his observation of the heated debate over American involvement in Southeast Asia and over the civil rights movement in which demonstrators used violence as a tactic to attract the attention of the major media. Barron wondered if society could afford such a destructive system of debate.

The Government,
the Public, and the
Regulation of the
Mass Media

264

Barron urged a new interpretation of the First Amendment:

There is an anomaly in our constitutional law. While we protect expression once it has come to the fore, our law is indifferent to creating opportunities for expression. Our constitutional theory is in the grip of a romantic conception of free expression, a belief that the "marketplace of ideas" is freely accessible. But if ever there were a self-operating marketplace of ideas, it has long ceased to exist. The mass media's development of an antipathy to ideas requires legal intervention if novel and unpopular ideas are to be assured a forum—unorthodox points of view which have no claim on broadcast time and newspaper space as a matter of right are in a poor position to compete with those aired as a matter of grace.

. . .

Today ideas reach the millions largely to the extent that they are permitted entry into the great metropolitan dailies, news magazines, and broadcasting networks. The soap box is no longer an adequate forum for public discussion. Only the new media of communication can lay sentiments before the public, and it is they rather than the government who can most effectively abridge expression by nullifying the opportunity for an idea to win acceptance. . . .

What is required is an interpretation of the First Amendment which focuses on the idea that restraining the hand of government is quite useless in assuring free speech if a restraint on access is effectively secured by private groups. A constitutional prohibition against governmental restrictions on expression is effective only if the Constitution ensures an adequate opportunity for discussion. Since this opportunity exists only in the mass media, the interests of those who control the means of communication must be accommodated with the interests of those who seek a forum in which to express their point of view.[75]

THE TRADITIONAL REMEDY—REGULATION OF BUSINESS PRACTICES AND OWNERSHIP

When during the 1930s Governor Huey Long found himself the object of increasingly severe criticism, the Louisiana legislature passed a tax of 2 percent of gross receipts on all periodicals with more than 20,000 weekly circulation. It did seem more than coincidence that, of the 13 newspapers with 20,000 or more circulation, 12 were critics of the Long political machine. A unanimous Supreme Court found such discriminatory and punitive taxation "a deliberate and calculated device . . . to limit the circulation of information to which the public is entitled. . . ."[76]

The circumstances of the case illustrate why enthusiasm for government regulation of the business side of the news media should be tempered by a recognition that the power to affect the business side carries the power to affect editorial content. If government can undermine the business operations of a newspaper, it can sap the paper's editorial courage.

Nevertheless, the protection against arbitrary and repressive action by government does not include protection against nondiscriminatory taxation or business laws of general application. The antitrust laws—applicable, at least until the passage of the Newspaper Preservation Act in 1970, to shoe companies and media alike—have long been considered the government tool for maximizing the diversity of ideas that is least likely to be warded off by First Amendment arguments.

When the Associated Press refused membership to the new Chicago *Sun* in the early 1940s, the Justice Department brought suit against the AP. The AP, cooperatively owned, had long protected its members by refusing to sell its service to their competitors without the members' consent.[77] The *Sun* was unable to obtain AP service because its competitor in the morning field, the Chicago *Tribune,* would not waive new membership fees of $350,000 for the *Sun.* That the *Sun* supported Franklin D. Roosevelt against the Roosevelt-hating *Tribune* added emotional overtones. Robert Lasch described the struggle:

> Almost to a man, the publishers of America interpreted the filing of this action as a foul assault against the First Amendment, and with frightening unanimity exerted all their power to impress upon the public that point of view.
>
> "We see in this, not the end perhaps, but surely the greatest peril, to a free press in America," said the Detroit *News.* From the citadel of its monopoly position in a city of 600,000 the Kansas City *Star* cried: "This is the sort of thing that belongs in the totalitarian states, not in a free democracy." "In the event of a government victory," said the New York *Daily News,* "the press services of the United States will be under the thumb of the White House."
>
> These were not extremist positions. They represented a fair sample of the opinion handed down by the press . . . [78]

In retrospect the press outcry seems a bit silly. The government won the case, the *Sun* got AP service, the White House did *not* put its thumb on the wire services, and no newspaper was restrained or censored. The question was commercial: Whether a news service could be withheld from some newspapers for competitive reasons. And the outcome is ironic: While access to the AP service may have helped sustain the independent voice of the Chicago *Sun* for a time—in 1948 it merged with the Chicago *Times*— it also meant more newspapers were relying on the *same* source for national and international news.

The philosophical thrust of the government's antitrust actions against the media has been to promote diversity of ideas by promoting diversity of ownership. U.S. Court of Appeals Judge Learned Hand made the argument most memorably in the *AP* case:

> . . . [the newspaper] industry serves one of the most vital of all general interests: the dissemination of news from as many different sources, and with as many different facets and colors as is possible. That interest is closely akin to, if indeed it is not the same as, the interest protected by the First Amendment; it presupposes that right conclusions are more likely to be gathered out of a multitude of tongues than through any kind of authoritative selection. To many this is, and always will be, folly; but we have staked upon it our all.[79]

It has become increasingly apparent in the 1960s and 1970s that the antitrust laws, with their focus on concentration of ownership and anticompetitive practices within a particular market, are ineffective tools for inhibiting the growth of newspapers chains or the absorption of media outlets into national and international conglomerates.

Even within markets the force of antitrust laws for promoting indepen-

The Government,
the Public, and the
Regulation of the
Mass Media

266

dence has been gutted. When the Justice Department succeeded in forcing two newspapers in Tucson, Arizona, to separate their joint business operations that violated antitrust laws, the Congress rescued the Tucson papers and 21 other joint newspaper operations around the country, extending exemptions from key portions of the antitrust laws to all newspapers that kept their editorial voices separate and that refrained from engaging in anticompetitive practices such as predatory pricing. The ostensible intent of this Newspaper Preservation Act was the securing of two independent editorial voices where only one would survive the forces of the marketplace. New combinations were permitted if one of the newspapers could demonstrate it was in danger of financial failure. The law did not account for the impact on other newspapers' ability to compete against papers "preserved" by act of Congress.

From Professor Barron's perspective, however, the ineffectiveness of the antitrust laws in securing a diversity of owners is of only moderate importance. As he points out, in this society influence comes not from speaking, but from being heard. The objective is not to be able to start a new newspaper or to preserve an old one, but to gain access to the *audiences* of the significant existing forums—whether they be the New York *Times* or CBS for a national political discussion or the hometown newspaper for a local issue. For this reason cable television, which has often been suggested as the answer to the access problem because of its tremendous channel capacity, is really no answer at all. Getting on the cable may be soul-satisfying, but it doesn't guarantee an audience.

ACCESS TO THE PRINT MEDIA

Barron's arguments stimulated major efforts in the 1960s and early 1970s to mandate public access to established media. The intent was to have a direct impact on content. Barron looked to the courts to apply his new interpretation of the First Amendment and permit government-enforced diversity. For the most part, however, the courts were unhelpful. Access arguments were successful only in instances where it could be demonstrated that government or extensions of government were involved—in violation of the First and Fourteenth Amendment prohibitions on *government* action—in the denial of access. For example, the courts approved limited rights of access to students newspapers at *state*-supported universities or high schools and to bar journals operated by *state* bar associations, but not to *privately* owned newspapers.

The Tornillo Case

The firmest rejection of Barron's arguments came in a case ill-conceived to present the basic concern for opening the media to new voices and new ideas. In 1918 Florida had passed a law that made it a misdemeanor for a newspaper to "assail" the personal character or public record of any candidate for public office without giving that candidate a chance to reply free of charge. An offender was subject to jailing, a fine, or both. The statute   Diversity of Ideas

267

free of charge. An offender was subject to jailing, a fine, or both. The statute was limited to newspapers, it applied only to candidates, and it took no note of whether the charges were true or false, defamatory or not. In essence, newspaper editors could be jailed for publishing what they knew and could prove was true if no space was provided for reply.

In the fall of 1972 Pat Tornillo, Jr., a candidate for the Democratic nomination in a Florida state legislature primary, sought to use the law. Five days before the primary election Tornillo demanded from the Miami *Herald* a right of reply to a critical editorial the paper had run several days earlier. The *Herald* refused to give space for a reply to this or the next editorial it ran criticizing Tornillo. Tornillo took the paper to court.

The case record did not reflect several facts that nevertheless help us understand why the access issue has been the subject of such lively debate. As head of a local teachers' union, Tornillo had come under considerable criticism in the news and editorial columns of the Miami *Herald.* In the past he had written letters to the paper rebutting the criticism, and many of these, along with his paid political advertisements, had been published by the *Herald.* A benefactor of the Newspaper Preservation Act's approval of joint operating agreements between newspapers in the same community, the morning *Herald* operated a joint business department with the evening Miami *News,* which *supported* Tornillo's candidacy.[80]

Tornillo, with Jerome Barron as his legal counsel, convinced the Florida Supreme Court that the increasing economic concentration of the mass media worked an unfair hardship on the individual seeking to be heard in the marketplace. However, the United States Supreme Court opted for the more traditional view that editorial decisions were to be made by editors, not public officials. Without really denying the basic criticism lodged against the print media, the court ruled that "press responsibility is not mandated by the Constitution and like many other virtues cannot be legislated." In essence, the court recognized that the First Amendment extended the right to be irresponsible as well as responsible, unfair as well as fair—subject, of course, to the laws of libel, privacy, and all those other exceptions already carved out of the First Amendment by the court.

BROADCAST RESPONSIBILITY

In the *Tornillo* decision the Supreme Court quoted with approval a passage from one of its earlier decisions:

> The power of a privately owned newspaper to advance its own political, social, and economic views is bounded by only two factors: first, the acceptance of a sufficient number of readers—and hence advertisers—to assure financial success; and, second, the journalistic integrity of its editors and publishers.[81]

The focus on newspapers was not casually stated. Broadcasters use a scarce, publicly owned resource, the airwaves, and so continue to be less generously dealt with under the First Amendment.

The Government,
the Public, and the
Regulation of the
Mass Media

268

The Federal Communications Commission

The government agency with primary responsibility for focusing broadcasters' attention on their responsibilities is the Federal Communications Commission. There is nothing like it for the print media.

The commission is made up of seven members, each of whom is appointed for seven years by the President of the United States, subject to the approval of the Senate. No more than four of the seven may be members of the same political party, and their terms of office expire at different times. These provisions of the Federal Communications Act were designed to insulate the commission from partisan politics. They have succeeded, but not completely. Dean Burch, who was appointed commission chairman by President Nixon in 1970, remarked after an FCC decision that was not to his liking that the expiring terms of two FCC members would soon enable the President to appoint commissioners with more favorable attitudes.

The commission with its staff of almost 2,500 has responsibility for regulating broadcasting "in the public interest, convenience, and necessity." It is also responsible for a host of other things, including some aspects of cable television, interstate telephone and teletype, and communication satellites.

As an independent regulatory agency, the commission combines in one institution legislative, executive, and judicial powers. Under a broad grant of authority from Congress it has considerable scope to write rules and regulations, to administer those rules and regulations as well as the specific provisions of the Communications Act, to judge whether anyone has violated its rules or regulations or the act itself, and to punish those it finds in violation. All of its activities are subject to judicial review. Its power is circumscribed, of course, by the President's and Congress's control over the selection of members and over its budget. Congress can also rewrite or amend the Communications Act if it finds commission actions unacceptable. Indeed, Congress could abolish the commission if it chose.

The Licensing Authority

Congress has empowered the FCC to grant renewable broadcast licenses for periods of up to three years. While renewal has proven to be almost automatic, the renewal process was meant as an opportunity for the commission to keep check on whether the licensee is serving the public interest, and it has proved an important point for pressure from citizens' groups. Broadcasters are identified as trustees or fiduciaries, not owners, of a valuable, limited public resource. This fundamental principle has justified government insistence on a measure of responsibility from broadcasters that is not required of the print media.

Before granting a license the commission considers whether the applicant has the necessary legal, technical, financial, and character qualifications. For example, the applicant must be an American citizen who is capable of complying with the commission's technical requirements for broadcast service, who has enough money to operate the station, and who will observe the provisions of the Communications Act and the rules and regulations of the commission. Such qualifications are a source of continuing interest to the commission, and licensees who fail to continue to meet them can find themselves fined or may have their licenses revoked or renewed on a short-term basis.

Among other considerations that have interested the commission in the licensing and renewal processes have been the concentration of ownership of broadcast facilities, the cross-ownership of broadcast facilities with other media, commercial practices, the involvement of the owners in the management of the station, the equal employment opportunity record, and program proposals and performance.

Through its allocation of the spectrum—that is, the frequencies where broadcasting is feasible—and its exercise of the licensing authority, the commission has had a considerable impact on the shape of the industry. Some argue that it is the misallocation of the spectrum by the FCC that has made the resource seem more limited than it is.

In assigning frequencies to various services and locations, the commission's declared intent is to ensure that all parts of the nation have local television and radio service and that the number of such signals be fairly distributed among the states. The commission has also attempted by general policy statement, through its licensing of individual stations, and through its rule-making powers to maximize the diversity of control of broadcast outlets. Its rationale for focusing on ownership patterns closely parallels that advanced for antitrust law: Diversity of content is encouraged without direct regulation of content. The commission wrote in 1953:

> It is our view that the operation of broadcast stations by a large group of diversified licensees will better serve the public interest than the operation of broadcast stations by a small and limited group of licensees. . . . Simply stated, the fundamental purpose of this facet of the multiple ownership rules is to promote diversification of ownership in order to maximize diversification of program and service viewpoints as well as to prevent any undue concentration of economic power contrary to the public interest. . . . [W]e wish to emphasize that by such rules diversification of program services is furthered without any government encroachment on what we recognize to be the prime responsibility of the broadcast licensee.[82]

To secure diversity within markets the commission has adopted rules prohibiting all same-broadcast-medium combinations and many cross-media combinations. Thus an individual or group cannot own or control two radio or television stations within the same market, although AM-FM combinations are not prohibited because AM and FM radio are considered different broadcast services. Nor is anyone allowed to acquire such cross-media combinations as VHF television station–radio station, cable television service–television station, newspaper–radio station, or newspaper–television station.

Many of the commission's multiple-ownership-within-a-market rules are

The Government,
the Public, and the
Regulation of the
Mass Media

270

relatively new. With very few exceptions the commission has sought to avoid what it considers the harshness of requiring existing combinations to sell off properties in order to fall in line with its rules. When the commission in 1975 sought to break up same market newspaper–broadcast station operations, it "grandfathered" all but 16 of the existing combinations—that is, it exempted established combinations from the new regulations. The commission has been criticized for protecting existing owners and, thus, limiting the opportunities for new people, particularly minorities, to buy into the broadcast industry. In March of 1977 the U.S. Court of Appeals, D.C. Circuit, told the commission to break up all such combinations unless they could be demonstrated on a case-by-case basis to be in the public interest.

To discourage national concentration of broadcast ownership, the FCC prohibits ownership or control of more than seven AM radio stations, seven FM radio stations, and seven television stations (no more than five of which may be the more desirable VHF signal stations). Thus, a network such as NBC may not own more than seven television stations around the country. The networks reach their large audience by supplying affiliate stations with programing in markets in which they do not hold a license. It is this affiliate relationship, in which a network acts as a broker for programing for stations around the country, that has limited the impact of the commission's national ownership rules on diversity of programing. A viewer would find much the same fare on an ABC station in Texas as on an ABC station in Wisconsin.

The commission has not yet really come to grips with regional concentration of ownership of broadcast facilities or with the co-ownership of communications outlets and other business interests.[83]

Program Content

The Federal Communications Act denies the commission the power to censor broadcasters apart from such classes of speech as obscenity, indecency, profanity, fraud, and lottery information. The commission may not interfere with broadcasters' right of free speech. But the commission, under the umbrella of the public interest standard, has taken the position that it must necessarily concern itself with overall program content and in some instances with specific programing decisions.

Ascertainment   Broadcasters are expected to provide programing that serves the public interest, convenience, and necessity of their local communities. The commission requires new applicants to submit programing proposals based on a careful assessment of the needs and interests of the communities they seek to serve. Licensees seeking renewal have to demonstrate that they have followed the commission's procedures for ascertaining local community problems. Throughout the license period the broadcaster is expected to consult with a broad range of community leaders and each year designate "ten significant problems, needs, and interests ascertained during the preceding year" and "the programs broadcast in response to these problems."

Although localism has long been the bedrock of broadcast regulation, ascertainment rules were not formalized until 1971. During his tenure as a commissioner Glen Robinson disapproved of the procedures, noting "that more than half of a sample of network affiliate television stations that he examined *decreased* the amount of time devoted to local programing after the ascertainment rules went into effect."[84] Such a result seems hardly worth the administrative costs to the commission or the broadcasters, although the decrease would have been even greater without the rules. Nevertheless, the ascertainment requirements remain in effect.

Program Format   The commission expects television stations to provide a mix of programing that suits the particular characteristics of the local community. The commission said in its 1960 programing policy statement:

> The major elements usually necessary to meet the public interest, needs and desires of the community in which the station is located as developed by the industry, and recognized by the Commission, have included: (1) Opportunity for Local Self-Expression, (2) The Development and Use of Local Talent, (3) Programs for Children, (4) Religious Programs, (5) Educational Programs, (6) Public Affairs Programs, (7) Editorialization by Licensees, (8) Political Broadcasts, (9) Agricultural Programs, (10) News Programs, (11) Weather and Market Reports, (12) Sports Programs, (13) Service to Minority Groups, (14) Entertainment Programming.

In recent years there has been considerable discussion of whether the commission should set the percentages of time a station should devote to specific categories of programing, particularly news and public affairs. The commission has resisted doing so on a formal basis, but it allows the commission staff to renew licenses—all other things being acceptable—without full commission consideration if a station does meet certain minimum standards.

The commission has faced a particularly difficult problem of diversity of programing in a market when local groups have sought to keep particular radio stations from changing formats when they changed hands. For example, if the sole classical music station in a particular community is to be sold to someone who proposes an already widely available format of, say, "rock" music, can or should the commission prevent that change? The commission has been reluctant to try, even though the U.S. Court of Appeals, D.C. Circuit, has pushed it to consider doing so.

Networking   The commission does not license the networks directly, but its power over individual licensees—particularly those owned and operated by the networks—gives it considerable indirect influence over network practices. Broadcast licensees are responsible for everything that is broadcast through their facilities whether it is advertising or programing, whether its source is a network, an independent supplier, or the licensees themselves. The licensees cannot enter into a contract that would put such control in anyone else's hands—not in the hands of networks and not in the hands of citizens' groups. Thus, licensees who enter into affiliate relationships with networks cannot transfer control over programing.

There have been many examples of local stations preempting programs

The Government,
the Public, and the
Regulation of the
Mass Media

272

or episodes of programs of which they disapprove or rescheduling those they think unsuitable for particular audiences. For example, when episodes of CBS's "Maude" dealt with abortion, affiliates around the country refused to run them. As a practical matter, however, local stations rarely have the opportunity to see network programing sufficiently in advance to influence the content substantially. That lack of opportunity has been a central issue in a recent petition to the commission to conduct an inquiry into network dominance over local stations. The petitioner, Westinghouse Broadcasting Company, warned that the "networks are trying to change local stations into mere extensions of the national network program pipeline. . . . If this is allowed to continue, local affiliated stations will ultimately perform functions little different from cable TV outlets."

Prime Time Access Rule   The Prime Time Access Rule represents a direct assault by the commission on the networks' control of prime time programing. First announced in 1970, it has survived several court challenges and two FCC revisions. The rule, as it now stands, requires that stations in the top 50 markets broadcast no more than three hours of national network programing or programing previously shown on a network during the four evening hours designated as prime time (7 – 11 p.m. Eastern Time, 6 – 10 p.m. Central Time). (The FCC has exempted from the rule certain categories of programing, for example, public or documentary programs, programs for children, political broadcasts.)

The objectives of the commission are these:

> (1) to reduce network "dominance" over programming decisions, (2) to provide market opportunities to new creative talent which were presumed to be foreclosed by the network triopoly, (3) to re-establish local control of programming decisions which were presumed to have been increasingly appropriated by the networks [an increase in local programming was mentioned only incidentally as a benefit in the original order; however, it has since become an important rationale of the rule], and (4) to increase the supply of first-run syndicated programming.[85]

By the commission's own standards the rule had—at least in its early effects—to be considered unsuccessful. The fare offered during the access period generally took the form of low-budget game shows and animal shows. The court reviewing the third version of the Prime Time Access Rule offered this minimal hope:

> One may assume that in the long run game shows will pale to some extent and that independent producers will have to turn to more variegated fare if they wish to survive, but any prophecy on public taste, certainly by judges, would be hazardous indeed.[86]

The third version went into effect in September of 1975. It has had the longer run the court considered necessary. Viewers can judge for themselves whether it has been effective.

Equal Opportunity for Political Candidates   Section 315 of the Federal Communications Act states that if broadcasters permit their stations to be used by a legally qualified candidate for any public office, they must provide equal opportunities to all other candidates for that office. In essence, Congress is insisting that broadcasters be evenhanded—not a foolish requirement from the perspective of an *elected* public official.

If broadcasters give time to one candidate, they must give time, on request, to all other candidates for that same office. If they sell time to one, they need only be prepared to sell it to the others. If one candidate is sold five minutes during prime time, another candidate's commercial cannot be relegated to Sunday morning. The opportunities must be equal.

In 1959 Congress amended Section 315 to exempt bona fide news programing. Failure to do so would have forced broadcasters either to avoid covering political campaigns or to give equal time to the candidates of every other party—major or fringe, from the Republican Party to the Happy Birthday Party—whenever a candidate, even a candidate who is an incumbent, was covered. Imagine how much coverage a television station would give to a Democratic mayor before a Democratic primary in which five other Democrats were running if the station had to provide equal opportunities to all of them.

Broadcasters, in addition to being required to be evenhanded, are forbidden by Section 315 from censoring candidates. The time that candidates get under Section 315 is theirs to use as they please, as they think will most benefit their candidacy. They can make a political speech or they can do a soft shoe dance.

The original Section 315 required that broadcasters treat all candidates for the same office equally. It did not require that access be given to anybody. But in 1971 Congress amended the Federal Communications Act to say that it would be "unreasonable" for broadcasters to willfully and repeatedly refuse to sell or give time to federal candidates, and it required broadcasters who sold time to any candidates during specified periods before elections to charge the lowest commercial rate. Both changes were designed to make the air waves more accessible to candidates.

What may seem to be a straightforward principle—that broadcasters treat candidates equally—has generated a maze of FCC rulings that broadcasters find frustrating and confusing. For example, the categories of news programing that Congress exempted in 1959 include (1) bona fide newscasts, (2) bona fide news interviews, (3) bona fide news documentaries, if the appearance of the candidate is incidental, and (4) on-the-spot coverage of bona fide news events (including, but not limited to, political conventions and activities incidental to them). Nevertheless, Congress felt it necessary in 1960 to suspend Section 315 so that broadcasters could cover the Nixon-Kennedy debates in their entirety without incurring equal opportunity obligations to other candidates. In 1962 the commission ruled in two cases that coverage of debates in their entirety was not exempt even though the debates were clearly newsworthy. In 1964 the commission ruled that coverage of press conferences held by President Lyndon Johnson and the Republican challenger, Barry Goldwater, was not exempt but that time given to the President by the three networks to discuss two international

The Government,
the Public, and the
Regulation of the
Mass Media

274

events was exempt, even though the President appeared just a couple of weeks before the election. In 1972 the commission ruled that a debate between two leading candidates in the California Democratic primary aired on "Face the Nation," a regularly scheduled news interview show, was exempt from Section 315 even though the show was expanded from a half-hour to an hour. (At the insistence of the U.S. Court of Appeals, D.C., the commission reconsidered and ruled that a third candidate was entitled to a half-hour of time.) Then in 1975 the commission decided it had been *wrong all those years.* On-the-spot coverage of newsworthy press conferences was exempt from Section 315. Coverage of debates not controlled by the candidates or the broadcasters was exempt from Section 315.

The issue of what is exempt and what is not is of no small significance to broadcasters trying to predict what their obligations will be, to third-party candidates excluded from minutes or hours of free time during the campaign, to major candidates trying to plan their strategy, and to the rest of us trying to figure out what is going on during an election campaign.

The Fairness Doctrine From a very early date broadcasters have been expected to play fair. In 1929 the Federal Radio Commission expressed the view that the "public interest requires ample play for the free and fair competition of opposing views, and the Commission believes that the principle applies . . . to all discussions of issues of importance to the public." The Federal Radio Commission and its successor, the Federal Communications Commission, went so far as to deny license renewals to stations that disregarded the principle of fairness. In 1941 the FCC, taking note of the limited nature of the radio spectrum, forbade licensees to use their frequencies for partisan ends. They were not to editorialize. Then in 1949 the commission reversed itself, abandoned the prohibitions on editorializing, and announced the Fairness Doctrine, encouraging broadcasters to express their own views as long as they were a part of *balanced* coverage. As one television critic remarked, it was like letting the umpire play in the game.

The "rules" of the game have changed somewhat in the 30 years of experience with the Fairness Doctrine, but the basic principles remain constant: As part of their responsibility to program in the public interest, licensees have an affirmative obligation to provide coverage of controversial issues and to treat those issues in a fair and balanced manner. There are no exceptions to this general requirement of the Fairness Doctrine for news or any other programing. Only advertising can claim some exceptions.[87]

As the doctrine is currently administered, if one side of an issue is given the opportunity to make its arguments or if the licensee advances one side of a controversial issue, the licensee has a responsibility to the public to seek out competing views and to put them on the air without charge if they cannot afford or choose not to pay. Except in instances of attack on a specific individual or group, the broadcaster's obligations are not to particular spokesmen but to the public. It is the listener's "right to hear," as the Supreme Court has phrased it, that is paramount.

Except in the narrow circumstances of personal attacks made during discussion of controversial issues, the doctrine affords no right of access as Jerome Barron sought. The purpose is fairness, not access.

The judgments of what constitutes a controversial issue, what views should be aired, and who should voice them are all left to the discretion of the licensee. The only role for the commission to play is to determine whether the licensee's judgments have been "reasonable"—not whether they are right, but whether they are reasonable.

Of course, deciding what is reasonable is exactly what the government cannot do with the print media, and substantial challenges to the constitutionality of the Fairness Doctrine have been mounted. In 1969, in its *Red Lion Broadcasting* decision, the Supreme Court approved both the general terms of the Fairness Doctrine and the specific provisions of the commission's personal attack rules on the ground that, unlike the print media, broadcasting is a limited facility that not all can enjoy.[88] Thus, it is not inappropriate for the commission to require some accommodation of the public's First Amendment interest through the Fairness Doctrine.

In 1970 two organizations attempted to transform the Fairness Doctrine into a right of access, at least for those willing and able to pay for it. The Democratic National Committee (DNC) asked the FCC to rule that a broadcaster, as a general policy, could not refuse to sell time to "responsible entities" such as the DNC. The DNC wanted broadcast time for fund-raising and for comment on public issues. Another organization, Business Executives Move for Vietnam Peace (BEM), filed a complaint with the FCC against a Washington radio station for refusing to sell time to BEM for spot announcements on the Vietnam War.

The central issue presented was very much an access issue: Must a licensee sell time for discussion of a controversial issue to a particular entity? The commission said no. The U.S. Court of Appeals, D.C. Circuit, said yes. The Supreme Court said no.[89]

The choice was whether the public was better served by a common-carrier broadcasting system (all who can pay can ride) or a system that relies on the judgment of licensees acting as trustees for the public's right to see and hear. The Court of Appeals had thought it ridiculous that broadcasters could restrict purchase of air time to those who sold soap and shampoo, but the Supreme Court worried that public issue advertising could be dominated by those who had money. In the end the Supreme Court opted for the FCC's experience and judgment that the public was better served by a Fairness Doctrine that relied on licensee discretion than by a system of paid access.

The commission has not always accepted broadcasters' judgments as reasonable. Brandywine-Main Line Radio Co. earned the distinction in 1970 of being the first station to lose its license for violating the Fairness Doctrine. The commission administered the extreme sanction because the station had failed to provide response time to those attacked during its programs.

The Government,
the Public, and the
Regulation of the
Mass Media

276

ANATOMY OF A
FAIRNESS DOCTRINE COMPLAINT

THE FCC'S ROLE IN
FAIRNESS DOCTRINE
REGULATION:

THE FCC DOES NOT SIT AS A NATIONAL CENSOR BOARD BUT MERELY DETERMINES WHETHER A STATION'S (NETWORK'S) JUDGMENT WAS "REASONABLE." ANY BENEFIT OF THE DOUBT GOES TO THE STATION (NETWORK).

THE STATION'S (NETWORK'S) ROLE
IN FAIRNESS DOCTRINE
REGULATION:

THE STATION (NETWORK) IS OBLIGATED TO PRESENT DISCUSSIONS OF CONTROVERSIAL ISSUES OF PUBLIC IMPORTANCE, AND TO PRESENT A REASONABLE OPPORTUNITY FOR DISCUSSION OF CONTRASTING VIEWS WITHIN ITS OVERALL PROGRAMING. THE STATION (NETWORK) IS NOT REQUIRED TO AFFORD EQUAL TIME, TO BALANCE VIEWS WITHIN A GIVEN PROGRAM, OR TO AIR A PARTICULAR SPEAKER.

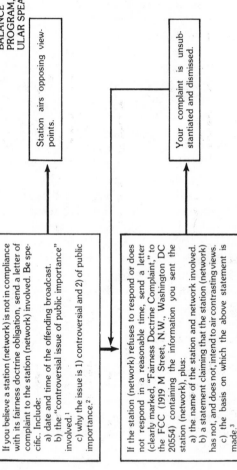

If you believe a station (network) is not in compliance with its fairness doctrine obligation, send a letter of complaint to the station (network) involved. Be specific. Include:
a) date and time of the offending broadcast.
b) the "controversial issue of public importance" involved.[1]
c) why the issue is 1) controversial and 2) of public importance.[2]

Station airs opposing viewpoints.

If the station (network) refuses to respond or does not respond in a reasonable time, send a letter (clearly marked, "Fairness Doctrine Complaint," to the FCC (1919 M Street, N.W., Washington DC 20554) containing the information you sent the station (network), plus:
a) the name of the station and network involved.
b) a statement claiming that the station (network) has not, and does not, intend to air contrasting views.
c) the basis on which the above statement is made.[3]
d) Copies of all correspondence with the station (network).

Your complaint is unsubstantiated and dismissed.

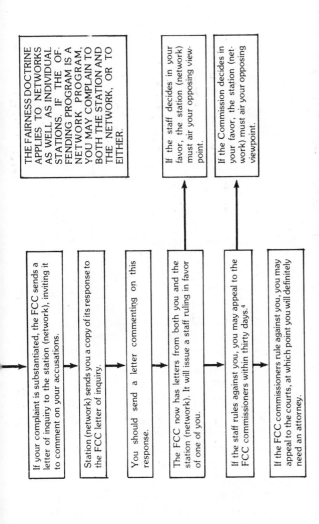

THE FAIRNESS DOCTRINE APPLIES TO NETWORKS AS WELL AS INDIVIDUAL STATIONS. IF THE OFFENDING PROGRAM IS A NETWORK PROGRAM, YOU MAY COMPLAIN TO BOTH THE STATION AND THE NETWORK, OR TO EITHER.

If the staff decides in your favor, the station (network) must air your opposing viewpoint.

If the Commission decides in your favor, the station (network) must air your opposing viewpoint.

If your complaint is substantiated, the FCC sends a letter of inquiry to the station (network), inviting it to comment on your accusations.

Station (network) sends you a copy of its response to the FCC letter of inquiry.

You should send a letter commenting on this response.

The FCC now has letters from both you and the station (network). It will issue a staff ruling in favor of one of you.

If the staff rules against you, you may appeal to the FCC commissioners within thirty days.[4]

If the FCC commissioners rule against you, you may appeal to the courts, at which point you will definitely need an attorney.

have not monitored, however, you must be prepared to certify, and so state in your complaint, that you have been a regular and frequent viewer of the station (network) for at least several weeks, particularly its news and public affairs programs, and have not seen viewpoints which contrast with those in the offending broadcast. It will help significantly to find others who can support this claim. You must also certify that you asked the station (network) to present such contrasting views and that it refused or did not reply within a reasonable time. The more substantiation your complaint provides, the better your chances for success. The complainant has the burden of proof; the station (network) is innocent until proven guilty.

[4]In this appeal, you must ask the FCC commissioners to review its staff ruling because (a) the ruling conflicts with other FCC cases or rules of Federal law, or (b) the ruling involves a novel question of policy or law not previously considered, or (c) the ruling involves existing law or policy that should be overruled, or (d) the ruling contains erroneous findings of fact on an important aspect of the case. If none of these grounds is present, the FCC commissioners can deny your request for review or it can accept your request for review and rule against you on the merits of the case.

FOOTNOTES

[1]You should be extremely specific about the nature of the issue. Vagueness only gives the station (network) and the FCC the opportunity to dismiss the complaint without even addressing the merits.

[2]The FCC's 1974 Fairness Report defines a "controversial" issue as one which is "the subject of vigorous debate with substantial elements of the community in opposition to one another." Concentrate on the amount of attention paid to the issue by government officials, community leaders, and the media. An issue is of "public importance" if a "subjective evaluation [reveals that] the issue is likely to have...a significant impact on society or its institutions." If you and the station (network) disagree on this, the FCC will decide on the basis of whether the station (network) was reasonable in its decision.

[3]Your complaint will be much more effective if you have monitored the station's (network's) programing over a period of time and can knowledgeably state that contrasting views have not been presented. If you

Reprinted with permission from *access*, 1028 Connecticut Ave. N.W., Washington, D.C. 20036.

The Government,
the Public, and the
Regulation of the
Mass Media

278

Up until 1976 most of the litigation and, indeed, all of the successful complaints brought under the Fairness Doctrine had dealt with whether licensees had treated controversial issues in a fair and balanced fashion. A long-overlooked requirement of the Fairness Doctrine was that broadcasters had an affirmative obligation to *provide* programing on controversial issues of public importance. This portion of the doctrine was particularly tricky to invoke when the concern was lack of coverage of a particular controversial issue rather than lack of coverage of *any* controversial issues. As long as the licensee provides some programing on controversial issues, the commission usually defers to the judgment of the licensee as to which issues should be programed. As the commission itself pointed out, "Licensees are not obligated to address each and every important issue which may be considered a controversial issue of public importance."

But in the mid-1970s the commission found an issue too critical to disregard even though the licensee had done so. In 1974 Congresswoman Patsy Mink and several citizens' groups complained that radio station WHAR, Clarksburg, West Virginia, had failed to provide adequate programing on strip mining, an issue of extreme importance to the Clarksburg area. The complainants had no difficulty in demonstrating the controversial nature of the issue, but that in and of itself would not have been enough to make it a "must cover" issue. In its renewal application the station had stated that mining was a major industry of the community and that "development of new industry" and "air and water pollution" were issues of great concern in the community.

The commission inquired of WHAR just what programing it had provided on the strip mining controversy. WHAR could not say for sure. The station relied heavily on network and wire-service news coverage, but did not know which items it had broadcast from them. Even more than it expects broadcasters to observe rules and regulations like the Fairness Doctrine, the commission expects broadcasters to know what they have done. WHAR didn't. As the commission pointed out, "[I]t is difficult to see how a broadcaster who is ignorant [of the programing he has presented on his station] . . . could possibly be making a conscious and positive effort to meet his fairness obligations."[90] The commission reminded broadcasters that it considered adherence to the Fairness Doctrine "the single most important requirement of operation in the public interest" and gave WHAR 20 days to tell the commission how it intended to meet its Fairness Doctrine obligations.

Legislation to repeal the Fairness Doctrine has been the subject of much discussion. The doctrine has throughout its history been one of the most controversial of FCC policies. It illustrates as much as any policy the substantial involvement of the commission in broadcast programing decisions. Despite its general deference to broadcaster judgment, the commission acts frequently enough to perform as a kind of erratic conscience. In that role it may serve to encourage blandness and timidity as well as fairness.

Public pressure on the media is often erratic, the effort of individuals asserting their rights as individuals. The broadcast media in recent years have learned however, that concerted citizen activity is a force to be reckoned with. Even if broadcasters win their battles with the public—as they often do—the expense, often in the hundreds of thousands of dollars, of dealing with the challenges of public-interest groups is sobering.[91] Just to win costs a lot of money. As a consequence, broadcasters have in many (but by no means all) instances accommodated citizens' groups' demands and requests in regard to employment practices, programing, advertising, and so forth rather than incur monumental legal fees.

Citizens' groups have been pressuring broadcasters at license renewal time, through the Fairness Doctrine, and through comments and petitions to the FCC. The commission has preferred to judge for itself what constitutes "the public interest," but the U.S. Court of Appeals, D.C. Circuit, has forced the commission to accord the public the legal standing to participate in license renewal proceedings,[92] and the public has long had the right to participate in rule-making and other FCC proceedings.

The FCC has been accused of being the handmaiden of the broadcast industry. That is hard to refute, but the commission's behavior can also be described as that of a compromiser. Instead of looking for the best solution to issues, it often looks to the best compromise between contending forces. Unless the public is contentious, it can easily be forgotten. Citizens' groups have by no means accomplished all that they wish, and they are not uniform in their wants, but they are now a force with which the commission and the broadcasters know they must deal.

THE MEDIA AND THE JUDICIARY

Those who own and staff the mass media are inclined to represent the legal pressures on their activities as part of a continuing struggle between Government and the Press, between Control and Freedom. The public is seen either in the role of spectator or ally of the media. In many instances, however, the government is not the adversary but the forum or the mechanism—whether it be the legislature or the courts—for dealing with struggles between the media and the public.

The frequency of those struggles may be testimony to no more than the inadequate education of the public to the importance of a truly free press. It may also be testimony to the arrogance or carelessness of some of those who own or staff the media. In any event the legal problems of the press cannot always be attributed to a repressive government.

Without overlooking the inclination of all branches of government to control the media or the power that government can exercise through the law to accomplish that control, one can temper that view by reflecting on the enormous contribution the American judiciary has made to the freedom of

The Government,
the Public, and the
Regulation of the
Mass Media

280

the press. Judges have not been uniform in their enthusiasm for a robust and free press, and they are as sensitive and aggressive as any government officials when the harsh spotlight turns on them, but these words from one judge to a 1975 conference of journalists and judges are worth consideration:

> Where, ladies and gentlemen, do you think these great constitutional rights that you were so vehemently asserting, and in which you were so conspicuously wallowing yesterday, where do you think they came from? The stork didn't bring them. [They] . . . came from the judges of this country, from these villains here sitting at the table. . . . It's not that it was done for you, or that it was done for ourselves. It happened because it is our understanding that that's what the Constitution provides and protects. But let me point out that the Constitution of the United States is not a self-executing document. . . .
>
> If you look at the literal language in the First Amendment . . . it says, "Congress shall [make] no law abridging the freedom of the press." That's all it says on this subject, absolutely all. It doesn't say a word about what a state can or can't do. It doesn't say a word about a reporter's privilege before a grand jury. . . . The very fact that these protections are available is attributable to the creative work of the judiciary over the last 190 years.
>
> If you say it's self-evident, that this was always clear, let me tell you that it wasn't always so clear. If you went back to the original understanding of our ancestors, back in the early years of the nineteenth century, you would find that their understanding of this clause and the Constitution in their judgment allowed them to enact the Alien and Sedition law[s]. And if those laws were still on the books, Richard Nixon would still be president of the United States, Spiro Agnew would still be vice-president of the United States and all of you people would probably be in prison.[93]

Notes

1. The details for this summary have been gleaned from a number of sources, but see Sanford J. Ungar, *The Papers & The Papers: An Account of the Legal and Political Battle over the Pentagon Papers* (New York: E. P. Dutton & Co., Inc., 1975); Peter Schrag, *Test of Loyalty: Daniel Ellsberg and the Rituals of Secret Government* (New York: Simon and Schuster, 1974), and "The First Amendment on Trial," *Columbia Journalism Review,* Special Issue, September/October 1971.
2. Ungar, p. 96.
3. *New York Times Co. v. United States,* 403 U.S. 713, 714 (1971).
4. *New York Times Co. v. United States,* pp. 718–719.
5. Thomas I. Emerson, *The System of Freedom of Expression* (New York: Vintage Books, 1971), p. 12
6. Emerson, pp. 6–7.
7. See *Chaplinsky v. New Hampshire,* 315 U.S. 568 (1942), and *Valentine v. Chrestensen,* 316 U.S. 52 (1942).
8. Chief Justice Fred Vinson, for the court, *American Communications Ass'n CIO v. Douds,* 339 U.S. 382, 394 (1950).
9. Treason is so narrowly defined in the Constitution that no activity engaged in for the purpose of publication to the general public is likely to be reached by it. Thus, our discussion is framed in more general terms.

10. *Schenck v. U.S.,* 249 U.S. 47, 52 (1919).

11. Chief Justice Fred Vinson, delivering the judgment of the court, *Dennis v. United States,* 341 U.S. 494, 509 (1951).

12. *Brandenburg v. Ohio,* 395 U.S. 444 (1969).

13. S. J. Archibald, "The Revised F.O.I. Law and How to Use It," *Columbia Journalism Review,* July/August 1977, p. 54.

14. The grand jury has a broad power to investigate all leads and rumors, even though they may eventually prove groundless, to determine if there is probable cause to indict anyone for criminal activity. To protect individuals against harm from leads and rumors that do prove groundless, the proceedings are held in secret.

15. Brief for Respondent Earl Caldwell, pp. 16–17, in *Branzburg v. Hayes,* 408 U.S. 665 (1972).

16. *Branzburg v. Hayes,* 498 U.S. 665, 697 (1972).

17. Norman E. Isaacs, "Beyond 'Caldwell'—1: 'There May Be Worse to Come from this Court,'" *Columbia Journalism Review,* September/October, 1972, p. 21. This issue of CJR contains two other articles on the Caldwell decision and the Supreme Court text.

18. *Editor & Publisher,* December 29, 1973, p. 16.

19. *Farr v. Superior Court,* 99 Cal. Rptr. 342 (1971); *Farr v. Pitchess,* 522 F.2d 464 (1975).

20. The Reporters Committee for Freedom of the Press, *News Media Alert,* August 1977, p. 7.

21. *Cherry v. Des Moines Leader,* 86 N.W. 323, 323 (1901).

22. *Gitlow v. New York,* 268 U.S. 652 (1925); *Near v. Minnesota,* 283 U.S. 697 (1931).

23. *Amici curiae* brief of the American Civil Liberties Union and the New York Civil Liberties Union, pp. 2–3, 5–6, in *New York Times Co. v. Sullivan,* 376 U.S. 245 (1964).

24. *New York Times Co. v. Sullivan,* pp. 279–280.

25. *New York Times Co. v. Sullivan,* pp. 270, 271–272.

26. *Rosenbloom v. Metromedia, Inc.,* 403 U.S. 29 (1971).

27. *Gertz v. Robert Welch, Inc.,* 418 U.S. 323 (1974).

28. *Gertz,* p. 345, cited in *Time, Inc. v. Firestone,* 96 S.Ct. 958, 965 (1976).

29. Samuel D. Warren and Louis D. Brandeis, "The Right to Privacy," *Harvard Law Review,* 4, 1890, p. 196.

30. William L. Prosser, "Privacy," *California Law Review,* 48, 1960, pp. 383–423.

31. *Sidis v. F-R Publishing Corp.,* 113 F.2d 806, 807, 809 (1940).

32. *Cox Broadcasting Corp. v. Cohn,* 420 U.S. 469 (1975). See *Oklahoma Publishing Co. v. District Court,* 97 S.Ct. 1045 (1977) for similar principle applied to name of juvenile.

33. Galella's behavior is described throughout *Galella v. Onassis,* 353 F. Supp. 196. Decision of the U.S. Court of Appeals, Second Circuit, can be found at 487 F.2d 986 (1973).

34. *Dietemann v. Time, Inc.,* 449 F.2d 245, 249 (1974). Another federal appellate court has ruled, however, that in an instance in which the reporters only *received* information that was gained by others' intrusion, without participating in or planning the intrusion themselves, the reporters could not be successfully sued for invasion of privacy for publishing the newsworthy information. *Pearson v. Dodd,* 410 F.2d 701 (1969).

The Government,
the Public, and the
Regulation of the
Mass Media

282

The Florida Supreme Court has accepted the notion that it is "common custom and usage" for reporters to accompany police and fire officials to the scenes of crime and disaster and that reporters do not commit a trespass when they do so unless they have refused a request to leave or unless they behave in some other offensive manner. *Florida Publishing v. Fletcher,* 2 Med. L. Rptr. 1088 (1976).

35. *MORE,* September 1977, p. 8.
36. *Time, Inc. v. Hill,* 385 U.S. 374 (1967).
37. The U.S. Supreme Court was able to avoid deciding this issue in *Cantrell v. Forest City Publishing Co., 419 U.S. 245 (1974), because the jury had determined that the reporter had known the information he published was false (he attributed quotes to Mrs. Cantrell without having interviewed her) and thus published the information with "malice." Because Mrs. Cantrell had won under the toughest standard, there was no need to decide whether she should be entitled to use an easier standard.*
38. *Zacchini v. Scripps-Howard Broadcasting Company,* 45 LW 4954 (1977).
39. *Griswold v. Connecticut,* 381 U.S. 479 (1965).
40. Quoted in Peggy Roberson, "What Are These LEAA Regulations and How Did We Get Into this Mess?" *The Quill,* July/August 1976, p. 21.
41. *Nebraska Press Association v. Stuart,* 96 S.Ct. 2791, 2794 (1976).
42. See Robert S. Warren and Jeffrey M. Abell, "Free Press-Fair Trial: The 'Gag Order,' A California Aberration," *Southern California Law Review,* 1972, pp. 51–99, for an effective statement of the media's role in the criminal justice system.
43. Marc Franklin, *The First Amendment and the Fourth Estate: Communications Law for Undergraduates* (Mineola, N.Y.: The Foundation Press, Inc., 1977), p. 185.
44. *Murphy v. Florida,* 421 U.S. 794 (1975).
45. *Nebraska Press Association v. Stuart,* p. 2805.
46. Material quoted scattered throughout *Sheppard v. Maxwell,* 384 U.S. 333 (1966).
47. *Nebraska Press Association v. Stuart,* 96 S.Ct. 2791 (1976).
48. *U.S. v. Dickinson,* 465 F.2d 496 (1972).
49. *Gannett Company v. Depasquale,* 2 Med. L. Rptr. 1215 (1976).
50. *Chicago Council of Lawyers v. Bauer,* 522 F.2d 242 (1975).
51. *Estes v. State of Texas,* 381 U.S. 532 (1965).
52. The Reporters Committee for Freedom of the Press, *Press Censorship Newsletter No. X,* September–October 1976, pp. 19, 35.
53. *Jacobellis v. Ohio,* 378 U.S. 184, 197 (1964).
54. *Roth v. U.S.,* 354 U.S. 476, 489 (1957).
55. *Cohen v. California,* 403 U.S. 15 (1971).
56. *Pacifica Foundation v. FCC,* 2 Med. L. Rptr. 1465 (1977). The U.S. Supreme Court has yet to rule on this issue.
57. *Miller v. California,* 413 U.S. 15, 24 (1973).
58. *A Book Named "John Cleland's Memoirs of a Woman of Pleasure" et al. v. Attorney General of Massachusetts,* 383 U.S. 413 (1966).
59. *Jacobellis v. Ohio,* 378 U.S. 184 (1964).
60. Robert Yoakum, "'An Obscene, Lewd, Lascivious, Indecent, Filthy, and Vile Tabloid Entitled SCREW,'" *Columbia Journalism Review,* March/April 1977, pp. 38–49; David M. Rubin, "Screw Gets Screwed," *MORE,* September 1976, pp. 34–35.

61. Quoted in Rubin, p. 35.

62. *U.S. v. Peraino,* 2 Med. L. Rptr. 1925 (1977).

63. The ad is reprinted in Robert Yoakum, "The Great Hustler Debate," *Columbia Journalism Review,* May/June 1977, p. 55.

64. Lewis H. Lapham, "Confusion Worse Confounded," *Harper's,* April 1977, pp. 12, 14.

65. *Young v. American Mini Theatres,* 96 S.Ct. 2440 (1976).

66. Helen Dudar, "America Discovers Child Pornography," *Ms.,* August 1977, p. 80.

67. The law provides for a different time limit for anonymous works, pseudonymous works, and works made for hire. It also sets out limits for various categories of works created before January 1, 1978. See 17 U.S.C.A. §§ 302, 303, 304 (1977).

68. Melville B. Nimmer, "Does Copyright Abridge the First Amendment Guarantees of Free Speech and Press?" *University of California at Los Angeles Law Review,* 17, 1970, p. 1193.

69. Quoted in Nimmer, p. 1191.

70. *Fortnightly Corp. v. United Artists Television,* 392 U.S. 390 (1968).

71. *Teleprompter v. Columbia Broadcasting System,* 415 U.S. 394 (1974).

72. Michael Botein, "New Copyright Act and Cable Television—a Signal of Change," *Bulletin of the Copyright Society of the U.S.A., 24, October 1976,* p. *17.*

73. *International News Service v. Associated Press,* 248 U.S. 215, 239–240 (1918).

74. *Time Inc. v. Bernard Geis Associates,* 293 F. Supp. 130, 146 (1968).

75. Jerome A. Barron, "Access to the Press—a New First Amendment Right," *Harvard Law Review,* 80, 1967, pp. 1641, 1655–1656.

76. J. Edward Gerald, *The Press and the Constitution 1931–1947* (Minneapolis: University of Minnesota Press, 1948), p. 100; *Grosjean v. American Press Co.,* 297 U.S. 233, 250 (1936).

77. *Associated Press et al. v. United States,* 326 U.S. 1 (1945).

78. Quoted in William L. Rivers, Theodore Peterson, and Jay W. Jensen, *The Mass Media and Modern Society,* Second Edition (New York: Holt, Rinehart and Winston, Inc., 1971), p. 154.

79. *United States v. Associated Press,* 52 F. Supp. 362, 372 (1943).

80. Walter Pincus, "Fairness in the News," *The New Republic,* March 23, 1974, pp. 11–14.

81. Quoting *Columbia Broadcasting System, Inc. v. Democratic National Committee,* 412 U.S. 94, 117 (1973), in *Miami Herald Publishing Co. v. Tornillo,* 418 U.S. 241, 255 (1974).

82. *Rules and Regulations Relating to Multiple Ownership,* 18 F.C.C. 288, 291–292 (1953).

83. The commission has been sharply criticized for excusing itself from addressing the conglomerate issue on a case-by-case basis on the grounds that it was conducting an inquiry into conglomerate ownership of broadcast outlets and then tersely terminating the six-year inquiry without devising any rule to deal with the issue. Howard Trickey, "Conglomerate Ownership: The FCC Shell Game," *access,* November 17, 1974, pp. 4–7 ff.

84. Commissioner Glen O. Robinson dissenting, *In the Matter of Ascertainment of Community Problems by Broadcast Applicants,* 35 RR2d 1555, 1580 (1975).

85. This summary is provided in the dissenting statement of Glen O. Robinson, *In*

The Government,
The Public, and the
Regulation of the
Mass Media

284

*the Matter of Consideration of the Operation of, and Possible Changes in, the
Prime Time Access Rule . . . ,* 32 RR2d 697, 728 (1975).

86. The court noted that in one season game shows constituted 41.9 percent of the
2,100 access half-hours on 150 stations. *National Association of Independent
Television Producers and Distributors et al. v. FCC,* 516 F.2d 526, 533 (1975).

87. In 1974 the FCC wiped out as a precedent its application of the Fairness
Doctrine to cigarette commercials and limited the application of the doctrine to
commercials that explicitly raise a controversial issue. The commission observed
that commercials that do no more than promote a product or service make no
contribution to meaningful discussion of a controversial issue of public importance and thus do not make necessary an opportunity for competing views.
"Fairness Doctrine and Public Interest Standards," *Federal Register,* Vol. 39,
No. 139, July 18, 1974, pp. 26372–26390.

88. *Red Lion Broadcasting Co., Inc. v. FCC,* 395 U.S. 367 (1969).

89. *Columbia Broadcasting System, Inc. v. Democratic National Committee,* 412
U.S. 94 (1973).

90. *In re Complaint of Representative Patsy Mink et al. against Radio Station
WHAR,* 37 RR2d 744, 751 (1976).

91. Joseph A. Grundfest, *Citizen Participation in Broadcast Licensing before the
FCC* (Santa Monica, Calif.: Rand, March 1976), pp. 97–98.

92. *Office of Communications of United Church of Christ v. FCC,* 359 F.2d 994
(1966); *Office of Communications of United Church of Christ v. FCC,* 425 F.2d
543 (1969); *Office of Communications of United Church of Christ v. FCC,* 465
F.2d 519 (1972).

93. Quoted in Howard Simons and Joseph A. Califano, Jr. (eds.), *The Media and
the Law* (New York: Praeger Publishers, 1976), pp. 36–37.

9

The Media and Government: Early Problems, Basic Patterns

Do you gentlemen who control so largely public opinion, do
you ever think how you might lighten the burdens of men in
power—those poor unfortunates weighted down by care,
anxieties, and responsibilities?

ABRAHAM LINCOLN TO A CORRESPONDENT

One day in 1690, a printer in a Boston printing shop,
using a deerskin swab tied to the end of a stick, inked some forms of type,
screwed down the wooden platen on a wooden press, and pulled off a copy
of Benjamin Harris's *Publick Occurrences*. That was the first newspaper
attempted in the American colonies. A two-column affair of four pages, one
of them blank, it was dedicated to recording "Memorable Occurrences of
Divine Providence."

Anticlimactically, *Public Occurrences* died with its first issue. Its quick
death resulted from ideas then current about the press. The paper offended
authorities, presumably with a story about brutalities committed by Indian
allies of the Colonial military forces. The authorities responded by forbidding publishers to bring out printed materials without first getting permission

from the government. Such censorship rested on the right of colonial governors to control the press on instructions from the English Crown. It was consistent with a firmly established authoritarian idea about the press: It should be controlled to serve the interests of the government in power.

Harris's experience is much more than a mere incident from history. It is central to understanding the American experience. For an important consideration in assessing the role of the mass media is the heavy hand of the official. It is by no means the only consideration, but it is among the most significant.

The need for newspapers in the new land was clear, but their growth was severely retarded by the attitude of government. Although the Colonies were originally established by trading companies and other independent groups, the trend was toward making them royal wards. Strong control over the press was exerted by governors and other authorities. Because the Puritans governed Massachusetts Bay, the first two presses in the Colonies were controlled by the church and turned out religious tracts and official printing. An effort to set up commercial papers in the middle of the seventeenth century resulted in a law providing for a board of three members to license the press and to examine all material before publication. In Philadelphia, where the Quakers were firmly in control, the first publisher was William Bradford, who published laws and almanacs—and showed everything to the authorities before publication. Then in 1689 he published a speech by a critic of Quaker policies. Although he was acquitted by a jury, Bradford's presses were for a long time kept in custody.

Not until 1704 was a publisher, John Campbell, able to establish and maintain a private paper of continuous publication. His Boston *News-Letter* succeeded only because Campbell promised never to offend the government.

Authoritarian Controls

The Colonial press was controlled by methods brought from England. Colonial newspapers sought government approval before publication for 30 years after the English Parliament allowed the Licensing Act to expire in 1694. Prosecution of criticism of Crown and government as treason, an offense punishable by death, seems to have been a potential although little used instrument in the Colonies. The threat of prosecution under the common law for seditious libel was also imported from England to the Colonies where it was administered by the royal courts. Seditious libel, a misdemeanor or less serious crime, "consisted of scandalizing the government, by reflecting on those who were entrusted with the administration of public affairs, by publishing material tending to breed in the people a dislike of their governors, or by alienating the affections of the people from the government in any way."[1] Its scope was wide, and truth was as offensive as falsity for truthful accounts, it was thought, would more likely breed discontent than false ones! The threat remained primarily a threat, however. Leonard Levy, a scholar of the period, suggests there were probably not more than a half dozen such prosecutions during the Colonial period.

In the most celebrated seditious libel case, John Peter Zenger was tried in 1735 for his criticism of the unpopular governor general of New York, William Cosby. Disregarding the judge's correct instructions in the law, the jury refused to bring in a verdict of guilty. Although this reluctance did not change the law, it did highlight the ineffectiveness of common law seditious libel as a means of control by the Crown. Under a jury system criticism of unpopular officials was protected from the law by public sentiment.

Publishers fared less well against another method of control imported from England: Parliamentary privilege. Seeking to enjoy the power exercised by their English model, the popularly elected provincial assemblies had little tolerance of criticism and a freer hand than the courts against offenders. As Levy describes the exercise of prerogative, "An assembly might summon, interrogate, and fix criminal penalties against anyone who had supposedly libeled its members, its proceedings, or the government generally."[2]

The assemblies sought to control reporting as well as opinion. The New York Assembly in 1747 under the banner of "the undoubted Right of the People to know the Proceedings of their Representatives!" insisted the colony's official printer, James Parker, print the Assembly's protest against Governor George Clinton's policies. But in 1753 it censured an apologetic printer, Hugh Gaine, for presuming to print reports of its proceedings without permission.

Taxation, used as a means of control in England, was never imposed extensively on the newspapers in the Colonies. It was tried primarily as a means of obtaining revenue, under the Stamp Act of 1765, but it met with strong resistance that contributed to the end of British rule in the Colonies—not so much because it impinged on freedom of the press but because the Colonists considered it taxation without representation.

During the Revolutionary period outspoken publishers had more to fear from lawless mobs than from the restrictions of the law. The adoption of the Constitution and the ratification of the Bill of Rights gave citizens of the new nation protection against the federal government although not always against the mob. Political passion did not end with the Revolution, and those rights were tenuously held. Within seven years the new Congress would pass the Alien and Sedition Acts to curtail criticism of the Federalist Party policies, but the repressive nature of those acts contributed to the Federalists' fall from power. When the Anti-Federalists assumed power, the acts were allowed to lapse.

The law, whether used to protect or repress the media, is only one element in the relationship between government and media, just one manifestation of the tensions generated by their evolution. And theory, although important, does not always account for experience. As important are the conventions and techniques the government and the media have

Thursday, *October* 31. 1765

THE

PENNSYLVANIA JOURNAL;

AND

WEEKLY ADVERTISER.

NUMB 1195

EXPIRING: In Hopes of a Resurrection to LIFE again.

I am sorry to be obliged to acquaint my readers that as the Stamp Act is feared to be obligatory upon us after the *first of November* ensuing (The Fatal To-morrow), The publisher of this paper, unable to bear the Burthen, has thought it expedient to stop awhile, in order to deliberate, whether any methods can be found to elude the chains forged for us, and escape the insupportable slavery, which it is hoped, from the last representation now made against that act, may be effected. Mean while I must earnestly Request every individual of my Subscribers, many of whom have been long behind Hand, that they would immediately discharge their respective Arrears, that I may be able, not only to support myself during the Interval, but be better prepared to proceed again with this Paper whenever an opening for that purpose appears, which I hope will be soon.
WILLIAM BRADFORD.

Taxation without representation: The Stamp Act of 1765 met with strong resistance that contributed to the end of British rule in the colonies. (New York Public Library)

developed for dealing with one another, the uses they make of each other, and the bargains they have struck between them.

It is often said that technology and patterns of ownership have changed the nature of the media and our society so substantially that the system provided by the Founding Fathers is inadequate, that their wisdom was based on a world that no longer exists. Yet many of the patterns for contemporary media-government relations can be found in earlier times. Although both the press and the government have changed substantially in 200 years, many issues remain constant. How can the public be kept informed of its affairs and the workings of its government. How much secrecy in government is tolerable in a representative democracy? When elected government officials determine that certain information should be kept secret for the good of the country, what should be done about those who disregard that judgment? Can government and its leaders maintain the confidence of the people under the weight of constant criticism? What responsibility does the press have for effecting the policies of an elected government? Is the press to be watchdog? Adversary? Ally?

These and other questions illustrate that we have much in common with the generation that wrote and adopted the American Constitution and its Bill of Rights. We are mistaken if we assume that the Founding Fathers could embrace the First Amendment because the press caused them and their society no problems. The experiences of American leaders tell us much about our system of government and the role the press plays in it. We will focus particularly on the relationship between the Presidents and the press.

The Public's Right to Know: How to Educate the Electorate?

From the beginning America's leaders saw the importance of information. They recognized the fundamental need in a democracy to inform the public. They recognized the need to use the press to provide that information. And, being realists—politicians as well as theorists—they could not resist the wisdom and folly of keeping some information from both press and public. The debate on how much to tell the public and how much to withhold echoes throughout American media-government history—the consequence of the conflict between our democratic origins and the authoritarian tendencies of almost every government.

The architects of American democracy wrote and spoke memorably of the need to inform the public and to use the press to do so. Madison told his fellow revolutionaries, "[A] people who mean to be their own governors must arm themselves with the power knowledge gives." In the debate in 1800 over what facilities should be provided the press by the House of Representatives Congressman Nichols argued [the use of the third person reflects the style of the period],

> [I]n a Government like ours, the theory of which is republican, and the practice of which he hoped would always continue to be republican, he considered the representatives of the people responsible to the people, by whom they were created. ... [T]he people, who were to judge, should possess the purest information, as to not only the acts, but the motives of the public agents. It was of little consequence to them to know what laws are enacted, compared with a knowledge of projects that were attempted or prevented, and the grounds on which they were supported or opposed. Nor could the merits of the acts themselves be understood, unless the reasons for them were stated. It was, therefore, of the highest consequence that the reasons for our conduct should be clearly understood, that our measures may be comprehended, and our motives also known, that our constituents may judge whether we have faithfully discharged our duty.[3]

Remarking on Shays's Rebellion, Jefferson wrote in 1787, "The way to prevent these irregular interpositions of the people is to give them full information of their affairs thro' the channel of the public papers."

It is clear not only that the Founding Fathers intended the press to serve as a continuing educator of the public but that they intended the press to operate independent of government. What they did not intend, apparently, was that the press operate independent of party or politician.

The desirability of an official, centralized government information system was debated during the Constitutional Convention of 1787. The idea failed to gain the necessary support, although some early government agencies had responsibilities for disseminating information about their particular functions.

It is hard to imagine a centralized information system in a government built on checks and balances as the government of the United States is. Which branch would concede control to another?

Indeed, the ability to use the press to influence public opinion has been an enormous resource in the struggle for power between different levels and branches of government. Nowhere is it more evident than in the modern struggle for power and authority between Congress and the Presidency.

For all George Washington's concern about faction, the new government had disagreement built into its basic processes. For the first four elections the runner-up in the Presidential balloting was elected Vice-President. Such a system would have made Barry Goldwater Vice President in Lyndon Johnson's Presidency, Hubert Humphrey in Richard Nixon's and Gerald Ford in Jimmy Carter's. A curious system that guaranteed division within the executive branch far more difficult to contend with than that within the legislative with its mechanisms for resolving disputes.

Nevertheless, the Founding Fathers, as individual politicians, did not leave the informing of the public to chance or the opposition. The press of the period was not an official arm of government, but it most definitely was an unofficial extension of political and government leaders. And government leaders have always understood that the accessibility of information to the press and thus to the public could affect public opinion in important ways.

From the earliest days members of Congress sought to protect their public image by controlling access to Congressional proceedings and accommodation in its facilities. The Constitution requires that each house of Congress, "keep a journal of its proceedings, and from time to time publish the same, excepting such parts as may in their judgment require secrecy. . . ." Beyond the Congress is under no Constitutional obligation to accommodate the curiosity of the public or press, but Congress wrestled from its earliest days with the practical problems of accommodating reporters in such ways as would encourage the fullest and most accurate account of their proceedings. Rendering an accurate and comprehensive account was a formidable task for early reporters dependent on stenography and presented with the difficulty of hearing each member in the chambers Congress then used. Not six months after the organization of the House, during a debate on a resolution that inaccurate reporting had violated that body's privileges, a representative from South Carolina reported that while he had found the errors great, he believed them caused by "the hurry in which business of this kind is conducted." Representative Smith illustrated his point:

[I]t was said, that the House had appointed a committee for the regulation of the *barbers* of the United States; this struck me as a very gross misrepresentation, for I could hardly believe, that the Legislature of the Union, would, at so early a day, attempt to usurp an authority not vested in them by the Constitution, and that, too, over a body of men, who could at any time put an end to the tyranny with the edge of the razor; but on searching the minutes of this case, I found that a bill was brought in for the regulation of the *harbors* of the United States.[4]

The South Carolinian urged that the offending reporter be "restored to his former situation behind the Speaker's chair, from whence he could both see and hear distinctly everything that passed in the House."

In the same debates, however, Representative Gerry found a curious distribution of errors in the reports. He promised charity and supposed the errors "arose from inability or inadvertency in the reporters." But he found it remarkable given that gentlemen on both sides spoke in comparably low tones "that all the arguments on one side were fully stated, and generally took up some columns in the newspapers; while the arguments of the other side were partially stated, and condensed to a few solitary lines."

The Senate did not open its doors to the press and public until 1795, and not until 1801 did it make special, if limited, provision for the press. From 1839 to 1841 the Senate provided floor privileges to Washington papers to the exclusion of non-Washington papers. Under assault from James Gordon Bennett of the New York *Herald* this manner of favoritism was ended; but for another 18 years Senate rules permitted Washington dailies two seats in the reporters' area while papers from outside the capital were allowed no more than one.

Not surprisingly the problems of accommodation of the news media and the selectivity of coverage of so diverse and complicated an institution as Congress continue.

The Party Press

At times in our history, government and press have been the most savage adversaries imaginable, and at other times they have been so cooperative that elements of the press have been incorporated into the machinery of power. Frequently there has been division within the press, some members of the press applauding and some bitterly attacking the same government. In this early period the divisions within the press mirrored the divisions within government.

Realizing that they cannot win popular support without a communication system, our officials have always sought to use the press. In the early decades their method could be best designated as "the party press." When one faction established a newspaper as its party organ, another retaliated by imitation.

While a member of President Washington's Cabinet, Jefferson led the opposition to Alexander Hamilton's Federalists, who had already established the *Gazette of the United States* at the new capital in Philadelphia. Eager to develop an editorial voice for Anti-Federalism, Jefferson tried to enlist Philip Freneau, a talented journalist who had become famous as "the Poet of the Revolution."

Freneau declined the first offer. Lamenting the rejection, Jefferson revealed in a letter to Madison how much favoritism he was ready to bestow on an editor who would echo Jefferson's own views: "I should have given him the perusal of all my letters of foreign intelligence & all foreign newspapers; the publication of all proclamations & other public notices within my department, & the printing of all laws. . . ."

Later the itch for a newspaper that would speak for him led Jefferson to woo Freneau by letter again: "The clerkship for foreign languages in my office is vacant; the salary, indeed, is very low, being but two hundred and fifty dollars a year; but it also gives so little to do as not to interfere with any other office one may chuse. . . ."

The sinecure lured Freneau. He established the *National Gazette,* which immediately became the loudest Anti-Federalist voice and the most incisive critic of President Washington. The attacks were "outrages on common decency," President Washington protested. He questioned Jefferson closely regarding Freneau's reason for coming to Philadelphia. Jefferson replied that he had lost his translating clerk and had simply hired Freneau to replace him. "I cannot recollect," Jefferson told Washington, "whether it was at that time, or afterwards, that I was told that he had a thought of setting up a newspaper." In any case, Jefferson pointed out, he could control his employee in the clerkship, but Freneau was a free agent in editing the *National Gazette.*

Washington did not ask that Freneau be fired, but he could not control his anger. Jefferson described a scene that developed during a Cabinet meeting shortly after Freneau had published a scalding satire:

> The President was much inflamed, got into one of those passions when he cannot command himself, ran on much on the personal abuse which had been bestowed on him, defied any man on earth to produce one single act of his since he had been in the government which was not done on the purest motives, that he had not repented but once the having slipped the moment of resigning the office, and that was every moment since, that *by God* he had rather be in his grave than in his present situation. That he had rather be on his farm than be emperor of the world and yet they were charging him with wanting to be king. That *that rascal Freneau* sent him three of his papers every day as if he thought he would become the distributor of his papers.[5]

When Jefferson left the Cabinet, Freneau lost his position and the *National Gazette* ceased publication.

Jefferson seized the publicity initiative as soon as he became President-elect in 1800. The nation's capital was being moved from Philadelphia to Washington, and Jefferson persuaded young Samuel Harrison Smith to set up his newspaper shop there by luring him with printing-contract patronage. It was a blatant exercise of news management, but there was provocation for it. Jefferson was so vilified by the opposition press that he once suggested editors categorize the contents of their papers under four chapters: Truths ("The first chapter would be very short"), Probabilities, Possibilities, and Lies.

The party press dominated political journalism during Jefferson's Administration. The President had other favorites—he once wrote to William Duane, editor of the wild *Aurora,* asking for "an exact list of the prosecutions of a public nature against you, & over which I might have controul"—but Smith's *National Intelligencer* was the dominant source of Presidential news, although less partisan than many other papers of the period. It was an efficient system. There were no Presidential press conferences and no Presidential interviews. Other editors were forced to rely for information on partisans like Smith.

How effectively such tactics worked is suggested by the success of the party organ, the *National Intelligencer,* when Jefferson became President. The editor of a rival newspaper, the *United States Telegraph,* announced that he had hired a Washington correspondent:

> We congratulate the readers of the *United States Telegraph* upon an arrangement by which the editor is able to obtain earlier, and he trusts *more full and accurate* information of the proceedings of Congress and the measures of government, than can be had from the Washington papers. We have hitherto been obliged to depend principally upon the *National Intelligencer* for reports of the proceedings of Congress; a paper which is conducted with very considerable ability, but with very little candour, inasmuch as the wishes of the president and his particular friends must be consulted in whatever representations are there made. . . . [6]

The minimal value of Washington-based newspaper correspondents in the country's early days is suggested by the fact that the *Telegraph's* man lasted only a few months. He could report on Congress, but could find no avenue to the Presidency, and he was soon reduced to reading the *National Intelligencer* to determine what Jefferson was up to.

None of the next three Presidents—James Madison, James Monroe, or John Quincy Adams—could manage the news as astutely as Jefferson.

Madison was much criticized by the Federalist partisans for his conduct of the War of 1812. As journalism historian John Tebbel observes, "Reading their papers, it could scarcely be told whether the President or the British were the enemy. . . ."[7] But Madison, an important voice in American libertarianism, resisted whatever urge he might have felt to suppress the inflammatory Federalist press—despite the available excuse of wartime.

There were newspapers that supported Madison, of course, and they were as nearsighted in his favor as others had been in opposition. As can happen when the law seems to withhold rather than impose appropriate punishment, a mob without sanction from the President and, no doubt, to

his dismay, attacked the *Federal Republican,* a Federalist organ. The mob
twice destroyed the paper's presses and building and attacked the staff,
killing General James M. Lingan, a hero of the Revolution.

Though not as effectively as Jefferson had, Madison and James Monroe
continued to use the *National Intelligencer* as party organ. Because the
Intelligencer had encouraged the candidacy of another for the Presidential
election of 1824 (sectionalism rather than party distinguished the four
Republican contenders), John Quincy Adams used a new paper edited by
Peter Force, the *National Journal.* Adams revealed the extent of his control
over the paper in this entry in his diary: "P. Force called to say that Mr.
McLean, the Postmaster-General, was desirous of publishing in the *National
Journal* an article in answer to a published letter addressed to him by J.
Binns in the Democratic Press. I told him I could have no objection to
this. . . ."

Rule by Newspaper

Presidential control of information and patronage reached its zenith under
President Andrew Jackson. He subscribed to 20 newspapers, dictated to
almost as many, and led "King Mob" to the capital, elevating journalism to a
visible force in government. In the judgment of historian James Schouler,
"Jackson was the first President who ruled the country by means of the
newspaper press."

President Jackson surrounded himself with newspapermen who had
supported his election, among them Amos Kendall, an able Kentucky editor
who became the leader of the "Kitchen Cabinet." One Congressman later
said of him, "He was the President's thinking machine, his writing machine,
aye, and his lying machine." In 1835 he was rewarded with an appointment
as postmaster general. Another newspaperman, Duff Green, had proved his
friendship for Jackson during the 1928 Presidential campaign by fabricating
a story that President and Mrs. John Quincy Adams had had premarital
relations.[8] Jackson asked Green to "remove to Washington and become the
organ of the party."

Green's *United States Telegraph* was the first Jacksonian organ, and for
a time it served the President well. But Green developed a strong liking for
the ambitious and magnetic John Calhoun, Jackson's party rival. Kendall
persuaded Jackson to bring in Francis P. Blair to establish another administration paper, the Washington *Globe.* The party faithful were strongly
encouraged to subscribe and administrative officials to send patronage
contracts. The *Globe* prospered.

For a time there were 57 journalists on the government payroll, and both
Green's *Telegraph* and Blair's *Globe* carried the administration line.[9] But it
was soon apparent that Blair was to be *the* official spokesman. A rival editor
described him as "one who must be believed when professing to act by

authority." Only six weeks after the establishment of the *Globe,* there was no doubt that Jackson would be a candidate for re-election; Blair had written: "We are permitted to say that if it should be the will of the nation to call on the President to serve a second term in the Chief Magistracy, he will not decline the summons."

Blair visited the White House almost daily, usually bringing a jug of milk from his farm at nearby Silver Spring. He and Jackson would lounge and drink and discuss administration policy and *Globe* strategy. They shared the direction of both. Back in his office, Blair would translate the President's ideas into fiery editorials. In the White House an assistant who came to the President with a sticky problem was likely to be directed to "take it to Bla'r" or "Give it to Frank Bla'r—he knows everything."

Anti-Jackson factions feared the cruel hook of Blair's satire. In time they learned to fear his devious system for spreading the influence of his paper. Blair would write pro-Jackson essays and editorials, plant them in small rural newspapers, then reprint them in the *Globe* as "indications of public opinion."

Government Patronage

Although contracts for local and state legal notice advertising are valuable accounts still much sought after by the modern press, such contracts do not compare with the financial support government once provided. Well into the nineteenth century government patronage and sinecure were substantial elements in the economics of newspapering. It had been common in Colonial times for publishers to be postmasters. The position of postmaster gave an individual special advantage not only from the salary earned but also from easy access to the intelligence of the day exchanged by post and to a system of distribution.

In the early nineteenth century federal government printing contracts were an important source of income for private newspaper enterprises. The disposition of those contracts gave the government officials who controlled them considerable influence over the press. When the seat of the federal government was moved in 1800 from Philadelphia to Washington, newspapers were lured to the new capital by the prospect of printing contract patronage not only from the executive branch but from Congress as well.

The fates of newspapers in the early nineteenth century depended in no small measure on their ability to "pick a winner." Winners had control over government printing contracts that losers did not share, and winners had a common habit of rewarding their own and not their rivals' supporters. And, as in the case of Green's *United States Telegraph,* a party organ that supported a rival party leader could lose its favored position. To win the patronage of Congress, newspapers faced the added strain of having to accommodate themselves to a majority of its members.

Decline of the Party Press

Two events of 1860 dealt the death blow to the party press. The Government Printing Office was established, all but destroying the printing-contract patronage that fed so many Washington newspapers and President-elect Abraham Lincoln arrived in the capital. Lincoln listened civilly to several editors who tried to persuade him that their papers should be his official journals. Then he rejected all offers. This was altogether characteristic of his shrewd approach to shaping opinion through the press. Lincoln refused to adopt an Administration organ because he saw that the Washington papers were impotent and because he realized that tying himself to one newspaper would restrict his dealings with others.

In fact, the beginning of the decline of the party press came in the 1830s with the publication first of Benjamin Day's New York *Sun* and then James Gordon Bennett's New York *Herald.* Day provided the financial formula for the first successful penny newspaper: Sensational news—some of it more likely fiction—sold for a penny an issue to large numbers of people who were attractive to advertisers. Bennett added to the formula—without neglecting the sensational stories—a zeal for news of significance. He organized his reporters in a beat system, covering Wall Street and the financial news himself; he sent correspondents to Europe to cover foreign news and by 1841 he was spending $200 a week to maintain a corps of Capital correspondents that was abler than the entire staff of any newspaper published in Washington. Bennett, who had earlier been a Washington correspondent himself, conducted the first recorded Presidential interview, a conversation with Martin Van Buren. The dyspeptic publisher of the powerful *Herald* was not a man a President could ignore.

Bennett's interest in political news and his independence of political favor signalled a new era in political coverage. In his prospectus for the *Herald,* Bennett wrote:

> Our only guide shall be good sound practical common sense, applicable to the business and bosoms of men engaged in everyday life. We shall support no party, be the organ of no faction or coterie, and care nothing for any election or any candidate from President down to constable. We shall endeavor to record facts, on every public and proper subject, stripped of verbiage and coloring, with comments suitable, just, independent, fearless and good tempered. . . . [10]

He did not keep his promise of objectivity, but his allegiance was not to party or politician but to his readers and to his own view of what was news and what was right. The difference between a party organ and such a *news*paper is profound. The party press was an adversary press to be sure. It would be hard to find more bitter, aggressive papers than the partisans of the early nineteenth century, but only with a financial base of large circulations and an attention to news was it possible for newspapers to become representatives of the public rather than representatives of party.

The Associated Press also contributed to the decline of the power of the

Washington party press. The AP installed its first Washington correspondent
Abraham Lincoln
and the Press

297

Washington party press. The AP installed its first Washington correspondent
in 1848 and its first formal Washington bureau in 1856. When the colorless
Presidents who followed Andrew Jackson named their party organs, these
little Washington dailies and weeklies were powerless in competition with
the Washington bureaus and the AP reports. It was a situation made to
order for the stentorian editors of nineteenth-century America.

Abraham Lincoln and the Press

Abraham Lincoln owed political debts to many newspaper publishers,
having used the press from the beginning of his political career—even
working anonymously as a correspondent for the Sangamon *Journal* while
serving in the Illinois legislature.

He was most deeply in debt to Joseph Medill of the Chicago *Tribune*.
Their relationship dated back to 1854, when Lincoln appeared personally at
the office of the *Tribune* to pay four dollars for a subscription. Medill met
Lincoln then and, over the years, came to think of him as a great man.
When the debates with Stephen Douglas made Lincoln famous, Medill
circulated through Congress a ringing letter endorsing Lincoln for President.
He pushed his candidate so relentlessly in the *Tribune* that Lincoln himself
was disturbed. "See here," he said to Medill, "you boys got me up a peg
too high. How about the Vice Presidency—won't that do?" Medill was
adamant: "Now it is the Presidency or nothing."

As one of the founders of the Republican Party and the publisher of its
strongest newspaper, Medill was in a unique position to promote Lincoln.
He persuaded other party leaders to hold the nominating convention in
Chicago in 1860, then took over the pivotal arrangement himself. He
distributed all the available spectator seats to Lincoln's supporters and
manipulated the delegate seating so that those who favored William H.
Seward could not affect the votes of the undecided.

Medill confessed later with satisfaction,

> It was the meanest trick I ever did in my life. New York was for Seward. . . . It
> followed that the New York delegates were seated at one end of the vast hall,
> with no state for a neighbor that was not hopelessly for Seward. At the other end
> of the hall, so far away that the voices of the Seward orators could scarcely be
> heard, was placed Pennsylvania [the most important of the doubtful states].
> Between Pennsylvania and New York were placed the Lincoln delegates from
> Illinois; also those of Indiana and New Jersey.[11]

Medill himself sat with old friends in the Ohio delegation and tried to win
them for Lincoln. At the end of the third ballot—before the totals were
announced—it was clear that Lincoln was still three and a half votes short of
the nomination. Medill coaxed an Ohioan: "If you throw Ohio to Lincoln,
Salmon Chase can have anything he wants." Ohio switched four votes from
Seward to Lincoln, and the nomination was in hand.

President Abraham Lincoln cultivated Horace Greeley, the influential editor of the
New York *Tribune*. (Library of Congress)

It is an unfortunate fashion in historical writing to picture Lincoln at bay, the press bent on bringing him down. And it is easy to find slashingly negative comments on his great speeches, the First and Second Inaugurals and the Gettysburg Address, in the partisan journals of that time:

New York *Express:* The President holds out, except in words, mere words, very, very little of the olive branch. . . .

Richmond *Enquirer:* . . . couched in the cool, unimpassioned, deliberate language of the fanatic.

Trenton *American:* It is very evident . . . that he feels all the perplexity of his position and his incompetence to shape his own course.

Hartford *Times:* . . . this wretchedly botched and unstatesmanlike paper. . . .

But it is also easy to find examples of high editorial praise for the same addresses:

Philadelphia *American:* Its language is so direct, its tone so patriotic, its honesty so unmistakable, that all will feel the earnestness of its author and the significance of his words.

Buffalo *Republic:* . . . certainly one of the most important addresses ever issued from Washington.

New York *News:* . . . an able and statesmanlike document.

Washington *Star:* . . . a state paper of great force and reasoning.

New York *Courier & Enquirer:* The address is a noble one. . . . [12]

The truth is that in a time of a strong and savage press—a time of unavoidable and deep controversy for the American people—Lincoln came off quite well, largely because of his own insight. He knew the extent of the political power that resided in the great editors of the midnineteenth century, and he pointed out: "In this and like communities, public sentiment is everything. With public sentiment, nothing can fail; without it, nothing can succeed. Consequently, he who moulds public sentiment goes deeper than he who enacts statutes or pronounces decisions."

Lincoln was especially sensitive to the criticism of the greatest editor of the time, Horace Greeley of the New York *Tribune.* Greeley was often critical; the President was usually conciliatory. Lincoln once asked a Washington correspondent for the *Tribune* why the impatient Greeley—who often wanted what the President wanted, but faster—could not "restrain himself, and wait a little." The answer was noncommittal. The President sighed, "Well, I don't suppose I have any right to complain. Uncle Horace is with us at least four days out of seven."

Lincoln went to surprising lengths to win Greeley's cooperation. For a time the *Tribune* had a secret inside line to the White House. The President would give information to Robert J. Walker, a special adviser in the Department of the Treasury, and Walker would pass it on to Greeley "for the use or guidance of the *Tribune.*" Later, when the Civil War campaign of 1864 began and Greeley's editorial tone became sharp, Lincoln wrote to him: "I have been wanting to see you for several weeks, and if I could spare the time I should call upon you in New York. Perhaps you may be able to visit me. I shall be very glad to see you." There was no response. Lincoln turned to a mutual friend, praising Greeley and expressing regret that he had not named the editor postmaster, adding that he could have the position if Lincoln was reelected. The editorial tone of the *Tribune* promptly became more favorable.

Lincoln also went far out of his way to placate the arrogant James Gordon Bennett, whose New York *Herald* was influential in Europe as well as in the United States. The President sent as emissary to Bennett an editor named Thurlow Weed, who had a profound sense of political journalism. Weed persuaded Bennett to slant his editorials in Lincoln's favor. Later, when a *Herald* reporter who had been refused a pass down the Potomac by Secretary of the Navy Gideon Welles went over Welles's head to the President himself, Lincoln was in haste to oblige; he wrote Bennett a "private and confidential" letter of apology.

None of this should suggest that Lincoln made the basic mistake of surrendering to the powerful editors. He granted many of their requests and demands, but just when it appeared that he had capitulated, he would refuse a favor and ignore their editorials. Few editors realized how subtly Lincoln used them. The celebrated Emancipation Proclamation, for example, was as much a publicity weapon as it was a declaration of the national conscience, a fact that is emphasized by Lincoln's own account of having issued it two months after it had been written:

> Things had gone from bad to worse, until I felt that we had reached the end of our rope on the plan of operations we had been pursuing; that we had about played our last card, and must change our tactics, or lose the game. I now determined upon the adoption of the emancipation policy. . . . [13]

During the Civil War the press had unusual opportunity for wartime to report on events in ways that would seem to put the military effort in jeopardy. Arthur Schlesinger, Jr., has noted that

> the Civil War was fought to a remarkable degree in the open. Lincoln's government, it is true, suspended *habeas corpus,* intercepted the mail, suppressed newspapers and so on; but there was no effective censorship, no Sedition Act, no Espionage Act. The Confederates got more information from northern reporters than they did from southern spies.[14]

Lincoln himself remarked in his Second Inaugural, "The progress of our arms, upon which all else chiefly depends, is as well known to the public as to myself," and Lincoln was on any number of occasions mightily upset with the premature disclosure by the press of Union military activity.

While obviously uncomfortable with suppressing opposition newspapers, Lincoln seemed prepared to do with freedom of the press as he was prepared to do with the issue of slavery—whatever was necessary to save the Union. The question of whether the extraordinary circumstances of wartime justify extraordinary measures against the press has never been resolved and comes up for reexamination each time the country becomes involved in war.

None of the nineteenth-century Presidents after Lincoln could match his command of the press. During the period from his death to the beginning of the twentieth century, as the country continued to expand and develop, there were many centers of governmental and press power other than the nation's capital. It was left to the Spanish-American War of 1898 to thrust the United States into international affairs and the magnetism of Theodore Roosevelt to place the Presidency again at the center of national attention.

The Presidents and the Press in the Early Twentieth Century

THEODORE ROOSEVELT

As Colonel Roosevelt, firing the horseless "Rough Riders" into their dash up San Juan Hill, Theodore Roosevelt had demonstrated how a leader with a flair for drama could overshadow the comic-opera flavor of an absurdity like the Spanish-American War. (Years later, Roosevelt himself commented, "It wasn't much of a war, but it was the best war we had.") As Governor of New York, he had promoted his many causes through twice-a-day meetings with the small corps of Albany correspondents. Then he was maneuvered into accepting the Vice Presidency, where the Old Guard of his own Republican Party was happily certain that his political career would die. But President William McKinley was assassinated in 1901—"Roosevelt luck," one of his despairing detractors called it—and TR, who had been chafing in the tranquillity of presiding over the U.S. Senate, was suddenly thrust into his sternest test as a shaper of public opinion.

The new President fixed shrewdly on two important facts. First, the great press associations, which served many papers of varying political persuasions, had during the latter part of the nineteenth century developed "objective reporting" so that any paper could safely use any story. Except for the few remaining yellow journals, the giant dailies that used dispatches from their own reporters in Washington had been shamed into reporting most political news with relative impartiality. The partisan publishers were relying largely on acid editorial pages to shape opinion. That was ideal for the theatrical Roosevelt, who knew quite well that a strong President can promote an indelible image through the news, whatever the editorials may say about him.

Second, the Age of the Reporter had been ushered in by romantic figures like Richard Harding Davis and by Lincoln Steffens, Jacob Riis, and the other "muckrakers"—a term Roosevelt himself had coined—with the result that some of the power that had resided in the thundering editors and publishers back home was passing to the correspondents on the scene. The political reporters of TR's day were much more independently powerful than the newspaper "agents" of nineteenth-century Washington.

And so Theordore Roosevelt set about managing the news more adroitly than any President before him. The thrust of his method was high-level press agentry: both courting the correspondents and commanding them. One day he saw a small group standing outside the gates interviewing departing visitors and ordered an anteroom set aside for reporters. This became the White House Press Room. He developed a subtly effective press conference, long before Woodrow Wilson established it on a formal basis, by regularly calling in the three correspondents whose reports were most widely circulated: David Barry of the New York *Sun's* Laffan Agency, Charles Boynton of the Associated Press, and Ed Keen of the Scripps-McRae Press Association (now United Press International). Everything the President said was deep background, which allowed him a maximum range of comment and no responsibility for anything they used. The day Keen joined the group, Roosevelt loosed an especially virulent view of his own party's Old Guard, then made the system clear to the newcomer with: "If you even hint where you got it, I'll say you are a damned liar."

Roosevelt's press relations were always a fascinating mixture of apparent impulsiveness and tight control. He was, one correspondent wrote, "the master press agent of all time." He sometimes gave reporters the run of the White House and often overwhelmed them with news. When Lincoln Steffens had completed his exposés of corruption in municipal and state governments and turned to Washington, he was given open access to the executive offices and a daily appointment with Roosevelt at the barber's hour. "I always came into the room," Steffens wrote, "primed with a question that I fired quick; and he went off." But one thoughtful correspondent, Charles Willis Thompson of the New York *Times,* has written,

> [H]e was never interviewed, in any proper sense. . . . He gave out many statements, some of them in the form of interviews, and sometimes, too, he was actually interviewed, but in such cases he always dictated the form the interview should take. . . . [H]e never said one word more than he had already decided to say. . . . Impulsive? The thousand reporters who have tried to catch Roosevelt off guard and make him say something he did not expect to say will laugh. . . . [15]

WILLIAM HOWARD TAFT

It was one of the perplexities of American politics at the beginning of the Administration of William Howard Taft that he did nothing to win the Washington correspondents. Ponderous but genial, Taft was TR's hand-picked successor, with a full opportunity to learn from Roosevelt. Moreover, Taft had once worked as a reporter in Cincinnati and, when serving in Roosevelt's Cabinet, had been the favorite news source of many correspondents. While he was Secretary of War, they developed the habit of "going Tafting" every afternoon at 4 o'clock, and he often helped them dig news out of other Executive departments. An unguarded spokesman in those days, Taft sometimes had to be protected from himself. Once, when Taft had been especially outspoken, Arthur Wallace Dunn of the Associated

Press urged him "to place the injunction of secrecy on us" to prevent
"disastrous consequences to yourself." Taft was grateful then and again
when he became the Republican Presidential nominee in 1908 and saw that
many correspondents were passing up stories that might have hurt his
chances. But his new relations with his old friends were forecast on Inauguration Day. Several correspondents called at the White House to pay their
respects. A secretary said that Taft would not see them then and was not
likely to be seeing them very often in the future.

Much later it became clear that this was no simple case of a new
President going high-hat. To put it plainly, Taft was afraid. Always envious
of Roosevelt, he knew that he could not match TR's confident command,
and so he took the worst possible course—doing nothing. Archie Butt, who
was an aide to both Roosevelt and Taft, wrote:

> There are a good many leaks about the White House. Neither the President nor
> his secretary gives out anything of real interest, nor do they understand the art of
> giving out news. In consequence, the papers seek their information from what-
> ever source they can find and therefore print rumors which, if printed a month
> ago [during the Roosevelt Presidency] would have resulted in a clean sweep of
> the Executive offices. Not able to find out much of the political intentions of the
> President or his Cabinet, they are turning their attention to the class of news
> known as bedroom politics. . . . [16]

Into the vacuum came that which Taft feared most—criticism. TR,
dismayed by his successor's floundering, prepared for what some correspondents termed "The Return from Elba." And for a time Taft's chief
pleasure was reading the New York *Sun's* lampoons of Roosevelt. He
would not even look at the critical papers. One night in 1911 when he asked
for the New York papers and Mrs. Taft handed him the *World,* he snapped,
"I don't want the *World.* I have stopped reading it. It only makes me
angry."

"But you used to like it very much," said Mrs. Taft.

"That was when it agreed with me, but it abuses me now, and so I don't
want it."

"You will never know what the other side is doing if you only read the
Sun and the *Tribune,*" she rejoined.

"I don't care what the other side is doing," Taft said.

It is easy to suspect that the turbulent Presidential politics of 1912, which
had Taft opposed for reelection by TR as well as Woodrow Wilson, are a
monument to his bewilderment about the network that forms public
opinion.

WOODROW WILSON

Wilson's Presidency began with loud applause from the Washington
press corps. Wilson inaugurated the formal Presidential press conference
and announced this credo: "I, for one, have the conviction that the government ought to be all outside and no inside. I, for my part, believe that there

ought to be no place where anything can be done that everybody does not know about. . . . Secrecy means impropriety."

It was a laudable theory, but those correspondents who had experienced the shrewd manipulations of Theodore Roosevelt wondered whether a President following Wilson's policy of "pitiless publicity" could compete effectively with a Congress operating outside this enlightenment.

Wilson was not naturally suited to the public relations role he had established for his Administration. Actually, he was warm and human, a lover of vaudeville who once confessed that he also liked fishing, baseball, wrestling, and such intimate sports as running to fires behind clanging engines, gossiping with police officers on their beats, reading grisly crime stories, and watching dogs fight in the street. But none of this came across to the public. Wilson was outwardly a cold man, whose only apparent excitements were intellectual. His approach to the Presidency was unrelaxed. He shielded his family from publicity and went to extravagant lengths to avoid informal pictures of himself. Photographers were not allowed on the White House grounds and were rebuffed when they sought to picture the President playing golf. Annoyed by their persistence, Wilson's Secret Service chief seemed one day to acquiesce, took them out to a "shack full of knotholes" near one of the greens where the President would be putting, and crowded them in. When their eyes became accustomed to the darkness, the photographers found that there were no knotholes and the door was padlocked. The President played undisturbed—and many a voter continued to think of Wilson as the epitome of austerity.

Meanwhile, the National Press Club, which at that time had rooms over Affleck's Drug Store, was becoming an informal home for members of Congress as well as correspondents. Great powers—among them Senator Thomas Gore of Oklahoma and Senator Boies Penrose of Pennsylvania— were letting their hair down in antic Press Club debates like the one that examined the question, "Resolved: That bow-legs are a greater menace to navigation than knock-knees." Later 14 Senators and Representatives engaged 14 correspondents in a spelling bee at the Press Club, and won. It was a time of growing comradeship between the men of the press and the men of Capitol Hill.

Many reporters retained their high regard for Wilson, but he soon demonstrated that he was not really willing to practice his theory of pitiless publicity. Like Taft he was supersensitive, and he blamed the correspondents for reporting criticisms of his Administration voiced by Congress. Resentment grew in the press corps when it became known that the President was, in private, a harsh critic of the reporters. "I am so accustomed to having everything reported erroneously," Wilson told Senator J. W. Stone of Missouri, "that I have almost come to the point of believing nothing that I see in the newspapers." He gradually withdrew into a shell of persecution. Press conferences were more widely spaced; then, as the United States was drawn into World War I, they were no more.

Because he was the President who began press conferences, then ended them during World War I, it is too often forgotten that President Wilson also

created the Committee on Public Information. It began on April 13, 1917, and lasted a little more than two years under the chairmanship of George Creel, a newspaper editor. Creel, a long time supporter of Wilson, corresponded with him frequently. When the United States entered the war on April 6, 1917, and news that some form of censorship would be imposed was reported, Creel protested to Wilson that what was needed was "expression not repression, and urged a campaign that would carry [American] war aims and peace terms not only to the United States, but to every neutral country, and also in England, France, and Italy." Creel insisted that secrecy could be accomplished by voluntary methods.

Although the President had long before assessed the ability of newspapermen harshly, he trusted Creel completely and established by executive order the Committee on Public Information with Creel as its chairman. The President had to choose one of two methods of handling public opinion during the war, one negative, the other affirmative. He could establish ironclad censorship with a huge bureaucracy that was to try to judge the loyalty of every item in newspapers, magazines, or books. That was, of course, negative, and Creel thought such a system "would inevitably stir demoralizing fears in the heart of every [soldier's] father and mother and open the door to every variety of rumor."

Creel instead emphasized the affirmative path, filling the channels of communication with official, approved news and opinion. He was engaged in what he called "the fight for the *minds* of men, for the 'conquest of their convictions' and the battle-line ran through every home in every country." It was, in his words, "a vast enterprise in salesmanship, the world's greatest adventure in advertising." Creel estimated that more than 150,000 Americans provided service in one form or another to the committee. Boy Scouts delivered copies of Wilson's speeches by hand to the homes of America. The committee furnished 200,000 lantern slides for illustrated lectures. Periodicals with the President's message were sent every two weeks to 600,000 teachers. Among the most ingenious of Creel's techniques was the mobilizing of 75,000 "Four Minute Men" who made an estimated 1,000,-000 four minute speeches during the intermissions at movie theaters around the country. In these and other activities Creel showed considerable enterprise at getting President Wilson's message to the nation, unfiltered by the press, in the days before radio was available for such an effort.

Creel did not limit himself only to providing information, however. He also sought to quell rumors that might result in panic, and he set out "Regulations for the Periodical Press of the United States during the War," which James Pollard describes:

> [Under the regulations] news fell into three classifications—dangerous, questionable, and routine. In case of doubt, the CPI urged editors and writers to submit such copy to it for prompt decision. At the same time editors were reminded that it was still their duty to police all local copy, including advertising, against possible abuses. . . . Most publications did their best to comply with this

code, but there were bound to be a few recalcitrants. The San Francisco *Examiner* and the Washington *Post* were among the newspapers which offended.[18]

Added to the bite of such "self-regulation" was the pressure from state and federal espionage and sedition laws. President Wilson urged Congress to provide a "mild form of censorship" to fix something "more than a moral obligation upon any newspapers that might tend to print news by which the enemy might profit,"[19] although he promised he would never use censorship to protect himself. The Espionage Law that Congress passed in 1917 and the Sedition Act of 1918 proved to be far more than a mild form of censorship. Zechariah Chafee, Jr., reported that as the federal district courts interpreted those statutes,

> It became criminal to advocate heavier taxation instead of bond issues, to state that conscription was unconstitutional though the Supreme Court had not yet held it valid, to say that the sinking of merchant vessels was legal, to urge that a referendum should have preceded our declaration of war, to say that war was contrary to the teachings of Christ. Men have been punished for criticising the Red Cross and the M.C.A. . . . [20]

Under these and other laws the Postmaster General had enormous power for censorship through control of what material could be carried by the postal service. Creel himself was appointed to a federal Censorship Board, which had considerable power over the foreign language press. As Pollard has observed, these and other examples of government control made clear that "censorship was more real than voluntary." And Creel had sharp critics in the press and Congress.

After the war when Wilson attempted to mold public opinion in support of the League of Nations, it became apparent that neither his understanding of the press nor his willingness to work closely with it had increased. In Paris he had violated his own instruction, "open covenants of peace, openly arrived at," by negotiating for peace in secret. He may himself not have seen the contradiction because he seemed to feel that there was nothing to be reported until decisions had been made. Also, he used an intermediary to deal with the press instead of seizing the publicity initiative himself.

When Wilson returned to the United States, he was straightforward in promoting the League; some members of Congress and some of the newspaper correspondents were not as straightforward in their opposition. Columnist Ray Tucker has described the way a small group of correspondents

> . . . conspired hourly with the "irreconcilables" and performed service far beyond the call of newspaper duty. They tipped off most of the Congressmen to Wilsonian statements and maneuvers, and started Congressional counterattacks before the War President could unlimber his orators. They wrote phillipics for the Borahs, Johnsons, and Reeds, cooked up interviews . . . carried on research into the League's implications, dug up secret material. Their dispatches bristled with personal hostility to the League, and carbon copies which they distributed to pro-Wilson writers affected even the latter's supposedly favorable articles. The

covenant was defeated by the Senate press gallery long before it was finally rejected by the Senate.[21]

It is easy, and perhaps right, simply to condemn the correspondents. But David Lawrence, Wilson's best friend and most devoted admirer in the press corps of the time, suggests that the President was largely at fault for his bad relations with the press. "They constituted a series of misunderstandings and unfortunate clashes," Lawrence has written. "The growing tendency in recent years in America to anticipate the news and to discuss future events or the processes by which conclusions are reached, was deeply resented by Mr. Wilson. His theory was that nothing is news until it was completed."

Wilson's health broke during his personal appearance campaign for the League. Some have questioned whether history might not have been quite different if he could have reached the public through radio.

HARDING AND COOLIDGE

The Harding era was epitomized by the Pulitzer Prize-winning chronicle of corruption written by brilliant, erratic Paul Y. Anderson (who was later to descend into an emotional whirlpool and commit suicide). First, Anderson's reports in the St. Louis *Post-Dispatch* pushed the Senate into a full-dress investigation of Teapot Dome. By executive order in 1921 President Harding had transferred control of the federal oil fields of Teapot Dome, Wyoming, from the Navy Department to the Department of the Interior. In 1922 Secretary of the Interior Albert Fall leased the fields to private individuals without competitive bidding. Then, during the hearings in 1923, Anderson and other correspondents supplied many of the searching questions used by Senators Thomas Walsh and Burton Wheeler to cut through evasions in the testimony of Administration officials. Fall resigned, and was later convicted of accepting bribes, sentenced to a year in prison, and fined $100,000. In the end Warren Harding's name became almost synonymous with Presidential ineptitude.

This was, in a way, a surprising denouement. Harding, an Ohio newspaper publisher and U.S. Senator who liked being around reporters, was protected better by the press during his early days in the White House than any other President. He began well by restoring the press conference to the place it had held during the early months of the Wilson Presidency. If he was a bit pompous in answering questions during the formal conferences, he won the correspondents with warmth and an openly friendly feeling after hours. He was an attractive man—"No one ever looked more Presidential," one reporter wrote—who privately confessed his limitations; he told the correspondents that he knew he could not be the greatest President but that he wanted to be the best loved.

Unfortunately Harding did not always know what he was talking about. He had been in office only a short time when he was asked during a press conference whether the Four Power Pacific Pact drawn up during the famous Washington Conference for the Limitation of Armaments involved the protection of the Japanese Islands. The President said that it did not.

Actually it did, and Harding's answer raced around the world, creating an international sensation. Secretary of State Charles Evans Hughes, his chin whiskers bristling, rushed to the White House to get an official correction. Then he prevailed upon Harding to agree that only written questions submitted well in advance of press conferences would be answered. It was a crushing backdown for a President who was warmest and most expansive in talking to journalists.

Toward the end, as the correspondents and the Congress revealed more of the scandals of his subordinates, Harding seemed to withdraw from life. He died in 1923, a man who had only gradually become aware that he had surrounded himself with thieves.

The Administration of Calvin Coolidge was a frustrating time for the Washington press corps. It is doubtful that Coolidge, the inert beneficiary of national prosperity, could have been affected by anything. He presided over a time of repose, napping often and boasting of sleeping soundly for 11 hours every night. It was dismaying for reporters on the lookout for an angle. As Leo Rosten put it. "The most striking characteristic about the new President was his lack of a striking characteristic."

Although the President was a little huddle of a man—Coolidge conquering the tense and controversial times that enveloped his successor is almost unimaginable—it is also true that he calculated his actions. Much later he revealed in his autobiography that a kind of philosophy dictated his tight-lipped image:

> Everything that the President does potentially at least is of such great importance that he must be constantly on guard. . . . Not only in all his official actions, but in all his social intercourse, and even in his recreation and repose, he is constantly watched by a multitude of eyes to determine if there is anything unusual, extraordinary, or irregular, which can be set down in praise or blame.[22]

Coolidge did little, and many correspondents simply ignored him. Raymond "Pete" Brandt of the St. Louis *Post-Dispatch* said that his group "never covered Washington in the Twenties. We covered the Senate. You wasted your time downtown." Those who were responsible for covering Presidential news inadvertently built the image of a man of strength and silence. Henry Suydam, who was then a correspondent for the Brooklyn *Eagle,* has written that President Coolidge would observe laconically, "with respect to a certain bill, 'I'm not in favor of this legislation.' The next morning Washington dispatches began as follows: 'President Coolidge, in a fighting mood, today served notice on Congress that he intended to combat, with all the resources at his command, the pending bill, etc.'"

Thus did the correspondents divert themselves in the quiet days of the Coolidge era.

HERBERT HOOVER

The press corps reawakened during the Administration of Herbert Hoover, and for a time it mastered both President and Congress. It had been the custom in the Senate since the time of George Washington for reporters and spectators to leave the chamber during votes on nominations made by the President. But Paul Mallon the the United Press and his assistant, Kenneth Crawford (later a columnist for *Newsweek*), decided to destroy the system. They began checking with friendly Senators after the executive sessions and publishing the secret roll-call votes.

In 1929 President Hoover sent up to Capitol Hill a highly controversial nomination: Senator Irvine Lenroot of Wisconsin to be a federal judge. The senatorial votes on Lenroot's nomination were certain to affect the elections in a number of states in 1930; the Senate took extraordinary precautions to ensure secrecy. But Mallon made his usual rounds afterward and published the complete senatorial box score, which showed that several senators had been talking one way in public and voting quite another way behind closed doors. Mallon was subpoenaed and questioned sharply by a Senate committee, but he would not reveal the sources of his information. The Senate gave up and has since virtually abolished executive sessions, having gone into executive sessions fewer than a dozen times in the last four decades.

Hoover's own relations with the correspondents were a carbon copy of Taft's. As Secretary of Commerce under Harding and Coolidge, Hoover had been the best news source in Washington, and he and the correspondents formed a mutual-aid society. Hoover gave the reporters what Paul Y. Anderson described as "a perfect gold mine of graveyard stuff"; and the reporters gave Hoover a national stature that no Secretary of Commerce since has been able to attain. Gradually, Anderson has written, newspaper editors and the American people came to believe "that Hoover knew more about the affairs of government and the actual condition of the country and the world than any other man in the administration." Hoover entered the White House on a wave of respect and liking—and promptly changed. Instead of continuing his impartial news policies, he began to play a few favorites among the correspondents—Mark Sullivan was a particular pet—and he did it so blatantly that they became known as "trained seals."

One Sunday afternoon when Hoover was relaxing at his mountain retreat on the Rapidan, news of a sudden development sent him racing back to the White House at 60 miles an hour—dangerous speed on the Virginia roads of those days. The White House correspondents, who were not allowed to stay at the camp, were at an inn several miles away and learned of Hoover's trip too late to catch up with him. But the next day the New York *Times* carried a front-page story on the President's breakneck run to the White House. Convinced that there had been a leak from his staff, Hoover ordered the Secret Service to investigate. Then it became known that Turner Catledge of the *Times* had simply worked a problem in arithmetic involving the distance covered and the time consumed in making the trip and had written the story merely to emphasize the foreign affairs emergency—but Hoover's fury strengthened in the correspondents their growing belief that the President had become a sour and resentful man.

Through much of his Presidency, Hoover's relations with the men who covered his actions were strained and humorless. The President invited publishers to the White House to complain about their Washington correspondents and caused several correspondents to be transferred or fired. When leaks from his disenchanted subordinates reached print, Hoover announced that "only such news as is given out through the stated channels of the executive offices should be printed by the newspapers of the country." This was actually an effort to cut down on the leaks, but it had the clear implication that the Chief Executive should rule the press as well as his Administration.

Finally, unable to exert any control, Hoover resorted to clumsy lies. He required that press conference questions be submitted 24 hours in advance. Then, when he bypassed pointed questions and was asked about them, he would say that he had not received them.

The most damning incident came in 1931, when Hoover denied knowledge of a letter from Governor Franklin Roosevelt of New York on negotiations with Canada for a St. Lawrence waterway project. Roosevelt promptly announced that he would make public his copy of the letter. Then Hoover admitted that the letter had been received but denied that he had denied knowledge of it and denied that there had been any negotiations. At this point many of the few friends he had left in the Washington press corps deserted him.

When panic grew after the Great Crash of 1929, Charles Michelson, a former New York *World* correspondent who had become publicity director of the Democratic National Committee, fired broadside after broadside at the hapless Hoover. Considering the President's ragged relations with the people who wrote about him day by day, it is not at all surprising that, having the option of using Michelson's charges or ignoring them, the reporters played them up. In Hoover's abortive reelection campaign of 1932, crowds booed him, people ran into the streets to thumb their noses at him, and the most widely repeated remark ran, "If you put a rose in Hoover's hand, it would wilt." The President became morose. He said not a word to his successor as they drove to the Capitol on Inauguration Day.

Notes

1. Leonard W. Levy (ed.), *Freedom of the Press from Zenger to Jefferson: Early American Libertarian Theories* (Indianapolis: Bobbs-Merrill, 1966), p. xxxi.
2. Levy, p. xxxv.
3. "Access for the Official Press: A Debate, 1800," reprinted from *Annals of Congress* in Robert O. Blanchard (ed.), *Congress and the News Media* (New York: Hastings House, 1974), p. 18.
4. "The Reporter's Place in the House: A Debate, 1789–90," reprinted from *Annals of Congress* in Blanchard, pp. 14–15.
5. Quoted in James E. Pollard, *The Presidents and the Press* (New York: Macmillan, 1947), p. 15.
6. Quoted in William L. Rivers, Theodore Peterson, and Jay W. Jensen, *The Mass Media and Modern Society,* Edition (New York: Holt, Rinehart and Winston, 1971), p. 108.

7. John Tebbel, *The Media in America* (New York: New American Library, 1974),
   p. 151.
8. Pollard, p. 150.
9. Douglass Cater, *The Fourth Branch of Government* (Boston: Houghton Mifflin,
   1959), p. 76.
10. Quoted in Tebbel, p. 182.
11. Quoted in Rivers, Peterson, and Jensen, p. 112.
12. Pollard, pp. 384–386.
13. Quoted in Rivers, Peterson, and Jensen p. 114.
14. Arthur M. Schlesinger, Jr., *The Imperial Presidency* (Boston: Houghton Mifflin,
    1973), p. 335.
15. Quoted in Pollard p. 579.
16. Quoted in Pollard, p. 607.
17. George Creel, *How We Advertised America* (New York: Arno Press, 1972), pp.
    3–4. For another account by Creel of the Committee on Public Information see
    George Creel, *Rebel At Large: Recollections of Fifty Crowded Years* (New
    York: G. P. Putnam's Sons, 1947).
18. Pollard, p. 666.
19. Quoted in Pollard, p. 662.
20. Zechariah Chafee, Jr., *Free Speech in the United States* (New York: Atheneum,
    1969), p. 51.
21. Quoted in Rivers, Peterson, and Jensen, p. 119.
22. Quoted in Pollard, p. 715.

10

The Media and Government: The Modern Presidency

Robert G. Spivack of the New York Post: "[D]id you feel that reporters had been fair to you . . . in their questions?" President Dwight D. Eisenhower: "Well, when you come down to it, I don't see what a reporter could do much to a President, do you?"

The whole concept of a return to secrecy in peacetime demonstrates a profound misunderstanding of the role of a free press. . . . The plea for security could well become a cloak for errors, misjudgments and other failings of government.

RICHARD M. NIXON, 1961

Government . . . [differs] from other ships in leaking most at the top.

WASHINGTON JOKE REPORTED BY ARTHUR SCHLESINGER, JR.

Franklin Roosevelt

Modern political persuasion began with Franklin Roosevelt. Leo Rosten describes Roosevelt at his first press conference:

312

His answers were swift, positive, illuminating. He had exact information at his fingertips. He showed an impressive understanding of public problems and administrative methods. He was lavish in his confidences and background information. He was informal, communicative, gay. When he evaded a question, it was done frankly. He was thoroughly at ease.[1]

Henry M. Hyde, one of the oldest and most respected of the correspondents, termed it "the most amazing performance the White House has ever seen." At the end the correspondents applauded spontaneously—for the first time in Presidential history.

Eventually, however, Roosevelt's instruments of persuasion seemed to deteriorate. He was occasionally waspish during press conferences, assigning low percentages of accuracy to columnists with national fame, labeling two reporters as dunces and inviting them to stand in the corner, paying tribute to the educational value of radio and movies and ignoring newspapers—all in public. Arthur Krock wrote that the Roosevelt Administration used "more ruthlessness, intelligence, and subtlety in trying to suppress legitimate unfavorable comment than any I know."

But Raymond Clapper, the most respected columnist of the time, pointed out that the working press judges Presidents as men, not as archangels. If the reporters were only 60 percent for the New Deal, he wrote, they were still 90 percent for the President personally. Clapper gave specific reasons for Roosevelt's continuing high standing with the press corps: Their personal contacts were usually pleasant and intimate; Roosevelt's press conferences were almost certain to yield live news; the correspondents admired the President's political skill and craftsmanship, and even when they disagreed with his purposes, they generally believed in his sincerity, courage, and readiness to experiment. Finally the Rooseveltian theme of rescuing the forgotten man was a powerful lure for those who had investigated the real conditions of American society.

The accuracy of Clapper's insight became clear early in 1936. Several Republicans were jockeying for the opportunity to oppose Roosevelt in the Presidential election. Leo Rosten asked the correspondents: "Of the current candidates for President, who is your choice?" Roosevelt received 54 votes. His closest opponents, Governor Alfred Landon and Senator Arthur Vandenberg, received eight votes each.

Too little has been made of his relationships with reporters and too much of the "fireside chats." The President was stunningly effective over the radio—those full, confident tones that John Dos Passos called "the patroon voice, the headmaster's admonishing voice, the bedside doctor's voice that spoke to each man and to all of us." But there were few fireside chats: four in 1933, two in 1934, one in 1935, one in 1936. Roosevelt actually preferred to reach the people through the Washington correspondents. During that four-year period, when the President appealed to the people over the radio exactly eight times, he held 340 press conferences.

More should be made, too, of Roosevelt's shrewd use of his own

President Franklin Roosevelt was stunningly effective in his use of the mass media, both in speaking directly to the American public by radio and in dealing with reporters. (Wide World photo)

expressive features. The 1930s, one photographer has said, "marked the opening of a golden era for Washington cameramen. Roosevelt had a perfect sense of the dramatic and unusual." Newspaper and magazine editors clamored for any shot of that mobile and animated face. On occasion Roosevelt punished the newspapers for opposing him by restricting pictures. In 1935 he furiously banned all pictures for a short period because a birthday photo that was snapped when he had taken off his glasses and was rubbing his eyes had been captioned, "President Ponders Farm Problem."

As a rule only one kind of picture of the polio-crippled President was forbidden: He was never to be photographed in pain or discomfort. Once, with dozens of photographers around him, Roosevelt fell full-length on the floor. Not a picture was taken. (One can only wonder if the same restraint would be shown today.)

Otherwise anything went. The President was shown eating hot dogs, munching peanuts at a baseball game, kissing his wife when she returned from a tour, playing with his pet Scotty, and—especially in the days ately before he ran for a fourth term, when rumors were persistent that he was a very sick man—with his big jaw thrust forward, cigarette-holder clenched in his teeth at a jaunty angle.

There was much more to Roosevelt's domination of the news. At least part of the success of his Administration sprang from the work of his press secretary, Stephen Early. Unlike Herbert Hoover's inept and hesitant press men, Early was a seasoned wire-service reporter, who was given, according to another Presidential assistant, "one of the most important voices in the government." He not only worked with the President but also presided over a large and growing apparatus of public relations and information that was spread throughout the federal departments and agencies. The Roosevelt Presidency marked the firm establishment of government by publicity.

Federal press agentry had begun in a small way in 1910. Some of the members of a Congressional committee looking into the operations of the Census Bureau had been startled when the director confessed that "for about six months now we have had a person whose principal duty is to act as what might properly be called, I suppose, a press agent." This had been Whitman Osgood, a former reporter whose work had been thoughtfully disguised under the title "Expert Special Agent."

Soon after this disclosure, members of Congress themselves had begun to hire assistants whose principal duty was to act as what might properly be called press agents. Members of Congress had always emphasized publicity, but it had been personal and somewhat erratic; Senator Pat Harrison of Mississippi was given to reminding his staff nervously, "Every day we don't get in the papers is a day lost." Congress had begun to fear that public-relations expertise in the Executive branch would help make the President dominant. And so in 1913 a bill had been passed, providing: "No money appropriated by this or any other Act shall be used for the compensation of any publicity experts unless specifically authorized for that purpose." The immediate target had been President Wilson, and the proviso had hampered him and his successors. But during the Roosevelt era it was little more than an invitation to subterfuge. Executive departments and agencies hired no "publicity experts"; they took on specialists in "public information" and "editing."

In the mid-1930s the fighting became intense, and a bit petty. Senator Vandenberg proposed that Senate approval be obtained before any Executive agency could use color printing in annual reports. Senator Harry Byrd of Virginia headed an investigating committee that turned up 270 public-information employees under the President's control. Others were hired, one correspondent wrote, even as Byrd made his report.

All in all, by putting adroit emphasis on government publicity and by catering, cajoling, and lecturing the Washington correspondents in 998 press conferences, Franklin Roosevelt managed the news more artfully than any other President before him.

Harry Truman

It was not in FDR's successor to be either artful or devious. Harry Truman was so open and obvious that even the correspondents who respected his crusty strength sometimes found it difficult to remember that they were

questioning the President of the United States. As Douglass Cater, author of
The Fourth Branch of Government, has observed, the language of a
reporter tends to take on the flavor of the Chief Executive being questioned.
Truman's meetings with the Washington press corps resulted in some of the
testiest press conference prose in history.

> REPORTER: Could you tell us anything about your conference with the Secre-
> tary of State and the Secretary of the Treasury?
> TRUMAN: No, it's none of your business.
> REPORTER: Would that mean, sir, that you would shake up the individual
> civilian end, service heads of the Navy Department, if this fight continues?
> TRUMAN: Not necessarily. I think it would work itself out. Just wait a little.
> REPORTER: I'll bet you two to one.
> TRUMAN: I'll take you on that. I'll take you on that.

Almost everything Harry Truman said emphasized his one great quality
as President: he was positive. If he had an abrasive personality, and if he
sometimes seemed to suffer from an inability to think consecutively, he
always gave the impression of believing devoutly in himself, in his friends,
and in his program. And his hardheaded and repetitious emphasis on his
beliefs made news. He spoke, as one reporter put it, "the language of Main
Street, and Main Street understands it—even to the grammatical errors and
slurred words." The editorials were overwhelmingly against him, but a
columnist who had no great admiration for President Truman noted sagely
that the President had demonstrated one endearing quality: "He has more
guts than a fiddle factory."

Specialists in the ghostly science of political measurements have laugh-
ingly criticized the press by listing all the newspapers and magazines
opposed to Truman in 1948, adding up their circulation figures, and
capping it all with a triumphant number: Truman's 2 million-vote margin
over Thomas E. Dewey. This seems convincing enough as common-sense
evidence, but it takes account only of *editorial* opposition to the President,
ignoring the hurdy-gurdy, news-making campaign, in which Truman captured the information initiative.

While Dewey, the confident Republican nominee, was holding vaguely
that "our streams must abound with fish," Truman attacked "the do-
nothing Eightieth Congress." Only the most violently partisan newspapers
gave their splashiest headlines to Dewey's platitudes. Most of the others,
including a great many that promoted Dewey in long-winded editorials,
played up Truman's salty speeches on page 1. This is not necessarily
paradoxical; some Republican publishers have an appreciation of news
values that transcends their biases, and the counting-house mentality that
afflicts others told them that "our streams must abound with fish" would not
sell newspapers.

Throughout the campaign of 1948, Dewey, unaware that he was running way behind, seemed satisfied with his resounding victories on the
editorial pages. Truman, who, like Roosevelt, often paid tribute to working

Many newspapers and news services were embarassed the morning after President Harry Truman's surprise reelection by stories and headlines of *President* Thomas Dewey's victory. (United Press International photo)

reporters in the same breath he used to damn their publishers, preferred the news victories on the front page, and he continued the string of Democratic victories of 1936, 1940, and 1944, all secured in the face of enormous editorial support for the Republican opposition.

The focus on Truman the man was so relentless during his seven years as President that few noticed what was happening to the publicity apparatus he had inherited from Roosevelt. One who was alarmed by it was Congressman Christian Herter of Massachusetts, who wrote: "During the recent session of Congress our federal bureaucracy revealed itself as the most powerful and potentially the most dangerous lobby of all. It fought, bureau by bureau, every Congressional move to curb its innate desire to expand. Backed by its vast, tax-supported propaganda machine. . . ."

By the end of Truman's Presidency, the machine had doubled. The executive branch had 3632 employees working in the "Information" and "Editorial" Civil Service classifications, plus an unknown number whose titles were "Deputy Assistant Secretary for Public Affairs," "Administrative Assistant," "Executive Assistant to the Assistant Secretary," and the like. Senator Byrd, despairing of trying to decide who should stay and who should go, simply called for a general reduction of 25 percent, hoping that such a cut would result in "more news and less bull from the federal publicity mill." Characteristically, President Truman ignored him.

Of as much concern was Truman's decision to extend to all federal agencies the authority to withhold and classify information in the interests of national security. Secrecy was obviously not something new in American government. The American system of government was born behind the closed doors of the Constitutional Convention of 1787. The *bureaucracy* of secrecy, however, was a phenomenon of the Cold War. The world situation after World War II, unlike that after World War I, made secrecy seem a pressing concern. As historian Arthur Schlesinger, Jr., describes the late 1920s, "[s]o unimportant did the protection of secrets seem to the State Department . . . that Henry L. Stimson, as Hoover's Secretary of State, disbanded the code-breaking section on the celebrated ground that gentlemen did not read other gentlemen's mail."[2] In the 1950s Americans did not think Communists were "gentlemen."

Although a military secrecy system existed before the involvement of the United States in World War II, not until 1951 was the authority to classify information extended to non-military agencies. Truman's vague executive order authorized all executive agencies to safeguard documents the "disclosure of which would or could harm, tend to impair, or otherwise threaten the security of the nation." President Dwight Eisenhower's Executive Order 10501 of 1953, described by some as "the bible of security stamping," limited the agencies and personnel who could wield security stamps, but until 1961, such agencies as the Migratory Bird Conservation Commission and the Indian Arts and Crafts Board had authority to classify documents.

Sometimes the national security seems to reside in curious information. The government has felt compelled to withhold from the American people reports on "silent flashless weapons" (the Pentagon's term for bows and arrows), newspaper clippings already published and read by thousands, and at least one memo with a Top Secret classification noting that too many papers were being classified Top Secret.

Almost unnoticed by everyone but the correspondents and a few of Truman's assistants were the changes in press conferences during the Truman Administration. Unlike Roosevelt, President Truman adopted the practice of addressing the country through a statement delivered at the beginning of the press conference. These were careful statements put together by many of his assistants and officials from the State Department.

Moreover, the press conference itself gradually became institutionalized and formal. Instead of just calling together the correspondents as President Roosevelt had, President Truman began to prepare with his staff as the time of the weekly press conference approached. At first, only his press secretary, Charles Ross, helped him. Soon, though, the press conference became more demanding because the questions were aimed at asking more than the press secretary could possibly know. Staff sessions were started at the White House, a collective effort to tell the President what kinds of questions were likely to be asked and in many cases the kinds of answers he must use.

When Roger Tubby became President Truman's press secretary late in the Truman Administration, he instituted another kind of refinement. Tubby had worked for Secretary of State George Marshall, who had relied on written briefings from his assistants. In the White House, Tubby asked *his* assistants to prepare about 40 questions that were likely to be asked of the President. He would gather them two days before the press conference, then farm them out to government officials. The night before the press conference was to be held, Truman would be given a notebook containing the information. A half-hour before the press conference, White House assistants and departmental representatives would gather around the President's desk and go over the tougher questions with him.[3]

Beginning on April 27, 1950, President Truman made another highly significant change. To accommodate the increasing number of reporters attending his press conference, he shifted the site from his oval office to the Indian Treaty Room in the Executive Office Building nearby. So it was that the intimate atmosphere of the Roosevelt press conferences was changed to a much more formal atmosphere. The day when banter was exchanged between some of the correspondents and the President in the early minutes had passed.

Dwight Eisenhower

How astute press agentry can overwhelm the Washington press corps is best revealed by the Eisenhower Presidency. Although it is doubtful that the President himself was responsible for many of the shrewd ploys made on his behalf, it is a mistake to assume that he was altogether unaware of the publicity methods used. Eisenhower had served for decades in the U.S. Army, where the struggle for status is often fierce and where the stakes are huge for an officer who can create a favorable image. With regard to military custom, it is revealing to cite the difference between an editorial as it was originally written for a military newspaper controlled by General Douglas MacArthur and the same editorial as it actually appeared in that paper. The writer, who apparently did not know of the rivalry between Eisenhower and MacArthur, wrote the version that appears at the left. The published version, as edited by officers more sensitive to MacArthur's wishes, appears at the right:

The words of General Eisenhower Tuesday at a dinner honoring the men of Russia, Britain, and the United States who fashioned victory in Europe illustrate something fundamental about this war.

The words were spoken by a man who commanded the most powerful, the most destructive army ever put on the field by the western allies. Yet not a single line extolled the glories of war. . . .

The words of American generals, who along with their Russian and British colleagues, helped fashion victory in Europe, illustrate something fundamental about this war.

The words were spoken by men who commanded the most powerful, the most destructive armies ever put on the field in Europe. Crowds in London, in Paris, in Washington, in Chicago, in Los Angeles thronged to pay tribute to their achievements. Yet, in none. . . .

When the Eisenhower Administration took over in 1953, it inherited most of Truman's publicists, who were secure in their Civil Service positions. Not trusting them with the Republican merchandising, Eisenhower's lieutenants added their own people. During Eisenhower's first four years, executive information personnel nearly doubled: In 1957 the Civil Service Commission listed 6878 "Information and Editorial Employees." The increase continued during the second term, and Christian Herter, who had been aghast at the size of the Truman Administration's propaganda machine, eventually became Eisenhower's Secretary of State and presided unprotestingly over one of the largest cogs in that machine.

"Press agent" is too weak a word to describe the Eisenhower Administration's chief publicist, James Hagerty, just as the description of Hagerty by another correspondent as "the best Republican President who was never elected" is too strong. But Hagerty certainly demonstrated how a canny PR man creates an image for his employer.

Hagerty often made subtle decisions about which stories should involve the President. The news of the first successful U.S. satellite was released not from the launching site but from Augusta, Georgia, where the President was vacationing. Later, when White House reporters asked where they could learn whether an Army satellite that had been fired that morning had gone into orbit successfully, Hagerty answered, "If it is in orbit, we will have an announcement." A correspondent who had grown wise in the ways of the press secretary then asked whether the White House would release the news if the satellite failed. "No," Hagerty replied. The satellite did not orbit. The Army announced the failure.

Eisenhower's many vacations were common knowledge, but Hagerty blunted the edge of criticism by making it appear that each trip away from Washington was a working vacation. Once, when the President was golfing in Augusta, the press secretary announced the appointments of three ambassadors. The decision to appoint them had been made three weeks earlier, and the nominations were not to be sent to Congress until 10 days later, but Presidential news was scarce, and Hagerty always aimed to keep

Eisenhower on the front pages. It worked. Later in Augusta, Hagerty announced that Secretary of Labor James Mitchell would visit the President to discuss a bill protecting labor welfare funds. The bill had been introduced in Congress four months earlier, but the President again made the headlines.

Eventually all the correspondents who covered the White House during the Eisenhower Presidency became aware of Hagerty's methods, but there was little they could do. As Russell Baker of the New York *Times* pointed out,

> Hagerty's enduring contribution to the White House was his demonstration of how to exploit the weakness of the American newsgathering system for the promotion of his boss. . . . If editors demanded a Presidential story a day, it follows that reporters will be found to satisfy them one way or another. On days when there is no news, they will poke around darkened rooms, look under the carpet, or start staring at the west wall and adding two and two in news stories. When that sort of thing happens, the White House is in trouble. Hagerty prevented this by seeing to it that there was rarely a newsless day. If there was no news, he made a little.[4]

One innovation by Hagerty needs underlining. He convinced President Eisenhower that his press conferences should be televised. The first conference covered by television cameras came on January 19, 1955. Conferences were filmed so that the networks could edit them for use during evening news shows. (The televising of press conferences had had to await advances in film processing that made it possible to develop and edit the film for a same-day deadline.) Hagerty would not allow direct *live* televising because of the potential for the careless remark, and he kept for himself the right to edit if necessary. Only when Eisenhower's successor, John Kennedy, took over, was there a President willing to take a chance on direct live television.

John Kennedy

In the spring of 1963, a newspaper publisher who had just received the latest Gallup Poll showing the country's attitudes toward its President exclaimed bitterly: "I just can't understand it. We've *exposed* Kennedy. We've shown that he's been failing and lying to the American people . . . And yet they're making a god of him!"

It was an understandable reaction, and not only because the publisher had been a whole-souled supporter of Richard Nixon. President Kennedy had just experienced the winter of his deepest discontent. His Administration was failing the task it had set for itself in Laos and Vietnam. It had failed to get the country moving, while adding hugely to the national debt. Perhaps most important, government officials had admitted that, to put it gently, they had told less than the truth about the Cuban crisis of October

President John Kennedy enjoyed the company of reporters, whom he once described as "the last of the talented poor." (Wide World photo)

1962. The whole orchestra had fallen downstairs at once; the critics were in full cry. And yet less than one-fourth of the American people—exactly 24 percent—disapproved of the way John F. Kennedy was performing as President.

A full view of the facts deepens the paradox, especially in view of the Administration's heavy-handed guides to reporting the Cold War. Secretary of Defense Robert McNamara set the tone shortly after he began his rule at the Pentagon. He had this plaintive question for correspondents who were revealing flaws in American weaponry: "Why should we tell Russia that the Zeus developments may not be satisfactory? What we ought to be saying is that we have the most perfect anti-ICBM system that the human mind can devise." That McNamara was simply arguing for false reports became clear when, shortly after suggesting that correspondents describe the Nike-Zeus program glowingly, he scrapped the program.

Then came the abortive Bay of Pigs invasion in 1961, only three months after Kennedy's Inauguration. Reporters were told at the height of the invasion that 5000 patriotic refugees were penetrating Cuba, when, in fact, a force of 1400 was involved. Like McNamara's guideline on Nike-Zeus, this was designed to mislead the enemy by misleading everybody.

In August 1962, Senator Kenneth Keating of New York made his sensational charge that Russia was arming Cuba. In October he said that the Russians were building intermediate-range ballistic missile sites for Castro.

But White House, State Department, and Defense Department officials held that there was nothing to Senator Keating's charges. Only when the buildup in Cuba had gone so far that President Kennedy announced a quarantine on Cuba and issued an ultimatum to Russia did the Administration admit that Keating had been right all along.

News management, and mismanagement, did not mar the Kennedy image, and there is no doubt John F. Kennedy was one of the most sophisticated shapers of public opinion in Presidential history.

Kennedy's information policies were complicated—and sometimes contradictory—but their thrust was not to be found in the blunders of the beleaguered Defense Department. The center of information was the White House, and there the policy was the precise reverse of censorship. Never before had Washington correspondents been given so full a view of the President and the Presidency; they were invited to feel with Kennedy the crushing responsibility, and to be enveloped in the aura, of the greatest center of leadership in the Western world.

The value of this policy was that the stark view of the Presidency overwhelmed the reporters' critical perspective. Talking to a President who has charm and toughness and keen intelligence, few reporters will fail to admire him. More than anything else, the open White House enabled Kennedy, who had the awesome responsibility of deciding when or whether the world would end, to become the dominant source of news, explanation, and opinion.

Kennedy revolutionized the reporting of the Presidency. Before 1961 the White House had been largely a closed preserve. Information was usually channeled through the President's press secretary, and some White House correspondents never so much as met some of the President's chief assistants. The almost invariable reply of Eisenhower assistants who were asked for interviews was "See Hagerty." One correspondent who arranged an interview with a Presidential speech writer without going through the press secretary was so elated that he telephoned his editor to say, "I broke around behind Hagerty!" The important news was not the substance of the interview but the fact that he got one.

When Kennedy took over in 1961, correspondents wandered through the White House offices in such numbers that they created a traffic problem.

President Kennedy's staff did much to influence favorable press coverage, but the President was his own most effective promoter. He practiced personal salesmanship with the *élan* of one accustomed to establishing the rules of the game. Franklin Roosevelt granted one exclusive interview, to Arthur Krock of the New York *Times*. Harry Truman granted one, also to Krock. In both cases the storm of protest blowing up among other correspondents was so violent that neither President ever again granted such an interview. (Anne O'Hare McCormick of the *Times* spoke to Roosevelt privately and obtained authoritative views, but she produced nothing that could properly be described as an interview story. Krock has written that Truman granted one other exclusive interview but required that the source be veiled.) Eisenhower observed the protocol. But Kennedy, from the beginning, made such a fetish of giving exclusive interviews that his press secretary, Pierre Salinger, once observed that he often had to go to the President's office to get to see the White House correspondents.

Kennedy, James Reston wrote, broke every rule in the book:

> When he came into the White House, he was warned by his newspaper friends about all the wicked ways of the press, particularly their jealousy and their hostility toward anyone who gives special advantages to any individual reporter.
>
> The President indicated how seriously he took this warning at the very beginning of his Administration. After his Inaugural Ball, he suddenly showed up at Joseph Alsop's house. . . .
>
> A few days later he drove around to Walter Lippmann's house for a talk, went to dinner at the house of Rowland Evans of the New York *Herald Tribune* and later had his old friend Charles Bartlett of the Chattanooga *Times* up to Hyannis Port for the weekend.
>
> When some of the President's associates asked the President whether this was wise, he took the original view that reporters were also members of the Human Race, and added that he proposed to see anybody he liked and even some reporters he didn't like.[5]

Reston warned his fellow correspondents of the lure of the new order: "It is hard to go into that House that means so much to us historically and not be impressed with it and with the terrible burdens the President has to carry. How could you help but be sympathetic? Once you become sympathetic it becomes increasingly difficult to employ the critical faculties." Yet Reston himself, who had once boasted that he had never talked alone with a President during 20 years in Washington—having feared, he explained, that he might get "tied up"—yielded often to the lure of exclusive Presidential interviews. It is doubtful, however, that Reston, an exceedingly tough-minded man, got tied up for long.

Lyndon Johnson

The only law requiring that Presidents hold press conferences, Arthur Krock once observed, is the political law of self-preservation. Nothing better illustrates the point—or makes it more obvious that Presidents use the mass media for their own ends—than the stark difference between the press conferences of John Kennedy and Lyndon Johnson.

Kennedy was slender, handsome, magnetic, with a quick mind and an articulate tongue. He was ideally equipped for the mass conferences staged in the State Department auditorium—an auditorium so large that, to give the impression of a packed house, the television cameras were placed not at the rear but at the halfway point, with the correspondents crowded in between the cameras and the President. In the words of one correspondent, "Kennedy glittered—he positively glittered—up on that platform. No wonder he wanted live television!"

Johnson, whose political acumen in this instance curbed his ego, knew better than to match himself against the fresh memory of Kennedy's performances. Johnson was attractive in person, but he was also earthy, with more than a strain of vulgarity. In the company of sophisticates, he sometimes became aware of his cattle-and-tumbleweed manner. He once asked a friend, "When are you going to help me wipe this tobacco stain off my jaw?"

The kind of press conference Johnson preferred was apparent from the first. Two weeks after he became President, 25 of the regular White House correspondents went to the office of Press Secretary Pierre Salinger for what had been announced as a routine briefing. Suddenly they found themselves ushered into the President's office. It was a highly informal conference. Navy mess attendants served coffee; the President sat in a cushioned rocking chair at the head of two semicircular couches; the correspondents sat on the couches, sipping coffee and asking occasional questions to further the rambling flow of Johnson's conversation.

Ten days later Johnson held another surprise press conference that was almost as informal as the first. Then, during an extended work-vacation at the LBJ Ranch in Texas, he held no fewer than four impromptu conferences, one of them beside a haystack, another at a party given by the correspondents. He became wildly experimental. There was a conference in the old White House theater, another in the spacious East Room, another on the south lawn. The conferences became mobile: seven laps around the White House grounds. They became expansive: the reporters' wives and children were invited. Finally the Baltimore *Sun* asked somewhat plaintively, "Will the next press conference be tonight, tomorrow, or next week? Will it be held on horseback? In the White House swimming pool? Will the public be invited and the press excluded?"

The great value for Johnson of his spur-of-the-moment press conferences was that he faced only the White House correspondents, avoiding questions from the specialists who cover the rest of Washington—specialists who do not have a vested interest in remaining on good terms with the President. Another was that the intimate atmosphere of small conferences discourages embarrassing questions. Bobby Baker was secretary to the Senate Democrats when he became the central figure in an influence-peddling scandal in the fall of 1963, and he had long been a protégé of Johnson. The Baker case was the height of interest during Johnson's first weeks as President, yet he was asked nothing about it during his first two meetings with the press. Perhaps the chief value of an informal conference for the President is that he can control it. Instead of submitting himself to a half hour of questioning in the Kennedy-type conference, which gives some control to the correspondents, with an informal conference the President can start and end as he likes. The importance of this factor became evident one Saturday two months after Johnson took office, when a rumor ran through the press corps that another impromptu conference was likely. By 2:30 that afternoon, more than 100 reporters were milling about. The

President waited until 5 p.m. to call them in. He alluded to the fact that he had heard complaints about "quickie conferences" and invited questions with what sounded like a warning: "I never enjoy anything more than polite, courteous, fair, judicious reporters, and I think all of you qualify." Then, after responding to a tentative question, he swerved into the Bobby Baker case and explained that his own involvement was innocent. Before the correspondents could pin down his exact relationship to Baker's deals, the President turned and walked out.

Not until his hundredth day in office did he schedule a traditional mass conference, after which James Reston commented: "President Johnson achieved his major objective in his first live television press conference: He survived."

It is not surprising that Johnson favored intimate, face-to-face meetings. Naturally inclined to earthy language and manner, he was acutely uncomfortable in the formal setting. His biographer Doris Kearns describes him this way: "Terrified of making slips swearing or using ungrammatical constructions, Johnson insisted on reading from formal texts. Facial muscles frozen in place, except for the simpering smile, he projected an image of feigned propriety, dullness, and dishonesty."[6]

By contrast, Johnson was overpowering up close. As Ted Lewis of the New York *Daily News* pointed out: "Johnson is formidably ingratiating—in private or semi-private gatherings. He easily dominates any group where he can look a man in the eye, grab lapels, poke chests, and talk about what happens to be on his mind." Columnist Jack Anderson describes the experience this way:

> Lyndon Johnson was a hard man to resist. When . . . he got you into the back rooms, he would smother you. First place he was a big guy. You came in looking up at him. And you put the prestige of the Presidency on top of that overpowering, physical fellow and you came in at a disadvantage. And then he would throw that great ham of an arm around you and he would hug you to his bosom. And he'd get about two inches from your ear and he was persuasive.
>
> And his pockets were usually stuffed with, with documents. He had papers, polls. He could prove anything with a poll. He had polls that he'd pull out of his vest. And classified doc[uments]. He was the worst security violator we've ever had. He'd lay them before your astonished eyes. And he would talk and you wouldn't get a word in edgewise. And you would go out of there saying, "Yes, Mr. President, yes, Mr. President."[7]

Johnson could be a blizzard of information. But more fundamentally he had a passion for secrecy and for absolute control over the release of information. To be predictable was to be weak. William Small has written in *Political Power and the Press,* "It was a common joke that the best way to kill a presidential appointment in advance was to leak it to the press because LBJ would never make an appointment first mentioned in print."

Partly because Kennedy was reasonably successful at it, his handling of the press was called "news management." It is a measure of Johnson's style that *his* Administration was plagued with a "credibility gap." Johnson's undoing was the Vietnam War, but his dissembling was not limited to American policies and actions in Southeast Asia. It infected foreign and domestic issues. His efforts to pressure the media—to influence them as if they were just another special interest group—were so bold, so immediate, and so frequent that his purposes were usually transparent.

In March of 1968 Johnson surprised almost everyone by declaring he would not run for, nor accept another term as, President. In its 1968 Freedom of Information report, Sigma Delta Chi summed up what many others felt: "President Johnson is leaving office with perhaps the worst record for credibility of any President in our history."[8] It is amazing how rapidly events can conspire to challenge such superlatives.

Richard Nixon

At an investigative reporters' conference in 1976 Jack Anderson, the dean of investigative reporters, was questioned by someone who had obviously already forgotten the "credibility gap" of the Johnson Administration. The questioner asked if the press would have gone after Nixon if he had been a "charming Democrat." Nixon, like virtually all new Presidents, had enjoyed a honeymoon with the press immediately after he took office in 1969—a honeymoon that was sweetened by a press exhausted from the bitterness of the Johnson Vietnam War years. Anderson's reply tells a great deal about why Nixon's press relationships degenerated into open warfare:

> I don't think that he was investigated because of his politics. I think probably that there were some of us that reacted to his personality. I think that that may have had something to do with our vigilance and our vigorousness. In my own case I have written . . . about more Democratic scandals than Republican scandals. Maybe because there are more Democrats than Republicans. But I think if Richard Nixon had been a Democrat, we would have conducted the same kind of investigation, the same kind of an inquiry.
>
> But Richard Nixon hated the press. It was, in my opinion, a fatal flaw in his character. He hated it with a neurotic passion and I think we sensed it, and I think it is possible that we reacted to that.

For Nixon the press was as much the enemy as any Democrat, and he showed himself willing to go to great lengths to subvert a free press as well as undermine other democratic institutions.

Ironically, Nixon's initial political experience in the 1940s was sheltered by the press. He began his public life in Southern California under the umbrella of the Los Angeles *Times,* now applauded as one of the best papers in the country but then considered one of the worst. He was friendly to reporters in his first years as a congressman and a senator in Washington and was a ready source of "leaks" during his pursuit of Alger Hiss.[9] However, the pattern for his Presidential press relations was set in 1952, the year he first ran for Vice President on the Eisenhower ticket.

When the press gave enough coverage to make the "Nixon fund," $18,235 in contributions from Southern California businessmen, a national scandal, Eisenhower considered dropping Nixon from the ticket. To save himself Nixon bypassed the journalists and editors of the press and used television to appeal directly to the public. In his "Checkers" speech, he defended his acceptance of the money: "Not one cent of the $18,000 or any other money of that type ever went to my personal use. Every penny of it was used to pay for political expenses that I did not think should be charged to the taxpayers of the United States." What gave the speech its name was his defense of one other gift:

> We did get something, a gift, after the nomination. . . . It was a little cocker spaniel dog . . . black and white, spotted, and our little girl Tricia, the six-year-old, named it Checkers. And you know, the kids, like all kids, loved the dog, and I just want to say this, right now, that regardless of what they say about it, we are going to keep it.

The response to Nixon's televised appeal was overwhelmingly in his favor, and he kept his place on the ticket. But he came out of the 1952 campaign identifying the press as *an* enemy, if not *the* enemy, and he had learned that he could reach the public very effectively through television because he could avoid the filtering processes of professional journalists.

Even in what seemed at the time his final defeat, Nixon spoke of broadcasting with approval. After his narrow defeat by John Kennedy in the Presidential election of 1960, Nixon retreated to California to run for governor against Democratic incumbent Edmund (Pat) Brown. Nixon lost, and this defeat in his home state seemed to spell the end of his political career. In his "last" press conference he vented his anger at the press. It had been decided that his press secretary, Herb Klein, would make the concession speech, but Nixon strode into the ballroom of the Beverly Hilton Hotel and interrupted Klein with these words:

> Good morning, gentlemen. Now that Mr. Klein has made his statement, and now that all the members of the press are so delighted that I have lost, I'd like to make a statement of my own.

And he closed with these words:

> One last thing. At the outset I said a couple of things with regard to the press that I noticed some of you looked a little irritated about. . . . Never in my sixteen years of campaigning have I complained to a publisher, to an editor, about the coverage of a reporter. I believe a reporter has got a right to write it as he feels it. . . . I will say to a reporter sometimes that I think, well, look, I wish you would give my opponent the same going over that you give me. . . . I think that it's time that our great newspapers have at least the same objectivity, the same fullness of coverage, that television has. And I can only thank God for television and radio for keeping the newspapers a little more honest. . . . But as I leave you, I want you to know—just think how much you're going to be missing. You won't have Nixon to kick around any more, because, gentlemen, this is my last press conference. . . .

It was, of course, *not* his last press conference, and he would in time include television in his denunciations of the press.

Despite his bitterness toward the press, Nixon enjoyed the support of the nation's publishers until close to the end of his Administration. Publishers are businesspeople and quite frequently Republicans. Nixon was a logical choice for them over Democrats Hubert Humphrey and George McGovern. In 1972 more than 70 percent of the daily newspapers endorsed Nixon, only 5 percent endorsed McGovern, and the rest expressed no preference. The calls for resignation in 1973 had all the more impact because so many came from publications that had previously supported Nixon: the Baltimore *Sun,* the Detroit *News,* and the Denver *Post. Time* magazine, in its first editorial in 50 years, also asked Nixon to resign.

As President, Nixon avoided contact with the working press as much as he could. His strategy for relations with the mass media became apparent during his successful Presidential campaign of 1968. James Reston made clear what that strategy was:

> His television performances are masterpieces of contrived candor. He seems to be telling everything with an air of reckless sincerity, but nearly always in a controlled situation, with the questioners carefully chosen, the questions solicited from whole states or regions, but carefully screened.
>
> He is now complaining publicly about how he and Mr. Agnew are misrepresented in the columns of the New York *Times,* but he has been refusing to be questioned on the record by editors of the *Times* and most other major newspapers ever since the very beginning of the campaign.
>
> Mr. Humphrey and Mr. Wallace submitted to questions by CBS, but Mr. Nixon sent tapes of replies made in his carefully prepared broadcasts. And his refusal to debate Mr. Humphrey on television is merely one more incident in a long campaign of packaged broadcasts. . . . [10]

Another Reston column of about the same period pointed to an attitude that afflicted Nixon throughout his career in public life:

> Mr. Nixon has had more than the normal share of trouble with reporters, because, like Lyndon Johnson, he has never really understood the function of a free press or the meaning of the First Amendment.
>
> Ever since he came into national politics, he has seemed to think that a reporter should take down and transmit what he says, like a tape recorder or a Xerox machine. He has learned to live with interpretive journalism more comfortably in this campaign [1968] than he did in the campaign of 1960, but he still suffers from this old illusion that the press is a kind of inanimate transmission belt which should pass along anything he chooses to dump on it. [11]

When he became President, Nixon demonstrated the accuracy of Reston's judgments. He did not often submit himself to the adversary relationship of the news conference. Indeed, according to a 1975 study by Lewis W. Wolfson for the National News Council, Nixon held a press conference about once every two months (his five predecessors had held them on the average of once every two weeks or more frequently). Wolfson reports that

Nixon went as long as "14 months without a televised press conference"
and as long as five months without holding any press conferences at all. He
preferred to go on national television with statements and not to respond to
questions.

Unfortunately for the credibility of the Nixon Administration, reporters
soon began to fix on its methods. When they were misled, they would quote
Nixon's campaign attacks on the credibility gap of the Johnson Administration: "It's time we once again had an open Administration—open to ideas
from the people and open in its communications with the people—an
Administration of open doors, open eyes, and open minds."

But Nixon the President said in 1970: "Our plan to end the fighting in
Vietnam as rapidly as possible consistent with achieving our basic objective
of self-determination for the South Vietnamese people is well under
way. . . . Because of the need to maintain the security of this plan, certain
information included in recent budgets does not appear this year."

By mid-August of 1969, so much doubt had arisen that *Newsweek*
published a long catalogue of cases proving that Nixon's "open administration" was "suffering from an advanced case of closed doors."

There were signs, too, of a rebirth of the tough stance many reporters
had adopted years before. After watching the Administration bow in quick
succession to the American Medical Association, the American Pharmaceut-
ical Association, and the Automobile Manufacturers Association—actually
reversing decisions already made—one journalist remarked that Nixon
would be in trouble with working reporters for a reason that has always been
at the root of his politics: "He worries too much about the problems of
people who own yachts."

Late in 1969 it became apparent that Vice President Spiro Agnew was to
be the Administration's champion in its battles with the mass media. The first
speech was delivered little more than a week after President Nixon
attempted to explain his Vietnam policy on national television. Agnew's
basic complaint was that liberal TV commentators had muted the effect of
Nixon's address during the half-hour discussions that immediately followed
the President's speech. Agnew's speech was vintage Nixon, emphasizing
James Reston's point that Nixon believed the news media should act as an
inanimate transmission belt, carrying anything he chose to dump on it. In
this case the networks had acted as a transmission belt carrying what Nixon
had to say, and in a live broadcast. But the television reporters were hardly
inanimate. It was this that aroused Agnew's—and Nixon's—ire.

There is rich irony in all this. For the "instant analysis" by the network
reporters that seemed to Agnew so reprehensible was born, in part, of
complaints from Richard Nixon and his friends. This can be traced back to
June 1957, when CBS broadcast an interview with Nikita Khrushchev, who
was then the Soviet premier. So outraged were Eisenhower Administration
officials that Khrushchev had been allowed to speak directly and at length to
the American people that broadcasters, ever mindful of their precarious
relationship to the federal government, took the advice of the most influen-

tial television critic, Jack Gould of the New York *Times.* He suggested that CBS had "many able and thoughtful commentators" and that "they should have been used immediately to analyze Khrushchev's words." Thus began the system of instant analysis that would cause Agnew such anguish.

Nonetheless, Agnew's attack was effective. While his words were still reverberating, President Nixon appeared on national television for one of his infrequent news conferences. Immediately after the conference the commentators and analysts for commercial television appeared, talked at length, and said nothing. Instead of supplying the usual background information on the President's words and the closely reasoned analyses of those words, the commentators simply cited what Nixon had said.

What the television people should have been doing was demonstrated strikingly the next day by Tom Wicker of the New York *Times.* In response to criticism of reporters, Wicker asked: "What of the responsibility of Presidents to inform the American people accurately and fully?" He then cited the President's statement that the Marines had built this year "over 250,000 churches, pagodas, and temples" for the people of Vietnam and reported that the Marines had actually built 117 churches and 251 schools. The President misled the people again, Wicker said, when he answered a question about Laos by saying that there are no American "combat troops" there. In fact, as Wicker made clear, this was true only if one interpreted "combat troops" to mean those who fight on the ground. "There are Air Force pilots who drop bombs, and plenty of CIA agents and Army personnel who organize, train, accompany, and support native armies."

Wicker's catalogue of President Nixon's misleading statements went on, but that is enough to demonstrate the point. Such revelations seemed only to excite new efforts to counter criticism from the media, especially television. It soon became known that White House staff members were carefully monitoring and judging television news shows. They even rated the networks:

> Most fair to the Administration: CBS (51 percent of the time). Least fair: NBC (40 percent). In the middle: ABC (41 percent).
> Most favorable to the Administration: ABC (29 percent of the time). Least favorable: NBC (15 percent). In the middle: CBS (24 percent).
> Most unfavorable: NBC (44 percent of the time). Least unfavorable: CBS (25 percent). In the middle: ABC (29 percent).

NBC, according to the judgments of White House staffers, was the only network that "periodically becomes crusading and generates news tending to reflect unfavorably on the Administration." Reuven Frank, president of NBC News, commented, "My reaction to all this noise is that we ought to be doing more of it. I view it as a compliment."

Another dimension of news from government was revealed shortly after President Nixon sent American troops into Cambodia in 1970. So bitter was the reaction from the nation's campuses that the Administration decided to counter it by inviting expressions of opinion from any American who wanted to call the White House. Early one morning United Press International (UPI) reporters in New York made four calls to the special White House number that had been set up to record the votes for or against. Two UPI reporters who announced that they wanted to cast votes favorable to the President's action were switched immediately to someone who answered "White House." The other two callers, who said that they opposed the President's action, never got past the switchboard. The calls ran:

UPI—"I'd like to register a vote for the President.
WHITE HOUSE—"Yes, you certainly can."
UPI—"This is the White House, I hope."
WHITE HOUSE—"Yes, where do you live?"
UPI—"New Jersey."
WHITE HOUSE—"All right, thank you very much for your call."

UPI—"Listen, are you taking votes?"
WHITE HOUSE—"No, I'm not taking votes. Are you taking votes?"
UPI—"I'd like to register a vote against President Nixon."
WHITE HOUSE—"You're way late, where have you been?"
UPI—"You're not taking votes?"
WHITE HOUSE—"I'm not taking any votes and haven't been taking any votes."

UPI—"I'd like to register a vote for President Nixon's policy, please."
WHITE HOUSE—"You certainly can. Can I have your name, please?"
UPI—"James Coburn, Weehawken, New Jersey."
WHITE HOUSE—"I'll take a message if you want to give me one. Give it to me."
UPI—"I don't want to say too much except that I am thoroughly in agreement with everything the President has said."
WHITE HOUSE—"Okay, James, and we really appreciate that now, and I can tell you that he does too. Thank you very much."

UPI—"I understand you are taking votes and I'd like to say I'm against the President and Vice President Agnew too, and the policy. Can I register that please"
WHITE HOUSE—"You want to vote on the President?"
UPI—"Yeah, I'm against the President and against what he has been saying."
WHITE HOUSE—"This poll is being taken on the extension of troops into Cambodia and not on whether or not you're against the President."
UPI—"I'm against the extension of troops into Cambodia and against any more American troops going anywhere in southeast Asia."
WHITE HOUSE—"Where are you calling from?"
UPI—"New York City."
WHITE HOUSE—"From New York. Well, this office is closed here in Washington; it's almost six o'clock."

Nixon's antagonism towards the press and his determination to control public opinion engaged him and his staff in strange enterprises. Charles

Colson, who at one time was special counsel to the President, has described
some of the milder techniques Nixon used to harass the press:

> Once [Nixon] called me after a TV interview in which Dan Rather of CBS had stung him with a string of snidely worded questions. "Get a hundred people to call Rather and complain," he commanded. Then he proceeded to dictate precise messages which these callers should convey.
>
> He was blowing off steam. I knew it; but I also followed his orders. Soon we had one Republican Committee employee assigned full time to carrying out such assignments, which included carefully orchestrated "letters to the editor" campaigns across the country. (The technique was not invented by Mr. Nixon. I'd seen similar devices employed in the six political campaigns I'd worked in since 1956.) Nixon asked for and received weekly reports on our success.

On another occasion Nixon asked Colson to get Edith Efron's *The News Twisters* on the best-seller list. (Efron's book charged the TV networks with anti-Nixon bias in their coverage of the 1968 campaign.) Colson's technique for carrying out Nixon's order was both ingenious and elementary, and it was possible because Colson could figure out how the media operated.

> At my staff meeting . . . I asked if anyone knew how to get a book on the best-seller list. One enterprising staffer discovered that some best-seller lists were based on weekly phone surveys of several key New York bookstores. Once we knew that, it was only a matter of logistics. I sent $8,000 in campaign funds to a stalwart supporter in New York. He recruited several young volunteers who roamed the streets, buying out one by one that total supply of a dozen stores. The following Monday, I proudly strode into the Oval Office and laid *Time* magazine on Mr. Nixon's desk. There on the best-seller list was *The News Twisters*. The Commander-in-Chief's orders were carried out, and an excited publisher rushed into a second printing (which doubtless resulted in the largest book-remainder sale in history).[12]

Some, but not all, of the more serious methods the Nixon Administration was to consider or try were described in an October 17, 1969, memo, entitled "The Shot-Gun versus the Rifle," to H. R. Haldeman from Jeb Stuart Magruder, then an aide to Haldeman and deputy director of White House communications. Magruder wrote,

> The real problem . . . is to get to this unfair coverage in such a way that we make major impact on a basis which the networks-newspapers and Congress will react to and begin to look at things somewhat differently. . . . The following is my suggestion as to how we can achieve this goal:
>
> 1. Begin an official monitoring system through the FCC as soon as Dean Burch is officially on board as Chairman. . . .
>
> 2. Utilize the anti-trust division to investigate various media relations to anti-trust violations. Even the possible threat of anti-trust action I think would be effective in changing their views in the above matter.
>
> 3. Utilizing the Internal Revenue Service as a method to look into the various organizations that we are most concerned about. Just a threat of an IRS investigation will probably turn their approach.
>
> 4. Begin to show favorites within the media. Since they are basically not on

our side let us pick the favorable ones as Kennedy did. I'm not saying we should
eliminate the open Administration, but by being open we have not gotten
anyone to back us on a consistent basis and many of those who were favorable
towards us are now giving it to us at various times. . . . [13]

Such bitterness and hostility would eventually generate an increased
aggressiveness from the media. One of the great ironies of the Nixon
Presidency is, as Theodore White has pointed out, that it has spawned the
era of the investigative journalist. In White's words: "The pursuit of Richard
Nixon . . . made folk heroes out of investigative reporters."

Because Nixon was aloof and reserved and because he resisted contact
with reporters, those who covered the President dealt primarily with Ron
Ziegler and his staff. Timothy Crouse in a description of the 1972 Presidential campaign explained Ziegler's significance: Reporters "usually couldn't
get in to see anyone else on the White House staff, and Nixon didn't like to
give press conferences. So Ziegler was the only President they had, and they
tried very hard to like him."[14] Crouse may be overstating the media's efforts
on Ziegler's behalf, but it is clear that by the end of the Nixon Presidency
there was nothing but dislike and distrust of Ziegler.

Ziegler was a public relations agent. He had served in a minor role in
Nixon's unsuccessful bid for the governorship of California in 1962.
Recruited by H. R. Haldeman, he joined the Los Angeles office of the
advertising agency, J. Walter Thompson, where his clients included 7-Up,
Disneyland, and Sea World. Both Haldeman and Ziegler worked for
Nixon's election to the Presidency in 1968, and Ziegler eventually replaced
Herb Klein as Nixon's chief press officer.

Ziegler's allegiance to Nixon was complete, and he had no feel for news
except as it served the Administration. He never answered a question he
didn't want to answer. His responses ranged from "I just have no comment
this morning" to this statement on the safeguarding of Watergate tapes,
which won him a National Doublespeak Award from the National Council of
Teachers of English:

> I would feel that most of the conversations that took place in those areas of
> the White House that did have the recording system would, in almost their
> entirety, be in existence, but the special prosecutor, the court, and, I think, the
> American people are sufficiently familiar with the recording system to know
> where the recording devices existed and to know the situation in terms of the
> recording process, but I feel, although the process has not been undertaken yet
> in preparation of the material to abide by the court decision, really, what the
> answer to that question is.

The best known of Ziegler's answers is probably this one:

> The way to assess the previous comments is to assess them on the basis that
> they were made on the information available at the time. The President refers to
> the fact that there is new material. Therefore, this is the operative statement. The
> others are inoperative.[15]

After Ziegler made this statement, Clark Mollenhoff of the Des Moines *Register* challenged Ziegler: "Do you feel free to stand up there and lie and put out misinformation and then come around later and just say it is all inoperative? That is what you are doing. You are not entitled to any credibility at all when you do that."

Gerald Ford

On August 9, 1974, Gerald Ford, a Michigan Congressman for 24 years, including 9 as House Minority Leader, became the thirty-eighth President of the United States—the first to reach that office without benefit of a national election. Without ever running for the Presidency or, it appears, without ever really wanting it, Ford had the responsibilities of the office to fulfill and the legacy of Richard Nixon to overcome. Just about everyone wanted Ford to do well. The prolonged trauma of Watergate had left the nation exhausted and the press spent.

In addition to the natural goodwill that flowed from the nation's hopes for Ford and the almost automatic honeymoon afforded each new President, Ford had several assets that seemed to cheer the country. For one, he was a "nice guy." For another, he seemed genuinely committed to establishing integrity, honesty, and candor as characteristics of Presidential conduct. And for a third—which was probably more meaningful to the media than anyone else—he had chosen a journalist as his press secretary.

Ford's choice for press secretary, Jerald ter Horst, was a much-respected, well-liked reporter for the Detroit *News*. He had covered the White House for 16 years and had a comfortable relationship with his colleagues in the White House press corps. The contrast with Ziegler and his public relations background was striking.

The selection of ter Horst was a welcome return to the tradition of using someone with news experience as a liaison with the media. But perhaps, in part, because of ter Horst's background, the good fellowship of the Ford honeymoon with the media was ended abruptly. On September 8, less than a month after he'd become President, Ford granted "a full, free, and absolute pardon" to Richard Nixon—and Jerald ter Horst resigned as press secretary.

There were reports that ter Horst resigned because "he was being kept in the dark about important White House decisions" and because "he had been misled by high administration officials on a number of different matters, and that this caused him to issue misleading statements to the news media." But Al Martinez has reported that it was not the handling of information that precipitated ter Horst's resignation, but the pardon itself. Martinez quotes ter Horst: "I knew that giving a pardon in advance of any confession or accusation of a crime flew in the face of the Constitution. . . . Critics have said I turned my back on the President at a time when he

needed me most. But I would have made his problem worse in the long run
by trying to defend something I could not possibly defend. An act of mercy
to me just represented an act of favoritism."

Ter Horst's situation points up the fundamental dilemma faced by any
press secretary of good conscience. How closely must the press secretary's
views mirror the President's? What does the press secretary do when they
don't? How far should he go to put the best face on the President's words
and actions? What obligations does he owe the public to deliver *unvar-
nished* truth? Ter Horst accepted that the allegiance of the press secretary
must be to the President and that the press secretary is necessarily an image
maker. "But," ter Horst said, "in order to do that you must pretty much
believe in what you're doing. I couldn't be an image maker to the extent of
pretending a problem didn't exist when it did.

"That's what got Ziegler into trouble—trying to put a good face on
something that only had a bad face."[16]

Ford replaced ter Horst with another journalist, Ron Nessen, an NBC
correspondent. Nessen lacked ter Horst's phlegmatic personality and the
necessary thick skin, and in June 1975 White House press relations again
broke into open warfare between the White House press corps and the
press secretary. Dennis Farney described in *The Wall Street Journal* one
particularly heated encounter:

> . . . last Friday's briefing, an unusually acrimonious affair, found angry reporters
> calling Mr. Nessen "a liar," accusing him of a "coverup" and, after 55 minutes of
> unproductive questioning, informing him that they didn't want to listen to him
> any more that day. Whereupon Mr. Nessen spun on his heel and left in a huff.[17]

Before the month was out Nessen, in a prepared statement, accused
unnamed reporters of "blind, mindless, irrational suspicion and cynicism
and distrust" of him. He warned that unless the atmosphere at the daily
press briefings improved, he might not continue to hold them.

Although Nessen was often taking the heat for the blunders of administration officials, the speculation after the press-Nessen confrontations centered not on whether *Ford*'s press relations were beyond repair, but
whether Nessen had jeopardized his own job. Nessen survived, but he
continued to face the legacy of Richard Nixon and Lyndon Johnson
although the relations between Nessen and the White House press corps
were conducted in a more civil manner thereafter.

Ter Horst, who returned to write for the Detroit *News* as a syndicated
columnist after his resignation from Ford's staff, addressed Nessen's problem in a column:

> . . . [T]he men and women who cover the White House . . . have lived through
> the Johnson and the Nixon years and feel they were regularly misinformed, even
> duped, by previous press secretaries, on Vietnam and Watergate. Thus burned,
> they are not about to take this president or any president on faith alone. So every
> day in the White House press room, Mr. Ford and Ron Nessen are subjected to a
> series of litmus tests as to their veracity, their credibility, their trustworthiness.

Meeting that kind of test is a responsibility this president and this administration cannot hope to escape. A presidential spokesman in these times must not only be loyal to his chief but he also must prove himself to be loyal to the public—through the press.[18]

Some of Nessen's problems can be explained, too, by the White House press corps' hurt pride. The men and women who cover the White House find themselves in a particularly strange situation. They include some of the best talent that American journalism has produced. And though they have the most prestigious beat in the country, they can find themselves the conduit for the earth-shaking news that the President lunched on cottage cheese with ketchup. The public needs to know what the President is saying, what he is thinking, whom he is seeing, what he is doing. But the embarrassment for the members of the White House press corps is that they spent so much time trying to break through to Nixon that they virtually missed the Watergate story. The investigative work that contributed to the unraveling of the Nixon Administration was undertaken by Carl Bernstein and Bob Woodward, then on the Metropolitan desk of the Washington *Post,* and perhaps 13–18 other reporters.[19] The White House press corps seems determined not to let another Watergate mushroom in its home territory— at least not unreported.

The problem for the White House press corps—talented and dedicated though its members may be—is that it devotes so much time to rituals that produce little information the President is reluctant to release.

Every day the press secretary's office holds a briefing at which reporters can ask whatever they wish. One might want details on travel arrangements for the press pool. Another might ask for the President's views on the death sentences handed down to American mercenaries by the Angolan government. It's the press secretary's job to guess in advance what will be asked that day and to have the answers. Ziegler would wing it without reference to notes. Nessen and his staff each day prepared answers to possible questions. The answers were arranged in a looseleaf notebook which Nessen took into the briefing. Obviously such preparation is time-consuming, and Nessen fumed publicly over reporters' *failure* to ask questions the answers to which he had prepared. Problems also arose when reporters asked the "wrong" questions on the right topic or questions for which Nessen had not prepared or questions that he had no intention of answering.

In these briefings reporters often seem to have short memories and little apparent independence of mind—from one another. Farney described in *The Wall Street Journal* how Nessen had been asked on one occasion "no fewer than 85 questions on whether or not the Central Intelligence Agency is now, or has ever been, in the business of assassinating foreign political leaders." Nessen avoided answering any of them. He was prepared to give some answers on Cambodia, but nobody asked any questions on it. The next day he got 59 questions on Cambodia, but not one on the CIA until he brought up the subject.[20]

The press is sometimes, quite literally, the captive of the White House. The most extreme case in recent memory came the evening of Richard Nixon's televised resignation. *Newsweek* reported that reporters were locked "in the White House press room for 23 minutes to insure Nixon's privacy while he walked from the Executive Office Building to the White House." More commonly, the press will find itself the captive of circumstances. Ben Bagdikian provides this example:

> [W]hen White House press agents handed out a presidential statement on drugs that attacked courts for worsening the problem, it made headlines all over the country [September 1972]. . . . It is possible that this made such a big display because it was filed from the campaign plane by the eighty-eight correspondents "accompanying" the President on a trip to Texas. The eighty-eight correspondents never spoke to the President. They were in another plane and were handed the press release by the White House press agents while their plane was in the air; on landing they rushed to phones to dictate stories based solely on the handout. As Richard Reeves commented in *New York* magazine, it would have been nice to ask the President which judges he meant and what he thought judges could do about the drug problem."[21]

When Ford took on the Presidency he promised greater accessibility as almost every President does. One minor way he sought to accomplish this was to allow reporters and photographers an unrestricted view of his arrivals and departures from the White House by helicopter. During Nixon's Administration, the press had been restricted on such occasions to a portico, screened by flowering crab apple trees. The result of Ford's policy was a series of photos of him bumping his head as he got in or out of the helicopter. The President did not seem any more concerned with these photos than with the ones of him stumbling down stairs. But AP reported when Mrs. Ford bumped her head on the helicopter doorway, the press found itself back on the portico behind the crab apple trees.

The Presidential Press Conference

The Presidential press conference is a highly ineffective way of gathering information, but it serves other functions. Television coverage of press conferences has given the public the opportunity to see their Presidents in a situation that is less orchestrated than a speech. The clamor of a press conference provides its vitality, but it also, in no small measure, demeans its participants. As the President winds down his answer to one question, reporters jump to their feet, shouting, "Mr. President, Mr. President." What might seem to a journalist a good, tough, probing question can appear to the folks back home a disrespectful or unfair jab at the President. In the end, it is always the President's show. He can answer a question with a speech. He can razzle-dazzle with statistics. He can avoid the tough question by answering the question he wants to answer even if it wasn't the one asked.[22]

Nevertheless, although there is no requirement that the President ever hold a press conference, we begin to worry when they come too infrequently. The press may get very little hard information from them, but the President's willingness to engage in them is symbolic of his willingness to submit to public inquiry, of his regard for public participation in government. George Reedy, President Johnson's first press secretary, has been reported as saying that although Johnson hated press conferences, Johnson—unlike Nixon—submitted to them because fundamentally he was "in awe of such democratic institutions." (Johnson's "awe" is all the more remarkable because he was not in awe of the press. It was just one more constituency to be dealt with.)

There are other benefits, too. Regular press conferences force a form of public accountability on the President. He cannot repeatedly obfuscate issues without the public recognizing his evasiveness. And press conferences along with other press-President exchanges give the press an opportunity to influence the agenda the President sets for the nation. The press cannot ignore what the President wants placed on the agenda, but neither can the President comfortably ignore the press's choices. The hit-and-miss structure of the press conference forces the President to prepare on a wide range of issues. Nessen, at least, saw this as valuable: "Before you can answer a question, you have to have a policy. Anticipating questions forces the White House to make decisions that might get delayed or not made (at all.)"

Unlike one-on-one interviews the formal press conference denies the President some of his ability to discriminate. While the information may not be as coherent or useful as what is ferreted out in an interview, the news produced at a press conference is everybody's news, no matter who asked the questions.

Ford did make a number of changes in the conduct of press conferences. It had been the practice in formal Presidential press conferences for each questioner to have the opportunity to ask just one question. When the conferences were televised, there was a temptation for reporters to grandstand—to make a speech or make a point. The questions and the questioners sometimes seemed more important than the President and his answers. For some it became paramount to be *seen* asking a question. But even the best reporters were trapped by the fragmentation that such random questioning produced. If the President only half answers another reporter's question, should the next reporter follow up on the same topic, or should he ask the question he prepared? Ford gave each reporter the opportunity to ask two questions, thus easing though not eliminating the problems of fragmentation. Ford also held press conferences outside of Washington, dividing the opportunity for questions between the regulars and local reporters.

Unlike those of his predecessor, Ford's relations with the press remained personally harmonious to the end. Where Richard Nixon animatedly disliked the press, Ford took obvious pleasure in the company of reporters and they in his. Where Nixon had been compared to a used car salesman, Ford was described as the kind of person whom everyone would like as a neighbor. The question to be answered was, did this "neighbor" have what it took to be President? A curious question to ask perhaps after the man had held the office for almost two years. Would anyone actually *vote* for Gerald Ford for the job?

Consistent with his neighborly image, Ford had difficulty exciting the voters in his reelection bid. Ronald Reagan, even as Ford defeated him—barely—for the Republican nomination, could electrify the convention more easily than the party's chosen standard-bearer.

Ford's strategy for the 1976 campaign was to be Presidential, rather than political, to wear the mantle of the office visibly—in the Rose Garden and around the nation. In the end, despite some memorable gaffes, Ford offered stability. As he had done so often coming out of the Presidential helicopter, Ford tripped himself in the second of the three campaign debates and told the world that Eastern Europe was not dominated by the Soviet Union. Still, despite such unintended surprises, Ford was a known commodity. The media and the public understood him as they still do not understand his opponent.

Jimmy Who?

In the December after Jimmy Carter's election to the Presidency, Gerald Johnson wrote in *The New Republic:*

> Even before it takes office the Carter administration has to its credit one accomplishment that is definitely worthwhile to the average American. It has given him a reason for wishing to live four years longer, for by so doing he may have a chance to see how it all comes out. . . . [23]

Curiosity and a sense of risk accompanied many votes for Carter in November 1976. What would this gamble on the unknown produce? Reporters struggled to get Carter in focus.

Introducing its controversial interview with Carter in its November 1976 issue, *Playboy* wrote,

> To many Americans, the old charge that [Carter] was "fuzzy" on the issues may be less accurate than the persistent feeling that he is fuzzy as a personality. Even this late in the campaign, Carter remains for many an unknown quantity.

Richard Nixon had been a figure in American national political life forever, or so it seemed. For some the episode of Watergate was only a confirmation of what they had believed of Nixon all along. Others felt they had missed seeing or reporting on the fatal flaws in Nixon's character that made the acts associated with Watergate—if not the downfall of Nixon's Presidency—inevitable. James David Barber's book, *The Presidential Character: Predicting Performance in the White House,* was cited as must reading for the nation's political reporters.

Reporters learn from their old mistakes even as they make new ones. As they hit the campaign trail, they vow not to repeat past errors. Thus, they worried over Carter's character as much as his policies. The candidate himself invited such scrutiny by advancing his character as his strongest qualification and wearing his religion on his sleeve. He set standards for himself that reporters considered impossible for a politician. Carter promised the nation that he would never lie.

It is rarely an advantage for a politician or a public official to be caught lieing, but to promise *never* to lie demands skepticism. For Carter, even a white lie or a lie delivered in good faith to protect the nation would be a black mark on his credibility and character. Not so much a promise, his statement was a challenge to reporters to catch him out.

Attempting to get a fix on Carter, the media mined the details of his life: his religion, his small-town Southern origins, his experiences as a peanut farmer and a nuclear engineer. He eluded them. In an article entitled, "Jimmy We Hardly Know Y'all," run as a companion to his *Playboy* interview of Carter, Robert Scheer wrote,

> The problem is that one's judgments about Carter are necessarily fragmented, because we have no sense of the depth of the man, of his experience and roots. He just came to us a winner. . . .
>
> * * * * *
>
> Reporters covering Jerry Ford or Ronald Reagan or Scoop Jackson soon stop looking for the "real" person behind the campaigner, because they realize that if they should happen to find him, he would be boringly similar to the one they've seen all along. But I have yet to meet a reporter who feels that way about Carter. He is intriguing, baffling and perpetually confounding.[24]

As President he continued to be so.

Carter campaigned on being someone who was not part of the old crowd, not one of the time-worn Washington politicians who had failed to live up to the goodness of the American people. He promised an open Administration in which the public would again participate in their own governance. As Barry Jagoda, his special assistant for media and public affairs, phrased it, "President Carter asked us to open up the government through television."

In his march to the Presidency Carter perhaps came to understand the media better than they understood him. For his own campaign he read such books as Timothy Crouse's detailed analysis of campaign reporting in 1972, *The Boys on the Bus.* Although he stumbled along the way, Carter put his reading to good use. That he could not always control the media or himself was evident as his lead in the polls began to slip away with the approach of the election. But as a newcomer to national politics, an outsider and an unknown, he would never have won the Democratic nomination if he had not understood a great deal about how the media operate.

As one example, Carter knew that the way to "win" a primary was to do better than the media expected. Coming in second when the media expected you to be fifth is a victory; winning narrowly is a defeat if you had been expected to win big. He predicted his own chances accordingly.

When he became President, Carter did not forget what he had learned—and experienced—as a campaigner. David Broder of the Washington *Post* in March of 1977 wrote that Carter had "transformed himself from the very shaky winner of a bungled campaign into a very popular President, whose mastery of the mass media [had] given him real leverage with which to govern." George Reedy, one-time press secretary to Lyndon Johnson, described Carter as "the first real television President." Although others have made that claim for Kennedy because of his wit and charm before the cameras and for Nixon for his calculated selling of himself in 1968 and for his extensive use of television during his 5½ years in office, Reedy had a subtle point to make. Where Kennedy had a command of words and could use television to give them wider currency, Carter "is sending complicated messages by purely symbolic means," Reedy said. "When he wore a sweater [during the fireside chat of February 1977], it was more than a stunt. He told people there was no magic solution to the energy problem, that they should dress warmly. And when he walked down Pennsylvania Avenue with his wife, he announced the end of the imperial Presidency."

Carter used symbols and the media skillfully. He insisted on the less formal "Jimmy Carter" in preference to "James E. Carter." During the campaign he carried his own garment bag on and off airplanes, knowing that cameras would be there to record the common-man gesture. The reviewing stand for the inauguration was heated with solar energy—a much publicized fact—although a conventional heating system was installed as a backup. He and his family walked rather than rode the 1½ miles down Pennsylvania Avenue from the Capitol to the White House—his vulnerability a symbol of his trust of the American people. In the first week of February 1977 Carter confronted the energy crisis brought on by severe winter weather with a fireside chat that echoed the radio performances of Franklin Roosevelt. For almost 30 minutes Carter, wearing a beige cardigan sweater and sitting beside a glowing fire, lectured the American public in mild tones on the sacrifices the country must make and discussed his domestic agenda. What he said was perhaps less important than the confidence with which he said it.

In early March of that year Carter participated in a radio call-in show suggested by CBS and hosted by Walter Cronkite. In two hours Carter responded to 42 calls—out of an estimated 9½ million attempted. Later the same month Carter answered questions for 90 minutes at a televised New England town meeting in Clinton, Massachusetts. In April NBC took its turn with a prime-time special on a day in the life of the President. In May, KNXT-TV, Los Angeles, staged "The People Talk to President Carter: A Television Meeting." For a little more than an hour Carter answered questions from audiences in five different locations in the Los Angeles area. The meeting gave 24 people the opportunity to ask questions and many more the chance to watch and listen. The program was carried in other parts of California, Oregon, Washington, and Nevada. In July in the sweltering heat of Yazoo City, Mississippi, Carter took off his jacket, rolled up his sleeves, and talked to a crowd of 1400 jammed into the high school gym in a televised Southern-style town meeting.

For these events and for his regular press conferences—many of them televised—Carter appeared comfortable as President and star. Television seemed, as NBC anchorman John Chancellor suggested, to help Carter maintain "an almost mystical relationship with the American people." His standing in the polls reflected his successes.

Could he keep it up? Would the public become bored? His staff looked for signs of overexposure. Reporters still searched for clues. Despite all the hours he had logged in the public view, Carter remained elusive, just out of the grasp of journalism's analysts. What would happen when Carter was really tested? When his hand was forced by events over which he had no control? If his standing with the public slipped, would he lose his composure as he did in the mistake-ridden days at the end of his campaign?

Carter will no doubt face many crises during his Presidency and some, if not all, will be complicated by media coverage. Carter, however, did demonstrate considerable public restraint when Bert Lance, his long-time personal friend and fellow Georgian, was forced to resign as director of the Office of Management and Budget (OMB).

When, in the late spring and summer of 1977, the news media and eventually the Senate began to unravel the personal finances and past business practices of Lance, Carter stood by his closest friend in Washington long after that course seemed prudent. Lance was accused of unsound banking practices that included large overdrafts by himself and members of his family, the use of the same collateral for two loans, the use of his bank's plane for personal and political trips, and many other actions that at best did not seem to recommend Lance's judgment or ethics. Serious charges, including suggestions of illegality, were given wide currency by the press, even though some were easily discredited. During the controversy no one questioned Lance's performance as director of OMB, but his past banking practices and inability to keep his own personal finances in order raised questions about his credibility as head of the nation's budget. As serious were the questions raised about Carter's apparent willingness to waive the high ethical standards he had set for his Administration—probably his greatest political asset—in a situation involving a close personal friend.

After the comptroller of the currency reported in mid-August that Lance had stayed within the law, Carter presented that barely positive finding as an endorsement of Lance and added his own, "Bert, I'm proud of you," at an August 19 press conference. The Administration seemed to expect that if the President called the comptroller's report a clean bill of health, the public and the Senate would accept the President's judgment. They did not, and the allegations continued. On Labor Day weekend Democrat Abraham Ribicoff, chairman of the Senate Governmental Affairs Committee, and Charles Percy, the ranking Republican on the committee, went to the President to ask for Lance's resignation for the good of the country. The incident was

President Jimmy Carter and his Press Secretary Jody Powell (left) defended fellow
Georgian and Director of the Office of Management and Budget Bert Lance (right)
long after that course seemed prudent. (Wide World photo)

striking in no small measure because only a few weeks before Ribicoff had
accused the media of smearing Lance and Percy had told Lance, "I'm
satisfied completely with your answers."

Lance insisted, however, on his "day in court." During three days of
testimony before Ribicoff's committee in mid-September, Lance's performance was extraordinary. Lance took the offensive, charging members of
the committee and the press with denying his basic human right not to be
judged guilty before he had had an opportunity to respond to the charges
against him. By the end of the first day Washington was asking, only partly
in jest, "Will Bert Lance ask the committee to resign?"

But in the end Lance could not overcome all the doubts and suspicions.
In a September 21 press conference notable for the obvious emotion the
President felt and for the illogic of his comments, Carter announced Lance's
resignation. Carter said that Lance had answered all questions "adequately," that he had restored his reputation, but that Lance was right to
resign. Carter suggested that Lance's ability to clear his name demonstrated
that the American system works. In essence, Carter seemed to say, Lance
has demonstrated he is blameless but he should resign.

The press, like the Senate, had given Lance's credentials no more than
perfunctory scrutiny at the time of his appointment to the Cabinet. When
the press did begin to examine Lance's background in detail, the thrill of
pursuit seemed to induce some to lose a sense of judgment and proportion.

The legacy of Watergate had not yet been spent, and the term, "Lance-gate," surfaced. Mercifully, it was not widely used. Unsupported and untrue charges were fed to the public along with serious charges that needed careful examination, complicating and confusing even further an already complicated and confusing situation. Whatever, if any, charges were made to stick against Lance, the situation reached crisis proportions if for no other reason than that it was being treated as a crisis. As Russell Baker of the New York *Times* observed, "The papers were covering it like a crisis, television was displaying it like a crisis, reliable sources were leaking at crisis rates and normally sensible men were behaving with crisis foolishness. . . ."[25]

Many reporters, columnists, and editors had played the watchdog role we expect of them, focusing public attention—albeit somewhat belatedly—on Lance's qualifications, but in the end the targets of public disapproval were not only Lance and Carter. Some members of the public read the episode as tarnishing the President's "ethical purity" image, but others saw it as an instance of the press hounding a good man out of office. Russell Baker was not the only one asking, was this a "molehill made a mountain by an energetic press caught in a dull summer with no one but Lance to exercise on? A press determined to show it can be just as beastly to Democrats as to the Nixonites?"

Despite his obvious sense of personal loss, Carter did not lash out at the media. When asked about their role in the Lance affair, Carter responded that he thought with a few exceptions the media had been fair. He did not detail the exceptions. It is too early to judge whether his response was genuine or merely politic.

The larger question for Carter was whether his handling of the Lance affair would jeopardize his special, fragile relationship with the public. As he faced Congress over the Panama Canal Treaty, energy legislation, governmental reform, and other issues of comparable significance, he needed public support to effect his policies. Any erosion of that support was a handicap.

The Presidency and Its Access to Television

Over the past 25 years Congress has grown jealous of the President's easy access to television airtime. It has not focused so much on the news coverage given the President but on the President's opportunity to address the public directly, virtually at his request. A 1976 report prepared for Speaker of the House Carl Albert by the Congressional Research Center of the Library of Congress found that "[f]rom January 1966 through December 1976, President[s] Johnson, Nixon, and Ford sought simultaneous television network time to address the Nation on 45 occasions and received it 44 of those times . . ." Only Ford, for an October 1975 message on a tax cut proposal, was turned down by two out of the three networks. The report

also suggested that when the Presidents did go to the public through
television, the impact on public opinion could be substantial:

> With Presidential access to the airways comes the power to reach millions of
> people and the potential to influence their views on national issues. Polls taken
> after various televised addresses suggest that ready access to the television
> networks often enabled Presidents Johnson, Nixon and Ford to rally public
> opinion to their points of view.
>
> In mid-summer 1964, for example, the Harris Survey found that 42 percent
> of persons polled supported the Johnson Administration's Vietnam policies. But
> after the President announced in an August 4 nationwide television address that
> he had ordered air strikes against the North Vietnamese to retaliate for their
> attacks against U.S. destroyers, public support of the President's policies rose to
> 72 percent in the following Harris Survey. Similarly, during a pause in the
> American bombing of North Vietnam in January 1966, Harris found 61 percent
> of the public favoring resumed bombing. But after LBJ announced and
> explained in a January 31 television address a resumption of the bombing,
> public support for a bombing resumption rose to 73 percent in the next Harris
> Survey.[26]

That analysis, of course, assumes that it is the use of television, not the
content of the message, that the changes in public opinion reflect.

In 1970 Senator William Fulbright, an outspoken opponent of the
Administration's conduct of the Vietnam War, laid considerable blame for
the support the President's policies had received on the availability of
television. Fulbright said:

> Unfortunately, Congress is at a great disadvantage in the war powers debate,
> as it is in discussing most issues, because the Executive has a near monopoly on
> effective access to the public attention. The President can command a national
> television audience to hear his views on controversial matters at prime time, on
> short notice, at whatever length he chooses, and at no expense to the Federal
> Government or his party. Other constitutional officeholders are compelled to rely
> on highly selective newspaper articles and television news spots, which at most
> will convey bits and snatches of their points of view, usually selected in such a
> way as to create an impression of cranky carping at an heroic and beleaguered
> President.
>
> The problem for a Senator or Senate Committee is not simply one of being
> heard. Anything that has the color of scandal, sensation, accusation or prediction
> will command eager attention from the media. What you cannot easily interest
> them in is an idea, or a carefully exposited point of view, or an unfamiliar
> perspective or a reasoned rebuttal to a highly controversial Presidential
> statement.
>
> • • •
>
> Communication is power and exclusive access to it is a dangerous,
> unchecked power. If Roosevelt had had television, he might have been pro-
> claimed emperor by acclamation. . . . [27]

Fulbright asked for, but did not get, legislation to require broadcasters to
give free time to Congress as well as the President.

This analysis of Presidential power is not only held by government officials who feel themselves denied fair access to the public. Fred Friendly, Ford Foundation executive and former president of CBS News, has written:

> The drafters of the American Constitution strove diligently to prevent the power of the president from becoming a monopoly, but our inability to manage television has allowed the medium to be converted into an electronic throne.
>
> No mighty king, no ambitious emperor, no pope, or prophet ever dreamt of such an awesome pulpit, so potent a magic wand. In the American experiment with its delicate checks and balances, this device permits the First Amendment and the very heart of the Constitution to be breached, as it bestows on one politician a weapon denied to all others.[28]

However, reflection on the experiences of the Presidents of the television age suggests that even the most skillful of these have not been able to use television to impose their will or secure their own positions. Life and politics are more complicated than that. Kennedy, who "positively glittered," had difficulty getting his programs through Congress. Johnson, who lacked the glitter, got programs through Congress, but squandered his public support on a foreign war. Nixon, who never had a request for time refused by the networks, addressed the nation on all three networks 32 times in 5½ years. But he could not preserve his Presidency. Ford could not capitalize on his incumbency to win the Presidency in his own right. Carter, so skilled in his use of television, has not convinced the country that the energy crisis is real, nor that his stamp of approval on Bert Lance was enough.

While it is an advantage to be able to use television—and other media— skillfully, the ebb and flow of public approval depend on substance as well as image. If television is an "electronic throne," "an awesome pulpit," "a magic wand," then it is curious, is it not, that with the exception of Eisenhower no President of the television age has served a full eight years.

Television has not necessarily eased the task of governing, for not only has it given the President greater access to the public, it has also given the public greater access to the President, a greater opportunity to see the flaws as well as the grandeur.

Notes

1. Leo C. Rosten, *The Washington Correspondents* (New York: Arno Press, 1974), p. 49.
2. Arthur M. Schlesinger, Jr., *The Imperial Presidency* (Boston: Houghton Mifflin, 1973), p. 338.
3. Elmer E. Cornwell, Jr., *Presidential Leadership of Public Opinion* (Bloomington: Indiana University Press, 1966), p. 172.
4. Russell Baker, *An American in Washington* (New York: Alfred A. Knopf, 1961), p. 81.
5. Quoted in William L. Rivers, Theodore Peterson, and Jay W. Jensen, *The Mass Media and Modern Society,* 2nd edition (New York: Holt, Rinehart and Winston, 1971), p. 134.

6. Doris Kearns, *Lyndon Johnson and the American Dream* (New York: Harper & Row, 1976), p. 303.

7. Speech at Investigative Reporters and Editors conference, June 18, 1976.

8. William J. Small, *Political Power and the Press* (New York: Norton, 1972), p. 119.

9. Theodore H. White, *Breach of Faith: The Fall of Richard Nixon* (New York: Dell, 1976), p. 92.

10. Quoted in Rivers, Peterson, and Jensen, pp. 136–137.

11. Quoted in Rivers, Peterson, and Jensen, p. 137.

12. Charles W. Colson, "The Richard Nixon I Know," *Family Weekly,* March 28, 1976, p. 4.

13. The full text of the memo is available in William E. Porter, *Assault on the Media: The Nixon Years* (Ann Arbor: University of Michigan Press, 1976), pp. 244–249.

14. Timothy Crouse, *The Boys on the Bus* (New York: Ballantine Books, 1974), p. 229.

15. Israel Shenker, "How's That Again?", New York Times News Service, Louisville *Courier-Journal,* November 29, 1974.

16. Al Martinez, "Press Secretary," Los Angeles Times-Washington Post Service, Louisville *Courier-Journal,* October 11, 1974.

17. Dennis Farney, "Uh, Ron Was that One English Muffin or Two? Any Jelly?", *The Wall Street Journal,* June 13, 1975.

18. Jerald ter Horst, "Credibility of Nessen Questioned," Bloomington, Indiana, *Herald-Telephone,* June 30, 1975.

19. Ben Bagdikian found that of the 433 reporters employed by Washington news bureaus with 10 or more correspondents, fewer than 15 were assigned fulltime to Watergate—some for only two weeks. "All organizations of any size apparently had a total of only twenty reporters on the case fulltime and most of these not from the start." "The Fruits of Agnewism," *Columbia Journalism Review,* January/February 1973, p. 12.

20. Farney.

21. Bagdikian, pp. 10–11.

22. Washington *Post* columnist David Broder has suggested that Presidential press conferences would be much more effective if fewer reporters attended. Questions would be less scattershot and the questioning process more civilized.

23. Gerald W. Johnson, "Carter on Trial," *The New Republic,* December 4, 1976, p. 9.

24. Robert Scheer, "Jimmy, We Hardly Know Y'All," *Playboy,* November, 1976, pp. 92, 96.

25. Russell Baker, "But What's It Really All About?", New York Times News Service, Baltimore *Evening Sun,* September 22, 1977.

26. Denis S. Rutkus, *A Report on Simultaneous Television Network Coverage of Presidential Addresses to the Nation* (Washington, D.C.: Library of Congress, January 12, 1976), p. 18.

27. Communications Subcommittee, Senate Commerce Committee, "Equal Time for Congress: Congressional Hearings, 1970," reprinted in Robert O. Blanchard (ed.), *Congress and the News Media* (New York: Hastings House, 1974), pp. 104–105.

28. Fred Friendly, "Foreword," in Newton N. Minow, John Bartlow, and Lee M. Mitchell, *Presidential Television* (New York: Basic Books, 1973), pp. vii–viii.

11

News

A people without reliable news is, sooner or later, a people without the basis of freedom.

HAROLD J. LASKI

A journalist is a man who possesses himself of a fantasy and lures the truth towards it.

. . . what about all newspapers carrying a notice, on the front page, just below their names, saying: "Warning! The selective attention to data herein contained may warp your view of the world!"

FROM *THE JOURNALISTS* BY ARNOLD WESKER

The journalist is controlled by that uncontrollable nonsense we call news.

REED WHITTEMORE

Who and how?	Men armed with knives, chains and guns
What and where?	invaded the B'nai B'rith building in Washington, D.C., and took hostages,
When?	at about 11 a.m., Wednesday, March 9, 1977.
Who?	Informed of the occupation of the B'nai B'irth headquarters, Israeli Prime Minister Yitzhak Rabin
What and where?	left under reinforced security from the Kennedy Center in Washington, D.C., where he had accepted an honorary degree from American University, rushed through a lunch-

	eon address at the Shoreham Hotel, drove under heavy guard to Andrews Air Force Base, and flew to New York,
When?	on Wednesday, March 9, 1977.
Who and how?	Men armed with knives and shotguns
What and where?	invaded the Islamic Center in Washington, D.C., and took hostages,
When?	at about 12:30 p.m., Wednesday, March 9, 1977.
Who and how?	Men armed with a shotgun and a handgun
What and where?	took over a fifth-floor office of the Washington, D.C., city hall, killing a radio news reporter, and wounding a guard, a city councilman, and a city council aide, and taking hostages,
When?	at about 2:15 p.m., Wednesday, March 9, 1977.
Why?	For hours the hundreds of Washington police surrounding each building, and the dozens of FBI agents that President Carter had ordered into the operation, did not know who the gunmen were, how many were involved, or whether the three attacks were connected.

Objective Journalism

The conventions of objective reporting prescribe that reporters confine themselves to facts such as these. Their role is to observe or gather "the news" objectively, to fashion a clear and concise "straight" news story, starting typically with the who, what, when, where, and how of an event, placing factual details in descending order of interest and importance. They are to hold a mirror up to an event to show its surface. Explaining why it had occurred and brooding over what should be done about it are left to the editorial writers and columnists. The conventions of objective journalism prescribe that reporters who had to meet deadlines during the first hours of the Washington, D.C., events and who wished to raise the possibility that the events were connected, must find a source to raise it and must attribute the speculation to the source.

The resistance of these conventions to change cannot be overestimated. Whenever new or revived journalistic forms, such as advocacy or new journalism, challenge the ascendancy, indeed the sanctity, of objective reporting, the ensuing debate generates extraordinary heat among journalists. Typically these forms recalled a bohemian, not quite respectable, past over which objective reporting had triumphed but which it had not fully repudiated. The techniques of objective reporting suggested something of the dispassion and rigor of scholarship, important values in an age of science and methodology; the conventions of journalism, particularly those of speed and of the scoop, preserved the vitality of a brasher age. These conventions are at the root of many of journalism's ethical dilemmas, and their tenacity checks the promise that new technologies offer for more analytical reporting.

The conventions of reporting derive mainly from the effect on journalistic practice of communications technology. The invention of the telegraph in Definitions of News

351

the 1840s forced a terse, fact-oriented style on journalists long accustomed to indulging their personal writing styles, interpretations, and views. The technology itself was vital to the development of the modern wire services, which reinforced the use of the concise, objective style because they strove to offer as neutral and objective an account of the day's events as possible so as not to offend the diverse political and social dispositions of their clients all over the country. "As often happens in the newspaper business," Washington *Post* reporter Lou Cannon observes, "a technique became a value." Cannon describes how the value has affected journalistic tradition:

> When editors and reporters make their practical decisions in the newsroom, they do so within the context of a long tradition which has determined that some kinds of happenings and stories constitute news while others do not. In explaining the workings of their craft to others, people in the news business often accept this tradition without much reflection and behave as if news was a finite body of information ready to be set in type or related to the television viewer.[1]

Former New York *Times* editor Lester Markel has pointed out how selective and subjective the workings of the journalistic craft are:

> The reporter, the most objective reporter, collects fifty facts. Out of the fifty he selects twelve to include in his story (there is such a thing as space limitation). Thus he discards thirty-eight. This is Judgment Number One.
>
> Then the reporter or editor decides which of the facts shall be the first paragraph of the story, thus emphasizing one fact above the other eleven. This is Judgment Number Two.
>
> Then the editor decides whether the story shall be placed on Page One or Page Twelve; on Page One it will command many times the attention it would on Page Twelve. This is Judgment Number Three.
>
> This so-called factual presentation is thus subjected to three judgments, all of them most humanly and most ungodly made.[2]

But Markel himself seems to share an assumption that Cannon identified. For Markel, Judgment Number One is the journalist's selection of 12 out of the 50 facts collected. But what of the judgment made earlier? Fifty facts about what? Why did the journalist choose to cover that particular event or "story" in the first place, and why choose those 50 facts rather than others? Suggested is an assumption characteristic of many journalists: that they do not select news, that news is an independent entity beyond journalists' control. It is simply out there, its features and attributes almost palpably obvious to trained journalists even though they may have endless trouble defining what news is.

Definitions of News

Consider this effort by John Masterman, a former NBC correspondent, to describe news:

Real news is chewy. Not like bubble gum. It's chewy like the end of a new black copy pencil is chewy. It gives off an odor. Pungent. Like whisky barrels and bad breath and cooking turnips. It has a mean, lean look to it when you get a glimpse of it skimming through the treetops. News catches the bus to go downtown on rainy Sundays to play dominoes with Max America's cast-off girlfriend. You know Max, the wrestler? Sometimes news squats in mud puddles, grinning, and says "Come get me. Meet me across town." It sings when it feels like it. Soprano. It'll come up behind you while you're standing on a street corner and pinch the nape of your neck and you shout at it and grab it and throw it down and smear it around on a piece of paper and watch the colors run and that's a damn fine feeling, and you wouldn't trade places with Sparky Anderson, the canny manager of the series-winning Cincinnati Reds. That's real news. Wrap much more of a definition around it and you'll frighten it away.

Is news, then, therapy for journalists? Masterman seemed to be saying as much in this excerpt from a speech he made in October 1975. Masterman's rendering of the poetry of news rather than defining news is a familiar reaction. Some journalists argue that news cannot be defined, that the best journalists are born with a nose for news. Others rationalize their behavior, saying that news is what is printed or broadcast, or is what the public will pay for. Nevertheless, concerned scholars and journalists have grappled with definitions in the conviction that definition matters, that a clearer understanding of what we think news is will affect what news we gather, how we gather it, and how we present it. And that understanding is vital if we recall the comment by Ben Bagdikian discussed in the first chapter: "For most of the people of the world, for most of the events of the world, what the news systems do not transmit did not happen. To that extent, the world and its inhabitants are what the news systems say they are." In this view, news is our reality. Not surprisingly, therefore, concerned journalists and scholars consider it of paramount importance to try to define and understand what news is.

Willard Bleyer, a reporter who later became a pioneer in journalism education, defined news as "anything timely that interests a large number of persons, and the best news is that which has the greatest interest for the greatest number."[3] Note that Bleyer did not restrict his definition to important events. What is interesting to one reader, listener, or viewer may not be to another; but information that interests and affects many—even though it may be a trivium in the great march of events—can be considered news.

One problem with Bleyer's definition is a failure to distinguish between the reporter's account of an event and the event itself. As Curtis MacDougall has noted, "At any given moment billions of simultaneous events occur throughout the world. . . . All of these occurrences are potentially news. They do not become so until some purveyor of news gives an account of them. The news, in other words, is the account of the event, not something intrinsic in the event itself."[4] A more useful definition of news, therefore, is this: News is the timely report of events, facts, and opinions that interest a significant number of people. But this definition is discouragingly imprecise and inclusive; and some will criticize it for what it excludes. The definition takes no account of information that should be of interest to the public. Scholars and journalists concerned to see the press communicate information that citizens need to know to fulfill their roles as citizens in a democracy and to protect their own interests argue that news must balance interest and significance.

Frustrated in their efforts to define satisfactorily what news is or what it should be, journalists and scholars have analyzed news stories to try to determine which qualities are common to events that arouse the greatest attention. Typically they list these qualities: conflict, proximity, prominence, unusualness, human interest, timeliness, and probable consequence. Reporters celebrated for their "nose for news" have the ability to recognize one or more of these qualities in an item of information or event. This intuitive skill is central to the workings of the journalist's craft that Cannon described. But his description makes no very clear distinction between news and the workings of the journalist's craft. That is because there is none. The norms and conventions of journalists' behavior influence profoundly what news is. Variations in conventional behavior, like those involved in advocacy journalism and the new journalism, for example, change what news is. As Herbert Altschull, a former AP and New York *Times* reporter and now professor of journalism at Indiana University, has observed: " . . . [N]ews is a dynamic phenomenon and hence cannot be fitted into a traditional, static definition. Like communication itself, news is a process."[5]

That is why studying the attitudes and behavior of sources, journalists, and their audiences and the context in which all interact—that is, the process of news—is likely to tell us more than analysis of news content alone. Warren Breed showed in 1955, for example, how reporters were socialized in the newsroom to the values, preferences, and policies of their senior colleagues, their editors and publishers, and lent some support to a widely held view that journalists write less for general readers than for other journalists.[6] In 1949 David Manning White studied the decisions of "Mr. Gates," the wire editor on a nonmetropolitan newspaper, and concluded:

> It is only when we study the reasons given by Mr. Gates for rejecting almost nine-tenths of the wire copy (in his search for the one-tenth for which he has space) that we begin to understand how highly subjective, how reliant upon value-judgments based on the "gate keeper's" own set of experiences, attitudes and expectations the communication of "news" really is.[7]

If meaningful definition of news finally eludes us, and that seems to be the state of the art, the importance of understanding how news is selected, gathered, and reported survives, particularly because of empirical evidence that demonstrates the media's success under certain conditions in setting the agenda, in telling their audiences what to think about.

In any society there are individuals, groups, and institutions with vested interests in what the public thinks about and, if possible, how the public thinks about the agenda before it. Their concern manifests itself in a number of ways—in censorship, secrecy, news management, public relations, and advertising. Thus in the absence of any understanding of what they think news is, or perhaps more important, of what they think news should be, journalists are vulnerable to manipulation—by their sources, their employers and editors, their commercial sponsors, their professional peers, and their audiences. Journalists are particularly vulnerable to the norms and conventions of their profession—to the cruel and arbitrary pressure of deadlines, to the competitive requirement that they get the news first and fast. These conventions subvert serious analysis.

In the controlled panic just before deadline, which pumps adrenalin through journalists' veins and for many is journalism's most exquisite pleasure, contemplation of what they are doing, why, and with what likely consequences is a luxury few have leisure to indulge. Masterman's rendering of news conforms to Wordsworth's definition of poetry: It is emotion recollected in tranquillity. And it tells us far more about journalists than it does about news.

The refusal by many journalists to "wrap much more of a definition around" news or to analyze the news process has contributed to the fluctuating emphases in journalistic forms such as advocacy journalism, new journalism, and investigative reporting, emphases that seem inevitably to be taken to extremes because they come upon the profession with the force of revelation. Each form has the appearance of newness, invariably generates controversy, then is absorbed into professional practice if it was not there already or fades as a professional fad. Consider the last two decades.

During the 1950s professional commitment to straight, so-called objective reporting was an approach that Senator Joseph McCarthy shrewdly exploited. Because he was a colorful and controversial public official with a flair for the sensational, McCarthy was news. His charges that there were X number of Communists in the State Department and elsewhere made headlines. In his biography of McCarthy, Richard Rovere noted that the New York *Times*

> . . . admitted that there turned out to be no truth in any of these stories, but it explained that it had seen no alternative to publishing them. "It is difficult, if not impossible, to ignore charges by Senator McCarthy just because they are usually proved false. The remedy lies with the reader." To many people this was rather like saying that if a restaurant serves poisoned food, it is up to the diner to refuse it.[8]

Nevertheless, Rovere endorsed the stance of the *Times*, thereby rejecting a Hutchins Commission recommendation to the press in 1947: "It is no longer enough to report the fact truthfully. It is now necessary to report the truth about the fact." The commission was recommending interpretative reporting, but failed to persuade major papers in the 1950s. McCarthy and his accusations possessed the qualities of news—prominence, conflict, and timeliness. No matter that his charges were false and terribly damaging to innocent individuals; they were news. They gave off an odor. Pungent. And news was objective fact, value free.

Advocacy Journalism

The willingness of the *Times* and other influential newspapers to serve as the neutral transmission belt for prominent, official sources like McCarthy reflected an institutional stance of the press that later enraged civil rights and antiwar activists in the 1960s and contributed to the flowering of the underground press. To underground journalists belief in objective reporting was hypocritical and delusory. In 1970, Raymond Mungo, a founder of the Liberation News Service, which served many underground papers, wrote:

> We were not sticklers for accuracy—neither is the underground press in general, so be advised. . . . *Facts* are less important than *truth* and the two are far from equivalent, you see; for cold facts are nearly always boring and may even distort the truth, but Truth is the highest achievement of human expression. . . . I'm saying that the distinctly Western insistence on *facts* (and passive faith in science and technology) betrays our tragically, perhaps fatally, limited consciousness of life. The facts, even if he can get them, will never help a man realize who and what he is or aspire to fulfill his natural role in the universe. Ain't it the truth? All we say: tell the truth, brothers, and let the facts fall where they may.[9]

Mungo had the same objective for truth as Walter Lippmann had had in 1922 when Lippmann wrote that

> . . . news and truth are not the same thing, and must be clearly distinguished. The function of news is to signalize an event, the function of truth is to bring to light the hidden facts, to set them in relation with each other, and make a picture of reality on which men can act.[10]

Underground journalists wanted a picture of reality on which people could act but were by no means as concerned as was Lippmann, and later the Hutchins Commission, to bring to light the hidden facts. Most were propagandists, advocates of a cause, and in those polarizing years their journalistic approach was contagious, particularly among younger journalists who wished to abandon what they saw as the illusion of objectivity in favor of advocacy and activism. They wanted to break down the separation of news from opinion, and the argument tended to rage in extremes—either straight news or advocacy, activist reporting. One must replace the other.

In the 1970s the journalism of advocacy had a firm hold on only a small part of the newspaper world. Although many reporters on conventional newspapers were angrily denouncing objectivity and fighting over it with their editors, another kind of newspaper affords a better view of the future of advocacy. This is the investigative paper, which is usually published weekly or monthly. One of the most valuable is the San Francisco *Bay Guardian*. Editor Bruce Brugmann explains its purpose:

> I aim my derringer at every reporter and tell him, by God, that I don't want to see an objective piece of reporting. . . . But this is not dishonest journalism; it is "point of view" journalism. Our facts are as straight as we can make them! We don't run a story until we feel we can prove it or make it stick; we always talk with the adversary and try to print his side as part of the story; he always gets the

chance of reply in the next issue (rarely do they, even when I offer in letter or by phone). We run almost all the critical reaction we get to stories; but the point is we don't run a story until we think it is in the public interest to do so.

How do you talk about our major stories, environmental pollution, Vietnam, the Manhattanization of San Francisco, saving the Bay, unless you do some "point of view" reporting? We're not just covering meetings. We're not just checking in with the official sources. We're going after stories, hopefully before they become certifiable facts. . . . Along with this come different forms of the new journalism; letting participants write their own stuff, using experts with special knowledge, more literary writing, the use of irony, poetry, impressionistic writing—everything really, that has relevance, and merit, and readability—and goes for the jugular.[11]

Whatever one thinks of "point of view" journalism, the stance of Brugmann's paper—and others such as the *Texas Observer* and *Cervi's Journal* in Denver—suggests a missing dimension in conventional newspapers. Much of the conventional press will take an adversary stance toward government, at least on occasion. The *Bay Guardian* and its counterparts look deeper into American society and recognize that rather than a relatively simple military-industrial complex, the United States is a military-industrial-labor-education complex that is eager to make an ally of the media of mass communication. These little journals strike an adversary stance toward all the powerful institutions.

New Journalism

At the same time as the United States split over the Vietnam War, many Americans were experimenting with different life styles. To capture the variety and flavor of these styles and prominent exponents of them, writers such as Tom Wolfe and Gay Talese began to experiment with what was called the "new journalism" or new nonfiction, adapting the literary techniques of the novel and short story to journalism.

Tom Wolfe defined the new journalism as the use in "nonfiction of techniques which had been thought of as confined to the novel or the short story, to create in one form both the kind of objective reality of journalism and the subjective reality that people have always gone to the novel for." The writers of the new journalism used many of the reporting and writing techniques common to most journalism. Beyond the conventional techniques, Wolfe singled out four central devices:

1. Scenic construction, moving from scene to scene and resorting as little as possible to sheer historical narrative.
2. Recording dialogue in full.
3. Presenting scenes through the eyes of a character by interviewing him about his thoughts and emotions at the time of the event the writer describes (also known as interior monologue).

4. Recording everyday gestures, habits, manners, customs, styles of clothing, decorations, styles of traveling, eating, keeping house— everything, Wolfe said, "symbolic, generally, of people's *status life.*"[12]

Gay Talese argues that new journalism "is, or should be, as reliable as the most reliable reportage, although it seeks a larger truth than is possible through the mere compilation of verifiable facts, the use of direct quotations, and adherence to the rigid organizational style of the old form." To Talese, the new journalism "allows, demands in fact, a more imaginative approach to reporting, and it permits the writer to inject himself into the narrative, if he wishes, as many writers do, or to assume the role of detached observer, as other writers do, including myself."[13]

Again the approach was contagious and controversial. Again dispute within journalism tended to split into either-or argument and again the old order perceived a threat to its norms and conventions. Timothy Crouse describes how a representative of the old order, Walter Mears of the Associated Press, the dean of the political wire service reporters, felt about the new journalism: "The problem with a lot of the new guys is they don't get the formula stuff drilled into them," Mears told Crouse in 1972. "If you don't learn how to write an eight-car fatal on Route 128, you're gonna be in big trouble." A reporter of the new journalism school described Mears to Crouse in a way that sharpens the distinctions between old and new journalism: "At what he does, Mears is the best in the goddam world. He can get out a coherent story with the right point on top in a minute and thirty seconds, left-handed. . . . In the end, Walter Mears can only be tested on one thing, and that is whether he has the right lead. He almost always does. He watches some goddam event for a half hour and he understands the most important thing that happened—that happened in public, I mean. He's just like a TV camera, he doesn't see things any special way."[14] What is happening beneath or behind the public surface and seeing that in a special way are at the heart of the new journalism.

INVESTIGATIVE REPORTING

Although the Washington *Post* was early committed to supporting the investigations of Carl Bernstein and Bob Woodward into the ramifications of the Watergate break-in, the rest of the American press was slow to see the significance in their stories. Then reporters rushed to catch up with and to scoop the *Post.* The initial response to Seymour Hersh's revelations in the New York *Times* in 1975 about the illegal activities of the CIA and abuses in the intelligence community was cool and skeptical. Then again a rush to catch up ensued. The investigative urge among reporters was irresistible.

In 1976 it found release in exposés of the sexual activities of members of Congress and former Presidents with what seemed to many a reckless disregard for privacy, for distinguishing between private and public interest. The either-or tendency—straight news reporting or investigative reporting—was not as apparent this time, but in February 1975 reporters and editors formed a national organization, Investigative Reporters and Editors (IRE), to develop a system to help investigative reporters do a better job. The objectives of the organization were admirable; its exclusivity was puzzling. In 1976 IRE proposed a directory of experienced investigative reporters, determined that not just any reporter should be listed. Not surprisingly, IRE struggled to define criteria for listing reporters in the directory, but agreed on these general principles:

> Reporters listed in the IRE directory should be (1) reliable, (2) accurate and (3) have extensive knowledge of the records and human news sources available within his/her field.

How to implement those vague principles with appropriate exclusivity was the problem; they describe desirable qualities in *any* reporter. What was curious about IRE, then, was its concern to institutionalize a distinction between reporter and investigative reporter, a concern that echoed the either-or controversies surrounding advocacy journalism and the new journalism.

Looking back on the professional disputes about advocacy, activist journalism, and the new journalism of the late 1960s and early 1970s, one is struck by what now seems their inordinate heat. Both forms, and the content they emphasized, were seductive to younger journalists, questionable to older ones. To a lesser extent, the investigative urge was taking on a similar character in the mid-1970s. None of the forms is essentially new. All have been practiced at different times since journalism began and all now find a place in the media mix. The controversies surrounding them served mainly to stress what had long been clear, that objectivity is an unattainable ideal, one that most American journalists consider worth seeking nonetheless.

Paradoxically, however, electronic technologies, which potentially narrow the gap between actual practice and the ideal, were causing concern in the late 1970s precisely because they can be more "objective" than print journalism. Although placement of equipment affects the view of reality presented, the ability of electronic technologies to record and transmit the sights and sounds of events live can reduce the selective process of "objective" reporting or restrict the ability of journalists to edit spontaneous events. It is unlikely, for example, that anyone could have reacted in time to edit Jack Ruby's shooting of Lee Harvey Oswald, the alleged assassin of President John F. Kennedy, out of the live television broadcast of police taking Oswald from the Dallas police station to the county jail on November 24, 1963.

The hours of confusion surrounding the events in Washington, D.C., on March 9, 1977, were ended when Hamaas Abdul Khaalis, the leader of the Hanafi Muslim sect, called WTOP-TV reporter Max Robinson and issued his demands live during the station's 6 p.m. newscast. Khaalis said that the 12 armed Hanafi Muslims would release the 134 hostages that they were holding in the three buildings if "Mohammed, Messenger of God," a movie about Islam premiering that day in Los Angeles and New York, were taken out of the country and the Black Muslims who had killed five of his children in 1973 were delivered to him at the Islamic Center. Khaalis told Robinson to inform Secretary of State Cyrus Vance and the ambassadors of all Muslim countries that the Hanafis were going to kill foreign Muslims at the Islamic Center and create an international incident.

The editorial control yielded or lost to newsmakers in situations of live coverage such as these alarmed some critics, who would in no way dissent from the principle that the press has a responsibility to serve truth. For various reasons, however—concern for standards of taste and decency, for minors, for the national security, for the rights of defendants to a fair trial and of individuals to privacy, and for the fact, as T. S. Eliot observed, that "human kind / Cannot bear very much reality"—they did not always approve of unedited "truth." In the 1970s new technologies that readily enabled live coverage were severely testing journalists' ability to respond quickly enough to critics' and their own perceptions of what the public should see and hear on its television screens.

Professional Responsibilities and Ethics

The Canons of Journalism adopted by the American Society of Newspaper Editors (ASNE) in 1923, and revised in 1975, and the Code of Ethics adopted by the Society of Professional Journalists (Sigma Delta Chi) in 1973 define as journalists' ultimate responsibility the duty to serve the truth. In more concrete terms, the 1923 canons specified: "The primary function of newspapers is to communicate to the human race what its members do, feel, and think." The 1973 code placed the journalists' function in a constitutional context:

> We believe in public enlightenment as the forerunner of justice, and in our Constitutional role to seek the truth as part of the public's right to know the truth. . . . The public's right to know of events of public importance and interest is the overriding mission of the mass media.

Journalists' responsibilities derive from their perception of their constitutional role in American democracy. The canons and the code are mainly concerned to define rules of conduct for journalists in carrying out these responsibilities. Their ethics include the responsibility to be accurate, thorough, objective, and fair. Furthermore, journalists must, among other ethical responsibilities, protect confidential sources of information, must guard against invading a person's right to privacy, must not pander to morbid curiosity about details of vice and crime, and must make prompt and complete correction of their errors.

But admirable and eloquent though the canons and the code are as statements of objectives and standards, they have neither the force nor the mechanism of regulation. And journalistic conventions, particularly the requirement to be first and fast, have always strained journalists' ethics.

At the turn of the century, when newspaper competition was intense, press and public were none too fussy about ethics. Their ambivalence was revealed in Joseph Pulitzer's ideals for the New York *World,* which illustrate the tension between journalists' competitive and ethical instincts.

Introducing his second of four ideals, Pulitzer asked his editors:

> What is the one distinctive feature, fight, crusade, public service or big exclusive? No paper can be great, in my opinion, if it depends simply upon the hand-to-mouth idea, news coming in anyhow. One big distinctive feature story every day at least. One striking feature each issue should contain, prepared before, not left to chance.

Pulitzer's fourth, and last, ideal was:

> Accuracy, accuracy, accuracy. Also terseness, intelligent, not stupid condensation.[15]

To produce one big, distinctive, exclusive story every day, reporters could not always be fastidious about accuracy. The order of Pulitzer's ideals does not seem accidental, and, despite the adoption of codes of conduct, journalists have found it hard to reorder his priorities. Now both press and public alike are much more inclined to question journalists' ethics. Through citizens' groups, press councils, ombudsmen, letters to the editor and station manager, and opinion polls, the public maintains its critical scrutiny of the press.

Still in the grip of their traditions and conventions, however, journalists are vulnerable to ethical compromises. Their desire to beat out the opposition has survived the dramatic decline in newspaper competition; they now work in the competitive mix of newspapers, news magazines, wire services, and broadcast news programs. They compete intensely not only against other media but also against one another. For newspaper reporters, getting their stories on the front page is the measure of professional success. For television journalists, it is getting their stories on the nightly news, preferably at the top of the program and as more than a headline item. Basic to most good journalists is the drive to be first, fast, and on the front page or at the top of the program, and that drive often triumphs over ethical niceties.

MEETING THE DEADLINE

The deadline is the cut-off point in the day's work. It is absolute, inflexible for the broadcast journalist; the print journalist can bend it some but not much. Because the media abhor a vacuum, most of the time journalists must cut their losses at this point and go with whatever information they have. The print media will not go to press with empty space; broadcast news programs will not go with dead air.

No daily news medium lacks information, of course. It pours in over the wires of Associated Press and United Press International, from other wire services and news syndicates, from distant correspondents and local reporters. Editors discard much of it quickly, choose among the AP, UPI, and other international wire service versions of the same events or combine their accounts, check stories for accuracy and spelling and typographical errors, edit lightly for conciseness and elegance, and find suitable cutting points for stories. They write headlines, decide the page and place on the page where the stories will go, and select and place the pictures they want.

On metropolitan daily papers the news editors and their assistants will sift hundreds of thousands of words daily, using perhaps no more than 10 percent of them. During a single working day, then, they edit the rough equivalent of a small book. (In contrast, after a book manuscript is in hand, a publishing house customarily devotes at least six months, and often a year or more, to its editing and production.)

Because they are constantly making judgments at high speed, editors rarely have leisure to ponder the ethical implications of any of them. Typically they decide in terms of what their professional experience tells them is newsworthy, accords with their perceptions of what is important and interesting to readers. Editing is a reactive rather than a reflective process. Most of the questionable decisions editors make are errors of news judgment rather than of ethical judgment. That is, their selection and placement of one story over another, of certain facts over others, may be questioned in terms of importance and interest. A headline may distort the actual content of a story or bear little or no relation to it.

Some of these decisions have ethical implications, of course, but typically these are not consciously considered. Much of the work is routine. Reporters gather and present information in accordance with the same norms and conventions about news that editors use. Many of the sources on whom reporters rely are attuned to these norms and conventions and shape their information accordingly. Sources time the release of information—in the form of handouts, speeches, hearings, press conferences, and briefings—to meet the deadlines of the media that they consider most desirable.

An essentially similar process occurs in television news: Reporters and editors make judgments at high speed about more information than they can possibly use in the limited and finite time available—a half-hour for network news, perhaps an hour for local station news. But the technology and its cost make for different norms and conventions. The day's events, the "news," have much more effect on the content of a daily newspaper than they do on the content of a television news program. The cost and logistics of deploying camera crews and correspondents require television news editors to plan the news in advance far more than newspaper editors need do. A newspaper can usually respond to haphazard events whenever and wherever they occur; a television news operation must anticipate and to some extent control events. "The news you present is actually the news you cover," Edward Jay Epstein quotes a network vice president as saying.

In his study of television network news, Epstein explains why:

The cost for gathering and producing news programing is controlled mainly by the deployment of camera crews and correspondents. Aside from costing about

CBS News, just before broadcast: At deadline, journalists must cut their losses and go with the information they have. (CBS photo)

$100,000 a year to maintain salaries and overtime, each camera crew generates a prodigious amount of film—about twenty times as much as is used in final stories—and this has to be transported, processed, edited and narrated. NBC accountants, in using a rule-of-thumb gauge of $14 in service for every foot of film used in the final story (or $504 a minute), have estimated that in 1968 each film crew accounted for about $500,000 annually of the budget of NBC News.[16]

The increasing shift from film to reusable videotape and videocamera equipment that has occurred since Epstein's study in 1968 and 1969 has speeded up the news process and cut some costs. But costs are still high.

Epstein found that each network selected no more than 20 or 30 possible film stories a day on the basis of advance information gathered through the wire services, newspapers, and its own correspondents. Film crews were sent to cover these stories and a small proportion of their exposed film, usually less than 5 percent, was edited into stories for broadcast.

From a four-month analysis of the logs of the NBC Evening News, Epstein found that

... only 47 percent of the news film depicted events on the day they occurred, while 36 percent of the news film was more than two days old, and 12 percent was more than a week old. None of the news stories during that period were live, and on some days as much as 70 percent of the filmed news was more than a day old. A similar proportion of news film on the CBS and ABC Evening News was also delayed; only 50 percent on CBS and 46 percent on ABC depicted events on the day they occurred.[17]

Epstein made these findings in 1968, when the Vietnam War dominated the news, so the time for transporting and processing film from Southeast Asia to New York explains much of the delay. When domestic and less far-flung foreign news dominates the news, higher proportions of news film of the day's events are shown on the day they occur. Nevertheless, his findings illustrate an important technological and logistical difference between print and televised news.

There is a difference, too, in form and content between print and televised news. Reuven Frank, former executive producer of NBC Evening News, describes it this way:

> The highest power of television journalism is not in the transmission of information but in the transmission of experience. . . . joy, sorrow, shock, fear, these are the stuff of news.

In 1963 Frank had instructed his staff:

> Every news story should, without any sacrifice of probity or responsibility, display the attributes of fiction, of drama. It should have structure and conflict, problem and denouement, rising action and falling action, a beginning, a middle and an end.[18]

One reason for this narrative form, argues Sharon Sperry in "Television News as Narrative," is the context in which a network news program occurs. It is important to recognize, she says:

> . . . that the national television news shows stand at the front of prime-time programming each evening, and the networks expect the news to capture an early audience which will stay tuned for the rest of the evening's programs. Consequently, the networks pour their resources into the half-hour news shows with an eye to building an audience as well as to fulfilling their responsibilities for news coverage. This policy, in turn, sets the parameters for the form the news assumes: half an hour's worth of news *stories*. Television news is a blend of traditional, objective journalism and a kind of quasi-fictional prime-time story-telling which frames events in reduced terms with simple, clear-cut values.[19]

Typically, spontaneous events do not fall into narrative form which stresses simple, clear-cut values. Events must be edited into that form. And yet the popular impression survives that television news is an accurate mirror of reality, that "the camera never lies." But to meet the requirements of the narrative form Reuven Frank and other television executives have prescribed for television news, a story line must often be imposed on the confusion of spontaneous events.

In his study of the television editing process, Epstein identified three main procedures to achieve the narrative effect:

1. Editors eliminate all technically inferior film footage and reduce visual noise or disconcerting elements.

2. Editors concentrate scenes of action so as to heighten the visual effect. They cut scenes with little visual interest and compress the remaining fragments into "one continuous montage of unceasing action."
3. Editors use only the portions of the film that fulfill the agreed-upon story, that most exactly illustrate the script.

Print news reporters and editors also impose a logic and order that spontaneous, confused events do not naturally possess, and they also prefer action and conflict in the news. Both the print and the broadcast media, then, try in their different ways to reduce the "great, blooming, buzzing confusion" of the day's events to some orderly, understandable, and often entertaining, form. But partly because of television's existence and news approach, the print media feel more responsibility for keeping the historical record, for reporting the often dull and complex activities of government at all levels and of human beings and their organizations in general.

Newspapers' greater tolerance for dullness and complexity makes them less liable than television to ethical pitfalls in their routine work. Although newspapers prefer action and conflict in the news, they will go to press without them. But television wants its pictures to move, and, wherever possible, to move vigorously, even violently.

Activists and minority groups seeking access for their views to mass audiences via the media have mastered television news values and have sometimes behaved violently in order to attract the television cameras. Calm, rational statement of their views has less visual interest than violent confrontation with the authorities these groups are trying to persuade. The effect of feeding television's preference for the visually dramatic has not always furthered their purposes, however. The women's movement of the 1960s, for example, is still dogged by its early bra-burning protests. The dramatic gesture appealed to television's desire for heightened visual effect, but the memorable symbolic action has fixed itself in many minds and has not proved helpful to women trying to argue the depth and complexity of their cause.

In 1968 and 1969 Epstein found no television editors troubled by the distortion of reality that their "process of distilling action from preponderantly inactive scenes" entailed. Because of the criticism of television's concentration on violence during the turmoil and protest of the late 1960s and particularly during the 1968 Democratic Convention in Chicago, television editors are more inclined now to consider the ethical implications of their preference for vigorous action. Their preference survives, as it does for newspaper reporters and editors. Action and conflict, after all, are in many respects the essence of what journalists call news, and under the press of the deadline these elements emerge more often than others at the top of television news and on the front pages of newspapers.

Radio and television quickly displaced the newspaper's function of feeding readers up-to-the-minute bulletins of breaking news. Now newspapers and magazines complement radio and television's headline service, by providing the background detail and analysis of the news. But newspaper reporters have not abandoned breaking news to broadcasting. The competitive urge to scoop other reporters, whatever medium they work for, is very much alive in all journalists. And it is particularly when this urge bumps against the deadline that reporters have ethical problems. Then they must decide whether to go with the perhaps unchecked, unexplained fragments of a possible exclusive story or let the deadline pass, use the extra time to check and explain what facts they have, gather more information, and run the risk that another reporter will come out with the story before them. If they publish or broadcast their unchecked information, they run the risk of disseminating wrong information that can severely damage the reputations and careers of persons involved in the story.

Once inaccurate information gets into the public's bloodstream, corrections and clarifications rarely wash it out, so tenacious are first impressions. Moreover, the news media are notoriously defensive about their errors. Corrections almost never receive the space and prominence given the original error. Regrettably, for some reporters and editors the publish-and-be-damned philosophy still has the appealing appearance of courage rather than of arrogance or irresponsibility.

Consider, for example, the contrasting behavior of journalists in covering the "Eagleton Affair" in July 1972.

THE EAGLETON AFFAIR

Senator George McGovern of South Dakota won the Democratic Presidential nomination at the party's convention in July 1972. At 9 a.m., July 13, his advisers met to select a Vice Presidential candidate, who had to be named by 4 o'clock that afternoon. Among candidates discussed was Senator Thomas Eagleton of Missouri, but two advisers recalled rumors about alcohol or psychiatric problems. Although the advisers tended to dismiss the rumors as unfounded, by early afternoon they did not regard Eagleton as a serious contender.

At 3:25 p.m., 35 minutes before deadline, the meeting still had no candidate. McGovern reviewed a report that Eagleton had been hospitalized in the 1960s for what he had publicly announced were stomach ailments, although "reliable sources" felt he had problems with alcohol. At 3:40 p.m. McGovern called Eagleton and offered him the Vice Presidential candidacy. Eagleton accepted, and in the early hours of July 14, the convention chose him as McGovern's running mate.

On July 17 an anonymous caller told the Detroit *Free Press,* a Knight newspaper, of Eagleton's medical record. John S. Knight, III, a grandson of the owner, asked the caller for details that reporters could check. On July 19 the caller reported details which were passed on to Clark Hoyt of the Knight newspapers' Washington bureau, who was already in St. Louis checking rumors of an Eagleton drinking problem. For almost a week Hoyt pored over newspaper clippings and interviewed key sources.

On July 20 Eagleton finally told McGovern's top advisers that he had been hospitalized three times between 1960 and 1966 and that treatment had included shock therapy on two of those occasions.

At midnight on July 22 Hoyt and Robert Boyd, chief of the Knight newspapers' Washington bureau, put before the Senator and his staff what they had learned about Eagleton. The reporters said that they wanted to publish the story after seeing the medical records and talking to the physicians and Eagleton himself. James Perry describes the reaction of Frank Mankiewicz, a McGovern campaign manager:

> Mankiewicz is one of the great dramatic actors of our time, and he turned it all on now. He appealed to the Knight reporters' patriotism. He promised them news breaks. He stalled and he fudged. One way or another, Boyd and Hoyt agreed to delay the publication of their findings.[20]

Mankiewicz promised them an exclusive interview with Eagleton on July 25. At breakfast on July 25 Eagleton and McGovern decided that Eagleton would stay on the ticket and would reveal his medical history at a press conference that morning.

Then Eagleton told reporters, "On three occasions in my life I have voluntarily gone into hospitals as a result of nervous exhaustion and fatigue." He admitted that he had twice received electroshock therapy. At last the nation knew the facts, or some of them, and Boyd and Hoyt lost their exclusive. The early and flattering accounts of Eagleton's career and character were replaced by efforts to probe the nature and effect of his psychiatric problem and by editorials urging his removal from the ticket. The most slipshod of these efforts came from syndicated columnist and investigative reporter Jack Anderson.

On his daily radio show the Pulitzer Prize-winning Anderson broadcast on July 27 that "Eagleton has steadfastly denied any alcoholism, but we have now located photostats of half a dozen arrests for drunken and reckless driving."[21] Anderson had no such photostats nor has he ever located them. Why, then, had he broadcast such a damaging claim? Like Boyd and Hoyt, Anderson had received a tip; unlike Boyd and Hoyt, Anderson had not checked it out adequately.

He defended his rush to broadcast the information on two grounds:

1. Because of competitive pressure before deadline—he suspected that other reporters had received the same tip and he wanted to be the first to release it; and
2. Because he had found the source of the tip to be reliable in the past and so saw no reason to check the information on this occasion.

Anderson was correct in one respect. A source had also informed Maxine Cheshire, gossip columnist for the Washington *Post*. Cheshire, however, spent 10 hours checking the story out. She noted that her source, True Davis, a bank manager in Washington, had been defeated by Eagleton for Senator in the 1968 Democratic primary in Missouri, and concluded that the charges could not be substantiated. Eagleton himself denounced them as a "damnable lie."

The damage to Eagleton had been done. Most of it was self-inflicted. He had lacked candor and judgment. The McGovern staff had been irresponsibly careless in checking the credentials of a candidate for high office. And the press, by a combination of the best and most responsible of its investigative skills and of the worst and most reckless had done its share, too. On July 31, three weeks after being nominated, Senator Thomas Eagleton resigned from the ticket.

Boyd and Hoyt won the 1973 Pulitzer Prize for National Reporting for their investigation, but it may not have given them the same intensity of satisfaction as scooping other reporters would have done. It is a satisfaction on which Anderson thrives—and for which most journalists yearn—but, because of the daily deadline, one earned only at some risk.

THE NEWS SOURCE AND THE DEADLINE

Depending on when a story breaks, a weekly or monthly publication may have days or weeks to gather and check information. The remorseless dailiness of the other news media has them in a vice that, in situations like Jack Anderson's, tests their willingness to reorder Joseph Pulitzer's priorities and place accuracy before a scoop. Boyd and Hoyt had time to check their information partly because no other reporters seemed interested in checking the rumors about Eagleton. Woodward and Bernstein could be meticulous in their Watergate investigations partly because few other reporters recognized the implications of the break-in. A relative absence of competitive pressure, then, freed these reporters to some extent from the tyranny of the daily deadline. Once other reporters became interested in the Eagleton and Watergate stories, instances of inaccurate reporting occurred, and reporters matched Anderson's careless use of unverified information from a by no means disinterested source.

When big, complex stories break, a vital journalistic ethic—the journalist's responsibility to preserve the confidentiality of his or her sources—is open to abuse. In such situations the principle of objectivity can also be abused. Journalists eager to scoop rivals are inclined to argue that inquiry into the motives of sources who reveal information damaging to others is outside the purview of objective reporters; their responsibility is to report who said what, where, and when—and no more. Analysis of motive, they say, is the province of the psychologist, not the reporter; "motive" is too elusive—or inconvenient—a concept to fit into the objective reporter's definition of a news "fact."

Context, too, is a notion that often dissolves when an objective reporter is in the presence of a potentially controversial, and therefore newsworthy, "fact." For example, during the 1976 Presidential campaign *Playboy* magazine published an interview with Democratic candidate Jimmy Carter that many felt gave the most complete and insightful picture of this skillfully elusive politician available before the election. For three months Robert Scheer traveled with Carter, recording hours of conversations with the candidate that were concerned to reveal what kind of person he was. Scheer condensed these into 26 full-page columns presented in *Playboy*'s question-and-answer interview format. Scheer's last question of Carter was: "Do you feel you've reassured people with this interview, people who are uneasy about your religious beliefs, who wonder if you're going to make a rigid, unbending President?"

Scheer reported: "Carter then delivered a long, softly spoken monologue that grew in intensity as he made his final points."

Among them, Carter tried to explain that as a Baptist he had had drummed into him not to commit the sin of pride, not to think he was better than anybody else. In the final paragraphs of his lengthy response, Carter said:

> I try not to commit a deliberate sin. I recognize that I'm going to do it anyhow, because I'm human and I'm tempted. And Christ set some almost impossible standards for us. Christ said, "I tell you that anyone who looks on a woman with lust has in his heart already committed adultery." I've looked on a lot of women with lust. I've committed adultery in my heart many times. This is something that God recognizes I will do—and I have done it—and God forgives me for it. But that doesn't mean that I condemn someone who not only looks on a woman with lust but who leaves his wife and shacks up with somebody out of wedlock.[22]

Playboy released previews of the interview to the press before the November issue of the magazine was available to the public. Almost without exception, reporters selected Carter's candid statement that he had committed adultery in his heart many times as the major news "fact" of the interview. Virtually none of the particular context of that comment, let alone the varied and perhaps more enduringly significant insights into Carter revealed elsewhere in the interview, survived the objective reporting process. The reporting was, in fact, almost a caricature of a comment on the press Carter had made early in the *Playboy* interview. The traveling press, said Carter,

> . . . have zero interest in any issue unless it's a matter of making a mistake. What they're looking for is a 47-second argument between me and another candidate or something like that. There's nobody in the back of this plane who would ask an issue question unless he thought he could trick me into some crazy statement.

The press' selection and manner of treatment reduced the *Playboy* interview to essentially that: a crazy statement.

Pressures of time and space necessarily make the news process reductive. That is partly why Walter Lippmann saw news as having such a limited function: to signalize an event. But the ASNE Canons of Journalism and the Society of Professional Journalists' Code of Ethics define a more expansive function for journalists: the constitutional role to seek the truth as part of the public's right to know the truth. For Lippmann the function of truth "is to bring to light the hidden facts, to set them in relation to each other, and make a picture of reality on which men can act." In 1922 he doubted, however, that journalists had the expertise to perform that function. He looked instead to political scientists.

Our examples might seem to vindicate his doubt, but they do not illustrate inadequacies inherent in journalism. They show individual and collective failures in responsibility and ethics caused by the pressure of journalistic convention on journalistic principle. They show also that when journalists are partly relieved of the conventional requirement to be fast and first—as were Boyd and Hoyt, Woodward and Bernstein—they can meet the responsibilities journalists have defined for themselves, and make a picture of reality in time for people to act upon it. Political science, like most scholarship, does not try to meet such a demanding deadline.

New Technology and the News

New technology may offer some relief from the tyranny of the deadline. For newspapers the move from linotype and hot metal to computerized photo-composition and cold type can save an hour or more in composing and printing. For television the move from the film camera and film to the video minicamera and videotape virtually eliminates the hours once needed for transporting and processing film. In 1977 the news media were in various stages of transition from the old to the new. Briefly, here is how the extremes differ.

NEWSPAPERS: THE OLD TECHNOLOGY

Typically a newspaper has been produced in four main stages:

1. Copy goes from the reporter's typewriter to a copy editor and then to a compositor at a linotype machine. The compositor types out the story on a huge keyboard and the machine produces slugs from hot metal equivalent to lines of type of column width in the newspaper. An inked roller is put over the type to produce a proof of the story for copy editors to check. Corrections are inserted in type on the linotype machines, pictures and advertisements are made into blocks, and the made-up page is set on a flat bed.
2. In the foundry the page is impressed onto a solid mold which is then curved to fit the rotary presses. Hot metal is poured into the mold to make the plate from which the paper is finally printed.
3. Huge rotary presses print the papers.
4. The papers are then sorted and bundled, ready for dispatch to newspaper distribution points by truck, train, or airplane.

The schedules of these delivery systems and the time taken for printing the papers determine the reporter's deadline.

Technological developments in electronic newsgathering have given television greater speed and flexibility in covering events live. (CBS photo)

NEWSPAPERS: THE NEW TECHNOLOGY

The new technology eliminates steps 1 and 2; no type is made at all. Reporters type their stories directly into a computer via a video display terminal (VDT). The VDT is a computer-linked television screen for viewing the copy in the computer and has a keyboard much like a typewriter's so that reporters and editors can type and edit the copy directly into the computer. The end product for the printing plant, then, is not hot metal but a set of computer instructions on paper or magnetic tape for a machine that turns them into a photocopy of type.

Steps 3 and 4 may also be eliminated one day. Technology already exists to deliver newspapers electronically directly into the home where readers can receive on a television screen whatever they want from the available news of the day.

TELEVISION: ELECTRONIC NEWS GATHERING (ENG)

Although the initial investment is high—in 1977 an ENG camera cost about $50,000, a film camera only $15,000—ENG had certain major advantages over film.

Because videotape is reusable, and is therefore much cheaper than film, reporters can cover events comprehensively without concern for cost, although clearly they must be concerned about time for editing. But use of tape cuts out the time it takes to transport and develop film and allows more time for editing. Moreover, the instantly available tape can be edited electronically as opposed to the comparatively time-consuming cut-and-splice process of film editing.

ENG increases the capability of covering events live. In 1977 many television stations had mobile vans fully equipped with ENG apparatus and able to move quickly to the scene of breaking news, so permitting more spontaneous, less programed news reporting than typically occurs with use of film. The story can be transmitted three ways:

1. It can be videotaped directly for later use;
2. It can be fed live by cable into a rented telephone line to the television news studio; or
3. It can be relayed live by microwave from a mobile van to a receiving station.

The speed and flexibility of ENG have opened new problems of responsibility that were dividing television news executives and reporters still unsure of ENG's appropriate use.

In August 1977 KPRC-TV in Houston happened to have a mobile unit near a four-story building from which a man was threatening to jump. He did, but cameraman Ken Cockroft decided not to let the camera follow the man down. He switched on his camera again once the man was on the ground. Cockroft may have been influenced in his decision by the controversy surrounding the series of photographs taken by Boston *Herald American* photographer Stanley Forman in July 1975 of a young woman and a two-year-old child plunging five stories from a collapsed fire escape. AP and UPI picked up the pictures and within a short time they appeared on the front pages of more than 250 newspapers in the United States and abroad. Readers reacted violently, accusing the newspapers of voyeurism, poor taste, irresponsibility, and invasion of privacy. KPRC-TV received dozens of complaints for showing the man on the building and then on the ground. Nevertheless, Cockroft's boss, KPRC-TV's news and public affairs director Ray Miller, felt that Cockroft should have captured the whole event on tape and allowed Miller to make the editorial decision. Despite the complaints, Miller said he probably would have shown the jump.

In February 1977 Anthony Kiritsis wired a loaded shotgun around the neck of a mortgage company executive and took him across town in Indianapolis to Kiritsis' apartment, an event that WRTV's mobile unit captured on tape. Kiritsis held the executive hostage for three days, during which he demanded that the mortgage company apologize for its treatment of him. The prosecutor asked WRTV to carry the firm's apology live so that Kiritsis, who was watching television in his apartment, could watch. WRTV did so. After three days, Kiritsis emerged with the shotgun still wired to the executive's neck and held a press conference. He delivered a tirade against the mortgage company, using violent and foul language. WRTV covered the conference live. WTHR, a competitor, which had set up its live mobile unit outside Kiritsis' apartment and camped there for three days, did not because

How Local Television Covers the News

Coverage of fast-breaking news stories of major importance requires quick action and coordination. When Chicago Mayor Richard Daley died Dec. 20, 1976, WBBM-TV there pulled out all stops, fighting against time in its attempt to provide Chicagoans with complete, factual and in-depth coverage on its 6 o'clock newscast. The following chronicle gives the account of how the station mobilized its news team to meet that challenge.

2:30–3:00 p.m. Assignment editor hears message on citywide fire band: "Get the doctor here quick [900 North Michigan Avenue] with surgical kit."

Assignment editor hears order to all patrol cars on city-wide police band to control traffic in area of 900 North Michigan.

Assignment editor diverts minicam, on another story, to scene.

Assignment editor gets call: "It's the mayor; he's had a heart attack."

Another minicam sent to scene; Bill Kurtis leaves studio from 900 North Michigan. Reporter John Drummond and film crew sent to city hall.

Bill Kurtis broadcasts live from 900; says it looks bad for the mayor.

3:00–3:30 p.m. By 3:05 five minicams and all film crews are covering mayor's death. Reporter Bob Faw and film crew leave for the mayor's neighborhood.

Silent camera and sound crew dispatched to the scene.

Reporter Harry Porterfield sent to Wesley hospital with minicam and film crew. Interviews paramedics who treated the mayor.

Mayor Daley's press secretary tells Kurtis the mayor is dead; city hall officials tell John Drummond the mayor is dead.

Bob Faw and crew sent to funeral home in the mayor's neighborhood.

Reporter Chuck Gomez researches mayor's medical history.

Reporter Burleigh Hines makes contact with black leaders.

Phil Walters, WBBM,-TV's Washington correspondent, calls Illinois congressmen.

3:30 p.m. Donna LaPietra, 6 p.m. news producer, starts machinery to cancel all other news for that evening and commercial inserts.

Kathryn Kiefer gives in-studio bulletins from the time the news of the death is received. Gives that job over and goes to taped man-on-the-street interviews.

Producer Bob Harris begins to put obit together with writers Chris Chandler and Marshall Rosenthal.

Tape is fed continuously (from minicam crew) during afternoon to studio. Editors and writers develop scripts for 6 o-clock news.

5:00–5:30 p.m. Bill Kurtis goes on the air, with no script, drawing information from his own and other reporters' on-the-scene reports.

6:00–7:00 p.m. Bill Kurtis reports, anchors news, including:

Peter Nolan interview with Alderman Vito Marzullo—live.

Kurtis interview with Governor Jim Thompson in studio—live.

John Drummond report on the law concerning succession when a mayor dies.

Phil Walter interview—by phone—with Congressman Don Rostenkowski in Washington.

Kathryn Kiefer live from mayor's fifth-floor city hall office.

Harry Porterfield recap of what happened at scene of death; film of interview with doctor.

Kurtis interview with Cardinal Cody at Cody's home—live.

Reprinted, with permission, from *Broadcasting*, August 22, 1977, p. 46.

of the possibility that Kiritsis would kill the hostage on live television. Some persons criticized WRTV for permitting Kiritsis through the prosecutor to use the station as WTOP in Washington had allowed itself to be used by Hanafi leader Khaalis. Others criticized WRTV for broadcasting Kiritsis' foul language and for risking a killing live on television. Others criticized WTHR for "censoring" its live coverage.

As with many dilemmas of responsibility and ethics in journalism, those that ENG posed in its infancy divided the profession. The dilemmas were not essentially new. The speed of electronic technologies merely gave them particular intensity, and they will surely survive the industry's growing pains with its new technologies. For what these new print and audiovisual technologies mainly permit is the gathering and transmission of more information, faster. In that respect, a technological revolution was occurring in the 1970s comparable in nature and impact to that brought about in the 1830s by improvements in transportation and communications and by the steam-driven rotary press. James Gordon Bennett harnessed the new technologies not only to intensify competition between newspapers by gathering and disseminating more information faster, but also to alter and enlarge the concept of news. The new technologies offer similar opportunities.

Electronic wizardry plays, however, to the reporter's respect for the most up-to-the-minute fact—the latest news is always "better" than the news of five minutes ago. Thus reporters are tempted to use the measure of relief from the deadline that the speed of electronic technology affords to gather and disseminate more of the latest information faster, rather than to reflect on new ways of defining and reporting the news, or simply to reflect on the information that they already have.

A minority of reporters, referred to as "precision journalists," has been sensitive to the potential of electronic—particularly computer—technology, however, and has been trying to adapt the research techniques of the social sciences to journalism so as to supplement the journalist's use of observation and interview, both valuable methods but particularly vulnerable to human error. The techniques of survey analysis, for example, produce information that is more valid than that produced by reporters' traditional reliance on haphazard man-on-the-street interviews. Although the planning and execution of surveys take more time than is usually available to reporters with daily deadlines, precision journalists' use of computers increases the speed and sophistication of analysis. Precision journalists also advocate more use by their colleagues of computer access to and analysis of the information stored in a variety of data banks maintained by government agencies, universities, industry, and commerce. A mass of information that can provide the context that gives meaning to the day's events can be at reporters' fingertips, no farther away than the press of a button.

These new technologies, then, can add significantly to the thoughtful journalist's efforts to refine the techniques of observation and interviewing in a way that reduces the validity of Walter Lippmann's reservations in 1922 about the reporter's training and expertise in analysis and interpretation. Ironically, because of their commercial concern to please consumers of the mass media, publishers and station owners were more excited by scholarly techniques, albeit applied to audience research, than were the journalists they employed. In its use of new technologies and techniques, management was leaping from the late nineteenth into the late twentieth century. Captivated still by the lore and conventions of news, most journalists seemed to be lagging behind.

Notes

1. Lou Cannon, *Reporting: An Inside View* (Sacramento: California Journal Press, 1977), pp. 35–36.
2. Quoted in William L. Rivers, *The Mass Media,* 2nd edition (New York: Harper & Row, 1975), p. 169.
3. Quoted in Rivers, p. 74.
4. Curtis D. MacDougall, *Interpretative Reporting,* 6th edition (New York: Macmillan, 1972), p. 12.
5. J. Herbert Altschull, "What Is News?", *Mass Comm Review,* December 1974, p. 18.
6. Warren Breed, "Social Control in the News Room," in Wilbur Schramm, *Mass Communications,* 2nd edition (Urbana: University of Illinois Press, 1960), pp. 178–194.
7. David Manning White, "The 'Gate Keeper': A Case Study in the Selection of News," *Journalism Quarterly,* 27 (1950), pp. 385–386.
8. Richard H. Rovere, *Senator Joe McCarthy* (Cleveland: World Publishing Company, 1960), p. 166.
9. Raymond Mungo, *Famous Long Ago: My Life and Hard Times with Liberation News Service* (New York: Pocket Books, 1971), pp. 67–68.
10. Walter Lippmann, *Public Opinion* (New York: Free Press, 1965), p. 226.
11. Quoted in William L. Rivers, Theodore Peterson, and Jay W. Jensen, *The Mass Media and Modern Society,* 2nd edition (New York: Holt, Rinehart and Winston, 1971), p. 214.
12. For a full discussion of his experiments in the new journalism, see Tom Wolfe, *The New Journalism* (New York: Harper & Row, 1973), pp. 3–52.
13. Gay Talese, *Fame and Obscurity* (New York: Bantam Books, 1971), p. vii.
14. Timothy Crouse, *The Boys on the Bus* (New York: Ballantine Books, 1974), p. 21.
15. Quoted in Willard Grosvenor Bleyer, *Main Currents in the History of American Journalism* (Boston: Houghton Mifflin, 1927), pp. 349–350.
16. Edward Jay Epstein, *News from Nowhere: Television and the News* (New York: Random House, 1973), pp. 100–101.
17. Epstein, p. 15.
18. Epstein, pp. 4–5.
19. Sharon Lynn Sperry, "Television News As Narrative," in *Television as a Cultural Force* (New York: Praeger Publishers, 1976), p. 131.
20. James M. Perry, *Us & Them: How the Press Covered the 1972 Election* (New York: Clarkson N. Potter, Inc., 1973), p. 195.
21. Quoted in Perry, p. 198. See also Donald S. Kreger, "Press Opinion in the Eagleton Affair," *Journalism Monographs,* August 1974, and Barbara Demick, "Greatest Blunders Ever Told," *MORE* November 1977, p. 37.
22. *Playboy,* November 1976, pp. 63–86.

12

The Professional Persuaders

I'm a professional. This is a professional job [preparing TV commercials for Richard Nixon]. I was neutral toward Nixon when I started. Now I happen to be for him. But that's not the point. The point is, for the money, I'd do it for almost anybody.

EUGENE JONES

The codfish lays ten thousands eggs,
The homely hen lays one.
The codfish never cackles
To tell you what she's done.
And so we scorn the codfish,
While the humble hen we prize,
Which only goes to show you
That it pays to advertise.

Editorial Writers, Columnists, and Reviewers

Story has it that a veteran Western journalist retorted to someone who was lamenting that, in view of its outstanding and informed comment on public affairs, the New York *Evening Post* under the editorship of Edwin Godkin from 1881 to 1899 did not have a larger circulation:

"You idiot," [the journalist] exclaimed with profane emphasis, "don't you know that there isn't a decent editor in the United States who does not want to find out what it has to say on any subject worth writing about, before getting himself on record in cold type?"[1]

In 1866 Godkin himself had rejected the arguments of critics who insisted that the influence of the editorial was declining. He wrote in *The Nation,* which he had helped found in 1865:

> When the world gets to be so intelligent that no man shall be more intelligent than any other man, and no man shall be swayed by his passions and interests, then there will be no need of editorial expressions of opinions, and editorial arguments and appeals will lose their power.[2]

The world has not reached the level of intelligence Godkin described, yet editorial appeals do not have the power that they had in the nineteenth century. This is so partly because personalities such as Horace Greeley, Edwin Godkin, and Joseph Pulitzer no longer dominate a news medium, partly because the FCC requires broadcast licensees to be fair, because a sense of responsibility impels most publishers to offer their publications as forums for the exchange of ideas by printing a range of opinion, much of it syndicated, in addition to their own editorial views.

Syndication had begun in Godkin's time; in 1884 Samuel S. McClure started the first newspaper syndicate. In 1977 about 300 syndicates were selling 10,000 features—columns, articles, comics, and cartoons—for an estimated $100 million a year. The most popular—columnist Jack Anderson, humorist Art Buchwald, and cartoonist Garry Trudeau, creator of the "Doonesbury" strip—each earned about $200,000 a year from the 400 to 600 publications that carried them in 1977. Nevertheless, they usually had to share the page with editorials, with other columns, local and syndicated, and with letters to the editor.

Although much respected and widely read, columnists such as James Reston, David Broder, George Will, Meg Greenfield, Mary McGrory, William F. Buckley, Jr., and James Kilpatrick probably have less influence on public opinion than the media's strictly informational content. That is, news stories may be a greater force in shaping public attitudes than editorials and political columns. And the influence of the columnists is often dependent less on the persuasiveness of their analysis or opinions than on their exclusive access to high levels of government and on the information they are able therefore to report. Political commentator Joseph Kraft observed in 1958, for example: "On some big matters the State Department informs [James Reston] almost automatically, as it would the representative of a major power."[3] The access of individual columnists to such information fluctuates with changes in administration—Reston was cut off during the Nixon Presidency. Invariably, however, top officials find it useful to feed information to favored columnists.

Skillful politicians are more subtle in their use of reporters. Timothy

Crouse has described how President John F. Kennedy cultivated a rising young generation of reporters, most of them college-educated:

> Kennedy played on the values he shared with these young reporters in order to engage their loyalty. He knew many of them socially, and he was careful to treat them with respect and affection. . . . Because they were so obviously in tune with the youthful, "intellectual" atmosphere of the New Frontier, the young reporters who had covered Kennedy's campaign in 1960, and now covered him in office, found their stock soaring. It was no coincidence that many of them—reporters like David Broder, Ben Bradlee, Bob Novak, Rowland Evans, Mary McGrory, and Russell Baker—would become leading journalists in the sixties and seventies, and would help to change the techniques of campaign coverage.[4]

All became successful syndicated columnists, except Bradlee, who became editor of the Washington *Post* and directed the *Post's* investigation of the Nixon Administration's Watergate scandal.

Although their individual influence on public opinion may not be direct, the best of them wield an indirect influence similar to that wielded by Godkin through the respect that they command from their colleagues and from other opinion leaders in society. Crouse quotes a reporter's comment on Pulitzer Prize-winning columnist David Broder that echoes the judgment of the veteran Western journalist in Godkin's time: "Broder's the mark . . . You have to measure your own stuff against what he writes."[5]

In this way, then, leading editorial writers, columnists, and political analysts shape the climate of political opinions which filter through opinion leaders and groups in society. The public is so bombarded by blatant and subtle efforts at persuasion, however—by the outright pitch of advertising, the special pleading of public relations and political rhetoric, and the advocacy, commentary, and criticism of editorials, columns, and reviews—that it is more sophisticated and skeptical and less pliable than it was in the 19th century. Columnists, therefore, have more limited expectations of their power than Godkin had in 1866. John Fischer, a former occupant of "The Easy Chair" in *Harper's,* the oldest column in American journalism (it was started in October 1851), described his function this way in 1970:

> The columnist's job . . . calls for something more than responsible reporting. It requires taking a position. It is not enough for the writer to say, "Here is a bunch of facts. Make what you can out of them." He is obligated to go a step further and say, "I have examined these facts as best I can, discussed them with other knowledgeable people, and arranged them in some kind of order. Here, then, is a conclusion which common sense might draw from them, and a course of action which a reasonable man might follow". . . . The real function of such analytic reporting is to help readers arrive at conclusions of their own. . . . Whether they agree with the columnist's interpretation doesn't much matter. . . . Here, I believe, is the chief justification for any column, in newspaper or magazine. It offers the reader a chance to become familiar enough with a given point of view so that he can use it to work out his own intellectual bearings.[6]

Most editorial writers and columnists would probably agree with Fischer.

So, too, would most reviewers. The influence of reviewers, however, particularly reviewers of the performing arts, on the public's decisions, although not necessarily on the public's opinions, may be greater than that of editorial writers and columnists. Some think reviewers on major newspapers such as the New York *Times* have the power of life and death over a play or an artist's career. Lehman Engel, a composer and conductor in the musical theater, is adamant: the daily reviewer "is the Dow Jones of the theater and it is rare when his judgment, justified or not, fails to coincide with or to cause the end or the beginning of a show's life span."[7] Engel, who is writing here about New York, exaggerates. No single critic in a city with three daily newspapers and several magazines and broadcast stations has such power. Sensitive to this potential power, moreover, most reviewers try to avoid too authoritative a tone. New York *Times* dance and drama critic, Clive Barnes, for example, developed a technique for diminishing the omnipotence of his judgments by "adroitly conveying two things at once, of sometimes both praising and criticizing a production in a single sentence, thus preserving his own integrity and a bit of the box office."[8]

Ultimately the analysis and opinions of reviewers may matter less than the agenda they set. That is, the necessity to choose certain books, films, plays, and musical and other entertainment events for discussion and to ignore others probably·has as much, if not more, effect on what the public knows and thinks about the arts and entertainment than any of the reviewers' words of praise or contempt.

Although perceived as professional persuaders, editorial writers, columnists, and reviewers perform more of an informational and analytical function than a persuasive one. The measure of agreement that they win from their readers and viewers no doubt flatters their egos. Their object, however, is to make the public think rather than to make it think as they do. In that way they differ from advertisers and public relations experts, who have a vested interest in persuading the public to agree with them, specifically to buy the goods and services that they sell and to accept the images that they purvey.

Advertising and Public Relations

Because every major enterprise with a shred of sensitivity now engages experts to build a favorable image through public relations or advertising or both, it was probably inevitable that image building would become a large and sensitive enterprise and that the experts would set about constructing a favorable public image for themselves. So it is that public relations specialists in the United States have been turning ever more assiduously to developing general respect for their craft, and the respectability the men and women in advertising are equally concerned with promoting of their own calling.

A few advertising and PR people have confessed in their memoirs that they did work they detested for money they didn't earn to buy things they didn't need to impress people they didn't like. With most of them, however, to ask for a definition of public relations or advertising invites a lofty response. When one advertising trade paper asked a number of the leading public relations firms to define their role, the typical answer was: "Public relations is the skilled communication of ideas to the various publics with the object of producing a desired result." The most widely repeated definition, which was offered by Cyril W. Plattes, manager of the department of public services for General Mills, ran:

> Public Relations is that responsibility and function of management which (1) analyzes public interest and determines public attitudes, (2) identifies and interprets policies and programs of an organization, and (3) executes a program of action to merit acceptance and good will.

Perhaps the most widely accepted definition of the role of advertising was written by Frederick R. Gamble, former president of the American Association of Advertising Agencies:

> Advertising is the counterpart in distribution of the machine in production. By the use of machines, our production of goods and services multiplies the selling effort. Advertising is the great accelerating force in distribution. Reaching many people rapidly at low cost, advertising speeds up sales, turns prospects into customers in large numbers and at high speed. Hence, in a mass-production and high-consumption economy, advertising has the greatest opportunity and the greatest responsibility for finding customers.[9]

Gamble's insight is valuable, but it fails to point up the essential similarity of public relations and advertising. Although advertising certainly does accelerate distribution, and it is most obviously at work in pushing particular brands, like public relations it is centrally concerned with winning acceptance and goodwill—for products, for people, for companies, for ideas. The difference between advertising and public relations is in method, and this difference dictates a different use of the mass media. Martin Mayer, author of *Madison Avenue, U.S.A.,* makes the distinction:

> Advertising, whatever its faults, is a relatively open business; its messages appear in paid space or on bought time, and everybody can recognize it as special pleading. Public relations works behind the scenes; occasionally the hand of the p.r. man can be seen shifting some bulky fact out of sight, but usually the public relations practitioner stands at the other end of a long rope which winds around several pulleys before it reaches the object of his invisible tugging. . . . The advertising man must know how many people he can reach *with* the media, the public relations man must know how many people he can reach *within* the media.[10]

Essentially public relations and advertising are selling devices. Their basic aims are so alike that they are, in fact, often linked—some advertising agencies have public relations departments, some public relations firms have advertising departments, many corporations place advertising and public relations in a single department—and they are linked, too, in the public consciousness.

Public Relations

To increase the sale of garbage cans for a client, one public relations firm drew up a model ordinance ostensibly designed to protect public health by preventing or controlling the spread of diseases carried by rats. Among other things the ordinance provided that all garbage must be deposited in containers of galvanized steel or other nonrusting material. After the ordinance had been approved by the U.S. Public Health Service, the public relations firm sent copies of it, along with promotional kits, to every city and county health officer in the United States. Within a year more than 300 cities had adopted the ordinance. The sales of substantial garbage cans multiplied.

Edward J. Bernays, noted public relations expert, used a different approach to stimulate the sale of bacon for a client: He got physicians to advocate hearty breakfasts. To promote the sale of luggage, he arranged for society leaders to come forth with the statement that a woman should take at least three dresses along on even the most informal weekend visit. The public relations department of the Pan American Coffee Bureau once set out to make the employees' coffee break, which had become common during World War II, an American institution. It surveyed top management on the benefits and drawbacks of the coffee break, then publicized the findings. It sent forth a flood of publicity about companies that had found that the coffee breaks improved morale, increased efficiency, and reduced employee fatigue. And in the 1960s, when coffee sales slumped, one public relations firm tried to increase consumption among soft-drink-conscious young people by encouraging the establishment of coffee houses.

The difference between these approaches and a national advertising campaign to promote sales is obvious. And Martin Mayer's point about the PR man who "stands at the other end of a long rope which winds around several pulleys" should be equally obvious.

But public relations practitioners are often concerned with much more than the sale of products. Their objective may be to change the public image of an individual or corporation or to alter public attitudes toward company policies. The Illinois Central Railroad, slicing north to south across mid-America, was once stigmatized as being controlled by Wall Street. In 1938 the company made three changes to remove conditions that contributed to that impression. It moved its financial offices from New York to Chicago, replaced its directors from the East with businessmen from along its route, and began to hold its monthly directors' meetings in Chicago instead of New York.

OBJECTIVES

Public relations are those aspects of our behavior that have social consequences. As Harwood L. Childs puts it:

Our problem in each corporation or industry is to find out what these activities are, what social effects they have, and, if they are contrary to the public interest, to find ways and means of modifying them so that they will serve the public interest.[11]

What is the public interest? In effect, says Childs, it is what the public says it is.

Because American business persists in emphasizing words rather than deeds, it is wasting enormous sums of money on ineffective efforts to convert the public, according to Bernays. Public relations, he believes, must emerge as a form of social statesmanship. Its practitioner, with the full cooperation of his clients, must attempt, as his four objectives:

To define the social objectives of his client or to help him define them.

To find out what maladjustments there are between these objectives and the elements in our society on which his client is dependent. These maladjustments may be distortions in the mind of the public due to misinformation, ignorance, or apathy, or they may be distortions due to unsound action by the client.

To attempt to adjust the client's policies and actions to society so that the maladjustments may be resolved.

To advise the client on ways and means by which his new policies and actions, or old policies and actions, if it is deemed advisable to retain them, may be understood by the public.[12]

HISTORY

The term public relations seems first to have been used in its modern sense in the closing years of the nineteenth century. One of the first to use it was Dorman Eaton of the Yale Law School in 1882 in an address, "The Public Relations and Duties of the Legal Profession." In 1906 and again in 1913 it turned up in talks by executives of the Baltimore and Ohio Railroad about railroads and their problems of "public relations." It was fairly common by the 1920s, when Bernays coined the expression "public relations counsel," although it was ridiculed as an absurdly pompous synonym for the use of press agents.

Shortly before World War II the term became imbedded in the vocabulary of American business. In its issue of March 1939, *Fortune* observed:

The year 1938 may go down in the annals of industry as the season in which the concept of public relations suddenly struck home to the hearts of a whole generation of businessmen, much as first love comes mistily and overpoweringly to the adolescent. Indeed, during 1938 there was scarcely a convention that did not feature an address on public relations, scarcely a trade magazine that did not devote some space to the subject, scarcely a board of directors that did not deliberate weightily on the powers of the new goddess. And they found that the sphere of this Mona Lisa was all of industry and that she presided over its most bewildering and least tangible aspects.

But if the term is fairly recent, the practice is certainly not new in this country. Some historians say that public relations in America expanded after the Civil War, gained ground as a result of the onslaughts on big

business at the turn of the century, emerged as a new profession in the
1920s when it began to tap the techniques of the social sciences, and came
of age in the 1930s when the Depression convinced management of its
need.

Publicists in the early days were press agents for politicians, stage shows,
and circuses, and later for hotels, railroads, and shipping interests. They
tricked, cajoled, and bribed newspapers into giving them space in the news
columns. Some of them used techniques and tools employed by present-
day public relations counselors. P. T. Barnum, that master promoter, had a
fine talent for creating events that became legitimate news. Thus he
arranged for one of his major attractions, General Tom Thumb, to have an
audience with Queen Victoria. Here is an example of creating news on the
one hand and of obtaining the testimonial of a prominent figure on the
other. But Barnum's public relations went beyond mere words. To build
goodwill for himself, he gave lectures for charity and contributed to welfare
societies. To overcome church opposition to his shows, he emphasized their
Christian character and admitted clergymen and their wives free.

Several historical developments sharpened the interest of business and
industry in public relations. One may have been the reaction to the robber
barons who dominated the period of headlong industrial expansion after the
Civil War. As they felled their forests, took their oil and ore from the earth,
and built their railroads and factories, they held labor in close check,
squeezed out their competitors, manipulated corporations and stocks, and
bought legislation for their own benefit. They took the view that what they
did and how they did it were their own concerns. Their attitude was
exemplified in the public mind by Vanderbilt's phrase, "The public be
damned!"

As abuses mounted, so did public criticism. Critics and reformers
shouted against corruption in business and politics. Muckraking magazines
exposed the evils perpetrated by the railroads, packing companies, oil
companies, insurance firms, patent-medicine manufacturers, and political
bosses. The government investigated antilabor practices and passed legislation regulating lobbies, monopolies, and the food and drug trade. For a time
the individualistic entrepreneur passed from public hero to public villain.

Business and industry seem to have begun showing a conscious—
perhaps a self-conscious—regard for the effects of their policies on the
public in the last years of the nineteenth century. The acknowledged
pioneer was the Bell Telephone Company under Theodore Vail, who saw
as early as 1883 that sound policies were as important as pious words. That
year, requesting a report from an affiliate in Iowa, he asked, "Where there
has been any conflict between the local Exchange and the public, what has
been the cause of the difficulties, and what has been the result?" When Vail
saw that male telephone operators lacked the necessary tact and patience,
he replaced them with women. In 1908 the company launched a campaign,
which has continued down to the present in its basic approach, to give the
public facts about the telephone system, to tell how calls should be made,

and to urge subscribers to answer their telephones promptly. The company schooled its employees in dealing politely and sympathetically with the public. Sensitive to charges of monopoly, the company recognized that the impressions people got about it were from contacts with its employees. As one vice president of the company said in 1909, "They know us as a monopoly, and that creates hostility at once because the public does not like monopolies. They have no opportunity to see us or know us. . . ." It is probably significant that the telephone companies, leaders in public relations, have emerged virtually unscathed from governmental investigations. In fact, telephone companies have had an amazing record. Not until telephone service became erratic in many urban areas in 1969 and 1970—a consequence of inadequate forecasts of needs for service—was there widespread dissatisfaction.

A second cause of the interest in public relations no doubt was World War I, in part because the war itself was charged by many to the influence of Eastern business, especially Wall Street. Then the vast outpouring of war propaganda on an unprecedented scale demonstrated the efficacy of words in shaping public attitudes. This intensified a general concern with the whole broad subject of public opinion on the part of scholars and laymen alike. And it gave experience in opinion manipulation on a large scale to some people who, with the peace, were to use their skills on behalf of business.

A third factor affecting the course of public relations was probably the Depression of the 1930s. Public faith in the free enterprise system declined, and thousands of Americans listened attentively to new prophets with their share-the-wealth plans and other cures for economic ills. Besides selling products, American business had to resell itself to the public. Its task was complicated by labor troubles and unrest. Words might still be an indispensable tool of public relations, but policies in accord with the public interest seemed even to the less public-spirited to take on an increased importance.

By 1949, according to *Fortune*, 4000 corporations had public relations departments or programs; in addition, there were 500 commercial public relations firms, supported mainly by business. Today churches, schools, colleges, medical associations, philanthropic organizations, social-welfare agencies, and government bodies all have public relations departments. Because of the difficulty of defining a professional public relations person, it is impossible to estimate their number. Not all people working in public relations are members, but in 1970 The Public Relations Society of America, Inc., had about 7000 members. (To qualify for associate membership, a person must have worked one year in public relations activities. Full members must have worked five years in public relations and must take an examination.) By 1977 membership had risen to about 8500.

CRITICISMS

Public relations people—who helped transform robber barons into benign philanthropists in the public image—ironically have never enjoyed good public relations themselves. Today journalists, from whose ranks

Campaigns to win the support of the public for American efforts in World War I gave experience to some people who with the peace were to use such public relations skills on behalf of business. (United Press International photo)

many public relations specialists are recruited, tend to look down on them— perhaps a little in envy of their higher salaries, perhaps much more in disdain of their "selling out to the special interests." Intellectuals scorn them as insincere hired manipulators, sometimes sinister, sometimes no more than offensive. The very term "public relations counsel" suggests the status seeking that led undertakers to call themselves morticians, janitors to call themselves maintenance engineers, and garbage collectors to call themselves sanitary haulers. The fact is that today's public relations worker has inherited a legacy of criticism. The criticism goes back to the press agents of the nineteenth century, whose tactics aroused the enmity of editors, publishers, and just plain casual observers. From 1908 through the 1920s, the American Newspaper Publishers Association conducted a campaign against free publicity and free advertising. The trade press repeatedly denounced

Public Relations

385

press agents, with which public relations people were regarded as synonymous. In 1913 there were even attempts to make the use of press agents a legal offense.

Recognizing some criticisms, the Public Relations Society of America stated in its 1969 booklet, *An Occupational Guide to Public Relations:*

> Because it is a young field which does not enjoy full understanding, public relations is sometimes not as well accepted as most other basic functions of management. This may detract from the status and security of its workers. While the work is allied to professionalism, it suffers from the absence of standards and definite boundary lines. Because it is concerned with influencing public opinion, it is often difficult to measure the results of performance, and, therefore to "sell" the worth of public relations programs. In the consulting field, competition is keen and if a firm loses an account, some of its personnel may be affected.
>
> Because of the dangers inherent in the exercise of persuasion and because of questionable tactics of fringe operations, all public relations has received considerable criticism. Public relations involves much more hard work and less glamour than is popularly supposed. The demands it makes for continual tact and for anonymity will be considered by some as less inviting features.

MODERN PUBLIC RELATIONS

Public relations is a large umbrella that covers many specialists, and the great majority of them protest that they should not be equated with the press agents who follow in the Barnum tradition. Indeed, they contend that publicity is only one facet of modern public relations—one among many tools used in many media. A news story, a speech, a film, a photograph—each is a tool of public relations. The channels that carry the tools—a newspaper, a club meeting at which a film is shown, a magazine—are media.

There is much more to the modern concept of public relations than the simple creation of publicity. Bernays and others began bringing a degree of respectability to a much-maligned craft by promoting the Total Program. They argued that public relations must run deeper than mere publicity. Bernays pointed out:

> The (company) president's acceptance of membership on advisory boards of national importance—indicates corporate interest in the national welfare. Speaking engagements of plant managers before local service groups highlight management's civic mindedness. .... All of these symbol-projected themes—civic mindedness, interest in education and youth and the like—gradually form a composite and favorable picture in the public mind.[13]

How the Total Program works and how it has been developed over the years is illustrated by the experiences of Paul Garrett, who was the only public relations employee of General Motors when he joined the company in 1931. When Garrett arrived at company headquarters in Detroit, he was asked, "How do you make a billion dollars look small?" Acutely sensitive about the company's size and visibility in troubled times, the management's chief aim was to grow inconspicuously. Garrett said not only that he could not answer the question; he did not think providing an answer was part of his job. Public relations is the practice of winning confidence, he argued, not putting on an act. As a consequence of his prodding, General Motors has engaged over the years in a wide-ranging permanent program calculated to win acceptance and goodwill. The program resulted eventually in the company's setting up related departments known as Plant City and Field Relations, Educational Relations, Speakers Bureau, and Institutional Advertising—all designed to persuade everyone that General Motors is a desirable, if huge, concern. When Garrett retired as a vice president after 25 years, General Motors was spending more than $1 million a year on a public relations program that involved more than 200 employees. The strength of this program may help to explain how GM was able to resist so successfully the challenges to its policies that developed in 1970. Part of a movement against destruction of the environment, the campaign was primarily devoted to convincing institutional owners of GM stock, especially universities, that they should help reform the company.

It is a measure of the importance of PR in the modern economy that public relations specialists are holding scores of corporate vice presidencies and that many are serving as company directors. The atmosphere has proved so heady that PR people speak increasingly of their "profession" and its fast-developing "prestige." One leading counselor, E. Edward Pendray, even holds that "To public relations men must go the most important social engineering role of them all—the gradual reorganization of human society piece by piece and structure by structure."

There is reason to doubt this sweeping role, and even more reason to question some of the methods of modern PR. This became especially clear when the firm of Carl Byoir & Associates undertook to defeat a bill that would have allowed increased size and weight limits for trucks on Pennsylvania roads. Byoir was paid $150,000 by the Eastern Railroads Presidents Conference. The firm earned the money in devious ways, primarily by setting up front organizations—the New Jersey Citizens Tax Study Foundation, the Empire State Transport League—to feed publicity unfavorable to truckers into Pennsylvania. The governor vetoed the bill, but the truckers brought a suit that eventually disclosed methods the presiding judge summed up as "the big lie." He commented, "This technique, as it appears from the evidence in this case, has been virtually adopted *in toto* by certain public relations firms under the less insidious and more palatable name of the third-party technique."

Perhaps more important is the case of the attempted takeover of the American Broadcasting Company (ABC) by the International Telephone and Telegraph Company (ITT). It was a friendly takeover in that ABC wanted to merge with ITT, a huge conglomerate with 433 separate boards of directors operating in more than 40 countries. But some senators and representatives, the Department of Justice, and especially three members of the FCC—Commissioners Robert Bartley, Kenneth Cox, and Nicholas Johnson—feared the takeover. Commissioner Johnson explained:

The merger would have placed ABC, one of the largest purveyors of news and opinion in America, under the control of one of the largest conglomerate corporations in the world. . . . Consider simply that the integrity of the news judgment of ABC might be affected by the economic interests of ABC—that ITT might simply view ABC's programming as a part of ITT's public relations, advertising, or political activities.

Events of 1967 indicated that Commissioner Johnson's fears were justified. He has written:

During the April, 1967, hearings, while this very issue was being debated, the *Wall Street Journal* broke a story . . . that ITT was going to extraordinary lengths to obtain favorable press coverage of those very hearings. Eventually three reporters were summoned before the examiner to relate for the official record the incidents that were described in the *Journal's* exposé.

An AP and a UPI reporter testified to several phone calls to their homes by ITT public relations men, variously asking them to change their stories and make inquiries for ITT with regard to stories by other reporters, and to use their influence as members of the press to obtain for ITT confidential information from the Department of Justice regarding its intentions. Even more serious were several encounters between ITT officials and New York *Times* reporter Eileen Shanahan.

On one of these occasions ITT's senior vice president in charge of public relations went to the reporter's office. After criticizing her dispatches to the *Times* about the case in a tone which she described as "accusatory and certainly nasty," he asked whether she had been following the price of ABC and ITT stock. When she indicated that she had not, he asked if she didn't feel she had a "responsibility to the shareholders who might lose money as a result of what she wrote." She replied, "My responsibility is to find out the truth and print it."[14]

Leading spokesmen for public relations argue that only a small percentage of the practitioners use devious methods and that the entire profession should not be tarred with the same brush.

William A. Durbin of Hill and Knowlton noted in March 1975, however, that the problem was larger than mere incidents of scurvy behavior by isolated individuals:

Unfortunately, many businessmen—including several who retain outside PR counsel or employ PR staffs—look on public relations as a magic wall to shield them from public view, or as a cosmetic that improves their company's image, or as a kind of deodorant spray that kills odors without disturbing germs. Or they look on communications as a means of telling *their* side of the story, rather than a way of hearing out their critics, of learning more about the other person's grievance or of getting a deeper understanding of the opposition's point of view. This is *also* communication, perhaps the more important part of the total process.

Durbin also indicted journalists for their shortcomings in reporting about the increasingly complex public issues of the 1970s:

As the news becomes less amenable to exposition and evaluation, competent personnel may not always be available or equal to these tasks, because of false economies imposed on media staffing. . . .

Quantitative and qualitative shortcomings of media staff can result in an unhealthy dependence, by underprepared and overworked communicators, on handouts from the very same factions on whose arguments and accusations the public wants to be guided or, at least, objectively informed. The harsh realities of communications *as a business* have come to place a premium on shallowness masquerading as succinctness and on glibness masquerading as expertise.

A wall has traditionally divided public relations and journalism. Journalists expect PR practitioners to try to manipulate them, PR practitioners expect journalists to be suspicious, even hostile. Durbin recommends one bridge in what is properly a somewhat adversarial relationship:

[T]he businessman must at least level with the public about all aspects of his business that affect the public welfare. He must reach toward the public, working as best he can through the appropriate opinion leaders: media people, educators, environmentalists, consumerists, even militant "public advocates" to the extent that they are reachable by frankness and the facts.[15]

Durbin's prescriptions are by no means new. In preparing *Crystallizing Public Opinion* in 1923, one of the first book-length discussions of public relations, Edward Bernays surveyed newspaper publishers and editors among other opinion leaders and reported:

The journalist of to-day, while still watching the machinations of the so-called "press agent" with one half-amused eye, appreciates the value of the service the public relations counsel is able to give him.

Bernays added:

It is because he acts as the purveyor of truthful, accurate and verifiable news to the press that the conscientious and successful counsel on public relations is looked upon with favor by the journalist.[16]

Political PR

As the mass media have moved to a pivotal position in elections, political public relations, which includes political advertising, has grown important. This became especially apparent in 1968, when Richard Nixon won the Presidency partly because of shrewd use of television. The three men who guided Nixon—Roger Ailes, Harry Treleaven, and Al Scott—were soon besieged with other offers.

In 1970 Treleaven was the chief strategist for senatorial campaigns in Florida, Tennessee, Michigan, and Texas. In some cases the fee for this kind of management can range as high as 10 percent of the campaign advertising budget—a budget close to a million dollars in a big state.

Men who know how to use the mass media have been working in political campaigns for decades, but they became the central figures only in 1952. The election of Dwight Eisenhower marked the grand entrance into politics of public relations and advertising specialists. Now the task of reaching the electorate has become so complex and technical that politicians must recruit communications specialists to wage a campaign that will achieve significant exposure.

The campaign audience consists of two groups. The members of one group use and believe the print media, although they are likely to attend to television as well. They are concerned and informed about issues and already have moderate to strong loyalties to one of the parties. They are more likely to vote than are others, probably for a candidate they decide upon early in the campaign. The aim of the candidate in appealing to them is to reinforce the commitments of those who favor him. He is unlikely to be able to convert the others.

The second group, which is larger—and growing—relies primarily on television and radio. The members of this group command most of the attention of the professional persuader, for they are not very well informed. Although people of all backgrounds are represented, within this group are large numbers of those of low to moderate income, little education, little interest in politics, and much more experience with TV, film, and recording personalities than in deciding public issues. This is the audience that Robert MacNeil described as "moderately more sophisticated and somewhat better informed than that of a generation ago, but it is basically conservative and, from its reading habits, passive and incurious about the world. Because it is not particularly interested in many subjects and issues, it will apparently accept what it is told about them more or less trustingly."[17] Such an audience is made to order for the political persuader.

Or it was in 1968 when MacNeil wrote his book. Largely because of the impact of Joe McGinniss's account in *The Selling of the President, 1968* of public relations and advertising methods in Richard Nixon's campaign, the press was alert to these methods in the 1972 election. How candidates were "sold" became major news stories in coverage of the campaign. Whether such exposure of political advertising contributed to public cynicism about the political process is not really clear, but the turnout for the 1972 Presidential election was the lowest in 20 years. In 1948, 51.1 percent of the voting-age population voted in the Presidential election; over 60 percent voted in 1960, 1964, and 1968; in 1972, 55.4 percent of those eligible voted. The 1972 voting-age population included 18-year-olds for the first time, but young voters proved to be even more apathetic than older voters. The political dirty tricks of the 1972 campaign revealed in the Watergate exposures seem to have deepened public cynicism. In the 1976 Presidential primaries, only about a third of those eligible voted; only 53 percent voted in the Presidential election itself. Polls during the primaries revealed familiar reasons for not voting—nonvoters did not consider voting an effective way to achieve change, they did not think their vote would mean much. But some nonvoters gave a new reason—they did not want to feel responsible for the result.

Despite the apparent apathy of voters, perhaps because of it, politicians spend mind-boggling sums of money on their campaigns. Approximately

$138 million was spent in the 1972 Presidential campaign and $425 million altogether for the Presidential, Congressional and other elective offices that year. Because of the way much of this money was misused in 1972, a campaign finance law was passed in 1974 putting a ceiling on campaign spending and contributions and authorizing public funds for part of the cost of the 1976 primaries and most of the cost of the general elections. Since 1972 Americans have had the option of checking off $1 contributions on their income tax forms for the Presidential campaign, and the Internal Revenue Service estimated that about $100 million had accumulated for the 1976 election. In the primaries about $11 million was made available to qualified candidates and about $22 million to each major party for the campaign after the party conventions.

It is to deploy these huge sums most effectively that candidates hire communication specialists. The 1976 campaign of President Gerald Ford, for example, was managed by Campaign '76 Media Communications, Inc., an ad hoc agency created for the purpose, drawing its specialists from the advertising industry. Peter Dailey, the chairman, was a Los Angeles advertising man who had helped manage Richard Nixon's 1972 campaign; executive vice president and manager of Campaign '76 was Bruce Wagner, on leave from Grey Advertising, Inc., in New York. SFM Media Services Corp., New York, handled local buying for the Ford campaign. Ronald Reagan, Ford's opponent in the Republican primaries, hired Ball & McDaniel of Nashville as the agency for his campaign. Harry Treleaven, who had directed Nixon's campaigns in 1968 and 1972, was Reagan's creative director. Ruth Jones, Ltd., was the campaign's media time buyer. Gerald Rafshoon Advertising, Inc., of Atlanta, which had handled Jimmy Carter's campaigns for 19 years, handled all of the Democratic Presidential candidate's media work in the 1976 campaign.

The names of the agencies and individuals are less important than what they suggest about the nature of modern political campaigns. No longer do candidates rely on the wisdom of political cronies and advisers for campaign management; professionals, almost all of them from the advertising industry, are now in charge. But for all the money and professional media expertise, voters survive as a relatively unmanageable lot. One of the misleading conclusions that Joe McGinniss's account dictated was that Nixon won in 1968 because of the wizardry of his media professionals, Ailes, Treleaven, and Scott. The reasons for his victory were much more complex, among them being the crippling disarray and internal bitterness of the Democratic Party, the nation's majority party. As Democrats pulled themselves somewhat together in the final weeks of the campaign, Senator Hubert Humphrey narrowed the gap, and some observers have argued that had the election been held a week later Humphrey would have won.

In the 1976 primaries George Wallace had one of the richest campaign chests of the Democratic contenders. In 1972 he had been a disconcerting force in the Democratic Party primaries, with a mesmerizing effect at political rallies. But the assassination attempt in 1972 that confined him to a wheelchair changed his campaign style for 1976. He stayed clear of crowds and committed most of his considerable funds to the media, particularly to television. While the other candidates were out pressing the flesh, Wallace blitzed audiences with 30-second commercials 15 days before each primary. Six days before the voting, he added 30-minute television shows to his 30-second spots, sometimes four in the final week—a staggeringly expensive form of campaigning that none of his rivals could afford to anything like the same extent. But in 1976 Wallace turned out to be no threat whatsoever.

Because broadcast advertising is so expensive, most candidates in the 1976 primaries used 30- and 60-second commercials, which have long been criticized as wholly inadequate for giving the voter anything more than a notion of the candidate's "image." WGN Continental Broadcasting Co. in Chicago shared this view, and since 1956 had refused to sell time for political advertising in less than five-minute periods. Thus when Campaign '76 Media Communications, Inc., President Ford's campaign advertising agency, tried to buy 30- and 60-second spots before the Illinois primary in March 1976, WGN refused. Campaign '76 appealed to the FCC. The commission overturned the WGN policy, a majority saying that they respected the WGN position but did not believe that Congress intended to allow broadcasters to overrule a candidate's determination that his political interests would be better served by spot announcements than by five-minute broadcasts. Congress had also specified that a candidate should receive treatment equal to that afforded a broadcaster's "most favored commercial advertiser." So if WGN was willing to sell spot time to commercial advertisers, it could not deny spot time to candidates wanting to buy it. Then in one of those reversals that bewilder and infuriate broadcasters, the FCC decided in May 1977 that its ruling in the WGN case had been wrong. By a 4-to-3 vote, the FCC held that Congress intended political candidates to have parity with advertisers only as to price, not as to length of the commercials that they might buy.

No matter how scientifically prepared, political advertising is no more successful than commercial advertising. Each year thousands of new products come on the market promoted with elaborate and ingenious advertising. Each year some sell, many do not, for reasons that are not necessarily clear. And the same process occurs with political candidates. Obviously, skillfully and professionally managed media campaigns are important to a candidate's success, but we need to keep their persuasive power in perspective. McGinniss showed how Nixon had been packaged and sold like soap or detergent in 1968. Most candidates are similarly handled by their campaign media agencies. The point is that the public knows it.

The content and purposes of political advertising, like those of commercial advertising, are transparent. Although often more ambiguous and subtle, the content and purposes of PR are also fundamentally transparent. At root these forms of persuasion offer information of potential value to appropriately skeptical journalists and citizens. Because the information is invariably selective does not mean that it is dishonest or worthless. The journalist's professed disdain for PR is, for the most part, no more than hypocritical posturing. Most journalists acknowledge that the honest practice of PR by government, industry, and commerce is an invaluable service. Without it, journalists would have to spend precious time digging up or merely gathering routine information. Or perhaps they, and therefore the public, would never know of genuinely newsworthy information. When the public is fed PR in the guise of news, however, journalists are responsible, not PR people.

Advertising

In 1923 Claude Hopkins wrote: "The time has come when advertising has in some hands reached the status of a science."[18] Hopkins, who was reputed to be the best of the copywriters, was referring only to mail-order advertising, which involved printing coupons in ads that consumers could clip and send in with a dollar or so to receive a product. It was possible to gauge roughly the effectiveness of mail-order advertising by the numbers of returns, as Hopkins demonstrated in his 20,000-word book and in hundreds of mail-order campaigns.

Mail order is still an important facet of advertising, but, as the mass media show every day, there are many other kinds, and it is seldom possible

THE NUMBER ONE KILLER OF YOUNG AMERICANS IS YOUNG AMERICANS.

You march against war. You fight for clean air and clean water. You eat natural foods. You practice yoga. You are so much for life. And you are so much against killing.

It would be unthinkable for you to kill another human being on purpose.

So then, why is this happening?

You don't mean to be. But you are. The numbers are simpl...

DRUNK DRIVER...

Advertisers have adapted their techniques to public interest ad campaigns.

to measure the effect of each with any real precision. Nonetheless, the methods of the behavioral sciences are so evident throughout the structure of the advertising world that it is clear that modern merchandising is attempting to make Hopkins's prescriptions apply to all advertising. Nearly every major agency spends a large share of its annual budget on research and on continuous efforts to take some of the guesswork out of appealing to masses of consumers.

Research in advertising is far too complicated to discuss in detail, but some understanding of the broad aims is available through considering the four major kinds of appeals, which have been described by Albert Frey, an expert in marketing:

> Primary: those aimed at inducing the purchase of one *type* of product.
> Selective: those aimed at inducing the purchase of a brand.
> Emotional: (sometimes termed *short-circuit* and *human-interest*
> appeals): those aimed at the emotions rather than the intellect.
> Rational: (sometimes termed *long-circuit* and *reason-why* appeals): those
> directed at the intellect.[19]

Advertising specialists at *The Reader's Digest* developed a detailed list of appeals, which they called an "Index of Human Emotions Which Will Actuate the Greatest Number of Prospects to Buy." It is a useful list, but there is, of course, a distinct limit to the value of analyzing appeals, in part because selling depends on so many other influences.

General analysis is limited, too, by the fact that leading figures have some highly individual notions as to how advertising should be presented. One example is Rosser Reeves, a sometimes frenetic and always enthusiastic proponent of technical authority. Reeves described the doctor who advised the Ted Bates & Company agency on drugs as "the man we believe to be the world's greatest pharmacologist." Another doctor, who offered advice on a soap campaign, Reeves said was "conceded to be one of the three leading experts in the United States on dermatology."

Reeves's chief contribution to advertising theory is known as USP:

> We can't sell a product unless it's a good product, and even then we can't sell it unless we can find the Unique Selling Proposition. There are three rules for a USP. First, you need a definite proposition: buy this product and you get this specific benefit. Pick up any textbook on advertising and that's on page one— but everybody ignores it. Then, second, it must offer a unique proposition, one which the opposition *cannot* or *does not* offer. Third, the proposition must sell. Colgate was advertising "ribbon dental cream . . . it comes out like a ribbon and lies flat on your brush." Well, that was a proposition and it was unique, but it didn't sell. Bates gave them "cleans your breath while it cleans your teeth." Now every dentifrice cleans your breath while it cleans your teeth—*but nobody had ever put a breath claim on toothpaste before.*[20]

Nearly every advertising specialist agrees with Reeves about the necessity for keeping everlastingly at it, for continuing the repetition. One agency man holds, "When the client begins to tire of an ad, you know it's beginning to catch on with the public." But there is considerable difference of opinion about Reeves's basic philosophy. David Ogilvy of Ogilvy, Benson & Mather acknowledged the value of USP for advertising some products but held that it was limited. Ogilvy, the high priest of brand-image advertising, specializing in building an aura of sophistication, has written: "It pays to give your brand a *first-class ticket* through life. People don't like to be seen consuming products which their friends regard as third-class."

Ogilvy is noted for choosing models who reflect elegance. He hired Baron George Wrangell of the Russian nobility to pose, black eye-patch prominently shown, as "the man in the Hathaway shirt." Commander Edward Whitehead became the symbol of Schweppes. In a speech at a meeting of the American Association of Advertising Agencies, Ogilvy pronounced his major theme: "Let us remember that it is almost always the total *personality* of a brand rather than any *trivial product difference* which decides its ultimate position in the market."

Still another approach was promoted by Norman B. Norman of Norman, Craig & Kummel. Although most agencies rely to some degree on the power of unconscious suggestion, Norman, who was trained as a social psychologist, had a distinctively Freudian orientation. His agency aimed at empathy, seeking to involve consumers at deep levels; motivational research is basic. Some of the ads were highly suggestive but the key was often subtlety. An ad campaign for Ronson lighters was built on research showing that flame is a sexual symbol.

One of the most admired agencies, Doyle Dane Bernbach, shunned all rules, relying instead on originality. In effect, William Bernbach simply hired the most creative copywriters and artists he could find, then encouraged them to work together. He is one of the few agency presidents who think little of market research, holding that advertising is not a science but an art. Speaking to other advertising specialists, he has said:

> Why should anyone look at your ad? The reader doesn't buy his magazine or tune in his radio and TV to see and hear what you have to say. . . . What is the use of saying all the right things in the world if nobody is going to read them? And, believe me, nobody is going to read them if they are not said with freshness, originality, and imagination.[21]

Few of the other large agencies promote anything that can be properly described as a philosophy, but there is general agreement on the goal: to reach the maximum number of users or potential users of a product at a minimum of cost. One authority, Otto Kleppner, has outlined three basic plans for using the mass media: the zone campaign, the cream campaign, and the national campaign. With the zone plan the advertiser puts maximum effort into a definite and restricted geographic area—a city, state, or recognized trading territory—gets what business can be obtained there, then passes on to another. With the cream plan the advertiser goes after the best prospects first, no matter how widely scattered, then goes after the next best, and so on down the scale. The national campaign combines the others on an enormous scale to get maximum sales from all possible prospects.

Selecting Media

Whichever sales strategy advertisers select, they choose media carefully. Long books have been written about media selection, but it is possible to set forth here the general guidelines.

GEOGRAPHIC SELECTIVITY

Selecting prospects geographically involves several choices of media for reaching them. Newspapers can carry a message to the cities advertisers are most interested in reaching. They can limit advertising to the cities where the product has adequate distribution, where they think it has the greatest sales potential, where weather or seasonal conditions promise demand for it, where employment is high and the economic picture bright. Furthermore, the speed with which newspapers are produced allows flexibility.

Radio and television, through their spot commercials and through programs that advertisers can sponsor in cooperation with local dealers, also enable them to reach prospects on a geographical basis. Even with network facilities they need buy only a part of the entire national market.

Magazines also enable advertisers to seek out customers and potential customers in definite regions. Some magazines concentrate their circulations in specific areas. *Sunset* circulates primarily in the western states, for instance, and *New Hampshire Profiles* has chosen a single state for its major concentration. *Successful Farming* draws the bulk of its audience from the rich agricultural heart of the Midwest.

Some magazines circulate nationally and offer advertisers a widely scattered but homogeneous body of readers sharing common tastes, interests, or even occupations. They are ill suited for geographical selectivity. In recent years especially, however, a number of large-circulation national magazines have given advertisers the option of buying either their entire circulation or a part of it. In 1959 *Look,* with a total circulation of nearly 6 million, inaugurated a Magazone Plan, under which advertisers could use any one or any combination of editions reaching seven standard marketing areas. Now magazines as diverse as *Sports Illustrated* and *Farm Journal* also are published in several geographic editions.

PROSPECT SELECTIVITY

But what of advertisers who want to reach only the most likely prospects for their product or service?

If products are found in most households—as, for example, soaps, detergents, deodorants—and especially if they are comparatively inexpensive, the advertisers may feel that they are reaching the market without undue waste if they get the sales message before as many persons as possible. Sheer numbers may suit their purpose, then, and they can use the big-circulation national magazines, network television shows, Sunday supplements, and a combination of dailies. But if the product appeals to some distinct body of purchasers or if it is relatively expensive, then they must carefully screen the audience for their sales pitch.

Magazines, because of their high selectivity of readers, are an excellent medium for such advertisers. There are magazines for people with similar concerns, such as rearing children, protecting health, or homemaking; with similar hobbies, such as stamp collecting, skin diving, hunting, fishing, yachting, or driving a hot rod; with similar interests, such as music, literature, science, fashions, or foreign affairs; and with similar occupations. There is scarcely a vocation, an interest, a facet of the personality that is not appealed to by some magazine.

The screened audience attracted by editorial content is magazine publishers' stock-in-trade. Condé Nast once likened magazine publishers to name-brokers. Publishers bait their pages with reading matter intended to attract either a large number of readers or a special class of readers, sell those pages at less than cost, and make a profit by charging advertisers for the privilege of addressing the distinctive audience they have assembled. Nast's own magazines reached a wealthy, sophisticated few, and Ilka Chase in *Always in Vogue* repeats the allegory Nast used to explain his publishing rationale:

> If you had a tray with two million needles on it and only one hundred and fifty thousand of these had gold tips which you wanted, it would be an endless and costly process to weed them out. Moreover the one million, eight hundred and fifty thousand which were not gold-tipped would be of no use to you, they couldn't help you, but if you could get a magnet that would draw out only the gold ones what a saving!

But now even some magazines which appeal to a broad range of consumers offer advertisers the opportunity to target particular demographic groups. *Time,* for example, in addition to many regional, state, and city editions, has a *Time B* edition ("subscribers who are primarily identified as business executives"), a *Time College* edition, a *Time Doctor's* edition, a *Time T* edition ("*Time* subscribers in top management"), a *Time Elite* edition, and so on.

In addition, there are research organizations which spend considerable time and money determining such specific information as whether readers of *The New Yorker* or readers of *Esquire* are more likely to be scotch drinkers—a piece of information of great interest to scotch advertisers.

Broadcasting and newspapers, attracting large, heterogeneous followings, do not permit the degree of audience selectivity that magazines do. Nevertheless, broadcasting advertisers can focus on an audience with some of the characteristics they are looking for by selecting particular programs or particular airtimes. Audience research firms such as the A. C. Nielsen

Company can give some detail on the types of people who watch particular programs, but broadcasting does not offer a magnet to draw out a group of, say, only electrical engineers. A magazine, on the other hand, can control its circulation so that its audience is made up solely of electrical engineers.

By their choice of newspapers, advertisers can reach populations that are predominantly rural or predominantly suburban. One metropolitan newspaper may deliver an audience different from that of another. The New York *Times* is addressed to quite a different segment of the population than the New York *Daily News,* although each offers a good market for a specific purpose. Nevertheless, newspapers cannot generally deliver as specifically defined an audience as some magazines do.

Criticism of Advertising

Before the development of our modern industrial economy's national markets to which mass-produced, packaged goods are transported by a network of trucks, trains, and airplanes, markets were local. They were served by the farmers and artisans of the immediate neighborhood, or goods were brought in from areas no farther than a day's journey by horse and wagon. Although advertising occurred, it was not essential. Most customers would not buy until they had inspected the wares and discussed their merits with the seller. The advertisers' main purpose, then, was to attract attention— which they did for the most part without feeling restraints of truth and accuracy. Outrageous and absurd promises were made; they were part of the game. To contrast the qualities of his Pennsylvania Fireplace, for example, Benjamin Franklin claimed that his competitors' fireplaces created drafts that made

> . . . women get cold in the head, rheums and defluxions which fall into their jaws and gums, and have destroyed many a fine set of teeth.

Today advertising is still a device for attracting attention, and some of it has not outgrown its vivid past. But now the customer cannot inspect the wares and ask the manufacturer searching questions about the merits of the merchandise. As people have become more dependent on advertising for information, their dissatisfaction with it has increased. Advertising, they say:

1. Stresses inconsequential values, lowers taste, and turns society into one dominated by style, fashion, and status-seeking;
2. Often bewilders rather than informs about the merit of products;
3. Lowers ethical standards by the insincerity or fraudulence of its appeals;
4. Corrupts and distorts the news;
5. Promotes economic waste and retards the growth of thrift by emphasizing immediate expenditures; and
6. Fosters monopoly.

In the 1970s advertising's effects on children were an increasing source of concern to social activists and reformers. Ralph Nader blamed advertising for children's ignorance of nutrition, and criticized the "Pepsi Cola-Pretzel-Frito-Lay's Potato Chip syndrome." Thousands of children are growing up, he said, "believing that Pepsi or Coke are prerequisites of a life of health and vigor."

In 1975, for example, according to Television Bureau of Advertising figures both Coca-Cola and Pepsi Cola ranked among the top 10 spot advertisers on television. Coca-Cola ranked fifth in spot television advertising, spending $24.8 million; Pepsi ranked ninth, spending $21.4 million. The two fastest-growing spot television categories in 1975 were games, toys, and hobbycraft, up 45 percent from the previous year to $67.5 million; and candy and gum, up 40 percent to $25.5 million. Much of this advertising is concentrated in Saturday morning programing, the so-called Saturday morning ghetto of children's programing. And with good reason. A representative of Oscar Mayer and Co. was quoted in a 1965 issue of *Advertising Age* as saying: "When you sell a woman on a product and she goes into the store and finds your brand isn't in stock, she'll probably forget about it. But when you sell a kid on your product, if he can't get it, he will throw himself on the floor, stamp his feet and cry. You can't get a reaction like that out of an adult." In a 1975 issue of *Advertising Age* another salesperson had this advice: "If you truly want big sales, you will use the child as your assistant salesman. He sells, he nags, until he breaks down the sales resistance of his mother."

The Boston-based Action for Children's Television (ACT) has been particularly alarmed by the amount of advertising directed at children. It has been estimated that children ages 2 to 5 view about 30 hours of television a week on the average; ages 6 to 11 see about 27 hours. The average child, then, will have seen about 8000 hours of television by the time he or she enters school; the moderate viewer will have seen about 25,000 commercials a year, 5000 of them telling the child what to eat. By the time the child is 12, he or she will have seen on the average about 300,000 commercials. ACT successfully petitioned the FCC to reduce the time allowed for commercials on children's television from 16 minutes an hour to 9½ minutes. It prompted an end to children's television hosts selling products and in 1972 persuaded the leading vitamin manufacturers to take their commercials for candy-flavored vitamins off children's television. ACT's goal was to see commercials directed at children eliminated in five to seven years.

Whether or not ACT will ever be able to achieve that goal, advertisers have good reason to be concerned about the kind of pressure ACT has been able to mobilize. They may also be concerned by a study published in 1976 by the *Harvard Business Review*. Children may not be as gullible as we think. Researchers interviewed 48 New Jersey children between 5 and 12 to assess their reactions to the years of commercials they had viewed. By age 11, the study concluded, "most children have become cynical—ready to believe that, like advertising, business and other social institutions are riddled with hypocrisy." The older children were particularly skeptical. The 7- to 10-year-olds "showed tension and anger over their inability to cope effectively with what they believe to be misleading advertising." Three-quarters of the 11- and 12-year-olds felt that "advertising is sometimes designed to 'trick' the consumer, and two-thirds believed that they could discern misleading advertising at least part of the time."

A sample as small as 48 may not permit such generalizations, but linked to the findings of a nationwide poll by *Intellect* magazine, the New Jersey study raises important questions for society. In a poll of 22,300 junior and senior high school leaders, *Intellect* magazine found that 64 percent of them had very little confidence in advertising. Society may approve the development of a certain amount of healthy skepticism among its children—most adults are not inclined to take literally every commercial message they see or hear. But children's belief that because advertising is deceptive and hypo-critical, other social institutions are, too, is the kind of precocious cynicism no stable society can endure.

FOSTERS MATERIALISTIC ATTITUDES

The loud voice of advertising, trumpeting the wonders of worldly posses-sions, has forced Americans, some critics have charged, to place undue emphasis on material values to the detriment of more enduring values.

In their own land Americans tend to measure their neighbors by the size of their income and automobile, by the elegance of their home, and by the number of possessions in it. Abroad they tend to judge foreign lands by the extent of such material comforts as modern plumbing and electrical refriger-ation. They put the dollar above principle, the material above the spiritual. So say the critics; and although they do not put the sole burden on advertising, they insist that it must share a substantial part of the blame.

FOSTERS MONOPOLY

Advertising also has been condemned because it can encourage monop-olies. Manufacturers have the potential to monopolize markets, according to a few critics, for, by an incessant barrage of advertising, they are able to convince consumers that their product serves them better than any similar product. Take aspirin, for a hypothetical example. Although all aspirin tablets are nearly alike, because they must meet certain minimum specifica-tions set by the government, one manufacturer might so dominate the advertising picture as to convince consumers that there is no really effective aspirin but his own. As sales increase, so does the manufacturer's economic power. It becomes increasingly difficult for competitors to get a share of the market.

On the other hand, C. H. Sandage has pointed out that such a monop-oly rests on control of human attitudes, not of supply, and that, because of consumers' shifts from brand to brand, it is highly uncertain. Moreover, he adds, the chief aim of such control is increasing sales rather than prices,

because any significant price increase might send customers flocking to
competitors' products.

A cooler and subtler analysis of advertising than that of most has been
made by David Potter in his book, *People of Plenty*. Potter points out that
advertising has become a powerful institution. And yet it is unlike other
institutions of society in that its view of people is solely commercial. The
church conceives of people as immortal souls; schools conceive of them as
being guided by reason; business and industry conceive of them as produc-
tive agents who can create goods or render services that are useful to
humanity. But advertising conceives of people as nothing more than consumers. In contrast with the other institutions, Potter has written:

> [A]dvertising has in its dynamics no motivation to seek the improvement of the
> individual or to impart qualities of social usefulness, unless conformity to material
> values may be so characterized. And, though it wields an immense social
> influence, comparable to the influence of religion and learning, it has no social
> goals and no social responsibility for what it does with its influence, so long as it
> refrains from palpable violations of truth and decency. It is this lack of institu-
> tional responsibility, this lack of inherent social purpose to balance social power,
> which, I would argue, is a basic cause for concern about the role of advertising.
> Occasional deceptions, breaches of taste, and deviations from sound ethical
> conduct are in a sense superficial and are not necessarily intrinsic. Equally, the
> high-minded types of advertising which we see more regularly than we some-
> times realize are also extraneous to an analysis of the basic nature of advertising.
> What is basic is that advertising, as such, with all its vast power to influence
> values and conduct, cannot ever lose sight of the fact that it ultimately regards
> man as a consumer and defines its own mission as one of stimulating him to
> consume or to desire to consume.[22]

The Regulation of Advertising

Although the Supreme Court has gradually drawn advertising within the
protection of the First Amendment, it is unlikely that advertising will ever
enjoy the full protection afforded "more respectable" forms of speech such
as political debate or even political advertising. The change in First Amendment status is based on the idea that the public has a right to commercial
information that advertisers are willing to provide. In a case dealing with the
constitutional right of the public to receive prescription drug advertising
when such advertising was forbidden by state statute, the Supreme Court
observed, "So long as we preserve a predominantly free enterprise economy, the allocation of our resources in large measure will be made through
numerous private economic decisions. It is a matter of public interest that
those decisions, in the aggregate, be intelligent and well informed. To this
end, the free flow of commercial information is indispensable."[23]

The court considers advertisers an especially hardy breed who will not
be chilled or discouraged from communicating by requirements that they

ensure that their advertising is truthful. The court described advertising as

"the *sine qua non* of commercial profits" and noted:

> Advertising, however tasteless and excessive it sometimes may seem, is none-
> theless dissemination of information as to who is producing and selling what
> product, for what reason, and at what price. . . .
>
> [T]he greater objectivity [in the sense that it is more easily verified than news
> reporting or political commentary because the advertiser knows more about his
> product than anyone else] and hardiness of commercial speech, may make it
> less necessary to tolerate inaccurate statements for fear of silencing the
> speaker. . . . They may also make it appropriate to require that a commercial
> message appear in such a form, or include such additional information, warn-
> ings, and disclaimers, as are necessary to prevent its being deceptive. . . . They
> may also make inapplicable the prohibition against prior restraints.[24]

The court has clearly stated that there is no protection for advertising of
illegal commercial activity, but the distinctions the court is willing to make
between "protected" advertising and other forms of protected speech leave
open the question of how the court will treat other government bans on
advertising of legal goods and services. In 1972 the Supreme Court affirmed
the constitutionality of a Congressional ban on the advertising of cigarettes
on broadcasting even though cigarettes were then, and continue to be, a
legal—if dangerous—commodity. But that decision predates the major shift
in the court's approach to commercial advertising. An interesting question is
how it would treat, say, a ban on the advertising of saccharin products in all
or any of the media, if Congress chose to impose such a ban on advertising
instead of prohibiting the sale of saccharin products. (Such products are
suspected of causing cancer but are also considered by some as great aids
for individuals suffering from diabetes or heart disease in which overweight
is a contributing factor.)

In any case, the court has left open the possibility of such bans and has
left intact the legislation and machinery of advertising regulation.

The Federal Trade Commission

There are many state and local and more than 20 different federal agencies
that regulate advertising in one way or another. The most important of these
is the Federal Trade Commission (FTC).

Under the original Federal Trade Commission Act (1914), false advertising was considered harmful not because it deceived consumers but because
it took customers from truthful competitors. The public interest resided in
the opportunity for fair competition. As late as 1931 the Supreme Court told
the commission that the act did not forbid the deception of consumers
unless the advertising injured competing businesses in some way—even
though the court had been presented with a case involving an "obesity
cure" containing "desiccated thyroid" that the FTC thought could cause

actual physical harm to those who consumed it without medical supervision.[25]

Since that time the court and Congress have become more solicitous of the interests of consumers. In 1938 Congress declared that "unfair or deceptive acts or practices in commerce" were unlawful. Advertisers were not to misrepresent their products and services by using confusing description, ambiguous words, or outright fraud.

The FTC has required that advertising be not just literally true but true in all its implications. For example, the FTC declared in 1970 that two claims made by Firestone Tire & Rubber Co. were deceptive and unfair. Firestone had advertised that "when you buy a Firestone tire . . . you get a safe tire." The FTC argued that even the most sophisticated testing and control methods could not guarantee that each and every tire produced by any manufacturer is free from defects. Firestone had also claimed that its Super Sports Wide Oval tire "stops 25% quicker." The FTC concluded that the claim was "without substantial scientific test data to support it." Such hyperbole or puffery can deceive consumers as Firestone's own survey demonstrated: 15.3% of a scientifically drawn sample of tire buyers thought the "Safe Tire" ad meant every Firestone tire was *absolutely* safe under *all* conditions.[26]

In 1971 the commission began the practice of requiring that advertisers in selected industries substantiate their advertising claims. The commission was not contending that any particular claims were false; it was putting the burden on the advertisers to demonstrate that all their claims were true. The program was justified in part as a benefit to consumers who could then examine the evidence advertisers offered for their claims. In many instances, however, advertisers overwhelmed the agency with highly technical information. For example, Renault was reported to have submitted 72 pages of documents, including some in French, to back up a gas mileage claim. Renault also sent along a five-page letter from a satisfied owner, only one sentence of which related to the mileage claim.[27] In 1974 the commission began to ask advertisers to provide summaries that the general public could understand to accompany technical or scientific documentation.

The FTC has required corrective advertising of some of those found guilty of deceptive and unfair advertising. For example, the FTC found that ITT Continental Baking Co. had falsely represented Profile bread as lower in calories than ordinary bread and as a special and significant product in weight control diets. In fact, a slice of Profile had fewer calories than slices of other breads because Profile was sliced thinner, and at that a slice of Profile had only 4.5 fewer calories than a slice of enriched white bread.

The FTC ordered ITT to cease and desist from this false advertising. The commission also required that ITT devote not less that 25 percent of its advertising budget for each medium in each market to correct the false impression it had created.[28]

The FTC went a step farther with the makers of Hawaiian Punch. To overcome the impression conveyed by past advertising that Hawaiian

Punch beverages consist predominantly of fruit juices, the commission required RJR Foods, Inc., to disclose in a clear and conspicuous manner in all advertisements the actual percentage of fruit juice in their beverage products. The corrective advertising was to run for a minimum of a year and beyond that until the company could demonstrate that specified percentages of its customers recognized that Hawaiian Punch contained no more than 20 percent natural fruit juice.[29]

A more ambitious objective of the FTC has been to make advertisers disclose negative information about a product that would be directly relevant to an informed purchasing decision. The FTC has been particularly concerned that food advertisers disclose the nutritional content of their products and that manufacturers of products potentially hazardous to health or safety, such as pesticides or nonprescription drugs, disclose the hazards. Cigarette manufacturers are, of course, required to put warnings on the cigarette packages themselves and in advertisements. There are obviously still many smokers who are not deterred by the reminders that the Surgeon General has determined that cigarette smoking is dangerous to their health.

In early 1972 the commission tried to enlist the FCC's support for the concept of counter-advertising whereby organizations or individuals would be given the right to free or purchased time in which to reply to advertisements that directly or indirectly raised controversial issues of public importance, that relied on scientific premises which were the subject of controversy within the scientific community, or which failed to disclose negative aspects of a product or service. Broadcasters and advertisers strongly opposed the suggestion and the Supreme Court gave some support to their opposition when it ruled in 1973 that broadcasters who meet their obligation to provide full and fair coverage of public issues are not required to accept editorial advertisements. In 1974 the Federal Communications Commission did its best to close the door on the idea entirely when it said that broadcasters' Fairness Doctrine obligations in regard to advertising were limited to commercials which *explicitly* raise a controversial issue of public importance (for instance, commercials in which an oil company specifically says its explorations for oil have not disturbed the ecology).

To some extent advertiser opposition to the counter-advertising concept has backfired. The energy crisis of 1973 and 1974 led to considerable criticism of the oil industry. Oil companies, particularly Mobil Oil, tried to place with the networks ads that dealt directly with the issue of responsibility for the energy crisis. The networks rejected the ads, and Mobil Oil claimed that this rejection constituted censorship and a violation of Mobil's First Amendment rights.

In fact, however, the media have long policed the advertising they carry. They no doubt do as much as the government to keep advertising honest, and they impose standards of taste that will, of course, not match the standards of everyone but that go beyond the power of government. The control that media have over what advertising they will carry means, in some instances, that people with ideas and information likely to be of interest to the public—maybe Mobil Oil's side of the energy controversy, maybe a citizens' group's warning against an unsafe toy—cannot buy their way to the audience of their choice.

The Federal Trade Commission has been criticized by some for being the tool of Ralph Nader, the public interest advocate, and by others for being totally inefficient in protecting consumer interests. The commission has been an outspoken advocate of consumer interests, but the clumsiness and slowness of its operations weaken its effectiveness. It has accumulated greater powers in recent years (for instance, the authority to issue trade regulation rules defining for an entire industry which acts and practices the commission considers unfair and deceptive and, thus, unlawful) which may help it deal with unfair and deceptive advertising more consistently and more quickly. But a moment's reflection on the volume of advertising flooding the American public—even if most of that advertising is fair and responsible—should serve to emphasize the enormity of what is only one of the commission's tasks.

Self-regulation and Public Service

Advertisers themselves have attempted to impose some measure of self-regulation on their own industry to meet their own sense of responsibility, to enhance the credibility of the industry, and no doubt to stave off even greater government regulation than now exists. The advertising industry's efforts in self-regulation have included most notably the formation in 1970 of the National Advertising Review Board, which has 30 advertiser, 10 advertising agency, and 10 public members. The board investigates complaints against national advertisers and is concerned mainly with deceptive and unfair practices. At the local level Better Business Bureaus respond to complaints and monitor local advertising.

The advertising industry's efforts to promote the public interest through its advertising expertise are led by the Advertising Council, formed during World War II. Each year the council conducts advertising campaigns through public service announcements for a number of groups, such as the Red Cross, the United Negro College Fund and U.S. Savings Bonds. The FCC defines a public service announcement as one for which no charge is made and which promotes programs, activities, or services regarded as serving community interests. Typically, hundreds of groups ask for the council's help each year, many more than it can handle.

David Potter would presumably applaud FTC, FCC, media, and advertising industry efforts to eliminate deceptive and unfair practices. Clearly, however, that was not his main concern. He was talking about the kind of activity that the Advertising Council and other public service groups are pursuing. Admirable though their activity is, it does not negate his major criticism. The industry still lacks an "inherent social purpose to balance social power." Its fundamental purpose is to sell, and selling has always carried a stigma. Anarchus said, "The market is the place set aside where men may deceive each other," and there have been echoes of that statement through the centuries.

Two authorities who have conducted searching examinations of professional persuasion through public relations and advertising have fashioned cogent defenses. In a study of public relations, Robert L. Heilbroner, a respected writer on economics, did not overlook the chicanery characteristic of some PR, but he summed up by quoting a public relations specialist who holds that the large corporation gets nervous unless people say what wonderful public relations it has: "So it has to *have* wonderful public relations. It has to *act* lovable. It has to *be* progressive." Heilbroner concluded:

> Hence, by an unexpected twist, public relations has become a weapon whose recoil is greater than its muzzle blast. Good Public Relations has come to be something very much like the corporate conscience—a commercial conscience, no doubt, but a conscience none the less.[30]

Martin Mayer is also unstinting in criticism of advertising, but he, too, finds a value not generally recognized:

> Any realistic approach . . . ought to start with the premise that successful advertising *adds a new value to the product*. . . . [A] lipstick may be sold at Woolworth's under one name, and in a department store under another, nationally-advertised name. Almost any teen-age girl will prefer the latter, if she can afford to pay the difference. Wearing the Woolworth's brand, she feels her ordinary self; wearing the other, which has been successfully advertised as a magic recipe for glamor, she feels a beauty—and perhaps she is.[31]

The public as a whole, however, tends to be ambivalent about the precise worth of this added value contributed by advertising. The trends in attitudes toward advertising between 1964 and 1974 presented in a paper at the annual meeting of the American Association of Advertising Agencies (AAAA) in 1975 do not reflect specifically on the notion of added value, but a sense of the public's attitude toward it emerges from the table below. The table shows the percentage of positive responses from comparable samples of approximately 1800 people in 1964 and 1974 to these statements:

	1964	1974
Advertising is essential	78%	88%
Advertising results in better products for the public	75%	59%
Advertising helps raise our standard of living	71%	57%
Advertising often persuades people to buy things they shouldn't buy	65%	83%
Most advertising insults the intelligence of the average listener	42%	59%
In general, advertising presents a true picture of the product advertised	41%	41%
In general, advertising results in lower prices	40%	29%

The only information of some comfort to advertisers in the study, then, is that 10 percent more people in 1974 thought that advertising is essential. Virtually every other response showed a more than 10 percent decline in favorable judgments toward advertising over the 10-year period. Perhaps advertisers were able to derive a measure of satisfaction from the fact that more people think advertising is essential, results in better products for the public, and helps raise our standard of living than do not think so. But given the effort by government and the industry itself to make advertising a more responsible social institution, the attitudes revealed in 1974 seem scant reward.

Nor had the advertising industry been able to combat its negative image by 1977. Louis Harris and Associates in collaboration with the Marketing Science Institute, a nonprofit research organization associated with Harvard Business School, surveyed a national sample of 1510 American adults in late 1976 and early 1977 and reported these responses:

	All	Most	Some
How much, if any, TV advertising do you consider seriously misleading?	9%	37%	39%
How much, if any, newspaper and magazine advertising do you consider seriously misleading?	4%	24%	50%

Asked which of 25 specific industries "do a good job in serving consumers," six percent named advertising, which put it in 22nd place. Twenty-five percent said that advertising "does a poor job"; only car manufacturers, garages, auto-mechanics, the oil industry, and used-car dealers were rated lower.

Often in surveys, the precise meaning of respondents' answers is not necessarily clear. Interpretation, therefore, can be a nebulous process. Why, for example, did more persons in 1974 than in 1964 think that advertising is essential even as, apparently, they felt less warmly toward advertising? It would be satisfying to learn that the public valued advertising's role in subsidizing the mass media of communication, the marketplace of information and ideas so vital to democracy. But then journalists themselves, who typically scorn advertising and all its works, have scarcely even grudging appreciation for this role. The table opposite illustrates the significant fact that the mass media received $20.8 billion, almost 62 percent, of the $33.6 billion of U.S. advertising revenues in 1976.

These advertising revenues for the mass media mean, for example, that readers can buy newspapers for less than the cost of publishing them, and sometimes for less than the cost of the raw materials themselves, and can watch television programs without paying directly for them at all. The important finding in this context may be, however, that only 29 percent of those in the AAAA survey thought that advertising results in lower prices. The public's sophistication about economics is hard to assess—it is somewhat less than that of journalists—but the majority of survey respondents

Table 12.1 Comparison of Advertising in Major Media in 1975 and 1976

		1975[1]		1976[2]	
		Millions	% of Total	Millions	% of Total
Newspapers	*Total*	$ 8,442	29.9	$10,205	30.0
	National	1,221	4.3	1,525	4.4
	Local	7,221	25.6	8,680	25.6
Magazines	*Total*	1,465	5.2	1,775	5.3
Television	*Total*	5,263	18.6	6,575	19.7
	Network	2,306	8.2	2,785	8.3
	Spot	1,623	5.7	2,125	6.4
	Local	1,334	4.7	1,665	5.0
Radio	*Total*	1,980	7.0	2,228	6.7
	Network	83	0.3	104	0.3
	Spot	436	1.5	488	1.5
	Local	1,461	5.2	1,636	4.9
Farm Pubs		74	0.3	85	0.3
Direct Mail		4,181	14.8	4,725	14.1
Business Papers		919	3.3	1,020	3.0
Outdoor	*Total*	335	1.2	388	1.2
	National	220	0.8	255	0.8
	Local	115	0.4	133	0.4
Miscellaneous	*Total*	5,571	19.7	6,602	19.8
	National	2,882	10.2	3,418	10.2
	Local	2,689	9.5	3,184	9.6
Total	*National*	15,410	54.6	18,305	54.6
	Local	12,820	45.4	15,298	45.4
GRAND TOTAL		$28,230	100.0	$33,603	100.0

[1]Revised
[2]Preliminary
Source: McCann Erickson, Inc., Newspaper Advertising Bureau

Reprinted with permission from "Facts About Newspapers: 1977," American Newspaper Publishers Association, April 1977.

Share of Advertising Dollar

Newspapers 30.0%
Magazines 5.3%
Television 19.7%
Radio 6.7%
Other 38.3%

may have concluded that they were paying for their mass media through the products and services that they buy.

It is probable, finally, that advertising was a victim of an apparent discontent with, even hostility toward, almost all American institutions in the late 1960s and in the 1970s. But advertising's task in overcoming that discontent and hostility is more formidable than the task for other American institutions, because, as Potter argued, advertising has no clear social goals or social purpose. The vital role that it plays in the commercial life of the nation and in supporting the communications media was not only inadequately understood but apparently not highly valued at a time when materialist values were heavily under attack.

Notes

1. Rollo Ogden in *The Nation,* July 8, 1915, quoted by Willard Grosvenor Bleyer, *Main Currents in the History of American Journalism* (Boston: Houghton Mifflin, 1927), pp. 290–291.
2. *The Nation,* May 8, 1866; quoted in Bleyer, p. 277.
3. *Esquire,* November 1958; quoted in Bernard C. Cohen, *The Press and Foreign Policy* (Princeton, N.J.: Princeton University Press, 1969), p. 143.
4. Timothy Crouse, *The Boys on the Bus: Riding with the Campaign Press Corps* (New York: Ballantine Books, 1974), p. 33.
5. Crouse, p. 91.
6. John Fischer, "What am I doing here? (apologia pro februa sua)," *Harper's,* May 1970, pp. 23–28.
7. Lehman Engel, *The Critics* (New York: Macmillan, 1976), p. xiv.
8. Gay Talese, *The Kingdom and the Power* (New York: Bantam Books, 1970), p. 582.
9. Quoted in William L. Rivers, Theodore Peterson, and Jay W. Jensen, *The Mass Media and Modern Society* (New York: Holt, Rinehart and Winston, 2nd edition, 1971), p. 236.
10. Quoted in Rivers, Peterson, and Jensen, p. 236.
11. Quoted in Rivers, Peterson, and Jensen, p. 238.
12. See Edward L. Bernays, *Crystallizing Public Opinion* (New York: Liveright Publishing Corporation, 1961), and *The Engineering of Consent* (Norman, Ok.: University of Oklahoma Press, 1955).
13. Quoted in Rivers, Peterson, and Jensen, p. 243.
14. Nicholas Johnson, *How to talk back to your television set* (New York: Bantam Books, 1970), pp. 47–48.
15. William A. Durbin, "Public Relations—A Magic Wall?", in Hill and Knowlton Executives, *Critical Issues in Public Relations* (Englewood Cliffs, N.J.: Prentice-Hall, 1975), pp. 223, 220–221, 226.
16. Bernays, *Crystallizing Public Opinion,* pp. 178, 182.
17. Robert MacNeil, *The People Machine: The Influence of Television on American Politics* (New York: Harper & Row, 1968), p. 17.
18. Claude C. Hopkins, *Scientific Advertising* (Chicago: Lord & Thomas, 1923), p. 1.
19. For a full discussion, see Albert Wesley Frey, *Advertising* (New York: Ronald Press, 1947), pp. 151–184.

20. Quoted in Martin Mayer, *Madison Avenue, U.S.A.* (New York: Harper & Row, 1958), p. 49.

21. Quoted in Mayer, p. 66.

22. David M. Potter, *People of Plenty: Economic Abundance and the American Character* (Chicago: University of Chicago Press, 1954), p. 177.

23. *Virginia State Board of Pharmacy v. Virginia Citizens' Consumer Council,* 96 S. Ct. 1817 (1976). The recent changes in the First Amendment status of advertising can be traced in these cases: *Pittsburgh Press Co. v. Pittsburgh Commission on Human Rights,* 93 S. Ct. 2553 (1973), *Bigelow v. Virginia,* 94 S. Ct. 2222 (1975), *Virginia State Board of Pharmacy* (cited above), and *Bates and O'Steen v. State Bar of Arizona,* 97 S. Ct.—(1977).

24. *Virginia State Board of Pharmacy,* pp. 1830–1831.

25. *Federal Trade Commission v. Raladam Co.,* 283 U.S. 643 (1931).

26. *Firestone Tire & Rubber Company v. Federal Trade Commission,* 481 F.2d 246 (1973).

27. *Broadcasting,* November 12, 1973, p. 38.

28. In re *ITT Continental Baking Co.,* 79 FTC 248 (1971).

29. In re *RJR Foods, Inc., et al.,* 83 FTC 7 (1973).

30. Robert L. Heilbroner, "Public Relations: The Invisible Sell," *Harper's,* June 1957, p. 31.

31. Martin Mayer, "What is Advertising Good For?", *Harper's,* February 1958, pp. 27–28.

13

Entertainment, the Media, and American Culture

I will run the risk of asserting, that where the reading of novels prevails as a habit, it occasions in time the entire destruction of the powers of the mind: it is such an utter loss to the reader, that it is not so much to be called pass-time as kill-time. It conveys no trustworthy information as to facts; it produces no improvement of the intellect, but fills the mind with a mawkish and morbid sensibility, which is directly hostile to the cultivation, invigoration, and enlargement of the nobler faculties of the understanding.

SAMUEL TAYLOR COLERIDGE

What is one going to say about *Petticoat Junction* anyway— beyond making a few arch, superior little cultural leaps into the air, and then jumping on its stomach? Who wants to spend his time jumping on *Petticoat Junction?*

MICHAEL J. ARLEN

It's summertime, and the movies are easy. The big-money hits like *The Deep, The Other Side of Midnight* and *Star Wars* all deal in one way or another with the simple things that seem to make for family entertainment—things like lust, abortion, murder, voodoo, sunken treasure and interplanetary warfare.

Newsweek critic Jack Kroll's wry comment on what was titillating movie-goers in the summer of 1977 suggests the transience of popular taste. Next summer "the simple things" will be different. By contrast, two attributes of great art are said to be its universality and timelessness, its genius for capturing something elemental in the human condition that reaches across the centuries. But it may reach very few people and that is a luxury the mass media entertainment industry cannot afford. For, unlike the artist who may labor for a lifetime and produce a single lasting work, the creators of mass media entertainment are continually investing hundreds of thousands, even millions of dollars in works to feed the mass media's voracious appetite for material, works they hope will please as many people as possible *now.* But they do not gamble recklessly; they prefer to bet on reasonable certainties.

Neil Shister reports: "Each season each [television] network airs between five and ten new series. These have been scheduled from approximately 2,000 story ideas proposed, 125 scripts commissioned and 40 pilots taped each year. Taping a half-hour pilot can cost as much as $500,000 and is not a move quickly made. Giving a show a slot in the prime-time schedule is an even more serious commitment, involving millions of dollars in production costs and potential revenues."[1] The networks spend thousands of dollars on audience research, hiring professional polling organizations to survey public response to story ideas and testing services to sample audience reaction to pilots, the test shows from which series may be developed.

Impressed with the success of Time Inc.'s *People,* a magazine of pictures and brief profiles of personalities, and with the public's apparent obsession with celebrities, the New York Times Co. spent more than $3 million to launch *Us,* its biweekly imitation, in May 1977 after two test issues in 11 cities. The fortuitous pretest for both magazines had been the successful change in formula of the weekly tabloid newspaper, the *National Enquirer.* Notorious in the late 1960s for sex and gore, for headlines like "I Cut Out Her Heart And Stomped On It" and "Mom Boiled Her Baby And Ate Her," the *Enquirer* shifted in the early 1970s to personality features, medical developments, self-help items and purported firsthand accounts of psychic or extraterrestrial phenomena, a formula captured in this spoof of an *Enquirer* lead paragraph concocted by Washington *Star* writer John Holusha: "A panel of psychics actually predicted Farrah Fawcett-Majors' astounding cancer cure! Top scientists said it was due to her ride in a UFO during which she learned 10 ways to become a better person." The *Enquirer's* change in formula jumped circulation from 1 million in the late 1960s to 5 million in 1977. The *Enquirer's* "audience research" was to post the latest Nielsen ratings of top-rated television shows in the newsroom. Once a show dropped below a certain point, its stars disappeared from the pages of the *Enquirer.*

The *National Enquirer's* crude measure of the public's interest illustrates a major problem for the mass media: the fickleness and unpredictability of their audiences in a society which, so Daniel Boorstin argues in *The Image,* is "ruled by extravagant expectations." One expectation is of "our ability to make art forms suit our convenience, to transform a novel into a movie and vice versa, to turn a symphony into mood-conditioning." Boorstin continues:

> By harbouring, nourishing, and ever enlarging our extravagant expectations we create the demand for illusions with which we deceive ourselves. . . . And we demand that there be always more of them, bigger and better and more vivid.[2]

The Difficulty of Definition

Because of individuals' different uses of mass media content, entertainment is not easily defined. Conventional distinctions between news or information, education, and entertainment will not necessarily help if by entertainment is meant whatever engages attention agreeably, whatever makes the time pass pleasantly. The content of the televised Watergate hearings in 1973 was clearly news. For thousands of viewers the hearings were also enthralling drama, what some would call "pure entertainment." The political novels of 1976 and 1977 about Washington by leading protagonists, officials, and journalists, in the Watergate affair—by Vice President Spiro Agnew, senior Nixon aide John Ehrlichman, CBS correspondent Marvin Kalb and former Nixon speech writer and New York *Times* columnist William Safire, to name a few—were labeled fiction and intended to entertain. But unquestionably solid "news" was buried—and avidly mined as fact or serious analysis by some readers—in these semi-fictional accounts.

After increasing the circulation of the New York *Post* by a claimed 122,000 in two months in 1977 with a brash sensationalism that is his trademark on three continents, Australian press baron Rupert Murdoch felt qualified to lecture U.S. publishers. After all, newspaper circulations across the country had been declining for three years. To compete with television, he told publishers, newspapers must resist the lure of the "minority quality audience" and appeal to the masses. For Murdoch this approach meant increasing the space and prominence in the *Post* for stories on crime, celebrity gossip, television trivia, and the racetrack. The message from readers and advertisers, if not from Murdoch, had not been lost on the nation's most comprehensive newspaper, the New York *Times.* During the second half of 1976 and the first half of 1977, the *Times* added three new life-style sections—previews of entertainment events, a food and shopping guide, and features on decorating and gardening. A growing emphasis on "soft" news and features was widespread in newspapers in the late 1970s, signifying, it seemed, a yielding of responsibility to tell the people what they should know in favor of giving them what they apparently wanted.

For thousands of viewers the Watergate hearings, chaired by Senator Sam Ervin,
were enthralling drama, what some would call "pure entertainment." (CBS photo)

Television itself, invariably decried as the villain responsible for corrupting public wants and causing the shift in the balance between information
and entertainment, had brightened its newscasts with short, visually exciting,
fast-paced stories, many concerned with sex and violence, and with "happy
talk," a breezy conviviality among the newscasters themselves. Television
news, in fact, seemed well on its way to realizing Paddy Chayevsky's satirical
vision in the movie *Network* of ruthless and tasteless exploitation of whatever increased the ratings.

These examples must be kept in perspective. The New York *Times* and
other newspapers and television news departments were not abandoning
information and analysis. Nor was the inclusion of entertaining content in
predominantly news media by any means new. Entertainment has always
been a significant part of news media content. Nevertheless, the apparent
triumph of entertainment over information in these experiments in responsiveness to the mass audience in the late 1970s alarmed many critics of the
mass media. Their assumption has been that news is mainly information
people need to know in order to protect their own interests and to participate as responsible citizens in governing themselves, that entertainment is
mainly material people attend to merely for momentary gratification, and
that mixing the two usually debases news. But people's use of and gratification from mass media content is not so clear cut or predictable. One
person's news is another's entertainment and vice versa. Even though critics

grant the individual's unpredictable use of mass media content and the difficulty therefore of satisfactorily separating news and entertainment, they still insist on the conventional distinction between them.

Difficulties of Presenting Quality Entertainment

The entertainment function of the media was intensified and in other ways affected as the media changed from a comparatively restricted audience to a broad-based popular one. In the nature of the communications system, one can find an explanation for critics' complaints that the mass media at best have made small contributions to art and at worst have debased popular culture and enlightenment. Both art and education are predicated upon a critical and discriminating reception; the conditions under which the mass media operate make such a reception difficult.

Intended for mass consumption, the media usually strive for mass appeal. Few find it economically feasible to consider the tastes of the individual members of their audiences, and most must play to the average tastes of large numbers. Nor can owners of media often indulge in the luxury of satisfying their individual tastes. They must produce whatever it is profitable to give great numbers of other people.

With the object of momentarily engaging the busy masses, the transient products of the media issue forth in an endless torrent, the significant cheek by jowl with the trivial, the good and the substantial emphasized little more than the bad and the shallow. The media must compete with themselves, with other claims on the individual's time and attention, with the individual's own lethargy. Somehow they must get through to their readers, listeners, and viewers. The nature of their task dictates their approach to content, and the approach to content contributes to their blending of entertainment with enlightenment. To capture and captivate their audiences, the media generally try to enliven and simplify their messages.

Newspapers have done so since the days of the penny press. According to sociologist Robert E. Park, newspapers exist in their modern format in part because a few publishers discovered in 1835 that people prefer news to editorial opinion and that they prefer being entertained to being edified. "This, in its way, had the character and importance of a real discovery," he says. "It was like the discovery, made later in Hollywood, that gentlemen prefer blondes. At any rate it is to the consistent application of the principle involved that the modern newspaper owes not merely its present character but its survival as a species." In short, the newspaper came to emphasize the interesting rather than the important, to use William Randolph Hearst's distinction.

This is not to say that newspapers ignore serious content seriously presented. They are certainly doing a better job on that score than they were when Park made his comment in 1940. It is true, however, that in undertaking serious discussion or in presenting information newspapers must always reckon with their reception. Because of the heterogeneous nature of the readers, reporters must not only translate complex issues and complex subjects into terms intelligible to the masses but must do so interestingly. The chief aim of the reporter, after all, is to get stories read. The aim of the deskman is to arrest attention with a headline. If the handling of a story and the headline that surmounts it attract readers to serious fare, that in itself is justification.

Especially among the magazines leading in circulation, the pressures to find and keep a large audience have sometimes contributed to a fusion of the functions of entertainment and enlightenment. Since World War II many magazines have shortened nonfiction articles on the assumption that readers no longer have the patience for long ones. But it is difficult to treat some subjects more than superficially in the allotted space and a few magazines— notably *The New Yorker, Esquire, Harper's,* and *Atlantic*—have devoted some of their columns to longer and more serious presentations.

Network broadcasters feel obliged to offer something for everybody. As CBS executive Richard S. Salant expressed it:

> For the fact is that broadcasting is truly a mass medium; it has to be. Unless it can enlist and hold the interest of most of the people a good part of the time, it is just too expensive to survive. It must, in its spectrum of programming, have some- thing—even the great majority of its material—that will appeal not just to the thousands or hundreds of thousands but to millions and tens of millions.[3]

A medium that is compelled to interest the tens of millions, one that counts most first-graders among its regular users, usually finds its common denomi- nator in entertainment.

In its entertainment fare, broadcasting must make certain compromises in subject matter and treatment as a result of the demands of the market. Although in the movie *Network* Paddy Chayefsky cruelly satirized the compromises television news makes to hold or enlarge the audience, he has acknowledged from personal experience the compromises a serious televi- sion playwright must make in entertainment. Chayefsky once said that he had never encountered sponsor or network interference with his television dramas, thanks to a producer who took a firm position. But he added:

> On the other hand, every one of us, before we sit down and write a television show, makes that initial compromise of what we're going to write. We don't sit down and write for television or conceive a television idea that we know is going to be thrown out the window. That's the compromise. I have never, never written down in television in my life, but I have never aimed very high. . . . You make that same compromise in the movies, and you make it on the stage too, but in a relatively less degree.[4]

What Chayefsky recognized was that television playwrights must accom- modate themselves to a mass audience and to advertisers who regard almost any controversy in the shows they sponsor as bad business. Limita- tions on dramatic subject matter arise partly because advertisers do not wish to offend anyone. Several advertising agency executives who testified at

FCC hearings agreed that programs that displease a substantial number of viewers represent a misuse of the advertising dollar. When fundamentalist groups protested a two-part Easter Week telecast on the life of Christ, "Jesus of Nazareth," in 1977, General Motors withdrew its sponsorship. Because sponsors want to leave their audience with a favorable impression, they usually avoid dramas that treat socially taboo subjects, portray extremes of misery or desolation, leave the viewer sad and depressed or deal with politics—politics being controversial and capable of alienating customers.

Although mass media economics make the presentation of quality entertainment difficult, the mass media can transcend the limitations of a mass audience or sensitive sponsors to produce works that are not only entertaining but have the lasting qualities of art. No contemporary movie or television performer, except perhaps actors in daytime television serials, rivals the extraordinary productivity of Charlie Chaplin who made 35 films in his first year for Mack Sennett's Keystone in 1913. Yet even though Chaplin was churning out entertainment for a mass audience with little time to dwell on aesthetic refinements, intellectuals soon began to write of his work as art, later of the film medium as a serious art form. Television has inherited the early prejudices against film, but occasional shows have overcome these and convinced skeptical critics of their lasting quality. ABC television's remarkable adaptation of Alex Haley's best-selling novel "Roots" for presentation in eight episodes on successive nights in 1977 not only attracted the largest audiences in television history but persuaded some critics that the production was more than mere entertainment.

The "Problem" of Entertainment

A disapproving tone invariably colors discussion of mass media entertainment in American society. When distinctions are made between news or information and entertainment, between entertainment and art, whatever is finally categorized as entertainment seems somehow less worthy than information or art. Why? Several reasons suggest themselves.

Traditional libertarian theory has given little attention to the entertainment functions of the mass media. Entertainment has no constitutional or philosophical rationale as does news. In the United States entertainment has never been considered important to the successful functioning of political institutions, as it has been under certain modern totalitarian systems, although radical critiques posit that entertainment is the opiate of the people, the establishment's device for diverting the masses from the flaws and contradictions of the American capitalist system. What weakens the radical critiques is the history of official suspicion and censorship of entertainment which has often been thought to threaten allegiance to the state, corrupt morals and debase the natural good taste of the public. Only

ABC's television adaptation of Alex Haley's best-selling novel *Roots* was not only a success in the ratings but also won considerable critical acclaim. (Wide World photo)

gradually has entertainment been allowed the freedom accorded informational content.

The first widely accepted legal definition of obscenity, the Hicklin test of 1868, was a legal transplant from Britain. It specified that the test of obscenity was "whether the tendency of the matter charged as obscenity is to deprave and corrupt those whose minds are open to such immoral influences, and into whose hands a publication might fall," and it was not repudiated in the United States until 1934. Then a U.S. court of appeals declared that James Joyce's *Ulysses* was not obscene and set a new test, that of "dominant effect." The objectionable parts had to be considered in the context of the work as a whole and in terms of literary and social values. Although, as constitutional scholar C. Herman Pritchett notes, the "abandonment of the Hicklin test permitted more civilized judgments on literary works,"[5] the Supreme Court still holds that obscenity is not constitutionally protected speech. To enjoy that protection, disputed matter must be shown to have serious literary, political or social value. Nevertheless, official tolerance of sexually explicit material has significantly expanded.

Although sexual content in mass media entertainment does not necessarily enjoy First Amendment protection, the Supreme Court decided in *Winters v. New York* in 1948 that entertainment per se does. The court ruled:

We do not accede to appellee's suggestion that the constitutional protection for a free press applies only to the exposition of ideas. The line between the informing and the entertaining is too elusive for the protection of the basic right. Everyone is familiar with instances of propaganda through fiction. What is one man's amusement, teaches another man's doctrine.[6]

Movies did not enjoy First Amendment protection until 1952. State and local boards of censors regulated the exhibition of movies with the approval of the Supreme Court, which had ruled in 1915 that movies were simple commercial products and not a constitutionally protected medium of speech. Then in *Burstyn v. Wilson* in 1952 the Supreme Court held that movies "are a significant medium for the communication of ideas" and brought movies within First Amendment protection.[7]

Although these court decisions gradually brought more forms of expression within First Amendment protection, the nature of that protection differs from medium to medium. Each mode of dissemination or method of expression, the courts have acknowledged, has its own problems to which the law has responded. Thus when broadcast technology was developed, its First Amendment protection was affected by these factors: the scarcity of spectrum space, children's potentially unsupervised access to radio and television receivers, and broadcasting's potential invasion of the privacy of the home.

The courts' wrestling with the elusive line between information and entertainment, between what should and should not be protected communication, indicates society's problem in dealing with material that has no obvious motive to educate or inform. Libertarian theory regards these functions as central to the operation of democracy. Lacking these explicit libertarian functions, entertainment continues to be controversial as Americans spend more and more time with the mass media, much of whose content is avowedly entertainment. As people dominated nature with machines and reduced the hard labor and chores of life with electrical appliances, as legislation reduced the work week from as much as 70 or 80 hours at the turn of the century to 40 hours today, and as the majority of Americans came to enjoy a middle-class income, particularly after World War II, so more and more leisure and income have been spent on the mass media. Wilbur Schramm reported these figures in 1973:

> The approximately 75 percent of American adults who read newspapers regularly spend an average of 35 minutes a day on them; the approximately 40 percent of Americans who read magazines regularly spend an average of 33 minutes per day on them; the one-third of Americans who read books regularly spend an average of 47 minutes a day on them. The television receiver in an average American home . . . is turned on more than 6 hours a day during the winter months, and all the media together absorb more than 5 hours per day of an average American's time . . . —more than he allocates to anything else except work and sleep.[8]

The media industries have responded to this demand with a pluralism and diversity of media offerings that, on the one hand, provide the range of choice libertarian theory requires for the pursuit of truth and the proper performance of citizenship and, on the other, enable citizens to choose entertainment rather than information. With every new communications technology, the opportunity to avoid explicitly educational and informational material has expanded, so offending the strictures of generations of civics teachers.

Although its own respectability tends to fluctuate, the "Puritan ethic" still affects the reputation of entertainment. Even as American society progresses to a shorter work week, the value of the work ethic seems not to decline nor entertainment to shrug off its aura as a creature of easy virtue, of gaudy frivolity. Furthermore, even as Americans show unfathomable interest in the trivia of entertainers' lives, so sustaining media industries that respond to their fascination, the huge salaries of leading entertainers offend many critics as obscene and soil the reputation of entertainment. Critics of this phenomenon are fond of pointing out that whereas Robert Redford can earn $2 million for four weeks' work in the movie *A Bridge Too Far,* William Safire can sell the paperback rights for his potboiler novel *Full Disclosure* for $1,375,000, and network news celebrities like Walter Cronkite and Barbara Walters can earn between $400,000 and $500,000 a year for reading 23 minutes of news-entertainment five nights a week, the President of the United States earns only $200,000 a year, a U.S. Congressman $59,700 a year, and a justice of the Supreme Court $66,000 a year. The apparent discrepancy in social values these salaries suggest tends to focus unflattering attention on entertainment and to reinforce a certain social unease with the time and money spent on entertainment.

Effects of Entertainment

The reasons suggested thus far for that social unease have been largely speculative and derive from a concentration on what entertainment is and how much time and money are spent on it. Both the content and the time spent on it have been described as escapist, a term that tends in this society to have negative connotations. Some years ago Joseph T. Klapper reviewed the different meanings that social scientists had given the term "escapist," and fashioned a common-denominator definition: "that communication which provides emotional release by diverting the reader from his own problems or anxieties."[9]

What is escapist for one person, then, is not necessarily so for another. If one uses media content primarily for pleasure, it is escapist no matter what else it is. Thus a businessman who relaxes with a magazine article about science or a scientist who takes refuge in the sports page of his newspaper is using the mass media for diversion. Under that concept all media fare is potentially entertainment. Whether it is or not depends upon the use to which the reader, viewer, or listener puts it.

One must be properly hesitant in generalizing about anything so nebulous as a national character or ethos, but American society seems particularly unwilling to approve anything smacking of escapism. Certainly the impulse for the early research of American social scientists into the effects of the mass media was rooted in concern that the effects were undesirable, that so much exposure to mass media content was leading to antisocial behavior.

Persuasive Powers

Research shows that entertainment is capable of affecting the way people think and act. Indeed, the assumption that entertainment can influence people's minds underlies a good deal of censorship. Fear of the persuasive and corruptive possibilities of entertainment lies behind much of the public concern over comic books, paperback novels, violence on television, and sensationalism in newspapers.

Convinced that entertainment is subtly forceful in propaganda, people have been using it for centuries. During the Revolutionary War newspapers, almanacs, and broadsides sought to lighten the burden of battle with anecdotes, jests, parodies, satires, and songs, which were also designed to promote the cause of freedom. The popular novel has been a widely used form of social protest, and cartoons have been a frequent weapon of crusaders at least since *Harper's Weekly* ran pictures by Thomas Nast to break the political power of the Tweed Ring in New York in 1870–1871.

Some of the findings of empirical research involving the persuasive powers of entertainment are contradictory. Studies do show, however, that certain types of entertainment—the soap opera, for example, and magazine stories—are effective. It is reasonable to suppose that entertainment has some effects similar to those of informational and avowedly persuasive content. That is, entertainment works outright conversion only rarely; more often it slightly modifies existing attitudes. Little by little, over a long period, it probably contributes to the attitudinal prism through which people perceive their environment and with which they interpret the multitudinous messages reaching them.

Much magazine fiction in the 1930s and 1940s emphasized the conventional virtues and idolized the little man, according to a study by Patrick Johns-Heine and Hans H. Gerth. While ostensibly preaching racial equality, it subtly perpetuated discrimination against minority groups and glorified the white Protestant American of Anglo-Saxon stock, according to another study by Bernard Berelson and Patricia Salter. Television producer Norman Lear has argued that the presentation of socially relevant material in his popular situation comedy, "All in the Family," has made bigoted people aware of their prejudices and given them an insight into how undesirable these are. In a review of research on "All in the Family" and similar television comedies—"Sanford and Son," "The Jeffersons" and "Good

Times"—Stuart Surlin reported in 1976, however, that persons with strong prejudices tended to have them reinforced rather than reduced by watching these programs.[10]

POSSIBLE VALUES AND DANGERS OF ESCAPISM

In his study of mass media effects, Klapper reported that people sometimes use entertainment to escape from feelings of inferiority and insecurity by identifying themselves with successful characters in stories, articles, films, and broadcasts. By enabling them to share vicariously in the good life and triumphs of others, identification provides a sense of prestige. At worst this is harmless, Klapper concluded; at best, helpful.

Some observers think that media entertainment offers a safety valve for pent-up aggressions and aberrant impulses and consequently performs a useful social function. This argument is at least as old as John Milton's *Areopagitica,* in which, to be sure, it took a somewhat different cast. Although Milton no doubt would be appalled at being cited to justify comic books, he nevertheless argued that reading is the best way to learn of evil. No man can be virtuous without a knowledge of evil, he said, and it is far better to learn vicariously through reading than through experience.

Some students of mass communication fear that overexposure to escapist material, by diverting people from the problems of daily living and by encouraging their retreat into a dream world, may promote individual and group apathy and thus inhibit social progress. But Klapper sees little reason for believing that escapist material diverts people from serious media fare. True, some people overindulge, he concedes, but they might be more dangerously preoccupied if the media were not so readily available. He grants that those who make heavy use of the media for escape probably have little interest in serious social problems, but he submits that their lack of interest is more likely to be the cause rather than the result of their tastes. A related concern because people spend so much time with the media, particularly television, is that conversational and creative skills have declined.

Other observers are concerned because some users of the mass media depend upon entertainment for information and advice. This can work harm in any of several ways. For one thing the advice is usually so superficial or impractical that it is likely to be futile; or it may be just plain wrong. For another it can lead people to a passive acceptance of whatever ills and misfortunes befall them in the confident hope that everything will work out all right sooner or later.

Still other authorities believe that certain types of media entertainment can seduce the weak-willed and the immature into lives of crime or immorality. The codes of performance for the comic-book, motion-picture and broadcasting industries all recognize this danger by urging that criminals never be glorified, crime never be portrayed attractively, and sin never be glamorized. In evaluating studies of these seductive effects, Klapper concluded, "The evidence they adduced, however, cannot substantiate any cause-and-effect relationship, and can be easily accounted for by the more established thesis that mass media material tends to further the development of already existing personality traits." Authorities sharing Klapper's view contend that the media do not teach transgressors their bad impulses, which arise from a complexity of causes; at worst, they may teach them the methods of carrying out those impulses.

Because adults bring to their encounters with the mass media a lifetime of socialization and experience from a welter of sources—home and family, school and church, work and social groups, friends and peers—researchers face an almost impossible task in trying to tease out the particular effects that specific media content may have on them. Even in rigorously controlled experimental conditions, researchers can rarely demonstrate with complete confidence cause-effect relationships between media content and attitudes and behavior.

CHILDREN AND TELEVISION

Studies of children confront similar difficulties, although the younger the children, the less socialization they have experienced, and the more vulnerable they are to the influences of media content. Research findings on children therefore tend to be more persuasive than those on adults. And there have been thousands of studies on children because of mounting concern about statistics like these:

According to A. C. Nielsen, children under 5 were watching an average of 23.5 hours of television a week in 1977. By high-school graduation, then, the average 17-year-old will have watched 15,000 hours of television during which he will have seen 350,000 commercials and 18,000 murders.

Studies have shown that so much television watching stifles children's creative imagination, instills attitudes of spectatorship rather than of participation, produces a low tolerance for the frustrations of learning, reinforces sex role stereotypes, and develops exaggerated fears of the danger of violence in their lives. The television industry challenges much of the research's assertion of causality on the one hand and blames parents for failing to regulate children's viewing habits on the other. But even the industry has acknowledged that some children under certain conditions will imitate violent and antisocial acts seen on television.

After analyzing the findings of 23 related studies on the effects on children of televised violence supported by his office at a cost of more than $1 million, the U.S. Surgeon General reported in 1972 to the Senate Commerce Subcommittee:

> The overwhelming consensus and the unanimous scientific advisory committee's report indicates that televised violence, indeed, does have an adverse effect on certain members of our society. . . . The data in social phenomena such as television and violence and/or aggressive behavior will never be clear enough for all social scientists to agree on the formulation of a succinct statement of

By high school graduation the average 17-year-old will have watched 15,000 hours of television during which he will have seen some 350,000 commercials and 18,000 murders. (Kenneth Karp)

causality. But there comes a time when the data are sufficient to justify action. That time has come.[11]

Studies show further that for most American children television is a major socializing agent. Eleanor Maccoby, professor of psychology at Stanford, summarized several studies:

> The nature of the effects depends upon many limiting conditions. . . . But the impact of the media is real. What the child absorbs while he is being 'entertained' he uses in the interpretation of his real-life experiences, and in preparing himself for roles that he will play in the future, as well as for immediate action. And the media may influence moods (e.g., produce moods of pessimism) or transmit persuasive beliefs (e.g., that the world is a threatening place), as well as present bits of information or bits of action for imitation.[12]

In 1973 Wilbur Schramm summarized research findings showing the "startling amount" of incidental information from media content intended to entertain rather than inform that children learn directly and indirectly:

> For many children entertainment media (especially television) provide a kind of social map. They learn what the distant world is like, who and what is worth looking at, what kind of behavior is valued. And this map is extremely vivid because children give themselves to entertainment media. The media attract them, excite them, arouse them.[13]

The Culture Debate

What effect does all the emphasis on entertainment have on American culture? No final answer is possible, but a clear focus on the questions can be derived from an interesting debate between Bernard Rosenberg and David Manning White.

Rosenberg's beliefs about the effect of mass communication on the fabric of culture are summarized here:

> There can be no doubt that the mass media present a major threat to man's autonomy. To know that they might also contain some small seeds of freedom only makes a bad situation nearly desperate. No art form, no body of knowledge, no system of ethics is strong enough to withstand vulgarization.[14]

The center of Rosenberg's argument is that mass culture is made to seem effortless. Dumping Shakespeare on the market along with Mickey Spillane, Rosenberg argues, places a master of world literature on the same level with a lickspittle—and suggests to readers that the same preparation is required for each.

White is almost equally vehement on the other side:

> The xenophilic critics who discuss American culture as if they were holding a dead vermin in their hands seem to imply that in some other, better age the bulk of people were fair copies of Leonardo Da Vinci. No critic shudders more audibly when discussing the vulgarities of American life than T. S. Eliot. Yet it is only realistic to note that in the England which became Eliot's haven, one of the most popular of diversions for nearly 700 years was bear-baiting. I do not cite this to demean the contributions to our world culture of a Chaucer, a Reynolds, a Thomas Tallis, or any English artist who added to the world's treasury, but only to draw the point that art was no more important to the mass of the people of their day than the goings-on at Paris Garden in Southwark, the chief bear-garden in London.[15]

White is not a blind defender of the media. He admitted that there are aspects of mass culture that are "banal, dehumanizing, and downright ugly." But he also pointed out that even though the media are Big Business and must show a profit, they bring valuable fare to millions.

ALEXIS DE TOCQUEVILLE'S VIEW

The response of the critics to such defenses of the media is often to recall the observations of an insightful foreign visitor, Alexis de Tocqueville. If his gloomy analysis was accurate, there is little reason to speculate about culture in the United States; a democracy cannot develop a culture of high quality and unquestioned merit. In a closely argued section of *Democracy in America,* which was published in 1835, de Tocqueville began by discussing artisanship. Aristocratic nations, he pointed out, gradually segregate workers until each craft forms a distinct class. Within each class the workers are known to each other and reputations are built on quality of workmanship. The aim of artisans is to stand high among their colleagues, only secondarily

In democracies, de Tocqueville argued, no such pride of workmanship is possible. The classes and professions are ever shifting. Every craft is open to everyone; the artisans are not necessarily known to one another; artisans stand in relationship to their customers rather than to their craft. Customers, unlike the privileged classes in aristocratic nations, are themselves creatures of mobility. If they are rising on the social scale, their desires are likely to grow faster than their fortune, and they try to acquire the objects of wealth before they can afford them, usually by shortcuts that create a demand for objects of synthetic value. Customers who are sinking on the scale retain the desires that were nurtured in the days of their affluence, and they, too, satisfy themselves surreptitiously. Artisans, too, wish to rise on the scale, and they perceive that wealth derives from selling many items at relatively low cost. Quality deteriorates.

De Tocqueville believed that the effect of democracy runs still deeper:

> Something analogous to what I have already pointed out in the useful arts then takes place in the fine arts; the productions of artists are more numerous, but the merit of each production is diminished. No longer able to soar to what is great, they cultivate what is pretty and elegant, and appearance is more attended to than reality.
>
> In aristocracies a few great pictures are produced; in democratic countries a vast number of insignificant ones. In the former, statues are raised of bronze: in the latter, they are modeled in plaster.[16]

DWIGHT MACDONALD

"The conservative proposal to save culture by restoring the old class lines," Dwight Macdonald has written, "has a more solid historical base than the Marxian hope for a new democratic, classless culture, for, with the possible (and important) exception of Periclean Athens, all the great cultures of the past were elite cultures." But Macdonald adds that the conservative solution "is without meaning in a world dominated by the two great mass nations, U.S.A. and U.S.S.R., and becoming more industrialized, massified all the time."

Macdonald sees three different cultures in America: High Culture, Mass Culture, and Folk Art. He is actually as gloomy about American culture as de Tocqueville was. For the appeal and the rewards of Mass Culture (which the Germans derisively term *Kitsch*) have been gradually affecting High Culture and Folk Art:

> If there were a clearly defined cultural elite, then the masses could have their *kitsch* and the elite could have its High Culture, with everybody happy. But, the boundary line is blurred. A statistically significant part of the population, I venture to guess, is chronically confronted with the choice of going to the movies or going to a concert, between reading Tolstoy or a detective story, between looking at old masters or at a TV show: i.e., the pattern of their cultural lives is "open" to the point of being porous. Good art competes with *kitsch*, serious

ideas compete with commercialized formulas—and the advantage lies all on one side. There seems to be a Gresham's Law in cultural as well as monetary circulation: bad stuff drives out the good, since it is more easily understood and enjoyed. It is this facility of access which at once sells *kitsch* on a wide market and also prevents it from achieving quality.[17]

Macdonald thus argues that Mass Culture is not just bad in and of itself; it homogenizes all culture and debases the entire spectrum. Clement Greenberg agrees, holding that *kitsch* "predigests art for the spectator and spares him effort, provides him with a shortcut to the pleasures of art that detours what is necessarily difficult in genuine art."[18]

It is a curious commentary on the validity of these criticisms that Dwight Macdonald's own career seems to bear out his chief contention. Writing in 1953, Macdonald listed *The New Yorker* among the magazines that debase High Culture. Its short stories, he wrote, are "smooth, minor-key, casual, suggesting drama and sentiment without ever being crude enough to actually create it;" *New Yorker* editors developed the style by skillfully selecting in the same way a gardener develops a new kind of rose. Then, a few years later, almost as though he were proving his point that High Culture is gradually enveloped in Mass Culture, Macdonald became a writer for *The New Yorker*.

WALT WHITMAN

If one accepts the premises of these critics, it is extraordinarily difficult to avoid their conclusions. But there is, of course, another side of the coin, which is not likely to be seen without looking at the conditions that obtained in the last century. As they were presented by Walt Whitman, the conditions set forth entirely different premises.

Much of the acclaim for Whitman springs from his poetry celebrating The People—the great, ill-defined masses that were beginning to loom on every side after the middle of the nineteenth century. A similar contribution may have come with the writing of *Democratic Vistas* in 1871, in which he argued for a clean break with the art of aristocratic nations:

> I should demand a program of culture, drawn out, not for a single class alone, or for the parlors or lecture rooms, but with an eye to the practical life, the west, the workingman, the facts of farms and jack-planes and engineers. . . . I should demand of this program or theory a scope generous enough to include the widest human area. It must have for its spinal meaning the formation of a typical personality of character, eligible to the uses of the high average of men . . . and not restricted by conditions ineligible to the masses. The best culture will always be that of the manly courageous instincts, and loving perceptions, and of self-respect—aiming to form, over this continent, and ideocrasy of universalism.[19]

GILBERT SELDES

The rapid development of urban life in the twentieth century has, of course, dictated quite different conditions from any Whitman could have imagined. Whitman's appeal for a democratic culture to reflect the pioneer spirit seems quaint in these times. But some modern observers have provided modern echoes of the original call for a democratic culture. In *The Great Audience* Gilbert Seldes laments that the artist in America has often gone abroad to seek recognition:

> . . . from the time of James Fenimore Cooper to the day of Sinclair Lewis, writers have found some way to attack the average American, not in loving correction but in contempt. In all that time perhaps two dozen men and women have been artists so great that they were misunderstood; the rest were good, but not good enough to separate themselves from their fellow men; they made little effort to understand what was happening in America, were incapable of helping or guiding or comforting. . . .

The "misunderstood" artist of the past has given way to the one who no longer cares whether

> he is understood or not, since he is not trying to communicate anything in the traditional sense of the word.[20]

Although there are stark differences between the critics who argue that only an aristocratically oriented culture is viable and those who contend that there is a deep need for democratic culture, they are united in criticism of the mass media. This is entirely understandable: Aspects of art—some drawings, paintings, and music, for example—exist quite apart from the modern instruments of communication, but the great bulk of Mass Culture is carried by the mass media. In fact, the most severe criticisms of American culture from both factions center on the world of newspapers, magazines, radio, television, books, and films. Were they not so pervasive, the critics argue, Mass Culture would not be so overwhelming. And were the rewards of the mass media not so alluring, Mass Culture would not find it so easy to subvert High Culture and Folk Art.

It must be obvious, however, that those who argue for an aristocratic culture are the more caustic critics of the mass media. Among the most caustic is Ernest van den Haag, who has written:

> The circumstances which permit the experience of art are rare in our society anyway and they cannot be expected in the audience of mass media. That audience is dispersed and heterogeneous, and though it listens often, it does so intermittently and poised to leave if not immediately enthralled and kept amused. . . . And the conditions and conditioning of the audience demand a mad mixture of important and trivial matters, atom bombs, hit tunes, symphonies, B.O., sob stories, hotcha girls, round tables and jokes.[21]

Even so acclaimed an educational program as public television's "Sesame Street," which is designed mainly to teach preschoolers their numbers and alphabet, has been criticized for contributing to the kind of conditioning van den Haag condemns. Some educators are concerned that, outstanding though "Sesame Street" is in many respects, it works so hard to keep children enthralled and amused with its brilliant puppetry and electronic wizardry that they are being conditioned to expect all learning, all information and art to be accompanied by visually exciting entertainment.

Culture and Public Policy

The media policy implications of the "aristocratic" critics' attacks are particularly offensive to students of media uses and gratifications. Harold Mendelsohn summarizes the reaction of uses and gratifications researchers this way:

> It is precisely because numerous publics with varieties of social and psychological attributes, and with differing interests, motivations, expectations and tastes, come away from the media with varying experiences, that formulating media policies on any given predetermined catalogue of audience needs will be self-servingly unrealistic. In this respect, the attacks on popular culture by elitist humanists stand out as rather presumptuous hollow assertions regarding human needs (mostly alleged aesthetic needs) as well as human behavior. To the elitist critic of popular culture, the mass media serve but one fundamental need (and, one might add, an evil need), the need for passive escape.[22]

Mendelsohn is particularly critical of the tendency of the elitist critics to want to determine media content rather than permit audiences to determine it. That is, says Mendelsohn, "the needs, uses, and gratifications of the critics, rather than those of the audiences, would serve as the bases for the neo-Platonic media policies of the elite humanistic critics of popular culture."[23] Certainly any reading of these critics will reveal their impatience and frustration with the slow and haphazard processes of formal education and of professional reviewing and criticism in raising public taste and appreciation of what they consider aesthetically satisfactory.

Public policy toward the arts was not really a lively issue in the United States until the establishment of the National Endowment for the Arts and Humanities in 1965 and the passage of the Public Broadcasting Act in 1967, both of which committed the federal government to supporting culture with tax revenue. Until then Congress had resisted pressure to help finance the arts, arguing that that was an improper role for government, one which had the potential for developing a state-controlled culture. While it was an attitude appropriate to a society founded on profound suspicion of government, the artistic community felt excluded, without a respected role in society. Nobel Prize winning novelist William Faulkner told the American Academy of Arts and Letters in 1957: "The artist has no more actual place in the American culture of today than he has in the American economy of today, no place at all in the warp and woof, the thews and sinews, the mosaic of the American dream."[24]

The cultural explosion of the late 1950s and early 1960s and President John F. Kennedy's visible commitment to the arts helped change these views of the role of the arts in society. Kennedy's symbolic gesture of inviting the poet Robert Frost to read a poem at the Inauguration and of inviting more than 50 writers, composers, and painters to attend was instantly effective. "What a joy that literacy is no longer prima facie evidence of treason," said Nobel laureate John Steinbeck. Archibald MacLeish wrote to President Kennedy, "No country which did not respect its arts has ever been great and ours has ignored them too long. . . . I heard the inaugural address. . . . It left me proud and hopeful to be an American—something I have not felt for almost twenty years."[25] Although Kennedy felt that "government can at best play only a marginal role in our cultural affairs,"[26] he established the Advisory Council on the Arts by executive order in 1963 following recommendations in a report on "The Arts and the National Government" that he had commissioned.

The sudden prominence of artists in the social life of the Presidency and of the arts in discussion of national policy finally persuaded Congress that it was appropriate for government to support American culture. But in administering the distribution of tax revenues for the arts, the National Endowment and the Corporation for Public Broadcasting, established by the 1967 Public Broadcasting Act, have necessarily been involved in aesthetic issues, specifically in the culture debate Rosenberg and White have so admirably presented. Who is to get how much of government's increasing appropriations for the arts—$170 million for the National Endowment and $103 million for public broadcasting in 1977—and in terms of what criteria will these questions be decided?

Advocates of high or elite culture argue that the funds are best spent on a few established centralized sources of public television programing and on established institutions like opera companies, symphony orchestras, dance companies, and museums, institutions which they argue are being crippled by rising costs and inflation. A 1974 Ford Foundation survey of 166 non-profit theaters, symphony orchestras, and opera and dance companies for the six seasons 1965–66 to 1970–71 found that the organizations taken together had a gap between earnings and expenses of $62 million for the 1970–71 season and a cumulative six-year operating loss of $8.4 million. Extrapolating from the survey's trends and assuming an inflation rate of 7 percent, the Ford Foundation projected a gap between earnings and expenses of $335 million for the 1980–81 season that it strongly urged government to help fill.[27]

Advocates of mass, popular, or grass roots culture argue that the funds should be spent more democratically, on state and local public broadcasting stations and on state and local arts councils and through them on local artists and arts activities. As is usual in the political process, funding has been distributed in a way that tries to satisfy both groups but does not fully satisfy either.

Another group still holds that government has no business funding culture. Tom Bethel, a Washington editor of *Harper's,* articulated this view in August 1977:

Unfortunately, however, this notion of culture as something that everyone
could enjoy—and therefore as something that needed no government funding
because it was so popular—never did appeal particularly to those who . . . saw
in art an opportunity to stake out a claim to superior sensibility. And that, I fear, is
the unstated intention behind federal funding of the arts. It is a fairly blatant
attempt to restore (or at least preserve) European conceptions of culture that are
either obsolete . . . or else frankly elitist.

Federal funding of the arts thus also involves a subtle denigration of American culture. What it really boils down to is an appeal to tax the mobs listening to
country-and-western, or rock, or soul, because *we*, the wonderful ones, have
something rather more elevated on our minds that *deserves* your subsidy.[28]

Bethel's view, however, at least for the moment, has been defeated. A
bill cosponsored by about 50 Congressmen was introduced to the House in
1977 proposing an income-tax checkoff system on tax returns that, if
enacted, would produce a projected $1.7 billion a year for the arts. Observ-
ers judged that the bill had an excellent chance of passage.

Part of the justification behind government funding of the arts is that it
redresses some of the damage thought to have been inflicted on public taste
by mass media entertainment. The impact of government funding cannot be
measured, but supporters of that funding quote statistics like these for the
decade since government involvement began: dance audiences up from 1
million to 15 million, major symphony orchestras up from 50 to 110 and
their audiences in 1977 reaching 26 million, museum attendance up to 50
million persons a year. Defenders of mass media entertainment claim a
share of responsibility for those statistics, arguing that high quality media
content has stimulated increasing public interest in the arts. They point to
such instances as NBC television's "Tut: The Boy King," an hour-long
prime-time special narrated by Orson Welles in July 1977 on treasures from
the tomb of Pharaoh Tutankhamun that were part of an exhibit touring U.S.
galleries and museums in 1977 as evidence of the mass media's role in
raising public taste.

The defenders of mass media entertainment argue furthermore that
even in their less ambitious content they no longer provide only escapist
entertainment. They argue that television entertainment, which has taken
the brunt of the attack for undesirable effects on culture and on social
behavior, has dealt consistently with socially relevant issues since the mid-
1960s. The women's movement in particular affected prime-time television.
Whereas actresses complained bitterly in the mid-1970s that there were no
good movie roles for women, prime-time situation comedies were dominated by the predicament of black and white, working- and middle-class
women, single, married, widowed, and divorced, several with fatherless
families, and all struggling to manage the often conflicting demands of
homes, social lives, and careers.

Not surprisingly, television's intrusion into social and political relevancy
did not please everyone, no matter how flattering the Nielsen ratings. In a
wide-ranging analysis of television in the conservative journal, *The Public*

sympathies by the way he characterized the trend:

> From 1953 through 1966, not a single program in this list [of the top prime-time
> shows] could have been regarded as politically or socially "relevant." But by
> 1972, five of the top 10 could have conceivably been so regarded—and their
> themes were always "establishment-liberal" or "establishment-swinger."[29]

No survey of the roles, values, and effects of mass media entertainment
can overcome a pervasive inconclusiveness. Nor in trying to convey the
diversity of opinions and research findings can it avoid creating the impression that preoccupation with the "problem" of mass media entertainment
was in the nature of a national neurosis. As final perspective, therefore, note
that in spite of the increasing amount of time average Americans were
spending with the mass media in the 1970s, they were somehow finding
more and more time outside working and sleeping hours to attend live
performances of the arts and of sporting events and to engage in such
increasingly popular outdoor activities as golf, tennis, skiing, jogging, and
backpacking, for which healthy enthusiasms the mass media also claimed
partial responsibility.

Notes

1. Neil Shister, "Polygraphs and Wires: TV Research Guys Mean Business,"
   MORE, December 1976, p. 38.
2. Daniel J. Boorstin, *The Image: A Guide to Pseudo-Events in America* (New
   York: Harper Colophon Books, 1964), pp. 5–6.
3. Speech at the Stanford University–*TV Guide* Broadcasting seminar, Asilomar,
   California, June 21, 1966.
4. Quoted in a UPI report, Palo Alto *Times,* May 17, 1970.
5. C. Herman Pritchett, *The American Constitution,* 2nd edition (New York:
   McGraw-Hill, 1968), p. 493.
6. *Winter v. New York,* 333 U.S. 507 (1948).
7. *Joseph Burstyn, Inc. v. Wilson,* 343 U.S. 495 (1952).
8. Wilbur Schramm, *Men, Messages, and Media* (New York: Harper & Row,
   1973), p. 173.
9. Joseph T. Klapper, *The Effects of Mass Media* (New York: Bureau of Applied
   Social Research, 1949), p. III–5.
10. Stuart H. Surlin, "Five Years of 'All in the Family': A Summary of Empirical
    Research Generated by the Program," *Mass Comm Review,* Summer 1976,
    pp. 2–6.
11. Proceedings of the U.S. Senate Commerce Subcommittee, March 21, 1972,
    Washington, D.C.: U.S. Government Printing Office, 1972.
12. Quoted in William L. Rivers, Theodore Peterson, and Jay W. Jensen, *The Mass
    Media and Modern Society,* 2nd edition (New York: Holt, Rinehart and Win-
    ston, 1971), p. 266.
13. Schramm, p. 163.
14. Bernard Rosenberg, "Mass Culture in America," in Rosenberg and David
    Manning White (eds.), *Mass Culture: The Popular Arts in America* (New York:
    Free Press, 1957), p. 5.

15. David Manning White, "Mass Culture in America: Another Point of View," in Rosenberg and White, p. 14.
16. Alexis de Tocqueville, "In What Spirit the Americans Cultivate the Arts," in Rosenberg and White, pp. 29–30.
17. Dwight Macdonald, "A Theory of Mass Culture," in Rosenberg and White, p. 61.
18. Rosenberg and White, p. 61.
19. Walt Whitman, "From 'Democratic Vistas,'" in Rosenberg and White, p. 38.
20. Gilbert Seldes, "The People and the Arts," in Rosenberg and White, pp. 78, 79.
21. Ernest van den Haag, "Of Happiness and Despair We Have no Measure," in Rosenberg and White, p. 516.
22. Harold Mendelsohn, "Some Policy Implications of the Uses and Gratifications Paradigm," in Jay G. Blumler and Elihu Katz (eds.), *The Uses of Mass Communications: Current Perspectives on Gratifications Research* (Beverly Hills: Sage Publications, 1974), p. 304.
23. Mendelsohn in Blumler and Katz, p. 304.
24. Quoted in Arthur M. Schlesinger, Jr., *A Thousand Days: John F. Kennedy in the White House* (Greenwich, Conn.: Fawcett, 1965), p. 669.
25. Schlesinger, p. 671.
26. Schlesinger, p. 674.
27. "The Finances of the Performing Arts," Vol. I, The Ford Foundation, 1974.
28. Tom Bethell, "The Cultural Tithe: An Argument Against Federal Funding of the Arts," *Harper's,* August 1977, p. 25.
29. Michael J. Robinson, "Television and American Politics: 1956–76," *The Public Interest,* Summer 1977, p. 32.

14

Epilogue

Where is the wisdom we have lost in knowledge?
Where is the knowledge we have lost in information?

T. S. ELIOT

By 1978 much of the new technology whose potential
had so excited people for more than a decade was in use. Most American
newsrooms, print and broadcast, were electronic or in process of becoming
electronic. Videocassette units that enabled people to record for later viewing programs shown at inconvenient times were on the market—expensive
(they cost about $1000 a unit), but available. New technology was realizing
something of democracy's fabled town meeting. For $300 subscribers to the
cable television system in The Woodlands, a new community 30 miles north
of Houston, Texas, could buy a home terminal unit that connected them to
the system's central computer. This two-way cable television system enabled them to participate from their living rooms in the community's monthly
town meetings. By pushing buttons they could vote on issues or direct
speakers to talk louder, to go faster or slower, or to change the subject.

In Britain the newspaper was being delivered electronically to home
television screens by both the British Broadcasting Corporation and the
Independent Television Authority. Moreover, viewers could select from the
available teletext (type on the screen) what they wanted. In New York the
British-owned Reuters news agency was offering a similar service to broker
age and financial houses. Reuters promised to extend this service to businessmen in their own homes, and to the general public by spring 1978.
Reuters proposed to use the satellite system that a national pay cable

service, Home Box Office, was using to beam its services to earth stations and from these via cable into American homes.

Because Americans are fascinated with new gadgetry and find "progress" irresistible, it seems likely that these information and entertainment services will become widespread. But just how many people will shift from largely passive communication roles, with editors and directors selecting, organizing, and assessing the relative significance of information and entertainment for them, to active, selective roles is by no means clear. Nor is it clear that if they do shift, they will use their opportunities responsibly.

Abundant Information

Asked once what he and his American Federation of Labor wanted, Samuel Gompers replied, "More!" His response is not only characteristic of a people of plenty, but is in the nature of a panacea. The new technologies of communication offer opportunity for wider, faster distribution of more information and entertainment. They feed an assumption that more is better and more faster is better still. But more of *what* is always the question. More recipes, garden tips, and gossip of the kind filling up special sections of the *new* New York *Times?* Or news and commentary more thoughtfully and interestingly presented?

It is doubtful that more information, when combined with an increased opportunity to select information, will necessarily improve the state of general public knowledge. As psychologist George Miller has observed, "the span of absolute judgment and the span of immediate memory impose severe limitations on the amount of information that we are able to receive, process and remember."[1] *What* we select will be our measure.

To the extent that journalists have not allowed only what interests the public to define the limits of reporting, the public may now be confronting information that it would not seek but is too lazy to avoid. But the greater control over the selection of information that the new technologies offer the audience may be no more than an expanded opportunity for many to avoid the information they find uninteresting but which they nevertheless need. The challenge to those who staff the new media is to make important information interesting.

Information/Power

In every society there are people who *seek* information. For some, especially the naturally curious, information is its own reward. For others, information may help them in problem solving, or it may mean advancement—economic, occupational, social. These are the people who learn how to seek and process information through whatever means exist. And among these people, of course, are those who seek information to enhance or employ their power. The potential of the new media for wider distribution of information could bring about a redistribution of power in society. But the more likely course is that the segment of the society that now seeks information to secure power will maintain its elite status with the new technologies. As long as the use of the new technologies remains expensive, the distance between people rich in information and the rest of society is likely to increase. But even as costs go down, some distance will remain until such time as more people learn to seek and value information of significance. The poor are poor not only because they lack money, but also because they have not been educated in information skills.

The Public(s) Interest(s)

Walter Lippmann has written that "the public interest may be what men would choose if they saw clearly, thought rationally, acted disinterested and benevolently."[2] The definition is appealing, but it presupposes that informed, rational, disinterested, benevolent people would agree, and it implies that if there is disagreement it is caused by some inadequacy on the part of at least one of the parties. That denies the individuality of reason, experience, and wisdom. In a society which values and protects the individual, there can be no single, uniform public interest. The function of "the public interest" is to act as our conscience and as a warning to beware of the uninformed, the irrational, the self-interested, and those of evil intent.

The First Amendment guarantees a large measure of independence from government. It offers no guarantee of independence from the pressures of economics and some in the mass media have the habit of defining the public interest by the standards of the counting-house, ratings, and circulation figures. It has been said that no one went broke underestimating the taste or the intelligence of the public, but no nation progresses by consumption alone. We are a pluralistic, not a homogeneous society and the purchasing power of the majority or the affluent is no measure of the public good.

In 1962 the Pilkington Commission studied the British Broadcasting Corporation and its audiences. Its observations are as pertinent to the United States as to Britain, to the print media as to broadcasting, to the 1970s as to the 1960s.

> "To give the public what it wants" is a misleading phrase; misleading because as commonly used it has the appearance of an appeal to democratic principle, but the appearance is deceptive. It is in fact patronizing and arrogant, in that it claims to know what the public is, but defines it as no more than the mass audience; and in that it claims to know what it wants, but limits its choice to the average of experience.
>
> . . .
>
> No one can say he is giving the public what it wants, unless the public knows the whole range of possibilities which television can offer, and from this range,

chooses what it wants to see. For a choice is only free if the field of choice is not unnecessarily restricted. The subject matter of television is to be found in the whole scope and variety of human awareness and experience. If viewers—the public—are thought [of] as "the mass audience," of "the majority" they will be offered only the average of common experience and awareness; the "ordinary"; the commonplace—for what all know and do is, by definition, commonplace. They will be kept unaware of what lies beyond the average of experience; their field of choice will be limited. In time they may come to like only what they know. But it will always be true, that had they been offered a wider range from which to choose, they might and often would have chosen otherwise, and with greater enjoyment.[3]

Responsibility for "the public interest" has been affixed to broadcasting by statute, but no medium of mass communication can excuse itself from its responsibility to serve the public interest, it can only abdicate its responsibility. To ask the media to reflect on the public good as well as private profit is not to dictate the definition of what constitutes the public good or to sacrifice the individual to "the public." The public interest may well best be served by protection of the individual against majority will. Certainly the First Amendment would suggest as much. And the First Amendment offers those in the mass media great freedom to define the public interest according to their own consciences.

The Public Contribution

The freedom of the First Amendment shields those in the mass media who harbor an arrogance towards the public and who are unwilling to see members of the public as anything but members of an audience or as nuisances or worse. If that arrogance became contagious, the First Amendment would be a fragile shield.

In the 1960s civil rights leaders took complaints of racial prejudice to the National Association of Broadcasters and asked for a policy statement encouraging broadcasters to deal fairly with blacks in programs and in employment practices. The head of the NAB was friendly but no policy statement was forthcoming, and Reverend Everett Parker, director of the Office of Communications of the United Church of Christ, recalls, "It's an interesting fact that all the troubles the broadcasters have with their license renewals came about because the directors of the NAB were such reactionaries. If they'd given us our statement, we probably wouldn't have gone further."[4]

It's hard to agree that people moved by a deep seated sense of grievance such as propelled the civil rights movement would have been satisfied for long with nothing more than a policy statement, but Parker went from his experience with the NAB to a course of action that established the public's legal *right* to participate in the broadcast license renewal process, the determination of whether a station will retain the privilege of operation. The

FCC was reluctant to open the license renewal process to media consumers because the commission feared it and the broadcasting industry would be overwhelmed by a "host of parties" motivated not by the public interest but by private, selfish interests. But it seemed apparent to the U.S. Court of Appeals, D.C. Circuit, that members of the public were as likely to be as motivated by the public interest as anyone else and that accommodation should be made in the license renewal process for "responsible representatives" of the public. The lesson that citizens learned in the 1960s and 1970s was that one of the most effective ways to get the attention of broadcasters was through legal action. (It can take years to defeat a citizen's petition to deny a license renewal and the costs of litigation have been estimated at anywhere from $100,000 to $1.5 million.[5])

In 1971 Clay Whitehead, then Director of the White House Office of Telecommunications Policy, remarked on what he considered "the ultimate perversion of the intent of the Communications Act," the development of an adversary relationship between citizens' groups and broadcasters, the transformation of the licensee "from public trustee to public enemy."[6] It is curious that the media can be so slavish to the public as consumers, and yet so intolerant of the public as critics.

The Mass Media in American Society

Great power is daily ascribed to the mass media. It is said that they distort our world, warp our children, hound our public officials from office, revise the distribution of power among our branches of government. The list seems neverending. But in so complex a society as ours no single institution can wield such power. To credit so much to the media discredits our schools, our families, our democratic institutions. Unless we admit to being fools, we must take some responsibility for the shape of our society, and we must parcel the rest to a wide range of institutions, ideas, and people. As columnist George Will has written,

> The contours of history are not determined by communications technology, however much it pleases people to think that history is what, and only what, can be seen at home. To see the rise of blacks, or the fall of [Lyndon Johnson], as primarily a consequence of television is to hollow out history. It discounts the noble and ignoble ideas and passions, heroes and villains and common people who make history.[7]

Notes

1. George A. Miller, "The Magical Number Seven, Plus or Minus Two: Some Limits on Our Capacity for Processing Information," *The Psychological Review,* Vol. 63, March 1956.
2. Quoted in Donald L. Guimary, *Citizens' Groups and Broadcasting (New York: Praeger, 1975), p. 8.*

3. Ronald H. Coase, "The Economics of Broadcasting and Public Policy," in Paul W. MacAvoy (ed.), *The Crisis of the Regulatory Commissions* (New York: Norton, 1970), p. 97.

4. Quoted in Martin Mayer, "The Challengers," *TV Guide,* February 3, 1973, p. 7. See Mayer's "Can They Get a TV Channel Worth $60,000,000 for just $400,000?" (February 10, 1973) and "Has the Public Benefited from 'Public Participation'?" (February 17, 1973), both in *TV Guide,* for more on the subject of citizens' license challenges.

5. Joseph A. Grundfest, *Citizen Participation in Broadcast Licensing Before the FCC* (Santa Monica, Calif.: Rand, March 1976), pp. 97–98.

6. Quoted in Guimary, p. 107.

7. George F. Will, "The Not-So-Mighty Tube," *Newsweek,* August 8, 1977, p. 84.

Suggested Readings

Chapter 2

Berelson, Bernard, and Morris Janowitz (eds.), *Reader in Public Opinion and Communication,* 2nd edition. New York: The Free Press, 1966.

Blumler, Jay G., and Elihu Katz (eds.), *The Uses of Mass Communications: Current Perspectives on Gratifications Research.* Beverly Hills, Calif.: Sage Publications, 1974.

Boorstin, Daniel J., *The Image: A Guide to Pseudo-Events in America.* New York: Harper & Row, 1964.

Boulding, Kenneth, *The Image.* Ann Arbor, Mich.: University of Michigan Press, 1968.

Carey, James W., "Harold Adams Innis and Marshall McLuhan," *Antioch Review,* 27, Spring 1967, 5–39.

Chaffee, Steven H. (ed.), *Political Communication: Issues and Strategies for Research.* Beverly Hills, Calif.: Sage Publications, 1975.

Clarke, Peter (ed.), *New Models for Mass Communication Research.* Beverly Hills, Calif.: Sage Publications, 1973.

Cohen, Bernard C., *The Press and Foreign Policy.* Princeton, N.J.: Princeton University Press, 1969.

De Fleur, Melvin, *Theories of Mass Communication,* Second Edition. New York: McKay, 1970.

Innis, Harold A., *The Bias of Communication.* Toronto: Toronto University Press, 1964.

Innis, Harold A., *Empire and Communications,* revised edition. Toronto: University of Toronto Press, 1972.

Lippmann, Walter, *Public Opinion.* New York: The Free Press, 1965.

McLuhan, Marshall, *The Gutenberg Galaxy.* Toronto: University of Toronto Press, 1967.

McLuhan, Marshall, *Understanding Media: The Extensions of Man.* New York: McGraw-Hill, 1965.

Mills, C. Wright, *The Power Elite.* New York: Oxford University Press, 1965.

Schramm, Wilbur, *Mass Communications: A Book of Readings.* Urbana, Ill.: University of Illinois Press, 1960.

Schramm, Wilbur, *Men, Messages, and Media: A Look at Human Communication.* New York: Harper & Row, 1973.

Schramm, Wilbur, and Donald F. Roberts (eds.), *The Process and Effects of Mass Communication,* Revised Edition. Urbana, Ill.: University of Illinois Press, 1971.

Shaw, Donald L., and Maxwell E. McCombs, *The Emergence of American Political Issues: The Agenda-Setting Function of the Press.* St. Paul, Minn.: West Publishing Co., 1977.

Stearn, Gerald E. (ed.), *McLuhan: Hot & Cool: A Primer for the Understanding of & a Critical Symposium with a Rebuttal by McLuhan.* New York: The Dial Press, 1969.

Wright, Charles R., *Mass Communication: A Sociological Perspective,* 2nd edition. New York: Random House, 1975.

Chapter 3

Ben H. Bagdikian, "Newspaper mergers—the final phase," *Columbia Journalism Review,* March/April 1977.

Bleyer, Willard Grosvenor, *Main Currents in the History of American Journalism.* Boston: Houghton Mifflin, 1927.

Boorstin, Daniel J., *The Image: A Guide to Pseudo-Events in America.* New York: Harper & Row, 1964.

Cunliffe, Marcus, *The Age of Expansion, 1848–1917.* Springfield, Mass.: G. & C. Merriam Company, 1974.

Emery, Edwin, *The Press and America: An Interpretative History of the Mass Media,* 3rd edition. Englewood Cliffs, N.J.: Prentice-Hall, 1972.

Fish, Carl R., *The Rise of the Common Man.* New York: Macmillan, 1927.

Galbraith, John K., *The New Industrial State.* New York: New American Library, 1968.

Mott, Frank Luther, *American Journalism: A History, 1690—1960,* 3rd edition. New York: Macmillan, 1962.

Nossiter, Bernard, *The Mythmakers.* Boston: Houghton Mifflin, 1964.

Parrington, Vernon L., *Main Currents in American Thought,* vols. 1 & 2. New York: Harcourt, 1927.

Peterson, Theodore, *Magazines in the Twentieth Century,* 2nd edition. Urbana, Ill.: University of Illinois Press, 1964.

Potter, David M., *People of Plenty: Economic Abundance and the American Character.* Chicago: University of Chicago Press, 1968.

Rucker, Bryce W., *The First Freedom.* Carbondale, Ill.: Southern Illinois University Press, 1968.

Schlesinger, Arthur M., *The Rise of the City, 1878–1898.* New York: Macmillan, 1933.

Schramm, Wilbur, and Donald F. Roberts, *The Process and Effects of Mass Communication,* revised edition. Urbana, Ill.: University of Illinois Press, 1971.

Tebbel, John, *The Media in America.* New York: New American Library, 1974.

Chapter 4

Ault, Philip, H., *News Around the World: Press Associations in Action.* New York: Dodd, Mead, 1960.

Bagdikian, Ben H., *The Information Machines: Their Impact on Men and the Media.* New York: Harper & Row, 1971.

Dann, Martin E., *The Black Press, 1827–1890: The Quest for National Identity.* New York: Putnam, 1971.

Dessauer, John P., *Book Publishing: What It Is, What It Does.* New York: R. R. Bowker, 1974.

Ford, James L. C., *Magazines for the Millions.* Carbondale, Ill.: Southern Illinois University Press, 1970.

Forsyth, David P., *The Business Press in America, 1750—1865.* Philadelphia: Chilton Books, 1964.

Gramling, Oliver, *AP, The Story of News.* New York: Farrar & Rinehart, 1940.

La Brie, Henry G., III, *The Black Newspaper in America: A Guide,* 3rd edition. Kennebunkport, Me.: Mercer House Press, 1973.

Mott, Frank Luther, *A History of American Magazines.* Cambridge, Mass.: Harvard University Press, 1957.

Peterson, Theodore, *Magazines in the Twentieth Century.* Urbana, Ill.: University of Illinois Press, 1964.

Rucker, Frank W., and Herbert Lee Williams, *Newspaper Organization and Management,* 4th edition. Ames, Ia.: Iowa State University Press, 1974.

Tebbel, John, *The American Magazine: A Compact History.* New York: Hawthorn Books, 1969.

Wolseley, Roland E., *Understanding Magazines,* 2nd edition. Ames, Ia.: Iowa State University Press, 1969.

Wolseley, Roland E., *The Black Press, U.S.A.* Ames, Ia.: Iowa State University Press, 1971.

Chapter 5

Aspen Series on Communication and Society, *The Future of Public Broadcasting*. New York: Praeger Publishers, 1976.

Balio, Tino (ed.), *The American Film Industry*. Madison, Wisc.: The University of Wisconsin Press, 1976.

Barnouw, Erik, *A History of Broadcasting in the United States*. New York: Oxford University Press, 1966 (Vol. I), 1968 (Vol. II), 1970 (Vol. III).

Barrett, Marvin (ed.), *Survey of Broadcast Journalism*. New York: Grosset & Dunlap, 1969, 1970, 1971, 1972.

Bluem, A. William, and Jason E. Squire (eds.), *The Movie Business: American Film Industry Practice*. New York: Hastings House, 1972.

Brown, Les, *Televi$ion: The Business Behind the Box*. New York: Harcourt, 1971.

Carnegie Commission on Educational Television, *Public Television, a Program for Action*. New York: Bantam Books, 1967.

Friendly, Fred W., *Due To Circumstances Beyond Our Control*. New York: Vintage Books, 1968.

Head, Sydney W., *Broadcasting in America: A Survey of Television and Radio*. Boston: Houghton Mifflin, 1956.

Le Duc, Don R., *Cable Television and the FCC: A Crisis in Media Control*. Philadelphia: Temple University Press, 1973.

Noll, Roger G., Merton J. Peck, and John J. McGowan, *Economic Aspects of Television Regulation*. Washington, D.C.: The Brookings Institution, 1973.

Owen, Bruce M., Jack H. Beebe, and Willard G. Manning, Jr., *Television Economics*. Lexington, Mass.: Heath, 1974.

Sloan (Alfred P.) Foundation Commission, *On the Cable: Television of Abundance*. New York: McGraw-Hill, 1971.

Smythe, Ted C., and G. A. Mastroianni, *Issues in Broadcasting*. Palo Alto, Calif.: Mayfield Publishing, 1975.

Tuchman, Gaye (ed.), *The TV Establishment*. Englewood Cliffs, N.J.: Prentice-Hall, 1974.

Chapter 6

Becker, Carl L., *Freedom and Responsibility in the American Way of Life*. New York: Alfred A. Knopf, 1945.

Becker, Carl L., *The Heavenly City of the Eighteenth-Century Philoso-*
phers. New Haven, Conn.: Yale University Press, 1932.

Berns, Walter, *Freedom, Virtue & the First Amendment.* Baton Rouge, La.:
Louisiana State University Press, 1957.

Brinton, Crane, *The Shaping of Modern Thought.* Englewood Cliffs, N.J.:
Prentice-Hall, 1963.

Chafee, Zechariah, Jr. *Free Speech in the United States.* New York:
Atheneum, 1969.

Ebenstein, William, *Great Political Thinkers: Plato to the Present,* 3rd
edition. New York: Holt, Rinehart and Winston, 1963.

Hamilton, Alexander, John Jay, and James Madison, *The Federalist: A
Commentary on the Constitution of the United States.* New York: Modern Library.

Hook, Sidney, *Heresy, Yes, Conspiracy, No.* New York: John Day Co.,
1963.

Laski, Harold J., *Liberty in the Modern State.* London: Faber and Faber
Ltd., 1930.

Levy, Leonard W. (ed.), *Freedom of the Press from Zenger to Jefferson:
Early American Libertarian Theories.* Indianapolis, Ind.: Bobbs-Merrill,
1966.

Levy, Leonard W., *Legacy of Suppression: Freedom of Speech and Press
in Early American History.* Cambridge, Mass.: The Belknap Press of
Harvard University Press, 1960.

Meiklejohn, Alexander, *Free Speech and Its Relation to Self-Government.*
New York: Harper & Row, 1948.

Meiklejohn, Alexander, *Political Freedom.* New York: Galaxy Books, 1965.

Milton, John, *Areopagitica and Other Prose Works of John Milton.* New
York: E. P. Dutton & Co., 1927.

Mott, Frank Luther, *Jefferson and the Press.* Baton Rouge, La.: Louisiana
State University Press, 1943.

Nelson, Harold, *Freedom of the Press from Hamilton to the Warren Court.*
Indianapolis: Bobbs-Merrill, 1967.

Parrington, Vernon L., *Main Currents in American Thought,* Two Volumes.
New York: Harcourt, 1954.

Rossiter, Clinton L., *Seedtime of the Republic.* New York: Harcourt, 1959.

Sabine, George H., *A History of Political Theory,* 3rd edition. New York:
Holt, Rinehart and Winston, 1963.

Siebert, Fredrick S., Theodore Peterson, and Wilbur Schramm, *Four Theories of the Press.* Urbana, Ill.: University of Illinois Press, 1956.

Smith, James Morton, *Freedom's Fetters: The Alien and Sedition Laws and
American Civil Liberties.* Ithaca, N.Y.: Cornell University Press, 1966.

Somerville, John, and Ronald E. Santoni (eds.), *Social and Political Philosophy: Readings from Plato to Gandhi.* Garden City, N.Y.: Doubleday,
1963.

Wolff, Robert Paul, Barrington Moore, and Herbert Marcuse, *A Critique of
Pure Tolerance.* Boston: Beacon Press, 1969.

Chapter 7

Blanchard, Margaret A., "The Hutchins Commission, The Press and the Responsibility Concept," *Journalism Monographs*, 49, May 1977.

Brown, Lee, *The Reluctant Reformation: On Criticizing the Press in America*. New York: McKay, 1974.

Commission on Freedom of the Press, *A Free and Responsible Press*. Chicago: University of Chicago Press, 1958.

Gerald, James Edward, *The Social Responsibility of the Press*. Minneapolis: University of Minnesota Press, 1963.

Gross, Gerald (ed.), *The Responsibility of the Press*. New York: Fleet Publishing Corporation, 1966.

Hocking, William, *Freedom of the Press: A Framework of Principle*. Chicago: University of Chicago Press, 1947.

Johnstone, John W. C., Edward Slawski, William W. Bowman, *The News People: A Sociological Portrait of American Journalists and their Work*. Urbana, Ill.: University of Illinois Press, 1976.

Merrill, John C., *The Imperative of Freedom: A Philosophy of Journalistic Autonomy*. New York: Hastings House, Publishers, 1974.

The National News Council, *In the Public Interest*. New York: The National News Council, Inc., 1975.

Nelson, Harold L. (ed.), *Freedom of the Press from Hamilton to the Warren Court*. Indianapolis, Ind.: Bobbs-Merrill, 1967.

Rivers, William L., and Wilbur Schramm, *Responsibility in Mass Communication*, revised edition. New York: Harper & Row, 1969.

Siebert, Fredrick S., Theodore Peterson, and Wilbur Schramm, *Four Theories of the Press*. Urbana, Ill.: University of Illinois Press, 1956.

The Twentieth Century Fund Task Force, *A Free and Responsive Press*. New York: The Twentieth Century Fund, Inc., 1973.

U.S. Commission on Civil Rights, *Window Dressing on the Set: Women and Minorities in Television*. Washington, D.C.: U.S. Government Printing Office, August 1977.

Chapter 8

Barron, Jerome, A., *Freedom of the Press for Whom?* Bloomington, Ind.: Indiana University Press, 1973.

Chafee, Zechariah, Jr., *Free Speech in the United States*. New York: Atheneum, 1969.

Dorsen, Norman, and Stephen Gillers (eds.), *None of Your Business: Government Secrecy in America*. New York: Viking Press, 1974.

Emerson, Thomas I., *The System of Freedom of Expression*. New York: Vintage Books, 1970.

Emerson, Thomas I., *Toward a General Theory of the First Amendment.*
New York: Vintage Books, 1966.

Francois, William E., *Mass Media Law and Regulation.* Columbus, Ohio: Grid, Inc., 1975.

Franklin, Marc A., *Cases and Materials on Mass Media Law.* Mineola, N.Y.: The Foundation Press, Inc., 1977.

Franklin, Marc A., *The Dynamics of American Law.* Mineola, N.Y.: The Foundation Press, Inc., 1968.

Franklin, Marc A., *The First Amendment and the Fourth Estate.* Mineola, N.Y.: The Foundation Press, Inc., 1977.

Friendly, Fred W., *The Good Guys, the Bad Guys and the First Amendment: Free Speech vs. Fairness in Broadcasting.* New York: Random House, 1976.

Gillmor, Donald M., and Jerome A. Barron, *Mass Communication Law,* 2nd edition. St. Paul, Minn.: West Publishing Co., 1974.

Grundfest, Joseph A., *Citizen Participation in Broadcast Licensing Before the FCC.* Santa Monica, Calif.: Rand, March 1976.

Guimary, Donald L., *Citizens' Groups and Broadcasting.* New York: Praeger Publishers, 1975.

Jones, William K., *Cases and Materials on Electronic Mass Media: Radio, Television and Cable.* Mineola, N.Y.: The Foundation Press, Inc., 1976.

Kahn, Frank J. (ed.), *Documents of American Broadcasting,* Second Edition, New York: Appleton-Century-Crofts, 1973.

Kohlmeier, Louis, *The Regulators.* New York: Harper & Row, 1969.

Krasnow, Erwin G., and Lawrence D. Longley, *The Politics of Broadcast Regulation.* New York: St. Martin's Press, 1973.

Krislov, Samuel, *The Supreme Court and Political Freedom.* New York: The Free Press, 1968.

Lawhorne, Clifton O., *Defamation and Public Officials: The Evolving Law of Libel.* Carbondale, Ill.: Southern Illinois University Press, 1971.

Le Duc, Don R., *Cable Television and the FCC: A Crisis in Media Control.* Philadelphia: Temple University Press, 1973.

Miller, Arthur R., *The Assault on Privacy: Computers, Data Banks, and Dossiers.* Ann Arbor, Mich.: University of Michigan Press, 1971.

Nelson, Harold L., and Dwight L. Teeter, Jr., *Law of Mass Communications,* 2nd edition. Mineola, N.Y.: The Foundation Press, Inc., 1973.

The Report of the Commission on Obscenity and Pornography. New York: Bantam Books, 1970.

Pember, Don R., *Mass Media Law.* Dubuque, Iowa: Wm. C. Brown Company Publishers, 1977.

Pember, Don R., *Privacy and the Press.* Seattle, Wash.: University of Seattle Press, 1972.

Schmidt, Benno C., Jr., *Freedom of the Press vs. Public Access.* New York: Praeger Publishers, 1976.

Schrag, Peter, *Test of Loyalty: Daniel Ellsberg and the Rituals of Secret Government.* New York: Simon & Schuster, 1974.

Shapiro, Andrew O., *Media Access: Your Rights to Express Your Views on Radio and Television.* Boston; Little, Brown and Company, 1976.

Simons, Howard, and Joseph A. Califano (eds.), *The Media and the Law.* New York: Praeger Publishers, 1976.

Symposium: Nebraska Press Association v. Stuart. Stanford Law Review, Vol. 29, No. 3, February 1977.

Twentieth Century Fund Task Force on the Government and the Press, *Press Freedoms under Pressure.* New York: Twentieth Century Fund, 1972.

Ungar, Sanford J., *The Papers & The Papers: An Account of the Legal and Political Battle over the Pentagon Papers.* New York: E. P. Dutton & Co., 1975.

Westin, Alan F., *Privacy and Freedom.* New York: Atheneum, 1967.

Chapter 9

Blanchard, Robert O. (ed.), *Congress and the News Media.* New York: Hastings House, Publishers, 1974.

Boorstin, Daniel J., *The Americans: The Colonial Experience.* New York: Random House, 1958.

Cornwell, Elmer E., Jr., *Presidential Leadership of Public Opinion.* Bloomington, Ind.: Indiana University Press, 1966.

Graber, Doris A., *Public Opinion, the President, and Foreign Policy: Four Case Studies from the Formative Years.* New York: Holt, Rinehart and Winston, 1968.

Hargrove, Erwin C., *Presidential Leadership: Personality and Political Style.* New York: Macmillan, 1966.

Levy, Leonard W. (ed.), *Freedom of the Press from Zenger to Jefferson: Early American Libertarian Theories.* Indianapolis, Ind.: Bobbs-Merrill, 1966.

Levy, Leonard W., *Jefferson and Civil Liberties: the Darker Side.* Cambridge, Mass.: The Belknap Press of Harvard University Press, 1963.

Levy, Leonard W., *Legacy of Suppression: Freedom of Speech and Press in Early American History.* Cambridge, Mass.: The Belknap Press of Harvard University Press, 1960.

Marbut, F. B., *News from the Capital: The Story of Washington Reporting.* Carbondale, Ill.: Southern Illinois University Press, 1971.

Mott, Frank Luther, *Jefferson and the Press.* Baton Rouge, La.: Louisiana State University Press, 1943.

Pollard, James E., *The Presidents and the Press.* New York: Octagon Books, 1973.

Rossiter, Clinton L., *Seedtime of the Republic.* New York: Harcourt, 1959.

Rosten, Leo, *The Washington Correspondents.* New York: Arno Press, 1974.

Smith, James Morton, *Freedom's Fetters: The Alien and Sedition Laws and American Civil Liberties.* Ithaca, N.Y.: Cornell University Press, 1956.

Chapter 10

Barber, James David, *The Presidential Character: Predicting Performance in the White House.* Englewood Cliffs, N.J.: Prentice-Hall, 1972.

Blanchard, Robert O. (ed.), *Congress and the News Media.* New York: Hastings House, Publishers, 1974.

Cater, Douglass, *The Fourth Branch of Government.* Boston: Houghton Mifflin, 1959.

Chafee, Zechariah, Jr., *Government and Mass Communications.* Chicago: University of Chicago Press, 1947.

Chittick, William O. *State Department, Press, and Pressure Groups.* New York: Wiley, 1970.

Cornwell, Elmer E., Jr., *Presidential Leadership of Public Opinion.* Bloomington, Ind.: Indiana University Press, 1966.

Crouse, Timothy, *The Boys on the Bus: Riding with the Campaign Press Corps.* New York: Ballantine Books, 1974.

Gilbert, Robert E., *Television and Presidential Politics.* North Quincy, Mass.: The Christopher Publishing House, 1972.

Hargrove, Erwin C., *Presidential Leadership: Personality and Political Style.* New York: Macmillan, 1966.

Hiebert, Ray Elson, and Carlton E. Spitzer (eds.), *The Voice of Government.* New York: Wiley, 1968.

Kraus, Sidney (ed.), *The Great Debates.* Bloomington, Ind.: Indiana University Press, 1962.

MacNeil, Robert, *The People Machine: The Influence of Television on American Politics.* New York: Harper & Row, 1968.

McCamy, James L., *Government Publicity: Its Practice in Federal Administration.* Chicago: University of Chicago Press, 1939.

Mendelsohn, Harold, and Irving Crespi, *Polls, Television and the New Politics.* Scranton, Pa.: Chandler Publishing Company, 1970.

Minow, Newton N., John Bartlow Martin, and Lee M. Mitchell, *Presidential Television.* New York: Basic Books, 1973.

Perry, James M., *How the Press Covered the 1972 Election.* New York: Clarkson N. Potter, Inc., 1973.

Pollard, James E., *The Presidents and the Press.* New York: Octagon Books, 1973.

Pollard, James E., *The Presidents and the Press—Truman to Johnson.* Washington, D.C.: Public Affairs Press, 1964.

Porter, William E., *Assault on the Media: The Nixon Years.* Ann Arbor, Mich.: University of Michigan Press, 1976.

Reston, James, *The Artillery of the Press: Its Influence on American Foreign Policy.* New York: Harper & Row, 1967.

Rivers, William L., *The Opinionmakers.* Boston: Beacon Press, 1967.

Rivers, William L., *The Adversaries: Politics and the Press.* Boston: Beacon Press, 1970.

Rosten, Leo, *The Washington Correspondents.* New York: Arno Press, 1974.

Schlesinger, Arthur M., Jr., *The Imperial Presidency.* Boston: Houghton Mifflin, 1973.

Small, William J., *Political Power and the Press.* New York: W. W. Norton & Company, 1972.

Strouse, James C., *The Mass Media, Public Opinion, and the Public Policy Analysis: Linkage Explorations.* Columbus, O.: Charles E. Merrill, 1975.

White, Theodore H., *Breach of Faith: The Fall of Richard Nixon.* New York: Dell, 1975.

Wise, David, *The Politics of Lying: Government Deception, Secrecy and Power.* New York: Vintage Books, 1973.

Witcover, Jules, *Marathon: The Pursuit of the Presidency, 1972—1976.* New York: The Viking Press, 1977.

Chapter 11

Bernstein, Carl, and Bob Woodward, *All the President's Men.* New York: Simon & Schuster, 1974.

Cannon, Lou *Reporting: An Inside View.* Sacramento, Calif.: California Journal Press, 1977.

Dennis, Everette, and William L. Rivers, *Other Voices: The New Journalism in America.* San Francisco: Canfield Press, 1974.

Epstein, Edward Jay, *News From Nowhere: Television and the News.* New York: Random House, 1973.

Epstein, Edward Jay, *Between Fact and Fiction: The Problem of Journalism.* New York: Vintage Books, 1975.

Journal of Communication, "What IS News?" Autumn 1976, Vol. 26, No. 4, pp. 86—123.

Lippmann, Walter, *Public Opinion.* New York: The Free Press, 1965.

McCombs, Maxwell, Donald Lewis Shaw, and David Grey, *Handbook of Reporting Methods.* Boston: Houghton Mifflin, 1976.

Meyer, Philip, *Precision Journalism: A Reporter's Introduction to Social Science Methods.* Bloomington, Ind.: Indiana University Press, 1973.

Mungo, Raymond, *Famous Long Ago: My Life and Hard Times with Liberation News Service.* New York: Pocket Books, 1971.

Sigal, Leon V., *Reporters and Officials: The Organization and Politics of Newsmaking.* Lexington, Mass.: D. C. Heath, 1973.

Wolfe, Tom, *The New Journalism,* with an anthology edited by Tom Wolfe and E. W. Johnson. New York: Harper & Row, 1973.

Chapter 12

Bernays, Edward L., *Crystallizing Public Opinion*. New York: Liveright Publishing Corporation, 1961.

Bernays, Edward L., *The Engineering of Consent*. Norman, Okla.: University of Oklahoma Press, 1955.

Bloom, Melvyn H., *Public Relations and Presidential Campaigns: A Crisis in Democracy*. New York: Thomas Y. Crowell Company, 1973.

Cohen, Bernard C., *The Press and Foreign Policy*. Princeton, N.J.: Princeton University Press, 1963.

Hill and Knowlton Executives, *Critical Issues in Public Relations*. Englewood Cliffs, N.J.: Prentice-Hall, 1975.

Mandell, Maurice I., *Advertising*, 2nd edition. Englewood Cliffs, N.J.: Prentice-Hall, 1974.

Mayer, Martin, *Madison Avenue, U.S.A.* New York: Harper & Row, 1958.

McGinniss, Joe, *The Selling of the President, 1968*. New York: Trident Press, 1969.

Nimmo, Dan, *The Political Persuaders: The Techniques of Modern Election Campaigns*. Englewood Cliffs, N.J.: Prentice-Hall, 1970.

Pimlott, John Alfred Ralph, *Public Relations and American Democracy*. Princeton, N.J.: Princeton University Press, 1951.

Potter, David M., *People of Plenty: Economic Abundance and the American Character*. Chicago: University of Chicago Press, 1954.

Reeves, Rosser, *Reality in Advertising*. New York: Alfred A. Knopf, 1961.

Rivers, William L., *The Opinionmakers*. Boston: Beacon Press, 1967.

Rotzoll, Kim B., James E. Haefner, and Charles H. Sandage, *Advertising in Contemporary Society: Perspectives Toward Understanding*. Columbus, Ohio: Grid, Inc., 1976.

Simon, Julian L., *Issues in the Economics of Advertising*. Urbana, Ill.: University of Illinois Press, 1970.

Chapter 13

Arlen, Michael J., *Living-Room War*. New York: Tower Publications, Inc., 1969.

Baxandall, Lee (ed.), *Radical Perspectives in the Arts*. Baltimore: Penguin Books, 1972.

Blumler, Jay G., and Elihu Katz (eds.), *The Uses of Mass Communications: Current Perspectives on Gratifications Research*. Beverly Hills, Calif.: Sage Publications, 1974.

Brown, Ray, (ed.), *Children and Television*. Beverly Hills, Calif.: Sage Publications, 1976.

Cater, Douglass, and Stephen Strickland, *TV Violence and the Child: The*

Evolution and Fate of the Surgeon General's Report. New York: Russell Sage Foundation, 1975.

Jacobs, Norman (ed.), *Culture for Millions? Mass Media and Modern Society.* Boston: Beacon Press, 1961.

Hammel, William M. (ed.), *The Popular Arts in America: A Reader.* New York: Harcourt, 1972.

Klapper, Joseph T., *The Effects of the Mass Media.* New York: Free Press, 1960.

Lowenthal, Leo, *Literature, Popular Culture and Society.* Englewood Cliffs, N.J.: Prentice-Hall, 1961.

Macdonald, Dwight, *Against the American Grain.* New York: Random House, 1962.

Mendelsohn, Harold, *Mass Entertainment.* New Haven, Conn.: College and University Press, 1966.

Nye, Russel, *The Unembarrassed Muse: The Popular Arts in America.* New York: Dial Press, 1970.

Rissover, Fredric, and David C. Birch, *Mass Media and the Popular Arts.* New York: McGraw Hill, 1971.

Rosenberg, Bernard, and David Manning White (eds.), *Mass Culture: The Popular Arts in America.* New York: Free Press, 1957.

Rosenberg, Bernard, and David Manning White (eds.), *Mass Culture Revisited.* New York: Van Nostrand Reinhold, 1971.

Warshow, Robert, *The Immediate Experience: Movies, Comics, Theatre & Other Aspects of Popular Culture.* New York: Atheneum, 1971.

White, David Manning, and Robert H. Abel (eds.), *The Funnies, an American Idiom.* New York: Free Press, 1963.

Winn, Marie, *The Plug-In Drug.* New York: The Viking Press, 1977.

Chapter 14

Clor, Harry M. (ed.), *The Mass Media and Modern Democracy.* Chicago: Rand McNally, 1974.

Dahl, Robert A., *A Preface to Democratic Theory.* Chicago: University of Chicago Press, 1964.

Federal Communications Commission, *Public and Broadcasting; Revised Edition.* Federal Register, Vol. 39, pp. 32288—32296, September 5, 1974.

Johnson, Nicholas, *How to Talk Back to Your Television Set.* New York: Bantam Books, 1970.

Kristol, Irving, *Republican Virtue vs. Servile Institutions.* Bloomington, Ind.: The Poynter Center, Indiana University, May 1974.

Lippmann, Walter, *Essays in the Public Philosophy.* Boston: Little, Brown, 1955.

Periodicals About Mass Media

compiled and annotated by

Frances Goins Wilhoit
Head, Journalism Library
School of Journalism
Indiana University

Journals and yearbooks annotated in this bibliography range from directories of media organizations to social science journals about media influence. The items selected were judged to be useful for beginning and intermediate study of mass communication. Other criteria for inclusion were these: Does the periodical consistently provide authoritative and/or unique information about mass media?

Public affairs magazines are excluded from the bibliography. Those which frequently have articles on the mass media include *Atlantic, Commentary, Harper's, The Nation, National Review, The New Republic, Newsweek, The New Yorker, The Progressive, The Public Interest, Saturday Review,* and *Time.*

An excellent guide to the study of the mass media is the *Aspen Handbook on the Media,* 1977-1979 Edition, edited by William L. Rivers, Wallace Thompson, and Michael J. Nyhan (New York: Praeger Publishers, 1977). This directory of media organizations, action groups, and research institutions also includes bibliographies and a guide to federal agencies, commissions, and Congressional committees involved in mass media policy.

©Frances Goins Wilhoit, October, 1977. Reprinted by permission of Frances Goins Wilhoit.

access, 1975 –   This is a monthly report on the broadcast industry, with occasional items on cable-TV, published by the National Citizens Committee for Broadcasting, a Washington, D.C.-based group, for other media action groups in the United States.

Access Reports, 1975 –   A bi-weekly newsletter service, *Access Reports* reports primarily on actions related to access to federal government files under the Freedom of Information Act. See also *Media Law Reporter* and *FOI Digest.*

Advertising Age, 1930 –   A weekly news magazine for the advertising industry, *Advertising Age* reports marketing strategies of major advertisers and agencies. The annual survey of the 100 leading national advertisers describes the corporate advertising rationale, itemizes the budget by each medium used, and lists the corporations' advertising personnel. It is indexed in *Business Periodicals Index.*

Alternative Press Index, 1969 –   The journals indexed by the *Alternative Press Index* vary from *Black Panther* and *Ramparts* to *Insurgent Sociologist* and the *St. Louis Journalism Review.* The index is over a year behind the publication date of the periodicals indexed, but it is a unique service, published by the Alternative Press Center, Baltimore, Md.

Ayer Directory of Publications, 1869 –   The directory lists the title, names of publisher and editor, address, and circulation of newspapers and magazines published in the United States, Canada, Panama, the Philippines, Puerto Rico, and the West Indies.

Billboard, 1894 –   The magazine correctly promotes itself as the "international music-record-tape newsweekly." *Billboard* reports news of recording stars, promotional strategies of recording companies, union meetings, and sales. The weekly rating charts for music—soul, country, pop, and easy listening—are published for the U.S. and selected world markets. *Billboard* is indexed in *Music Index.*

Broadcasting, 1931 –   *Broadcasting* reports weekly on news of the broadcasting and cablecasting industries. The coverage is dependable and comprehensive: programing, network policies and personnel changes, FCC decisions, changes in station ownership, Congressional hearings, the impact of recent legislation, research reports, court decisions, court cases pending, code revisions, media policy positions of national organizations and interest groups. The journal's own index, recently issued for 1972–1975, lists entries by personal name and specific stations and events, as well as by general topic. The journal is also indexed in *Business Periodicals Index.*

Broadcasting Yearbook, 1931 –   The annual directory for information about television and radio stations, *Broadcasting Yearbook* also lists changes of station ownership for the previous year, personnel for the networks, the FCC, and other media groups. The yearbook is a handy source for current FCC rules and regulations and a summary of statistics indicating the impact of radio and television on the U.S. economy.

Broadcasting Cable Sourcebook, 1972 –   Similar in content and format to *Broadcasting Yearbook,* the *Cable Sourcebook* is an annual directory of the cable systems in each state and the provinces of Canada. The yearbook includes FCC rules, state regulations, government agencies, equipment manufacturers, program suppliers and a brief history of cable regulation.

The Bulletin, 1923 –   Issued nine times a year, *The Bulletin* of the American Society of Newspaper Editors is an important chronicle of current professional thinking. Each issue of *The Bulletin* focuses on a single problem, for example, the decline of newspaper readership among young adults, the quality of newspaper editorials, balanced newspaper coverage of the President of the United States, the role of comics in the newspaper. See also the society's annual report, *Problems of Journalism.*

CATV, 1964 –   A weekly journal published in Englewood, Colo., *CATV* reports on business, financial, and legal news about community antenna television. See also *Broadcasting.*

CBS News Index, 1975 –   Issued quarterly, this index is a subject guide to all news and public affairs programming including *CBS Reports* and *60 Minutes.* See also *Television News Index and Abstracts.*

CBS News Almanac   In addition to the standard fare of statistical, geographical, and historical information, this extensive almanac offers more—a review of the year's events by CBS news correspondents, an atlas, a dictionary, and obituaries and who's who information. See also *Facts on File.*

Columbia Journalism Review, 1962 –   Published bi-monthly, the *Columbia Journalism Review* offers essays that assess media performance of national interest. The journal regularly reprints the deliberations of the National News Council. *Humanities Index* indexes the journal. See also *MORE.*

A number of regional media reviews have begun and some have ceased. Noteworthy among those publishing to date is the *St. Louis Journalism Review.* The *Washington* (D.C.) *Journalism Review,* to begin in 1977, promises to be a relentless critic of the Washington press corps. See also *Alternative Press Index.*

Congressional Quarterly Weekly Report   The most current information on the status of major legislation being considered by the U.S. Congress is digested in this report, which was started in 1945 as *Congressional Log.* It publishes summary articles on major bills of general interest: energy, defense, water, consumer interests, transportation, welfare. The voting records of individual members of Congress are printed regularly. The *CQ* weekly report is noted for its accuracy.

Editor & Publisher, 1884– The weekly trade magazine for newspaper management, *E&P* concentrates on news of economic and technological developments in the newspaper business and records changes in newspaper ownership. The magazine also reports on major legal, political, and legislative developments affecting newspapers. Summaries of practical research are included. Important among the frequent special issues are the syndicate directory, published annually in July, and the advertising linage report in May. The magazine is indexed in *Business Periodicals Index.*

Editor & Publisher International Year Book Detailed information is given for daily newspapers published in the United States and Canada: circulation, advertising rates, time of publication (morning or evening), newspaper group affiliation if applicable, and the names of the publisher, editors, and department heads. Directory information is also included for state press associations, weekly newspapers, the black press, and syndicated services.

FOI Digest, 1957– A good source for current information about state laws and court rulings on access to public information, this digest is a bimonthly newsletter published by the Freedom of Information Center at the School of Journalism, University of Missouri. The center also regularly publishes longer reports, *FOI Reports,* on issues of press freedom, such as the fairness doctrine in broadcasting, privacy rights, and state "sunshine" laws.

Facts on File, 1940– A weekly almanac of news events as reported by the press. It is cumulated annually. See also *The New York Times Index* and the *CBS News Almanac.*

Folio, 1972– A monthly trade journal for magazine management, *Folio* records the events of magazine publishing, for example, how many new magazines were started last year, how many ceased publication, the advertising income of leading magazines, new color printing technology, and circulation problems.

Gallup Opinion Index Report, 1965– A monthly compilation of the published polls from the American Institute of Public Opinion, this report also has topical articles on the problems of polling. It is indexed in *Public Affairs Information Service.* See also *Public Opinion Quarterly.*

Gazette: International Journal for Mass Communication Studies, 1955– Published quarterly in The Netherlands, *Gazette* is a scholarly journal that prints articles of a cross-cultural, comparative nature on press, radio, television, propaganda, public opinion, advertising, and public relations.

IPI Report, 1952– A monthly report of events significant to the world press community published by the International Press Institute based in Zurich, *IPI Report* has news of censorship, incarcerated reporters and editors, and national newspaper developments, country by country. See also *Index on Censorship.*

Index on Censorship, 1972 –   This journal publishes summary articles on the history of censorship, essays on the definition of censorship,
and articles on international incidents of censorship. The publisher is a
non-profit company, Writers & Scholars International Ltd., based in
London. Among those dozen persons listed as "patrons" of the journal
are Henry Moore, Iris Murdoch, and I. F. Stone.

Index to Legal Periodicals, 1908 –   Articles about mass communications law—libel, privacy, obscenity, free press/fair trial, broadcast regulation—are included among the subjects in this comprehensive index
to the legal literature.

Journaliam Quarterly, 1924 –   *JQ* is a journal of research articles
and notes that are not limited to the print media. Articles on television,
public opinion polls, advertising, and international communication also
appear. Much of the research is about newspaper content, the reporting and editing process, newspaper readership, journalism history, and
communications law. Extensive bibliographies are included in each
issue. It is indexed in *Humanities Index, Public Affairs Information
Service,* and *Sociological Abstracts.*

Journalism Studies Review, 1976 –   This annual publication from
Great Britain is the British counterpart to the *Columbia Journalism
Review.* The essays, which discuss British journalism, are more com-
parative and international in scope than those in the *CJR.*

Journal of Broadcasting, 1956 –   A quarterly journal of research
articles on broadcasting, this scholarly publication often groups articles
under topics, such as children and television, broadcast journalism, and
broadcast education. The journal is indexed in the *Humanities Index*
and occasionally in *Public Affairs Information Service.*

Journal of Communication, 1951 –   This quarterly journal presents
a wide variety of scholarly articles about communication. Organized
thematically, the journal publishes a symposium of articles varying from
issues of international law and satellites to such popular culture topics
as humor and the media. The journal is indexed in *Sociological
Abstracts, Film Literature,* and *Current Index to Journals in Education.*

Journal of Popular Culture, 1967 –   Popular culture is broadly
defined as entertainment and art in everyday life without limits of
period, culture, or country. Some articles are about the mass media, for
example, Edward R. Murrow and radio news, early American magazines, television entertainment programs, and newspaper comic strips.
The journal is indexed in *Humanities Index* and *Film Literature.*

Mass Comm Review, 1973 –   The articles in this journal, issued three
times a year, range over topics such as political advertising, film history,
shield laws for reporters, the definition of news, and the National News
Council.

Matrix, 1915 –   A professional journal for women in communications,
Matrix features articles on general topics of politics and the media,
professional codes of behavior, and issues of press freedom. The

activities and problems of women working in the media are emphasized. See also *The Quill*.

Media Law Reporter, 1977 –   Currently the only comprehensive
reporting service for legal developments in communications, this
weekly loose-leaf service provides texts of decisions by courts and
administrative agencies and news notes about relevant events and new
cases. A bibliography of current journal articles on communications law
is often included on the inside back page of the weekly report.

Media Report to Women, 1972 –   This monthly newsletter empha-
sizes factual information about women and the mass media: brief
research reports about the image of women, news items of women's
action groups, litigations, the employment of women, announcements
of new magazines, and dates of conferences.

MORE, 1971 –   A critical, sometimes satirical monthly media review,
MORE has broadened its coverage from the New York area press and
television networks to include any journalistic or entertainment topic or
event worthy of national attention. Although most articles are keyed to
specific media events, the journal offers analysis of broader topics, such
as professional ethics, political reporting, and terrorism and the media.
See also *Columbia Journalism Review*. *MORE* is occasionally indexed
in *Public Affairs Information Service*.

The New York Times Index, 1851 –   An extensive subject guide to
the contents of the New York *Times,* the index is a valuable chronology
and summary of world events. The computerized index, the *New York
Times Data Bank,* which indexes many other publications in addition to
the New York *Times,* is only one week behind the news events; the
printed index is several months behind. The computerized data bank is
now available in many large university and state libraries. See also
Facts on File.

The News & The Law, 1977 –   Published by The Reporters Committee for Freedom of the Press, *The News & The Law* reports on legal
matters of interest to persons working in the media. The first issue has
articles on gag orders, ownership of the Nixon tapes, freedom of
information actions, confidentiality of news sources, privacy, libel, and
prior restraint. This journal, to be issued eight times a year, replaces the
Press Censorship Newsletter (Nov. 1973 – Oct. 1976), which was also
a project of The Reporters Committee.

Nieman Reports, 1947 –   A collection of essays on problems in journalism written by Nieman Fellows, journalists who are or were on a
sabbatical study at Harvard University, *Nieman Reports* offers a
thoughtful review of a wide range of journalistic issues.

PTR: Public Telecommunications Review, 1973 –   This journal
concentrates on problems, issues, and successes of noncommercial
television. It is indexed in *Current Index to Journals in Education*.

Problems of Journalism, 1923 –   This publication reports the annual
proceedings of the convention of the American Society of Newspaper
Editors. It is valued for the committee reports which offer positions on

issues of journalism—ethics, newspaper codes, news councils, shield laws, and university education for journalists. See also the society's *The Bulletin.*

The Public Opinion Quarterly, 1937–   *POQ* is a scholarly journal of academic research on the nature and effects of the formation of public opinion. The articles often discuss the role of the mass media and public opinion. The journal is indexed in a variety of indexes; among them are *Social Sciences Citation, Social Studies Index,* and *Sociological Abstracts.*

Public Relations Review, 1975–   This scholarly quarterly carries research and comment on the functions, techniques, responsibilities, and ethics of public relations.

Publishers' Auxiliary, 1866–   This journal, the oldest trade journal for newspaper publishers, serves the interest of those persons involved in publishing small daily and weekly newspapers. The articles are primarily about financial and practical problems of publishing and occasionally about legal and ethical problems. See also *Editor & Publisher.*

Publishers Weekly, 1872–   This trade journal chronicles the book publishing industry, reporting trends in publishing, the annual production volume and sales, and legal developments, for example, the 1978 copyright law. It also calendars the promotional tours of authors. A weekly review of the new book titles is a substantial part of the magazine.

The Quill, 1912–   A monthly journal published for members of the Society of Professional Journalists, Sigma Delta Chi, *The Quill* has articles on various aspects of print journalism—court restraints on reporters, investigative journalism, the newspaper job market, and the press coverage of terrorists. See also *Matrix.*

Television News Index and Abstracts, 1972–   The evening news programs of the three television networks are taped and filed in an archive at Vanderbilt University. The news programs are abstracted, usually a single line describes each news item in the program, and indexed by subject in the quarterly *Television News Index and Abstracts.* See also the *CBS News Index, The New York Times Index,* and *Facts on File.*

Television Quarterly, 1962–   Essays written by established members of the television industry on various subjects—television news and the social effects of broadcasting—are published quarterly in this journal from the National Academy of Television Arts and Sciences.

Television/Radio Age, 1953–   A bi-weekly trade journal, *Television/ Radio Age* covers broadcast advertising. Topics usually discussed are selling advertising, creating commercials, trends in advertising, Wall Street, sales statistics, and agency news. Each issue features an article about a general topic of interest in broadcasting—live-coverage of the courtroom, broadcast stations as an investment, television violence.

Television, 1973–   A bi-monthly publication devoted to alternative uses of television, *Television* offers a lively look at the activities of the industry and the Federal Communications Commission from the consumer point of view.

TV Guide, 1953 –   In addition to its primary fare of the weekly schedule of television programs, *TV Guide* has solid articles treating issues such as citizens' groups' challenges of broadcast license renewals, funding for public television, television coverage of the energy crisis, and news judgment by television journalists. It is indexed in *Popular Periodicals Index* and *Topicator.*

Variety, 1905 –   A weekly newspaper, *Variety* reports in entertaining style the news of all mass entertainment with an emphasis on the film industry. A regular feature is the listing of the gross earning of the 50 top films. For more news about the music industry, see *Billboard.* *Variety* is indexed in *Film Literature, Media Review Digest,* and *Topicator.*

Name Index

Adams, J. Q., 293, 294
Agnew, S., 2, 3, 7, 8, 10, 217, 280, 329–331, 412
Ailes, R., 388, 390
Albert, C., 345
Ali, Muhammad, 102
Allbritton, J. L., 44, 45, 47
Allen, F., 111
Alsop, J., 324
Altman, R., 134
Altschull, H., 353
Anderson, J., 217, 218, 326, 327, 366, 367, 376
Anderson, P. Y., 307, 309
Appleton, N., 51
Archibald, S. J., 219
Arledge, R., 116
Arlen, M. J., 196, 410
Arnold, M., 99
Arthur, W. B., 202
Bagdikian, B., 3, 74, 75, 83, 184, 198, 200, 201, 338, 352
Baker, B., 325, 326
Baker, R. S., 59
Baker, R., 181, 321, 345, 377
Barber, J. D., 340
Barnard, H., 49
Barnes, C., 378
Barnouw, E., 105, 111, 128
Barnum, P. T., 382, 385
Barrett, S., 203
Barron, J., 182, 263, 264, 266, 267, 275
Barry, D., 302
Bartlett, C., 324
Bartley, R., 386
Beard, C., 146
Becker, C. L., 149
Bellow, S., 71, 257, 258
Bennett, J. G., 55, 56, 78, 291, 296, 300, 373
Benny, J., 111
Berelson, B., 420
Bernays, E. J., 380, 381, 383, 385, 388
Bernbach, W., 394
Bernstein, C., 5, 43, 223, 337, 357, 367, 369
Bethel, T., 429, 430
Bingham, B., 196
Bishop, R., 68
Black, H., 165–167, 213, 214, 253
Blackstone, W., 157, 158
Blair, F. P., 294, 295
Bleyer, W., 352
Bok, E., 66, 90
Boorstin, D. J., 58, 412
Botein, M., 261, 262
Bower, R. T., 13
Boyd, R., 366, 367, 369
Boynton, C., 302

Bradford, A., 46, 47
Bradford, W., 286
Bradlee, B., 377
Brandeis, L. D., 164, 165, 232, 233
Brandt, R., 308
Branscomb, A., 131
Branzburg, P., 223, 225
Breed, W., 353
Brennan, W., 252, 253
Breslin, J., 94
Brinkley, D., 116
Broder, D., 2, 342, 376, 377
Brown, E. (Pat), 328
Brown, H. G., 90
Brown, L., 101, 118
Browne, M., 3
Brugmann, B., 355, 356
Buchwald, A., 376
Buckley, W., 181, 376
Bullard, W. H. G., 105
Burch, D., 261, 268, 333
Burger, W., 252
Bush, C., 200
Butt, A., 303
Byrd, H., 315, 318
Caldwell, E., 223–225
Calhoun, J., 294
Calley, Lt. W. L., Jr., 4, 5, 241
Camden, E., 158, 159
Campbell, J., 286
Cannon, L., 351
Capote, T., 88
Carrington, E., 1, 48
Carson, J., 98
Carter, J., 12, 131, 254, 290, 340–345, 367, 368, 390
Cater, D., 14, 316
Catledge, T., 309
Chafee, Z., 259, 306
Chamberlain, N., 112
Chancellor, J., 343
Chandler, C., 372
Chandler, R. W., 201
Chapin, D., 5
Chaplin, C., 416
Chase, I., 396
Chase, S., 297
Chayefsky, P., 116, 413, 415
Cheshire, M., 366
Childs, H. L., 380, 381
Clapper, R., 313
Cleland, J., 252
Clinton, G., 287
Cockroft, K., 371
Coleridge, S. T., 410
Colson, C., 332, 333
Conrad, F., 105
Coolidge, C., 307–309
Cooper, J. F., 48
Coppola, F. F., 134, 427
Coren, M., 195

Subject Index